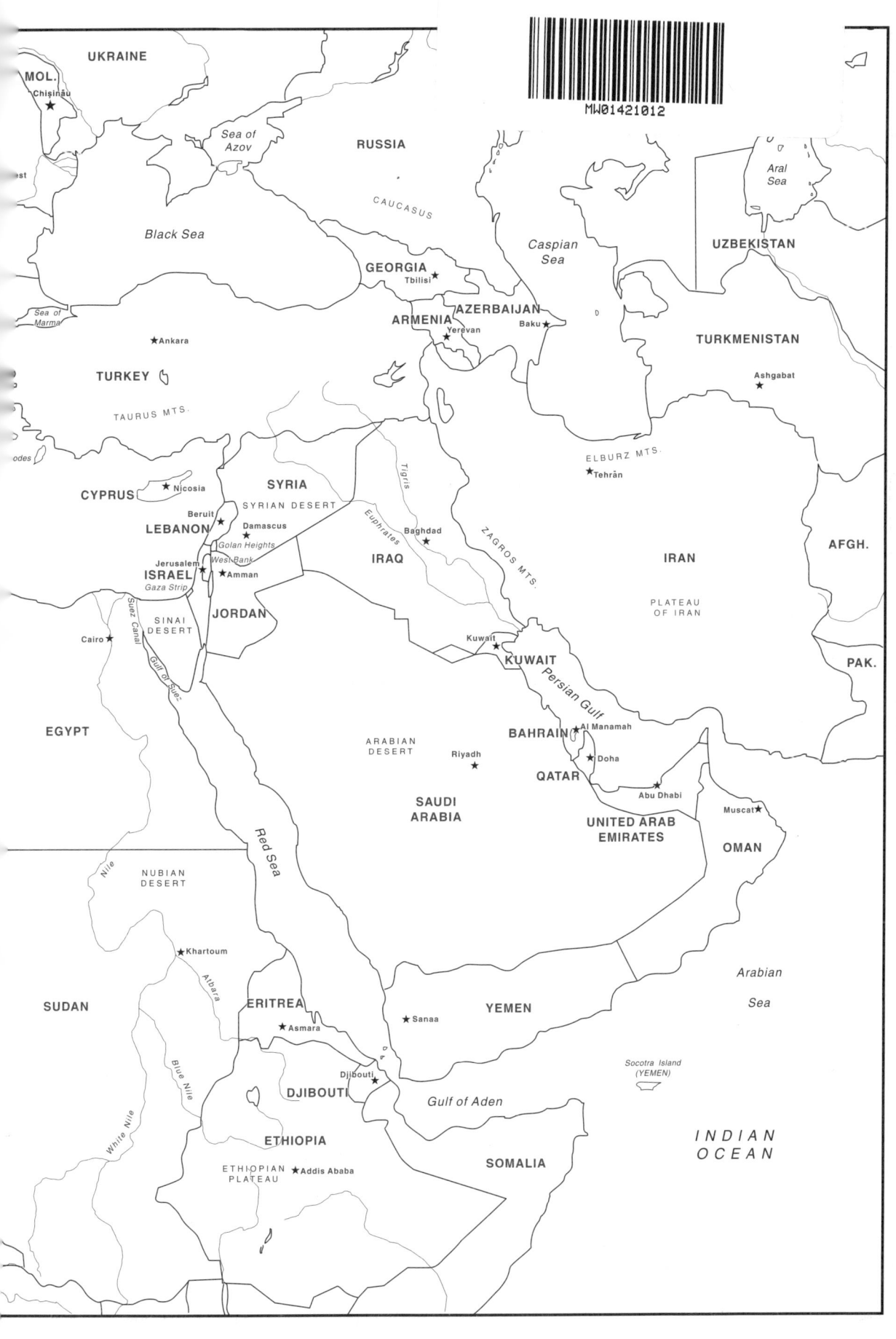

The Greenwood Encyclopedia of
Women's Issues
Worldwide

Editor-in-Chief

Lynn Walter
University of Wisconsin, Green Bay

Volume Editor

Bahira Sherif-Trask
University of Delaware, Newark

Contributors

Naji Abi-Hashem
Seattle, Washington

Sima Aprahamian
Simone de Beauvoir Institute, Concordia University, Montreal, Quebec

Brigitte H. Bechtold
Central Michigan University, Mount Pleasant

Susanne Dahlgren
University of Helsinki, Finland

Nancy Mataraso Fitzgerald
Kansas City, Kansas

Angel M. Foster
Harvard Medical School, Cambridge, Massachusetts

Chava Frankfort-Nachmias
University of Wisconsin, Milwaukee

Stephanie Hargrave
Wichita State University, Kansas

Mary Hegland
Santa Clara University, Santa Clara, California

Amy J. Johnson
Berry College, Mt. Berry, Georgia

As ad Abu Khalil
California State University, Stanilaus

Julie M. Koivunen
University of Delaware, Newark

Sandra Lee
University of Southern California, Los Angeles, California

Kim Shively
William Paterson University, Wayne, New Jersey

Ghoncheh Tazmini
University of Kent, Canterbury, United Kingdom

Carolyn I. Wright
Syracuse, New York

THE GREENWOOD ENCYCLOPEDIA OF Women's Issues WORLDWIDE

THE MIDDLE EAST AND NORTH AFRICA

Editor-in-Chief
Lynn Walter
Volume Editor
Bahira Sherif-Trask

GREENWOOD PRESS
Westport, Connecticut • London

Library of Congress Cataloging-in-Publication Data

The Greenwood encyclopedia of women's issues worldwide : The Middle East and North Africa / Lynn Walter, editor-in-chief ; Bahira Sherif-Trask, volume editor.
    p. cm.
    Includes bibliographical references and index.
    ISBN 0-313-32787-4 (set : alk. paper) — ISBN 0-313-31888-3 (alk. paper)
    1. Women—Middle East—History. 2. Women—Africa, North—History. I. Title: Encyclopedia of women's issues worldwide. II. Walter, Lynn, 1945– III. Sherif-Trask, Bahira.
HQ1726.5.G74 2003
305.4'0956—dc21   2003044818

British Library Cataloguing in Publication Data is available.

Copyright © 2003 by Lynn Walter and Bahira Sherif-Trask

All rights reserved. No portion of this book may be reproduced, by any process or technique, without the express written consent of the publisher.

Library of Congress Catalog Card Number: 2003044818
ISBN: 0-313-32787-4 (set)
       0-313-32087-X (Asia and Oceania)
       0-313-32129-9 (Central and South America)
       0-313-31855-7 (Europe)
       0-313-31888-3 (The Middle East and North Africa)
       0-313-31852-2 (North America and the Caribbean)
       0-313-32145-0 (Sub-Saharan Africa)

First published in 2003

Greenwood Press, 88 Post Road West, Westport, CT 06881
An imprint of Greenwood Publishing Group, Inc.
www.greenwood.com

Printed in the United States of America

The paper used in this book complies with the
Permanent Paper Standard issued by the National
Information Standards Organization (Z39.48–1984).

10 9 8 7 6 5 4 3 2 1

Volume map cartography by Mapcraft.com. Country map cartography by Bookcomp, Inc.

CONTENTS

Set Foreword ... vii

User's Guide ... ix

Glossary ... xiii

Introduction ... 1

1. **Algeria** — Brigitte H. Bechtold ... 15
2. **Bahrain** — Sandra Lee ... 43
3. **Egypt** — Bahira Sherif-Trask ... 67
4. **Iran** — Mary Hegland ... 105
5. **Iraq** — Ghoncheh Tazmini ... 149
6. **Israel** — Chava Frankfort-Nachmias ... 169
7. **Jordan** — Nancy Mataraso Fitzgerald ... 189
8. **Lebanon** — Sima Aprahamian and Julie M. Koivunen ... 239
9. **Libya** — Amy J. Johnson ... 259
10. **Morocco** — Kim Shively ... 281
11. **The Occupied Territories** — Stephanie Hargrave ... 313
12. **Saudi Arabia** — As ad Abu Khalil ... 337

CONTENTS

13. **Syria** Naji Abi-Hashem 355

14. **Tunisia** Angel M. Foster 381

15. **United Arab Emirates** Carolyn I. Wright 411

16. **Yemen** Susanne Dahlgren 437

Index 467

The Six-Volume Comprehensive Index begins on page 569 of the final volume, Sub-Saharan Africa

SET FOREWORD

The Greenwood Encyclopedia of Women's Issues Worldwide is a six-volume set presenting authoritative, comprehensive, and current data on a broad range of contemporary women's issues in more than 130 countries around the world. Each volume covers a major populated world region: Asia and Oceania, Central and South America, Europe, the Middle East and North Africa, North America and the Caribbean, and Sub-Saharan Africa. Volumes are organized by chapters, with each focusing on a specific country or group of countries or islands, following a broad outline of topics—education, employment and the economy, family and sexuality, health, politics and law, religion and spirituality, and violence. Under these topics, contributors were asked to consider a range of contemporary issues from illiteracy and wage discrepancies to unequal familial roles and political participation and to highlight issues of special concern to women in the country. In this way, the set provides a global perspective on women's issues, ensures breadth and depth of issue coverage, and facilitates cross-national comparison.

Along with locating women's agenda in specific national and historical contexts, each chapter looks at the cultural differences among women as well as the significance of class, religion, sexuality, and race on their lives. And, as women's movements and their non-governmental organizations (NGOs) are among the most worldwide forms of civic participation, their effectiveness in addressing women's issues is also examined. In addition to focusing on national and local organizations, many authors also highlight the major role the United Nations has played in addressing women's issues nationally and in supporting women's networks globally and point to the importance of its 1979 Convention on the Elimination of All Forms of Discrimination Against Women (CEDAW), which is still the most comprehensive international agreement on the rights of women.

Contributors were chosen for their expertise on women's issues in the country or area about which they write. Each contributor provides an authoritative resource guide with suggested reading, web sites, films/videos, and organizations as well as a selected bibliography and extensive references. The chapters and resource guides are designed for students, scholars, and engaged citizens to study contemporary women's issues in depth in specific countries and from a global perspective.

This ambitious project has been made possible by the work of many scholars who contributed their knowledge and commitment. I want to thank all of them and especially the other volume editors, Manisha Desai, Cheryl Toronto Kalny, Amy Lind, Bahira Sherif-Trask, and Aili Mari Tripp. Thanks also to Christine Marra of Marrathon Productions and Wendi Schnaufer of Greenwood Publishing Group for their editorial assistance.

As I read the many chapters of this series what struck me most was the sheer force and determination of the many women and men who are seeking solutions to the problems of inequality and poverty, discrimination, and injustice that lie at the root of women's experiences worldwide. I hope this series will further their vision.

Lynn Walter, Editor-in-Chief

USER'S GUIDE

The Greenwood Encyclopedia of Women's Issues Worldwide is a six-volume set covering the world's most populated regions:

Asia and Oceania

Central and South America

Europe

The Middle East and North Africa

North America and the Caribbean

Sub-Saharan Africa

All volumes contain an introduction from the editor-in-chief that overviews women's issues today around the world and introduces the set. Each volume editor broadly characterizes contemporary women's issues in the particular region(s). The volumes are divided into chapters, ordered alphabetically by country name. A few chapters treat several countries (e.g., Tajikistan, Kazakhstan, Turkmenistan, and Kyrgyzstan, which are grouped together as Central Asia) or a group of islands (e.g., the Netherland Antilles).

The comprehensive coverage facilitates comparisons between nations and among regions. The following is an outline showing the sections of each chapter. In rare instances where information was not available or applicable for a particular country, sections were omitted.

Profile of [the Nation]
A paragraph on the land, people(s), form of government, economy, and demographic statistics on female/male population, infant mortality, maternal mortality, total fertility, and life expectancy.

USER'S GUIDE

Overview of Women's Issues
A brief introduction to the major issues to be covered, giving the reader a sense of the state of women's lives in the country.

Education
Opportunities
Literacy
Statistics on Female Literacy

Employment and Economics
Job/Career Opportunities
Pay
Working Conditions
    Sexual Harassment
Support for Mothers/Caretakers
    Maternal Leave
    Daycare
    Family and Medical Leave
Inheritance and Property Rights
Social/Government Programs
    Sustainable Development
    Welfare and [or] Welfare Reform

Family and Sexuality
Gender Roles
Marriage
Reproduction
    Sex Education
    Contraception and Abortion
    Teen Pregnancy

Health
Health Care Access
Diseases and Disorders
    AIDS
    Eating Disorders
    Cancer
    Depression

Politics and Law
Suffrage
Political Participation
Women's Rights

Feminist Movements [Women's Movement]
Lesbian Rights
    Marriage
    Parenthood
Military Service
Religion and Spirituality
Women's Roles
Rituals and Religious Practices
Religious Law
Violence
Domestic Violence
Rape/Sexual Assault
Trafficking in Women and Children
War and Military Repression
Outlook for the Twenty-first Century
Resource Guide
Suggested Reading
Videos/Films
Web Sites
Organizations
Selected Bibliography

    A regional map is in the inside cover of each volume. Additionally, each chapter has an accompanying country or mini-region map. Each volume has an index consisting of subject and person entries; a comprehensive set index is included at the end of the Sub-Saharan Africa volume.

GLOSSARY

Allah. Arabic word for God.

Bedouin. Nomad who travels with camels.

Burqua. Women's head-to-toe caftan with only a slit left open for the eyes.

Chador. Specifically Iranian veil for women.

Copt. Egyptian Christian.

Hadith. Statement or deeds attributed to the prophet Muhammad or one of his followers of which he (Muhammad) approved.

Hajj. Pilgrimage to Mecca that all Muslims should make at least once in their lifetime.

Hijab. Head scarf worn by Muslim females.

Hijrah. Emigration in 622 of Muhammad and his followers from Mecca to Medina; marks the Muslim New Year.

Imam. Muslim religious leader.

Islam. A religion that is followed by more than 1 billion people, primarily in the Middle East and parts of Africa and Asia; defined by the belief in one God, revealed to a series of prophets ending with Muhammad.

Mahr. Dowry; sum of money or valuables that the husband pledges to his wife as part of the marriage contract.

Muhammad. Prophet and founder of Islam.

Muslim. Person who subscribes to Islam, the belief in one God and that Muhammad was the last prophet.

Qur'an. The collection of revelations that Muslims believe were transmitted to the prophet Muhammad from God; the legal and ethical basis of life for Muslims.

GLOSSARY

Ramadan. Period of twenty-eight days of fasting (one lunar cycle) from sunrise to sunset that all adult Muslims are expected to observe once a year.

Shari'a. Islamic religious law; believed to be sacred.

Sheikh. Term applied to a tribal leader, religious teacher, or ruler.

Shi'ism. A major tradition in Islam; its followers are found primarily in Iran and part of Iraq.

Sufism. Mystic and ascetic branch of Islam.

Sunna. Practice attributed to the prophet Muhammad; the idea to be imitated by all Muslims.

Sunni. Branch of Islam to which most Muslims belong.

Talaaq. Unilateral right of a man to divorce his wife; repudiation.

Umma. Community of believers.

INTRODUCTION

This volume seeks to give readers an accurate picture of the lives of women in North Africa and the Middle East. It dispels many misconceptions that Westerners have about the lives of these women and introduces them to the highly diverse nature of the societies that are found in this part of the world. In the countries of North Africa and the Middle East, there are very wealthy women who wear the latest Western fashions, travel, and are highly educated; there are less well-to-do women, some of whom work outside the home and some of whom stay home; there are women who work on farms; and there are women who live their whole lives as nomads, moving from place to place with their families and animals. There is also a great deal of religious diversity: some women are Muslim, some are Christian, some are Jewish, some are Zoroastrian, and some are secular. Furthermore, North African and Middle Eastern women represent an array of races, including African, Caucasian, and Asian.

While the two regions covered in this volume are bound by strong geographical, linguistic, religious, and historical ties, the areas are highly heterogeneous when it comes to women's issues, ways of life, subsistence and economies, and political systems. As will be seen throughout the volume, women's lives and the issues they face vary from country to country. North African and Middle Eastern women live in oil-rich nations such as Saudi Arabia and the United Arab Emirates and in countries with much poorer economies such as Egypt and Lebanon. Women's lives are heavily influenced by the socioeconomic conditions in their respective countries. But there are other differences as well: women live under an array of political systems that include governments modeled on the French system as well as political dictatorships and monarchies. Furthermore, while these two regions are primarily associated with Islam, as will be seen, there are multiple versions and interpretations of Islam that again affect the rights, issues, and lives of women in their respective societies.

NORTH AFRICA AND THE MIDDLE EAST

North Africa and the Middle East stretch from Morocco to Iran and encompass a distance of approximately 3,400 miles, equal to the distance from New York City to Fairbanks, Alaska.[1] There are various conceptions of what constitutes North Africa and the Middle East. Included in this volume are the North African countries of Morocco, Algeria, Libya, Tunisia, and Egypt and, in the central Middle East, Lebanon, Syria, Jordan, Israel, the Occupied Territories, Saudi Arabia, Bahrain, the United Arab Emirates, Yemen, Iraq, and Iran. Afghanistan and Pakistan are included in the Asia and Oceania volume of this series, and Turkey is covered in the Europe volume.

The geographic position of North Africa and the Middle East has made them crossroads for many different peoples over thousands of years. Most of the stories of the Old and New Testaments as well as those in the Qur'an, the holy book of Islam, took place here. This is the area with some of the oldest civilizations. It is also the region with the world's primary reserves of oil. It is estimated that at least 70 percent of the world's known reserves of oil can be found in the central Middle East.[2]

Most of the land in North Africa and the Middle East is desert or semiarid and characterized by the prevalence of urban areas, irrigation agriculture, and pastoral nomadism. However, the whole region is not clearly delineated by natural frontiers. While the region is partially cut off from sub-Saharan Africa and from the Indo-Pakistani subcontinent by mountains and deserts, the northern boundaries with some of the former Soviet Muslim republics are political borders and not geographic ones.[3]

It is interesting to note that even though these regions are characterized by similar religious, historical, and linguistic experiences, this has not led to a common identity (an issue that is often glossed over in discussions in the West). For example, over the last half century, Turkey, a largely Muslim country with strong historical ties to the Arab world, has openly stressed its ties with Europe rather than its Muslim neighbors, which is why Turkey is included in the Europe volume. Other countries have also faced identity issues that are often linked to their historical experiences of having been colonized.[4] For example, it is still not uncommon to find well-to-do upper-class Egyptians who insist on speaking only French or English. Israel is faced with its own unique challenges, as the only Jewish state surrounded by Arab Muslim countries.

While most of the region is Arabic speaking, there are many dialects, which makes communication difficult. Written Arabic is relatively standard, but the many variations of spoken Arabic can make it virtually impossible, for example, for someone from Morocco to understand someone from Iraq. Also, in Israel, people speak, read, and write Hebrew, and in Iran the dominant language is Persian.

Most inhabitants of North Africa and the Middle East share a common religious heritage: Jews, Christians, and Muslims all trace themselves back to the Old Testament and share some of the same holy places in the central Middle East, such as Jerusalem. While there is a great deal of diversity with respect to lifestyles, political situation, and economics, all of these societies do share some common roots in terms of religion, beliefs, and social practices. We find, for example, throughout North Africa and the Middle East, women who veil who are not Muslim or aspects of the marriage contract that are the same among Muslims and Jews. As will be seen throughout the chapters in this volume, many of the divisions and boundaries that exist today are the result of colonialism and constantly changing political and economic contexts.

ISLAM

While there exists much more diversity in North Africa and the Middle East with respect to religion, culture, and class than most people from other parts of the world realize, it is important to point out that Islam *does* play a very significant role in this region of the world. The word "Islam" is an Arabic word meaning "submission to the will of God." A Muslim is anyone who follows the religion of Islam.[5] While Islam is one of the youngest religions in the world (its inception dates to 622 A.D.), it is the fastest-growing religion, with currently approximately 1.3 billion adherents, most of whom live in Pakistan, India, and Southeast Asia.

Islam is a monotheistic religion that is very similar to Judaism and Christianity. All Muslims believe that there is only one God and regard the Old and New Testaments as revelations that came from God (Allah). Much of the moral code with respect to human behavior is identical in Islam, Judaism, and Christianity. A primary difference, however, is that Islam does not accept the Christian concept of the Trinity or Jesus as the Son of God. Instead, Jesus is regarded as a prophet who was then followed by Muhammad, the last prophet. This makes Muhammad the most important prophet to Muslims. Furthermore, there are two major strands of Islam: Sunni Islam and Shi'a Islam, their distinction resulting from a crisis of succession after the death of Muhammad.

Islam is more than a set of beliefs and ritual practices. It constitutes a system of thought and includes rules of behavior that were transmitted to the prophet Muhammad from God. These rules are understood to be a series of commands in order to assist individuals in every aspect of their lives. Thus every pious Muslim has to fulfill the five "pillars of Islam": the proclamation that there is no God but Allah, and Muhammad is his prophet; five daily prayers performed in the direction of Mecca; the fast of Ramadan, during which Muslims may not eat or drink from sunrise to sunset for a whole month; charitable giving; and the pilgrimage to the Holy City of Mecca (*hajj*) that every Muslim is expected to perform once in his or her lifetime. Furthermore, every Muslim is expected to be moderate and may not drink alcohol, eat pork, or gamble.

The commands found in the Qur'an are thought to be divine; they were revealed once and hence may not be changed in any form. God's will is also expressed in the sunna, containing the traditions about and the sayings of the prophet Muhammad. The canon law or shari'a is composed of the Qur'an as well as the sunna. It is the sunna that provides the basis for interpretations of the Qur'an and for an adaptation of its commands to present-day societies. A prominent piece of the shari'a is the laws dealing with family issues, especially marriage, divorce, and succession. Thus family roles and responsibilities can be identified in the law.[6] The link between the law, the religion, and God's will explains why in all Islamic North African and Middle Eastern countries changes to the personal status law raise such concern and outrage. A parallel situation is found in Israel where the orthodox rabbinical courts have complete jurisdiction over issues of personal status. An important aside about religious law is that, historically, the interpretation and transmission of the shari'a and of Jewish personal status law has always been in the hands of male lawyer-theologians. This has had major implications for women when it comes to legal rulings with respect to gender issues.[7]

WOMEN AND ISLAM

Women's roles and status and gender relations in North Africa and the Middle East must be understood within a full spectrum, not only in terms of religion. While Islam has always played a very important role in the lives of many individuals in this area, it is not the only or necessarily the primary influence. In fact, Islam shares the same views as the other major religions of the area, Judaism and Christianity, when it comes to the role of women as primarily wives and mothers. Islam is, therefore, not more or less patriarchal than these other religions.[8] In addition, many North African and Middle Eastern women are not Muslims. As will be seen in the various chapters included in this volume, North Africa and the Middle East are characterized by a multiplicity of religions and cultures, coexisting side by side. As well, the issue of women's rights cannot be explained purely through religious and cultural terms. Many of the topics and movements associated with the contemporary Middle East are the product of historical, political, and economic forces that pervade the inhabitants' lives.

VEILING AND THE SECLUSION OF WOMEN

The topics of veiling (the wearing of a head and face cover in public) and the seclusion of women are examples of social traditions exclusively associated with Islam. However, historical evidence exists that veiling was prevalent in pre-Islamic Arabia. With respect to the seclusion of women, evidence in the Qur'an itself indicates that women just prior to and in the early days of Islam in Arabia played an active role in the social and political life of the religious community. Multiple studies of the Qur'an and the Hadith show that there is no particular injunction stipulating that women should be veiled or forbidden from active participation in public life. Veiling and the seclusion of women were only introduced in the century after the prophet Muhammad's death. It was at that point that seclusion came to refer to the practice of encouraging women, after puberty, not to interact with men and instead of confining them to private spaces such as the household. Veiling was the symbolic expression of this seclusion. The practices of veiling and seclusion were for the most part urban phenomena that were practiced to varying degrees by Muslims as well as Christians and Jews up through the twentieth century. However, as some studies have illustrated, only middle- and upper-class families could afford a system where women were kept out of the public sphere.[9] The majority of the population, the working classes and the rural, agrarian population, could not put either veiling or seclusion into practice. Families needed their women to work in order to contribute to their economic survival (as is still the case).[10]

During the eighteenth century, when North Africa and the Middle East became increasingly dominated economically by the West, veiling started to have more of a symbolic meaning than just indicating the economic or political status of a woman. While neither veiling nor the seclusion of women was ordained by the Qur'an or Islam, both practices now became forced on women in the name of religion. Moreover, these practices were increasingly tied to deeply held traditional sexual and moral beliefs about gender roles. Women's innate active sexuality was perceived as dominating their lives, in contrast to men, who were only partially defined by their sexuality. Further, women were believed to possess a more powerful sexual drive than men, posing a threat to society because of the chaos (*fitna*) they could unleash.[11] The force of women's sexuality was thought to be so powerful that the mere presence of a woman would force a man to want sexual relations with her.[12] To complicate matters, women's sexual purity was linked to the honor of men and the family. Segregating women to their homes and covering them with veils when they went out in public were deemed necessary to the preservation of their sexual purity and maintaining the honor of their men and families.[13]

By the close of the nineteenth century, the veil became more of a political symbol as the French and the British began to play an important political role in the Arab world and, in particular, Egypt. Colonial interpretations of the status of women in North Africa and the Middle East concluded that Islam innately oppressed women and that the veil and segregation epitomized that oppression. These images, placing veiled women at the center of the dialogue, were used in part to justify the creation of an image of a less developed society that needed to be introduced to Western ways of thinking.[14] The colonialists advocated that only by removing the veil and changing the position of women could the developing societies of North Africa and the Middle East modernize.[15]

The role of the colonialists, in part because of their focus on women and Islam, evoked several national responses, particularly in Egypt. Beginning in the twentieth century, several new oppositional forces arose. These movements provided the basis for some of the ideological forces we now find in the contemporary Middle East. The first movement was based on a modern intellectual approach. It advocated the liberation of women through the removal of their veils and the reform of marriage and divorce laws in order to advance the nation. In contrast, however, a new nationalist conservative force arose simultaneously that turned to and defended Islamic practices. This opposing force, in particular, insisted that women must veil in order to demonstrate their national pride. Adherents of this movement felt that the traditions that had come under colonial scrutiny, the customs relating to women, needed to be revived as a means of resisting Western domination.[16] Eventually the veil came to symbolize the colonial resistance movement and no longer the inferiority of North African and Middle Eastern culture. In the 1920s, Egyptian women were the first to remove their veils and were quickly followed by their other North African and Middle Eastern peers. By the second half of the twentieth century, a third ideological orientation, the Islamic fundamentalists, appeared throughout North Africa and the Middle East, often in opposition to the governments in power. Like the conservatives of the first part of the century, they have emphasized women's "natural" role in the home and as wife and mother.[17]

The new fundamentalist movement stresses the supposedly religiously ordained view of the separation of the sexes, the "traditional" hierarchy between husbands and wives, and the importance of marriage and motherhood for women. If these beliefs and practices are not actively supported, adherents of the fundamentalist movements predict the demise of society. This fundamentalist discourse has made major inroads in many of the countries of North Africa and the Middle East and has become part of the mainstream dialogue about the "appropriate" roles of men and women in society. It is reflected primarily in debates about whether women should work outside of the home, the rights women have when it comes to divorce, and the extent to which women need to submit to their husbands. It is important to point out that the basis for these debates is interpretations of religious doctrines and not the actual Qur'anic injunctions and is, therefore, subject to time and context.

As part of these changes, many societies in North Africa and the Middle East have seen a resurgence of veiling among women. In a time of globalization and rising fundamentalist fervor, conflicting values have pervaded many North African and Middle Eastern countries. There are strong sentiments about the ills of postcolonization, perceived Western imperialism, and the economic problems that beset many of these nations. As the various societies struggle with finding a sense of national identity, women and their appropriate roles have been caught in the middle as part of those national dialogues. As a response, many North African and Middle Eastern women have returned to wearing varying versions of the veil. However, today, they are veiling as a different type of symbolic statement. The new veiling suggests that these women are conservative, that they are Muslim, and that they are not Western. For many of these women, veiling has become a statement of identity in societies that are often in political and economic flux. Thus what we find is that at the beginning of the twenty-first century, North African and Middle Eastern women and their place in society and within Islam have become intertwined in the political and economic discourses of their respective countries.

RESEARCH ON NORTH AFRICAN AND MIDDLE EASTERN WOMEN

The complex issue of who is a North African or a Middle Eastern woman is reflected in the limited geographic range of studies in these regions. In studying women's issues, research has focused primarily on women in Egypt, Iran, Morocco, and Yemen. Furthermore, the situation of women in Israel is often not included in works on the Middle East. There is also not a widespread inclusive literature in terms of the topics that have been studied. Much of the work on North African and Middle Eastern women has been conducted in three distinct arenas: (1) anthropological studies specifically of villages or tribes that may include a chapter on women and family; (2) health surveys of women in certain countries; or (3) writings by Muslim feminists explaining their societies through Western theoretical perspectives.[18] Due to the lack of more comprehensive research on this part of the world, there is little awareness of the multiple, complex gender issues that have differentially affected women.

The lack of a more inclusive scholarship can be understood, in part, by taking a somewhat historical perspective on the broader research that has been conducted on North Africa and the Middle East as a whole. In the United States, post–World War II government support of area studies had the unintended result of separating and marginalizing research on North Africa and the Middle East (as well as other parts of the world such as the Soviet Union and the Indian subcontinent). Area studies concentrated on the uniformity of an area, particularly with regard to religion, language, and social customs.[19] This focus furthered the image of the homogeneity of geographic entities where all of the inhabitants had similar lives and experiences. Only in the last several decades have Western academics begun to acknowledge more broadly the complexity of other cultures, including North Africa and the Middle East. Today, there is much more recognition of the diversity that exists in North Africa and the Middle East and among

Muslims themselves. There is increasing awareness that interpretations of Islam as well as its followers are varied and that, in fact, religion is only one of many factors that pervade people's lives.

Feminists in the Arab world have been diligently working to separate Islamic beliefs from the patriarchal forms of social organization that have been a part of the heritage of North Africa, the Middle East, and the Mediterranean area. Their works illustrate that gender relations and the status of women in the Muslim world cannot be attributed solely to Islam but are part of an array of social traditions, varying interpretations of religious texts, and ever-changing political and economic conditions. It is important to note that the activities of these native feminists are not antireligious, but instead focus on the underlying forms of patriarchal social organization and its development over the centuries.[20]

The specific study of women's roles and rights in North Africa and the Middle East is hampered by its own set of issues. Until about thirty years ago, men primarily conducted most research on women (of which, as has been mentioned, there was very little). Due to the gender-segregated nature of societies in North Africa and the Middle East, this led to a distorted dissemination of information, as male academics accessed information through contacts with male informants who emphasized the patriarchal features of their cultures. This created the image in the West that North African and Middle Eastern women had virtually no rights either in their families or in the public sphere.

The feminist movement that began in the 1960s and that was extremely influential with respect to research on Western gender issues had a profound effect on studies of women in North Africa and the Middle East. In particular, it raised criticism that women in this part of the world had been neglected or sparsely portrayed, primarily through the writings of men and through stereotypical images. Western feminist studies transformed this situation. An initial effect was that the concepts by which the status of women in North Africa and the Middle East was viewed were revised. A new wave of studies introduced innovative ways of thinking and understanding about taken-for-granted concepts such as power, identity, and women's own agency.[21] Feminist academics and writers also introduced the concept of gender to research on North African and Middle Eastern women. These studies stressed that cultural, social, political, and economic factors influenced relationships between men and women and that these relations were constantly changing. (Ironically, it has proven difficult if not impossible to translate the term "gender" into Arabic and Persian.)[22] An important impact of the feminist movement was to shift research on North African and Middle Eastern women to the realities of their lives and the complex contexts in which they were making their choices and decisions. It stressed the importance of listening to women's voices about their situations instead of relying on textual interpretations. This new perspective also encouraged researchers to examine the macro influence of issues such as nationalism, colonization, and economics on women's lives.

While, on the whole, there has been a positive shift in academic studies on North African and Middle Eastern women's issues, several important factors still contribute to the uneven and, at times, controversial body of research. As was mentioned earlier, there are certain countries and cultures that are heavily represented in the academic literature, while other areas are virtually absent. The difficulty of learning foreign languages compounded by local dialects, the intricacies of studying Islam and its relationship to other religions, and the varied sociopolitical contexts add to the complexity of research in this region and also make some Western research methods (such as surveys, for example) ineffective. Further, it is at times extremely difficult if not impossible to conduct fieldwork and archival research in certain countries that may officially discourage or even forbid any type of Western social scientific research. This may explain, in part, why, for example, there is a heavy proliferation of research on women in Egypt but not in Libya. Due to a long-term historical association between Egypt and the colonial powers of France, England, and more recently the United States, there is a variety of materials easily accessible to researchers in Cairo and in European libraries and archives. In contrast, it is extremely difficult to conduct field research on women in Algeria, Iraq, Libya, Saudi Arabia, and many of the smaller countries on the Arabian peninsula.[23] This is an important point because interested individuals as well as researchers of North African and Middle Eastern women must be careful not to draw conclusions about the lives of women about whom we know very little, compared to the lives of the women about whom we have a great deal of information.[24] Further, it is important to remember that the various societies of North Africa and the Middle East are, for the most part, composed of three groups with respect to subsistence: those individuals who live in urban areas, those who live on rural agricultural lands, and those who make their living as pastoral nomads. These groups are also often clearly delineated by class differences. The lifestyle and issues that an upper-class woman in Cairo is facing will be radically different from the experiences of a Bedouin nomadic woman living in the Western Desert of Egypt. Women in North Africa and the Middle East, therefore, live in a variety of contexts and regions and may have completely different experiences and issues to deal with, even in the same society.

THE CONTEMPORARY CONTEXT OF WOMEN'S ISSUES

The chapters in this volume illustrate that the status of women, their rights and duties with respect to ownership over property, control over their own bodies, and position in their families, and the degrees of seclusion and veiling vary considerably throughout North Africa and the Middle

East. They also differ across class lines and across ethnic and religious affiliations. Even in highly conservative societies such as Saudi Arabia and Iran, there are enormous variations in women's influence in domestic and political affairs. These chapters illustrate, moreover, that religious laws do not necessarily determine the behavior of the sexes and the position of women. There is a considerable range of interpretations of laws and traditions within each society as well as over time.

Many of the chapters also show that women in the contemporary Middle East are oftentimes at the center of apparently contradictory discourses and interests. These tensions are characteristic of dilemmas facing many postcolonial societies and are brought on through globalizing influences. Many of these issues are rooted in modernization, its relation to Westernization, and contestations of "authentic" national culture and traditions.[25] Many North African and Middle Eastern societies are characterized by clashing ideologies and unequal access to resources. This has led to conflictual relationships between classes, genders, and religious and ethnic groups. Women at times become the scapegoat and/or symbol for ideological struggles that are actually the result of other deep-rooted issues in their respective societies.

The chapters in this volume also indicate that in many contemporary North African and Middle Eastern countries, growing Islamist and other conservative religious movements have influenced the options available to women.[26] That said, a fascinating new development has been the rise of a new feminist movement rooted in the principles of Islam. Women are turning to religious writings and historical records in order to find a culturally authentic basis for their rights. A major difference is that the new authentic feminism does not emphasize the equality of the sexes, as Western feminism does. Instead, the new Islamic feminism is based on the concept of the complementarity of the sexes and a search for rights based on religious traditions. This is a response by feminists, as well as other concerned women, to hold off conservative populist Islamist forces that are encouraging women not to work outside the home and emphasizing their primary role as mothers. As a counterforce, indigenous activists are focusing on issues that are relevant to the lives of contemporary women and their daughters.[27]

SCOPE OF THIS VOLUME

The purpose of this volume is to explore the diversity of issues that women in the contemporary Middle East face. The issues touched upon earlier, as well as others, will be addressed, analyzed, and interpreted in various ways by the contributors. The chapters do not present a uniform view of the historical, current, and future lives and rights of North African and Middle Eastern women. Nor do the authors necessarily agree with each other about the roots of certain movements or the impact of certain forces on the women who live in the societies of North Africa and the Middle East. Yet while the emphasis on issues differs somewhat from chapter to chapter, all of the authors share a commitment to present women living in North Africa and Middle Eastern societies as active agents who are not governed by severe religious beliefs or never-changing cultural traditions. Oftentimes, the authors also illustrate that the pictures presented to the outside world may differ greatly from the realities of women's lives. While, at this point, women's rights in many places around the world are fairly well documented, this cannot be said of North African and Middle Eastern women. Hence another purpose of this volume is to illustrate through examples that despite stereotypical images, ideological struggles, and social, economic, and political constraints, women in this part of the world are striving to understand, advocate, and advance their rights.

A glossary preceding this introduction defines terms that occur frequently in the chapters. The spelling of these terms has been standardized.

NOTES

1. D. Eickelman, *The Middle East: An Anthropological Approach* (Englewood Cliffs, NJ: Prentice-Hall, 1981), 2.

2. T. Kavunedus and H. Hammond, *The Middle East: History, Culture, People* (New York: Globe Book Company, 1985), 15.

3. See Eickelman, 1981, 1–16, for a more extensive discussion of these issues.

4. Ibid., 5.

5. Note that Islam and Muslim are based on the same Arabic root: *slm*.

6. J. Esposito, *Women in Muslim Family Law* (Syracuse, NY: Syracuse University Press, 1982), 13.

7. Historically, Islam arose in a tribal society in Arabia, organized along patrilineal principles of descent, inheritance, and succession. In a brief period of time after its rise in the seventh century, Islam developed into a civilization founded on traditions that were prevalent in ancient Arabian and other North African and Middle Eastern societies. These traditions, along with the religion, then spread with the Arabs through North Africa to other parts of the continent and eastward to Asia. D. Bates and A. Rassam, *Peoples and Cultures of the Middle East* (Englewood Cliffs, NJ: Prentice-Hall, 1983), 31–55.

8. D. Chatty and A. Rabo, eds., *Organizing Women: Formal and Informal Women's Groups in North Africa and the Middle East* (Oxford and New York: Berg, 1997), 13.

9. M. Badran, *Feminists, Islam and Nation* (Princeton: Princeton University Press, 1995).

10. Ibid., 15.

11. I. Nicolaisen, introduction to *Women in Islamic Societies: Social Attitudes and Historical Perspectives*, ed. B. Utas (London: Curzon Press, 1983), 7.

12. See in particular Fatima Mernissi, *Beyond the Veil: Male-Female Dynamics in a Modern Muslim Society* (London: Schenkman Pub. Co., 1975). In this book, Mernissi describes the historical and religious writings that led to this concept of an active female sexuality.

13. Badran, 1995, 5.

14. One still sees a similar mechanism working in the modern media, where often

news stories on North Africa and the Middle East feature a woman in a full-length black veil as part of the visual picture.

15. Badran, 1995, 6.
16. Chatty and Rabo, 1997, 15.
17. Ibid.
18. H. Bodman and N. Tohidi, eds., *Women in Muslim Societies: Diversity within Unity* (Boulder, CO: Lynne Rienner, 1998), 1.
19. Ibid., 2.
20. Chatty and Rabo, 1997, 13.
21. D. Kandiyoti, ed., *Gendering the Middle East* (Syracuse, NY: Syracuse University Press, 1996), 12.
22. R. Roded, ed., *Women in Islam and the Middle East: A Reader* (London: I.B. Tauris, 1999), 14.
23. Bodman and Tohidi, 1998, 2.
24. For example, we cannot say that just because we know a great deal about the lives of white middle-class American women, we know a lot about the African American female experience.
25. Chatty and Rabo, 1997, 15.
26. Azza Karam, *Women, Islamisms, and the State: Contemporary Feminism in Egypt* (New York: St. Martin's Press, 1998), 13.
27. Badran, 1995, 24.

SELECTED BIBLIOGRAPHY

Ahmed, L. *Women and Gender in Islam: Historical Roots of a Modern Debate*. New Haven, CT: Yale University Press, 1992.

Badran, M. "Independent Women: More Than a Century of Feminism in Egypt." In *Arab Women: Old Boundaries, New Frontiers*, ed. J. Tucker, 125–48. Bloomington: Indiana University Press, 1993.

Bates, D., and A. Rassam. *Peoples and Cultures of the Middle East*. Englewood Cliffs, NJ: Prentice-Hall, 1983.

Bodman, H., and N. Tohidi, eds. *Women in Muslim Societies: Diversity within Unity*. Boulder, CO: Lynne Rienner, 1998.

Chatty, D., and A. Rabo, eds. *Organizing Women: Formal and Informal Women's Groups in North Africa and the Middle East*. Oxford and New York: Berg, 1997.

Eickelman, D. *The Middle East: An Anthropological Approach*. Englewood Cliffs, NJ: Prentice-Hall, 1981.

Esposito, J. *Women in Muslim Family Law*. Syracuse, NY: Syracuse University Press, 1982.

Kandiyoti, D., ed. *Women, Islam, and the State*. London: Macmillan, 1991.

———, ed. *Gendering the Middle East*. Syracuse, NY: Syracuse University Press, 1991.

Karam, Azza. *Women, Islamisms, and the State: Contemporary Feminism in Egypt*. New York: St. Martin's Press, 1998.

Kavunedus, T., and H. Hammond. *The Middle East: History, Culture, People*. New York: Globe Book Company, 1985.

Moghadam, V. *Modernizing Women: Gender and Social Change in the Middle East*. Boulder, CO: Lynne Rienner, 1993.

Nicolaisen, I. "Introduction." In *Women in Islamic Societies: Social Attitudes and Historical Perspectives*, ed. B. Utas, 1–11. London: Curzon Press, 1983.

INTRODUCTION

Roded, R., ed. *Women in Islam and the Middle East: A Reader*. London: I.B. Tauris, 1999.

Shaaban, B. *Both Right and Left Handed: Arab Women Talk about Their Lives*. London: Women's Press, 1988.

I

ALGERIA

Brigitte H. Bechtold

PROFILE OF ALGERIA

Algeria is a North African country that can be described from a variety of perspectives. It can be seen as a nation that has survived a lengthy war for independence from colonial domination by France and a brutal civil war—both of which claimed thousands of human lives—to become a society with fairly respectable levels for its socioeconomic indicators, compared with the other oil-producing developing nations. However, when women's development is considered in contrast to men's, a very different picture emerges. Women fully participated in obtaining independence from colonial rule in 1962, but they do not enjoy equal citizenship with men, and their social status declined further with the passing of the Family Code of 1984, based on an interpretation of Islam, which is the dominant religion.

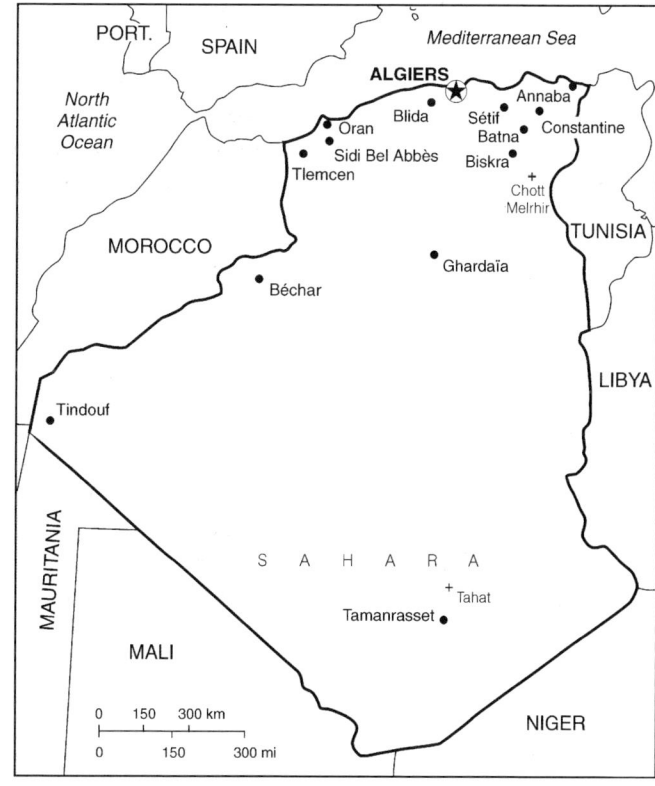

Algeria comprises 2.4 million square kilometers[1] and thus is the second-largest country in Africa. It forms a large part of the Maghreb, a vast rectangular region in northern Africa that is parallel to the equator. It is bordered on the north by the Mediterranean Sea, and its largest cities, the capital of Algiers and Oran, are situated on the Mediterranean coast. Most of the coastline is characterized by steep mountains dropping off into the sea. The country's closeness to the sea is further accentuated by the fact that on its east and west it is bordered by the north-south-oriented nations of Tunisia and Morocco, which themselves have long borders, respectively, with the Mediterranean and the Atlantic. Between two chains of the Atlas Mountains lies a region of high plateaus, suitable for raising livestock. The southern region of the nation is part of the Sahara Desert and borders Mauritania, Mali, Niger, and Libya, moving from west to east. Algeria thus offers many physical contrasts. It has also historically been a place of contacts of the civilizations of Africa, Asia, the Middle East, and Europe and has a population that reflects these influences. Perhaps it is for this reason that Algeria is generally considered as part of the Middle East, rather than a foremost African nation.

Only 17 percent of Algeria's total land area was domesticated in the mid-1990s. Even so, permanent pastures, forest, and woodland are in decline. Since the discovery of natural gas and oil, fields of gas and oil extraction now occupy a circle in the middle of the nation and are interspersed with oil fields in the east. Economic activities span cultivation of dates and grapes, raising livestock, and industrialization around the petroleum sector. The real gross domestic product (GDP) expanded at average growth rates of 5.5 percent in 1975–1984, but at less than 1 percent per year from the mid-1980s to the mid-1990s.[2] Gross national product (GNP) per capita declined by 1.6 percent each year between 1988 and 1998, which is a dismal performance in comparison with its neighbors in the Maghreb. Neighboring Morocco and Tunisia saw respective GNP per capita increases of 0.7 percent and 2.4 percent over the same time span.

Today, Algeria has a population of approximately 31 million, nearly two-thirds of whom live in urban areas—4 million in Algiers alone. Ninety-nine percent is of Arab-Berber origin, while the remaining 1 percent is European (mostly French). The average annual population growth has slowed from 3.1 percent annually in the 1975–1984 decade to 2.8 percent in 1985–1989 and further to 2.3 percent in the mid-1990s.

The female population comprises 49.4 percent of the population, well below the overall African ratio of 50.2 percent.[3] The birth sex ratio (the ratio of males to females) is 104, which is somewhat high, and remains at that level for children aged 0–14. Middle Eastern nations possess sex ratios that generally exceed those in European and American nations: female infanticide is a possible explanation. After age 65, the number of women significantly surpasses that of men, for two reasons. First, in Algeria, as everywhere else, males die at greater numbers than females due to natural causes, beginning since conception, and second, violent deaths of older women are not as frequent as they are for younger age groups.

Life expectancy at birth has risen to seventy years of age for both sexes, up from sixty only fifteen years earlier. The total fertility rate is now below 3, while the crude birth rate and death rate are 27.1 and 4.9 per 1,000, respectively. Infant mortality was 32 per 1,000 in 1997, down sharply from 88 per 1,000 in 1982. Maternal mortality per 100,000 live births is 140.

OVERVIEW OF WOMEN'S ISSUES

In the years since independence from France, Algerian women's status has changed from freedom fighters in the war for liberation (*moudjahidates*) to that of nonemancipated minors in the charge of husbands and brothers, as outlined in the Family Code. All postindependence governments in Algeria have adopted a formal concept of citizenship for women that fosters a dual status for women in which they lack agency and are placed in the custody of their male relatives, who see themselves as acting in the name of God.

As a result of the dual concept of women's citizenship, violence against women, occurring in an environment of politicized Islamic fundamentalism, is the most pressing social issue. The *Shadow Report on Algeria* states that Algerian women suffer from discrimination and are subjected to ongoing, and indeed increasing, threats of "politicized, violent religious fundamentalism." The fundamentalist violence and oppression that have targeted women are characterized in the report as equivalent to war crimes and crimes against humanity, including sexual slavery.[4] It is indeed impossible to paint a picture of women in relation to their employment, their family life, their participation in public life, their intellectual pursuits, and their political movements without understanding the ongoing indiscriminate violence they and their children suffer at the hands of men. Even though violence has been greatly reduced since the government changeover of 1999, its threat remains, and so does the Family Code.

It is difficult to avoid Western feminist terms such as "domestic violence," "private and public sphere," and "subordination" when describing African women, including Algerians. Ethnocentric bias is further exacerbated by European and U.S. popular opinions that invite the description of violence against women as "Islamic" female victimization without exploring explanatory factors that are rooted in politics and economics. In the same vein, focus on the veil (*hijab*), which Algerian women and girls wear, as a symbol of women's subordination may be misplaced.[5]

EDUCATION

The history of education in Algeria contains periods of frenchification followed by periods of arabification. The ideological battles have left Algeria with a school system that is patterned on the French model. More recently, emphasis has shifted to provision of equal access and government-subsidized free schooling to children aged six to sixteen, and there is draft legislation specifying sanctions for a parent who would prevent access to education for children in that age category.

Opportunities

A high percentage of girls are attending elementary school. According to the Ministry of Education, rates of enrollment of girls have increased significantly since the 1970s. When expressed as the ratio of children of all ages enrolled in primary school to the population of children of primary-school age, primary-school enrollment equals 108, while the secondary-school enrollment ratio is 63. The combined primary- and secondary-school enrollment ratio is 82 percent for girls and 90 percent for boys, and girls' share of second-level enrollment is 48 percent. Compared to other North African countries, this ratio is identical to that of Tunisia and exceeds comparable ratios in Morocco, Egypt, and Ethiopia. Recent trends in the provision of secondary education include increasing the number of boarding schools, secondary institutions in rural areas, and availability of small school buses, thus increasing schooling opportunities for children of nomadic groups in the Sahara. The Ministry of Education recently pointed to plans to purchase several hundred small school buses, with the goal of reducing families' educational expenses and fostering school attendance by girls.[6]

At the higher education level, however, enrollment drops off sharply: only 10 women and 14.7 men per 1,000 are enrolled in institutions of higher learning in Algeria, which compares favorably with neighboring Morocco, but is lower for both sexes than enrollment rates in Tunisia and Egypt.[7] Algeria's forty-eight provinces have a total of twenty-eight universities. Scholarships are available for needy students, but no government effort is applied to increase the percentage of women obtaining access to a university education.

There are several positive indicators of women's importance in providing education to others and obtaining education in fields related to communication. Nearly half of Algeria's schoolteachers are female: 45 percent of primary-school teachers and also 45 percent of secondary-school teachers. Furthermore, women constitute nearly four-fifths of the higher education graduates in the traditional media and information fields.[8] These skills are important when one considers the need for Algeria's women to acquire increased agency and egalitarian citizenship.

Literacy

Illiteracy among Algerian women is still quite high: while only 27 percent of males were illiterate in 1997, the illiteracy rate for women, at 52 percent, was nearly double that.[9]

EMPLOYMENT AND ECONOMICS

Toward the beginning of the third millennium, the Algerian labor force totaled 9.4 million. Of these, 26 percent are agricultural workers, 31 percent are in the industrial sector, and 43 percent are in services. The percentage of women in the labor force rosen from barely 20 percent in 1970 to 21.4 percent in 1980 and 25.7 percent in the mid-1900s.[10] At the same time, the percentage of children aged ten to fourteen has declined from 7.4 percent to only 1 percent of the labor force. Although Algerian women certainly work in the home and perform most of the tasks related to child rearing, food preparation, and housekeeping, the official numbers of unpaid family workers as the share of active workers reflect mostly the work of men (5.6 percent of economically active male workers are unpaid family workers, while less than 1 percent of economically active women are registered as unpaid family workers). Women work mainly in agriculture (57 percent), followed by activity in services (36 percent) and very low participation in industrial jobs (7 percent).[11]

Job/Career Opportunities

Economic opportunities for women in various occupational groups are still quite limited. In 1990, only 6 percent of administrative/managerial positions were held by women. Women made up 38 percent of professional and technical workers, 13 percent of clerical/sales workers, and 23 percent of service workers.[12] Extreme examples of the limitation of opportunities for Algerian women and the denial of their achievements are those of noted author Assia Djebar and Algeria's well-known first Olympic gold medalist, Hassiba Boulmerka.

The international award-winning author Assia Djebar writes autobiographical novels and short stories that reveal the condition of women in her native land, from which she is effectively banned. In her own words, she writes about "women of the Algerian darkness, the new women of contemporary Algiers."[13] In one story, "Blood Does Not Dry on the Tongue," she recounts the murder of Mina, a teacher of French, who received threatening phone calls in 1995 and thought nothing of them. However, teaching French was considered her crime, and several days later she was brutally murdered: "Two unknown men accost her, blocking her way, one on the right and one on the left. Each takes out a gun. Each takes aim, and from very close range, fires at her temple. Mina's head is blown off."[14] Djebar herself has turned to French as the language of her writing. In the preface to her book *Women of Algiers in Their Apartment*, Djebar explains that she translates the voices of the women she has listened to since 1958 from the nonstandard Arabic they spoke into French, which becomes the women's language and stands in opposition to the standard Arabic spoken by the patriarchy.[15]

Despite the repression of women chronicling women's experience during the two Algerian wars and the time between these wars, many women have turned to writing and have revealed women's history in Algeria. Their work shows Algeria as a society that has been to some extent deserted by its men, who went to the front or to prison or were engaged in civil war, and where women have taken things in hand. Their "writings mark the affirmation of women who are freeing themselves from under the authority of men. For women, the tragedy born of the war has been a formidable accelerator of hi/stories."[16]

From the time she was a schoolgirl, Hassiba Boulmerka was determined to set track records. Her dream was realized when she competed in Tokyo and became the world women's 1,500-meter track champion in 1991. She thus became the first African woman to win a world championship gold medal. Upon her return to Algeria, she found not welcome celebrations but a public condemnation (*kofr*) issued by the Islamic fundamentalists for having run the race barelegged.[17] The next year, she captured a gold medal at the Olympic Games in Barcelona, the first in Algeria's history. This did not sway the fundamentalist threat to her safety, and Boulmerka does not go to public places without her bodyguard. She does most of her training abroad these days. She has become a role model for young Algerian and other Arab women and is a frequent public speaker promoting women's sports. Until the late 1990s, however, government funding for women's sports was nonexistent.

Women's employment opportunities are receiving increased attention since Algeria subscribed to the Convention on the Elimination of All Forms of Discrimination against Women (CEDAW). Some temporary measures have been taken recently to increase the presence of women in traditionally male professions, notably a program to increase the number of women in the police force and the armed forces.[18] While such programs are definitely an improvement over the situation in the mid-1990s, they have two continuing shortcomings. First, the effort to create a presence of women in the police force is linked to providing a listening ear for the concerns of battered women, thus relegating such concerns to the realm of "women's"—that is, "less important"—social problems. Second, the policy ignores the historical fact that Algerian women have very much been part of combatant armed forces, but have been denied citizenship and agency in more recent decades.

Pay

According to the permanent representative of Algeria to the United Nations, Algeria is determined to make the equality of women a reality and acknowledges that the Convention on the Elimination of All Forms of Discrimination against Women (CEDAW), which was ratified by Algeria in 1998, has absolute primacy over domestic laws, including the Family Code.[19] However, there are "shortcomings, particularly in the field of employment,"[20] and the poor performance of labor-market participation and pay are blamed on the fact that women "appeared in the marketplace, as in politics, late in the game."[21]

ALGERIA

The 1989 constitution addresses the right to work in Article 52 for all "citoyens," the French word denoting either "all citizens" or "all male citizens," which is not sufficiently strong to ensure women's legal right to work. Nadia Mohand Amer, assistant director for women at the Ministry of Solidarity and the Family, stresses that women are "entitled to the same salaries, rest periods and pensions as their male counterparts" and that those who feel that they have been discriminated against regarding the CEDAW provisions may "address the courts with their complaints." The choice of words demonstrates the reality that first, gender equality in work and pay is far from the reality in Algeria, and second, the courts are not likely to redress these inequalities. The less than equal status of women in relation to both types of work done and pay received is also present in the subtext of the following summary of *Farida Kerkbeb*.

Equal pay, provided by law, has been rigorously and *effectively* applied. Work at home was an income-generating activity which was *not based on a traditional classical work relationship. Statistics, therefore, were not available*, but the Government had noted an increase in the number of women working at home, and had regulated that practice since last December. That type of employment had allowed many women to participate in the economy and reap the *resulting* social and monetary benefits [italics added].[22]

Working Conditions

There is no de jure differential treatment of men and women in the workplace. However, management positions are routinely held by men, and it is unlikely that women in the workplace completely escape the second-class citizenship to which they are relegated in the Family Code. Some social measures have been taken to provide daycare for children of working women.

Sexual Harassment

The legal code addresses the issue of exploitation of human beings, but the reference is to exploitation of "man by man." The Algerian Penal Code provides for the punishment of women's exploitation, and this could also cover sexual harassment and attempts to harass, both of which may be subject to fines or imprisonment.[23] However, due to the double meaning of the terms *hommes* (men or people) and *citoyens* in the French language—they can refer to human beings in the plural or to men only—coupled with the Family Code that subjects women to men in private life, Algerian women do not enjoy full freedom from sexual harassment and assault.

Support for Mothers/Caretakers

No law prevents married women and mothers from working, and the Family Code, while implicitly discouraging women's labor-market participation, does not regulate women's activities in public life. Discrimination according to a person's marital status is prohibited by secular law, but not by religious law.

Maternal Leave

A law provides salary compensation for fourteen weeks of maternity leave.

Daycare

Child-care centers are provided to working women, but primarily in urban settings. The centers are available to all working mothers, including single parents, who represented more than half of Algeria's working women in the late 1990s. Women are also allowed to employ certified daycare personnel in a home-care setting. Moreover, school cafeterias provide opportunities for working women to reconcile work and family obligations.

Family and Medical Leave

No legal act regulates family and medical leave.

Inheritance and Property Rights

The shari'a, the Islamic law, discourages accumulation of wealth and excessive spending. In fact, disaccumulation is encouraged, among other measures, by an inheritance law under which equal shares go to all heirs, with women heirs receiving half shares.[24] Women may own land and wealth under the ruling. In rural Algeria, women may also own and herd camels and small ruminants.

Social/Government Programs

Sustainable Development

The United Nations country report on Algeria, prepared on the occasion of the Johannesburg Summit of 2002, provides detailed information on initiatives that are in the process of being implemented in the various areas of sustainable development. While many of these involve planning for the first several years of the new millennium and have not yet been implemented, several are noteworthy in that they touch upon the daily lives of women and children. Several of the initiatives are the responsibility of the Ministry for Social Affairs and National Solidarity and are part of the economic revitalization plan covering the years 2000–2004. Priority will be given to local and human development, focusing on measures that improve the quality of life of Algerian citizens, such as access to clean water, improvement of the environment, and promotion of women's issues, especially in the area of reproductive health. The provision of 500 school buses for impoverished regions is mentioned as one of the measures that will improve the lives of the rural population.

Welfare

Welfare for women and their families is provided under the auspices of the Ministry of Solidarity and the Family. Funding is provided under the special national solidarity fund. Programs were initiated in the late 1990s to aid in family planning and to provide access to contraception for women who are in a socially vulnerable position. The ministry also manages a number of programs to combat poverty and to provide access to housing for economically deprived families, generally with assistance by local communities.[25]

FAMILY AND SEXUALITY

Evaluation of family life, women's sexuality, their health, and their religion needs to be conducted in relation to the Algerian Family Code. In addition to a summary of the provisions of this code, it is also relevant to provide a statistical portrait of women's sexuality and health. A limited statistical portrait can be established using data from the United Nations and the World Bank.[26]

Gender Roles

Overall, gender roles and rights of ownership are dictated by the Algerian Family Code. Passed in 1984, the code was based on the principle of the shari'a and thus institutionalized inequality between men and women, in defiance of women's constitutional rights. The code essentially defined women's status relative to men's in a manner similar to (and in some ways more repressive than) the rights of Algerian natives during French colonial rule. Under the Family Code, women must have a male guardian (*iwalî*) for the purpose of contracting marriage, and the dowry is defined as a legal requirement to complete the marriage contract. Women can divorce men only under very specific circumstances, while men have much broader bases for divorce.[27] Albeit in an indirect way, the code also makes it possible for a man to divorce by renouncing his wife three times.

In the domestic sphere, women do the majority of the social reproductive work in the family, including cooking, cleaning, child care, and provision of family health. They are not full guardians of their children, and in the public sphere, they are effectively denied political citizenship rights, since the latter are not permitted under the shari'a. Since the passage of the Family Code, Algerian women have thus become subject to two sets of authorities, one secular and the other religious.

Marriage

The mean age at marriage was reported to be twenty-four years of age for women and twenty-eight for men by the World Bank.[28] However, a recent survey reports the mean age of marriage to be 27.6 for women and 31.3 for men, based on data for the year 2000.[29] Regardless of the source used, women definitely marry at a somewhat older age in Algeria than in neighboring countries (at age twenty-two in both Morocco and Egypt, for example). Fathers have custody of the children, although the work of child rearing is done by mothers, and women receive custody only upon the death of their husbands. Under a recent revision of the custody law, women can receive custody of their children when their father has disappeared or is known to have abandoned the family.

Although the shari'a-based Family Code specifies that women's role is in the domestic sphere, secular law does not require women to obtain authorization to look for a job and to be employed. Secular recruitment law provides equal access to women, including those who are married. Moreover, married women have access to social security protection.[30] However, the everyday reality is still that married women need to obtain the permission of their husbands or fathers to seek employment, obtain a loan, start a business, or engage in business travel.

Polygamy, the practice of having more than one mate, seems to be practiced by fewer and fewer men. According to statistics from 2001, 95 percent of households had one married woman present, 4.1 percent had two married women present, and a minor percentage of households had three or four married women present. Not all of these represent polygamous relationships.[31]

Reproduction

The average number of births per woman in Algeria has fallen from approximately six to three in just twenty years. While one explanation of this dramatic reduction has been that women do not need children as much today to help with household tasks because of rising incomes in oil-producing nations,[32] additional factors help explain this decline in Algeria. A fairly high percentage (58 percent) of Algerian women receive prenatal care, and 77 percent deliver their babies with attendance by a skilled professional.[33] Forty-eight percent of babies are exclusively breast-fed until three months of age, and 21 percent are still breastfeeding at twenty to twenty-three months.[34]

Sex Education

No comprehensive data are available on the incidence of sex education in the public school system or by other public methods. The prevalence of AIDS has given rise to government campaigns to encourage the use of condoms as a method of prevention, thereby also providing a form of sex education.

Contraception and Abortion

Algerian women rely on both modern and traditional methods of contraception. As expected, contraception, especially by means of modern methods, is used somewhat more frequently by women in urban areas. A recent survey by the National Institute for Public Health (Institut national de santé publique) revealed that 53 percent of urban women and 48 percent of women in rural areas had used modern contraceptives, including intrauterine devices (IUDs), condoms, spermicidal creams, and oral contraceptives. Traditional methods, including protracted lactation, calendar (rhythm method), and coitus interruptus, had been used by 13.4 percent of urban and 14.5 percent of rural women. At the time of the survey, one out of every three women surveyed did not use contraceptives at all.

As of 1999, it was legally permitted for women to have a therapeutic abortion in three circumstances: to save the woman's life, to preserve her physical health, or to preserve her mental health. Therapeutic abortions must be prescribed by a physician and must be carried out in a medical facility. According to information provided by the Ministry of Health and Population, abortions can only take place with the consent of the "interested party," which may refer to consent by the husband, father, or other legal guardian.

Teen Pregnancy

Although no reliable national data are available on the prevalence of births among unwed teenagers, a survey conducted by the National Institute for Public Health found that 1 percent of married women were 15–19 years of age in the year 2000.

HEALTH

There are fewer women than men in Algeria. Women make up only 49.4 percent of the population, well below the overall African ratio of 50.2

percent, but only slightly below the ratio for the world as a whole (49.9 percent).[35] The slight deficit is likely due to discrimination and neglect of women's health, and to some extent to violence against women, including sexual crimes committed by medical personnel,[36] and female infanticide, although no reliable data exist for its prevalence in Algeria. The recent hearings on Algeria's compliance with the CEDAW mention, however, that discrimination against girls in the provision of vaccination against communicable diseases has lessened.

Health Care Access

Despite the fairly high percentage of women receiving prenatal care and attendance at the time they give birth, maternal mortality, at 220 per 100,000 live births in Algeria, is fairly high in comparison to that in other North African nations. Indeed, while fewer Egyptian women receive prenatal care and deliver in the presence of a qualified attendant, maternal mortality is only 170. Similarly, in neighboring Morocco, where fewer than half of pregnant women receive prenatal care and have a professional present while giving birth, the maternal mortality ratio is only modestly higher (at 230) than in Algeria.[37]

According to the 2001 survey conducted by the National Institute for Public Health (Institut national de santé publique),[38] 43 percent of Algerian women had at least one prenatal consultation with a physician at a public clinic, and 54 percent in a private clinic, while an additional 3 percent had both. The survey also found that 88 percent of women still deliver their babies without medical assistance, and 4 percent do so without any assistance.

Access to pharmaceuticals is still limited, even by prescription. Civil rights lawyer Mahmoud Khelili states, "I don't see the day yet when you can just buy medicine here and not have a friend sneak it into the country for you."[39] This statement also implies that such access is limited to the well-to-do.

Diseases and Disorders

AIDS

To some extent, the number of living adult women relative to men is also influenced by epidemic diseases notably AIDS. The estimated prevalence of HIV/AIDS in adults in 0.07 percent, but no reliable statistics have been published about the differences in the incidence of the disease in men and women. A recently instituted national awareness program alerting the population to the risk of sexually transmitted diseases, advertised both in the workplace and in rural areas, has led to 100 percent increase in condom use among men.

Eating Disorders

There are no nationwide data on eating disorders among Algerian women and girls. The National Institute for Public Health's 2000 survey of the health of mothers and children also did not address eating disorders. While it found that 10 percent of newborns had low birth weight in 1995, which is in part caused by malnutrition of the mother, this condition among mothers was attributed to improper diets due to poverty rather than to eating disorders.

Cancer

Algeria does not participate in the World Health Survey conducted by the World Health Organization, and data on diseases such as breast cancer and cervical cancer are not readily available for the nation as a whole.

Depression

Data on the incidence of depression among women are not readily available for Algeria as a whole. Indirectly, information can be gleaned from the novels of writers like Assia Djebar, whose creative nonfiction addresses personal struggles of women, including depression and its social causes.

POLITICS AND LAW

Algeria is a republic with a socialist legal system that is based on both French and Islamic law. It has a president and a prime minister, a cabinet of ministers who are appointed by the president, and a bicameral parliament, in which several political parties are represented.

Suffrage

Whereas women have the right to vote under the secular law, they are treated as wards without similar rights under religious law. "It is this lack of political personhood with its concomitant lack of agency that paves the way for the violence that has targeted women since 1992 and the redefinition of women's roles in the Islamist discourse since 1989."[40] Abolition of the Family Code can thus be seen as a vital part of women's struggle to obtain full citizenship.

Political Participation

Women are only minimally represented in government. In 1984 the first woman cabinet minister was appointed. In the 1990s several female deputies participated in various political realms but recent Islamic fervor has hampered any progress in this area. Evaluation of women's overall status in relation to the public arena, including their degree of participation in politics, is best conducted in the larger dimension of citizenship and focusing on political liberalization as one of several rights, including the right of cultural expression, freedom of speech, and the right to participate in domestic as well as international associations and organizations.

Women's Rights

Women's legal status and citizenship have changed over the years in relation to successive constitutions and the Family Code. Citizenship is a broad concept, referring to rights that define individual freedom, including the right to personal liberty, freedom of speech, freedom of belief, the right to engage in contracts, the right to own property, and the right to defend all of the aforementioned rights and liberties in an environment of equality with others.[41] This list implies that women's rights and women's agency are a prerequisite to political citizenship. In reviewing the period since Algeria's independence in 1962, it can be seen that all governments have incorporated a dual view of women's rights.[42] The forty-year period can be summarized as follows:

> The extension of formal citizenship to women enabled the state to disregard antinomy between the assertion of equality before the law, a secular requirement of (substantive) citizenship, and inequality between men and women as prescribed by the shari'a. This concept of citizenship simply masked the notion . . . that women are essentially subjects, lacking agency, who must be in the custody of males acting in the name of God.[43]

Gender differences in citizenship are present in the first political text published by the government of free Algeria, La Chartre d'Alger (Algerian Charter) of 1964; in the Code de la nationalité of 1963 and 1970 (Algeria's nationality law); in the successive constitutions (1969, 1976, and 1989); and especially in the Family Code of 1984.

Passed soon after independence, the Algerian Charter outlines Algeria's social and economic problems, as well as socialist policies to solve these problems. Referring to the Algerian people as the "masses," the charter promises that the Front of National Liberation (FLN) — the unifying party during the war for independence — will end exploita-

Algerian women count votes in a polling station in central Algiers, May 2002. AP/Wide World Photos.

tion of "man by man."⁴⁴ In this passage, the term "man by man" was a generic way to denote "human beings," since in the French language, the word for "man" (*homme*) is the same as the word for "human beings" (*les hommes*, plural). However, the charter goes on to describe the social position of Algerian women and thereby defines them as unequal. Women are described as having conducted their struggle for independence side by side with men, a description that validates their activities because men were present, not because of their own agency.⁴⁵ Where the charter addresses the need for women to become men's equals, it does so by means of a vague recommendation that women "should" be able to take part in public and economic activity, while simultaneously failing to guarantee women's civil rights. Furthermore, while the charter mentions the social prejudice against women in retrograde cultural interpretations of Islam, it does not redress these interpretations by legal means.⁴⁶ Women were thus shortchanged overall in the charter, and they also failed to gain egalitarian citizenship in the constitutions that were adopted in later years.

Under President Houari Boumédienne's regime (1965–1978), Algeria's socialism was qualified as being Islamic; that is, God's rule was upheld by the secular state. Women thus became de facto subjects not just of the state, but of the authority of the shari'a. Legislation built on the shari'a, which would eventually become the Family Code, was debated but not passed during Boumédienne's presidency. In 1981, women's rights to travel abroad were restricted, and unemployed women were denied access to passports.⁴⁷ While the 1989 constitution no longer considered women as a category and adopted the French words *citoyen* and *citoyenne* in describing civil rights, it specifically used only the masculine version in Article 52, where the right to work is affirmed, thus permitting an interpretation that only men have this right.

Feminist Movements

A number of political organizations have specifically addressed the needs of women and have served as vehicles of their political mobilization. Some have been more successful than others at achieving this goal. The Union nationale des femmes algériennes (UNFA, National Union of Algerian Women) was established in 1963, at the onset of Algerian independence, as the official agency addressing women's issues. Its stated objectives included the economic emancipation of women, participation by women in the political process, and social protection of mothers, children, and the disabled. In reality, however, it kept women's political emancipation in check, since it "was supposed to keep women informed of the views and decisions of the male leadership of the FLN" while simultaneously diverting their "political activities away from the main power structures which remained male-dominated."⁴⁸

Organized efforts by women to defeat the passage of the Family Code were initiated in 1981 after draft legislation of the code was presented. This led to the formation of Isis, a group that organized street demonstrations and propelled women into political visibility. Its leadership included women who had fought in the independence war (*moudjahidates*), trade-union leaders, and women intellectuals, notably teachers and students. Insisting on a political voice, women's groups staged protests at the entrance to the National Assembly. Although the Family Code was passed nevertheless, these groups were important steps in the political mobilization of women.[49]

More recently, in 1989, the Association pour l'égalité devant la loi entre les hommes et les femmes (Society for the Equality of Men and Women before the Law) was formed. Referred to in abbreviated form as Égalité, this nongovernmental organization (NGO) consolidated thirty women's organization and seeks to eliminate all forms of discrimination.

In September 1995, the Fourth World Conference on Women was held in Beijing, and the Algerian government adopted several measures to improve the lot of women. However, these measures appoint committees to study issues rather than implement true changes. A standing committee was set up, chaired by the minister in charge of national solidarity and the family. The four subcommittees established under the standing committee show the emphasis of policy makers. They were charged with the following areas: legal protection and policy; education, training, and history; health, social affairs, and development; and information, communication, and culture.

The first of these subcommittees was to investigate amending the Family Code of 1984. True empowerment of Algerian women requires abolishment of the code altogether. Instead, the standing committee endeavored to make amendments that "do not conflict in any way with our values or the teachings of our true religion; rather, they derive their strength from these liberal teachings, which are aimed at promoting equality between women and men."

Overall, women's organizations in Algeria suffer from an institutional lack of agency in that they are typically affiliated with some political party. Not only does this lead to a tendency for these organizations to become mouthpieces for more than women's social issues, but they also have to limit the scope of their political activities to those that are sanctioned by their sponsoring political party. As such, several women's associations have packaged their demands for abolition of the Family Code with a demand for adoption of a Kabyle-Berber dialect as a national language of Algeria.[50] Few women's organizations, however, have been able to secure alliances with powerful political parties that make it possible to incorporate socioeconomic issues into the organization's political "packaging," even though poverty, social security, housing, and access to clean water are vital components of women's socioeconomic betterment.

Lesbian Rights

While no laws specifically prohibit the open practice of lesbianism, including marriage and parenthood, the patriarchal nature of Algerian society and the continued influence of the Family Code, which defines women's existence relative to that of men, suggest that lesbian rights are nonexistent and that, at best, tolerance of lesbianism can be expected in time periods when religious fundamentalism is not in the political forefront.

Military Service

Algerian women do not have to serve in the military. They are, however, permitted by secular law to serve in positions in the police force and the military.

RELIGION AND SPIRITUALITY

Women's Roles

Since Islam is the ruling religion in Algeria, it permeates Algerian family life. The family is the basic unit of social life in all Islamic societies, and the family has a patriarchal structure of authority. While the Qur'an specifies that men and women have equal rights in marriage and divorce, it also implies that men are the head of the household, which can easily be interpreted as allowing women to be subjugated to men. According to Qur'anic scholars, the fact that there is no clergy in Islam and that each man can be the religious interpreter for his own household has gradually introduced traditions that permit privileges to men while simultaneously denying them to women.[51] These traditions include the interpretation of the veil as a symbol of men's ownership of women.

The Qur'an also forbids the private acquisition of public goods such as water and pastures. The shari'a fosters humility and moderation. Consumption should not reflect one's means but one's virtue. The lives of Algerian women are affected by the shari'a in two ways: through long-established tradition and through the Family Code of 1984, which subjects them to Islamic as well as secular law, thereby reinforcing the patriarchal structure of family life.

Rituals and Religious Practices

While the well-known rituals and religious practices of Islam are prevalent in Algeria as in other Muslim nations and involve only men, some rural practices related to maraboutism, a type of religious practice associated with mysticism, are conducted by women, especially where they relate to healing. Trance dancing is still performed by Islamic sects for purposes of healing and exorcism of evil spirits. Both men and women participate in the dancing, sometimes accompanied by drummers whose leaders may include elderly women who recite religious litanies.[52]

Religious Law

Today's Algeria is an Arab nation as well as an Islamic nation. This has not always been the case. When Arabs invaded this region of North Africa in the seventh century, they found a people that was under Roman rule and had largely adopted its state religion of Christianity.[53] The Berbers who lived in the Kabyle region in central Algeria did not convert to Christianity and instead practiced the religion of Donatism, which focused on egalitarianism and communalism. While this first Arab invasion introduced Islam as the new state religion, the later migrations into the region by nomadic Arab tribes were the ones that gradually Islamicized the Berber people, a nomadic tribe usually found in the Sahara. Berbers were taken by the Sufi (Muslim mystics and ascetics) brotherhoods, called *marabouts* in the Maghreb, who emphasized ecstatic worship. *Marabouts* and the descendants of the prophet Muhammad (*shurama*) gave rise to the rulers of Arab-Berber tribes.[54] Three centuries of Ottoman rule of the region ended in 1830 with the French invasion and concomitant dismantling of Muslim institutions. In 1881, the Code de l'indigénat, a collection of laws applying to Muslims, made several Muslim practices illegal, including the teaching of children without state authorization. Muslim education became strictly regulated and limited to only a few schools.[55]

Not surprisingly, a nationalist movement, called the Islamic Reform Movement, emerged after World War I under the leadership of Algerian Islamic scholars (*ulamas*). It stressed the need for Algeria to return to the roots of Islam while simultaneously adopting modernism under the motto "Islam is my religion; Arabic is my language; Algeria is my fatherland."[56] Following independence, only a minority of Algerians retained Christianity as their religion, and Islam again became the state religion. The main variant of Islam practiced in Algeria is Sunnism. Since the early years of independence, organized forms of political Islam have emerged. The Islamic Salvation Front (FIS), which became the major fundamentalist party in Algeria, evolved from the postindependence organization al-Qiyam (the values), which sought to eliminate all non-Islamic cultural influences and to establish a strict Islamic moral code as the foundation of the new Algerian legal system. Although this group was banned by Boumédienne in 1966, Islamic fundamentalism gained momentum in the years following the Islamic Revolution of Iran, which took place in 1979, and the FIS was established as a political party in 1989. Other religious political parties included the right-wing Movement of Islamic Resistance (Hamas) and the left-wing Armed Islamic Group (GIA), the latter of which is a party that broke away from FIS following the 1992 military coup. The GIA has declared war not only against the government, but also against members of the general population who are seen as lacking in dedication to Islam. Women who do not wear the veil or show modesty of dress (*hijab*) in public or who seem to be insufficiently Islamic in other ways—for example, in their employment—have especially been targeted.[57] Popular Islam in Algeria traditionally has also been strongly associated with maraboutism. Since the rise of Islamic fundamentalism in the late twentieth century, maraboutism has been attacked as anti-Islam and has retained importance mostly in the countryside.

VIOLENCE

Several types of violence against Algerian women have been documented: torture and killing during revolutionary and civil wars, mutilation and domestic repression at the hands of men, and relegation to second-class citizenship under the Family Code. Since the 1970s, the main threat of violence against women has come from the rise of politicized religious fundamentalism, which strives to theocratize the government by means of a campaign of violence and atrocities against the civilian population, particularly against women.[58] Attacks against women are not publicized, and the international community focuses its attention on attacks by the state against fundamentalist insurgents. Hence feminist movements are being progressively undermined. Since the 1970s, Algerian fundamentalists have strategically attacked female activists, female students, and women living without a male guardian (*iwalii*). They were successful in forcing the government to enact the regressive Family Code, which treats women as minors. Women's loss of citizenship resulting from the code has become a backdrop against which violence against women has been undertaken since 1992. Whereas Islamic militarized political factions have been blamed for the numerous massacres that have been committed, the murder of women has become almost sanctioned due to their lack of legal citizenship. That is, once women's political person had been "killed" by the Family Code, it became a relatively small step to also kill their physical person. It has been noted that "[the] progression from lacking political personhood to being a subject in family law and, finally, to losing one's life for the establishment of the kingdom of God is both logical and inescapable. Women have become one of the wrongs to be righted as a matter of duty to God."[59]

Rape/Sexual Assault

A form of violence against women that has been enabled, though not fully legalized, by women's loss of citizenship is the practice of temporary marriage (*muta'a*) a shari'a Muslim practice that is common in Iran. It is used to effectively institute the practice of sexual slavery in Algeria. In the late 1990s, it was not uncommon for men to attack a village and abduct the most physically beautiful of the village's women to their hiding place. The French newspaper *Le Monde* has reported this form of violence against women and has condemned the violent political factions that engage in it, citing in particular the group Men Angry with God. The stated goal of this group is to punish God because he did not let them be victorious against the secular government. Since God cannot be punished directly, their violence is directed against human beings, especially women and children.

Threats of violence and second-class-citizen status under the Family Code have not served to transform all Algerian women into a mass of invisibles who work and hide in their homes. Many women continue to live their lives as professionals or in occupations that are not considered suitable for women by the religious patriarchy. In looking for suitable terms to describe these women, one may consider words like "maverick," "freedom fighter," or "feminist." It is difficult to categorize women who are like the woman cabby, the woman athlete, the rappers, and the writer of creative nonfiction, some of whose stories have been briefly mentioned in this chapter. They transcend violence and repression by living their lives as if these practices do not exist and hence practice liberation and emancipation of the Algerian woman.

One such woman is Soumicha, the subject of a recent documentary film directed by Belkacem Hadjadj.[60] Faced with the prospect of having to support her three children after her husband died, Soumicha became a taxi driver in Sidi Bel-Abbès, in defiance of the distinct possibility of being murdered by Islamic fundamentalists or political extremists. In the course of her visible job, driving a yellow French compact car, she interacts with other women, several of whom are political activists struggling to expand women's rights. Soumicha's story reveals some of the contradictions in today's Algerian society. While simultaneously criticizing working women, some men are relieved to have their wives and daughters ride in a taxi driven by a woman. Other men and women are openly supportive of Soumicha. At the end of the documentary, a rumor that the female cabby has been murdered turns out to be just a warning from extremists. Undaunted, Soumicha continues to drive passengers to destinations in Sidi Bel-Abbès and surrounding towns.

Trafficking in Women and Children

The practice of trafficking in women and children is illegal under the Penal Code. However, during the years of violence by Islamic fundamentalists in the 1990s, the temporary or trial marriage was used as a justification for the kidnapping and sexual exploitation of women and girls. Since Algeria has ratified the CEDAW, this illegal practice is counter to both domestic and international law.

War and Military Repression

Algerian women participated in direct combat during the Algerian war and were active in providing safe havens for guerrilla fighters. Many of those who were captured were tortured (by electrical shock and other methods) and guillotined in prisons. Others have been assassinated by their previous "brothers in combat," and all have been ignored in the recording of history, which is written by the survivors in general, and particularly by those holding social and political power. As was the case with women in the nationalist movements and wars in other countries, notably France in the 1789 revolution and in World War II and in Greece and Ireland in the nineteenth century, Algerian women have participated and yet have been excluded from egalitarian citizenship.

In a published selection of testimonies of eighty-eight women interviewed between 1978 and 1986, Danièle Amrane reveals shocking accounts of women who fought as guerrillas and were captured, tortured, and killed, or, if they survived, were forced back into a strictly domestic sphere, where they were ruled by husbands and brothers. This is what happened, for example, to Fatima Baichi, who, inspired by nationalist ideas, helped turn the house she shared with three brothers into a refuge for the revolutionaries (*feddayin*) in the Algerian war.[61] Arrested in 1957, she was imprisoned and tortured. When she was released three years later, she was forced by her own family into a traditional marriage. Even her younger brother, who had been her fellow combatant during the Algerian War, encouraged her husband to prohibit her from leaving the house. Only in the 1980s, after her two daughters became adults, did Baichi recapture some of her earlier independence, and she became reacquainted with other women who had shared a similar lot. She has since been active in movements to fight for women's rights and for the abolition of torture.

OUTLOOK FOR THE TWENTY-FIRST CENTURY

In some respects, the outlook for Algerian women in the decades to come hinges on global economics. It could be argued that the collapse of Algeria's oil revenues during the recessions of the industrialized nations in the last quarter of the twentieth century helped establish politicized Islamism and other movements reversing democratization, which in turn reinforced measures limiting women's citizenship. In a very real sense, then, globalization is at least partly to blame for diminishing Algerian women's civil rights. However, globalization may begin to exert a positive impact when the attention of the international community turns away from simplified interpretations of Muslim nations of the Middle East toward a more humanistic understanding of the Islamic world and its people. However, it would be wrong to see solutions to Algeria's gendered social problems as subject to international control. Rather, the international community needs to play a role that continues the efforts of Beijing+5 (a population conference on women), provides access for Algerian women and egalitarian men to nongovernmental organizations, and promotes opportunities for Algerian women to study, publish, travel, and perform outside as well as inside Algeria's borders. Most important, however, the courageous acts of women and men living their lives as equals despite the Family Code and the increasingly sophisticated and well-organized women's movements and feminist networking by Algerian women and men will be the main driving force leading to the acquisition of basic civil rights and political freedoms of Algerian women in this decade and the next.

NOTES

1. One kilometer equals approximately 0.6 miles.
2. Most of the statistical information available is from World Bank, *African Development Indicators 2000* (Washington, DC: World Bank, 2000) (hereafter cited as World Bank, *ADI 2000*), and United Nations, *World Economic and Social Survey 2001: Trends and Policies in the World Economy* (New York: United Nations, 2001).
3. Data for 1996 from World Bank, *ADI 2000*, 317.
4. *Shadow Report on Algeria to the Committee on the Elimination of Discrimination against Women*, report submitted to CEDAW by the International Women's Human Rights Law Clinic (IWHR) and by Women Living under Muslim Laws (WLUML), January 1999 (London: WLUML, February 2002), 3.
5. As a striking example, one may point to the fact that French charities in late-nineteenth-century Algeria would provide free oil and floor space to poor indigenous women, but under the condition that they remove their veil. Women who did this were not liberated from subjugation, but were used by the French colons (colonials) to interfere with Algerian customs. Nicole Gaouette, "Voices from behind the Veil," *Christian Science Monitor*, December 19, 2001.
6. Statement by Leila Boumghar, advisor to the Ministry of Education. See United Nations, press release WOM/1085, 412th Meeting (AM), January 26, 1999, 6–7.
7. United Nations, *The World's Women 2000: Trends and Statistics* (New York: United Nations, 2000), 103.
8. World Bank, *ADI 2000*, 325.
9. Ibid.
10. Ibid., 275–78.
11. Ibid., 275.
12. Ibid., 337.
13. Assia Djebar, "Blood Does Not Dry on the Tongue," *Research in African Literatures* 30 (fall 1999): 18–22.
14. Ibid., 1–2.
15. Assia Djebar, *Women of Algiers in Their Apartment*, trans. Marjolijn de Jager (Charlottesville: University Press of Virginia, 1992). First published in French in 1980.
16. Benjamin Stora, "Women's Writing between Two Algerian Wars," *Research in African Literatures* 30 (fall 1999).
17. Paul Gains, "Hassiba Boulmerka, Algeria," *Women's Sports and Fitness* 19 (October 1997): 65.
18. See comments by Hind Benhassine, deputy director for prospective studies,

Ministry of Civil Service and Administrative Reform, United Nations, press release WOM/1085, 412th Meeting (AM), January 26, 1999.

19. Abdallah Baali speaking to the United Nations committee considering compliance by Algeria with the Anti-Discrimination Convention, United Nations, press release WOM/1085, 412th Meeting (AM), January 26, 1999.

20. Ibid., 2.

21. Ibid., 3.

22. Inspector-General, Ministry of Labour, Social Protection, and Professional Training, replying to questions concerning equal employment, United Nations, press release WOM/1085, 412th Meeting (AM), January 26, 1999, 7.

23. Nadia Benabdellah, advisor to the Ministry of Justice, United Nations, press release WOM/1085, 412th Meeting (AM), January 26, 1999, 6.

24. The shari'a is an Islamic law, according to which men occupy a higher rung on the social hierarchy ladder than do women, and this superiority is transmitted to laws and regulations that make men into the legal guardians of women and impose limitations on the rights of women in relation to their own civic life and their children and family. Reliance on the shari'a effectively turns women into subjects.

25. Information provided by Nadia Mohand Amer, assistant director for women at the Ministry of Solidarity and the Family, United Nations, press release WOM/1085, 412th Meeting (AM), January 26, 1999, 4.

26. United Nations, *World Economic and Social Survey 2001* and *The World's Women 2000*; World Bank, *ADI 2000*.

27. This provision also existed in the Napoleonic Code, which has been the foundation for family law in France and Belgium. Until rather recently, a man could divorce his wife for a number of reasons, including adultery, while a wife could only obtain a contested divorce if her husband had committed adultery in their conjugal bed.

28. World Bank, *ADI 2000*.

29. Institut national de santé publique (National Institute for Public Health), *Enquête nationale sur les objectifs de la fin décennie: Santé mère et enfant* (Algiers: Institut national de santé publique, 2001).

30. United Nations, press release WOM/1085, 412th Meeting (AM), January 26, 1999, 6–7.

31. Institut national de la santé publique, 2001.

32. See the section on demographic transition in Economic Research Forum, *Economic Trends in the MENA Region* (Cairo, Egypt: American University in Cairo Press, 2002).

33. For North Africa overall, 65 percent of pregnant women receive prenatal care, 57 percent of deliveries take place in health facilities, and 66 percent of deliveries are attended by a skilled professional. United Nations, *The World's Women 2000*, 61.

34. World Bank, *ADI 2000*, 324.

35. Data for 1996, World Bank, *ADI 2000*, 317.

36. As mentioned by Nadia Benabdella, advisor to the Ministry of Justice, United Nations, press release WOM/1085, 412th Meeting (AM), January 26, 1999, 6.

37. United Nations, *The World's Women 2000*, 79.

38. Published in 2001.

39. Quoted in Suzanne Daley, "Algerians Seek Something More Than Survival," *New York Times*, December 14, 2001.

40. Marnia Lazreg, "Citizenship and Gender in Algeria," in *Gender and Citizenship in the Middle East*, ed. Sued Joseph (Syracuse, NY: Syracuse University Press, 2000), 65.

41. Ibid., 59.
42. Ibid., 60.
43. Ibid.
44. *La Chartre d'Alger* (Alger: FLN Commission Centrale d'Orientation, 1964), 63.
45. See, for example, Lazreg, 2000, 62.
46. *Chartre*, 1964, 82.
47. Lazreg, 2000, 64.
48. Catherine Lloyd, "Organising across Borders: Algerian Women's Associations in a Period of Conflict," *Review of African Political Economy* 26 (December 1999): 482.
49. Ibid., 483.
50. Lazreg, 2000, 69.
51. Ibid., 68.
52. One such ceremony is described by Boutheina Cheriet, "Gender, Civil Society, and Citizenship in Algeria," *Middle East Report* 198 (January–March 1996).
53. James Ciment, *Algeria: The Fundamentalist Challenge* (New York: Facts on File, 1997), 26.
54. Ibid., 27.
55. Ibid., 33.
56. Ibid., 35.
57. Ibid., 96.
58. *Shadow Report on Algeria*, 2002, 5.
59. As explained by Lazreg, 2000, 67.
60. *A Female Cabby in Sidi Bel-Abbès*, 2000.
61. Danièle Djamila Amrane-Minne, *Des femmes dans la guerre d'Algérie* (Paris: Editions Karthala, 1994), 111–27.

RESOURCE GUIDE

Suggested Reading

Amrane-Minne, Danièle Djamila. "Women and Politics in Algeria from the War of Independence to Our Day." *Research in African Literatures* 30 (fall 1999): 62–77.
Bennoune, Karima. "Algerian Women Confront Fundamentalism." *Monthly Review* 35 (September 1994): 26.
Bouatta, C. *Evolution of the Women's Movement in Contemporary Algeria: Organization, Objectives, and Prospects*. World Institute for Development Economics Research, Research Paper 124 (United Nations University, 1997).
Djebar, Assia. "Blood Does Not Dry on the Tongue." *Research in African Literatures* 30 (fall 1999): 18–22.
Joseph, Suad, ed. *Gender and Citizenship in the Middle East*. Foreword by Deniz Kandiyoti. Syracuse, NY: Syracuse University Press, 2000.
Lazreg, Marnia. "Citizenship and Gender in Algeria." In *Gender and Citizenship in the Middle East*, ed. Suad Joseph, 58–69. Syracuse, NY: Syracuse University Press, 2000.
Lloyd, Catherine. "Organising across Borders: Algerian Women's Associations in a Period of Conflict." *Review of African Political Economy* 26 (December 1999): 479–90.
Sylvester, Christine. "African and Western Feminisms: World-Traveling the Tendencies and Possibilities." *Signs* 20(4) (1995): 941–69. Reprinted in *Theorizing Femi-*

nism: Parallel Trends in the Humanities and Social Sciences, ed. Anne C. Herrmann and Abigail J. Stewart. 2nd ed. Boulder, CO: Westview Press, 2001.

Videos/Films

Algeria: Women at War. 1992. Video produced by Parminder Vir. 52 minutes, color, VHS (England). Produced for Channel 4 TV, this documentary combines interviews with archival footage to document the position of women in Algeria under the rise of Islamic fundamentalism and escalating political violence.

A Female Cabby in Sidi Bel Abbès. 2000. Documentary directed by Belkacem Hadjadj. 52 minutes, color. This film tells the story of Soumicha, a mother of three, who became a taxi driver to earn a living after her husband's death.

Love and Marriage. 2001. Filmmakers: Samia Chala (Algeria) and Muriel Aboulrouss (Lebanon). Producers: Deborah Davies, Daoud Kuttab, and Ilan Ziv. Arab Diaries Series. 26 minutes, color. In this film, the beauty salon is portrayed as a social sphere in Algeria where women can have free conversations about their lives.

Youth. 2001. Filmmakers: Samia Chala (Algeria) and Muriel Aboulrouss (Lebanon). Producers: Deborah Davies, Daoud Kuttab, and Ilan Ziv. Arab Diaries Series. 26 minutes, color. This film tells the story of the two female performers of the Algerian rap group called The Messengers, whose improvised lyrics are a vehicle for social and political dissent, carried out against the backdrop of Islamic violence.

Web Sites

Amazigh, www.amazigh.co.uk/.
General portal web sites dealing with Algeria, with special focus on Amazigh (Berber) culture.

Algeria Daily, www.algeriadaily.com.
A general web site for the latest news, current events, and general information about Algeria.

Algeria-Watch, www.algeria-watch.org.
A web site containing information and articles on human rights violations in Algeria since 1992.

Algeria Watch International, www.pmwatch.org/awi/.
Lists a variety of Algerian associations abroad, as well as news items, basic country facts, human rights reports, women's rights organizations, a great number of articles, and bibliographies. Algeria Watch International can be contacted at the following email address: awi@zworg.com.

Flamme, www.flamme.org/documents/algeria.html.
Summary of measures in Algeria in relation to the Fourth World Conference on Women.

International Planned Parenthood Federation, Algeria profile, http://ippfnet.ippf.org/pub/IPPF_Regions/IPPF_CountryProfile.asp?ISOCode=DZ.

Summarizes the state of sexual and reproductive health of the population and introduces Algeria's Association for Family Planning (Association algérienne pour la planification familiale, or AAPF).

Newstrove, www.newstrove.com/content/algeria.
In addition to providing an archive on current Algerian news, this web site also has useful links to other web sites and to books. It is not gender specific.

Women Living under Muslim Laws, www.wluml.org.
This web site describes the organization, posts calls for action, and provides useful links and a list of publications. See list of organizations for contact information.

Organizations

Arab Women Speak Out (AWSO)
111 Market Place, Suite 310
Baltimore, MD 21202, USA
Phone: (410) 659–6300
Fax: (410) 659–6266
Email: webadmin@jhuccp.org
Web site: www.jhuccp.org

An advocacy and training program, initiated in 1999 as a joint effort of the Johns Hopkins University Center for Communication Programs (JHU/CCP) and the Center for Arab Training and Research. AWSO empowers women in the Middle East to achieve their goals despite obstacles of lack of education, socioeconomic deprivation, and political opposition.

Association algérienne pour la planification familiale (AAPF, Algerian Association for Family Planning)
P.O. Box 107
Alger, Algeria
Phone: 213 (2) 540489
Fax: 213 (2) 540489
Email: aapf@wissal.dz

Founded in 1987, this organization focuses on disseminating information and education, directed especially toward young women in underprivileged rural areas. The organization collaborates with religious and political leaders to ensure their support.

Association indépandante pour le triomphe des droits des femmes
26 Boulevard Mohamed V
Alger 16000, Algeria
Phone: 213 (2)-736220

Femmes sous lois musulmanes, réseau international de solidarité (WLUML, Women Living under Muslim Laws)
Coordination office for Africa and the Middle East

P.O. Box 73630
Victoria Island, Lagos, Nigeria
Email: baobab@baobabwomen.org

An international solidarity network, providing information and support for women living in environments ruled by laws and customs said to be rooted in Islam. The network's goal is to empower women engaged in struggles in Muslim countries by providing them with direct support and a liaison for them with feminist organizations.

SEVE (Association savoir et vouloir entreprendre)
30 Rue Rahmoun Dekkars El Biar
Alger, Algeria
Phone: 213 (2) 799395
Fax: 2922498

Union nationale des femmes algériennes (UNFA, National Union of Algerian Women). This organization was created by the government in 1962 to mobilize the support of women for the socialist movement. It never became a union of feminists, nor did it attract many women from rural areas.

SELECTED BIBLIOGRAPHY

Best, Victoria. "Between the Harem and the Battlefield: Domestic Space in the Work of Assia Djebar." *Signs* 37 (spring 2002): 873–79.
La Chartre d'Alger. Alger: FLN Commission Centrale d'Orientation, 1964.
Cheriet, Boutheina. "Gender, Civil Society, and Citizenship in Algeria." *Middle East Report* 198 (January–March 1996): 22–26.
Ciment, James. *Algeria: The Fundamentalist Challenge*. New York: Facts on File, 1997.
Daley, Suzanne. "Algerians Seek Something More Than Survival." *New York Times*, December 14, 2001.
Djebar, Assia. *Women of Algiers in Their Apartment*. Translated by Marjolijn de Jager. Charlottesville: University Press of Virginia, 1992. First published in French in 1980.
Economic Research Forum. *Economic Trends in the MENA Region*. Cairo, Egypt: American University in Cairo Press, 2002.
Gains, Paul. "Hassiba Boulmerka, Algeria." *Women's Sports and Fitness* 19 (October 1997): 65–66.
Gaouette, Nicole. "Voices from behind the Veil." *Christian Science Monitor*, December 19, 2001.
Heradstveit, Daniel. *Political Islam in Algeria*. Oslo, Norway: NUPI, 1998.
Herrmann, Anne C., and Abigail J. Stewart, eds. *Theorizing Feminism: Parallel Trends in the Humanities and Social Sciences*. 2nd ed. Boulder, CO: Westview Press, 2001.
Joseph, Suad, ed. *Gender and Citizenship in the Middle East*. Foreword by Deniz Kandiyoti. Syracuse, NY: Syracuse University Press, 2000.
Lazreg, Marnia. 1994. "Algerian Women in Question." In *The Eloquence of Silence: Algerian Women in Question*, ed. M. Lazreg, 216–17. New York: Routledge, 1994.
Martinez, Luis. *The Algerian Civil War, 1990–1998*. London: Hurst, in association with the Centre d'études et de recherches internationales, Paris, 1998.
Nations Unies (United Nations). *Sommet de Johannesburg 2002: Profil de l'Algérie*.

United Nations Publications, no. CP2002. New York: United Nations, 2002. Available in English.

Philibert, Celine. "Memory Process and Feminine Desire in Claire Denis' *Chocolat* and Brigitte Rouan's *Outremer*." *Journal of Third World Studies* 13 (fall 1996): 173–87.

Shadow Report on Algeria to the Committee on the Elimination of Discrimination against Women. Report submitted to CEDAW by the International Women's Human Rights Law Clinic (IWHR) and by Women Living under Muslim Laws (WLUML), January 1999. WLUML, February 2002.

Stora, Benjamin. *Algeria 1830–2000: A Short History*. Ithaca, NY: Cornell University Press, 2001.

———. "Women's Writing between Two Algerian Wars." *Research in African Literatures* 30 (fall 1999): 78–94.

United Nations. Press Release WOM/1085, 412th Meeting (AM), January 26, 1999.

———. "Twelfth Periodic Reports of States Parties Due in 1995: Algeria (State Party Report)." In *International Convention on the Elimination of All Forms of Racial Discrimination (CERD)*. United Nations Publications, no. 05/06/06. CERD/C/280/Add.3. New York: United Nations, 2001.

———. *World Economic and Social Survey 2001: Trends and Policies in the World Economy*. United Nations Publications, no. E.01.II.C.1. New York: United Nations, 2001.

———. *The World's Women 2000: Trends and Statistics*. United Nations Publications, no. E.00.XVII.14. New York: United Nations, 2000.

World Bank. *African Development Indicators 2000* (ADI 2000). Washington, DC: World Bank, 2000.

French Bibliography

Algeria Watch. *Algerien, 10 Jahre nach dem Putsch: Eine erschreckende Bilanz der Menschenrechtslage*. Report of January 11, 2002.

Amrane-Minne, Danièle Djamila. *Des femmes dans la guerre d'Algérie*. Preface by Michèle Perrot. Paris: Éditions Karthala, 1994.

Auclert, Hubertine. *Les femmes arabes en Algérie*. Paris: Société d'Éditions Litéraires, 1900.

Belkaïd, Malika Lemdani. *Normaliennes en Algérie*. Paris and Montréal: Editions l'Harmattan, 1998.

Bretin, Hélène. *Contraception, quel choix pour quelle vie? Récits de femmes, paroles de médecins*. Paris: Institut national de la santé et de la recherche médicale: Documentation française, 1992.

Faulkner, Rita A. "Assia Djebar, Frantz Fanon, Women, Veils, and Land." *World Literature Today* 70 (Autumn, 1996): 847–55.

Gacemi, Baya. "Hopes and Lost Illusions." *Le monde diplomatique* (October 1997): 1–7. http:/MondeDiplo.com/1997/10/alger3.

Guedj, Eliaou Gaston. *L'enseignement indigène en Algérie au cours de la colonisation, 1832–1962*. Paris: Éditions des Écrivains, 2000.

Institut national de santé publique. *Enquête nationale sur les objectifs de la fin décennie: santé mère et enfant*. Algiers: Institut national de santé publique, 2001.

2

BAHRAIN

Sandra Lee

PROFILE OF BAHRAIN

Bahrain is a small archipelago composed of thirty-three islands located in the Persian Gulf. Six islands—Bahrain, Muharraq, Sitra, Nebih Salih, Jidda, and Umm an-Nasaan—are the principal islands of the group. The meaning of "Bahrain," or "al-Bahrain" in Arabic, is the "two seas." The capital is Manama, located on the main island of Bahrain. The al-Khalifa family has ruled Bahrain since 1782. The country gained independence from Great Britain on August 15, 1971. Islamic tradition and colonial influence are reflected in the legal system. The governing constitution and court system, for example, combine both Islamic law and English common law. The religion of the local population is Muslim. Seventy percent are Shi'i Muslims, and 30 percent are Sunni Muslims.

Bahrain is considered to be one of the more cosmopolitan countries in the region of the Gulf, and the discovery of oil and the resulting quickly expanding economy have dramatically shifted and influenced political and societal issues, traditional ways of life, job occupations, and the role of women in society. The country has attempted to modernize and industrialize while still trying to preserve its heritage and customs.

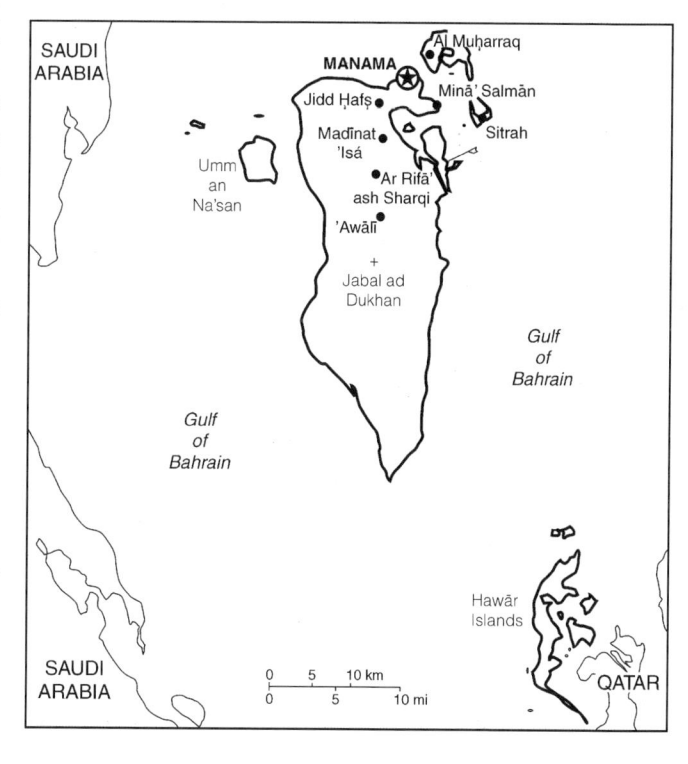

This has created obstacles for policies and economic development. These changes are currently affecting historical traditions and also the lives of many women.

According to recent information, the population of Bahrain is estimated to be 645,361. Of the population, 29.6 percent is below the age of fourteen (of whom 96,697 are male and 94,330 are female); 67.43 percent are between the ages of fifteen and sixty-four (of whom 257,360 are male and 177,839 are female); and 2.97 percent are sixty-five years of age or older (of whom 9,721 are male and 9,414 are female).[1] The infant mortality rate is 19.77 deaths per 1,000 live births, while the birth rate is 20.07 births per 1,000 people. The total fertility rate is 2.79 children per woman. Life expectancy in Bahrain is projected to be at an average of seventy-three years. The average life expectancy for men is seventy years, while the life expectancy for women is seventy-six years.

OVERVIEW OF WOMEN'S ISSUES

Women in Bahrain consist of nearly half of the national indigenous population. This also takes into account the number of foreigners that are currently living in the country.

Women in Bahrain have begun demanding political and civil rights. More women in Bahrain have been holding jobs and completing higher levels of education. Opportunities for receiving education have expanded since independence from Great Britain, but the presence of foreign workers has increased competition in the job market. Besides issues of employment, women in Bahrain have faced political constraints from the government.

Bahrain has undergone significant changes at a fast rate, such as population growth; the growing need for better education and job training; and disturbed family relationships as traditional roles and family patterns alter. In a small country such as Bahrain, such changes cannot occur without impacting the society and lifestyles of families and individuals.

EDUCATION

Public education began in 1919, earlier than in any other Gulf state. The first girls' school in the Gulf was established in Bahrain in 1928, although the first girls' primary school had been established in 1892 by the American Arabian Mission. Between 1931 and 1983, investment in public education increased dramatically, and the number of enrolled students increased.[2] The number of students enrolled in schools increased from 500 boys and 100 girls in 1931 to 1,750 boys and 1,288 girls in 1946. Education at the secondary and university levels expanded during the 1970s both for boys and girls. By 1974, the numbers had increased significantly to 30,302 boys and 23,459 girls, about a quarter of the total population at the time. The number of enrolled students kept rising until it reached a total of 78,797 (41,477 boys and 37,320 girls) aged six to twenty-one years in 1983–1984.[3] The University of Bahrain was founded on May 24, 1986, after Shaikh Isa Bin Salman al-Khalifa issued a decree merging the Gulf Polytechnic School, founded in 1968, and the University College of Bahrain, founded in 1978.

Although there was a significant rise in the number of students enrolled, inadequacies in the educational system have prevented it from being effective. For example, nearly half of the school-age population between five and twenty-four years of age did not attend school in 1971. One of the problems facing women has been that the standards of education have not been able to meet the standards needed for many jobs.

Opportunities

Women's education and the goal of increasing the number of educated women continue to be important issues for many women in Bahrain. Traditionally, education was not accessible for many women. The ability to receive a decent education is seen as one of the first and most crucial steps for liberating women and allowing them to function in society. There has been a large effort to try to find various ways for more women to receive an education.

Receiving an adequate education is crucial to enabling Bahraini women to change existing societal norms and political constraints. One of the most important benefits in receiving a minimal level of high-school education is the ability to participate and compete in the job market and thus become financially independent. Studies and data indicate that a strong correlation exists between the level of female literacy and the access of women to the labor market.

Several factors exist that prevent women from education. Females in Bahrain tend to marry early and are expected to look after family members and do a large share of housework. If there are financial constraints on a family, parents tend to prefer to provide education to the boys over the girls in the family.

Literacy

The illiteracy rate was 12.3 percent in 2001. The government was not able to eradicate illiteracy by the year 2000, as it previously announced it would do. Nationalization of thousands of foreigners with their families—most of whom are illiterates or non-Arab speaking—is the main factor causing this discrepancy.

Illiteracy in Bahrain is predominantly based upon class and gender. Eighty percent of illiterate people aged ten to forty-four years are females.[4] But women have been able to make substantial gains in education. The illiteracy rate fell from 41 percent in 1980 to 19 percent in 1998.

While the rate of illiteracy fell overall in the latter half of the twentieth century, it fell within the female school-age population. There is an apparent link between literacy and those women who are working. Illiterate females have the lowest rates of participation in the labor force, whereas those who complete basic educational programs or beyond have dramatically higher rates of participation.[5]

Illiteracy imposes many constraints on adults. It creates a large obstacle to the participation of large sections of society in development. Due to the realization that economic development and industrialization were in part affected by illiteracy, a group of volunteers started a literacy campaign in Bahrain in the early 1940s. They opened literacy classes for seventy adult students. In the 1960s, more classes were opened for males and females, and later, a committee was formed to evaluate and supervise literacy activities.

In 1971, the Ministry of Education took the responsibility for literacy education and since then has attempted to implement literacy programs. The ministry implemented a five-year plan from 1983 to 1989 with the main goal being to eradicate illiteracy for the entire population of Bahrain aged ten to forty-four years.[6] The literacy campaign was funded by three main sources: the Arab Gulf Program for UN Development Organizations, the Islamic Charity Funds (Waaf), and the Arabic Fund for Literacy and Adult Education. The funding received from these organizations was intended to build up necessary infrastructure, educational projects, and literacy programs.

Overall the program did not meet its objectives, and a survey done by An-Nadha Women's Association assessed the literacy program and formulated suggestions for its improvement. It was determined that the curriculum, especially math, English, and handicrafts, needed alteration. An-Nadha also suggested that transportation for students be provided and more extensive use of audiovisual aids be implemented.

A literacy program's success depends on the expertise and cooperation of those who are supporting the program—training staff, administrators, teachers, and field workers. A center for training staff for adult education was established in 1977 in Bahrain. This is the regional center for a literacy center based in Iraq and is part of the Arab League. Adequate training of personnel is important not only to ensure a better quality of education but also to make them aware of obstacles that face those who must learn how to read and write. People who work in the literacy program have to mobilize the learners and their community and to organize local resources for the program.[7] Motivation, participation, and coordination are very important in literacy programs and adult education. Those who work in literacy programs must learn or have knowledge of adult psychology and adult learning behavior.

Success depends on the efforts of citizens and nongovernmental organizations (NGOs) joining the work toward greater literacy. In addition to the government's efforts at eradicating illiteracy, women's associations have played an important role in the campaign as well. One of their main focuses has been on teaching illiterate females. Besides providing facilities or training personnel, these associations focus on raising awareness among illiterate females living in villages or providing classes that can be taught for women by women from these associations. Many women's organizations have participated in literacy programs since the 1960s. An-Nadha Women's Association opened literacy classes in 1961, followed in 1963 by the Child and Mother Welfare Association. The Awal Women's Association also joined in teaching illiterate women in 1970.

EMPLOYMENT AND ECONOMICS

Oil and trade currently contribute the most to the Bahraini economy. Bahrain has also become an important financial center, and the banking market has increased significantly. Although tourism is newer to the country, it has received increasing attention from the government.

Before the discovery of oil, Bahrain's economy mainly relied on pearl diving and agriculture, but its location in the Persian Gulf led to the development of a rich and historical tradition built upon trade. The cultivation of dates and boat building sustained Bahrain's economy for centuries. As early as the third millennium, records exist describing local tribes or villages subsisting on date cultivation, boat-building industries, and trade.

Pearling has always been important to Bahrain's heritage and economy and is probably the oldest industry in Bahrain. The diving season would last for approximately four months, from June until October. The dive groups would return home only a couple of times during the season to replenish food or supplies. Experienced divers could dive to great depths and remain submerged for approximately a minute. Bahrain's economy relied heavily on the exportation of pearls to various places such as Europe and Bombay. At the beginning of the twentieth century, the pearl trade constituted almost half of Bahrain's export business. As the pearling industry began to decline, Bahrain's economy was saved by the discovery of oil.

Bahrain was the first site in the Middle East for the commercial discovery of oil. The discovery at the beginning of the twentieth century significantly changed Bahrain's economy as it began to receive previously unheard-of revenue from oil production and oil refining. A strange man appeared in Bahrain in the 1920s. People noticed a man riding a white donkey under a large white umbrella with a green lining. "Altogether his garb was old-fashioned and slightly eccentric, as if his style of dress had crystalized in the 1890s, and remained unaltered ever since."[8] Frank Holmes was from New Zealand and would lead the beginning of a new age. In 1925, his company, the Eastern and General Syndicate, was awarded the first exploratory oil concession. On May 31, 1932, the first commercially productive well was brought to a depth of 723 meters.

Petroleum production and refining currently account for 60 percent of export receipts, 60 percent of government revenues, and 30 percent of total gross development production (GDP). Many multinational firms also exist in Bahrain and play an important part in the economic development of the country. As the economy began expanding, not only did the number and types of jobs increase, but the influx of workers coming from abroad began to increase as well.

Job/Career Opportunities

Women's employment has increased, as have career opportunities for women. The number of women in Bahrain who began to work jumped 86 percent between 1965 and 1971 and increased another 560 percent from 1971 to 1981. By the 1980s, the percentage of working women in Bahrain was higher than in any other Gulf state. The average age of the majority of Bahraini women who are working is between twenty and twenty-four, although this is changing as older women continue to remain within their occupation. Women are increasingly taking jobs previously reserved for men and now constitute approximately 20 percent of the workforce. Women tend to work outside the home after completing studies up until marriage.

More women continue to receive higher levels of education, but there remains a fundamental lack of employment for such women. Some of the more common jobs held by Bahraini women are teaching, nursing, or secretarial jobs and working in various women's organizations. Most women, however, work at different government agencies, and most of the women employed in government offices work as support staff. Very few of them occupy senior positions. No women serve in the Majlis or as the chief of a ministry. One woman serves as an ambassador to Europe.

Underemployment among women has been a rising concern, one of the problems being not enough women receiving adequate training or education. Although more women have begun to work, most still do not. Around 80 percent of Bahraini women do not hold jobs, whether because of education, family, or class. Significantly more women have been seeking employment.

Pay

The concept of equal pay for equal work is not found in the Labor Law, and women still earn less than men.

Working Conditions

Women also are discriminated against in the workplace in terms of lack of promotion. The Labor Law and the government do not discriminate against women. In fact, the government encourages women workers with specific laws designed to get them into the workforce. The government is also one of the top employers of women.

Sexual Harassment

Sexual harassment is currently prohibited; however, it is a widespread problem for foreign women. No specific information could be found on reported cases or incidents of sexual harassment.

Support for Mothers/Caretakers

Support for mothers and the establishment of health centers for mothers and for their children has increased significantly. The Ministry of Labour and Social Affairs offers several programs for the development of women and children. The various social development projects are implemented through a network of seven social centers located throughout the major regions of Bahrain. The social centers provide community centers such as nurseries for preschool children. The Ministry of Information has established a multidisciplinary advisory committee on family and child programs. This advisory committee evaluates the various programs that are directed to the family and delivered through radio and television.

Maternal Leave

Laws prohibit the dismissal of pregnant working mothers. As of 1998, the length of maternity leave for a working mother in Bahrain was forty-five days.[9] Full wages were to be covered during this period by the employer.

The laws are not upheld in many cases. Working women who become pregnant are faced with the threat of losing their job, suspended earnings, and increased health risks. Establishing strong maternity-leave protection for working women will alleviate some of the unequal treatment that occurs in employment as a result of women's reproductive role.

Daycare

The number of daycare facilities has increased over the years, and many facilities currently cater to children ranging from young infants to adolescents as old as ten or eleven. Daycare nurseries and kindergartens in Bahrain are a relatively recent occurrence. The first daycare nursery was established in 1995. Their number is still inadequate, but there have been increasing efforts to establish such facilities.

Increased support for working mothers has provided more options for them. Three departments in the government are responsible for planning and supervising the development of child-care services: the Ministry of Education, the Ministry of Labour and Social Affairs, and the High Council for Youth and Sports. The government in Bahrain subsidizes daycare nurseries and kindergartens, which are operated by women's associations.

Many public and private daycare centers receive funding from women's associations. Lack of funds, lack of planning, and lack of trained staff members, however, prevent such facilities from reaching their full potential and effectiveness. Daycare services lag behind the rapid social change that has brought the need for such services. The majority of the staff are neither well educated nor well paid. Many child-care centers are situated in modest buildings, sports clubs, private homes, health centers, or social centers. Overall, the quality and standard of health-care services does not appear to be high. Although progress has been made in supporting working mothers, there have been setbacks for women's groups attempting to push the government to issue a modern family law.

Family and Medical Leave

The International Labor Organization (ILO) has set standards for the maternity benefits that should be received by employed women. Due to the low number of married women working outside of the home, the government has introduced new labor legislation to assist mothers. All employers must grant new labor legislation to assist mothers. All employers must grant new mothers forty-five days of full-pay maternity leave. In addition, they must provide fifteen days at half-pay. Further, all employers must provide times for nursing for new mothers.

Inheritance and Property Rights

The Shi'i and Sunni branches of Islam allow women to own and inherit property, and they are entitled to represent themselves in all public and legal matters. If there is no direct male heir, Shi'a women inherit all, whereas Sunni women are apportioned the inheritance by Islamic law (shari'a), with the rest going to male relatives of the deceased.

Social/Government Programs

Sustainable Development

Due to its rapid economic change, Bahrain has had to meet the demands of its citizens in a quickly changing society. Bahrain not only was able to actively develop its oil industry, but also adapted and adjusted its economy to nonoil industries. It has been able to establish and maintain infrastructures that can sustain Bahrain's economic development. The government is involved in many aspects of sustainable development. Current ministries and government organizations involved are the Ministry of Health, the Ministry of Commerce and Agriculture, Water Resources, the Central Municipal Council, the Ministry of Finance and National Economy, the Ministry of Development and Industry, the Ministry of Information, the Ministry of Education, and the Bahrain Center for Studies and Research (BCSR).

Environmental issues have also been considered. Currently there is an Environment and Sustainable Development Authority to address these needs. The government has ratified the Conventions on Protection of the Ozone Layer, Biological Diversity, Climate Change and the Control of Transboundary Movement of Hazardous Wastes, and Wetlands. Bahrain has also participated in conferences at the Organization for Economic Co-operation and Development (OECD), with an eye to increasing the number of women.

Welfare

A social security system was implemented in 1976. Women working for companies with more than ten employees are eligible for pensions and compensation for injuries on the job.

FAMILY AND SEXUALITY

Family patterns and perceptions of gender and sexuality have changed in Bahrain. One of the characteristics of the Gulf societies is the importance placed on the existence of separate spheres for men and women. Islam has played a significant part in traditionally defining gender roles not only in Bahrain but in most other Middle Eastern countries. Tribal heritage also continues to play a role in defining societal norms. Although Bahrain is seen as relatively open compared to the other Gulf states, traditional values of maintaining separate societies for men and women have inhibited the pace of development in regard to women's issues. The increasing rate of women's participation in the labor force has affected traditional family life for reasons such as delayed marriages and reduced numbers of children. There also has been an increase in emphasis on the nuclear family and a diminishing role of the extended family. Women currently suffer from the absence of family civil law. Their rights in marriage, divorce, and child custody are frequently violated.

Gender Roles

Women have historically been confined to the private sphere. Nurturing family life has been their traditional role. More changes to this structure have been visible among urban women than among rural women in recent decades. Prior to the discovery of oil, women in Bahrain were veiled. Only the wives of fishermen and peasants worked outside the home. Their work would be to clean and sell fish or to help their husbands in the fields. Some people have noted that working wives and mothers have not only changed women's roles in society, but have also strained the husband's sense of identity and status within the family and in society.[10]

Traditionally, women live within a large kinship network: affiliation with one's kin was and still is defined by birth. Unlike Western practices, an Arab woman does not take her husband's last name. These kinsmen and family members are responsible for protecting and providing for the woman. Social pressure ensures that the importance of maintaining the reputation of the kinsmen or family members is always relevant.

Veiling

The veil was long considered a symbol of the confinement of women, and beginning in the 1950s, women became less restricted in covering their faces. In the 1960s, women began taking their veils off. Despite this increase of women taking off the veil, which to them represents "the roots of the past life deeper in the personality and culture of the present generation,"[11] many women still continue to wear the traditional black *abaya*, and many women still wear a piece of cloth or scarf around their hair. Thus the increasing interest in joining the labor force has not been balanced by an interest in changing traditions as quickly.

Marriage

Many long-held marriage customs, religious or cultural, have begun to change as more women become educated and hold jobs. Since independence, marriage patterns, especially among the elite, have shifted. Not only is the increased number of working women affecting the dynamics of families, but the fact that women are marrying at a later age also means that society and family are changing. One significant difference is that men and women have been able to play a more decisive role in the choice of whom they will marry. The tradition of family-arranged marriages is gradually giving way to prospective partners for marriage making arrangements and deciding on their own. The observance of the traditional custom of demanding a bride price from the prospective groom's family also has begun to diminish. Polygamy—the right of a man to marry more than one wife at the same time—is not as common in Bahrain as in the other Gulf states; such marriages were 5.4 percent of all marriages. This is a direct result of the advent of women working and becoming more educated.

Shi'a and Sunni women can initiate a divorce but religious courts can refuse to grant it. Shi'a women usually can obtain a divorce from a local religious court. If a case is out of the ordinary, travel abroad to receive one may be required.

Child custody of daughters younger than nine and sons younger than seven years is usually given to mothers. Fathers typically gain custody after this. However, the father always retains the right to make certain legal decisions for his children, for example, with regard to property belonging to the child, until the child reaches legal age. If a non-Bahraini mother divorces a Bahraini father, custody goes to the father. A Muslim woman legally may marry a non-Muslim man if the man converts to Islam. In such marriages, the children are automatically considered to be Muslim.

Reproduction

Females in Bahrain have normally exhibited a statistically high fertility rate, which historically has helped perpetuate the restriction of women. Women who have many children and are the primary caretaker of them are prevented from seeking higher education, economic independence, and participation in public life. As more women began participating in the work environment, however, one of the first changes in family patterns was a marked decline in the fertility rate.

Recent studies indicate that the general fertility rate dropped from 135.9 per 1,000 in 1982 to 111.2 per 1,000 in 1995. The highest fertility level is among women between twenty and twenty-nine years of age. From 1981 to 1995 the total fertility rate dropped from 4.8 to 3.1.[12]

Sex Education

No data are available in regard to whether formal programs or classes on sex education are offered in the school system. It can be assumed, however, that the probability of having sex education classes in Bahrain is extremely low to nonexistent. Information is offered through clinics to interested families.

Contraception and Abortion

Bahrain was the first state among the Gulf countries to provide official family-planning services. The Ministry of Health provides family planning in all health centers and medical hospitals as well as postnatal clinics and child welfare clinics. The Bahrain Family Planning Association (BFPA) was created in 1975 and provides information, education, and training. The BFPA also pressures the government to formulate explicit policy guidelines for effective programs. The Ministry of Health and the Ministry of Labour and Social Affairs support BFPA in its mission.

Sixty-two percent of women aged fifteen to forty-nine use contraception. Thirty-one percent from this group use modern methods of contraception, while the rest rely on traditional methods.[13] Statistics on abortion are lacking.

Teen Pregnancy

By 1995 about 8.8 percent of women under twenty gave birth. This represents a decline from 12.1 percent in 1988.[14]

HEALTH

No formal health service or program existed in any Gulf state in the early 1920s. Harsh climate conditions and low standards of living throughout the region contributed to a high incidence of diseases such as malaria, tuberculosis, dysentery, typhoid, and trachoma. Trained medical staff and adequate health facilities were lacking, as were the financial means to solve such problems. In 1925, Bahrain had only one physician.

Starting in 1925, the government provided free immunization, outpatient treatment, and hospitalization. With this advance, endemic and infectious diseases were nearly eradicated. Health facilities began to improve in the 1940s due to the revenues Bahrain was receiving from oil. The first hospital in Bahrain began operation in 1948 under the supervision of two medical officers. Now, maternal and pediatric care are free.

Health Care Access

There are twenty-seven nongovernmental agencies in Bahrain, out of which five are women's associations and one is a maternal and child-care association. These are very active in meeting the needs of Bahraini women and children and work closely with the Ministry of Health in Bahrain, especially in the area of health education programs.

Eighteen health centers deliver primary health care for families. The Maternal and Health Care program provides assistance and information to mothers and services for their children. A child-development screening program was started in all of the health centers in 1986: every child receives periodic checkups until the age of six. Home visits are made by nurses or doctors through the Maternal and Health Care program. Immunizations are also provided.

Diseases and Disorders

AIDS and cancer, among other diseases and disorders, remain prevalent concerns for most countries, but the greatest problem in Bahrain is bringing awareness of and education on such health concerns to the general public. Genetic and hemoglobin disorders as well as other genetic blood disorders have received increasing attention. The genetic center at the Salmaniya Medical Center initiated a premarital screening exam in 1985. When the Ministry of Health recognized the importance of its work, it expanded the center's medical and counseling services in 1992.

AIDS

Approximately 0.15 percent of the adult population of Bahrain has contracted HIV or has AIDS.[15] Numbers are not available for the number of people who are currently living with HIV/AIDS or for the number of deaths caused by AIDS. Recognition of the disease and support for those infected are growing, however. The *Bahrain Tribune Daily News* reported on December 1, 1999, that Bahrain would celebrate World AIDS Day with the theme "Listen, Learn, and Live: World AIDS Campaign with Children and Young People." The article stated that there would be health education activities through the media.

Cancer

Breast cancer is one of the most serious and prevalent diseases affecting the women of Bahrain. Hospitals such as the International Hospital of Bahrain advocate the early treatment and cure of breast cancer through regular screening and testing. The Bahrain Cancer Society established a cancer support group in 1993.

Depression

Many studies and articles have discussed the issue of depression among women in Bahrain. Most surveys and statistics state that anxiety and depression occur most commonly among older women, unemployed women, divorcées, widows, and women with a lower educational background.[16] The prevalence of psychiatric disorders among general hospital outpatients in Bahrain is 19.4 percent.

POLITICS AND LAW

A constitution was drafted and passed in 1973. On December 7, 1973, Bahrain males elected members of the National Assembly. On August 26, 1975, however, the National Assembly was dissolved because of its objection to the 1974 State Security Law, and the amir ended the "constitutional experiment" without setting a date for its reintroduction. He suspended the constitution and assumed direct rule over the country. In 1992, the government rejected various constitutional proposals and instead formed a Council of Shura.

On February 2001, Amir Hamad bin Isa al-Khalifa declared Bahrain a constitutional monarchy, and Crown Prince Sheikh Salman bin Hamad was appointed head of the committee to implement the charter. Amir Hamad is the main chief of state, and the current prime minister of Bahrain is Khalifa Salman bin Khalifa. Amir Hamad assumed power after the sudden death of his father, Sheikh Isa bin Salman, on March 6, 1999.

Amir Hamad has brought changes to the government, including his commitment to grant the right to vote to women. Beginning in March 1999, immediately after his succession, he released more than 800 political detainees and convicted prisoners in several stages from 1999 to late 2000. He refused to use state security courts and offered citizenship for the stateless minority of Bidoons, who are without citizenship. They are descendants of poor Persian, Afghan, and Baluchi immigrants. In October 1999, he announced the formation of a Human Rights Committee. At the same time, however, he has prioritized the preservation of the royal family and consolidation of his authority.

The government consists of nineteen ministries, and as many as seventeen government organizations currently exist in Bahrain. The political structure consists of twelve municipalities. Many citizens of Gulf countries began demanding rights shortly after the Gulf War, and in Bahrain people pushed for political liberalization.

Many organizations such as Human Rights Watch had noted the deteriorating situation of human rights in Bahrain. Deterioration escalated in the 1990s after the period of the Gulf War and particularly after 1994. Human rights violations have typically been placed under two categories: law enforcement, including the administration of justice, and the denial of civil and political rights such as freedom of expression, of association, and of assembly.[17] The media are controlled by the state, and newspapers and other print media exercise self-restraint and self-censorship. The government has to authorize public meetings and gatherings.

Bahrain's legal system stems from tribal law, Islamic law (shari'a), and modern law (mainly English common law). Shari'a courts in Bahrain and other Islamic societies mainly have jurisprudence over personal matters such as marriage, divorce, or inheritance.

Suffrage

Women in Bahrain may have become the first to have been granted suffrage rights, in 2001, in the Persian Gulf. Bahrain adopted a constitution that granted women the right to vote and also to hold office. The adoption of the National Action Charter (NAC) has probably been one of the most significant events in Bahrain's recent history. The NAC referendum for a European-style constitutional monarchy won 98 percent approval with a 90 percent turnout among the 217,000 registered voters. Under the NAC, all Bahrainis over twenty years of age are allowed to vote—including women for the first time. On February 14, 2002, the amir of Bahrain announced the first legislative elections, which would be held for the first time in almost twenty-five years. It is expected that women will participate in the election of the Municipal Councils and the National Assembly.

Suffrage rights for both men and women did not exist in Bahrain for most of the twentieth century. In December 1971, Sheikh 'Isa proposed the adoption of a constitutional form of government. The objective was to enhance the cohesion of Bahraini society and encourage a greater level of popular support and participation in the islands' affairs. The following June, the amir issued a decree mandating the creation of a Constitutional Assembly.

Bahrain's first national elections were held on December 1, 1972. Twenty-two representatives were chosen by the country's native-born male citizens twenty years of age and over who were grouped into nineteen electoral districts centered on the larger urban communities. The strongest supporters of the new electoral system were college-educated professionals, middle-income businessmen and trades people, and the owners of the country's newspapers.

Bahraini woman casts her vote in Bahrain's landmark municipal polls in Muharraq, May 2002. AP/Wide World Photos.

Women at this time began to demand their inclusion in the electoral process. Professional and middle-income women in the larger cities began mobilizing active protests against the disenfranchisement of female citizens. Several women's societies held public demonstrations to criticize their exclusion from the electoral process. The most active of these societies were the Bahrain Young Ladies' Association, the Awal Women's Society, and the Rifa' Women's Society. Sheikh 'Isa expressed his sympathies, but did nothing to alter the country's election laws at the time. It was not until after his son Sheikh Hamad ascended the throne that women gained the right to vote.

Political Participation

Political parties are prohibited in Bahrain, and political participation in general is prohibited as well. Political participation in Bahrain is generally as difficult for men as it is for women. The political or social actions of the government and people do not completely reflect the entire scope of attitudes, dispositions, or opinions of many of the women in Bahrain. Many still elevate the importance of culture, tradition, and religion over civil rights and thus have been caught between changing societal norms and accepting them. This is one of the fundamental problems with which many modernizing nations have had to deal.

The shift toward openness has posed problems for the religious clergy in Bahrain.

On August 22, 2001, Amir Sheikh Hamad bin Isa al-Khalifa announced the formation of a new Supreme Council for Women in Bahrain to advise the government on women's issues. The council consists of fourteen experts chaired by Sheikha Sabeeka bint Ibrahim al-Khalifa, the wife of the amir. Many women have been campaigning against domestic violence and to have the same rights that men hold.

Women played an active role in popular protests that erupted in 1994. These protests encompassed a wide variety of political groups, including secularists and Islamists. In 1995, political protests for reform turned into violent clashes. Thirty-eight deaths resulted, and 15,000 were arrested by the end of the demonstration. During that same year, 310 Bahraini women signed and circulated a petition asking the amir to resolve the increasing social inequalities and violence in the country. Some women have supported increasing women's rights, while others have promoted more conservative, Islamic values.

Women's Rights

The Ministry of Labour and Social Affairs is responsible for women's affairs within the government. The ministry does not currently have a national plan to implement the Plan of Action for the Fourth World Conference on Women or the Social Summit meeting. Recently the Consultative Council and the Cabinet of Ministers agreed in principle to sign the Convention on the Elimination of All Forms of Discrimination against Women.

Bahrainian women are free to travel abroad, get jobs, drive, and wear what they want. Women also have been persistently organizing in ways that allow them to discuss how to obtain rights, with respect to gaining political office and increased freedom in the personal realm. They have begun to form women's associations addressing the needs and concerns of working women. As more women are being educated, the desire to have a fulfilling career is increasing as well. It is significant that many women have also begun to seek more active roles in society by demonstrating their desire to have a voice in and to affect the change of government policies.

The first chapter of the National Action Charter begins by stating: "The State strives to consolidate the rights of women and to issue necessary legislation to protect the families." Personal freedom and equality are stated from the beginning of the charter. Not only is the charter of political importance, but it stipulates that the principles of equality and justice were sanctified by Islam. The principles and other enumerated rights come from law and from God. The first section under Chapter 1 states: "All citizens are equal before the law in rights and duties. There is no discrimination between them on the grounds of sex, origin, language, religion, or creed." The charter continues in section two to state that all personal freedoms are guaranteed, and section three states that no person will be subject to any moral or physical torture or to any "non-human, derogatory or humiliating treatment, under any circumstances." The point of the National Action Charter is to give equality and humane treatment all Bahraini citizens.

Feminist Movements

Since the 1970s, many women have formed and joined associations not only in order to address the growing needs and concerns of working women but also to provide facilities to address the issues of education, literacy, and health. Labor unions and formal political parties are banned in Bahrain. As a result, political activities take place in religious centers and cultural and sports clubs. What is significant about the formation of these women's associations is that they reflect the changing social and political attitudes of many women in Bahrain.

The An-Nadha Women's Association is considered the first of its kind in the Gulf. An-Nadha was established in 1955 by a wealthy merchant who donated land and financed the building of the association. His wife presided there for many years, and the organization confined its activities to cultural and educational programs such as eradicating illiteracy, opening daycare facilities for the children of working mothers, raising the awareness of women in general, and conducting research on issues such as problems created by divorce.

The Child and Mother Welfare Association consists mostly of well-off housewives. Established in 1960, the association has accomplished various projects such as the Amal Institution for the handicapped and has established kindergartens and nursery schools. Sheikha Hessa bint Salman Ebrahim al-Khalifa, the mother of Sheikh Hamad, is currently the honorary president. She is also currently the honorary president for other women's associations such as the International Ladies Association and the Bahrain Businesswomen Society. She is one of the many wives of leaders in the Gulf countries who have become more involved in their countries' affairs in the areas of education, child welfare, and health.

The Awal Women's Association (AWS) was established in 1967 in the city of Muharraq. AWS's main mission is to promote women's social and cultural status. The majority of its members are young working women who are concerned with organizing cultural and educational programs. They provide a number of lectures, programs, training missions, and workshops in order to increase rural women's awareness and upgrade their standard of living. AWS also coordinates and cooperates with women in and outside Bahrain, strengthens relationships with other local and international social organizations, and trains its members to hold administrative and organizational positions.

The Rafa' Cultural and Charity Association was established in the city of Rafa' in 1970. This association concentrates on cultural programs and charity work. It also runs and supervises kindergarten schools. The International Women Association was established in 1975 and is considered the only association that includes foreign females among its members. Most of its activities consist of charity work and other humanitarian projects such as visiting patients in hospitals.

More recent organizations include the Union of Bahraini Women and the Bahrain Women's Society. The Bahraini Young Ladies Association (BYLA) was organized in 1995 and works for the enhancement of women's cultural, educational, and social standards. Members also promote the political participation of women and take a role in the country's development. BYLA further works in advancing childrens' affairs and in promoting the concept of voluntary social work.

Lesbian Rights

The issue of homosexual rights and issues is rarely discussed in the public sphere in Bahrain, as in most other Middle Eastern countries. Little data are available on lesbian rights in Bahrain. Part of this can be explained by the government's strict control of the media from religious considerations. In certain Muslim countries that enforce the shari'a, a sexual relationship between two women is punishable by public flogging and even death. In 1999, the twenty-one-year-old niece of the ruling amir of Bahrain was reported to be hiding in a London "safe house" after coming out as a lesbian.

Military Service

Women currently are not allowed to join the military services in Bahrain.

RELIGION AND SPIRITUALITY

The women of Bahrain share an Arab-Islamic tradition with the women of the Gulf region. Many barriers have constrained the integration of women into the workforce, and the customs and norms extending from religious considerations remain as one. Islam continues to play a large role in Bahrain despite modernization and industrialization. Cultural and religious traditions remain deeply rooted in the country and society.

Women's Roles

In the Arab-Islamic tradition, the relative roles of the male and the female are unambiguous, and a strong demarcation between the two is enforced. This separation is continually emphasized through traditions and family and societal structures. Segregation and separation are "expressed in space, architecture, education and employment."[18]

Underlying this conceptual notion of a division in society is the recognition of the disruptive nature of strong active sexuality, which must be controlled and managed through acts such as the literal separation of men and women. Men rarely see another man's wife, sister, or mother when entering another's house.

An important traditional role for women was to reproduce so that lineage and family lines could be passed down through their children. As society and family patterns change, women have increasingly endeavored to change the perceptions that women should have about themselves.[19] Interpretation of the Qur'an and of the biases that extended from that interpretation and Islamic tradition, however, has made this particularly difficult.

Religious Law

Bahraini women's personal status is defined by Islamic law. Traditional Islamic laws concerning women and family can be considered one of the major barriers to women's integration into the labor force. Traditional Islamic law (shari'a) is still strictly observed in Bahrain, and all aspects of the family, such as marriage and divorce, are governed by it. Shari'a Islam is the state religion, but Christians, Hindus, Jews, and others are generally permitted to worship freely.

Laws regarding marriage, divorce, inheritance, and child custody in Bahrain are governed by Shari'a Islamic law. The right for women to dissolve their marriage is denied to most women in Muslim countries. Islamic law allows men to have up to four wives at any one time.

The process of change in Bahrain in regards to Islamic law and secular constitutional law will take a longer time, although the process of change has begun and progressed forward.

VIOLENCE

No government policies or laws exist that explicitly address violence against women, although the National Action Charter states that no undue violence or punishment should be enacted.

Domestic Violence

According to a U.S. report, "Women's groups and health care professionals state that spousal abuse is common, particularly in poorer communities." Society is closed on the subject, and the matter is kept in the family to save face. A few articles have appeared in the local press regarding violence against women and lack of laws to defend them against abusers. The report also states that "there are very few known instances of women seeking legal redress for violence. Anecdotal evidence suggests that the courts are not receptive to such cases."

It has been reported that foreign domestic workers are frequently the victims of beatings or sexual abuse. Courts allow victims to sue for damages and the cost of returning home, but most women do not feel empowered to challenge their employer.

Rape/Sexual Assault

Rape is a crime in Bahrain. However, because marital relations are governed by shari'a law, spousal rape is not a legal concept within the law. Statistics and data are not available on this subject.

Trafficking in Women and Children

The government has not yet made significant efforts to combat trafficking of women and children or to help victims. It does not recognize that trafficking is a problem because foreign workers travel to the country voluntarily, a fact that can be used as an excuse for ignoring the serious issue of victimization. A large reliance on the continuous influx of foreign workers in Bahrain and in many other Gulf states may be another reason why the issue has not been actively addressed by the government.

The law does not specifically prohibit trafficking in persons, and there are reports that some foreign female workers are recruited for employment on the basis of fraudulent contracts and then forced into domestic servitude or sexual exploitation. Workers from the Philippines, Ethiopia, India, Russia, and Belarus have reported such treatment.

Although prostitution is illegal, many foreign women, including some who work as hotel and restaurant staff, engage in it. Such women typically are locked in a communal house when not working and are driven to work in a van. Unskilled foreign workers in essence become indentured workers and are unable to change employment or leave the country without their sponsors' consent.

OUTLOOK FOR THE TWENTY-FIRST CENTURY

The recent political changes made under Amir Hamad have made prospects for the citizens and women of Bahrain look hopeful. The National Action Charter gives women various rights, including the right to hold office, and protects families. Bahrain has undergone many recent economic, political, and societal changes. Women have made significant efforts to change traditions and religious biases and have created associations and organizations to help working women. The continued efforts of the women in Bahrain will help them to make progress and effect changes that benefit not just them, but the society as a whole.

BAHRAIN

NOTES

1. Although reports issued by the Bahraini government contain information on population and demographics, the U.S. State Department and CIA have been relied on for this chapter.

2. Munira A. Fakhro, *Women at Work in the Gulf: A Case Study of Bahrain* (London: Kegan Paul International, 1990), 115.

3. *Statistical Abstracts/1984* (State of Bahrain, Council of Ministers, Central Statistics Organization, December 1985), 134.

4. Fakhro, 1990, 116.

5. Fred H. Lawson, *Bahrain: The Modernization of Autocracy* (Boulder, CO: Westview Press, 1989), 21.

6. For further details, see Fakhro, 1990.

7. Ibid., 137.

8. Molly Izzard, *The Gulf*.

9. Based on statistics from the United Nations Statistics Department. Trends and statistics measured maternity-leave benefits from 1998.

10. Fakhro, 1990, 66.

11. Ibid., 75.

12. www.emro.who.int/publications/EMHI/0601/20.htm.

13. Statistics from the International Planned Parenthood Foundation.

14. Ibid.

15. "Epidemiology of HIV and AIDS in Bahrain," *J. Comm. Dis.* 1997 (4) (December 29): 321–26.

16. For further information, the World Health Organization (WHO) has publications regarding aspects of health that exist in each country's profile.

17. Human Rights Watch/Middle East, *Routine Abuse, Routine Denial: Civil Rights and the Political Crisis in Bahrain* (New York: Human Rights Watch, 1997), 43.

18. Jeffrey B. Nugent and Theodore H. Thomas, eds., *Bahrain and the Gulf: Past Perspectives and Alternative Futures* (London: Croom Halm, 1985), 83.

19. For further details, see Leila Ahmed, *Women and Gender in Islam: Historical Roots of a Modern Debate* (New Haven, CT: Yale University Press, 1992).

RESOURCE GUIDE

Suggested Reading

Ahmed, Leila. *Women and Gender in Islam: Historical Roots of a Modern Debate*. New Haven, CT: Yale University Press, 1992.

Bulloch, John. *The Gulf: A Portrait of Kuwait, Qatar, Bahrain, and the UAE*. London: Century Publishing, 1984.

Clarke, Angela. *Bahrain Oil and Development, 1929–1989*. Boulder, CO: International Research Center for Energy and Economic Development, 1990.

Jenner, Michael. *Bahrain: Gulf Heritage in Transition*. London: Longman, 1984.

Khuri, Fuad I. *Tribe and State in Bahrain*. Chicago: University of Chicago Press, 1980.

Sadik, M.T., and W.P. Snavely. *Bahrain, Qatar, and the United Arab Emirates*. Lexington, MA: Lexington Books, 1972.

Web Sites

Arab NGO Network for Development, www.worldforumbeirut2001.org/english/anndmembe.htm.

Government of Bahrain, www.bahrain.gov.bh/english/.

Human rights organizations, www.sigi.org/Resource/hr_org.htm.

Middle East human rights organizations, www.ittijah.org/middle.htm.

Middle East Wire, www.middleeastwire.com/gender/stories/20020311_meno.shtml. Provides articles and stories in regards to human rights issues.

U.S. Department of State, www.state.gov/g/drl/rls/hrrpt/2000/nea/781.htm.

The Voice of Bahrain, www.vob.org/english/.

Organizations

The Embassy of the Kingdom of Bahrain
3502 International Drive NW
Washington, DC 20008
Phone: (202) 342-1111
Fax: (202) 362-2192
Email: info@bahrainembassy.org

SELECTED BIBLIOGRAPHY

Ahmed, Leila. *Women and Gender in Islam: Historical Roots of a Modern Debate*. New Haven, CT: Yale University Press, 1992.
Anderson, Lisa. "Absolutism and the Resilience of Monarch in the Middle East." *Political Science Quarterly* 106(1) (Spring 1991): 1–15.
Clarke, Angela. *Bahrain Oil and Development, 1929–1989*. Boulder, CO: International Research Center for Energy and Economic Development, 1990.
Cordesman, Anthony H. *Bahrain, Oman, Qatar, and the UAE: Challenges of Security*. Boulder, CO: Westview Press, 1997.
Fakhro, Munira A. *Women at Work in the Gulf: A Case Study of Bahrain*. London: Kegan Paul International, 1990.
Human Rights Watch/Middle East. *Routine Abuse, Routine Denial: Civil Rights and the Political Crisis in Bahrain*. New York: Human Rights Watch, 1997.
Jenner, Michael. *Bahrain: Gulf Heritage in Transition*. London: Longman, 1984.
Khuri, Fuad I. *Tribe and State in Bahrain: The Transformation of Social and Political Authority in an Arab State*. Chicago: University of Chicago Press, 1980.
Lawson, Fred H. *Bahrain: The Modernization of Autocracy*. Boulder, CO: Westview Press, 1989.
Nakhleh, Emile A. *Bahrain: Political Development in a Modernizing Society*. Lexington, MA: Lexington Books, 1976.

Nugent, Jeffrey B., and Theodore H. Thomas, eds. *Bahrain and the Gulf: Past Perspectives and Alternative Futures*. London: Croom Helm, 1985.

Sadik, Muhammad T., and William P. Snavely. *Bahrain, Qatar, and the United Arab Emirates: Colonial Past, Present Problems, and Future Prospects*. Lexington, MA: Lexington Books, 1972.

3

EGYPT

Bahira Sherif-Trask

PROFILE OF EGYPT

Egypt (also known as the Arab Republic of Egypt) is located in the northeastern corner of Africa and includes a small Asian peninsula between the Middle East and northern Africa known as the Sinai. Most of Egypt is arid, desolate, and barren, with hills and mountains in the east and along the Nile River. The majority of the population lives in the fertile valley by the Nile River, which stretches 550 miles from the eastern Mediterranean Sea south into the Sudan. Three percent of the land is arable; 2 percent is devoted to permanent crops; and 2 percent of the land is irrigated.

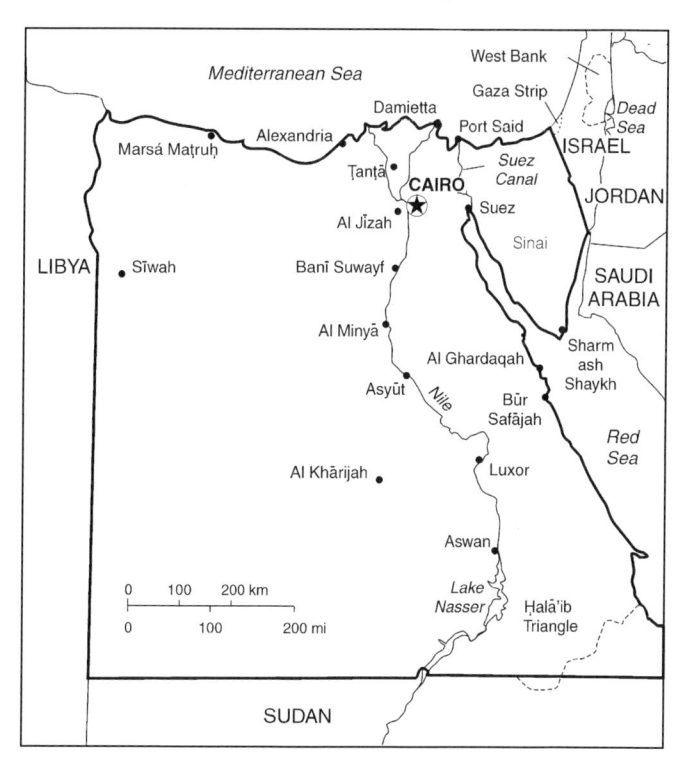

Egypt's estimated population in 2001 was 69,536,644, with 34.5 percent of the population being under the age of fifteen years, 61.6 percent between the ages of fifteen and sixty-five, and 3.8 percent over the age of sixty-five. Forty-five percent of the population lives in cities, a substantial portion in poverty and slums. Cairo (El-Qahira) has an estimated population of 9,690,000, and Alexandria (El-Iskandriyah) 3,584,000. Ethnically, 99 percent of Egyptians are of Eastern Hamitic stock or are Bedouin (Berber). According to official statistics, 94 percent of Egyptians are Muslim, primarily Sunni, with the remaining 6 percent adhering to either the Coptic Christian religion or other religions. Arabic is the official language, although French and English are widely understood and often used by the educated classes. The per capita gross domestic product (GDP) is about $1,400 per year. Official statistics show that 34.4 percent of wage earners work in agriculture. According to its constitution, Egypt is a social democracy with a legal system based on Islamic law, English common law, and Napoleonic codes. Islam is the state religion, and legislation is based on Islam. With respect to this aspect of the constitution, religious practices that conflict with Islamic law are forbidden. Christianity and Judaism do not fall under this umbrella and therefore do not conflict with religious law (the shari'a). In general, non-Muslim minorities are free to worship as they wish.

The average life expectancy (2001 estimate) was 61.9 for males and 66.24 for females. The birth rate in 2001 was 24.4 per 1,000 population, the death rate 7.5 per 1,000, and the infant mortality rate 58.6 per 1,000, for an annual natural increase of 1.89 percent. The 1999 total fertility rate (TFR) was 2.9 children per fertile woman, giving Egypt a rank of 89 out of 227 nations.[1]

OVERVIEW OF WOMEN'S ISSUES

Contemporary legal rights and issues impacting Egyptian women have been the subject of many scholarly and popular articles since the late 1970s, yet many of these works do not explore the importance of ideological movements or a constantly changing socioeconomic situation for the lives of Egyptian women. This is surprising since Egypt was the first country in the Middle East to experience the full impact of globalization and the subsequent exposure to various ideologies. Specifically, Westernizing influences and the resultant changes in the social balance have greatly affected gender issues, and specifically women's rights. The history of Egyptian women's rights and issues is characterized by two conflicting directions: (1) the promotion of women's emancipation because it is perceived to be crucial to the betterment of the society and the nation and (2) a belief that this is an alien Western concept detrimental to the health and traditional aspects of the society. Further, it must be noted that Egyptian women do not constitute a homogeneous group, with all individuals sharing the same experiences. Instead, great inequalities persist in Egyptian society based on class affiliation and access to social, educational, economic, and political opportunities, as well as vast differences between rural and urban areas.

EDUCATION

Opportunities

There are significant variations throughout Egypt with respect to opportunities for education for women. School enrollment figures differ most specifically according to rural-urban differences. Currently, approximately 80 percent of all school-age children are enrolled in schools, but there are various estimates for rural, poor, and village areas. The urban gap between boys and girls is approximately 1 percent, while the rural gap is 18 percent. This gap increases to 56 percent in poor villages in Upper Egypt.[2] In particular, poor and rural parents tend to take their daughters out of school as soon as they are old enough to be sent out to earn extra money or to work around the house.[3] Further, enrollment rates tend to go down as girls mature due to the lower social value of girls' education. As of 1990, by some estimates, twice as many girls dropped out of school as boys.[4] Cultural norms, particularly among the poor and in rural areas, favor continuing the education of boys over that of girls, most particularly in times of economic turmoil. As well, significant increases in the costs of education influence poor parents' decisions with respect to schooling for their children, especially for girls. The primary cultural belief among the poor and village dwellers maintains that girls will marry and bear children and, therefore, do not need to be as educated as boys. In contemporary Egypt, this view does *not* hold true among the middle and upper classes. Education for young women is perceived as a necessity for both self-fulfillment and future career preparation. Many middle-class Egyptians believe that an educated young woman has better marriage chances since her future husband will be interested in the earning potential of his future wife and will also think that she will make a better mother of his children. Among those middle- and upper-class men and women who married at a younger age, it is becoming common for the woman to continue her schooling anyway. This is a significant cultural shift for women.

Literacy

Although literacy among men and women has been increasing over the last three decades, the adult female population, as in many developing countries, is characterized by high illiteracy rates. Illiteracy is prevalent in various sectors of Egyptian society, again signifying the inequality of development opportunities within the society. According to the 1986 census, 62 percent of adult women were illiterate, compared to 38 percent for men; of that number, 76 percent of rural women were illiterate, compared to 45 percent of urban women. Illiteracy is also closely correlated with age: for ten- to fourteen-year-old girls it is 27 percent, for twenty-five- to twenty-nine-year-old women it is 66 percent, for forty-five- to forty-nine-year-old women it is 84 percent, and for sixty- to sixty-nine-year-old women it is 92 percent.[5] Again, these percentages are related to cultural norms that favor the education of boys over girls, especially, as has been pointed out, among the poor and uneducated.

EMPLOYMENT AND ECONOMICS

Job/Career Opportunities

There is a major discrepancy between the law and the real situation of women in employment issues. According to the law, all women should have equal opportunities with respect to employment and training options. This theoretically allows contemporary Egyptian women to study any field of their choosing and subsequently to work in every sphere, including government, medicine, law, the sciences, architecture, education, and business.

The law grants women equal employment opportunities, which are, on paper, sometimes even greater than those in developed countries. Nonetheless, these ideals are not accomplished in reality. According to recent government statistics, 17 percent of private businesses are owned by women, and one-fourth of executives at the four national banks are women. This is astounding given that women make up about 33 percent of the total number of university graduates.[6] Also, the statistics indicate that more than 50 percent of working women do not reach senior positions except after the age of fifty-five. It can be hypothesized from the figures that it is very difficult, especially for younger women, to attain levels of seniority in their respective workplaces. Current statistical representations of women's employment may be inaccurate. In particular, they do not account for unpaid work in agriculture, domestic work, and other participation in informal family enterprises. Although Egyptian women have officially had the right to work outside of the home since the 1950s, their actual contributions often go unnoticed and are also increasingly the focus of scathing criticism. Further, with a shifting economy and increasing fundamentalist pressures, women in the 1990s again became the focus of heated debates centering on the roles of men and women in society. A wider survey of women's economic activities and a more realistic picture of women's employment in Egypt can be found in a recent Labour Force Sample Survey. Women's labor-force participation is 35.4 percent, with rural-urban differences 32.5 percent and 18.8 percent, respectively.[7] Women's economic participation in the government is 29.5 percent, in other parts of the public sector 13.1 percent, and in the private sector 39.3 percent. Women's participation in agriculture is greater than men's, estimated at 53 percent.[8] Furthermore, women also carry out most household chores, especially in rural areas, and it is estimated that they may work up to sixteen to nineteen hours per day. Despite these figures, women are not recognized as playing a particularly important role in the labor force; therefore, they have limited access to government-sponsored training and educational opportunities. This discrepancy can be explained by the fact that even though families in Egypt increasingly need the incomes of both men and women to survive, the cultural ideal remains that working outside of the home and being the main breadwinner are still seen as the man's role.

The persistent view of men as the primary, or even only, breadwinners leads to unemployment being perceived as a significant problem only for males. This perspective persists despite statistics that show unemployment to be 10 percent for men and 25 percent for women. Viewing women as not as important to the labor force has repercussions for them. Due to the country's problems with unemployment, women are encouraged to retire early, and current legislation offers women half-time employment for half of their salary. Additionally, in the private sector, recruitment efforts focus almost completely on men. In contrast, women often are perceived as an economic liability to workplaces due to the concern that they may require maternal leave at some point during their employment. In the period between 1976 and 1986, the percentage of women employed in the private sector sank from 47 percent to 30 percent. However, by 1993, about 20 percent of all Egyptian households were primarily dependent on women's incomes.[9] Despite all of the statistical evidence with respect to women's employment outside of the home, increasingly conservative social attitudes advocate that women's "natural" role is in the home with their children. The discrepancy between the public discourse about women and the social and economic realities of their lives is most clearly reflected in the lack of social services and public policy provided for them.

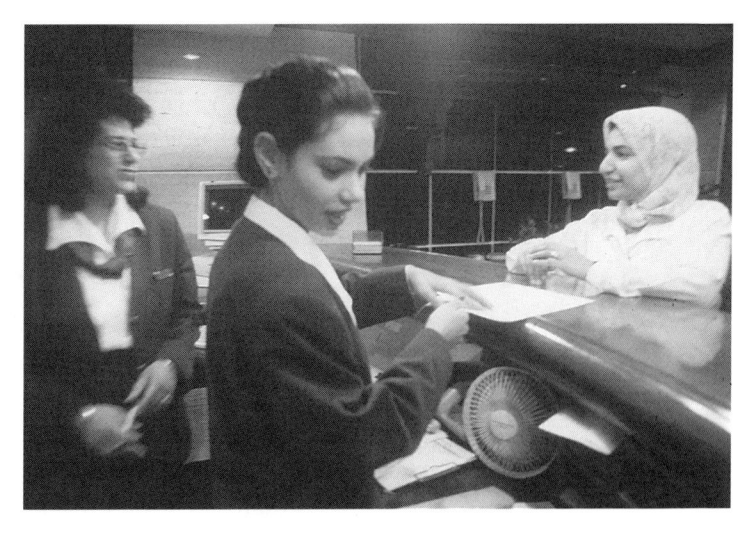

Women in Luxor working at a business center. Photo © TRIP/H. Rogers.

Pay

The Egyptian labor laws mandate equal rates of pay for equal work for both men and women who are employed in the public sector.

Working Conditions

Egyptian labor laws grant women a wide array of privileges and attempt to protect them against abuse or mistreatment by employers. For example, the labor laws prohibit the employment of women between 8 P.M. and 7 A.M. except in certain types of work, the nature of which requires night-time work (for example, hotels, restaurants, theaters, and hospitals). This exception also applies to women in senior executive positions. The laws also prohibit the employment of women in work that may require hazardous conditions, may compromise their morals, or is considered physically too strenuous (for example, bakeries, underground mines, and prostitution).[10]

Support for Mothers/Caretakers

Maternal Leave

Egyptian labor laws are relatively generous on the issue of motherhood, indicating the emphasis placed on mothering for women in the society. Women simultaneously have the right to paid maternity leave and unpaid child-care leave. For example, women who are employed in the government or the public sector may take up to two years' unpaid leave to look after their newborn child. This unpaid leave may be granted up to three times during the employee's period of service. During this child-care leave, the state is responsible for paying part of a woman's social insurance or for paying her an indemnity equivalent to 25 percent of her salary. The employed woman may make the choice herself as to which option suits her better. Women are paid during maternity leave for a period of three months, and upon return, a female employee must receive two fully paid half-hour rest breaks daily to breast-feed her infant during the eighteen months after the birth of her child.[11] According to the law, companies employing more than 100 female workers must provide nursery facilities or must participate in one if the number of employees is fewer than 100.

Inheritance and Property Rights

Laws pertaining to personal status are defined by one's religion. With regard to inheritance and property rights, Egyptian Muslim female heirs may receive only half the amount of a male heir's inheritance. Christian widows of Muslims have no inheritance rights under the law. A sole female heir receives half her parents' estate; designated male relatives receive the rest. In contrast, a sole male heir legally inherits all his parents' property. Part of the rationale for this division of property is that male Muslim heirs are expected, according to the traditions of the society, to take care of all needy family members, in particular dependent female relatives, but this tradition is not always upheld.

Social/Government Programs

Sustainable Development

The position and status of women are determined in part by the development strategy adopted by individual countries. In Egypt, an important marker for women was Sadat regime's (Anwar Sadat, president from 1970 to 1981) adoption in 1974 of the economic Open Door Policy, which encouraged the private sector to increase the productive capacity of the economy. This resulted in a decrease in women's participation in the labor force. As the government withdrew its commitment to guarantee employment to all college graduates (instituted after the 1952 revolution), unemployment increased. The expectation that women would enter the labor force thus became a liability to the state rather than an asset. The national dialogue about women's work started to shift, and the definition of women as primarily important in the domestic arena, as wives and mothers, became more popular. Social ideologies based on a sexual division of roles began to be more prevalent. These perspectives were widely supported by the newly emerging Islamic fundamentalist groups that advocated that women's place was in the home.[12] Further, a provision was added to Article Eleven of the 1971 constitution that declared the state's commitment to help by reconciling women's family obligations and their equality to men in the public sphere, "provided that this did not infringe on the rules of the Islamic shari'a." The new constitution represented an important shift away from the secular discourse of the 1960s and created opportunities for Islamic groups to oppose women's rights on the grounds that they were in opposition to Islamic principles.[13]

Throughout the 1980s, the Open Door Policy became increasingly institutionalized. While this policy has been relatively successful on a macro level, it has had negative consequences for the more vulnerable sectors of society, namely, the poor, and specifically poor women and their children.[14] As key resources, such as health care and education, become scarcer, lower-class women and children are least likely to have access to them. Also affected by the economic restructuring are individuals who would previously have been classified as middle class, namely, civil servants and unemployed college graduates.

Welfare

There is no formal welfare program in Egypt. Any discussion of women's rights must therefore raise awareness of the fact that priorities vary for the different classes of women. Poor women must be included in the women's rights dialogue in order to link all women in the society to the joint venture that allows them access to the structure of opportunities.

FAMILY AND SEXUALITY

Gender Roles

From all perspectives, the institution of the family, not the individual, is the basic unit of Egyptian society. While there is no such entity as "the Egyptian family" or even "the Islamic family," laws, religious principles, and social traditions all combine to provide the foundation for the fundamental workings of families. While families differ across regions, class, educational lines, and particular circumstances, most adhere to similar principles, especially with respect to gender issues. Egyptian society is organized on the fundamental concept that men and women are different from one another with respect to their nature, talents, and inherent tendencies. This becomes most apparent in the sphere of the family, where, according to dominant gender constructs, men and women each have a different part to play. Men's role is to move in the public sphere and to be responsible for providing financially for the family. Women are seen to be best suited for remaining within the domestic/family arena by caring for the home, the children, and the husband. Further, women's inherent sexuality is believed to be constantly endangering the social harmony of society (by tempting men) and is, therefore, best controlled through women's modesty and their remaining as much as possible within the private sphere of the family. This belief is reinforced through cultural and religious norms that are increasingly advocating that adhering to traditional roles of both women and men is fundamental to maintaining the societal structure. Increasingly, dominant public voices advocate that women's place is in the home and oppose women working and abandoning their primary roles.[15] In this social environment, contemporary images of women as economic assets and providers are rapidly coming into conflict with what are perceived as divinely inspired roles—roles that are advocated by God.

Another basic gender construct that is at times in contradiction to the reality of women's daily struggles in Egypt is the cultural and religious ideal that the sexes complement each other. According to this belief system, women are not devalued as persons who have inherently less value than men. Also, they are not thought to be lacking in any type of abilities or talents. Instead, Egyptians tend to emphasize that everyone—men, women, and children—is part of an interrelated community, and that gender balance or gender complementarity is part of the message of the religion. This concept of gender complementarity, particularly in the realm of the family, is an integral part of understanding the social structure of Egyptian society.

Gender constructs impact women in another important realm: the law. A Muslim woman's legal identity, like that of a man, begins at birth, but in contrast to men, her legal capacity and status undergo various changes throughout her life cycle. For a woman, her legal coming of age and her achievement of physical maturity do not necessarily coincide. She is a ward of her father or guardian as a child and, as an adult, is restricted in legal decision making. Her legal persona and social status depend on the state of her sexuality—whether she is a virgin, married, divorced, or widowed.[16] At different times in a woman's life, she is treated differently both by the law and by the society. Societally and legally, the young woman is the focus of a great deal of protection, and her freedom of movement is limited in order to protect her from the dangers of the society. In contrast, an old woman is able to move about publicly without evoking much interest or thought and may also go to places and participate in situations where a young woman would be forbidden. It is therefore very important to emphasize the fundamental difference between the stability of adult men's status under the law and the changing nature of adult women's status.

While women are clearly not always as much in the public arena as men are, they perform their duties in other ways. Women are perceived and valued as the first teachers of their children in the practices and beliefs of Islam. They are seen to accomplish this both through their instruction and by the way they live their daily lives outside of the home. Individuals in Egyptian society like to point to the many examples from Islam's historical record of women who have became leaders in their communities, including the spiritual realm. For example, the wives of the prophet Muhammad (the founder of Islam) are still upheld as paradigms of virtue and are used as examples of women who had a powerful presence in their community.

Nonetheless, in contemporary Egypt, these ideals of women are often at odds both with women's actual experiences and their own aspirations and desires. Through increased access to education, more and more women are receiving the chance to earn their own income and are thus wielding more formalized power in their families. This is occurring in an environment that increasingly is promoting a traditional division of labor. Meanwhile, by retaining their traditional informal access to power through strong same-gender associations, women are also increasingly becoming aware of their legal and social rights.

Veiling

One example of how women are dealing with the dichotomies in their lives can be found in the very public issue of the urban, educated woman's return to veiling in contemporary Cairo. The *hijab*, the wearing of a head veil and loose-fitting clothing, has come to symbolize all traditional institutions governing women's place in an "orderly" Islamic society. Thus in the ideological struggles surrounding the position of Islam in the modern world, the *hijab* has become a cultural symbol. This, in part, explains why an increasing number of women are choosing to adopt these new forms of Islamic dress, thereby literally covering themselves in tradition and modernity.

In Egypt, the return to the veil has provided women with an effective means of coping with the new pressures imposed by modern life. The veil allows women to negotiate their relationships both with their husbands and with men in the workplace. While the *hijab* has obvious religious and cultural connotations, it also has a very practical value. Through wearing a veil, women advertise their respectability. This enables them to venture into the public sphere without harassment or damage to their reputation.

In contrast, women who wear Western clothing are now often thought to be tempted by Western ills such as sexual immorality and are thus frequently harassed in the street, on public transportation, and in other outdoor spaces. Moreover, veiling has made it possible for women to interact with their male coworkers and men they may see outside of the home without any perceived sexual overtones.

For married working women, in particular, veiling sends a message to both their husbands and to the larger society. It conveys the social view that a woman can work outside of the home without losing her roles of wife and mother. Veiling becomes a means for women to take some control over the ambiguous moral situation created by new economic and social pressures. By wearing a veil, women can move in public spaces, go to work, use public transportation, and attend school without raising questions about their behaviors. In addition, for some women, the veil has become a means to advertise their religiosity, modesty, and good reputation. Veiling makes it possible for women to achieve the socially desired combination of education and income, in their marriages and the outer world, without the connotation of immorality that working outside of the home carries. For women, both within their families and in the wider community, wearing the veil makes a statement about what it is to be a "real Muslim woman."

Female Genital Cutting

In the West, the most highly publicized issue concerning women's health in the Muslim world and parts of Africa is female genital cutting (circumcision). This practice is extremely widespread in Egypt, especially among the poorer classes and in rural areas. It is considered an extremely important part of womanhood for girls to be circumcised. This is due to cultural norms that stigmatize uncircumcised girls and prevent them from marrying. Estimates of the percentage of all Egyptian women who are circumcised range from 50 to 90 percent, but precise figures are not known.[17] Female circumcision remains a common practice despite Western efforts to stop it and government proclamations to the contrary. In a 1995 survey, among women with one or more living daughters, 87 percent reported that at least one daughter had already been circumcised or that they intended to have the daughter circumcised in the future.[18]

Most circumcisions take place before puberty. The median age at circumcision for women of the older generation as well as their daughters has remained about 9.8 years. Among the older generation, traditional practitioners such as midwives were responsible for more than eight to ten percent of the circumcisions, while trained medical personnel performed more than half of the circumcisions among the daughters.

Most women surveyed (82 percent) were firmly convinced that female circumcision should be continued. Seventy-four percent believed that husbands prefer their wives to be circumcised, and 72 percent believed that circumcision is an important aspect of the teachings of Islam. A surprisingly low number of women recognized the negative consequences of circumcision, such as reduced sexual satisfaction (29 percent), the risk of death (24 percent), and the greater risk of problems in childbirth (5 percent).

Female circumcision is often presented as a practice advocated by Islam, but this is inaccurate. The issue of female circumcision was raised at the 1994 International Conference on Population and Development in Cairo, and much criticism was directed at the Egyptian government. Subsequently, the government issued a decree to stop the practice in hospitals. The government, however, refrained from completely outlawing the practice due to pressure by Islamic groups who advocated the importance of female circumcision as a traditional practice. Critics, however, point out that the prophet Muhammad's own daughters were not circumcised and that circumcision is not practiced in Saudi Arabia, the most conservative Islamic country in the Middle East. In 1997, under extreme pressure from Islamic fundamentalist groups, the government lifted the ban on this practice. Despite international efforts to publicize the physical and psychological dangers of circumcision, female circumcision is gaining legitimacy as fundamentalists attempt to popularize the belief that circumcision is mandated by Islam. The controversy around female circumcision is an excellent example of the conflict between ingrained cultural values with respect to gender, the fundamentalist Islamic movement's quest for "authenticity" and "tradition," and Western perspectives that advocate universal women's rights with respect to control of their bodies.

Marriage

Marriage remains at the center of contemporary Egyptian social life. It is the primary focal point in the lives of both women and men, followed only by the birth of a child. The rights and obligations of all husbands and wives are defined by Islamic law, the sexual division of labor, and Egyptian cultural practice and traditions.

A Muslim marriage gives a wife the unconditional right to economic support from her husband regardless of her own financial means. After marriage, women legally remain in control of their property, including inheritance or earned income. However, in case of divorce, the ex-wife is entitled only to three months' alimony and to those possessions that she brought with her at the beginning of her marriage. She may also keep everything that she acquired with her own income during the marriage, as well as any portion of her bride price (*mahr*) that is due her. The *mahr* is a sum of money or property that, according to Islamic practice, a husband agrees to pay to his bride at any time prior to or during the marriage or upon divorce. (For additional information regarding divorce, see the "Politics and Law" section.) Different social classes have varying practices with respect to the *mahr*, but the basic principles of exchange remain the same for all those who marry irrespective of education, class, and geographic location.

In return for the unconditional economic support of his family, a husband has certain rights within the marriage, the most important of which is his status as head of the household. As such, he has the right to restrict his wife's physical movements. This is often interpreted as the right of a husband to prevent his wife from working outside the home. The husband also has the unilateral right to end the marriage without the consent of his wife. In case of divorce, the husband legally receives custody of the children after they have reached the age of ten in the case of boys, and twelve in the case of girls. However, it is customary for girls to remain with their mother after a divorce. Recently, some of these rights have been curtailed by changes in the law that increasingly promote the rights of women. Primarily, women are now able to file for divorce, especially in cases of domestic disputes. A new law enacted in 2000 gives women similar rights to divorce as men. In particular, women do not need to prove "cause" anymore and may gain a divorce by giving uprights to the *mahr*, or dowry. Men must now formally file for divorce with the legal system and cannot just divorce a woman by uttering, "I divorce thee" three times, as is permitted by the Qur'an. It is important to note that maintenance cultural practices such as cross-cousin marriages and sizable sums of money allocated through the *mahr* have evolved to protect women and counterbalance the unequal rights of men and women with respect to divorce. The relatively low incidence of divorce in Egypt (2 percent, according to the last census), particularly after children are born, suggests that stable marriages remain an important aspect of Egyptian social life.

All Muslim Egyptian marriages, irrespective of class, are characterized by a formalized set of negotiations that begin once the suitability of a potential spouse has been determined by the respective families. The prelude to the composing of the marriage contract is the betrothal, which is the request by the man for the hand of a specific woman in marriage. It is at this point that the potential groom will approach the woman's family with the view of describing his status, job prospects, and family. He will then negotiate with them the marriage contract and their respective wishes. According to custom, in order for the betrothal to be valid, both parties need to be aware of each other's character and behavior as well as have some understanding of their respective economic situations. Much of this information is obtained through inquiries and investigations by members of each family as well as the direct contact of the couple in the presence of a chaperon. Once the man's offer is accepted by the woman, or by those who are legally entitled to act on her behalf, the betrothal is considered to have taken place. It is usual at the point of betrothal that the man offers his future bride a gift, which in Egypt is referred to as the *shabka*. In some instances, particularly if the man does not know the bride's family through previous contacts, or if he wants to make an extremely favorable impression on the young woman, the man will offer her the *shabka* before the signing of the contract, thereby illustrating his good will, his good intentions, and perhaps his good financial situation. The *shabka* is, by middle-class American standards, a very expensive gift of jewelry. It is important to note that betrothal does not constitute a marriage contract: It is merely a mutual promise of marriage between the two parties, and it is not legally binding for either party. In practice, the betrothal is easily dissolved. Its main purpose is for the couple to get to know one another in a respectable framework.

Among Egyptians, the betrothal becomes a public acknowledgment of the couple's right to spend chaperoned time together. It is a general rule that now the prospective bridegroom will join the woman's family for dinner on a regular basis, giving the couple an opportunity to get to know each other in the presence of others. In addition, other members of the two families will start visiting one another. In particular, the man's mother and sisters or female cousins will begin spending long periods of time with the prospective bride.

The Islamic Marriage Contract

The key to understanding any Islamic marriage (and 95 percent of all marriages in Egypt are Islamic) is the contract that is formed by the two families. From a legal standpoint, the marriage contract establishes a series of rights and obligations between a couple that have a long-lasting effect on most aspects of their future lives. In all schools of Islamic law, marriage is seen as a contract, the main function of which is to make sexual relations between a man and a woman legal. A valid and effective marriage contract outlines certain respective legal rights and duties for wife and husband, together with other rights and duties shared by both of them. This contract represents more than a mere exchange of money or material goods. It is a form of social exchange and is thus a legal, religious, economic, and symbolic transaction. The contract is constructed with great seriousness and is preceded by a set of lengthy negotiations, almost all of which center around the material protection of the woman and her unborn children once she is married. Nevertheless, the marriage contract may include conditions that are advantageous for either or both spouses. Conditions that are specified in the contract range from the woman's right to dissolve the marriage to an agreement that neither party may leave the town they agree to live in, and even that the husband may not marry another woman. The contract also acts as a bridge for bringing the various members of the two families together and provides them with the opportunity to discuss in detail the preliminary workings of the prospective marriage. Most important, the marriage contract symbolizes the public acknowledgment of the formation of a lawful sexual partnership. This coupling will be sanctioned religiously and socially and marks the beginning of the formation of a family. This family is then legally obligated to care for and raise the children. Marriage in Egypt remains the pivotal institution for channeling sexuality, founding a family, and joining two extended families into a reciprocal relationship of obligations.

Sexuality is considered a highly important part of marriage. Islam justifies sexual intercourse through the marriage contract but limits sexuality to the marital unit. The complete social prohibition of young people's sexual activities outside of marriage naturally leads to the near nonexistence of illegitimacy. A unanimously shared Egyptian belief is that reproduction belongs to the realm of the family and is thus, like sexuality, highly regulated by legal as well as social rules and responsibilities.

Polygyny

Although polygyny is allowed by the Qur'an, it is virtually nonexistent in Egypt. In contrast to the stereotypical Western image of Muslim men with multiple wives, Egyptian men bemoan the difficulties of supporting one wife in today's economy, and strong social sanctions work against their even considering polygyny as a viable option.

Male and female views on this topic can only be understood in light of a 1979 ruling, also known as "Jihan's law," so named after Sadat's modernist wife, who introduced a decree outlawing polygyny as an option for men. This law caused considerable debate in the media as well as among secular and religious elites concerning the Personal Status Laws and their relationship to the shari'a (Islamic law). The amendment was eventually partially changed on procedural grounds in 1985. However, in June of that year a similar law (Law No. 100) amending the 1925 and 1929 laws was put into place, where it still remains.[19] The new law stipulates that in the case of a polygynous union, the first wife retains the right to divorce her husband, but it is no longer her automatic right. Instead, she now has to prove that her husband's second marriage is detrimental to her either materially and/or mentally. Further, the first wife now only has the right to sue for divorce in the first year of the new polygynous marriage.

Reproduction

Family planning is a problematic area even though Egypt has the longest history of contraceptive initiatives in the Middle East. In 1996, the former Ministry of Population and Family Planning was abolished, and a new Ministry of Health and Population was created to highlight the renewed importance the government is giving to issues of population growth. Population growth is one of Egypt's most serious issues and has multiple aspects: rapid rates of population growth are related to high fertility and an unbalanced population distribution. The highest fertility level is found in rural Upper Egypt (5.2 births per woman), compared to a lower fertility level in urban Lower Egypt (2.7 births per woman).[20]

Infertility, even though it is barely acknowledged or studied, is also an important cultural problem that affects primarily Egyptian women. In a society where it is crucial for women of all classes to bear children and thus attain social status through motherhood, the inability to bear children leads to serious societal consequences. There are no dominant social alternatives to motherhood and domesticity for women, and adoption is not allowed under Islamic law. Thus for all women, biological parenthood is crucial to their social standing, especially since under Islamic law a man has the right to replace an infertile wife through divorce or polygynous marriage. While polygyny is not an option that is employed by upper- and middle-class men, the threat of divorce hovers over childless marriages. Among all classes and educational levels, women are typically blamed for not being able to bear a child, and they also bear the burden of overcoming this condition through prescriptions that are often traumatic and have no results.[21] Further, childless women face strict social judgment, for they are perceived as being less than other women, as depriving their husbands and their husbands' families of offspring, and as potentially endangering other people's children through their supposedly uncontrollable envy.

There is no sex education in schools in Egypt. Sex education only occurs within the framework of contraception advice from doctors or in clinics. There is some research on sexuality being conducted at Cairo University, but this information is not widely disseminated.

Contraception and Abortion

In order to help curb population growth, the government has consistently advocated the use of family-planning methods. However, the quality of family-planning services is often poor, contraceptives are not readily available, and poor and rural women are especially reluctant to use artificial birth-control methods, which they have heard rumored to be detrimental to women's health.

Many unwanted pregnancies end in self-induced abortions because abortion is prohibited in Egypt except in cases where pregnancy threatens the life of the mother. The 1995 Egypt Demographic and Health Survey, a nationally representative survey of 14,779 married women aged fourteen to forty-nine, shows a leveling off of the contraceptive-prevalence rate at around 48 percent from 1991 to 1995. Although contraceptive use in Egypt doubled between 1980 and 1995, from 24 percent to 48 percent, most of the increase happened in the 1980s, and there was no significant change in the overall rate of contraceptive use between 1991 and 1995.[22] The 1995 survey also revealed significant differences in the level of contraceptive use based on region, with women in Lower Egypt accounting for approximately 53 percent, compared to 24 percent in Upper Egypt. This high discrepancy can be attributed, at least in part, to lower socioeconomic conditions and traditional practices and beliefs.

A primary issue discussed during the International Conference on Population and Development held in September 1994 in Cairo was the relationship between religion, family planning, and women's rights. Abortion became the most controversial topic of that conference. Muslims vehemently argue against abortion as a means of family planning but believe that abortion should be tied to decisions and the situation of the family unit. They believe that abortion may be practiced in exceptional cases where the health of either the mother or the fetus is in danger. The government's position is that women must avoid abortion as a method of family planning whenever possible, but it will provide treatment and counseling to women forced to resort to this measure.

Teen Pregnancy

There is virtually no teen pregnancy outside of marriage in Egypt. Social norms forbid young girls from having sex. Thus, teenage girls only have children if they are married and today this is found primarily in rural areas.

HEALTH

Health Care Access

Increasingly, the relationship between women's status and women's health is being understood as a solid indicator of the status of gender issues. This is based on the observation that oftentimes women face disproportionately higher health risks because of their place in their respective societies. In the Egyptian situation, factors such as heavy work loads, multiple pregnancies, limited economic resources, and lack of access to good health care exacerbate the problems faced, in particular, by poor and rural women. Further, inadequate statistics on the health of women are themselves an indicator of the issues women may be dealing with.

Gender-based health risks begin for girls and women at birth. Because of cultural norms emphasizing the importance of sons, the birth of a daughter is often a disappointment to parents of all classes. Among the lower and rural classes in particular, girls face a higher risk of death because they are often nursed for shorter periods of time and are fed inadequately.[23] Statistics indicate that child mortality rates for children less than one year of age are 28 per 1,000 for girls and 24 per 1,000 for boys.[24]

The reproductive period of ages fifteen to forty-nine is generally considered the time of highest risk for mortality for women. Maternal mortality rates are 320 per 100,000, which is higher than the reported 15 per 100,000 in developed countries, but lower than the 590 per 100,000 found in some other less developed countries. Other risk factors that primarily affect women are early marriage and childbearing. While the legal age of marriage for girls is sixteen, they are often married off at younger ages in rural and poor communities since they are seen as a burden and risk to their families. Early marriage and accompanying early childbearing tend to have a negative effect on women's health as well as reducing their chances for subsequent education and employment. The rate of adolescent marriages is reported to be 15.3 percent, but it may be much higher given the practice of doctors issuing age-assessment certificates to allow families to marry off their young daughters.[25]

Diseases and Disorders

Information about sexually transmitted diseases (STDs) in Egypt is very difficult to obtain, often anecdotal, and taboo for most public discussions. Nevertheless, there is some evidence that sexually transmitted diseases may be more widespread in the general population than is reported. The only formal study that provides some indication of the prevalence of sexually transmitted diseases is research on reproductive morbidities, including reproductive-tract infections, conducted among 502 women in two villages in rural Giza, 1989–1990. Sixty-four of the women sampled had a reproductive-tract infection at the time of the survey, which may be in part because condoms are rarely used in Egypt. While solid data are lacking, the 1995 Demographic and Health Survey reported that only 14 percent of married women used condoms for family planning. It is, therefore, unlikely that condoms are commonly used in Egypt for disease prevention.[26]

Although information about prostitution in the religiously conservative nations of the Middle East is limited, prostitution is known to exist in most Arab countries, including the urban areas of Egypt.[27] As in many other countries of that region and sub-Saharan Africa, the migration-prostitution-STD triad is present in Egypt. Studies indicate that in particular, male labor migration (which is currently more than 2 million) brings with it a variety of social problems, including STDs. Given strict cultural norms regarding women's premarital virginity and marital fidelity, Egyptian women find themselves in the predicament of receiving a variety of sexually transmitted infections. Many of their husbands migrate for extended periods of time, contract gonorrhea, genital chlamydia, and other sterilizing infections, primarily from foreign prostitutes, and then bring the diseases home to their wives. Emerging studies from both rural and urban Egypt indicate that rates of various STDs are rising in proportion similar to those in the West. Often the men who contract STDs avoid seeing doctors due to the cultural stigmas that accompany extramarital sex. The infection may therefore become chronic in them, and they subsequently transmit the diseases to their wives. A number of incidents have been reported in which men may even transmit the diseases directly on the first wedding night to their new brides. Women thus at times start their marital lives with tubal infections that potentially lead to infertility. This has major societal implications because, as mentioned earlier, infertile women face their greatest danger from their husbands, who have the right under Islamic law to replace an infertile wife through divorce or a polygynous remarriage. Such actions are often encouraged by the husbands' families, who view an infertile wife as useless, damaged goods, and even potentially a threat to the continued social reproduction of their family.[28] Another factor that may influence the spread of STDs is the popularity of Egypt as a tourist destination, both for visitors to the ancient treasures and, more recently, for those seeking vacations at Red Sea resorts.[29] Nonetheless, given the private role of sexuality in this fundamentally Muslim country, very little formal knowledge exists about the prevalence of these behaviors. As a consequence, very few if any social supports are available for those individuals who do contract sexually transmitted diseases.

AIDS

According to United Nations statistics, North Africa and the Middle East account for less than 1 percent of the total number of individuals worldwide infected with HIV. As far as formal statistics reveal, in that whole region, 27,000 people have died from HIV-related illnesses, compared to 170,000 in Europe and 46 million in sub-Saharan Africa. The National AIDS Program in Egypt recently published the number of units of blood that have tested positive for HIV in each of the last seven years. This indicated that there is a low prevalence of infection and that there is no real evidence of an upward trend. For example, in 1990, 136,422 blood units were tested, and only 4 were positive for HIV; in 1996 a quarter of million units were tested, and only 3 were positive.[30] The data from blood donations are interesting because all blood collected in Egypt's public health facilities is donated on a voluntary basis by family members of patients. Egypt's medical surveillance of blood units provides a good indicator of the rate of HIV in the adult population.

Despite worldwide increases in the AIDS epidemic, AIDS has so far not spread in any major degree throughout the Egyptian population. Nonetheless, factors that could contribute to the spread of HIV exist. Scattered evidence suggests that other sexually transmitted diseases are widespread in the general population, and this indicates that AIDS may become a problem in the future. Reliable survey data, however, are not available. Egyptian medical experts claim that the low prevalence of HIV infection and AIDS in the general population is probably the result of a prevalent strict Islamic moral code that forbids adultery, sex before marriage, and homosexual practices. Widespread adherence to these beliefs and practices could mean that HIV infection may be prevalent in small groups practicing sexual behaviors that increase their chance of infection. However, only rarely do individuals in the general population come into contact with at-risk individuals. Increasing research into patterns of sexuality is needed in order to explain the low prevalence of AIDS in Egypt. Also, the lack of reliable data makes it difficult to determine the real situation and to compare it to that presented by official sources.

Eating Disorders

The traditional idea that in order to be attractive, women should be pleasantly plump still exists, though in the upper classes of Egyptian society this is changing through the impact of Western images and movies. Traditionally, being plump was associated with having a certain wealth and enough food to eat. The importance of being full figured can be found in popular expressions, where, for example, to call a woman skinny as a stick is commonly perceived an insult, or to say that she is "hilwa mirabraba" (pretty and plump) is a compliment. However, Western diet concepts are starting to become more popular, and it is now possible to find diet Cokes and fitness classes in Egypt. Also, obesity is now being treated in hospitals. There are no reported cases of bulimia or anorexia.

POLITICS AND LAW

In recent years, Egyptian women have been profoundly affected by changes in the political situation and subsequent revisions to the law. After the 1952 revolution that overthrew the monarchy, the Egyptian state defined promoting social justice and the self-reliance of all of its citizens as a primary goal. The new constitution introduced a secular approach that granted equal opportunities to all citizens, regardless of gender, ethnic origin, or religion. This perspective was adopted in order to realize the country's goals of development.[31] Although the revolutionary government attempted to improve women's participation on social, economic, and political levels, it remained reluctant to change the Personal Status Law. This has led to continuing inequality in the situation of women, particularly with respect to domestic issues. In turn, women's equal participation in the public sphere was restrained. Still, women did gain some economic, social, and cultural power through their increased access to education and employment.

Suffrage

Egyptian women were the first Arab women to acquire political rights. Article 32 of the 1956 constitution gave political rights to Egyptian women, including the right to vote. The legislature observed the principle of equal rights for all citizens, men and women. However, in deference to Egypt's cultural traditions, the law did not make women's registration for elections mandatory, as is the case for men.[32] Further, statistics indicate that only 18 percent of eligible women voters are actually registered to vote. An unusual development with respect to elections is that despite the higher rate of education in urban than in rural areas, there are more women registered to vote in the rural areas.[33]

Political Participation

Despite government efforts to ensure equal rights for men and women, there are still very few women who hold office in the government and politics. Women hold 11 of the 454 seats in the People's Assembly. The same low representation is found in the cabinet of the president, where two of thirty-two ministers are female. In the public domain, there are four main channels through which Egyptian women can participate in government and in the political decision-making process: registering in the electoral rolls, being elected to the People's Assembly, being elected to popular and local councils, and joining political parties. For the most part, however, most Egyptians, women and men, are politically apathetic. The lack of formal participation may be the historical result of long periods of colonization, a monarchy before 1952 and the subsequent regime of Gamal Abdel Nasser (1956–1970), which discouraged political dissent and frightened people away from heavy political involvement.[34]

Women's Rights

In order to understand the role of women's rights in Egypt, it is necessary to take a historical view of some of the issues they have been dealing with. The first public challenge to the traditional Islamic view of women and their proper role in society is generally associated with a modernist movement in Egypt. Beginning in the late nineteenth century, Egyptian male reformers and nationalist modernizers took up the question of women's status and role in society. This marks the beginning in Egyptian history of a struggle between those who sought to promote women's rights because they perceived them to be crucial to the development of the society and the nation and those who perceived women's freedoms as an alien Western concept, detrimental to the health of the society. This debate about the place and roles of women continues in the current struggle between fundamentalist and modernist groups.

The reform movement sought to modernize Egypt and bring it closer to the West by building a new society. This development was to be accomplished by abandoning adherence to the traditional formulations of the established schools of law (*taqlid*) in favor of a new interpretation (*ijtihad*) of the Qur'an and Islamic law (shari'a), based on the principles of Islam. The fundamental principles of this movement are associated with the social and religious reformer Shaykh Muhammad 'Abduh (1849–1905).

Shaykh ʿAbduh advocated educational and legal improvements, the emancipation of women, economic development, and governmental reorganization in order to move Egypt forward to compete with the technological and economic changes taking place in the Western world.[35] The most open and prominent advocate of women's rights was his associate, Qasim Amin (1863–1908), whose book *Tahrir al-marʾa* (The Liberation of Women, 1899) brought the issue of the status of women into the forefront of controversy. His writings provoked Egypt's first major journalistic debate on the issue of women. In this book, Amin advocated major reforms in education and divorce procedures for women, as well as arguing against their veiling and seclusion. He suggested the idea that women were at the heart of the progress or backwardness of a nation, and that change was part of the necessary order in life. Recent scholarship illustrates that alongside Amin's efforts, other female-inspired movements were already under way in Egyptian society but were at that time not given the same prominence due to cultural traditions that did not publicize women's debates and writings. These initial debates about women's issues and rights set the stage for a long, complicated dialogue about the appropriate roles of women that continues to the present time. Nonetheless, the issues in this debate have stayed fundamentally the same: do women belong at home in a fundamentally domestic role, or can they reconcile that role with a more public life that includes access to public educational and employment opportunities?

In the contemporary situation, Egyptian society is caught in a dichotomous place due to its dependence on Western aid on the one side and growing fundamentalist movements on the other. On the one hand, there is growing international pressure on the Egyptian government to adhere to United Nations conventions concerning women's rights. Due to economic dependence on the U.S. Agency for International Development (USAID) and other international donor organizations such as the International Monetary Fund and the World Bank, the current regime must show that it is complying with the values and ethos of Western-inspired human and women's rights.[36] This has led, in part, to informal governmental support of recent grassroots profeminist activists whose efforts center on such issues as women's political participation, women's equality in the workplace, women's reproductive rights, and violence against women in the family. Organizations focusing specifically on female-oriented issues such as the Women's Media Watch, the Female Genital Mutilation (FGM) Taskforce, and a network of groups dealing with women and violence have actually gained in momentum since 1994 when the International Conference on Population and Development (ICPD) was held in Cairo.[37] This development stands in direct contrast to the growing fundamentalist movement that either does not recognize these issues as central to women's lives or even advocates that some, like female circumcision, are an important part of traditional practice. These dichotomous movements have led to the boom of a new group of indigenous feminists who are seeking the answers to the situation of women in a reexamination of traditional texts and laws.

Many contemporary Egyptian feminists have become very concerned with those aspects of the law that clearly indicate discrimination against women. As mentioned earlier, most laws are concerned with promoting and protecting the equality of the sexes. However, several elements, when combined with traditional customs, discriminate against women. For example, according to the law, a father's permission is required for a single woman under the age of twenty-one to get a passport and to travel. Even all married women need their husbands' permission to travel. Another inequality in the law with respect to women is that only men may confer citizenship on their children. In effect, a child of an Egyptian mother and a foreign father who is not a citizen is also not a citizen. Although women are not legally prohibited from working as judges, in practice, there have been no female judges until recently. On January 22, 2003 Tahanyal-bebaly became the first woman in modern Egyptian history to be appointed a judge in the Supreme Constitutional Court. This symbolizes a major symbolic shift for Egyptian women.[38]

In Egypt, there is a direct relationship between laws affecting marriage and personal status (the Personal Status Law), and people's religions. Even in the contemporary conservative climate, laws favoring women's rights are being passed. For example, in January 2001, the Parliament passed a new Personal Status Law that made it easier for a Muslim woman to obtain a divorce without her husband's consent. Now a woman can get a divorce provided that she is willing not to take any alimony from her former husband and to return her dowry. (In contrast, divorce is not permitted by the Coptic [Christian] Orthodox Church.) She may also seek a divorce in the event of spousal abuse. Changes to the law, however, are not always approved. For example, an earlier version of the Personal Status Law that contained an amendment that would have made it easier for a woman to travel without her husband's or father's consent was rejected.[39] Another controversial aspect of the law allows a husband to forbid his wife to work outside of the home. In order to do this, he must prove that her employment interferes with her household duties. Women do have the option to protect themselves legally from such actions by their husbands through their marriage contracts. They can, for example, add a clause that stipulates that they may work outside of the home during their marriage. However, in practice, few women carry through with this option because of the cultural stigmas attached to such an action.

A legal area with blatant inequalities between men and women have been the divorce laws. Until 2000, husbands did not need to provide any explanation if they wished to divorce, while women had to prove an assortment of conditions in their claim. Legally, there were six conditions under which a woman may divorce her husband: if the husband is imprisoned for three years; if the husband stopped maintaining her financially; if the husband abandoned her for more than one year; if the husband was suffering from an incurable disease and if his wife was ignorant of his condition at the onset of their marriage; sexual impotence and sterility; and abuse and harm. All of these conditions had to be proven by the wife and/or witnessed.[40] According to Egyptian law, a husband who intended to divorce had to inform his wife through a public notary and deliver a copy of the papers to her or her attorney. After a divorce, the ex-husband had to provide economically for his former wife for a period of one year. The rationale behind these laws favoring the ease of divorce for men is that women are more emotional and, therefore, may seek divorce on irrational grounds. After a divorce, mothers retain custody of their sons until they reach the age of ten, while girls are required to remain with their mothers until the age of twelve (a judge may, at his discretion, extend this period until the marriage of the girl). Custody decisions are based on traditional concepts of gender roles and responsibilities. Maternal custody is based on the belief that women are better nurturers of young children and females, but that young men then need to be raised by a male role model. Also, with respect to custody, financial maintenance of the children is considered the father's duty until the marriage of his children, especially girls. In 2000, a new divorce law was passed in Egypt that gave women similar rights to divorce as men. In order to enact a divorce, if she does not wish to prove cause, a woman may choose to give up her right to financial maintenance by the man or give up her *mahr*, or dowry.

Feminist Movements

Egypt has a long and divided history with respect to feminist movements. As mentioned, these movements were promoted by both men and women starting in the nineteenth century, but they were motivated by different reasons and took place in separate arenas. In the nineteenth century, Egyptian men's profeminist sentiments were initiated by contact with European society. To these men, it was apparent that European women were prominent in the public sphere, and they assumed that these societies had made great developmental progress in part due to the increasing rights of women. They felt that in order for Egypt to move ahead and be able to compete with the Western world, women needed to be accorded more rights. In contrast, Egyptian women's feminism originated as an upper-class phenomenon between the 1860s and the early 1920s and grew out of women's own learning and observations.[41] These women determined that many so-called Islamic practices such as veiling, segregation, and seclusion were not ordained by Islam, as they had been brought up to believe. For example, the memoirs of Huda Sha'rawi's, one of the most pivotal women of that period and the forerunner of modern feminism in Egypt, reveal the existence of women's debates on Islam and veiling in a Cairo harem salon of the 1890s.[42] By 1914, Huda Sha'rawi, with the support of the princesses of the Egyptian royal family, initiated the Intellectual Association of Egyptian Women. She and other early Egyptian feminists asserted that through the correct understanding and practice of Islam, women could regain basic rights from which they, their families, and the larger society would benefit. This is a theme that has repeatedly recurred in the contemporary situation, particularly with the growing fundamentalist movement.

While the first Egyptian feminists based their growing consciousness in the teachings of Islam, they rapidly added nationalism as a new dimension to the debate. This is an aspect that clearly distinguishes Egyptian feminism from Western feminism. By 1919, these women were actively involved in the national debate to oust the British colonizers. Women's public participation, led by Huda Sha'rawi in a nationalist march is considered by many scholars to have been the turning point that brought the Egyptian feminist movement into the open.[43] Although these were nationalistic issues and were not inspired by feminist issues, women's participation empowered them to take a more public role with respect to issues relating to the condition of women.

In 1923, Huda Sha'rawi formed the Egyptian Feminist Union (EFU) and remained, throughout the 1920s and 1930s, a central figure in the women's movement. The union's program centered primarily on women's political rights, such as voting and qualifying for parliamentary representation. Increasingly, however, social issues with respect to women became part of the agenda as well. In 1924, the union and the Women's Wafd Committee presented the Egyptian Parliament with a set of demands for increased educational opportunities for women and girls. Included on the program were voting rights for women, parliamentary representation, the elimination of polygamy, and restrictions on divorce. Further, in 1924, after attending the International Conference on Women in Rome, Huda Sha'rawi cast off her veil and thus encouraged other middle- and upper-class women to follow her lead. This action represented a symbolic announcement to the society of the rejection of a whole way of life. For these women, the veil became the symbol of the exclusion and backwardness of women.

The EFU remained the primary means for women's activities throughout the 1920s and 1930s. At its pinnacle, membership reached 250 women. Members worked on setting up schools and health clinics, hosting a Conference for the Defense of Palestine in 1938 in order to show solidarity with Palestinian women, and held the first Pan-Arab Feminist Conference in 1944, which resulted in the establishment of the Arab Feminist Union. By the early 1940s, the EFU began to disintegrate into conflicting factions based, in part, upon class divisions within the group. While the original founders of the group tended to be upper class, French speaking, secular, and Western oriented, members who joined later were primarily middle-class women whose language of choice was Arabic and who saw themselves as rooted in local culture.[44] World War II led to new social and political conditions in Egypt that spawned a new nationalist resurgence and the formation of other secular and religiously based women's groups.

A recent focus for contemporary feminist groups is to find indigenous solutions to women's issues in Egyptian society. Their agenda has concentrated on further the rights of women as well as mobilizing them to assist in completely transforming the society. Contrary to Western assumptions, Muslim family law provides women certain rights, even while imposing certain limitations. Thus an important aspect of the new Islamic movements as well as the more secular groups is women's own explorations of these rights in order to reorganize society and advocate for their own issues. An increasing number of Islamic female activists have become important within dominant fundamentalist discourses by challenging their male counterparts for misinterpreting Islam with respect to women's issues. They emphasize Islam's compatibility with UN-stipulated standards of women's rights and, as evidence, point out those pre-Islamic traditions that lowered women's position in society. An important feature of these movements is their ability to reach women in various segments of the society. The fundamental principle of these movements is that women must take an active role in understanding the original principles of Islam that accord both women and men rights and obligations in the familial sphere.

All of the groups concerned with women's rights—whether secular, Muslim, or Islamist—focus specifically on the Personal Status Law (PSL) or family law, which is based on and derived from the shari'a religious law. While all other Egyptian laws are modeled after French civil law, the only law that is quite explicitly based on the shari'a is the PSL. Any attempts at reform of the PSL are seen by many Muslims as a direct assault on Islam and on Islamic groups. The rights of Egyptian women are directly related to the gender relations specified in the PSL.

The Egyptian PSL specifies, at least theoretically, the roles and interactions between men and women in the family. It regulates all laws relating to marriage, divorce, child custody, guardianship, and inheritance and defines women as legal subordinates to men. Egypt follows the Hanafi school of shari'a law according to which the husband is in charge of supporting his wife and children financially. In return, the man has the right to restrict his wife's movements, restrain her activities, and make decisions on her behalf. According to the law, for her part, the wife must care for her spouse and children and must obey her husband.[45] An explanation and understanding of the PSL is important because it reflects and legitimizes the patriarchal structure of the society, institutionalizes inequality with respect to roles in the family, and is used by men to validate their power over women.

The current PSL was proclaimed as law in 1920. It was amended in 1925 and remained consistent until 1979, when amid great controversy it was amended again. The latest revision included the right of the wife to keep the family home after divorce, the right of the first wife to be informed in case of the husband's marriage to another, and her right to demand a divorce on that basis. These amendments to the law became popularly termed as "Jihan's law," after the wife of then President Anwar Sadat, and were eventually partially changed on procedural grounds in 1985. However, in June of that year, a similar law (Law No. 100) amending the 1925 and 1929 laws was enacted and is now the current version.[46] The new law stipulates that if the husband becomes involved in a polygynous union, the first wife retains the right to seek divorce. However, it is no longer her automatic right. Instead, she now has to prove that her husband's second marriage is hurtful to her either materially and/or mentally. Further, the first wife now only has the right to sue for divorce in the first year of the new polygynous marriage. It needs to be pointed out that it is socially unacceptable among the middle and upper classes for men to engage in polygynous unions, and, in fact, they are not seen as an option. The revisions in the law are important on a symbolic level in terms of giving men certain legal rights over women in the context of the family. The new provision in the law stipulates that in cases of divorce, after the period of custody ends, the husband is entitled to the return of the spousal home, at which time the wife is required to leave. The revision in the law also altered the conditions of alimony, with the husband being responsible for only one year of financial maintenance of the wife. Further, under these provisions, the husband can now withhold alimony if his wife disobeys him, leaves the house without his consent, or works against his will, or if her work is perceived as jeopardizing family life. The amount of alimony a wife is to receive is determined by the judge of the case, based on his assessment of the man's financial situation. Judges have also been granted the power to enforce the child-custody stipulations that return boys to their fathers when they reach the age of ten and girls when they turn twelve.[47]

Poorer lower-class women are differentially affected by the PSL. While women of all classes often face problems petitioning for a divorce, claiming alimony, and contesting custody of children, lower-class women have even less access to judicial hearings and often are not taken seriously when they do get a hearing. Further, the decision whether a woman should be granted a divorce always rests with a male judge, since women are unable to reach the position of judge. Again, cultural beliefs about the innate natures of women and men come into play in these issues. Traditionally, it is believed that women should not hold positions that require "male" characteristics such as rationality and lack of emotion. While there have been fervent attempts by women's groups to provide access for women to judgeships, the current political climate advocates a much more domestic role for women, making such a possibility unlikely in the near future.

A major debate between secular and Muslim-oriented women's groups also concerns the vast divide between laws protecting the rights of women and their actual implementation. Many women, especially those from less privileged backgrounds, are unaware of their legal rights. In order to rectify this problem, in the last several years different programs have made strong efforts to raise consciousness among women by teaching them about their legal rights. Further, these programs attempt to educate women on these issues in light of cultural values and belief systems that legitimize men's domination over women's lives. Oftentimes these cultural beliefs prevent women from feeling justified to seek these rights. Despite the PSL, which is based on a very conservative interpretation of Islamic law, the Egyptian legal system has several favorable aspects for women. In 1981, Egypt became the first nation in the Arab world to ratify the Convention for the Elimination of All Forms of Discrimination against Women. Additionally, within the family sphere, the shari'a protects women's material possessions. All of a woman's possessions, including her jewelry, property, and earnings, are legally her own. Should a wife choose to share her possessions with her husband, it is her choice but not her obligation to do so. While in practice it is often difficult to maintain separate material spheres in a marriage, this provision in the law does give women a certain amount of financial independence. In contrast, men must by law provide materially for their family and any unmarried females in their extended circles. At this point, the strict gender hierarchy in families that is advocated by the PSL is under constant negotiation due to the large number of women in the workforce. In the intimate realm of the family, strict separation of wealth and of roles is impossible to maintain, especially in an economic climate where households are tied into a global economy that increasingly necessitates dual-income earners.

Lesbian Rights

No information is available on lesbian issues in Egypt or most of the Middle East.

Military Service

Military service is compulsory only for men in Egypt.

RELIGION AND SPIRITUALITY

Women's Roles

The teachings and principles of Islam have made a significant difference in the lives and beliefs of most Egyptian Muslims since the seventh century. Islamization has been a continual process in Egypt and has helped shape Egyptian identity, culture, and social and political relations. For most Egyptians, being Muslim is part of their understanding of the world, and experiencing Islam is a lifelong engagement. Gender roles in Egypt derive much of their legitimacy from the Qur'an. In particular, women are often the focus of quotations that supposedly refer to the appropriate roles and behaviors of women. Nonetheless, references to the roles of women are scattered broadly throughout the Qur'an and are subject to interpretation. Further, religion is by no means the sole determinant of women's issues and rights. In the contemporary context of postcolonial Egypt, women remain central as symbols of dominant ideological and religious beliefs. Women of all classes are perceived first and foremost as wives and mothers. To earn status, all women must marry and reproduce. The law gives first their fathers and then their husbands the power to control their ability to work or travel, and men hold unilateral rights of divorce. Children after a certain age are assigned to the husband's family and are often lost to the mother in the case of divorce. Family honor and reputation or, conversely, shame rely mainly on the public behavior of women, thereby reinforcing a high degree of sex segregation in the society.

Differences between men and women are prevalent in several aspects of Islamic law. Islamic law assigns certain rights and capacities to both men and women. A Muslim individual's legal capacity begins at birth and ends with death. His legal responsibilities are assumed under his legal capacity and are distinguished as a "capacity of execution" and a "capacity of obligations." According to the law, a free Muslim man who is sane and considered an adult has the highest degree of legal capacity. A Muslim woman, even though she has certain rights, generally is considered to have half the legal capacity of a man. This difference only becomes significant when men and women reach adulthood. According to the Islamic legal point of view, an adult is a "legally and morally responsible person, one who has reached physical maturity, is of sound mind, may enter into contracts, dispose of property, and be subject to criminal law. Above all, he is responsible for the religious commands and obligations of Islam."[48] When a Muslim man reaches maturity, his legal capacity becomes complete; neither his age nor his marital status influences his legal rights, responsibilities, or capacity of execution.[49]

Little is known about the lives of non-Muslim women in Egypt. Given the statistics that more than 90 percent of the population is Muslim, very few studies have been conducted on adherents of the Coptic Church, the small minority of Jews who live in Egypt, or the practitioners of other religious beliefs. It is known, however, that many of them share the same sociocultural beliefs and traditions. For example, Coptic Christian women veil just as Muslim women do and often observe strict premarital courtship behaviors. Coptic Christian men and women do not have the right to divorce. More statistics and studies are needed in order to ascertain the extent to which Islamic cultural traditions intersect with those of practitioners of other faiths in Egypt.

Rituals and Religious Practices

While both Muslim men and women are expected to be observant practitioners of religious rituals, the actual practice of Islam among men and women in Egypt varies. According to the official view of Islam, all believers have the same responsibilities to God and the same duties to perform. In one sense, the Muslim community is made up of equals, and this is supported by the belief that all humans, regardless of gender, ethnicity, race, or class, are equal before God. This belief is supported by reference to the Qur'an and serves as the foundation for the appeal that Islam is an egalitarian religion. In this community of believers, all adults are expected to carry out the five religious obligations. The first two obligations of a Muslim, recitation of the belief in one God and the validity of Muhammad's mission (the *shahada*) and the giving of alms, are not influenced by gender and can be practiced by all in a somewhat similar manner. In contrast, the other three obligations are influenced by the gender of the practitioner and are fulfilled quite differently in practice, even though they are supposed to be practiced by all believers equally.

The third obligation, Ramadan, the fasting time, falls within the ninth month of the lunar calendar.[50] This obligation affects men and women in a different manner because fasting requires ritual purity. A woman who is menstruating during this time or who has given birth recently cannot achieve ritual purity. It is therefore practically impossible for younger women to observe the thirty-day fast. The days that are lost to menstruation, like days that are lost to sickness, must be made up at a different time. In general, women make up this time either by attaching it to a particular sacred day (such as a Friday) or to the week preceding the next Ramadan. Thus even though the legal obligation to observe the fast applies equally to all believers, in reality it must, through necessity, be practiced differently by men and women. This leads to a clear differentiation between women and men based on the concept of purity. All believers are equal before God, but are separated by gender, practice, and their ability to fulfill this obligation in real life.

Women also are differentiated from men in trying to fulfill the fourth obligation, pilgrimage to Mecca (*hajj*). Again, menstruation plays a role. Only women past the age of menopause can maintain the ritual purity required for the ritual of the *hajj*. This forces most women to delay the pilgrimage until they no longer menstruate. It also leads to a division by age in terms of who has fulfilled the obligation of the pilgrimage and who has not. The importance of this difference lies in the fact that both men and women who have performed the pilgrimage are granted higher social status in the society. A woman who has performed the *hajj* is, from that point onward, referred to as a *hajja*, and people will not question her movements in the same manner as they may have before. Most women who have performed the pilgrimage will also choose to cover their hair upon returning, often wearing a turbanlike hat that signifies that they have participated in the *hajj*. Performing the *hajj* is for both men and women a rite of passage through which they publicly manifest their piousness and devotion as good Muslims.

The fifth obligation, prayer, is also impacted by the gender of the individual. In Egypt, one finds that men often pray in public spaces such as mosques, while women pray in private, usually in their homes. This becomes most apparent on Fridays, when more than 50 percent of Muslim men participate in the midday prayer at the mosque while the women stay at home to pray. The actual structure of prayer within the community is thereby affected by gender segregation and cultural beliefs.

Religious Law

Religious law is intertwined with civil law in Egypt specifically with respect to gender issues due to the prevalence of the Personal Status Law. See the discussions under "Politics and Law" on the role of the Personal Status Law.

VIOLENCE

Domestic Violence

Domestic violence against women is a significant but rarely acknowledged problem in Egypt. As in other places around the world, there is a tendency to blame the victim, and there are few, if any, social and economic supports for women who must deal with violence in their private lives. These issues are further exacerbated by rigid interpretations of Qur'anic law and culturally prevalent values that permit men to use violence against their wives as a legitimate form of discipline. There are, however, some limited data on domestic violence in Egypt. Most of this information comes from a national study conducted in 1995 that was part of a comprehensive demographic and health survey. This study revealed that 35 percent of Egyptian women have been beaten by their husbands at least once during their marriage.[51] Other, smaller studies support the notion that wife beating is prevalent and is actually considered by many as an intrinsic right of the husband in order to control his wife. Because family privacy is highly valued in Egypt, abuse, including wife beating, is not a public issue. However, it is known that violence of all kinds occurs in all social classes and among most occupational groups. Anecdotal evidence suggests that females with a spouse in a blue-collar or manual job are more likely to experience beatings resulting in disabling injuries or even murder. A troubling aspect of these forms of domestic violence is that many women, if not a majority, accept these behaviors as typical behavior on the part of men rather than as an aberration. Under recent changes to the law, spousal abuse is now accepted as the basis for divorce. Nevertheless, the woman must produce eyewitnesses, which is often difficult for women if not completely impossible. Even more problematic is that even with solid proof, many courts dismiss a majority of cases due to cultural beliefs based on issues of family honor, traditions, and provisions in the criminal code that allow husbands to "discipline" wives. Courts are male dominated and are also characterized by extreme sentencing disparities, with social class often playing a direct role in decisions. It is thus likely that poorer women are less able to get justice in their cases. Although there are no credible statistics, activists believe that despite cultural beliefs to the contrary, retaliation by women is not an unusual occurrence. This observation is substantiated by the increase in the number of women who kill their abusive husbands.[52] In order to assist in changing this situation, Egyptian female activists are increasingly turning to culturally and religiously based initiatives, including reinterpretation of Qur'anic law, recruitment of women into criminal justice agencies, and the development of support services to deal with these issues.

Another widespread problem, particularly in Cairo (much less so in villages and small towns), is the general harassment of women in public spaces. Groups of young men, mostly unemployed, roam the streets, visit religious sites and festivals, and ride public transportation as well as participating in outdoor activities while calling out to women and often trying to touch and fondle them. In 1996, 3,695 cases of verbal and physical harassment against women were reported.[53] Egyptian women explain this high level of harassment as evidence of the men being "morally corrupt" and "sexually frustrated." Men tend to explain their behavior as the result of the lack of economic opportunities that leaves them unable to find jobs and therefore marry, as well as having nothing to do with too much free time on their hands.[54] While the government has taken actions for stricter enforcement of laws, harassment is still very common, particularly in large urban areas.

Rape/Sexual Assault

There are no reliable statistics on rape in Egypt, nor is there any public discussion of this topic, but the recent strengthening of laws against rapists indicates its hidden existence in the society. Under the new strict laws, rapists now face life imprisonment or death. However, there are numerous barriers to reporting rape. Many of these barriers are based on cultural traditions that may bring great social dishonor to the woman and her family in the face of even the suspicion of rape. Further complicating this issue is that marital rape is not a legitimate concept in Egypt and is legal. In rural areas, honor killing—the murder of a woman because she is suspected of having potentially participated in illicit sexual relations—is known to occur. This concept is based on a cultural conception that the loss of a woman's virginity is a shame that can only be wiped out in blood. If a woman is raped, there exists the strong likelihood that she and her family will be forever shunned by their community. This stigma is even passed on to the family's offspring. Sentiments about rape are rooted in deep traditional beliefs about the importance of the sexual purity of women and the honor or shame that their behavior brings to their families.

Trafficking in Women and Children

Prostitution and sex tourism are illegal in Egypt. Nonetheless, there is some evidence that they can be found throughout the country. Poor prostitutes are particularly at risk because of exploitation by their clients and the outrage of their communities if it is revealed that they are engaged in illicit sexual activities. In contrast, high-class prostitutes have more security because they are often under the protection of a wealthy client who may rent or buy an apartment for them. However, under the law, prostitutes face imprisonment and even possibly the death penalty.[55] Punishment for prostitution contains another discriminatory aspect: male clients of female prostitutes cannot be punished if they are caught. Further, these men themselves may be used as credible witnesses in court against the prostitutes they have visited.[56] Again, as with all issues of sexuality in Egyptian society, there are few if any statistics, most evidence is anecdotal, and there is little public discussion of the cause or the possible solution.

OUTLOOK FOR THE TWENTY-FIRST CENTURY

Rights and issues pertaining to Egyptian women are complicated by social conditions that permit individuals of different classes to have varying access to knowledge, enforcement of their legal rights, and economic privileges. As part of an increasingly global community, various sectors of Egyptian society have differential access to opportunities. Middle- and upper-class women have much greater knowledge about social policies, informal and formal same-gender organizations, and the connections that family ties can bring. They are also the recipients of advances in educational opportunities, health-care options, and employment outside the home. Poor and rural women have only one option, survival, and this remains the most pivotal aspect of their lives. These women are for the most part ignored in most public discussions of women's issues and rights and, further, are taken advantage of by different groups and sometimes even their own spouses and families. This lack of awareness of differentiation by class is true of both secular and religious dialogues in Egypt on issues concerning women. In order to truly advance women's rights in Egypt, social policies and public dialogues must take into account the varied access of women to the structure of opportunities. The Western concept of feminism that emphasizes equality of the sexes, equality of opportunity, and a decreasing importance of gender in the definition of social roles takes as its starting point an arena where all individuals have equal chances and opportunities. Currently, this is not the case in Egypt. Furthermore, Egyptian women are part of a larger nationalistic debate that struggles between finding indigenous solutions to contemporary problems and negotiating Western concepts in order to remain viable in the global community. Interlinked is the issue that fundamentalist discourses on gender issues are gaining in popularity in Egypt because they originate not just from interpretations of religious texts but also from anti-imperialist beliefs that portray the West as a morally corrupt culture. In order to truly promote an atmosphere of equality between all individuals, all sides need to begin to understand each other's belief systems, ideologies, concerns, and positioning in the global system. Debates and implementation of women's rights take place in specific sociohistorical contexts. It is only by understanding the social, political, economic, and religious context of these discussions that we can begin to understand a particular society's women's movement as well as attitudes toward it.

NOTES

1. *The Worldfact Book 2002*, Central Intelligence Agency, Brasseys Inc.
2. Shahida el-Baz, "The Impact of Social and Economic Factors on Women's Group Formation in Egypt," in *Organizing Women: Formal and Informal Women's Groups in the Middle East*, ed. Dawn Chatty and Annika Rabo (Oxford: Berg, 1997), 151.
3. H. el-Nashif, *Basic Education and Female Literacy in Egypt* (Cairo: Third World Forum, Middle East Office, 1994), 1.
4. Ibid., 3.
5. el-Baz, 1997, 150.
6. U.S. State Department, *Country Reports on Human Rights Practices: Egypt — 2000* (Washington, DC: Bureau of Democracy, Human Rights, and Labor, 2001), 16.
7. CAPMAS, *Labour Force Sample Survey (LFSS)* (Cairo: 1990).
8. Ibid., in el-Baz, 1997, 152.
9. el-Baz, 1997, 153.
10. Azza Karam, *Women, Islamisms, and the State: Contemporary Feminisms in Egypt* (New York: St. Martin's Press, 1998), 160.
11. Karam, 1998, 159.
12. Ibid., 149.
13. M. Hatem, "Economic and Political Liberalization in Egypt and the Demise of State Feminism," *International Journal of Middle East Studies* 24 (1992): 241.
14. el-Baz, 1997, 149.
15. Arlene Elowe Macleod, *Accommodating Protest: Working Women, the New Veiling, and Change in Cairo* (New York: Columbia University Press, 1991), 85.
16. There is, of course, variation in different Islamic societies as to the perception of the different stages of femaleness.
17. A recent study conducted by researchers from Ayn Shams University found that 98 percent of all girls in the Egyptian countryside and poor girls in Cairo had been circumcised (both Muslims and Coptic Christians), while the estimate for upper-

class girls in Cairo was approximately 305. Selma Botman, *Engendering Citizenship in Egypt* (New York: Columbia University Press, 1999), 106.

18. Egypt Demographic and Health Survey (EDHS-95), 1995.
19. Karam, 1998, 145.
20. C. Chelala, "Egypt Faces Challenges of Population Growth," *Lancet* 348(9042) (1996): 1651.
21. Marcia Inhorn, *Quest for Conception: Gender, Infertility, and Egyptian Medical Traditions* (Philadelphia: University of Pennsylvania Press, 1994), 5.
22. Chelala, 1996, 1651.
23. UNICEF, 1990, 17.
24. *Beijing National Report* (Cairo: National Women's Committee, National Council for Childhood and Motherhood, 1995), 39.
25. el-Baz, 1997, 154.
26. C. Lenton, "Will Egypt Escape the AIDS Epidemic?" *Lancet* 349(9057) (1997): 1005.
27. M. Inhorn and K. Buss, "Infertility, Infection, and Iatrogenesis in Egypt: The Anthropological Epidemiology of Blocked Tubes," *Medical Anthropology* 15 (1993): 1–28.
28. Inhorn, 1993, 4.
29. Despite the growing conservative fundamentalist movement, Egypt is still more liberal than other Arab states.
30. Lenton, 1997, 1005.
31. el-Baz, 1997, 148.
32. Karam, 1998, 152.
33. Ibid.
34. Ibid.
35. Botman, 1999.
36. Nadje al-Ali, "Feminism and Contemporary Debates in Egypt," in *Organizing Women: Formal and Informal Women's Groups in the Middle East*, ed. Dawn Chatty and Annika Rabo (Oxford: Berg, 1997), 181.
37. Ibid.
38. U.S. State Department, 2001, 16.
39. Ibid.
40. Karam, 1998, 148.
41. Margot Badran and Miriam Cooke, introduction to *Opening the Gates: A Century of Arab Feminist Writing*, ed. Margot Badran and Miriam Cooke (Bloomington: Indiana University Press, 1990), xxvi.
42. Beth Baron, *The Women's Awakening in Egypt: Culture, Society, and the Press* (New Haven, CT: Yale University Press, 1994), 5.
43. Leila Ahmed, "Feminism and Feminist Movements in the Middle East, a Preliminary Exploration: Turkey, Egypt, Algeria, People's Democratic Republic of Yemen," *Women's Studies International Forum* 5(2) (1982): 160.
44. Botman, 1999, 41.
45. Ibid., 48.
46. Karam, 1998, 145.
47. Botman, 1999, 86.
48. Ira M. Lapidus, "Adulthood in Islam: Religious Maturity in the Islamic Tradition," *Daedalus* 105(2) (1976): 93.
49. Ibid.
50. During this time of fasting, nothing may enter the body, neither liquid, food,

nor smoke. It is also a time of daytime celibacy (Qur'an 2:186–87). At nightfall, the fast is broken with a simple meal and prayer, followed around midnight by a heavier meal.

51. N. Ammare, "In the Shadow of the Pyramids: Domestic Violence in Egypt," *International Review of Victimology* 7(1–3) (2000): 29.

52. Ibid.

53. F. Nawa, "Sexual Harassment of Women Is Commonplace on Cairo's Streets," *Cairo Times* (1)14: 1–4.

54. Ibid.

55. W. Zenie-Ziegler, *In Search of Shadows: Conversations with Egyptian Women* (London: Zed, 1988); N. el-Saadawi, *The Hidden Face of Eve* (London: Zed, 1980).

56. Karam, 1998, 151.

RESOURCE GUIDE

Suggested Reading

Atiya, N. *Khul-Khaal: Five Egyptian Women Tell Their Stories.* Cairo: American University, 1988.
Beck, L., and N. Keddie, eds. *Women in the Muslim World.* Cambridge, MA: Harvard University Press, 1978.
Bowen, D., and E. Early, eds. *Everyday Life in the Muslim Middle East.* Bloomington: Indiana University Press, 1993.
Hoodfar, H. *Between Marriage and the Market.* Berkeley: University of California Press, 1997.
Macleod, Arlene Elowe. *Accommodating Protest: Working Women, the New Veiling, and Change in Cairo.* New York: Columbia University Press, 1991.
Rugh, A. *Family in Contemporary Egypt.* Syracuse, NY: Syracuse University Press, 1984.
Singerman, D. *Avenues of Participation: Family, Politics, and Networks in Urban Quarters of Cairo.* Princeton, NJ: Princeton University Press, 1995.
Wikan, U. *Tomorrow, God Willing: Self-Made Destinies in Cairo.* Chicago: University of Chicago Press, 1996.
Zenie-Ziegler, W. *In Search of Shadows: Conversations with Egyptian Women.* London: Zed, 1988.
Zuhur, Sherifa. *Revealing Reveiling: Islamist Gender Ideology in Contemporary Egypt.* Albany: State University of New York Press, 1992.

Videos/Films

Arab Diaries. 2001. First Run Icarus Films. Four young women striving for independence and empowerment in Algeria, Egypt and Lebanon.
Covered: The Hejab in Cairo, Egypt. 1995. Women Make Movies. On the recent resurgence of veiling.
Four Women of Egypt. 1997. Women Make Movies. On Muslim, Christian, and atheist women in Egypt.
The Price of Change. 1982. First Run Icarus Films. Working women in Cairo (issues still pertinent).
A Veiled Revolution. 1982. First Run Icarus Films. Why women in Egypt are returning to veiling. A classic and still relevant film on this issue.

Web Sites

al-Ahram, www.ahram.org.eg.
The site of the official main weekly newspaper of Egypt.

Arab Infoseek, www.arabinfoseek.com/arab-women's_issues.
Debatabase on women's issues throughout the Arab world.

www.egypt.net.
A catchall site that allows viewers to access all types of information about Egypt.

United Nations Development Fund for Women, www.arabwomenconnect.org.

Organizations

Alliance for Arab Women
28 Adly Street, Apt. 74–75
Cairo, Egypt
Phone: (202) 3939899
Fax: (202) 3936820
Email: aaw@link.com.eg

Arab Women's Solidarity Association (AWSA)
4A Dareed Saad Street
Kasr el Ainy, Cairo, Egypt

Egyptian Women's Association
4 el Awhady Street
Menshiet El Bapri, Cairo, Egypt
Phone: (202) 83 5271

General Department of Women's Affairs
Ministry of Social Affairs
Mogama Building, 4th Floor
Tahrir Square
Cairo, Egypt
Phone: (202) 3543003

The National Council for Women
1113 Corniche el Nil, Tahrir
P.O. Box 11625
Maglis el Shoura
Cairo, Egypt
Phone: (202) 5748168
Email: ncwl@idsc.gov.eg

SELECTED BIBLIOGRAPHY

Abdel Kader, S. *The Situation Analysis of Women in Egypt*. Cairo: Central Agency for Population, Mobilization, and Statistics (CAPMAS) and UNICEF, 1992.

Ahmed, Leila. "Feminism and Feminist Movements in the Middle East, a Preliminary Exploration: Turkey, Egypt, Algeria, People's Democratic Republic of Yemen." *Women's Studies International Forum* 5(2) (1982): 153–68.

al-Ali, Nadje. "Feminism and Contemporary Debates in Egypt." In *Organizing Women: Formal and Informal Women's Groups in the Middle East*, ed. Dawn Chatty and Annika Rabo. Oxford: Berg, 1997.

Amin, Qasim. *Tahrir al-mar'a* (The Liberation of Women). Reprinted in Muhammad 'Imara, *Qasim Amin: Al-a'mal al-kamila*, vol. 2. Beriut: 1976.

Ammare, N. "In the Shadow of the Pyramids: Domestic Violence in Egypt." *International Review of Victimology* 7(1–3) (2000): 29–46.

Anderson, J.N.D. "The Eclipse of the Patriarchal Family in Contemporary Islamic Law." In *Family Law in Asia and Africa*, ed. J.N.D. Anderson, 221–34. London: George Allen and Unwin, 1968.

Badran, Margot. "Competing Agenda: Feminists, Islam, and the State in Nineteenth- and Twentieth-Century Egypt." In *Women, Islam, and the State*, ed. Deniz Kandiyoti, 201–36. Philadelphia: Temple University Press, 1991.

Badran, Margot, and Miriam Cooke. Introduction to *Opening the Gates: A Century of Arab Feminist Writing*, ed. Margot Badran and Miriam Cooke, xiv–xxxvi. Bloomington: Indiana University Press, 1990.

Baron, Beth. *The Women's Awakening in Egypt: Culture, Society, and the Press*. New Haven, CT: Yale University Press, 1994.

el-Baz, Shahida. "The Impact of Social and Economic Factors on Women's Group Formation in Egypt." In *Organizing Women: Formal and Informal Women's Groups in the Middle East*, ed. Dawn Chatty and Annika Rabo. Oxford: Berg, 1997.

Beijing National Report. Cairo: National Women's Committee, National Council for Childhood and Motherhood, 1995.

Botman, Selma. *Engendering Citizenship in Egypt*. New York: Columbia University Press, 1999.

CAPMAS. *Labour Force Sample Survey (LFSS)*. Cairo, 1990.

———. National Census. Cairo, 1986.

CAPMAS and UNICEF. *Women's Participation in the Labour Force*. Cairo, 1991.

Chelala, C. "Egypt Faces Challenges of Population Growth." *Lancet* 348(9042) (1996): 1651.

Hatem, M. "Economic and Political Liberalization in Egypt and the Demise of State Feminism." *International Journal of Middle East Studies* 24 (1992): 231–51.

Inhorn, Marcia. *Quest for Conception: Gender, Infertility, and Egyptian Medical Traditions*. Philadelphia: University of Pennsylvania Press, 1994.

Inhorn, M., and K. Buss. "Infertility, Infection, and Iatrogenesis in Egypt: The Anthropological Epidemiology of Blocked Tubes." *Medical Anthropology* 15 (1993): 1–28.

Karam, Azza. *Women, Islamisms, and the State: Contemporary Feminisms in Egypt*. New York: St. Martin's Press, 1998.

Lapidus, Ira M. "Adulthood in Islam: Religious Maturity in the Islamic Tradition." *Daedalus* 105(2) (1976): 93–108.

Lenton, C. 1997. "Will Egypt Escape the AIDS Epidemic?" *Lancet* 349(9057) (1997): 1005.

Macleod, Arlene Elowe. *Accommodating Protest: Working Women, the New Veiling, and Change in Cairo*. New York: Columbia University Press, 1991.

Najmabadi, A. "Hazards of Modernity and Morality: Women, State, and Ideology in Contemporary Iran." In *Women, Islam, and the State*, ed. Deniz Kandiyoti, 48–76. London: Macmillan, 1991.

el-Nashif, H. *Basic Education and Female Literacy in Egypt*. Cairo: Third World Forum, Middle East Office, 1994.
Nawa, F. "Sexual Harassment of Women Is Commonplace on Cairo's Streets." *Cairo Times* (1)14: 1–4.
el-Saadawi, N. *The Hidden Face of Eve*. London: Zed, 1980.
Talhami, Ghada. *The Mobilization of Muslim Women in Egypt*. Gainesville: University Press of Florida, 1996.
UNICEF. *Report on the State of Women and Children in Egypt*. Cairo: UNICEF, 1993.
U.S. State Department. *Country Reports on Human Rights Practices: Egypt—2000*. Washington, DC: Bureau of Democracy, Human Rights, and Labor, 2001.
Zenie-Ziegler, W. *In Search of Shadows: Conversations with Egyptian Women*. London: Zed, 1988.
Zuhur, Sherifa. *Revealing Reveiling: Islamist Gender Ideology in Contemporary Egypt*. Albany: State University of New York Press, 1992.

4

IRAN

Mary Hegland

PROFILE OF IRAN

Iran lies between Iraq and, further north, Turkey to the west and Afghanistan and Pakistan to the east. Armenia, Azerbaijan, Turkmenistan, and the Caspian Sea border Iran to the north, and the Persian Gulf to the south. Iran covers 636,293 square miles.

In the early decades of the twentieth century, many people lived by herding animals. Some of the Kurds and the Shahsevan in the northwest, Qashqai, Bakhtiary, Lurs, and Kamseh in the southwest, Baluch in the southeast, and Turkmen in the northeast lived in nomadic camps, traveling with their animals in search of water and pastures. Beginning in the 1920s, the two Pahlavi shahs, Reza Shah and his son, Mohammad Reza Shah, worked to pacify tribespeople and bring them under the control of the central government. Now, nomads have largely been settled and live in villages or migrate to urban areas.

In addition to tribal groups, Iranians are ethnically diverse. A large number of Turks or Azaris live in the northwest province of Azerbaijan, which lies on the border of Turkey and Azerbaijan and Armenia, newly independent states of the former Soviet Union. To the south of this Turkish area, also in Azerbaijan and then in villages and towns of provinces further south along the Iraqi border, live Kurds. Kurds have a centuries-long history of settled agriculture and urban living in addition to transhumance (nomadism). Kurds also live in contiguous areas across borders in Iraq and Turkey. In the southwest near the Persian Gulf and the Iraqi border live some people of Arab background who speak Arabic. About 85 percent of Iranians accept Shi'a Islam, but some adhere to Sunni Islam, including most Kurds and some Arabs. Christian Armenians and Assyrians live in western areas of Azerbaijan, for example, around Urmiyeh (Rezayeh). A large group of Armenians were settled in Julfa, next to Isfahan, and practiced handicrafts. Some Christians, and also Jews and Baha'is, left Iran in the years after the 1979 revolution and subsequent formation of the Islamic Republic of Iran, although many remain. Some Zoroastrians, descendants of people who managed to hold on to their religion after the Islamic conquest in the seventh century, still live in Iran.

As much of Iranian territory is desert or semidesert, agriculturalists commonly practice irrigation. Production depends to a large degree on access to water. As an exception, the Caspian Sea coastal areas receive a great deal of rain and produce rice, tea, and citrus fruits as well as many other crops. Until the 1960s, Iranians primarily worked in agriculture, trading, or handwork. Since the oil boom of the 1960s and even more the 1970s, the economy has relied primarily on the sale of oil and less on exported Persian carpets and fruits and nuts. Construction, factories, government service, education, health services, and businesses and services have expanded due to the oil money. In recent years, many agricultural products and manufactured goods have been imported.

Prior to the 1979 revolution, shahs (monarchs) ruled the country, largely through balancing and playing off against each other regional and tribal leaders. The last two shahs were able to take power away from such leaders and centralize power. With the help of concessions and then oil sales, the Pahlavi shahs strengthened the armed forces, police, rural gendarmerie, and secret police. Although they instituted modern services, improved infrastructure, education, and health services, and the economy boomed, they did not bring about political liberalization. In the 1970s, Iranians became increasingly dissatisfied with the government. People lacked political freedoms. Less well-off people resented their inequitable access to improved standards of living and financial gain. The clergy and traditional classes begrudged their lack of power and U.S. political and cultural influence.

On February 11, 1979, Iranians rose in massive marches, demonstrations, and strikes and overthrew the Pahlavi regime. No political groups, religious or secular, had been allowed to operate under the shah's regime. The clergy, though, had used religious spaces, gatherings, and organizations in the political struggle against the shah. They were thus well placed to take over leadership after the fall of the Pahlavi government. They held an election for the formation of an Islamic Republic. Since then, Iran has had a Shi'a Muslim government, largely manned by Shi'a clerics.

The leader of the revolutionary movement, Ayatollah Khomeini, became the first supreme leader. Upon his death in 1989, President Ali Khamene'i became his successor. Akbar Hashemi Rafsanjani was elected president in July 1989. Following him, Mohammad Khatami was elected in 1997 and reelected in 2001. Iranians elect their president, representatives to Parliament, and other officials from a roster of candidates approved by the government. The Supreme Leader, Ayatollah Ali Khamene'i, appoints six clerics to the twelve-member Guardian Council. The parliament (Majlis) elects the other six from candidates presented by the Supreme Judicial Council. The Guardian Council can veto bills passed by the Parliament. The Supreme Leader controls the army forces and the judiciary. Basically, conservative Shi'a Muslim clerics run the country. Reformists clerics and more liberal and secular-minded Iranians are struggling to put people into office who will bring about more political freedom and democracy and less control by the governmental Shi'a clerics over all aspects of life.

Out of a total population of about 68 million, males predominate, with some 105 males for each 100 females. Iranian men can expect to live for 66 years and women for 69 years. According to government reports, both infant mortality and maternal mortality have declined to 33 per 1,000 births. Fertility has been declining precipitously since the mid-1980s, down from 6.8 children per woman in 1984 to 6.3 in 1986, 5.5 in 1988, 2.8 in 1996, and 2.1 in 2000.

OVERVIEW OF WOMEN'S ISSUES

Iranian women are facing tremendous challenges. Despite barriers and disadvantages, they are finding ways to struggle for more influence in society and government and improved lives. Since the 1979 revolution, women have devised many subversive ways of resisting conservative clerics' definition of them and restrictions on their behavior. They have succeeded in bringing about many positive changes. Through their determination and untiring efforts, they have been able to erode restrictions. Faced with this mass of unwieldy disobedience, clerics have tired of constantly trying to police women, and their efforts have flagged. Iranian women stand at stage center of political dynamics and seem determined to go after economic success as well.

During the reign of the two Pahlavi shahs, government policies sought to bring women out of the anonymity of home and family life into the world of educated, working women. The shahs wanted to modernize women to become symbols and means of Westernizing Iranian society. Although Iranian women were largely targets of government policy rather than participants in policy formation, they enjoyed more access to education, and many joined the workforce during the Pahlavi era. Legal changes gave women improved rights and status in marriage and the family, at least on paper, and women were able to come out into public space. Then came the Iranian Revolution of 1978 and 1979 and the subsequent Islamic Republic of Iran. Iran became a theocracy. The Shi'a Islamic clerics in power saw Westernized Iranian women as symbols of moral corruption, Western control, and the decline of Islam. Although women had participated in the revolution in marches, demonstrations, strikes, and communication, clerics saw their political involvement as necessitated by the critical situation. Once the Islamic Revolution was successful, conservative clerics believed, women should go back to their rightful, God-ordained place as wives and mothers protected at home. God created women as emotional, compassionate creatures, fit to bear and raise children and to provide comfort for men, who, as rational, active people, were fit to work outside of the home. The physical differences between the sexes and their related natures fit them for different activities. This attitude toward women colored clerics' beliefs about women's rightful place in the family and in society. Islamic Republic officials attempted to change laws and policies to channel women's activities in what they saw as the right direction and to protect them from corruption. Men, too, should be protected from the irresistible temptation of women's sexuality out in the open, which could disrupt families and society.

In attempting to craft Iranian women to serve as symbols and means for an Islamic society, clerics faced several challenges. Religious figures in control of the government had benefited from women's heavy revolutionary participation. Women's involvement had swelled the numbers of demonstrators and had demonstrated the seriousness and determination of revolutionary activists. Leaders continued to enjoy women's support through allowing them to vote in the initial election to establish the Islamic Republic of Iran and in elections thereafter. To benefit from their support, they defined women as participants in political life and then found it difficult to openly deny women's political influence. Women, seeing themselves defined as political actors and given religious blessing for political participation, were encouraged and enabled to act politically. Once clerics had proclaimed women's duty to participate in politics and support the Islamic Revolution and the Islamic Republic, they could hardly deny the legitimacy of women's political pressure, even when they called for more rights for women and a more moderate political system. Most dramatically, women took advantage of their political rights to vote disproportionately for the liberal president, Mohammad Khatami, in the 1997 and 2001 elections, posing a threat to the conservative clergy.

Clerics in political power attempted to mold women into private persons, stationed in homes and under the control of male family figures. Women were to be defined by marriage and family relationships, and their primary roles were to be wife and mother. However, clerics were dealing with many women who had benefited from the shah's modernization and

Westernization program to become educated, working, more autonomous and individualized women. Such women did not readily accept the pronouncement that they were not able to deal with the public world, that their acquiescent and easily aroused natures would leave them susceptible to sexual advances, and that their emotional, compassionate natures made them incompetent to deal with the hard, rational requirements of the public world. Because of their work experiences, women knew that they could handle careers. Women resented the characterization of their natures as irrational and emotionally weak. They resented harassment and discrimination in their jobs and the efforts to push them back into dependent home life.

When political leaders ruled that the sexes must be segregated in order to maintain women's modesty and prevent the threat of their uncontrolled sexuality to society, ironically, they needed educated, trained females to work with women in order to accomplish sex segregation. Female doctors, nurses, teachers, and other service personnel had to be available to deal with women. Women therefore had to be provided with education and job opportunities. Such initiatives then cast doubt on the proclamation that women were fit only for homemaking and child rearing and that their compassionate, emotional, susceptible, and irrational natures should be guarded by seclusion at home.

Iranian women today face a struggle. The tremendous forces for change in the country—the press for modernization under the Pahlavi shahs along with their failure to institute political freedoms, the oil-boom economy, the Iranian Revolution of 1978–1979 and the subsequent formation of the Islamic Republic of Iran, and pressures against the clerical rule for political liberalization and improved women's rights—have produced a situation in flux. The conservative clerics and traditional, religious classes are battling to maintain control of Iranian society and the future against the moderate clergy and people who want more freedom, democracy, and equality between the sexes. Contention over gender and what it means to be an Iranian Muslim woman is taking place in many arenas: families, kin networks, communities, workplaces, religious gatherings and organizations, and politics. Wives are pushing husbands for change, and daughters are asserting themselves against fathers. As villagers migrate or commute to urban areas, and communication, transportation, media, and literacy reach previously remote villages, even rural women and lower-class urban females are acquiring new ideas and finding ways to try to improve their situations.

However, transgressions sometimes bring punishment. Many Iranian women realize this and do not risk open confrontation. Those women who do resist authoritarian men and Islamic policy sometimes find themselves more on their own rather than benefiting from the protection and support that other females hope to receive in return for submission. Today's women, though, have far more resources and opportunities than their mothers. At present, Iranian females can more often resist restrictions openly, rather than subtly attempting to manipulate and influence the men controlling their lives. Many women have become entrepreneurial and run their own businesses, sometimes fronted by a male relative. Many feisty, educated young females are carving out more independence and access to economic rewards for themselves. They are willing to do whatever it takes to earn their own money, especially since they see many young men as undirected and unsuccessful.[1]

EDUCATION

Opportunities

Before the establishment of public education, very few females could learn to read. While some boys could attend traditional religious schools (*maktabs*), girls could not. A few fathers might bring a tutor into the home to teach reading the Qur'an to a daughter under close supervision. Even those few girls who learned to read the Qur'an usually would not understand what they were reading, as the language was Arabic. When a girl did have the opportunity to learn to read Farsi, the modern Persian language, rarely was she taught to write. Girls might use the skill to write notes to boys, people feared, bringing scandal to the family. In the early twentieth century, several Tehran women began to open classes for girls in their homes. The shah's government established a public schooling system, although girls' attendance lagged far behind that of boys. The school system provided segregated schools for boys and girls. In order to cut down on improper interaction between the sexes, superintendents usually modified school schedules so that girls would reach home before the boys emerged on the streets. Because urban children had better access to schools than rural children, in 1964 the Pahlavi government formed the Literacy Corps. Thousands upon thousands of high-school graduates went out to villages to teach, greatly improving rural children's access to education.

After the revolution, the government produced new schoolbooks, featuring a more traditional sex division of labor and Islamically dressed females. The government continues to promote education, and girls' school attendance has risen, as has boys'. Because of the Islamic nature of the government and schools, traditionally conservative people feel more comfortable about girls' education. Before the revolution, most girls did not wear veils or scarves over their school uniforms. The Islamic Republic requires females, both teachers and students, to wear Islamic dress. Recently, education officials have announced that schoolbooks will be modified to show the diversity of women's roles in society, rather than presenting females as mothers and housewives only. In 2002, a pilot project in several girls' schools in the Tehran area allowed both students and teachers to attend class without scarves, although they were carefully hidden from outsider view.

Given the Islamization of the environment, dress, and universities, in recent years even conservative families have felt much less hesitant to send their girls to schools and universities. Families who during the shah period considered entrance to university an initiation into prostitution now feel comfortable letting their daughters attend universities. In addition to the transformation of institutions of higher learning into religious spaces, university education for girls has become physically easier. Many new university branches have opened throughout the country. Daughters can attend university while continuing to live under careful guard in their own family homes. Public transportation has improved and become segregated, also making parents more at ease about letting their daughters go out.[2] Even for the lower classes and rural females, attending undergraduate education has become the thing to do for females. Along with literacy, education, and women's journals, modernist ideas about women and their liberation are spreading to all sectors of the population. "Education for women is seen as the only road to later employment and an income without which a 'good life' cannot be had, either by the woman or by her family. It is now seen as an economic and liberating necessity, women themselves say."[3]

During the last shah's reign, some girls attended mixed-gender universities, although their attendance lagged behind that of males. In addition to the public universities, private institutions opened, increasing the relatively small number of slots. For the public universities, students took entrance exams (the *concur*). Relatively few could pass the exam. In the 1960s and 1970s, because of oil revenues, better-off parents could send their children abroad for university educations. By the 1970s, Iranians formed the largest foreign student population in the United States.

After the revolution, in April 1980 the government closed Iranian universities in order to restructure them into Islamic institutions. When they reopened, only professors with proper Islamic credentials and attitudes could teach. In addition to passing a religion test, students had to bring documentation about their piety and correct Islamic attitudes from neighborhood mosque organizations. Females had to wear a veil and modest dress, the proper Islamic covering, and avoid obvious interaction with male students. Although males and females sometimes attended the same classes, they sat in separate sections. Moreover, not all fields of education were open to women. The Islamic Republic did not allow unmarried females to go abroad for education, although this law has recently been rescinded. Married females had to be accompanied by their husbands. During both the Pahlavi period and the Islamic Republic, women have not been able to leave the country without the written permission of their husbands.

Sometimes sex-segregation rules result in lower-quality education for females. In 2000, students at a women's medical school in Qom went on strike to protest lower-quality education because of sex segregation; following segregation rules, officials had fired all male employees. More recently, the government has dropped restrictions for women in some fields of study. Although some decades ago males outnumbered females in universities, for several years now more females than males have been attending universities.

Literacy

Literacy rates have been climbing in the last several decades. The Iranian government claims that 65.8 percent of women are literate, although the UN Statistics Division reports 43 percent literacy for women compared with 70–78 percent of men.

EMPLOYMENT AND ECONOMICS

Job/Career Opportunities

During the Pahlavi era, more males than females gained education in the rapidly expanding public school system. Many more males than females found positions in government services, such as education, health, and the bureaucracy. However, boys and girls went to separate schools, and many positions therefore opened for female teachers. Other early career opportunities for women included midwifery and nursing. Sometimes, especially along the Caspian Sea coastal areas, females worked in agriculture on their family-owned land or as day laborers, harvesting and processing some crops. Girls and women did most of the tedious work knotting the famous Persian carpets and weaving gelims. Females from poorer families commonly worked as servants in households. In the earlier years of modernization and Westernization, men held secretarial and typist positions. Because traditional males' honor rested on supporting their wives and daughters so that they need not be exposed to unrelated men through work, even positions commonly held by women in Western countries, such as restaurant server and telephone operator, were not open to women.

In the 1960s and 1970s, more and more females attended universities, both inside Iran and abroad, and thus were able to take professional positions in government and private sectors. Iranians did not share the American view that females do not excel in such fields as math and engineering, and females did not feel constrained to avoid these areas of study and work. After the revolution and formation of the Islamic Republic, however, conservative clerics pushed for women's veiling. Feeling pressured about their dress and interaction style, many women chose to stay at home rather than undergo the rough scrutiny of lower-class females hired to guard entrances from inadequately covered females.

Conservative clerical leaders struggled to put women back at home where they belonged, caring for husbands and children and safe from potentially bringing temptation to males, thus disrupting society. Governmental clerics placed restrictions on women's employment, but because many Iranian men went to war with Iraq, and the economy had weakened, women were needed. Further, in order to segregate females from unrelated males, women were needed in education, medicine, and other services. In the face of inflation, families needed women's salaries to supplement men's. The government employed females to evaluate women's covering at the entrance of public buildings and in other relatively menial positions in female areas. Government clerics and religious leaders pointed to Islam as providing the best conditions for females. Iranian women used this clerical stance to struggle for improved women's rights and employment opportunities.[4]

Defending their perspective with the Qur'anic stipulation that two female witnesses are equal to one male, clerics barred women from working as judges. Eventually, pressured by women, the government appointed some women lawyers to work in the court system and then to become family-court judges. Now women have entered virtually every line of work, including taxicab drivers and airline pilots, although in small minorities in many fields. Men still dominate in construction, factory management, manufacturing, the modern employment sector, and business, although many women are opening their own businesses. Many women are becoming doctors, and women remain overrepresented in the nurturing professions, especially caring for other females. However, drawing on the tradition of elite women's imperious behavior toward both male and female underlings, Iranian professional women in supervisory positions do not shy from stern and straightforward behavior with employees. Apparently quite secure in their sexual identity, they do not anguish over trying to balance gentle and compassionate behavior to demonstrate their femininity with the need to be demanding and brusque to maintain hierarchical command.

Pay

In general, women receive the same pay as men in the same positions. Women employees complain, however, that through overtime and other means of getting extras, men manage to take home much more money than women in the same position.[5] Under both the Pahlavi government and the Islamic Republic, overt salary discrimination against women has not been much of a problem. Partly because education was scarce and valued, people tended to view the education and qualifications of females as more significant than their sex.

Working Conditions

Working conditions for females, as well as for males, have been quite abysmal in Iran. Girls, often from a very young age, as well as women who worked as servants, had to be ready at all times to work, received very little pay—and even that likely went to family males—often did not enjoy adequate nutrition, and could be mistreated and abused. Household males, a father or his sons, might well require sexual services of them. Girls and women who labored in carpet workshops or knotted carpets at home likewise worked very long hours for little pay, hunched in the same position, usually with inadequate light. Agricultural workers likewise worked hard for little pay. Like males, females did not earn any social security, enjoy legal protection over working conditions and environments, or receive workers' compensation if they were injured on the job. At present, the Social Security Organization and the State Welfare Organization provide insurance and many types of benefits for state employees and also reach out to private companies and individuals in need.

Sexual Harassment

During the Pahlavi period, males commonly bothered females on the streets, calling out improper comments or invitations and pinching or touching them. Males, although very sensitive about men insulting their honor by improper attention to their own wives, sisters, or daughters, did not feel constrained from bothering unrelated females themselves. Males particularly targeted professional or Westernized women and girls on their way to school who did not wear a veil, but also might handle veiled females. During the revolutionary period, men placed importance on respecting their "Muslim sisters." People made efforts to provide separate spaces for females in public areas, roping off aisles, for example. Harassment of women and girls on the streets declined dramatically for a period.

The Islamic Republic prides itself on fostering a society where pious Muslim women are protected and respected. To this end and to avoid arousing men's lust through the sight of females, females are required to wear clothing covering their body shape and hair. Such dress should signal to men that they are proper and pious Muslim women. They should thus be treated with respect rather than being viewed as immodest and thus susceptible to male attention. After the Islamic Republic government took over firm control, fear of sanctions and punishment made males hesitant to call out sexual comments or touch females on the street. Modesty requirements have eased somewhat in recent years. Now some girls and women may go without stockings under sandals, wear tunics that cover only to the knee or even higher, show some hair under a head covering, and wear makeup and nail polish outside of the home. However, young women still often fear sexual harassment or robbery on the streets and try to avoid going out.[6]

In spite of such public molestation of females during and after the Pahlavi period when more urban women began venturing outside of the home, Iranians did not hold a concept of sexual harassment. As in the West, where "sexual harassment" is a new term for a long-standing social problem, in Iran, if a girl or woman received unwanted attention, it was because she encouraged it or put herself in a position where this might happen. Bothering girls on the street was just something that boys did, and nothing could be done about it. Therefore, little is known about sexual harassment in the workplace at that time. Given the more formal interaction between unrelated males and females put together in the workplace, likely most women did not suffer much sexual harassment. If they did, fearing dishonor, they would not publicize it. Upon meeting a female and working with her, males would not feel as free to intrude on them as they might toward unknown women in the streets. Girls and women who worked as servants in other people's homes, however, might face employers' or their sons' sexual predation.

Because of much greater efforts to segregate males and females and the focus on proper behavior between unrelated males and females, overt sexual harassment on the job does not constitute a problem for most women in the Islamic Republic. During the earlier years of the Islamic Republic, however, women were in danger of harassment by relatively uncontrolled Revolutionary Guards as a punishment for improper covering or behavior. Men shopkeepers and women employed to check women's covering (*hijab*) at the entrances of government buildings scolded and turned away inadequately covered women. Males and females felt free to criticize inadequate covering of females and to order them to shape up. Under the Islamic Republic, people feel responsible for even unrelated females' dress and behavior and do not hesitate to exert pressure or force.

Support for Mothers/Caretakers

Iranians consider caring for children to be the mother's job in Iran. She may sometimes solicit assistance from her mother or other female relatives. In middle- and upper-class households, servants commonly took over care for children, although the mother retained final responsibility and was accountable for bad behavior. In better-off households, sometimes a maid was assigned to each child. Now that household servants are not as common as they were several decades ago, mothers do not as often have live-in women to help them out. The Islamic Republic emphasizes the traditional sexual division of labor and the mother's responsibility for children. Although in some cases, Iranian men have begun to spend time with children, in most families fathers still do not play much part in child care. The government's Social Security Organization and State Welfare Organization provide assistance for mothers and children and also supply grants to private organizations aimed at assisting mothers and children.

Maternal Leave

Iranian mothers may have ninety days of maternal leave. For childbirth and maternity leave, they can receive 66.7 percent of their pay for sixteen weeks from the Social Security Organization for up to three children.

Daycare

Daycare is a relatively new phenomenon in Iran. In past decades, men who could afford it supported their wives, enabling them to stay at home. For teachers and other professional women, grandparents, other female relatives, or maids could care for children until they began to attend schools. In recent decades, fewer couples have lived with parents. Middle- and upper-class households are smaller and employ fewer servants than several decades ago.

The government has opened some daycare facilities. Many large organizations, public and private, offer on-site daycare facilities. Iranians do not like to leave children with strangers or in a public daycare facility, however, if they can help it. Frightening stories about how badly children are treated by caretakers abound. Whether they are true or not, working mothers' greatest area of concern is child care. Sometimes women turn to the grandparents for assistance if they do not live far away and are willing to take on this responsibility. Some women care for children in their homes as a means of making an income, and working mothers may take advantage of such opportunities.

Family and Medical Leave

The government's Social Security Organization and State Welfare Organization provide assistance for employees needing family and medical leave assistance.

Inheritance and Property Rights

Females may own property. Female offspring inherit half the share of males. Typically, brothers expected or even took for granted that sisters turn over their share to the brothers. Through the 1970s, when most females had little or no education, they felt dependent on brothers should their husbands die or divorce them. They therefore wished to stay in the good graces of brothers. More recently, sisters have felt less reticence about going after their rights. It has been reported that "the courts are besieged by women who claim that their brothers cheated them in inheritance of the father's property."[7]

Social/Government Programs

Traditionally, private philanthropy provided such assistance to the needy as was available. People brought food and other resources to mosques and shrines for distribution and gave to the needy on a personal, individual basis. Giving alms is one of the five pillars of Islam. Ideally, a tenth of a person's income should be given to charity. Traditional bazaar merchants tended to give their required alms (*zakat*) to their chosen spiritual leader (*imam* or *ayatollah*) for him to distribute to followers. As Shi'a Muslims now run the government, people are all the more aware of this requirement. In addition to private donations and distributions at Shi'a sites, many people have joined philanthropic organizations either of the traditional charity type or newer, more modernly organized semi-government-connected nongovernmental organizations. The government's Social Security Organization and State Welfare Organization provide many types of support to people and also give grants to private philanthropic organizations. People may relatively easily take out bank loans to support their standard of living.[8] The government has developed a number of organizations and programs to assist women, such as the Office of Women's Affairs, Women's Social and Cultural Council, Department of Women and International Social Affairs, Women Villagers' Cooperatives, Women's Sports Organizations, and Women's Affairs Committee.

Sustainable Development

Due to the revolution, war with Iraq, political conflict and turmoil, inflation and a troubled economy, regional political instability, and large out-migration and brain drain to Western nations, among other problems, the government and Iranians in general have not yet focused on sustainable development. There is an environment section in the government, and some attention has been given to reforestation, relocating industry outside of cities, and developing alternative sources of energy. Some people have joined an Iranian Green Group, but governmental attention largely lies elsewhere.

Welfare

As mentioned, Shi'a Muslims are required to give alms as one of the five pillars of Islam. They may give coins to people on the street or discreetly provide for destitute families. Many people distribute food, particularly in conjunction with vows or pleas to the saints. Philanthropic organizations give assistance to special groups of people. Private organizations and the government run orphanages and more recently have opened old-people's homes. People receive pensions upon retiring from government employment, generally at the same salary as when they worked. Many government agencies, more modern nongovernmental organizations, and traditional charity groups provide assistance to the needy. The Imam Khomeini Relief Committee most actively extends assistance to economically deprived persons. The government has provided many benefits, such as housing, education, food, and jobs, to survivors of "martyrs" in the Iran-Iraq War.

FAMILY AND SEXUALITY

Gender Roles

Among nomads who guided their flocks on migration routes toward food and pasture, women carried heavy work loads. They packed and unpacked tents and other materials, milked animals and processed milk and wool into usable products, gathered and dried vegetables, cared for children, and prepared and distributed food.[9] In some areas, rural women did agricultural work. Otherwise, Iranian men preferred to have their wives and daughters at home, attesting to the men's honor through their seclusion and separation from unrelated men. Village women might milk and care for animals around the home and also might go out in groups to gather and then dry wild vegetables and fruit.

Islamic gender constructs view men as suited for the rough-and-tumble outside world of work and women's emotional, compassionate, and nurturing qualities as better suiting them for home life, caring for children and serving their husbands. Men held authority in the family and neighborhood, and women might attempt to manipulate and influence through subtle and subversive interpersonal strategies.[10] Women generally took on administrative and family relations duties in the home as they matured from young brides to mothers and then into midlife. Women from more comfortable households generally carried heavy social responsibilities. They handled hospitality; maintained social networks among relatives, neighbors, and associates through visiting; attended segregated life-cycle and religious rituals in homes and sometimes mosques or other religious spaces; and provided advice and guidance for other women.[11] Women were held responsible for children's behavior and training.

Although female roles supposedly are different but equally valued and important in the Muslim perspective, often this ideal did not translate into reality. From birth, people generally gave males more attention, resources, and leeway in behavior. Males grew up expecting to be favored and catered to and could often be self-centered and dismissive toward females. Males' parental roles and assistance to wives consisted of financial support. For many husbands and fathers, their perceived obligations to the rest of the family did not go much further than

Woman chats with her friends in Tehran while holding her little girl. Photo © TRIP/M. Cerny.

that. In turn, they expected women and children to give them deference, obedience, loyalty, and service. Such attitudes varied among families according to class, location, education, and family culture. They have changed over time as females have gained exposure to other possibilities and opportunities. With Iran's move toward modernization and women's increasing presence in the economic arena and social life, male authoritarianism has declined somewhat, at least among the educated.

After the 1979 Iranian Revolution, clerics wanted women to be under the control of their fathers and husbands in order to maintain social purity and stability. They succeeded in enforcing more measures to maintain women's modesty, control by family males, and economic dependence. However, pressure from women as well as economic necessity and the need for women workers have pushed them into reversing some of these measures. Women face the challenge of revising gender roles and ideas to allow them more rights and opportunities. They must find ways to do this without overt reference to Western feminism, but rather must appear to be operating within an Islamic framework.

Marriage

In Islam, marriage is considered to be a contract rather than a religious sacrament or vow of love, loyalty, and fidelity. Traditionally, parents arranged the marriages of their children. The prospective bridegroom's parents looked for a pretty, modest, obedient, and hardworking girl from a good family. The prospective bride's parents hoped for a young man with good financial prospects from a good family who could support their daughter and the children as well as possible. Parents negotiated the terms of the contract, with the fathers and often other male relatives of each side meeting to work out the details. The groom's family had to bring gifts to the girl and members of her family during the time leading up to the ceremony and had to provide a bride price (*mahr*). A stipulated part of this sum, in some areas called milk money (*shir baha*), should change hands at the time of the marriage. With the money given to him by the groom's family, the bride's father purchased the household furnishings that his daughter had to bring to the new union. Depending on the families' resources and the father's level of devotion to his daughter, these household furnishings could be quite ostentatious.

The rest of the negotiated amount of money, usually the larger part, was supposed to be given to the wife in the case of divorce. Often, however, a husband found ways of evading this obligation, perhaps making the wife's life so miserable that she became willing to give up her *mahr* to obtain her freedom. After marriage, a wife was supposed to obey her husband. Wives might have certain conditions put into the marriage contract, such as being provided with a separate home from the groom's family or the right to education and a career, but sometimes these conditions would not be upheld. Iranians saw marriage as a household partnership, a means of producing children, and a legitimate way to satisfy male and female sexuality more than as the way to structure companionship and love between husband and wife.

Men and women generally lived rather separate lives, with men busy at work in fields, shops, or businesses and women interacting with other women at home and in the neighborhood. Often women formed their most emotionally meaningful relationships with other women. Mothers generally formed deep bonds with children, and both males and females continued close connection with their mothers throughout adulthood. Sons expected mothers to cater to them and adore them and in turn often showed lasting devotion to their mothers. Mothers generally looked to daughters as companions and assistants, and daughters turned to mothers for support and deep friendship.

Women might feel quite unhappy in marriages, but usually tolerated the situation, given social pressure and the lack of alternatives. They might turn to their children to share their unhappiness and complaints against the husband. In the last twenty years, this has begun to change for some couples. With more women becoming educated and working in the modern public sector rather than staying at home and in the neighborhood, people often have chosen their own spouses. Husband-wife relationships in many families have become more companionate, and they have developed some common activities and interests. However, for many families in the lower classes, and even some middle- and upper-class ones, much has stayed the same.

In Islam, males are allowed up to four wives. There is no limit on the number of temporary wives (*sigheh*) they may take at one time. Although they should not marry multiple permanent wives if they cannot treat them all equally, this stipulation may be ignored. Fear of their husbands divorcing them or marrying another wife makes wives feel insecure and more willing to appease their husbands and tolerate their situations. Again, these attitudes have changed somewhat over time. Divorce does not bring as much scandal and loss of reputation to a woman and her family as it used to do, and women do not feel the same level of constraint against contemplating divorce. Although women are attempting to bring about change, men are still able to divorce their wives more easily than women can divorce husbands: they need not provide a reason for divorce. Women are allowed to divorce for such reasons as nonsupport, insanity, and impotence. Women and reformers in the Parliament have recently been working to grant women improved rights to divorce.

With the rising divorce rate, job migration, and war dead, single motherhood unfortunately is on the rise. Many single mothers struggle to provide for their children, perhaps seeking assistance from relatives in addition to working.[12] When men divorce their wives, they are supposed to return their marriage payment. Men often find ways of evading this financial obligation. Recently, a new law has decreed that when giving the marriage payment to divorced wives, men must adjust it for inflation since the agreement at the time of the marriage. Upon divorce for any reason, men are granted custody of boys at age two and girls at age seven. In May 2002, the Parliament passed a bill allowing mothers to keep custody of both boys and girls until age seven, at which time the courts would make a decision about custody. In order to put this bill into effect, which should give women improved custody rights, the Guardian Council must grant approval. In actuality, generally a father can get custody of his children if he really wants it. He can also withhold child support, causing the wife financial distress. As elsewhere, unless a single mother has a well-paying job, she and the children live in relative deprivation.[13]

Reproduction

Sex Education

Sex education basically has not existed in Iran. Traditionally, married women attempted to cull obvious sexual references from their talk when unmarried females were present. Mothers did not feel obligated to inform their daughters about sex or even about menstruation. Daughters remained unprepared for menarche and for abrupt sexual initiation on their wedding night. Sometimes an older woman might be stationed within or near the bridal bower to assist the marital act. Traditionally she carried a white cloth, or the bride was provided with one, to gather blood, documenting the bride's virginity and the groom's virility, to be displayed to visitors.

Most parents still shy away from discussions about sex with their teens. In 1996, two out of five girls had not received any information prior to their first menstruation, a government study found. Government education likewise has not provided sex education. Sex is supposed to be contained within the husband-wife relationship. Knowledge about sex therefore has no relevance to the unmarried. Upon marriage, the husband is expected to initiate sex and a woman to receive his sexual attention. Muslims see sexual activity and bearing children within marriage to be part of a well-lived and pious life, but they expect that married couples will go about this naturally, without guidance from outsiders. Classes about contraception now required for marrying couples may include some sex education. In the fall of 2002, government officials announced, AIDS education will become part of secondary-school education.

Contraception and Abortion

Traditionally, in-laws and husbands expected brides to become pregnant as soon as possible, hopefully with a boy. If a wife did not become pregnant, in-laws and the husband generally complained and tried to find solutions. People blamed the wife for infertility. The husband of a barren woman might divorce her or possibly bring in an additional wife. Both courses of action brought trouble and loss of status to a wife. In August 2002, Parliament passed a law authorizing in vitro fertilization for couples unable to have children. Several decades ago, although becoming pregnant when too old caused embarrassment, women continued to have children well into middle age, often bearing eight, ten, or more. High child mortality took about half of children born, although this has been improving during the last several decades.

As late as the 1970s, older women and traditional midwives tried to use herbs, magical practices, or attempts to harm the fetus to prevent conception and induce abortion for women who did not want children. Such home methods did not effectively or safely prevent pregnancy and induce miscarriage. During the 1960s and even more in the 1970s, modern contraceptives became more readily available. Males usually did not like to use condoms, and high-dosage birth-control pills sometimes caused discomfort and health problems for women. Birth rates did fall somewhat until Islamic Republic officials encouraged reproduction to increase population during the Iran-Iraq War.

In December 1989, recognizing the serious overpopulation problem and the swelling proportion of children and youth to the rest of the population, the government launched an ambitious family-planning program. Islamic clerics have energetically championed family planning, pointing to the higher standard of living and better provision for children that a smaller family allows. Fertility rates have dropped dramatically. More than half of childbearing-age women now use contraceptives, and the rates are as high as 80 percent in some urban areas. Birth control is provided free of cost. Maternity leave and other benefits are not available to women after their third child. Also, females are marrying later; young couples now often postpone pregnancy for a period after marriage; and older women are bearing fewer children. Fewer children are dying, which has lowered pressures to have more children. Parents also are developing higher aspirations for their children. Female education is climbing, and girls entertain higher expectations for themselves. For the last several years, more girls than boys have passed the entrance exams and have been admitted to the government universities.[14] All of these factors contribute to the dramatically lowered birth rates.

Although according to law, abortion may be performed for mothers whose doctors will testify danger to their lives, fearing problems with the authorities, doctors are hesitant to perform this operation. In general, women do not have access to legal abortions. In August 2002, several reform-minded members of Parliament introduced for debate a bill to allow abortions in cases where three doctors testify to a severely deformed fetus. Many articles have appeared in Iranian newspapers on the merits of vasectomy, and the government has encouraged it. Couples must have blood tests before marriage. Couples must also take a course in contraception that is supposed to include discussion about AIDS.

Teen Pregnancy

Because virginity is highly valued and protected, teen pregnancy outside of marriage has been much rarer in Iran than in the United States or European countries. However, as under Shi'a Muslim law, young girls can marry, teens very frequently became pregnant within marriage. During the reign of Mohammad Reza Shah Pahlavi, the Family Protect Laws of 1967 raised the legal age of marriage for girls to sixteen. Although the Islamic Republic clerics lowered it again to age nine, recently they have yielded to pressure and raised it again to fifteen. However, because of economic and educational reasons, because many men were killed in war or migrated abroad, and because there is less pressure on many girls to marry early, the average age of female marriage has risen above twenty-two. Teen pregnancy has declined.

Because of girls' increased mobility for schooling and some opportunities to interact with males in parks, hiking areas, or even homes, a small percentage of girls do become pregnant outside of marriage. Sometimes this pregnancy is the result of incest. It is difficult to learn much about this because of family shame. During the war with Iraq (1980–1988), government clerics successfully encouraged procreation, raising rates of teen pregnancy within marriage. Aware of the negative effects of overpopulation, especially in a shaky economy, since then, government officials have advertised and supported family planning, lowering teen birth rates dramatically.

HEALTH

Health Care Access

Access to health care has increased: urban people and 85 percent or more of rural residents have access to primary health care. The decentralized health network of Urban and Rural Health Centers and Health Houses serve people locally, and mobile units go out into more remote areas. University-affiliated hospitals in provincial capitals offer specialized care. The Social Security Organization of Iran, affiliated with the Health Ministry, provides health coverage for some 40 percent of the population: for government employees, employees of many private companies, and retired persons. Benefits include medical treatment, survivor's pension plans, subsidies to large families, disability pensions, unemployment compensation, subsidies for pregnancy periods, subsidies for marriage costs, retirement pensions, sick leave, and coupons for food. The expanding universal health insurance system and the growing number of doctors, some 108 per 100,000 people in 1997, also bring about better access to medical care.

Diseases and Disorders

AIDS

Numbers of AIDS and HIV-positive cases have been relatively low in Iran. However, since 2002, government health officials have warned about the rapidly increasing incidence of AIDS cases. Until recently, officials estimated the number of HIV-positive patients to be about 2,000. Recently, the disease control division estimated it to be much higher, about 19,000. Apparently more than 350 out of the more than 400 AIDS patients have died. Polygamy, prostitution, labor migration, and the Shi'a Muslim practice of taking temporary wives contribute to the AIDS problem, as does the use of dirty needles among drug addicts in the country, whose number is dramatically increasing. Officials have recently started a national AIDS awareness campaign that is especially active in the province of Sistan Baluchistan, on the Pakistani and Afghan borders. Beginning in the fall of 2002, the government has announced, AIDS education will be added to the secondary-school curriculum.

Eating Disorders

In recent decades, Iranian females have become increasingly concerned about body image. Although people formerly appreciated plumpness in girls and women, now more often females want a slender body. Some urban women go to gyms for aerobics and working out. Through videos, television, the Internet, and traveling, Western ideals of beauty have spread in Iran. Plastic surgery for smaller noses and other face and body modifications has become relatively common. Although females must cover their bodies in public and in front of nonrelated men, research in 2001 found that young females living in Iran are just as obsessed with losing weight as Iranian American young women living in the United States. They are just as likely to develop eating disorders.[15]

Cancer

Little research about cancer in Iranian women has been published. For the first time, a 1994–1995 preliminary study in Shiraz presented an estimate on breast cancer prevalence among women thirty-five years old and older. The research found about 6.6 breast cancer tumors per 1,000 women.

Depression

Young Iranian women suffer from depression due to lack of opportunities to get out of the house, restrictions, pressures to marry young, forced or unhappy marriages, or the threat of divorce or facing a second wife. Females suffer from depression four times more often than males, although for both sexes, depression has become almost an epidemic. A 1999 government study showed that females in Qom, the stronghold of Shi'a clergy, where rules about women's dress and behavior are applied more strictly, suffer depression more often than those in Tehran. In situations where females feel that they do not have the ability to refuse an unwelcome marriage or to try to change an unhappy situation, they may become depressed or attempt suicide.

Most suicides are committed by people between fifteen and twenty-four years of age. Young women are the most vulnerable to suicide and commit suicide at higher rates than young men. Since 1989, suicide rates for young women have been climbing. Rates of suicide for married women are higher than for married men, but rates of suicide for single men are higher than for single women. Having children mitigates rates of suicide for females to an extent. Most often, family and marriage issues influence women to attempt suicide. Early marriage, significant age difference with spouse, polygamy, spouse's addiction, problematic relationship with spouse, male domination, forced marriage, lack of children, mistreatment, and divorce issues may lead to young women's suicide. The most common female means of committing suicide is burning oneself.[16]

POLITICS AND LAW

Suffrage

Women as well as men were able to vote during Mohammad Reza Shah Pahlavi's reign, although this held little meaning. Only one political party, the shah's Rastakheez Party, was allowed to exist. The shah's government approved all candidates put on ballots. No dissent against the shah's government was allowed. People opposed to the shah's government could not become candidates, and if their attitudes became known, they were imprisoned.

Islam supposedly relegates women to the household and care of the family. Some clerics and religious groups had opposed women's suffrage when the shah initiated it. However, clerics included women in the voting for the establishment of an Islamic Republic and in subsequent elections. Under the Islamic Republic as well, only candidates approved by the government can stand for election.

Political Participation

Although men have held public leadership positions in Iran and have played roles in public political participation, women have exerted influence behind the scenes and during some periods have taken publicly recognized steps and crucial roles in political competition and conflict. In the 1905–1911 Constitutional Revolution, women demonstrated, wrote letters, influenced men, and became crucial political symbols.[17] In general, Iranian women seem to be aware of and interested in political conditions, events, and conflict that affect their lives. Even illiterate village women informally and sporadically participate in politics.[18] Some women excelled in gathering information from a variety of sources and developing political analyses concerning village-level politics as well as national trends and incidents during the 1978–1979 revolutionary period. Women could gather and spread information and perspectives, form and maintain political alliances, pressure their men, condemn violence and outrageous behavior, help to swing majority support, and rouse people to action through emotional displays and haranguing. Through their visiting, distribution of food, and talk, women developed and maintained political networks.

Women gathering at scenes of violence, wailing and beating themselves in mourning or distress, focused attention on the event and the seriousness of the political situation. Women could deny involvement in a current conflict, maintaining at least formal relations with women in hostile groups. They could try to pick up information this way or be in a position to mend relationships should a rapprochement be attempted.[19] As connections between families through marriage, women served to strengthen political alliances.[20] Although women had participated in politics in less publicly obvious ways, and a few had taken publicly recognized political action, the 1978–1979 revolutionary period marked the dramatic entrance of masses of Iranian women into political conflict. Ironically, the clerics who had earlier opposed women's voting rights now sanctioned women's participation in the movement against the shah as a religious duty. Although males usually served as leaders of the movement, women joined marches, demonstrations, strikes, and religiopolitical gatherings in mosques. Women listened to tapes and foreign radio broadcasts, such as BBC news, learned about and distributed information about events, read leaflets, and memorized revolutionary chants. Even professional women donned the veil (*chador*) as a symbol of support for the revolutionary movement and dissent against the shah's government.[21] After the February 11, 1979 revolution, capitalizing on women's activism and support during the revolution, clerics gave them recognition and praise.

During the last shah's reign, two women reached the position of minister: Farrokhroo Parsa, minister of education, and Mahnaz Afkhami, minister of women's affairs. Since the revolution, some women have been elected to the Parliament. Daughters and wives of high-ranking government clerics have sometimes become politically influential, winning seats in the Parliament and speaking out for women's advancement and other causes. Many women ran for office during the 2000 elections for local councils. Several women have gained important governmental positions. However, the Islamic Republic of Iran, like the shah's government before it, remains under male control.

Women's Rights

Since early in the twentieth century, a few women and their male supporters have been working toward improving rights and opportunities for Iranian women. They have faced social pressure, religious leaders' condemnation, and even legal and police action. During Mohammad Reza Shah Pahlavi's reign, the government promoted female education and Western dress and gave women better legal rights. After the 1979 revolution and the subsequent formation of the Islamic Republic, governmental clerics enforced women's "Islamic" dress, cut back on their legal rights and protections, and attempted to place them into home-based family roles. Since that time, women have struggled against great odds to bring about better rights for women.[22]

Feminist Movements

Women living in Iran have faced barriers in attempting to mobilize a women's movement or even to work for women's rights. In the early decades of the twentieth century, males saw even attempting to teach females to read as subversive. Nevertheless, women organized home-based schools for females, wrote newsletters, and founded journals.[23] Although such efforts reached only a tiny minority of females, some women began to be aware of potential alternatives to illiteracy and seclusion. During the Pahlavi era, the shahs wanted to present Iranian females as educated and Westernized to demonstrate how Iran was modernizing. Education for women was seen as enabling them to be good mothers and good citizens who could help their country, rather than assisting them in personal development for their own sakes. Mohammad Reza Shah appointed a minister of women's affairs and had women's groups organized. Many women worked hard to educate females and bring about improved considerations and opportunities for women. However, women could not form independent feminist organizations.

The government instituted improvements for women with national, political, and self-presentational aims in mind.[24] Although many women who are implementing policies and developing programs value women's contributions and wish to improve their conditions,[25] on the whole, the government-instigated and managed changes cannot be seen as a women's movement.[26] Even among the antishah activities in Iran and the antishah movement among Iranian students abroad, leaders discouraged women from attention to specifically female issues. Leaders both religious and secular assured women that when the government fell and democracy was instituted, women would automatically receive their rights. Working specifically for women's rights detracted from the main aim of overthrowing the shah's regime and would be divisive, they warned.[27] During the revolutionary period, clerics condemned "naked" and immodest Western women, who through their corrupt and promiscuous behavior had brought about the downfall of the Western family and the dissolution of society. They saw Western feminists as selfish, self-centered enemies of the family, community, and nation. Pious, modest Muslim women, in contrast, upheld the family and society and through their religiosity and dedicated service strengthened Islamic society.[28] Because of this attitude, women living in Iran do not feel it wise to overtly promote feminism or women's movements. Rather, they try to work within an Islamic framework, defending better rights and opportunities for women through application of Islamic traditional law and sources.[29]

Scholars debate the existence of a feminist movement in Iran and whether or not women working for improved women's rights within the Islamic Republic framework can be called "feminists."[30] As a patriarchal religion, Islam provides no space for women's rights, some scholars and activists argue. Trying to bring about improvements for women within an Islamic framework constitutes accommodation, they believe, and can have no permanent positive effects. Whether or not Muslim activists call themselves feminists—and they usually do not—others argue that if they work for women's improved conditions, they are in fact feminists and thus can be called "Islamic feminists." Clearly, many women have developed sensitivity toward gender issues; even what Iranian women are writing and reading testifies to growing awareness of feminist concerns.[31] Women's magazines and journals not only focus on fashion and interests traditional to women, but also publish materials about women's legal rights, political participation, and difficulties in patriarchal society and families. They pressure Islamic Republic officials for improvements. Women in Iran communicate with feminists outside the country.[32]

Many women and men in Iran are struggling in many different arenas to improve conditions for women. Women have organized minor protests, such as the march to protest enforced *hijab* shortly after the revolution. Many women are working in subtle and small ways to protest gender restrictions. Even some women from conservative Islamist families have become disillusioned about conditions for women under the Islamic Republic and have joined reformist Muslim women and secular women in strategies of different types to improve women's rights.[33] Outraged women from different points of the religious/political spectrum joined forces in 2002 to defeat a proposal for a government-run prostitution organization.

Although it was to be framed in the Shi'a tradition of temporary marriage (*sigheh*), women saw this possibility as humiliating and harmful to women.

Women's efforts are often sporadic, subtle, nebulous, subversive, informal, individual, and scattered.[34] Nevertheless, women and their supporters, through the Parliament, the media, elections, the educational system, and women of elite clerical families as well as through informal communicating and networking, have succeeded in forcing the conservative clerics to reinstate some rights and opportunities for women.

Lesbian Rights

In Iran, homosexuality is illegal and can be severely punished. Gays and lesbians do not have rights and are fortunate if they can avoid detection. Iranian tradition does, however, contain male homosexual eroticism and poetry. During the decades before the 1979 revolution, people looked the other way in the case of discreet male homosexuality as a premarital phase and expected it to end upon marriage. Although sex segregation likely served to encourage even heterosexually oriented men toward other males, sometimes sexual attraction for other males did not end upon marriage. Males sometimes married in order to camouflage their homosexual orientation and activity. Such a man's wife would be subject to lack of sexual attention and companionship from her husband and, since the 1980s, to the danger of AIDS. Sometimes men accustomed to anal sex with other males forced this type of sexual activity on their wives.

Other than close relationships between female relatives and intimate, apparently platonic friendships and open physical affection among females, Iranian culture does not recognize lesbians. Some females might take shelter in acceptable platonic friendships to hide their sexual attraction or activities. Very little research has been conducted on homosexuality in Iran, and even less is known about lesbian orientation and activity. Some of the Iranian females living abroad have come out as lesbians, but such a move would be socially reprehensible and dangerous in Iran. At least two Iranian lesbians have received political asylum in the United States because of their sexual orientation.

Military Service

During the Pahlavi era, women were not drafted and did not volunteer for the armed forces. They could become members of the Literacy Corps or Health Corps and be stationed as teachers or medical workers in villages. After the revolution, when Iraq attacked Iran in 1980, some women were recruited into the war effort and became trained to use weapons.[35] However, the government did not send women to the war front as soldiers. Since the war, males but not females have been subject to the draft.

RELIGION AND SPIRITUALITY

Although Sunni Muslims, Christians, Zoroastrians, Jews, and Baha'is also live in Iran, Shi'a Muslims form some 85 percent of the population. This section will therefore focus on women in Shi'a Islam.

Women's Roles

Women have played significant roles in Shi'a Islamic history, mythology, sainthood, and ritual. In 680 A.D., the reigning caliph's forces killed Imam Husein, grandson of the prophet Muhammad (the founder of Islam), and his small band of men on the plains of Karbala, in present-day Iraq. Imam Husein's sister Zaynab then supported the womenfolk as the victors marched them into captivity at Damascus.

Imam Husein and his followers differed from the caliph's supporters in that they believed that Muslim leadership should go to the Prophet's descendants. As the Prophet had no surviving son, all of the twelve Shi'a imams or leaders were descendants of the Prophet through his daughter, Fatimah Zahra. These women and also the bereft young daughters of Imam Husein, Sakineh and Roqayeh, are featured in mythology and mourning rituals commemorating the Karbala story. As Shi'a Muslims accept intercession between God and believers, women can talk to these female saints and beseech them for assistance. Women served as followers and supporters and then as mourners who wept and told the Karbala story, so that it lived on in believers' hearts and became the means of intercession and redemption. People often believe that the female saints are more emotional and compassionate and thus are more susceptible to pleas for assistance. Often women go to saints' shrines and commemorative gatherings to seek help from the saints on behalf of their menfolk.[36]

All of the twelve imams, leaders of the Shi'a, were men. The ayatollahs who serve as leaders in the absence of imams are also almost always men. Very few women have attained the religious knowledge to qualify them for the position of ayatollah. Shi'a clerics, ritual specialists and preachers (*mullahs* and *akhunds*), are male. Professors and students at the seminary in the city of Qom and other institutions of higher religious learning were also male until after the formation of the Islamic Republic of Iran in 1979. Generally, males attended mosques and went on the pilgrimage to Mecca (*hajj*), required of all Muslims who can afford it, more than women did. As more women now have their own and/or sufficient income and are thus eligible for the *hajj*, this is changing.

In religious spaces and organizations, generally women either stayed in separate areas, behind or out of sight of the men, or did not come at all. Often, less advantaged rural women, kept out of mosques and other public places, also did not enjoy the social networks of women's segregated religious rituals and seemed rather to receive only hurtful misogynous teachings.[37] Urban women, in spite of their lack of presence in mosques, seminaries, and public leadership positions, might participate actively and even hold leadership positions in women's segregated rituals.

Since the 1979 revolution, religion has become an increasingly significant arena and source of status for Iranians. Clerical leaders give political legitimacy to themselves because of their Islamic knowledge and practices. They require Islamic knowledge and certification of conforming behavior from Muslim figures or groups to anyone seeking a political position, university education, or government job. They provide models for women's behavior based on historical Muslim females.[38] In order to inform women about Islam and their place in religion and society, religious leaders encourage their religious education. They wish to inform women about the behavior required of them, encourage women's continued support of the Islamic Republic government, and demonstrate how Islam provides the best situation for women.

Together with women's crucial role in the 1978–1979 revolution, women's greater access to valued Islamic education and qualifications has given them more voice and status in the now central arena of Islam. Women attend seminaries and religious schools. Many women enjoy positions as teachers and preachers of Islam.[39] Sometimes women speak about religion even in front of men. As they are studying Islamic sources such as the Qur'an and the Hadith, traditions of the Prophet passed down through chains of authority, some women are beginning to give new interpretations of Islamic teachings about women and gender. Through women's neighborhood religious gatherings, female preachers are leading discussions that subtly question male religious authority.[40] However, male religious clerics and scholars still hold most Islamic power and authority, and women face great challenges in resisting their control over religious power. Given the existence of the Islamic Republic of Iran, one crucial route for improving women's rights, other than exerting political pressure and popular opinion, lies in finding ways to defend their rights and opportunities within the Islamic framework.

Rituals and Religious Practices

The five pillars of Islam include testifying belief in God and his prophet Muhammad, giving alms, fasting during the month of Moharram, offering five sets of prayer each day, and making the pilgrimage to Mecca if financially possible. Women are disadvantaged in performing these requirements. When women menstruate, deal with children's urine and feces, or engage in sexual intercourse, they are considered religiously impure. After these activities, and for forty days after giving birth, until they have washed in rituals of purification, women cannot touch the Qur'an, attend the mosque, fast, or pray. As they usually have less discretionary money than men, giving alms and making the pilgrimage to Mecca pose difficulty for them.

Although women have had more access to public religious spaces since the revolution and institution of the Islamic Republic, before that they were almost entirely limited to more informal, sex-segregated rituals. Women gathered in homes for meals donated to one of the saints (*sofreh*) and rituals (*rozehs*) including a story about one of the Karbala saints with mourning, perhaps some religious exhortation, and, finally, refreshments and chatter.[41] Women made pilgrimages to local shrines to ask for help from the saints.[42] In urban areas, some women might go to shrines as individuals, but often groups of women sought refuge in shrines. They might even stay overnight to form a closer relationship with the saint and thus hope for more compassion from her or him. Women attended mourning gatherings as a religious obligation, sitting in separate rooms or buildings from men. Generally, women did not accompany the body of the deceased and the grieving men to the cemetery. However, they actively attended mourning gatherings in homes or segregated public spaces on the third, seventh, and fortieth days after the death and on the one-year anniversary. Women also commonly went to the local cemetery on Thursday afternoons, the day before Friday. They used Thursday as the day of the week reserved for religion, to weep, talk to the deceased, and ask for intercession for them. At this time, they often distributed food or drink on behalf of the deceased and found opportunities to talk with other women. During Ramadan, the month of fasting, women cooked and served special foods before daylight and then to break the fast when darkness fell. Women prepared and distributed foods in honor of the saints at different times of the year.

In the years since the formation of the Islamic Republic of Iran, opportunities for women's participation in some types of rituals have increased. Although previously women, especially younger ones, generally did not attend mosques, now officials are more welcoming of their presence. Sometimes they take steps to allow even menstruating women or women otherwise in a state of impurity to attend by arranging for balconies or other separate areas not considered a part of the mosque and thus not in danger of pollution. At times, women may speak before mixed congregations, with the understanding that the message's significance can make an exception to the rule that women's voices should not be heard by unrelated men.

Government officials hold large gatherings for women as part of their policy of inviting women's support and participation in Islamic Republic activities. The government and government-connected companies organize in-country pilgrimages as well as trips to saints' shrines in Iraq and Syria. These religious-oriented tours have become very popular forms of recreation. Men and women travel in the same buses.[43] Generally, more females than males purchase these tours. These opportunities draw older women especially, who may travel without a male relative chaperone if they wish. Many older widows whose children have grown up and moved away now live by themselves. For such elderly ladies, these pilgrimages offer social and spiritual rewards.

In addition to participating in formerly popular rituals such as *sofrehs*, *rozehs*, and visiting saints' shrines to request assistance and intercession (*ziarat*), many women attend a newer form of women's religious ritual, the *majles*. Most often, a female preacher and teacher leads these community home-based gatherings, where women discuss holy sources and aspects of Islam, listening to and questioning their female leader. These sessions can be dynamic and thought-provoking. Through such discourse, women are involved in developing and reconstructing some interpretations of Islam and women's place in Islam.[44]

Although Islamic Republic officials have emphasized the importance of prayer and Islamic attitudes, behaviors, and rituals, many people, particularly the young, have become rather disinterested in Islamic attitudes and concerns and rather lax in fulfilling their prayer obligations, according to official commentary. Many females as well as males resist pressures to discipline their thoughts and activities into Islamic channels. Rather, they develop interests in secular orientations and areas of life.

Religious Law

Laws in Iran are supposed to be based on the religious law (*shari'a*). Government clerics say that requirements of modest dress for women are taken from the Qur'an. Marriage, divorce, inheritance, and custody laws all come from shari'a tradition, according to government clerics.

VIOLENCE

Domestic Violence

Religious conservatives defend domestic violence by pointing to men's obligation, as stated in the Qur'an, to guide disobedient wives. If they do not listen to admonishment or improve when they are denied access to the marital bed, husbands may physically punish them, but must not be so severe that they leave any mark on the body. Many husbands beat their wives for disobedience, in frustration, or because of family dynamics. To some extent, a woman's safety from battering depends on her own family's relative status and power.[45] Her own male relatives may offer her refuge or express their distress if a woman is beaten by her husband, but often her own family encourages her to return to her husband and tolerate the situation. Men may practice emotional and mental abuse as well as physical.

Rape/Sexual Assault

In Iran, those families that can do so pay much attention to protecting women and girls against potential sexual predation or activity. A girl who has lost her virginity will face great disadvantage in courtship. The preoccupation with virginity and a woman's chastity and loyalty to her husband after marriage serves to protect women from exposure to potential sexual aggressors. However, under certain circumstances, men have forced or pressured girls and women into unwanted sexual activity. Most commonly, because of the traditionally low age of girls' marriage, lack of contact between the couple, and sexual ignorance, the required consummation of marriage on the wedding night typically took the form of rape,[46] although women did not put it in such terms. Typically, sexual activity for the first period of marriage brought distress and discomfort to females.

No concept of marital rape exists in Iran; a wife does not have protection from unwanted sexual activity from her husband. Indeed, Iranian Muslim women are supposed to be available at all times for any type of sexual attention from their husbands. Males of the household may well force or pressure sexual attentions on girls and women brought into middle- and upper-class homes to work as maids.

During the political repression of Mohammad Reza Shah's regime, guards and interrogators sometimes raped female political prisoners. After the formation of the Islamic Republic of Iran, fanatic Muslim males apparently used rape as a political tool against raped females accused of plotting against the Islamic Republic before their execution in order to influence their afterlives.

Incest does take place at times between brother and sister, daughter and father, or with a father-in-law or other male relatives. However, shame prevents females and families from disclosing such incidents.

Girls run away from home, often from beatings or fear of beatings, early marriage, sexual abuse, and their father's use of them as prostitutes to take in money for themselves. Most runaways end up as prostitutes. The increase in men's drug addiction brings trouble to wives and daughters due to the men's tendency to abusiveness and need for cash. The 1999 opening of Rayhaneh House, a shelter for runaway girls, has brought this previously shrouded issue into the open to be addressed as a social problem. By 2000, twenty-two such temporary shelters had been established in Iran, most of them by the Social Services Organization.[47]

Trafficking in Women and Children

At times during Persian/Iranian history, especially if economically pressed, a relatively few fathers or other male guardians have sold females. In one infamous case, poor harvests and impossibly high fees required by landlords in the area of Quchan in northeastern Iran prompted fathers to sell daughters to Turkmen tribal people who then took most across the border into Russia for sale.[48] More often, fathers or male relatives from a village or poor urban neighborhood arranged to send a young girl for employment as a maid in a town or city home, where she might be subject to sexual predation. When females did not have much education or job opportunities, a divorced wife, if her own family would not take her in, frequently had few options other than becoming a prostitute.

During Mohammad Reza Shah's reign, prostitutes operated in a specific section of a settlement, such as Shahr-e No or the New City in Tehran. After the formation of the Islamic Republic, especially during and after the war with Iraq, clerics encouraged men to take females as temporary wives as a way of supporting war widows and as a means of channeling sexual desires of young people not yet in a position to commit to marriage. Shi'a Islam allows temporary wives (*muta'a* or *sigheh*). Under this arrangement, a woman agrees to become a man's sexual partner for a stipulated period of time and for a stipulated amount of money. Although this is allowed by Shi'a law, if a female becomes a man's temporary wife, she suffers a severe loss of status and will not be an acceptable wife in a good marriage.

In the last ten years, with the movement of girls and young women into public places for schooling and jobs, a few of them have apparently begun casual prostitution work as a way of picking up cash to buy clothes and other items. Temporary marriage makes it relatively worry free to engage in such activity. A couple or a female, if apprehended in the company of a nonrelated man, could hope to defend themselves by saying that they had made a *muta'a* contract and thus had temporarily become husband and wife.

Prostitution is illegal is the Islamic Republic and can bring women floggings or even execution. Nevertheless, prostitution has been increasing dramatically. It is no longer limited to a set-aside section of a city. Even government officials estimate that the number of prostitutes in Tehran has risen to more than 300,000. Recently, the government has begun cracking down on prostitution. Police have broken up several prostitution rings, some with international networks sending young Iranian girls to Arab countries in the Persian Gulf, Turkey, East Asia, and Europe. In the fall of 2002, police broke up some seventy brothels in the holy city of Qom. The press continued to publish reports of police raids on prostitution rings, many run by women, almost weekly. In order to cut down on sexual corruption, several clerics suggested the establishment of "chastity houses" where the government would channel access to women's sexuality through the permitted temporary marriage arrangements. Women and other groups reacted so violently against this possibility that it seems to have been defeated for the time being.

Parents arranged their children's marriages. Although a female is supposed to agree to a marriage, often fathers ignored this rule in reality. In Iran, Muslim law allowed marriage of girls at age nine. Fathers might arrange the marriages of girls even younger than this, although ideally, husbands were to wait until a young bride's menarche before consummating the marriage. Because such arrangements were legal, marriage actually constituted the main means of trafficking in women and children. Fathers might also arrange for daughters to become temporary wives of men in return for financial benefit. As females now have more educational opportunities, and the average age of first marriage has apparently risen above twenty-two, such marriages of young girls have declined, but still take place. Sometimes drug addiction prompts men to basically sell a daughter to support their habit.

War and Military Repression

In 1936, Reza Shah ordered Iranian women to remove their veils. Females had to wear Western clothing outside the house, stay at home, or attempt to sneak out in a veil. When police apprehended females wearing veils or scarves, they shouted at them and tore off their covering. Reza Shah later rescinded this order. Reza Shah abdicated in 1941, and his son Mohammad Reza Shah became ruler. Mohammad Reza Shah did not force women to leave veiling, but encouraged women to wear Western clothing.

In the late 1940s and early 1950s, Iranians actively participated in politics. People supported nationalization of oil and Prime Minister Mohammad Mossadeq, and the shah was forced to leave the country. The United States and England supported a coup d'état to overthrow popular Prime Minister Mosaddeq and reinstated the shah. Iranians saw the shah's return to power as illegitimate, reigniting the opposition. To gain control, the shah resorted to maximum forms of repression to curb opposition. Drawing on the anti-Communist rhetoric of the West, he arrested, imprisoned, and executed members of the pro-Soviet Tudeh Party and other political organizations. With increasing repression, the opposition either left the country or went underground. During the revolution, all of these forces reemerged and united to overthrow the government.

Mohammad Reza Shah continued the process of centralizing power that his father had begun and attempted to prevent any competing centers of power or any political activity outside his own organizations. The shah's government prevented women as well as men from expressing political dissent. Women became political prisoners along with men, although in fewer numbers, and suffered from torture, sometimes of a sexual nature, and death. During the antishah movement of the late 1970s, soldiers sometimes killed females among the marchers and demonstrators. Shortly after the revolution, some of the tribal/ethnic groups revolted—for example, the Kurds in the northwest and the Qashqai in the southwest—and then suffered the consequences of government attack and executions.

After the 1979 revolution, the new government imprisoned and executed female shah supporters—for example, the former minister of education,

Farrokhroo Parsa—and leftists. Females became members of the dissident Muslim group the Mojahedin and fought battles with Iranian forces, at times based within Iraq. The Islamic Republic government imprisoned, tortured, raped, and executed many female Mojahedin as well as males. Females also suffered during the Pahlavi regime, the revolutionary period, and the Islamic Republic because of imprisonment, torture, house arrest, or execution of male family members and relatives. The new Islamic government's strict policy about women's modesty, separation from unrelated men, and nature suited to the family and home rather than the outside world reduced women's freedoms and opportunities. Women could be harassed, fired, arrested, tortured, or executed for refusal to conform to Islamic modesty regulations. Governmental clerics saw women as important symbols of the purity of Muslim society, in contrast to the corrupt and promiscuous West; therefore, they required strict conformity from women. Many women were arrested and flogged or imprisoned for inadequate covering. In the years following the revolution, even a strand of hair peeking out from a scarf, lipstick, nail polish, or insufficiently opaque stockings showing beneath a veil could cause a woman serious trouble. Vigilante groups took it upon themselves to reprimand and punish improperly dressed females, as their motto *Ya rusari, ya tu sari* (Either the scarf or a blow on your head) indicates.

In 1980, neighboring Iraq attacked Iran. The revolutionary turmoil had weakened Iran and made it less able to defend its territories, Iraqi leaders believed. The subsequent devastating eight-year war brought destruction, death, and hardship. Iranian women suffered from bombing and missiles, loss of homes and dislocation, economic deprivation, fear and insecurity, and death or disability of male relatives fighting at the front. Some cities suffered great damage, such as Abadan in the southwest. Refugees from areas near the border with Iraq inundated some cities, such as Shiraz in the southwest. The war left thousands upon thousands of widows and their fatherless children to struggle for a livelihood in the postwar inflation and poor economy. During the years of political turmoil and war in Afghanistan, thousands of Afghan refugees, mainly males, entered Iran from the east. Many married Iranian women. When the United States overthrew the Taliban regime in 2002, many of these men left their Iranian wives to return to Afghanistan.

Iranians face political instability and possible war in the region. Internally, although repression has been mitigated by the 1997 election of moderate cleric President Mohammad Khatami, the Islamic Republic government continues to limit political freedoms. Elections are held, but the Council of Experts must approve candidates in order for them to be listed on ballots. As the government is a Shi'a Muslim theocracy, run by Shi'a Muslim clerics and supposed to be guided by Shi'a Muslim religious law, Sunni, Armenian, Assyrian, Jewish, Zoroastrian, and more secular women do not feel that the government is supportive of their interests. As

Shi'a Muslims consider Baha'is to be apostates, they have suffered brutal repression. Vigilante groups killed many Baha'is and burned their homes and shops not long after the revolution, and the government executed some Baha'i leaders. In the years since the revolution, several women have been stoned for sexual impropriety. Security has declined, leaving women to fear robbery, burglary, and attacks upon their persons.

Because of the formation of the Islamic Republic, the 1980–1988 Iran-Iraq War, and political repression under the Islamic Republic, thousands upon thousands of Iranians left Iran. Some of them were forced to flee clandestinely, paying high prices to smugglers to lead them across borders to Turkey or to Afghanistan and then Pakistan. Iranian immigrants, many of them from the middle or upper classes who held government and military positions under Mohammad Reza Shah Pahlavi's regime or prospered during the oil boom of that time, are now scattered throughout the United States, Canada, Europe, and elsewhere in the world. So many Iranians found homes in the Los Angeles area after the revolution that they call it "Irangeles" or "Tehrangeles." These Iranian immigrants in the United States and elsewhere suffer from being forced to leave their own country and culture and often family members and relatives.

Although many Iranians in the United States and elsewhere have prospered because of bringing money from Iran, becoming successful in business, or entering professional careers for which their often high levels of education qualify them, many Iranian women must take less prestigious work in order to help support their families. Their degrees are not recognized by American institutions. Additionally, their limited English may prevent them from working in their own fields. They have also suffered from the American public's hostility and discrimination, especially during some periods, such as when radical Muslim students took Americans at the embassy in Tehran hostage in December 1979 and held them for more than a year. Iranian women living in the United States and elsewhere abroad also face cultural dissonance with their children who have grown up in the new culture.[49]

Since the terrorist attacks in the United States on September 11, 2001, Iranians have faced regional insecurity and possible war. To the east, the new Afghan government under President Hamid Karzai does not fully control the entire country, and violence breaks out periodically. The recent war in Iraq has caused anxiety in the West about the role of the U.S. in the region. Further, American President Bush has included Iran in his "axis of evil," and Iranians fear that they may be next on the U.S. agenda. As the Shi'a Muslim Hizbollah active in threatening Israel from southern Lebanon is suspected of receiving assistance from Iran, Iranians' fears of being an eventual U.S. target are exacerbated. Regional political turmoil brings to Iranian women as well as men a sense of fear about the future and the possible effects of war for them.

OUTLOOK FOR THE TWENTY-FIRST CENTURY

Conservative clerics consider proper Muslim Iranian women to be an important marker of the Islamic Republic of Iran. Women's modest covering (*hijab*), separation from nonrelated men, and presence in the home as nurturing mother and obedient, supportive wife demonstrate Muslim society's superiority and smooth functioning. In their view, such women symbolize difference from the corrupt, dissolute West where women's promiscuity has harmed both family and society. As important symbols of Islamic identity, Iranian women face great pressures to conform to ideals. They are making great efforts to resist clerical definition and develop equality and self-determination. Their situation in the twenty-first century depends in large part on the outcome of the struggle between conservative Islamic Republic clerics, on the one hand, and reformist clerics, liberals, and secularists, on the other. More education and entrance into religious arenas provide women with employment and opportunities to exercise influence. However, the economic situation and females' greater access to the world outside the family also bring to some divorce, economic necessity of women working, and even additional chances for sexual aggression, premarital sex, physical and emotional assaults from threatened male family members, and prostitution. Since the 1979 revolution and the subsequent formation of the Islamic Republic, women have undergone war and severe restrictions on their dress and behavior, mobility, and opportunities. They are making headway in struggling for improved rights and opportunities for women. Economic and political conditions inside the country, the moderate versus conservative trends of the Islamic Republic, and regional stability or war will all influence developing rights and opportunities for women and the level of protection for women from violence and privation.

NOTES

1. Erika Friedl, personal communication.
2. Ashraf Zahedi, personal communication.
3. Erika Friedl, personal communication.
4. Haleh Afshar, "Women and Work in Iran," *Political Studies* 45(4) (1997): 755–68.
5. Erika Friedl, personal communication.
6. Ibid.
7. Ibid.
8. Ibid.
9. Lois Beck, "Women among Qashqa'i Nomadic Pastoralists in Iran," in *Women in the Muslim World*, ed. Lois Beck and Nikki Keddie (Cambridge, MA: Harvard University Press, 1978), 351–73; Erika Friedl, *Women of Deh Koh: Lives in an Iranian Village* (New York: Penguin Books, 1991); Erika Friedl, "The Dynamics of Women's Spheres of Action in Rural Iran," in *Women in Middle Eastern History: Shifting Bound-*

aries in Sex and Gender, ed. Nikki Keddie and Beth Baron (New Haven, CT: Yale University Press, 1991), 195–213.

10. Erika Friedl, "Sources of Female Power in Iran," in *In the Eye of the Storm: Women in Post-revolutionary Iran*, ed. Mahnaz Afkhami and Erika Friedl (Syracuse, NY: Syracuse University Press, 1994), 151–67; Erika Friedl, "Notes from the Village: On the Ethnographic Construction of Women in Iran," in *Reconstructing Gender in the Middle East: Tradition, Identity, and Power*, ed. Fatma Müge Göçek and Shiva Balaghi (New York Columbia University Press, 1994), 85–99.

11. Nancy Tapper (Lindisfarne), "The Women's Subsociety among the Shahsevan Nomads of Iran," in *Women in the Muslim World*, ed. Lois Beck and Nikki Keddie (Cambridge, MA: Harvard University Press, 1978), 374–98.

12. Ashraf Zahedi, personal communication.

13. Erika Friedl, personal communication.

14. Mohammad Jalal Abbasi-Shavazi, "The Fertility Revolution in Iran," *Populations and Societies* 373 (November 2001): 1–4.

15. P. Abdollahi and T. Mann, "Eating Disorder Symptoms and Body Image Concerns in Iran: Comparisons between Iranian Women in Iran and in America," *International Journal of Eating Disorders* 30 (2001): 259–68.

16. Somayeh Askari, "Women, Main Victims of Suicide in Iran," *Farhang-e Tose'e* [Culture of Development]: *Cultural, Social, Political and Economic (Monthly)*, February 21 to March 20, 1998 (Special Report on Women), 37–42.

17. Janet Afary, "On the Origins of Feminism in Early 20th–Century Iran," *Journal of Women's History* 1(2) (fall 1989): 65–87; Mangol Bayat-Philipp, "Women and Revolution in Iran, 1905–1911," in *Women in the Muslim World*, ed. Lois Beck and Nikki Keddie (Cambridge, MA: Harvard University Press, 1978), 295–308; Afsaneh, Najmabadi, "*Zanha-yi millat*: Women or Wives of the Nation?" *Iranian Studies: Journal of the Society for Iranian Studies* 26(1–2) (summer 1993): 51–71.

18. My own 1978–1979 anthropological fieldwork experience in a village near Shiraz in southwestern Iran.

19. Mary Elaine Hegland, "Political Roles of Aliabad Women: The Public/Private Dichotomy Transcended," in *Women in Middle Eastern History: Shifting Boundaries in Sex and Gender*, ed. Nikki Keddie and Beth Baron (New Haven, CT: Yale University Press, 1991), 215–30.

20. Paul Vieille, "Iranian Women in Family Alliance and Sexual Politics," in *Women in the Muslim World*, ed. Lois Beck and Nikki Keddie (Cambridge, MA: Harvard University Press, 1978), 451–72.

21. Mary Elaine Hegland, "Women and the Iranian Revolution: A Village Case Study," in *Women and Revolution: Global Expressions*, ed. M. J. Diamond (Dordrecht, Netherlands: Kluwer Academic Publishers, 1998), 211–25; G. Nashat, ed., *Women and Revolution in Iran* (Boulder, CO: Westview Press, 1983).

22. E. Sanasarian, *The Women's Rights Movement in Iran: Mutiny, Appeasement and Repression from 1900 to Khomeini* (New York: Praeger Publishers, 1982); P. Paidar, *Women and the Political Process in Twentieth-Century Iran* (Cambridge: Cambridge University Press, 1995).

23. Sanasarian, 1982.

24. Najmabadi, "Hazards of Modernity and Morality: Women, State, and Ideology in Contemporary Iran," in *Women, Islam, and the State*, ed. Deniz Kandiyoti (Philadelphia: Temple University Press, 1991), 48–76.

25. Mahnaz Afkhami, "A Future in the Past: The Pre-revolutionary Women's

Movement," in *Sisterhood Is Global*, ed. Robin Morgan (Garden City, NY: Anchor Books, 1984).

26. Sanasarian, 1982.

27. H. Moghissi, *Populism and Feminism in Iran: Women's Struggle in a Male-Defined Revolutionary Movement* (New York: St. Martin's Press, 1994); H. Moghissi, *Feminism and Islamic Fundamentalism: The Limits of Postmodern Analysis* (London and New York: Zed Books, 1999); Ashnaf Zahedi, *From Triumph to Despair: The Story of Women of the Confederation of Iranian Students' Movement Abroad*, forthcoming.

28. Najmabadi, 2001.

29. Hisae Nakanishi, "Power, Ideology, and Women's Consciousness in Postrevolutionary Iran," in *Women in Muslim Societies: Diversity within Unity*, ed. Herbert L. Bodman and Nayereh Tohidi (Boulder, CO: Lynne Rienner Publishers, 1998), 83–100.

30. Janet Afary, "The War against Feminism in the Name of the Almighty: Making Sense of Gender and Muslim Fundamentalism," *New Left Review* 224 (1997): 89–100; Ziba Mir-Hosseini, "Women and Politics in Post-Khomeini Iran: Divorce, Veiling, and Emerging Feminist Voices," in *Women and Politics in the Third World*, ed. Haleh Afshar (London: Routledge, 1996), 142–69; Minoo Moallem, "Transnationalism, Feminism, and Fundamentalism," in *Women, Gender, Religion: A Reader*, ed. E.A. Castelli (New York: Palgrave, 2001), 117–45; Moghissi, *Feminism and Islamic Fundamentalism*; S. Mojab, "Islamic Feminism: Alternative or Contradiction?" *Fireweed* 47 (1995): 18–25; Afsaneh Najmabadi, "Feminism in an Islamic Republic: Years of Hardship, Years of Growth," in *Islam, Gender, and Social Change*, ed. Yvonne Yazbeck Haddad and John L. Esposito (New York: Oxford University Press, 1998), 59–84; Parvin Paidar, "Feminism and Islam," in *Gendering the Middle East: Emerging Perspectives*, ed. Deniz Kandiyoti (Syracuse, NY: Syracuse University Press, 1996), 51–68; Parvin Paidar, *Gender of Democracy: The Encounter between Feminism and Reformism in Contemporary Iran*, Democracy, Governance, and Human Rights Programme Paper No. 6, United Nations Research Institute for Social Development (UNRISD) (2001); Nayereh Tohidi, "Modernity, Islamization, and Women in Iran," in *Gender and National Identity: Women and Politics in Muslim Societies*, ed. Valentine M. Moghadam (London: Zed, 1994), 110–47.

31. Kamran Talattof, "Iranian Women's Literature: From Pre-revolutionary Social Discourse to Post-revolutionary Feminism," *International Journal of Middle East Studies* 29(4) (November 1997): 531–59.

32. Nayereh Tohidi, "International Connections of the Iranian Women's Movement," in *Iran and the Surrounding World since 1501: Interactions in Culture and Cultural Politics*, ed. Nikki R. Keddie and Rudi Matthee (Seattle: University of Washington Press, 2002).

33. Mehranguiz Kar, "Women's Strategies in Iran from the 1979 Revolution to 1999," in *Globalization, Gender, and Religion: The Politics of Women's Rights in Catholic and Muslim Contexts*, ed. Jane H. Bayes and Nayereh Tohidi (New York: Palgrave, 2001), 177–201.

34. Shahin Gerami and Melodye Lehnerer, "Women's Agency and Household Diplomacy: Negotiating Fundamentalism," *Gender and Society* 4(4) (August 2001): 556.

35. Minou Reeves, *Female Warriors of Allah* (New York: E.P. Dutton, 1989).

36. Anne Betteridge, "The Controversial Vows of Urban Muslim Women in Iran," in *Unspoken Worlds: Women's Religious Lives*, ed. Nancy Auer Falk and Rita M. Gross,

(Belmont, CA: Wadsworth Publishing Company, 1989), 102–11; Anne Betteridge, "Women and Shrines in Shiraz," in *Everyday Life in the Muslim Middle East*, ed. Donna Bowen and Evelyn Early (Bloomington: Indiana University Press, 1993), 239–47.

37. Erika Friedl, *Women of Deh Koh: Lives in an Iranian Village* (New York: Penguin Books, 1991).

38. Erika Friedl, "State Ideology and Village Women," in *Women and Revolution in Iran*, ed. Guity Nashat (Boulder, CO: Westview Press, 1983), 217–30; Erika Friedl, "Legendary Heroines: Ideal Womanhood and Ideology in Iran," in *The Other Fifty Percent: Multicultural Perspectives on Gender Relations*, ed. Mari Womack and Judith Marti (Prospect Heights, IL: Waveland Press, 1993), 261–66; Erika Friedl, "Ideal Womanhood in Postrevolutionary Iran," in *Mixed Blessings: Gender and Religious Fundamentalism Cross Culturally*, ed. Judy Brink and Joan Mencher (New York: Routledge, 1997), 143–57.

39. Zahra Kamalkhani, "Women's Everyday Religious Discourse in Iran," in *Women in the Middle East: Perceptions, Realities, and Struggles for Liberation*, ed. Haleh Afshar (London: Macmillan, 1993), 85–96.

40. Mary Elaine Hegland, "Gender and Religion in the Middle East and South Asia: Women's Voices Rising," in *Social History of Women and Gender in the Modern Middle East*, ed. Margaret Meriwether and Judith Tucker (Boulder, CO: Westview Press, 1999), 177–212; Zahra Kamalkhani, *Women's Islam: Religious Practice among Women in Today's Iran* (London: Kegan Paul, 1998); Azam Torab, "Piety as Gendered Agency: A Study of *Jalaseh* Ritual Discourse in an Urban Neighbourhood in Iran," *Journal of the Royal Anthropological Institute* 2(2) (1996): 235–51; Azam Torab, "The Politicization of Women's Religious Circles in Post-revolutionary Iran," in *Women, Religion, and Culture in Iran*, ed. Sarah Ansari and Vanessa Martin (London: Curzon in association with the Royal Asiatic Society of Great Britain and Ireland, 2002), 143–68.

41. Betteridge, "Controversial Vows," 1989.

42. Betteridge, "Women and Shrines in Shiraz," 1993.

43. Erika Friedl, personal communication.

44. Kamalkhani, *Women's Islam*, 1997; Torab, "Piety as Gendered Agency," 1996; Torab, "Politicization," 2002.

45. Mary Elaine Hegland, "Wife Abuse and the Political System: A Middle Eastern Case Study," in *To Have and to Hit: Cultural Perspectives on Wife Beating*, ed. Dorothy Counts, Judith Brown, and Jacquelyn Campbell (Urbana: University of Illinois Press, 1999), 234–51.

46. Friedl, *Women of Deh Koh*; Mary Elaine Hegland, "Marital Rape and Power," paper presented at the panel on "Life Cycle Conflicts within the Family" at the Middle East Studies Association Conference, Research Triangle Park, North Carolina, November 11–14, 1993.

47. Ziba Mir-Hosseini, "Iran's Runaway Girls Challenge the Old Rules," *ISIM Newsletter*, International Institute for the Study of Islam in the Modern World, the Netherlands, January 2002, 23.

48. Afsaneh Najmabadi, *The Story of the Daughters of Quchan: Gender and National Memory in Iranian History* (Syracuse, NY: Syracuse University Press, 1998).

49. Mary Elaine Hegland, "Iranian Women Immigrants Facing Modernity in California's Bay Area: The Courage, Creativity, and Trepidation of Transformation," in *The Iranian Woman and Modernity: Proceedings of the Ninth International Conference of the Iranian Women's Studies Foundation*, ed. Golnaz Amin (Cambridge, MA: Iranian Women's Studies Foundation, 1999), 35–62.

RESOURCE GUIDE

Suggested Reading

Afkhami, M., and E. Friedl, eds. *In the Eye of the Storm: Women in Post-revolutionary Iran*. Syracuse, NY: Syracuse University Press, 1994.

Fathi, A., ed. *Women and the Family in Iran*. Leiden: E.J. Brill, 1985.

Friedl, Erika. *Children of Deh Koh: Young Life in an Iranian Village*. Syracuse, NY: Syracuse University Press, 1997.

———. *Women of Deh Koh: Lives in an Iranian Village*. New York: Penguin Books, 1991.

Haeri, S. *Law of Desire: Temporary Marriage in Shi'i Iran*. Syracuse, NY: Syracuse University Press, 1989.

Mir-Hosseini, Z. *Marriage on Trial: Islamic Family Law in Iran and Morocco*. London, New York: I.B. Tauris, 2000.

Moghissi, H. *Populism and Feminism in Iran: Women's Struggle in a Male-Defined Revolutionary Movement*. New York: St Martin's Press, 1994.

Najmabadi, A. *The Story of the Daughters of Quchan: Gender and National Memory in Iranian History*. Syracuse, NY: Syracuse University Press, 1998.

Tabari, A., and N. Yeganeh, eds. *In the Shadow of Islam: The Women's Movement in Iran*. London: Zed Press, 1982.

Videos/Films

The Circle. 2000. Directed by Jafar Panahi. Iranian Movies.com.

The Day I Became a Woman. 2000. Directed by Marziyeh Meshkini. Iranian Movies.com

Divorce Iranian Style. 1998. Directed by Kim Longinotto and Ziba Mir-Hosseini. Women Make Movies.

The Hidden Half. 2001. Directed by Tahmineh Milani. Iranian Movies.com

Runaway. 2001. Directed by Kim Longinotto and Ziba Mir-Hosseini. Women Make Movies.

Web Sites and Organizations

American Iranian Council, www.American-Iranian.org.
An educational organization that aims at "providing for a sustained dialogue and a more comprehensive understanding of US-Iranian relations." Among its many programs, this organization examines "the complex issues of Iranian women's role in the contemporary Iranian society." Email: aic@american-iranian.org.

Association of Iranian Women, www.aiwusa.org.
This association's objective is "to educate and empower Iranian women throughout the United States. It works toward building a network committed to the idea of advocating women's rights." Email: BehjatDehghan@aiwusa.org.

Bad Jens, www.badjens.com.
An online feminist magazine that aims "to improve links between activists of academics inside and outside Iran" and to enhance intellectual and cultural exchange between Iranians and non-Iranians. The site provides links to many organizations, including a list of nongovernmental organizations. Email: badjensletters@yahoo.com.

A Brief History of Women's Movement in Iran, www.payvand.com/women.
Offers a historical and analytical essay that examines the structural and ideological transformation in Iran and traces women's quest for rights and political participation. Email: massoume@mailandnews.com.

Forugh Farrokhzad, www.forughfarrokhzad.org.
This web site's aim "is to offer an international open forum for all those who have been touched by Forugh's poetry, life, and liberation." Email: info@forughfarrokhzad.org.

Homan, www.geocities.com/WestHollywood/Heights/3470.
Homan's vision "is to promote the creation of a safe community where Iranian lesbians, gays, and bisexuals can come together in celebration of both their cultural and sexual identities without hatred or prejudice." Email: homan-la@geocities.com.

Iranian Women Poets, www.art-arena.com/women.
Introduces many famous Iranian poets and provides a brief description of their lives. The introduction also includes a poem by each poet. Email: Katy@art-arena.com.

Iranian Women's Studies Foundation, www.iwsf.org.
The mission of this foundation is "to provide a forum for exchange of ideas on issues related to Iranian women, to disseminate information on Iranian women's achievements, and to establish a network of connection among communities of Iranian women the world over." Email: Iranianwsf@aol.com.

Karamah, www.karamah.org.
The organization of Muslim Women Lawyers for Human Rights. It is committed "to advancing an Islamic perspective on issues of human rights." The site provides articles on issues pertaining to women. Email: karamah@karamah.org.

National Committee of Women for a Democratic Iran, http://ncwdi.igc.org/index.html.
Devoted to "monitoring women's rights in Iran," the committee's objective is to "advocate observance and implementation of internationally accepted standards of human rights, in particular those pertaining to women." Email: ncwdi@igc.org.

Salam Iran, www.Salamiran.org.
Web site created by the Islamic Republic of Iran (Iranian embassy in Ottawa, Canada). The site is comprehensive and covers a wide range of topics including women. The section on women provides insights on organizations and committees that address different aspects of women's affairs in Iran. It contains reports and statistics on women as well as a list of nongovernmental organizations operating in Iran.

Women Living under Muslim Laws, www.wluml.org.
An "international Network that provides information, solidarity and support for all women whose lives are shaped or governed by laws and customs said to derive from

Islam." It aims at increasing women's autonomy and empowerment and has extensive links. Email: run@gn.apc.org.

Women's Voice (Avaye Zan), www.tvs.se/womensvoice/.
Covers a host of issues concerning women and has links to a number of informative sites. Email: Sholeh.irani@mailbox.swipnet.se.

Women, the Visual Arts, and Islam, www.skidmore.edu/academics/arthistory/ah369/Iranianfilm.htm.
Informs users about the role of women in the Iranian cinema. It provides an overview of internationally acclaimed Iranian films and has links to many informative sites.

Zan, www.zan.org.
An interactive directory with links to other organizations addressing women's issues. Its mission is "to break down negative stereotypes around Iranian women, as well as being a network channel connecting them globally." Email: Roya@zan.org.

SELECTED BIBLIOGRAPHY

Abbasi-Shavazi, Mohammad Jalal. "The Fertility Revolution in Iran." *Populations and Societies* 373 (November 2001).

Abdollahi, P., and T. Mann. "Eating Disorder Symptoms and Body Image Concerns in Iran: Comparisons between Iranian Women in Iran and in America." *International Journal of Eating Disorders* 30 (2001): 259–68.

Afary, Janet. "On the Origins of Feminism in Early 20th-Century Iran." *Journal of Women's History* 1(2) (Fall 1989): 65–87.

———. "The War against Feminism in the Name of the Almighty: Making Sense of Gender and Muslim Fundamentalism." *New Left Review* 224 (1997).

Afkhami, Mahnaz. "A Future in the Past: The Pre-revolutionary Women's Movement." In *Sisterhood Is Global*, ed. Robin Morgan. Garden City, NY: Anchor Books, 1984.

Afshar, Haleh. "Women and Work in Iran." *Political Studies* 45(4) (1997): 755–68.

Askari, Somayeh. "Women, Main Victims of Suicide in Iran." *Farhang-e Tose'e* [Culture of Development]: *Cultural, Social, Political, and Economic (Monthly)*, February 21 to March 20, 1998 (Special Report on Women), 37–42.

Bamdad, B. *From Darkness into Light: Women's Emancipation in Iran*. Hicksville, NY: Exposition Press, 1977.

Bayat-Philipp, Mangol. "Women and Revolution in Iran, 1905–1911." In *Women in the Muslim World*, ed. Lois Beck and Nikki Keddie, 295–308. Cambridge, MA: Harvard University Press, 1978.

Beck, Lois. "Women among Qashqa'i Nomadic Pastoralists in Iran." In *Women in the Muslim World*, ed. Lois Beck and Nikki Keddie, 351–73. Cambridge, MA: Harvard University Press, 1978.

Betteridge, Anne. "The Controversial Vows of Urban Muslim Women in Iran." In *Unspoken Worlds: Women's Religious Lives*, ed. Nancy Auer Falk and Rita M. Gross, 102–11. Belmont, CA: Wadsworth Publishing Company, 1989.

———. "Women and Shrines in Shiraz." In *Everyday Life in the Muslim Middle East*, ed. Donna Bowen and Evelyn Early, 239–47. Bloomington: Indiana University Press, 1993.

Friedl, Erika. *Children of Deh Koh: Young Life in an Iranian Village*. Syracuse, NY: Syracuse University Press, 1997.

———. "The Dynamics of Women's Spheres of Action in Rural Iran." In *Women in Middle Eastern History: Shifting Boundaries in Sex and Gender*, ed. Nikki Keddie and Beth Baron, 195–213. New Haven, CT: Yale University Press, 1991.

———. "Ideal Womanhood in Postrevolutionary Iran." In *Mixed Blessings: Gender and Religious Fundamentalism Cross Culturally*, ed. Judy Brink and Joan Mencher, 143–57. New York: Routledge, 1997.

———. "Legendary Heroines: Ideal Womanhood and Ideology in Iran." In *The Other Fifty Percent: Multicultural Perspectives on Gender Relations*, ed. Mari Womack and Judith Marti, 261–66. Prospect Heights, IL: Waveland Press, 1993.

———. "Notes from the Village: On the Ethnographic Construction of Women in Iran." In *Reconstructing Gender in the Middle East: Tradition, Identity, and Power*, ed. Fatma Müge Göçek and Shiva Balaghi, 85–99. New York: Columbia University Press, 1994.

———. "Sources of Female Power in Iran." In *In the Eye of the Storm: Women in Postrevolutionary Iran*, ed. Mahnaz Afkhami and Erika Friedl, 151–67. Syracuse, NY: Syracuse University Press, 1994.

———. "State Ideology and Village Women." In *Women and Revolution in Iran*, ed. Guity Nashat, 217–30. Boulder, CO: Westview Press, 1983.

———. *Women of Deh Koh: Lives in an Iranian Village*. New York: Penguin Books, 1991.

Gerami, Shahin, and Melodye Lehnerer. "Women's Agency and Household Diplomacy: Negotiating Fundamentalism." *Gender and Society* 4(4) (August 2001): 556–574.

Hegland, Mary Elaine. "Gender and Religion in the Middle East and South Asia: Women's Voices Rising." In *Social History of Women and Gender in the Modern Middle East*, ed. Margaret Meriwether and Judith Tucker, 177–212. Boulder, CO: Westview Press, 1999.

———. "Iranian Women Immigrants Facing Modernity in California's Bay Area: The Courage, Creativity, and Trepidation of Transformation." In *The Iranian Woman and Modernity: Proceedings of the Ninth International Conference of Iranian Women's Studies Foundation*, ed. Golnaz Amin, 35–62. Cambridge, MA: Iranian Women's Studies Foundation, 1999.

———. "Marital Rape and Power." Paper presented at the panel on "Life Cycle Conflicts within the Family" at the Middle East Studies Association Conference, Research Triangle Park, North Carolina, November 11–14, 1993.

———. "Political Roles of Aliabad Women: The Public/Private Dichotomy Transcended." In *Women in Middle Eastern History: Shifting Boundaries in Sex and Gender*, ed. Nikki Keddie and Beth Baron, 215–30. New Haven, CT: Yale University Press, 1991.

———. "Wife Abuse and the Political System: A Middle Eastern Case Study." In *To Have and to Hit: Cultural Perspectives on Wife Beating*, ed. Dorothy Counts, Judith Brown, and Jacquelyn Campbell, 234–51. Urbana: University of Illinois Press, 1999.

———. "Women and the Iranian Revolution: A Villlage Case Study." In *Women and Revolution: Global Expressions*, ed. M.J. Diamond, 211–25. Dordrecht, Netherlands: Kluwer Academic Publishers, 1998.

Hoodfar, H. "The Veil in Their Minds and on Our Heads: Veiling Practices and Muslim Women." In *Women, Gender, Religion: A Reader*, ed. E.A. Castelli, 420–46. New York: Palgrave, 2001.

Kamalkhani, Zahra. "Women's Everyday Religious Discourse in Iran." In *Women in the Middle East: Perceptions. Realities, and Struggles for Liberation*, ed. Haleh Afshar, 85–95. London: Macmillan, 1993.

———. *Women's Islam: Religious Practice among Women in Today's Iran*. London: Kegan Paul, 1998.
Kar, Mehranguiz. "Women's Strategies in Iran from the 1979 Revolution to 1999." In *Globalization, Gender, and Religion: The Politics of Women's Rights in Catholic and Muslim Contexts*, ed. Jane H. Bayes and Nayereh Tohidi, 177–201. New York: Palgrave, 2001.
Kousha, Mahnaz. "Ties That Bind: Mothers and Daughters in Contemporary Iran." *Critique: Journal for Critical Studies of the Middle East* 11 (fall 1997): 65–83.
Mir-Hosseini, Ziba. "Iran's Runaway Girls Challenge the Old Rules," *ISIM Newsletter*, International Institute for the Study of Islam in the Modern World, the Netherlands, January 2002, 23.
———. "Women and Politics in Post-Khomeini Iran: Divorce, Veiling, and Emerging Feminist Voices." In *Women and Politics in the Third World*, ed. Haleh Afshar, 142–69. London: Routledge, 1996.
———. "Women, Marriage, and the Law in Post-revolutionary Iran." In *Women in the Middle East: Perceptions, Realities, and Struggles for Liberation*, ed. Haleh Afshar, 57–84. London: Macmillan, 1993.
Moallem, Minoo. "Transnationalism, Feminism, and Fundamentalism." In *Women, Gender, Religion: A Reader*, ed. E.A. Castelli, 117–45. New York: Palgrave, 2001.
Moghadam, V. "Women's Employment Issues in Contemporary Iran: Problems and Prospects in the 1990s." *Iranian Studies* 28(3–4) (1995): 186–89
Moghissi, Haideh. "Women in the Resistance Movement in Iran." In *Women in the Middle East: Perceptions, Realities, and Struggles for Liberation*, ed. Haleh Afshar, 158–71. London: Macmillan, 1993.
Mojab, S. "Islamic Feminism: Alternative or Contradiction?" *Fireweed* 47 (1995): 18–25.
Najmabadi, Afsaneh. "Feminism in an Islamic Republic: Years of Hardship, Years of Growth." In *Islam, Gender, and Social Change*, ed. Yvonne Yazbeck Haddad and John L. Esposito. New York: Oxford University Press, 1998.
———. "Hazards of Modernity and Morality: Women, State, and Ideology in Contemporary Iran." In *Women, Islam, and the State*, ed. Deniz Kandiyoti, 48–76. Philadelphia: Temple University Press, 1991.
———. *The Story of the Daughters of Quchan: Gender and National Memory in Iranian History*. Syracuse, NY: Syracuse University Press, 1998.
———. "*Zanha-yi millat*: Women or Wives of the Nation?" *Iranian Studies: Journal of the Society for Iranian Studies* 26(1–2) (summer 1993): 51–71.
Nakanishi, Hisae. "Power, Ideology, and Women's Consciousness in Postrevolutionary Iran." In *Women in Muslim Societies: Diversity within Unity*, ed. Herbert L. Bodman and Nayereh Tohidi, 83–100. Boulder, CO: Lynne Rienner Publishers, 1998.
Paidar, Parvin. "Feminism and Islam." In *Gendering the Middle East: Emerging Perspectives*, ed. Deniz Kandiyoti, 51–68. Syracuse, NY: Syracuse University Press, 1996.
———. *Gender of Democracy: The Encounter between Feminism and Reformism in Contemporary Iran*. Democracy, Governance, and Human Rights Programme Paper No. 6, United Nations Research Institute for Social Development (UNRISD), 2001.
Razavi, Shahrashoub. "Women, Work, and Power." In *Women in the Middle East: Perceptions, Realities, and Struggles for Liberation*, ed. Haleh Afshar, 117–36. London: Macmillan, 1993.
Reeves, Minou. *Female Warriors of Allah*. New York: E.P. Dutton, 1989.

Talattof, Kamran. "Iranian Women's Literature: From Pre-revolutionary Social Discourse to Post-revolutionary Feminism." *International Journal of Middle East Studies* 29(4) (November 1997): 531–59.

Tapper (Lindisfarne), Nancy. "The Women's Subsociety among the Shahsevan Nomads of Iran." In *Women in the Muslim World*, ed. Lois Beck and Nikki Keddie, 374–98. Cambridge, MA: Harvard University Press, 1978.

Tohidi, Nayereh. "Gender and Islamic Fundamentalism: Feminist Politics in Iran." In *Third World Women and the Politics of Feminism*, ed. Chandra Talpade Mohanty, Ann Russo, and Lourdes Torres, 251–67. Bloomington: Indiana University Press, 1991.

———. "International Connections of the Iranian Women's Movement." In *Iran and the Surrounding World since 1501: Interactions in Culture and Cultural Politics*, ed. Nikki R. Keddie and Rudi Matthee. Seattle: University of Washington Press, 2002.

———. "Modernity, Islamization, and Women in Iran." In *Gender and National Identity: Women and Politics in Muslim Societies*, ed. Valentine M. Moghadam, 110–47. London: Zed, 1994.

Torab, Azam. "Piety as Gendered Agency: A Study of *Jalaseh* Ritual Discourse in an Urban Neighbourhood in Iran." *Journal of the Royal Anthropological Institute* 2(2) (1996): 235–51.

———. "The Politicization of Women's Religious Circles in Post-revolutionary Iran." In *Women, Religion, and Culture in Iran*, ed. Sarah Ansari and Vanessa Martin, 143–68. London: Curzon in association with the Royal Asiatic Society of Great Britain and Ireland, 2002.

Vieille, Paul. "Iranian Women in Family Alliance and Sexual Politics." In *Women in the Muslim World*, ed. Lois Beck and Nikki Keddie, 451–72. Cambridge, MA: Harvard University Press, 1978.

Zahedi, Ashraf. *From Triumph to Despair: The Story of Women of the Confederation of Iranian Students' Movement Abroad*. Forthcoming.

———. "Transformation through Tragedy: The Case of Iranian War Widows." *Gender and Society*. Forthcoming.

5

IRAQ

Ghoncheh Tazmini

PROFILE OF IRAQ

Iraq—officially the Republic of Iraq or in Arabic Al-ʿIraq, or Al-Jumhuriyah al-ʿIraqiyah—is a partially landlocked country in southwestern Asia. It is the easternmost country of the Arab world, located at about the same latitude as the southern United States. Iraq has an outlet to the sea on the Persian Gulf and is neighbored by Iran to the east, Turkey to the north, Syria and Jordan to the west, and Saudi Arabia and Kuwait to the south. Geographers explain Iraq's geography in terms of four main zones or regions: the rolling upland between the upper Tigris and Euphrates rivers (in Arabic known as the Dijilis and Furat, respectively); the desert in the west and southwest; the highlands in the north and in the northeast; and the central and southeastern alluvial plain through which the Tigris and Euphrates flow. Iraq's total land area is variously given as 433,970 and 437,520 square kilometres.

The climate is extreme, with dry, hot summers when temperatures may exceed 43 degrees Celsius (109 degrees Fahrenheit) and cold winters, particularly in the highlands. Summers are damp and humid near the Persian Gulf. Approximately 90 percent of the annual rainfall occurs between

November and April, most of it in the winter months from December through March. The remaining six months, particularly the hottest ones of June, July, and August, are dry. The summer months are marked by two kinds of wind. The southerly and southeasterly *sharqi*, a dry, dusty wind with occasional gusts of eighty kilometers (approximately 47 miles) an hour, occurs from April to early June and again from late September through November. It may persist for only a couple of days at the beginning and the end of the season but blow for several days at other times. The wind is often accompanied by severe dust storms that may rise to heights of several thousand feet, and that may close airports for brief periods. From mid-June to mid-September, the prevailing wind, known as the *shamal*, is from the north and northwest. It is a steady wind, absent only occasionally during this period. The arid air brought by the *shamal* permits intensive heating of the land surface by the sun, but the breeze does have a cooling effect. The combination of rain shortage and extreme heat makes much of Iraq a desert.

When Iraq became independent from Great Britain in 1932, the departing British officials estimated the population at roughly 3.5 million. The first census was carried out in 1947 and showed a population of about 4.8 million. The 1957 census recorded a population estimated at around 6.8 million, and the 1965 census gave a population figure of more than 8 million. According to the 1987 census, the annual population growth rate was 3.1 percent, placing Iraq among those countries with high population growth rates.[1]

Although data are not entirely reliable, the government estimates that 76 percent of the people are Arabs, 19 percent are Kurds, and the Turkmen-speaking population, Assyrians, Armenians, and other relatively small groups make up the rest. The official language is Arabic, spoken by 80 percent of the population.

About 95 percent of the population adheres to Islam. The Islamic body is divided into two groups: Sunni and Shi'a, the latter comprising the majority. Official figures set the number of Shi'as at 55 percent. However, members of the Sunni sect have dominated the regime that came to power in 1968, the Arab Ba'th Socialist Party. This centralized and highly disciplined party has been organized around an ideology of Arab socialism and pan-Arab nationalism.

OVERVIEW OF WOMEN'S ISSUES

Principles in Iraq state that women's rights should be maintained, that women are liberated, and that women are equal to men and should have equal opportunities. Over the past ten years, legislation established by the political leadership has helped women participate in national development. There has been a marked increase in women's education and literacy and female participation in public organizations, including government and military organizations. Nevertheless, in spite of the many successes achieved by the Ba'th Party, many limitations in its programs are also evident. In addition to the General Federation of Iraqi Women (GFIW), the Iraqi elite has created other organizations into which women are mobilized. Paramilitary organizations of boys and girls from elementary schools to college have been created through the school system. Sports groups, music and fine arts groups, literary clubs, scientific and professional associations, student organizations, hobby clubs, and youth hostels have been organized by the party and financed by the state.

EDUCATION

Opportunities

When the Ba'th Party assumed control of the state, its development agenda included a program for formal education. Article 45 of the Ba'th Party constitution declared that education was an exclusive function of the state. Accordingly, the party abolished foreign and private educational institutions. Article 48 of the constitution made primary (beginning at six years of age and lasting for up to six years) and secondary education (beginning at twelve years of age and lasting for up to six years) compulsory and education free to all citizens. It also stipulated that non-Arab citizens be barred from teaching in primary and secondary schools as part of the Ba'th Party's effort to retain ideological control over the youth.

Before the Ba'th Revolution, of the approximately 4 million females in the population, only 23,000 had achieved secondary certificates or their equivalents; 8,000 had acquired college or institute certificates; 200 had received graduate degrees or vocational diplomas; and 90 had received doctorates. Only a decade after Ba'th control began, females made up 43 percent of those in vocational schools. In the 1970s, female registration in primary schools increased 366 percent, in secondary schools 314 percent, and 210 percent in universities.

Iraqi women are encouraged to attend law school and to practice and even to teach law. Women from minorities, however, face open discrimination: they can attend schools, but they are prevented from practicing.

Only Arabic and Kurdish can be used in instruction. Public instruction in Syriac for Assyrian and Chaldean students who live in areas under government control is not allowed. Where the Kurds rule in the north, teachers have been able to use Syriac since an antigovernment uprising in 1991.

Literacy

At the time the Ba'th Party took control in 1968, about 67 percent of the female population was illiterate. Although the change was dramatic within a decade, the expansion of education was mostly effective for youths, not for adults. To remedy this problem, the Ba'th Party embarked on a literacy campaign in 1978. A law was promulgated requiring adults of both sexes aged fifteen to forty-five to participate for two years in one of the many literacy programs the government established. Literacy centers were constructed across the country, and penalties were levied against those who did not attend. Official statistics showed the success of these measures in recruiting both the youth and adults into educational programs.[2]

Statistics on Female Literacy

According to reports prepared by Arab experts and compiled under United Nations support, there is an 85 percent literacy rate among women.[3]

EMPLOYMENT AND ECONOMICS

Job/Career Opportunities

An article was added to the Constitution of the Iraqi Republic in 1970 that states that all citizens are equal under the law, that there is no distinction between the sexes, and that equal rights and opportunities in all fields are assured. The law of reforming the government system confirming equity in the economic and financial fields followed in 1977.[4]

The record of successes and limitations of the Ba'th/GFIW programmes for women is rather mixed. It is uncertain how many women have been affected by women's programs, or how profoundly or positively. On the other hand, some changes are evident for at least part of the female population. There has been a noticeable increase in the female labor force from 2.5 percent of the total labor force in 1957 to 12 percent in 1977 according to one report,[5] or an increase from 7 percent in 1968 to 19 percent in 1980 according to another report.[6] In fact, since the early 1980s, women have entered practically every profession, including the army. In 1980, 37 percent of oil-project planners working under the Ministry of Oil were women, and 30 percent of construction supervisors were women. By 1982, women comprised 46 percent of secondary-school teachers, 29 percent of physicians, 70 percent of pharmacists, 46 percent of dentists, 15 percent of accountants, 14 percent of factory workers, and 4 percent of executive or managerial positions in Iraq.[7]

Pay

A series of work laws instituted in 1987 confirm women's right to work and equal salary for the same jobs as men. Law No. 191 of 1975 confirms equity between women and men in rights and advantages.

In practice, women tended to receive lesser earnings than their male counterparts. For instance, studies show that government benefits to widows or female members of families of war heroes were significantly lower than sums received by the males in the family.[8]

Working Conditions

The GFIW staff has worked closely with the state-run industries to prepare women for factory work and to resolve problems when disputes arise on the job. They collaborated with the trade unions in educational and service programs and worked with the peasant cooperatives in the rural regions, where women formed a considerable portion of the labor force. Although trade unions did consciously attempt to recruit women, in 1977 only a nominal 4 percent of the membership and administrative leadership of the unions were female.[9]

There are discrepancies in the figures on the number of women in trade unions. The statistics are unreliable due to the nature of the regime and the fact that the government tried to downplay the role of trade unions and the working class.

Sexual Harassment

The Ba'th Party, in its efforts to bring women into the workforce, has repeatedly stipulated that sexual harassment will not be tolerated. Nevertheless, the extent to which this law has been enforced can be questioned. Often investigations are incomplete and perfunctory. Moreover, culturally, women are less inclined to report cases of sexual harassment. Often, the victim, for the sake of preventing scandal that could prove shameful and dishonorable in the eyes of her family, will remain silent about incidents.

Support for Mothers/Caretakers

The Ba'th Party has officially extended the same rights on the job to women as to men, including areas of training, pay, benefits, compensation, and retirement.

Maternal Leave

The social patronage law of women and widows among others gives maternity leave for one year and provides a supportive environment for working women by adopting methods of employment convenient to their situation and using material and social incentives to encourage their work and to increase their productivity. At the time when the Ba'th Party was attempting to encourage women to increase the population (before the worldwide economic embargo), it offered women generous maternity leaves—a month prior to delivery and six weeks after with full pay, followed by six months' leave at half pay. Women, like men, could qualify for child-allowance increases in their pay for additional children they had.

Daycare

The Ba'th Party has extended services of vital importance to women. For instance, child care is provided free of charge to working mothers, often adjacent to the workplace. The Ba'th Party also has given free meals to schoolchildren during school hours. Nursing mothers have been given time off work, mornings and afternoons, to attend to their infants.

While some working-class women have found the daycare centers helpful, many women refuse to put their children in the centers, opting instead for daycare by family members. Resistance is often expressed by absenteeism and what appears to be wastefulness and ineffectiveness.

Inheritance and Property Rights

The laws of pension and social insurance, of taxation and income, and of the estate bank and the civil law all state that women are equal to men in inheritance and property rights and advantages.

According to the Iraqi Women's Federation, with regard to inheritance, women as well as men get what the law says, even the land. However, the enforcement of these inheritance rights has varied. Empirical research suggests that in practice, Kurdish and Shi'te women do not receive the rights Sunni Iraqi women are granted.

Social/Government Programs

Sustainable Development

Weakened by decades of war and sanctions, the Iraqi economy is in tatters. Unemployment and inflation are rampant, and the economy is contracting rapidly. In 1991, a United Nations report described Iraq, in the early and mid-1980s, as a country rapidly approaching the standards of developed countries. UNICEF currently describes the situation as "an ongoing humanitarian emergency" and reports that "Iraq has experienced a shift from relative affluence to massive poverty. The national economy has not shown signs of recovery as hyperinflation, unemployment and the depreciation of the national currency continued unabated."[10]

Basic infrastructure, including electrical, water, and sanitation systems, continues to collapse. Sanctions against Iraq remain the single most decisive factor in the country's economy. Oil exports are limited, foreign assets remain frozen, and Iraq is saddled with a war debt of U.S. $70 billion (the equivalent of seven years of oil revenues). Iraq's industry, consisting of petrochemicals, textiles, steel, sugar, and cement, has been dramatically affected by both the bombing and the international embargo. The revenue generated from the sale of Iraqi oil cannot be used for local procurement or investment, and this has caused 70 percent of civilian industrial enterprises to go defunct or operate at significantly reduced levels, resulting in unemployment rates of 60–75 percent. Migration and the collapsing system of education have led to a deskilled or deprofessionalized population. The middle class, once committed to moving Iraq toward a more open society, has been reduced to destitution.

Over the period 1990–1999, agricultural production declined by an average of 4.1 percent per year; output declined by 14.1 percent in 1999.[11] The output of cereals fell from 3.45 million metric tons in 1990 to an estimated 1.60 million metric tons in 1999; estimates for 2000 assessed cereals production at only 0.8 million metric tons. Industry (including mining, manufacturing, construction, and power) employed 1.3 percent of the labor force in 1987 and provided only 1.1 percent of the gross national product (GNP). The services sector employed 19.1 percent of the labor force in 1987 and contributed to 52.2 percent of GNP (as compared to 46.7 percent in 1989).

Nevertheless, the Iraqi government has attempted to correct the grim economic circumstances. In a six-month emergency reconstruction budget announced in mid-1991, planned expenditure in the general consolidated budget was reduced from Iraqi dollars (ID) 14,596 million to ID 13,876 million, while the investment budget expenditure was reduced from ID 2,340 million to ID 1,660 million. The Iraqi government estimated that on January 1, 1991, its total external debt stood at ID 13,118 million (U.S. $42,320 million), and that the servicing of the debt over the period 1991–1995 would cost ID 23,388 million (U.S. $75,450 million). These estimates did not, however, take into consideration loans made to Iraq during the Iran-Iraq War by Saudi Arabia and Kuwait. In 1996, the average rate of inflation was a staggering 450 percent, compared with inflation averaging 24.4 percent per year in 1985–1989.[12]

This grim situation has forced the Iraqi leadership to mobilize all of its resources for development, particularly the female part of the population. In the past, Iraqi women had assumed the traditional tasks of being stay-at-home mothers and wives. To solve Iraq's severe shortage of manpower, women were integrated into the workforce. Iraq chose to train women rather than employ foreign guest workers, as did Kuwait, Bahrain, and Saudi Arabia in their initial stages of economic development. Presently, Iraq employs one million foreign workers, most of them Egyptian—a relatively smaller number than in to other Arab nations.[13]

Welfare

The state has subsidized low-income housing for workers, which women workers could apply for independently of their male kin. Free transporta-

FAMILY AND SEXUALITY

Economic realities have reinforced the dependence of individuals on their families. The assistance of the extended family has been necessary to support young couples as they work and try to raise children. Given the shortage of housing, young couples often begin their household by adding rooms onto the homes of their parents. Many have been turning to their families for child care, loans, labor exchange, and other economic assistance.

Gender Roles

Iraq is a patriarchal society, both at the macro level in the relationship of the government to citizens and at the micro level in the private sphere, where the father is at the helm of family life. However, veiling is not mandatory in Iraq as it is in neighboring Iran.

The attitude toward the role of women in the private domain and public sphere began to change in the 1970s. This shift in attitude was, in part, spearheaded by the Ba'th Party, which perceived women as an untapped resource with the potential of performing an array of nontraditional roles and functions. With this end in mind, the government moved to expand the role of women, particularly in the public sphere, through a vast series of benefits, incentives, and remunerative inducements.

The GFIW was also enthusiastic in promoting this trend. Albeit restricted, it began challenging the deep-seated stereotypes espoused by traditional Iraqi society. For example, it changed the illustrations on children's book covers to represent women beyond domestic surroundings. It also taught housework to boys as well as girls with the objective of emphasizing equality of the sexes. Members of the federation went into rural villages, identified women with leadership qualities, and instructed them on health care, nutrition, and hygiene. Some were trained to be educators who got a chance not only to disseminate this valuable information, but also to try out a role other than the conventional and traditional ones they had been performing most of their lives. The GFIW also assisted widows or women who were indigent with monetary help through training, including basic schooling, driving classes, and self-development programs, all with the aim of making women self-sufficient and improving their chances of being co-opted into society.[14]

However, the UN sanctions have undone these efforts and have reversed many of the gains of the 1970s. The shrinking job market brought about by poverty has forced women to resort to marriage as a means of survival. Often, families have been keen to wed their daughter to the highest bidder.

This state of extreme desperation has led to a gender imbalance and the restored practice of polygamy. Though Iraqi religious law sanctions polygamy, the government has strongly discouraged it. Aiming to assimilate women into society and to improve their status, the government has imposed difficult conditions on the practice of polygamy.[15]

Marriage

The family unit has continued to be strong in part because the Ba'th Party has subsidized families directly and indirectly. The pronatalism of the Ba'th Party and the emphasis on marriage has contributed to an idealization of the family. The nation has been represented as a large family with the president as the father. Article 38 of the Ba'th Party constitution stipulates that the state is responsible for protecting and developing the family, which is considered to be the basic cell of the nation. The article continues to note that the state must encourage and facilitate marriage, which is a national duty. Finally, it asserts that offspring are entrusted to the state immediately after the family.

Implicitly, Ba'th Party leaders have expressed the legitimacy of maintaining the solidarity of large family groups by their reliance on members of their own Tikriti clan to rule. Members who are blood related or distant kin of state leaders occupy a significant number of key state positions. In using their own primordial groups, they may have reinforced the legitimacy of such affiliations in general.

However, despite the apparently contradictory nature of direct and indirect support of "family" and the uncertainty as to the degree of success of its program, the Ba'th Party's project has been to curtail the connections between individuals and their large family/ethnic/tribal groups and to intensify loyalties to and identification with the state. In fact, the Ba'th Party has attempted to subordinate the family to the state by taking over family functions (women's programs, education, health care, and social control), transforming the family from a unit of production to a unit of consumption and subsidizing the nuclear family in order to win allegiance away from kin groups to the state.

In spite of the attempts of the Ba'th Party to emasculate the population's allegiance to the large family/tribal/ethnic groups, these primordial groups can still claim the allegiance of a considerable portion of the population. One explanation for this is the reaction to the repressive political atmosphere. The repression in the regime and the lack of legal political alternatives to the Ba'th Party have driven opposition underground or into silence. The persistent mistrust of the state generated by this political repression has reinforced the dependence of individuals on their families.

The Ba'th Party has been forthcoming about extending rights and services to them. Legislative reform programs, for example, included modest changes in the personal status laws in 1978. Ba'th elites merged what they argued were the more tolerant and progressive aspects of Sunni and Shi'a laws. For instance, in cases of divorce, mothers were given custody of their children until the age of ten (previously age seven for boys and nine for girls), at which time, at the discretion of a state-employed judge, custody could be extended to age fifteen. At the age of fifteen, the child could choose with which parent he/she wished to live. The code widened the conditions under which a woman could request a divorce. The law also made the consent of state-employed judges necessary before a man could remarry.

Reproduction

The system of male predominance in Iraqi society is reflected in intimate relations between male and female. Iraqi women are brought up to believe that sex is a duty for a wife, who must fulfill her husband's sexual needs under any circumstances. Studies have shown that men's expectations of sex are high, but that they have little interest in making sex enjoyable for their spouse. This is explained by the fact that most men believe that sexual enjoyment and fulfillment for a woman could lead to her becoming promiscuous.

The discrepancy between male and female sexuality begins at a young age: while girls are taught that sex is a sin outside of marriage and altogether a shameful act, young men are encouraged to seek out sexual encounters. As in the West, men proudly discuss their sexual encounters.[16] As is typical of developing countries, Iraq's population is young; in 1987, approximately 57 percent of the population was under the age of twenty.

Contraception and Abortion

The government does not seek to implement a birth-control program. This policy was reinforced by the Iran-Iraq War in an effort to offset losses in the fighting and to mitigate the threat from Iran, whose population is about three times that of Iraq. Over the period 1990–1998, the Iraqi population increased by an average of 3 percent per year.[17]

The government has generally celebrated women's reproductive role and has invariably encouraged women to reproduce through campaigns aimed at increasing the population. The shortage of manpower attributed to war, high infant mortality rates, disease, and starvation have compelled the government to launch campaigns encouraging women to have more children. This has been promoted through the use of incentives. Therefore, abortion, unless recommended by a doctor who deems a mother physically unfit for pregnancy, birth, and child rearing, is prohibited.

HEALTH

On August 2, 1990, the Iraqi army invaded its southern neighbor, Kuwait. Four days later the United Nations responded by imposing a complete trade embargo on Iraq. In the years since Iraq's attempted invasion of Kuwait, it has continued to be the subject of sanctions that affect almost every aspect of life for the average woman, man, and child. With imports of food and medicine severely restricted, malnutrition and disease are now endemic in what was once one of the healthiest countries in the world.

Health Care Access

Iraq's oil wealth led to swift economic and social development before the start of the 1991 conflict. Shortly before the start of UN sanctions, the health-care system reached approximately 97 percent of the urban and 79 percent of the rural population. Infant mortality—children born alive, but dying before their first birthday—had fallen to 47 per 1,000 live births between 1984 and 1989. When asked on U.S. television whether the death of 500,000 Iraqi children as a result of sanctions was justified, Madeleine Albright replied, "I think this is a very hard choice, but the price—we think the price is worth it." Marc Bossuyt, author of a UN-commissioned report released in August 2000, called the sanctions "a humanitarian disaster comparable to the worst catastrophes of the past decades." Bossuyt said that the Security Council's decision to continue sanctions while knowing they caused an untold number of Iraqis to die was "unequivocally illegal" under international humanitarian law.

Nutrition surveys carried out by UNICEF and other UN agencies in 2002 showed that in spite of the introduction of the UN's Oil for Food Program in 1996, the nutritional status of children had not improved. UNICEF reported that "one in five children in the south and center of Iraq remain so malnourished that they need special therapeutic feeding." A 1999 UNICEF report calculated that more than half a million children have died as a direct result of sanctions. On average, 200 hundred Iraqi children are dying every day. In September 1998, Denis Halliday, head of the UN humanitarian program in Iraq, resigned, claiming that he could no longer administer "an immoral and illegal" policy. His successor, Hans von Sponeck, also later resigned, along with the head of the World Food Program.

Research indicates that both infant and child mortality have more than doubled, rising well beyond 100 per 1,000 live births in many parts of the country. This puts Iraq, once a highly prosperous country with an advanced health system, on a par with some of the poorest developing countries in this index.[18] However, infant and child mortality in the autonomous, mainly Kurd region in the north of the country has actually fallen, perhaps reflecting the more favorable distribution of aid in that area.

Diseases and Disorders

The effect of the sanctions on the Iraqi civilian population has been truly disastrous. Food supplies are drastically low; sanitary equipment is often no longer functioning; water quality is seldom acceptable in towns; and resources to stop the spread of diseases are almost nonexistent.

POLITICS AND LAW

The political system in Iraq is democratic only in theory, as any political parties need the approval of the state to participate in elections. The president, who is elected by the Parliament, rules Iraq. However, opposition parties are illegal in Iraq, and the Supreme Council for the Islamic Revolution in Iraq (SCIRI) operates from Iran. Opposition groups operate under the Iraqi National Congress (INC), an umbrella organization based in Kurdistan and the United States.[19] The Patriotic Union of Kurdistan (PUK) is the second-largest party in the Kurdish parliament. The political system in Iraq is characterized by arbitrary rule, the absence of democratic institutions, and monopoly of the legislative, executive, and judicial powers by the Revolutionary Command Council (RCC), dominated by Saddam Hussein, who serves as its head, as commander of the armed forces, and as secretary general of the Ba'th Party.

All authority emanates from Saddam Hussein and is dispersed through an inner circle, whose members are chosen for their unquestioning loyalty to him. These members come from his immediate or extended family, were born in Tikrit, Hussein's hometown, or have risen through the ranks of the Ba'th Party with Hussein. To have any hope of succeeding, an attempt to oust Hussein would have to be at least abetted by one of these men, though it would also require the support of military commanders.

Iraq operates a dual legal system based on a combination of Shi'a and Sunni legal principles. There are three main sources of Iraqi law: Islamic law, constitutional law, and legislation and statutory law. In addition, the Iraqi legal system draws on some secondary sources such as usage, custom, and judicial precedents. The president of the Republic appoints all jurors.

The Iraqi court system can be divided into two categories. The first includes the judicial hierarchy that is administered by the Ministry of Justice; the second is composed of a number of courts and tribunals affiliated with, and supervised by, executive organs other than the Ministry of Justice. The Courts of First Instance, one of the subdivisions of the system, have jurisdiction in all civil and commercial matters of first instance and in personal matters of non-Muslims. The Courts of personal Status, another subdivision, have jurisdiction in all matters of first instance related to personal status of Muslims, including family, marriage, divorce, succession, and inheritance.

Suffrage

Under its constitution, Iraq has a democratic structure that includes parliamentary elections in which all citizens can vote. Due to the efforts of the GFIW branch of the Ba'th Party, in March 2000 women exercised the right to vote and run for office in national elections for the first time since 1980. Twenty-five women stood among 522 candidates for the National Assembly, which comprises 220 members.

Political Participation

Hussein's monopoly over power was sustained by a number of factors in his favor. The first is sectarianism, a crucial element in the Iraqi power structure. As a religious minority, the Sunni—Hussein's core support—are aware of the antipathy of the large Shi'a population in the south and the Kurdish population in the north toward the central government. The regime's second advantage was its increasing wealth. Rapid increases in Iraqi crude oil output in 1999 and 2000, combined with an upturn in oil prices, boosted export earnings considerably. The revenue generated by the regime from the smuggling of oil and oil products also multiplied with the rise in prices and the increase of throughput at Iraq's refineries. The third factor in Hussein's favor was the fear and terror generated by his regime. Countless stories depict the ruthlessness of the ruling clan in dealing with opposition, real or imagined. The final factor reinforcing the regime's strength was Hussein's own expertise. After twenty-five years in effective control of Iraq, his knowledge of the country's political system was unmatched. Knowing what type of concessions to grant a given clan or tribe, knowing which army units are trustworthy and which are not, and knowing which personalities have the most local weight and authority are necessary skills that can only be acquired with time.[20]

It was fundamental for Saddam Hussein and the Ba'th Party to secure women's allegiance for the leadership. The idea was that raising the social and political status of women would help consolidate support among an important sector of the population. Asked why the ruling class was so concerned with raising the status of women, Undersecretary of Foreign Affairs Nizar Hamdoon, a leading party member, explained that first, women had to be treated as equals, and second, the government needed to make women more productive members of society. By raising the level of benefits it offers women, the government has managed to alleviate the labor shortage and to create a strong base of support among the population. About 11 percent of Ba'th Party members are women.[21]

The Ba'th Party developed programs for mobilizing Iraqi women in the public sphere. One of the elite's most interesting mechanisms for the re-socialization of women has been the General Federation of Iraqi Women (GFIW). The GFIW, created by the Ba'th Party in 1968, was designed as the female arm of the party. The federation's leadership has been party members appointed by Ba'th members. Its ample budget has come directly from the state, and the party has been responsible for coordinating its programs. The GFIW's goals were outlined by the party as follow: to work for, and fight the enemies of, a socialist, democratic Arab society; to ensure the equality of Iraqi women with men in rights, in the economy, and in the state; to contribute to Iraq's economic and social development by cooperating with other Iraqi organizations and by raising the national consciousness of women; and to support mothers and children within the family structure. Toward those ends, by 1980 the GFIW had established 256 centers around the country and boasted a membership of 177,000 females aged fifteen to fifty-nine.[22]

With the support and legitimacy of the party and the state, women were encouraged to participate in an expanding public domain of social, cultural, political, and economic activities. The women received training and experience in organization, hierarchy, discipline, and service. These groups, however, were inculcated with the importance of commitment to the party, the state, the ruling elite, and the ideology of Arab socialism and pan-Arab nationalism. The organizational incorporation of women into party- and state-run agencies also offered women an alternative route for participation in the political structure.

Women's Rights

Under the Iraqi constitution, women are granted a wide range of rights. They are protected by many laws that pertain to marriage, divorce, inheritance, and employment. Although they are granted certain civil rights, dissent is not tolerated under Hussein's regime. However, in this dangerous area, women do not face discrimination, since this intolerance also applies to males. Compared with other Arab nations, the status of Iraqi women is far superior. Unlike other Arab nations such as Saudi Arabia, women are permitted to drive, to work in positions of management, to divorce, and to inherit property.[23]

Feminist Movements

The 1970s inaugurated an era of feminist activism, led by Bint al-Huda of Najaf. She was eventually persecuted and disappeared as the Ba'th Party became intolerant of all political and social movements. It appears that this intolerance was part of a larger strategy of stifling dissent through a policy of terror, censorship, and indoctrination. This move was highly ironic considering that on the one hand, the government was promoting women in the workforce, yet on the other, it was abrogating their civil rights.[24]

Lesbian Rights

The Iraqi society and government do not tolerate homosexuality, male or female. Although it is not mentioned in Iraqi law, Islamic law strongly denounces the practice. Society shuns homosexuals, and there is no support system for homosexuals.

Military Service

At the beginning of January 1998, the Iraqi Ministry of Defense called on Iraqi men and women to go to Ba'th Party headquarters and begin military training throughout all Iraqi provinces in February 1998.[25] The government's appeal to women was born out of necessity, as both men and women were needed for mobilization during the crisis over UN weapons inspections. Women are also encouraged to train for the police force because the country lacks manpower in every sector.

A substantial number of women capable of carrying weapons and undergoing training have responded to the government's pleas, though exact figures are not readily available. In 1997, a *Newsweek* issue ran a photograph of women in female commando training units in Baghdad. With the persistent American threat, it is probable that these units have proliferated.

RELIGION AND SPIRITUALITY

Women's Roles

Islam, as the state religion, is conducive to elevating the status of women. The prophet Muhammad stated that women and men are equal before God and that the same injunctions and prohibitions apply to both sexes. Overall, Islam treats women on an ethical and equitable basis, fosters their advancement, and ensures their protection under Islamic law of the Shari'a.[26]

Rituals and Religious Practices

Iraqi women actively engage in Islamic rituals, observing, for instance, the holy month of Ramadan (the ninth month of the year), during which the holy Qur'an was revealed to the prophet Muhammad. During this month, many women fast and partake of the festivities at the end of the fasting period. They celebrate the births of various disciples and commemorate the deaths of other religious notables by presenting feasts for relatives. They occasionally offer suppers to the neighborhood as acts of charity. This is a common practice, particularly following the celebration of a birth or marriage. Iraqi women have the option to veil themselves, unlike neighboring Arabs and Iranians. However, Islam permeates the life of Iraqi women because the laws governing society are modeled on Islamic law.

Women gather outside the Ali El Hadi Mosque in Samarra. Photo © TRIP/J. Sweeney.

Religious Law

Muhammad condemned oppression and degradation of women and gave women the right of inheritance and the right of individual, independent ownership, unhampered by father, husband, son, or brother. Islam also grants the right of a woman to reject a marriage proposal and to seek a divorce if she deems the marriage to have failed beyond repair. The husband undertakes polygamy only if each of the women involved consent to marriage and are treated equally. This was a practice that was encouraged during times of war in the eighth century. Polygamy requires the permission of a judge, and the husband must show that he has the financial stability to be able to support more than one wife. The government imposes imprisonment and fines on husbands who do not comply.

Veiling is not mandatory in Iraq, as it is in neighboring Iran. However, women are not permitted to marry outside of Islam. There is no law stipulating this principle, but it is general knowledge that non-Muslims are considered by the state as outsiders or disbelievers. Therefore, marriage between a Muslim and a non-Muslim is very rare in Iraq.

VIOLENCE

Domestic Violence

There have been disturbing reports about an increase in domestic violence, especially against women. Human rights organizations have provided credible evidence that since 1991, hundreds if not thousands of women have become the victims of so-called honor killings. The political parties have been rather slow to act against these crimes. Oft-heard disclaimers that honor killings are leftovers from an allegedly traditional Islamic or tribal mentality cannot hide the fact that in scale, scope, and tactics, this violence is largely a new phenomenon. It is at least in part a consequence of the social, economic, and political dislocations of the past four decades.

Apart from these honor killings, other violent acts of a more clearly political nature have been carried out, notably assaults against women and women's hairdressers. They have apparently mostly been carried out by some of the more radical Islamist splinter groups, although these groups have not claimed responsibility. The situation does not appear to be anywhere near as bad as in government-held territory, however; there are consistent reports of a much more serious breakdown in law and order in Baghdad. Apparently, the Iraqi government has not given up on the central tasks of its security apparatus, but rather, has been less eager to keep ordinary policing tasks on its agenda.

Rape/Sexual Assault

Human rights organizations and opposition groups often receive reports of women being raped or beaten. Although the government has made various pronouncements against rape and other violent crimes, it has not followed up with action. There is little public discussion of the subject, and the cultural reality is that a victim often keeps quiet in order to avoid a scandal that could bring shame and disgrace to her family. During the Anfal Campaign in 1988 in Iraqi Kurdistan, there were numerous reports that security guards raped Kurdish women—wives, daughters, or widows of insurgent Kurds. No official investigation was carried out.

OUTLOOK FOR THE TWENTY-FIRST CENTURY

Under Saddam Hussein, the country's sociopolitical, economic, and diplomatic situation had a wide range of implications for Iraqi women. With the deterioration of the economy and government cutbacks, women faced deficiencies, notably in health care and social benefits.

The country's international standing is inextricably linked to the fate of women in Iraq. For example, as a result of the sanctions imposed on Iraq, women are forced to marry at an older age because the gruelling economic situation has made it difficult for a suitor to provide support for a prospective spouse.[27] Paradoxically, this has also had a positive effect because women have opted to study and to work. Before the sanctions, women received relatively higher pay and were granted land and government housing. With cutbacks, salaries dropped and benefits halted.

Following the Anglo-American attack on Iraq, women have been severely disaffected. Pregnant women are lacking the medical attention they need as a result of the shortage of medical supplies and equipment. Military conflict has only served to further jeopardize the health of women who face enormous risks, including an increased likelihood of miscarriage, premature delivery, and complications of pregnancy and childbirth. The damage to the health care system, the effect of the sanctions, and the increasing scarcity of food and water have proven disastrous, particularly among those women displaced by the war. The present situation is one where health, nutrition, and shelter have become the vital issues confronting women.

The problem of lawlessness that has followed the war has made women more vulnerable. Some have lost brothers and husbands during the war and face a security issue. It is up to the two coalition forces to restore order and to assemble a sustainable peacekeeping force in post-war Iraq. Economically, it remains to be seen whether the Western powers will succeed in restoring the economy that will serve the interests of Iraqi men and women. Politically, if the external powers succeed in forging a democratic government, female participation in public life will most probably increase. If supranational and humanitarian organizations commit to fostering education at both the junior and university level, it is also likely they will yield a higher literacy rate among women and also promote female registrants in post-secondary institutes.

NOTES

1. www.photius.com/wfb1999/iraq/iraq_people.html.
2. Suad Joseph, "Elite Strategies for State-Building: Women, Family, Religion, and State in Iraq and Lebanon," in *Women, Islam, and the State*, ed. Deniz Kandiyoti (London: Macmillan, 1999), 181–82.
3. Women's Edge: The Coalition for Women's Economic Development and Global Equality. www.womensedge.org/ThewomenofIraq.htm.
4. Law no. 35 of 1977.
5. Ihsan Al-Hassan, *The Effects of Industrialisation on the Social Status of Women* (Baghdad: General Federation of Iraqi Women, 1980).
6. Amal Sharqi, "The Progress of Women in Iraq," in *Iraq: The Contemporary State*, ed. Tim Niblock (London: Croom Helm, 1982).
7. Andrea Laurenz, "Iraqi Women Preserve Gains Despite Wartime Problems," *Washington Report on Middle East Affairs*, July 1989, 4.
8. Helen Chapin Metz, ed., *Iraq: A Country Study* (Washington, DC: Federal Research Division of the Library of Congress, 1988).
9. Ministry of Planning, *Iraq Annual Abstract of Statistics* (Baghdad: Ministry of Planning, 1977).
10. *UN Report*, March 1999.
11. Estimates by the *Middle East Economic Digest* of London, December 1999.
12. *The Europe World Year Book*, vol. 1 (Old Woking, Surrey: Gresham Press, 2001), 2041–42.
13. Laurenz, 1989, 4.

14. "The Status of Iraqi Women," *Al-Raida* 17(2) (spring 1991): 59.
15. Barbara Nimri, "Sanctions Hurt Women More," *Women Envision*, July 12, 1998.
16. T.Y. Ismael, *The Arab Left* (Syracuse: Syracuse University Press, 1976), 134.
17. Deniz Kandiyoti, ed., *Women, Islam and the State*, 186–87.
18. Sana Al-Khayyat, *Honour and Shame: Women in Modern Iraq* (London: Saqi Books, 1990), 89–91.
19. www.worldpress.org/profiles/Iraq.cfm.
20. Noga Efrati, "Productive or Reproductive? The Roles of Iraqi Women during the Iraq-Iran War," *Middle Eastern Studies* 35(2) (April 1999): 27–44.
21. *UNICEF Press Release* (November 13, 2000).
22. Derek Hopwood, ed., *Iraq: Power and Society* (Reading: Ithaca Press, 1993), 43.
23. *Economist Intelligence Unit, Country Briefings: Iraq*, October 6, 2000.
24. "Iraqi Women," *The Review* XI(2) (June 10, 1996).
25. Andrea Laurenz, 1989, 4.
26. Manal Al-Alusi, Speech Delivered at the Ninth Conference of the General Federation of Iraqi Women (Baghdad, General Federation of Iraqi Women, 1980).
27. Marion Farouk Sluglett and Peter Sluglett, *Iraq Since 1958: From Revolution to Dictatorship* (London: KPI, 1987), 264.

RESOURCE GUIDE

Suggested Reading

Adams, Doris. *Iraq's People and Resources*. Berkeley: University of California Press, 1958.
Adams, Michael, ed. *The Middle East: A Handbook*. London: Blond Press, 1971.
Awni al-Kassir, Maliha. *The Woman's Status in Modern Iraq*. Baghdad: al-Tadamon Press, 1965.
Ingrams, Doreen. *The Awakened: Women in Iraq*. London: Third World Centre, 1983.
Kandiyoti, Deniz, ed. *Women, Islam, and the State*. London: Macmillan, 1991.
al-Khayyat, Sana. *Honour and Shame: Women in Modern Iraq*. London: Saqi Books, 1990.
Woodsmall, Ruth F. *Women and the New East*. Washington, DC: Middle East Institute, 1960.

Videos/Films

Hidden Wars of Desert Storm. 2001. Free Will Productions.
Iraq: Cradle of Civilization. 1991. Baltimore: Maryland Public Television.
Iraqi Women: Voices from Exile. 1994. Maysoon Pachachi.

Web Sites

The Iraqi Foundation, New York, iraq@iraqfoundation.org.
Dedicated to human rights and democracy within Iraq.

Photius Coutsoukis, www.photius.com/wfb1999/iraq/iraq_people.html.
Personal web page with information on Iraq and information and links to U.S. government sites for green card and citizenship information.

SELECTED BIBLIOGRAPHY

Abdulrahman, A.J. *Iraq*. Oxford, U.K.: Clio Press, 1984.
Ahmad, Khurshid, ed. *Islam: Its Meaning and Message*. London: Islamic Council of Europe, 1975.
al-Ani, Khaled, ed. *The Encyclopedia of Modern Iraq*. 3 vols. Baghdad: Arab Encyclopedia House, 1977.
Fernea, Elizabeth Warnock. *Guests of the Sheik. An Ethnography of an Iraq Village*. Garden City, NY: Doubleday, 1969.
Harris, George L. *Iraq: Its People, Its Society, Its Culture*. New Haven, CT: HRAF Press, 1958.
al-Hassan, Ihsan. *The Effects of Industrialisation on the Social Status of Women*. Baghdad: General Federation of Iraqi Women, 1980.
Iraqi Foundation. *Human Rights: Iraq*. New York: Iraqi Foundation, 2001.

6

ISRAEL

Chava Frankfort-Nachmias

PROFILE OF ISRAEL

The state of Israel has its roots in Zionism, the nationalist movement founded in 1896 to reclaim Palestine as a homeland for the Jewish people. Established by Eastern European Zionists who immigrated to Palestine early in the twentieth century, Israel emerged as a state in 1948 after it had won a war against its Palestinian Arab neighbors. Subsequently, Israeli society has become a homeland to millions of Jewish immigrants from different countries and diverse backgrounds. During the three years following the establishment of the state, mass immigration doubled the size of the Jewish population, which was approximately 600,000 in 1947. Today the Jewish majority makes up about 82 percent of the nation's population. The remaining 18 percent are non-Jews, mostly Arabs. Israeli Jews are evenly divided between those originating from Europe and those originating from Middle Eastern countries. Israel is an industrialized urban society, with about 90 percent of its population living in urban areas. It has a Western-style democracy with a multiparty parliamentary system. The parliament (Knesset) of 120 members is elected by proportional representation from party lists. Israel has a technologically advanced market economy with considerable government participation.

The total population of Israel in 2002 was 6,029,529. The ratio of males to females in the population is 0.99. The total fertility is 2.54 children per woman. The infant mortality is 7.55 deaths per 1,000 live births, and maternal mortality is 5 per 100,000. Life expectancy is 81.01 years for women and 76.82 for men.

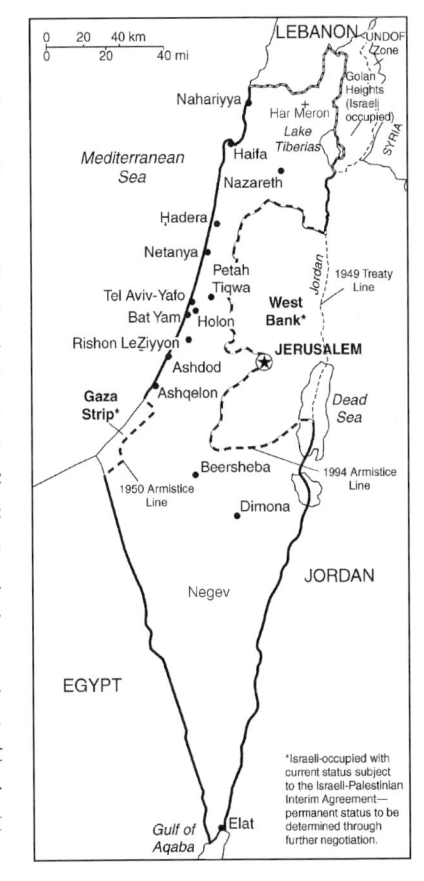

OVERVIEW OF WOMEN'S ISSUES

In 1991, *Calling the Equality Bluff: Women in Israel*, the first scholarly book on contemporary Israeli feminism, was published.[1] This title is symbolic of the most significant characteristic of feminism in Israel: the sharp contrast between legislation on women's equality and reality.[2] While the status of women has received attention since the establishment of the state, with some impressive landmarks, most efforts have been confined to the legislative but not always observed in practice.[3]

Despite progressive legislation, gender inequality is evident at all levels of society in Israel: in the family, the labor force, politics, and the military. Israeli women are excluded from the center of political power. They work in a highly segregated labor force and occupy a highly traditional role in the family. A paradox is how gender equality is manifested in the most central institutions of Israeli society: in education, work, family, health, politics, and the military. The framework used in this chapter to analyze gender equality in Israel applies only to Jewish women. Although Israeli Palestinian women are Israeli citizens, their gender status is not affected by the same forces that shape the status of Jewish women.

EDUCATION

Since the 1980s, increases in educational attainment in Israel have been dramatic for both men and women. Moreover, gender differences have narrowed considerably over time. In 1986, the median number of years of schooling was 11.3 for men and 10.9 for women. In 1996, the median increased to 12.1 for men and 12.0 for women. Overall, in the 1990s, the median number of years of schooling for both Israeli men and women was the same at 11.8 years.[4] The gender gap has also narrowed for those who completed thirteen to fifteen years of education. Whereas in 1986, 27 percent of men and 25 percent of women completed thirteen or more years of education, in 1996, 37 percent of both men and women attained this level of education.[5] Israel has among the highest percentage of women who are college graduates: In 1994–1995, 55 percent of all college graduates were women.

Opportunities

Despite these trends, there is a great deal of gender differentiation in fields of concentration. Women are predominant in the humanities and social sciences, while men are more likely to be concentrated in the physical sciences and engineering. These trends tend to reproduce the sex-segregated labor market. For example, the fields of electronics in Israel are almost exclusively male, while fashion design and nursing are predominantly female.[6] Gender differentiation is also manifested in Israeli universities. While women are in the majority among all graduate students, in 1997 they held only 22 percent of all faculty positions. Moreover, female academics are concentrated at the lowest rungs of academe and are underrepresented at the tenured top levels. However, partly as a result of the myth of gender equality, many university officials strongly deny that these distributions could be the result of discrimination.[7]

A gender-equality policy in education was formulated in 1994 following the election of a new and progressive government. The policy consisted of a variety of measures designed to increase gender equality in the public school system in Israel. Among the measures taken were the publication of new textbooks eliminating sexist language and the provision of workshops and training for teachers on gender issues.[8] To date, the policy has been only sporadically implemented, and it is too early to tell whether it has resulted in a significant change in gender inequality in education.

EMPLOYMENT AND ECONOMICS

The "myth of equality" in Israel and the sharp contrast between formal legislation and its implementation into action are best illustrated in the area of women and work. Israel is considered one of the most progressive nations in its labor legislation as it relates to women.[9] However, while Israeli enjoy economic equality before the law, they are employed in a highly segregated labor market where pay and other benefits are unequally distributed.

Job/Career Opportunities

From the mid-1970s through the early 1980s, a series of suits was brought before the courts to contest discrimination against women in the labor market. These efforts culminated in the Equal Employment Opportunity Law passed by the Knesset in 1988. The law made discrimination on the basis of sex in the workplace illegal. Specifically, the law prohibits discrimination in job advertising, conditions of employment, job training, and promotion as well as dismissal and severance pay.[10] A prohibition against sexual harassment was also included. In 1996, and the law was further expanded to define fringe benefits as income and to prohibit unequal allocation of these benefits for similar jobs.

Clearly, the unequal status of women in the labor market has been an important part of the legislative agenda in Israel. Beginning in the 1950s and culminating in the 1980s and 1990s, serious efforts have been made to fight gender discrimination in the workplace. Yet despite these legislative attempts to reduce inequality, Israeli women continue to be employed in a segregated labor market. Furthermore, women continue to have limited access to training and promotion opportunities and earn considerably less than men do. Feminist scholars have argued that recent legislation introduced to fight discrimination in the workplace has been ineffective because it does not include affirmative action in its definition of equality, nor does it have provisions for enforcement.[11] Another factor accounting for the ineffectiveness of the new legislation is the reluctance of women to sue employers. While there have been a few landmark cases fought in the labor courts, the majority of women are unwilling to pay the economic and psychological price involved in suing their employers.

Progressive legislation and general public support for women's employment outside the home contribute to a relatively high labor-participation rate of Israeli women. Between 1976 and 1996, the proportion of women in the labor force rose from 32 percent to 46 percent. Among women aged thirty-five to forty-four, the rate in 1996 was 68 percent. Education is highly correlated with women's labor-participation rate. Whereas 68 percent of women with sixteen years of education or more were in the labor force in 1996, the rate was only 28 percent for women with less than a high-school education.[12]

The upward trend in women's employment can also be attributed to restructuring of the Israeli economy and demographic trends in Israeli society. First, the expansion of the economy in the 1980s resulted in demand for qualified workers in education and financial and business services. At the same time, growing defense needs absorbed men from the civilian sector, thus opening new employment opportunities for women.[13]

Although women represent about 50 percent of the graduates of Israel's medical schools, only about 30 percent of woman physicians are specialists, compared with about 60 percent of the men. Women are especially underrepresented in prestigious specialties. In 1991, 19 percent of all male residents specialized in surgery, compared to only 7 percent of female residents. Women are also absent from decision-making bodies in the medical profession. Fewer than 20 percent of department heads in Israeli hospitals are women, and of the fifty to sixty committees in the Israeli medical association, only a handful are headed by women. In contrast, Israeli women are overrepresented among the less prestigious paraprofessions at 70 percent. In a sense, the traditional division of labor characteristic of Israeli society is manifested in the health-care system as in other workplaces, with women performing nurturing roles that are subordinate and undervalued.[14]

In societies where people's jobs and occupations determine their location in the status system in terms of income and prestige, gender segregation in the workplace contributes to women's lower pay and lesser social power.[15] Israeli women have "more limited career choices, fewer promotional opportunities, and inferior wages and fringe benefits."[16] Despite the fact that the proportion of women in management positions has almost doubled in the last twenty years, women occupied only 20 percent of management positions in 1996.[17]

Pay

Women in all positions earn considerably less than men. In 2000, the average hourly wage for women employed full-time was 83 percent that of men. The gender gap in earnings increases with level of education. In 1996, the hourly wage of women with only four years of education or less was almost equivalent (95 percent) to that of men with the same level of education. In contrast, educated women (sixteen years of education or more) earned 27 percent less than men with the same level of education.[18]

The income differentials in Israel are attributed not only to a segregated labor market but also to direct discriminatory practices of employers. In Israel, fringe benefits such as overtime pay, cars, and travel allowances account for about 40 percent of the take-home pay. Employers tend to differentially allocate such benefits to men and women in essentially similar jobs. Because of the weight of fringe benefits in the overall pay package, such practices tend to widen the pay gap between men and women.

Working Conditions

Labor legislation relating to women dates back to the 1950s. Labor law provisions reflected Israeli culture's dual commitment to a socialist philosophy in which everyone is engaged in productive labor, on one hand, and a strong family orientation in which women are perceived as homemakers and mothers, on the other.[19] This duality is manifested in legislation and institutional arrangements that support the working-mother model as long as the family is given priority.[20] Consequently, a strong legal foundation was created to ease the integration of family and work. Another factor accounting for the growth in the proportion of women in paid employment is the considerable increase—from 50 percent of the total in 1970 to 73 percent in 1990—in the proportion of women between the ages of twenty-five and fifty-four.[21]

The strong family orientation in Israel and the pressure exerted on women to put family obligations first have motivated many women to work part-time. In 1996, 36 percent of women were working part-time. Moreover, women constitute nearly 70 percent of all part-time workers in the labor force. It should be noted, however, that at least in the short run, part-time work is not penalized in Israel. In contrast to other countries, part-time workers receive the same workers' benefits and social security as well as the benefits of tenure as full-time workers.[22]

The legal infrastructures relating to women's work facilitate the integration of work and family. They contribute to a labor-force participation rate of Israeli women that is among the highest in the world. However, this infrastructure also perpetuates the stereotype of women as primarily homemakers and secondarily employees and ignores the need to guarantee equal opportunity for women in the labor market.[23] The current policies support a highly segregated system in which the majority of women are on career tracks where the opportunities for promotion and higher pay are often limited.[24]

Most Israeli women and men are concentrated in different jobs and occupations. However, gender segregation, the concentration of men and women in different occupations and jobs, is not unique to Israel. It is found in most other industrialized countries and accounts for women's poor position in the labor market. Women tend to be concentrated in a small number of "feminine" occupations. In 2000, Israeli women were heavily concentrated in education (75 percent) and social work and nursing (75 percent). In contrast, they constituted less than 30 percent of the workforce in agriculture, industry, and construction.[25]

Maternal Leave and Daycare

The main thrust of labor legislation relating to women is the provision of protection to working mothers. For example, women are given a three-month maternity leave and the right to take up to one year of leave without pay.[26] In addition, measures have also been taken to provide working mothers with publicly subsidized daycare and preschool services.

The availability of child-care facilities has made it possible for women with young children to be in the labor force.[27] In 1996, 59 percent of women whose younger child was less than one year old and 79 percent of women whose younger child was between the ages of ten and fourteen were in the labor force.

The perception of women as wives and mothers and thus as secondary breadwinners continues to reinforce the traditional stereotype of females as needing protection in the workplace even when this limits their ability to compete equally.[28] As is the case in other Western countries, without a fundamental change in social norms regarding women's equal status in the labor force, employment legislation will be limited to providing legal rights rather than promoting gender equality in the workplace.

FAMILY AND SEXUALTIY

There are several explanations for the centrality of the traditional family in Israeli society. The first explanation is the Jewish religious tradition, which historically has emphasized the family as a means of assuring individual and communal survival.[29] Most Israelis, orthodox, conservative, or secular Jews, adhere to the basic tenets of the Jewish tradition. These values have been sustained by contemporary historical events. After the Holocaust of World War II, most Israeli Jews found themselves with truncated families. Many first-generation Israelis had never known their grandparents. The family became a means to establish permanence and stability and create a "new" family history.

The second reason for the importance of the family is the centrality of the army and security issues in Israeli society. The family provides the "people" power necessary to man the armies. Since the establishment of the state in 1948, Israel has fought five wars and has been engaged in an ongoing conflict with its Arab neighbors. Consequently, soldiering, the army, and national security have dominated the public discourse.

Gender Roles

The Jewish religion and the institutionalization of security issues have been significant mechanisms sustaining the traditional family, the gendered division of labor within the family, and, consequently, gender inequality. Numerous studies have confirmed the unequal division of labor between men and women in the Israeli family.[30] Child care is considered the mother's responsibility; and although the founders of the state, influenced by socialist ideals, expected women to work, the assumption was that they would work part-time so that they could fulfill their duties as wives and mothers. Married women are expected to be home when their spouses and children come home between one and four in the afternoon. Husbands are rarely equal partners in managing the house and at best are expected "to give her a hand."[31]

Ironically, the centrality of the family in Israeli society and early socialist ideology have resulted in progressive legislation designed to protect women in their multiple roles as workers, wives, and mothers. However, despite these gains, the gendered division of labor and the perception that women's role is secondary to men have made Israeli women dependent on men and severely limit the choices open to them.

Marriage

Although Israel has been characterized as a developed, urban-industrial democracy, it is a family-oriented society with strong traditional-patriarchal elements more typical of agrarian societies. According to Jewish religious law (*Halakha*), the marriage ceremony is a unilateral ceremony where the woman is "purchased" by the husband. Moreover, a Jewish woman cannot get a divorce without the consent of her husband even when she is abused or abandoned by her husband.[32] It is estimated that there are approximately 10,000 women in Israel whose husbands will not grant them a divorce. The divorce rate in Israel in 1994 was four per 1,000, while a single parent headed only 6 percent of households.[33] Marriage and children are the norms for women in Israel and are not seen as choice. The pressures for women to find their identity and security in marriage produce a society in which approximately 98 percent of the women are or have been married.

Reproduction

The task of being a wife and a mother is seen as falling in the public, rather than the private, sphere. Having a family, preferably with many children, became a national priority encouraged and rewarded by state authorities. In the 1950s, David Ben-Gurion, the first prime minister of Israel and a leading proponent of a high birth rate, announced a prize for families with ten children or more. State subsidies are granted for large families (with four or more children) to cover the cost of daycare and summer camps, and a political lobby represents the rights and interests of large families.[34] The fertility rate, which was 2.62 for Jewish women in the years 1990–1994, is higher than in most urban industrialized countries.[35]

Contraception and Abortion

Judaism permits abortion if there is a direct threat to the life of the mother and recognizes psychiatric as well as physical factors as potential threats to the mother. Abortion is regularly practiced in Israel. In 1996, the abortion rate per 100 live births was 14.0. Since 1977, the law ensures a low-cost and sometimes free legal abortion to any woman who is between the ages of eighteen and forty; is carrying a fetus with a serious defect; claims that the pregnancy is a result of rape or incest; or shows that by continuing the pregnancy, her physical or mental health will be affected. Despite the seemingly liberal law, the termination of pregnancy is not entirely a woman's choice. Abortions are allowed under strict state supervision. A woman who seeks an abortion must appear before a committee consisting of two physicians and a social worker. At least one woman must be present on each committee. In 1999, 96 percent of 20,581 applications were approved and 91 percent of pregnancies resulted in terminations.[36] Abortions are often used as a form of contraception, especially among married women. Although modern contraception is widely available, the wide use of withdrawal and abortion as forms of contraception place women's reproductive health under the control of men and reveal the relatively powerless position of women in Israeli society.[37]

HEALTH

Health Care Access

Gender bias and the lack of awareness of gender differences compromise Israel's health services except for reproduction. The lack of attention to women's health-care needs is reflected in medical practice and in the lack of female medical students and physicians.

As is the case elsewhere, women in Israel live longer than men (with a life expectancy of 79.9 years versus 76.3 for men), but they suffer more than men from multiple health problems that significantly affect their quality of life.[38] Israeli women visit their family physicians 20 percent more often than men and their specialists 60 percent more often. Also, hospitalization rates are 33 percent higher for women.[39]

Diseases and Disorders

Women's symptoms are often not taken as seriously as men's are. For example, women with myocardial infarctions are consistently less likely than men to be admitted to coronary care units. Thus they often miss out on the lifesaving potential of thrombolytic therapy administered in coronary care units. This may contribute to the poorer prognosis of women heart patients.[40]

Cancer

Israeli women rank tenth highest in incidence of cancer among forty developed countries, whereas Israeli men rank thirty-third. In 1994, cancer accounted for 44 percent of all deaths in women aged fifty-five to sixty-four.[41] Despite the predominance of breast cancer as the leading cause of death in women under the age of fifty-five, national mammography screening programs begun only in 1994 still result in a relatively low response rate.

POLITICS AND LAW

Suffrage

Israel is considered among the few "first-wave countries," or contemporary societies, where women gained political rights, including the right to vote, in the last century.[42] The British government granted suffrage in the late 1920s, about twenty years before the establishment of the State of Israel.

Political Participation

The myth of gender equality in Israel has been reinforced by the image of Golda Meir, the late Israeli prime minister, who was considered "proof positive" that Israel had no need for feminism. However, Meir, who rose through the party ranks after years of hard work, was a glaring exception. As with other institutions, women's political representation is shaped by social and cultural forces and by the relative predominance of patriarchy. Major impediments to women's political representation in Israel are the preoccupation with national security and the influence of religion on public affairs.

In Israel, as in most other countries, women are underrepresented in elected bodies at all levels and branches of government, including the Knesset, the government on the local level, and the bureaucracy. Since 1948, when elections of the first 120-member Knesset took place, the number of women elected to the Knesset has fluctuated between a low of eight to a high of twelve women legislators. The 1999 elections brought a distinct improvement in the representation of women, whose numbers rose from nine women in the Fourteenth Knesset to fourteen women in the Fifteenth Knesset. Despite this improvement, the percentage of women legislators has remained consistently below 12 percent. In this respect, however, Israel does not differ much from most nations in the West, with the exception of the Scandinavian countries.[43]

Even when Israeli women are elected, they have very little power relative to men. Woman have seldom belonged to either the Foreign and Security Affairs Committee or the Finance Committee, the two most powerful committees in the Knesset. Similarly, women are underrepresented in the cabinet. For example, out a single woman was included in the 1980s cabinet, which had twenty-six ministers.[44] While the situation changed somewhat in the 1990s, the 1996 Netanyahu cabinet included only one woman. Even the 1999 elections, which brought a distinct improvement in the representation of women in the Knesset, resulted in only two women being included in the newly formed cabinet led by Ehud Barak.

In many countries, while women are excluded from the centers of power in national legislative institutions, their representation at the local level is considerably higher. The focus of local governments on matters of traditional concern to women, as well as family constraints, has attracted women to the local political arena. In Israel, the proportion of women elected to local political bodies gradually rose from 4.2 percent in 1950 to 10.9 percent in 1993.[45] However, despite this increase in their relative representation on the local level, women's representation is still very small, with only three women heading local councils out of a total of sixty-three and not a single female mayor prior to the 1998 elections. The public sector is another arena in which Israeli women are underrepresented. In 1995, women constituted 60 percent of those employed in the public sector, but 80 percent of those employed at the lower ranks were women, while they constituted barely 10 percent of the four highest ranks in the government bureaucracy.[46]

Finally, as in other countries, Israeli women's limited political power is correlated with their unequal gender status in other social and economic institutions. Israeli feminists agree that an increase in political representation at all levels of government is essential for removal of some of the major impediments to gender equality in Israel. However, despite the organization of a women's network that has been relatively successful in mobilizing broad coalitions of women, the predominant patriarchal culture and the increased influence of the orthodox religious parties remain serious obstacles to the political representation of women in Israeli society.

Women's Rights and Feminist Movements

The struggle for gender equality was led by a minority of revolutionary Jewish women who emigrated from Russia to form a new egalitarian society in Palestine. These women fought for the right to work and established the Women's Workers Movement, an important feminist force in the Jewish community. After independence in 1948, gender equality was inscribed in the Declaration of Independence, and in the 1950s, the Israeli Knesset passed the Women's Equal Rights Law, which entitled women to legal equality.[47] In the 1970s, a new women's movement developed, inspired by immigrants from the United States and other English-speaking countries. The movement led to the establishment of shelters for battered women, rape crisis centers, and other feminist organizations. During the 1970s, various steps were taken by the government to address women's issues. In 1975, Prime Minister Yitzhak Rabin appointed a commission on the status of women, which presented its findings and recommendations in 1978. Following the recommendations of the commission, various government agencies were established to promote women's equality. The 1980s were marked by the development of liberal feminism in Israel, with feminist organizations as well as more traditional women's organizations focusing on legislation and political participation. During this period, the Israel Women's Network (the Israeli equivalent to the American National Organization for Women) was established.

Lesbian Rights

The environment for lesbians and gay men in Israel improved dramatically in the early 1990s. The political and social turning point came in February 1993 at a conference in the Knesset. Convened by a member of the Knesset, Yael Dayan, the conference brought more than 100 lesbians and gay men to the Knesset to testify. Since then, public attitudes toward gays and lesbians as expressed in the media and as felt by lesbians and gay people themselves have markedly improved.[48] Israel is currently in the forefront of countries granting gays and lesbians freedoms as advanced as those in the Netherlands and Scandinavia. Highlights since 1993 include the inclusion of sexual orientation in Israel's sexual-harassment legislation, the passage of laws banning employment discrimination, and the granting of spousal benefits to gay El Al (Israel's national airline) employees and others. The equality that lesbians, gay men, and bisexuals are beginning to experience in Israel is not merely legally formal but has a culturally public aspect as well. For example, a national Pride Day began to be celebrated in June 1993, and like other lesbian, gay, and bisexual public events and issues, it generally was covered sympathetically by the Israeli media. In 1999, Haifa held its first pride festival, with 500 in attendance at a local park, and in Tel Aviv, the pride parade was funded by the Tel Aviv municipality under the slogan "From Tel Aviv with Pride."[49]

Military Service

The problem of national security has dominated the public discourse in Israel in the prestate era and since the establishment of the state in 1948. The unspoken consensus that Israel faces a constant external threat has made security the number one issue on the agenda for more than fifty years, and it continues to prevail despite Israel's military and economic resilience.[50] This siege mentality has reinforced the already strong family tradition in Israeli society. The family is seen as a safe haven for husbands, sons, and brothers who face a demanding and long military duty (usually three to five years plus one month a year until they turn fifty).

Female soldiers in Jerusalem. Photo © TRIP/A. Tovy.

The militarization of Israeli society has created a male-oriented culture in which women are expected to nurture their men who are called up to serve their country and who give their lives if necessary. The metaphor of the "crowded nest" has been used to describe the typical Israeli family where "the female hovers over the males, preoccupied with combating real and imaginary enemies and attending to their needs."[51] These "duties" have been internalized by women who are seen as the frontline "soldiers," serving their country by catering to the needs of men.

The family remains at the center of the Israeli woman's life even when her children leave home to serve in the army. During this period, the family is seen as an important source of support for its soldier. The woman is expected to nurture her soldier son or soldier daughter by laundering and ironing uniforms, preparing meals during family visits, and baking cakes for the children to take back to the army. This period only serves to reinforce the Israeli woman's traditional role in the family.[52]

In a nation preoccupied with security, the military has become a major institution. Israel was the first and still remains the only country with compulsory conscription of both Jewish men and women. Military service is perceived as both an obligation and a right and as a staple of the Israeli experience as well as a key to Israeli identity. The central role of the army in Israeli life has created a macho culture that fosters the myth of male superiority and female dependence and has contributed to the perpetuation of gender inequality. Although the image of women clad in uniform and carrying rifles on their shoulders has been touted by Israeli public opinion campaigns as proof of an egalitarian approach, this egalitarian image is a myth.

Despite compulsory conscription of both men and women, the Israeli Defense Force (IDF) is probably the most gendered institution in Israeli society. Women serve in the military for a shorter period than men and are automatically exempted from service due to marriage, pregnancy, or if they are religiously observant. All women who serve in the Israeli military belong to the Women's Corps, which is entirely separate from other units in the IDF. The acronym for the Women's Corps, CHEN, means "charm," suggesting the traditionally feminine characteristic emphasized in the corps. Women are expected to "raise the morale" of the male fighter and create for him "a home away from home."[53] Furthermore, during basic training, women receive cosmetic guidance to help them emphasize their feminine characteristics and neat appearance.

The prime illustration of women's unequal status in the IDF is their exclusion from all jobs involving combat. While women are sometimes on the front lines in various support positions, they are sent to the rear at the first sign of hostilities. The unequal status of women with their male counterparts begins with basic training, in which men shoot hundreds of bullets during three weeks of basic training, compared with only one clip of thirty-two bullets shot by women. A Jerusalem councilwoman put it this way: "A woman has a better chance of hitting a terrorist with her handbag than with a bullet."[54] Women's exclusion from combat duty severely limits their job opportunities in the military. Occupations in the IDF are severely segregated along gender lines. Most female soldiers are assigned to clerical or similar positions mostly providing support to male commanders. In 1976, only about 30 percent of all jobs in the IDF (about 700 jobs) were filled by women, and approximately 65 percent of women soldiers held secretarial, administrative, and clerical jobs.[55]

When the IDF was first established, the state recognized the right of women to serve in all jobs on a voluntary basis. As time elapsed, equality disappeared. The only considerations are army efficiency and economic ones. Jobs are opened and closed to women on these bases. As a result, the IDF lags behind other armies that are more resourceful in absorbing women. Following the recommendation of the Commission on the Status of Women, the range of jobs open to women expanded considerably from 30 percent to about 70 percent by the end of 1994. While nearly 90 percent of all combat jobs are still closed to women, the IDF has successfully experimented with assigning women as instructors in the artillery and tank corps. However, these jobs account for less than 4 percent of women conscripts.[56]

Despite the progress that has been made regarding women's status, the IDF remains a deeply gendered institution. Women soldiers are still the secretaries, the clerks, the nurses, the teachers, and the social workers of the IDF. As recently as 1981, the Israeli military attorney general ruled that coffee making and floor washing are considered legitimate duties of military secretaries, the majority of whom happen to be women.

Gender inequality in the IDF has far-reaching implications in Israeli society. Because of the dominance of national security in the public discourse, the military plays a central role in the formation and recruitment of political and economic elites. High-ranking officers, upon retirement at the age of forty-five, are routinely recruited for political posts and management positions in business and industry. In 1995, women constituted only 12.4 percent of the officers in the professional service.[57] Their small numbers and exclusion from combat duty severely limit women's opportunities for promotion on the military ladder and their ability to link into the old-boy network crucial to recruitment and advancement in postmilitary careers. Thus while men are able to translate their military service into better positions in the labor market, women are rarely in a position to do so.

The IDF, with its preferential treatment accorded to men and its highly segregated and gendered nature, reproduces and reinforces the gendered division of labor and the masculine-macho culture of Israeli civil society. Its centrality and dominance and the important role it plays in creating an Israeli identity render legitimacy to gender inequality and limit women's access to power.

RELIGION AND SPIRITUALITY

Religious Law

The strong religious influences on the Israeli family can be observed not only in the private sphere but in the public arena as well. In 1953, the state gave the orthodox rabbinical courts complete jurisdiction over matters of personal status such as marriage and divorce. Religious law takes priority over matters of personal status, and at present there is no mechanism under the jurisdiction of civil law that allows individuals to marry or divorce. This legislation had an adverse effect on the status of women in the family and in the larger society. The Jewish religion, with its patriarchal attitudes toward gender roles, does not consider men and women equal before the law.

The status of women in religious courts is no better than the status of the mentally deficient, the insane, or the convicted criminal. Women cannot sign documents, be witnesses, or testify.[58] Considering women's inferior status, it is not surprising that in a prayer recited by the orthodox Jew every morning, thanks are given to God for not creating him a woman.

VIOLENCE

Domestic Violence

It is estimated that between 5 and 10 percent of Israeli married women are subject in the course of their life to domestic violence. These figures are widely considered to be underestimates. Many Israeli women, especially new immigrants, do not know that battering is a crime. Battered women in Israel are remarkably similar to battered women in other parts of the world. They come from all ethnic groups, all social classes, and every level of education.

Until the late 1970s, violence in the family was invisible and unmentioned because it was incompatible with the dominant family halo in Israeli society. The notion that "Jews do not beat their wives"[59] underlined the definition of wife battering as a private family affair rather than a legal offense. Rarely did police authorities intervene, and even when a criminal file was opened, little effort was made to bring the case to trial.

Domestic violence was first articulated as a social problem in 1976, when Marcia Freedman, a feminist member of the Israeli Knesset, testified and moved that domestic violence be put on the agenda. In addition, the feminist movement created the first shelter for battered women in 1977. Subsequently, other shelters were established and won public recognition and legitimacy. The Justice Ministry began to investigate police handling of battering and to formulate legislation on violence in the family. In 1991, the domestic violence law for the prevention of violence in the family was passed in the Knesset. It established battering as a criminal offense and provided for a court injunction to remove the battering husband from the home.

OUTLOOK FOR THE TWENTY-FIRST CENTURY

Israel combines two worlds: on the one hand, it is a liberal society characterized by democratic institutions, principles of equality, justice, and freedom, and a relatively free flow of communication; on the other hand, it is characterized by a high level of familialism, the strong influence of religion and tradition, and military involvement in government and civil society. This duality has resulted in relatively progressive legislation in women's issues coupled with gender inequality, which is evident in all major institutions of society. Israeli women are discriminated against in the workplace and the military and are excluded from the center of political power. In the family, the role of Israeli women is similar to the role occupied by women in traditional and agrarian societies. With security at the top of the national agenda, gender equality has not been high on the list of priorities for most Israelis, who consider equality for women of secondary importance at best.

The election of a more progressive government in 1999 and its commitment to jump-starting the peace process gave many social observers and feminists cause for optimism. Certainly peace would have resulted in the diminished importance of the military, a decline in the centrality of the family, and the depoliticization of motherhood and mothering. However, since the beginning of the second Intifada in 2001, the hopes for peace between Israel and the Palestinians have all but died. As long as this ongoing conflict continues to dominate the national discourse, the combined influence of religion and the institutionalization of security issues will persist as powerful barriers to gender equality in Israel.

NOTES

1. Barbara Swirsk and Marilyn P. Safir, eds., *Calling the Equality Bluff: Women in Israel* (New York: Pergamon Press, 1991).
2. Yael Yishai, *Between the Flag and the Banner* (Albany: State University of New York: Press, 1997).
3. Yishai, 1997; Barbara Swirski and M. Hasan, "Jewish and Palestinian Women in Israeli Society," in *Women in the Third World: An Encyclopedia of Contemporary Issues*, ed. Nelly P. Stromquist (New York: Garland Publishing, 1998).
4. Calvin Goldscheider, *Israel's Changing Society: Population, Ethnicity, and Development* (Boulder, CO: Westview Press, 1996).
5. *The Israel Women's Network* (in Hebrew) (Jerusalem: Israel, 1997).
6. Roslyn Arlin Mickelson, Mokubung Nkomo, and Stephen Samuel Smith, "Education, Ethnicity, Gender, and Social Transformation in Israel and South Africa," *Comparative Education Review* 45 (2001): 1–35.
7. Haim Watzman, "Israeli Scholars Try to Focus Attention on Challenges Faced by Women in Academe," *Chronicle of Higher Education* 46 (1999): A77–A78.
8. Devorah Eden, "Israel's Gender Equality Policy in Education: Revolution or Containment?" *Urban Education* 35 (2000): 473–95.
9. Yishai, 1997.
10. Ibid.
11. Frances C. Raday, "Women Work and the Law," in *Calling the Equality Bluff: Women in Israel*, ed. Barbara Swirski and Marilyn P. Safir (New York: Pergamon Press, 1991); Yishai, 1997.
12. Central Bureau of Statistics (CBS), *Statistical Abstract of Israel* (Jerusalem: Office of the Prime Minister, 2000), table 12.5.
13. Yael Azmon and Dafna N. Izaeli, eds., *Women in Israel* (New Brunswick, NJ: Transaction Publishers, 1993).
14. Amy Avgar, "Women's Health in Israel Feminist Perspective," *Social Work in Health Care* 25 (1997): 45–62.
15. Barbara Reskin and Irene Padavic, *Women and Men at Work* (Thousand Oaks, CA: Pine Forge Press, 1994), 46.
16. Yishai, 1997, 154.
17. Central Bureau of Statistics (CBS), 2000.
18. Ibid.

19. Nitza Berkovitch, "Motherhood as a National Mission: The Construction of Womanhood in the Legal Discourse in Israel," *Women's Studies International Forum* 20 (1997): 605–19; Raday, 1991.

20. Azmon and Izraeli, 1993, 1–13.

21. Yishai, 1997.

22. Azmon and Izraeli, 1993, 11–13; Yishai, 1997.

23. Raday, 1991.

24. Dafna N. Israeli, "Women and Work: From Collective to Career," in *Calling the Equality Bluff: Women in Israel*, ed. Barbara Swirski and Marilyn P. Safir (New York: Pergamon Press, 1991).

25. Central Bureau of Statistics (CBS), 2000.

26. Raday, 1991.

27. Yishai, 1997.

28. Raday, 1991.

29. Galia Golan, "Militarization and Gender: The Israeli Experience," *Women's Studies International Forum* 20 (1997): 581–86; Yishai, 1997.

30. Marilyn P. Safir, "Religion, Tradition, and Public Policy Give Family First Priority," in *Calling the Equality Bluff: Women in Israel*, ed. Barbara Swirski and Marilyn P. Safir (New York: Pergamon Press, 1991); Yishai, 1997.

31. Safir, 1991; Yishai, 1997.

32. Swirski and Hasan, 1998; Yishai, 1997.

33. Central Bureau of Statistics (CBS), *Statistical Abstract of Israel* (Jerusalem: Office of the Prime Minister, 1994).

34. Safir, 1991.

35. Swirski and Hasan, 1998.

36. *Jerusalem Report*, February 12, 2001.

37. Goldscheider, 1996.

38. Avgar, 1997.

39. Eileen Hoffman and Amy Avgar, "Women's Health in Israel and the United States: A Cross-Cultural Perspective," *Journal of Gender-Specific Medicine* (1998).

40. Helen Scharyy Motro, "Women's Health Neglected in Israel," *Jerusalem Post*, April 13, 2000.

41. Hoffman and Avgar, 1998.

42. Yishai, 1997; Swirski and Hasan, 1998.

43. Azmon and Izraeli, 1993.

44. Yishai, 1997.

45. *The Israel Women's Network*, 1997.

46. Yishai, 1997.

47. Berkovitch, 1997; Frances C. Shalev Raday and M. Liban-Kooby, eds., *Women's Status in Israeli Law and Society* (in Hebrew) (Tel-Aviv, Israel: Schocken Publishing, 1995).

48. Tracy Moore, ed., *Lesbiot: Israeli Lesbians Talk about Sexuality, Feminism, Judaism, and Their Lives* (London: Cassell, 1995).

49. Lee Walzer, *Between Sodom and Eden* (New York: Columbia University Press, 2000), 258.

50. Hanna Herzog, "Homefront and Battlefront: The Status of Jewish and Palestinian Women in Israel," *Israel Studies* 3 (1998): 61–84.

51. Ibid.; Swirski and Safir, 1991; Yishai, 1997.

52. Azmon and Izraeli, 1993; Herzog, 1998.

53. Simona Sharoni, "Every Woman Is an Occupied Territory: The Politics of

Militarism and Sexism and the Israeli-Palestinian Conflict," *Journal of Gender Studies* 1 (1992): 447–62.

54. Sharon Beth-Halachmy, "Principles of Gender Equality in Israeli Law: The Military Example," unpublished paper, 1996.

55. Sharoni, 1992.

56. Anne R. Bloom. "Women in the Defense Forces," in *Calling the Equality Bluff: Women in Israel*, ed. Barbara Swirski and Marilyn P. Safir (New York: Pergamon Press, 1991).

57. *The Israel Women's Network*, 1997.

58. Swirski and Hasan, 1998.

59. Marcia Freedman, *Exile in the Promised Land: A Memoir* (Ithaca, NY: Fireband Books, 1990).

RESOURCE GUIDE

Suggested Reading

Azmon, Yael, and Dafna N. Izraeli, eds. *Women in Israel*. New Brunswick, NJ: Transaction Publishers, 1993.

Freedman, Marcia. *Exile in the Promised Land: A Memoir*. Ithaca, NY: Fireband Books, 1990.

Goldscheider, Calvin. *Israel's Changing Society*. Boulder, CO: Westview Press, 1996.

Hazleton, Lesley. *Israeli Women: The Reality behind the Myth*. New York: Simon and Schuster, 1977.

Swirski, Barbara, and Marilyn P. Safir, eds. *Calling the Equality Bluff: Women in Israel*. New York: Pergamon Press, 1991.

Yishai, Yael. *Between the Flag and the Banner*. Albany: State University of New York Press, 1997.

Yuval-Davis, Nira. *Israeli Women and Men: Divisions behind the Unity*. London: Change Publications, 1982.

Web Sites

American-Israeli Cooperative Enterprise/The Jewish Virtual Library, http://www.us-israel.org/jsource/Society_&_Culture/womentoc.html.

Americans for Israel and Torah (AMIT) Women, http://www.amitisrael.org/.

International Council of Jewish Women, http://www.icjw.org.uk/ijwhrw/jewish_law_agunot.htm.

Maven Search/The Jewish Web Directory, http://www.maven.co.il/.

New Israel Fund, http://www.nif.org/women/.

SELECTED BIBLIOGRAPHY

Avgar, Amy. "Women's Health in Israel Feminist Perspective." *Social Work in Health Care* 25 (1997): 45–62.

Azmon, Yael. "Women and Politics: The Case of Israel." In *Women in Israel*, ed. Yael Azmon and Dafna N. Izraeli. New Brunswick: Transaction Publishers, 1993.

Berkovitch, Nitza. "Motherhood as a National Mission: The Construction of Womanhood in the Legal Discourse in Israel." *Women's Studies International Forum* 20 (1997): 605–19.

Beth-Halachmy, Sharon. "Principles of Gender Equality in Israeli Law: The Military Example." Unpublished paper, 1996.

Bloom, Anne R. "Women in the Defense Forces." In *Calling the Equality Bluff: Women in Israel*, ed. Barbara Swirski and Marilyn P. Safir. New York: Pergamon Press, 1991.

Central Bureau of Statistics (CBS). *Statistical Abstract of Israel*. Jerusalem: Office of the Prime Minister, 1994.

———. *Statistical Abstract of Israel*. Jerusalem: Office of the Prime Minister, 1996.

———. *Statistical Abstract of Israel*. Jerusalem: Office of the Prime Minister, 2000.

Eden, Devorah. "Israel's Gender Equality Policy in Education: Revolution or Containment?" *Urban Education* 35 (2000): 473–95.

Fishman, Rachelle H.B. "Concern Grows over Domestic Abuse in Israel." *Lancet* 346 (1995): 174.

Freedman, Marcia. *Exile in the Promised Land: A Memoir*. Ithaca, NY: Fireband Books, 1990.

Golan, Galia. "Militarization and Gender: The Israeli Experience." *Women's Studies International Forum* 20 (1997): 581–86.

Goldscheider, Calvin. *Israel's Changing Society: Population, Ethnicity, and Development*. Boulder, CO: Westview Press, 1996.

Hazleton, Lesley. *Israeli Women: The Reality behind the Myth*. New York: Simon and Schuster, 1977.

Herzog, Hanna. "Homefront and Battlefront: The Status of Jewish and Palestinian Women in Israel." *Israel Studies* 3 (1998): 61–84.

Hoffman, Eileen, and Amy Avgar. "Women's Health in Israel and the United States: A Cross-Cultural Perspective." *Journal of Gender-Specific Medicine* (1998).

Israeli, Dafna N. "Women and Work: From Collective to Career." In *Calling the Equality Bluff: Women in Israel*, ed. Barbara Swirski and Marilyn P. Safir. New York: Pergamon Press, 1991.

The Israel Women's Network (in Hebrew). Jerusalem, 1997.

Israel Year Book and Almanac. Jerusalem: Israel Business, Research, and Technical Translation/Documentation, 1998.

Jerusalem Report Report. February 12, 2001.

Mickelson, Roslyn Arlin, Mokubung Nkomo, and Stephen Samuel Smith. "Education, Ethnicity, Gender, and Social Transformation in Israel and South Africa." *Comparative Education Review* 45 (2001): 1–35.

Moore, Tracy, ed. *Lesbiot: Israeli Lesbians Talk about Sexuality, Feminism, Judaism, and Their Lives*. London: Cassell, 1995.

Motro, Helen Scharyy. "Women's Health Neglected in Israel." *Jerusalem Post*, April 13, 2000.

Raday, Frances C. Shalev, and M. Liban-Kooby, eds. *Women's Status in Israeli Law and Society* (in Hebrew). Tel Aviv, Israel: Schocken Publishing, 1995.

———. "Women Work and the Law." In *Calling the Equality Bluff: Women in Israel*, ed. Barbara Swirski and Marilyn P. Safir. New York: Pergamon Press, 1991.

Reskin, Barbara, and Irene Padavic. *Women and Men at Work*. Thousand Oaks, CA: Pine Forge Press, 1994.

Safir, Marilyn P. "Religion, Tradition, and Public Policy Give Family First Priority." In *Calling the Equality Bluff: Women in Israel*, ed. Barbara Swirski and Marilyn P. Safir. New York: Pergamon Press, 1991.

Sharoni, Simona. "Every Woman Is an Occupied Territory: The Politics of Militarism and Sexism and the Israeli-Palestinian Conflict." *Journal of Gender Studies* 1 (1992): 447–62.

Swirski, Barbara. "Jews Don't Batter Their Wives: Another Myth Bites the Dust." In *Calling the Equality Bluff: Women in Israel*, ed. Barbara Swirski and Marilyn P. Safir. New York: Pergamon Press, 1991.

Swirski, Barbara, and M. Hasan. "Jewish and Palestinian Women in Israeli Society." In *Women in the Third World: An Encyclopedia of Contemporary Issues*, ed. Nelly P. Stromquist. New York: Garland Publishing, 1998.

Swirski, Barbara and Marilyn P. Safir, eds. *Calling the Equality Bluff: Women in Israel*. New York: Pergamon Press, 1991.

Walzer, Lee. *Between Sodom and Eden*. New York: Columbia University Press, 2000.

Watzman, Haim. "Israeli Scholars Try to Focus Attention on Challenges Faced by Women in Academe." *Chronicle of Higher Education* 46 (1999): A77–A78.

Yishai, Yael. *Between the Flag and the Banner*. Albany: State University of New York Press, 1997.

Yuval-Davis, Nira. *Israeli Women and Men: Divisions behind the Unity*. London: Change Publications, 1982.

7

JORDAN

Nancy Mataraso Fitzgerald

PROFILE OF JORDAN

Jordan occupies almost 92,000 square kilometers[1] east of Israel, an area known as the East Bank of the Jordan River. It shares borders with Israel, Syria, Iraq, and Saudi Arabia and is almost completely landlocked, with the exception of a small coastal area on the Gulf of Aqaba. The capital is Amman. In 1950, Jordan annexed the area west and northwest of the Dead Sea, known as the West Bank. Israel occupied this territory in the 1967 war, and the late King Hussein of Jordan renounced Jordan's claim to the West Bank in 1988.

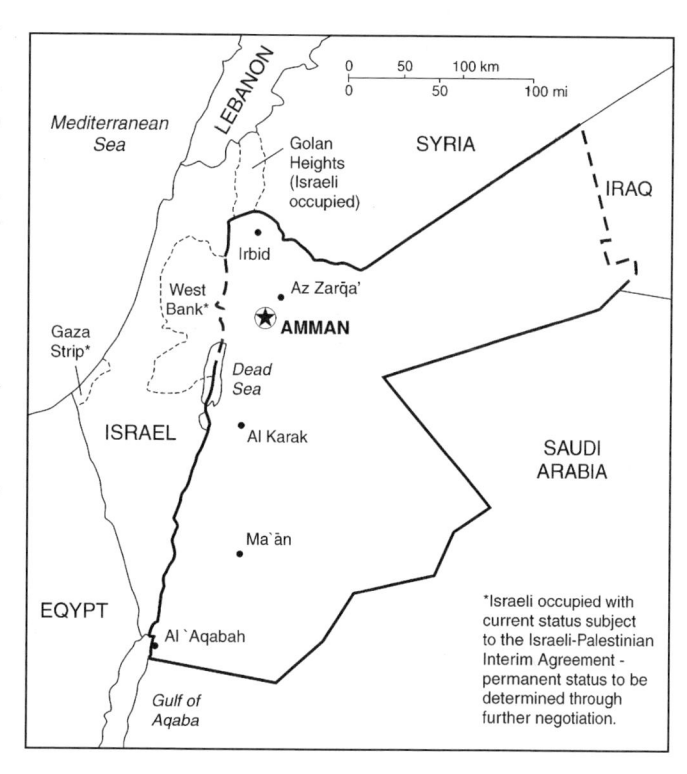

The population is predominantly Arab, with small non-Arab minority groups of Circassians, Chechens, Armenians, and Kurds, who originate from other parts of central Asia. The Arab population consists of those who are descended from the occupants of the former Palestine (West Bankers, from the west bank of the Jordan River) and Transjordanians (East Bankers, who are descended from the population of the Emirate of Transjordan [1921–1946], an area roughly the same as present-day Jordan). Many Palestinians are refugees from the wars in 1948 and 1967. Today there are approximately 1.4 million registered Palestinian refugees in Jordan. The distinction between the Transjordanian and the Palestinian populations permeates many aspects of Jordanian life, including the status of women. In the political arena, the ethnic heritage of a candidate is always known, and the cabinet has quotas for ministers who represent the Palestinian, Christian, and Circassian populations. Jordan also had a large influx of refugees during the Gulf War in 1990–1991. An estimated 275,000 Palestinians with Jordanian passports fled from Iraq and Kuwait to Jordan.

Most Jordanians are Sunni Muslim; various Christian denominations constitute a small minority. Islam is the state religion.

According to official information, the majority of the Jordanian population is descended from the nomadic Bedouins. The nomadic way of life was pastoralism, in which the Bedouins moved from place to place with their herds, leaving one area after it had been grazed to find another. Many of the remaining Bedouins have combined pastoralism with agriculture, and the Jordanian government has promoted their settling. The government acknowledges that to a certain extent the Bedouins are outside of the state's governing authority.

The Ottoman Empire controlled the area of present-day Jordan for about 300 years, until the time of the Arab Revolt against the Ottomans during World War I. In 1921, Britain divided the Palestine Mandate, establishing the Emirate of Transjordan. Jordan became completely independent from Britain in 1946 and was named the Hashemite Kingdom of Jordan. The late King Hussein ruled Jordan from 1953 until his death in 1999, when his oldest son, Prince Abdullah Bin al-Hussein, succeeded him. Upon his father's death, the new King Abdullah named his brother Prince Hamzah crown prince.

Jordan's government is a constitutional monarchy; Chapter Three of the constitution of 1952 gives the king both executive and legislative powers. The power vested in the king is quite significant; the king rules the country and is far from a figurehead monarch. There are many controls over individual liberties in Jordan. The constitution provides for the throne to pass through male heirs only. The legislative branch of government known as the National Assembly, frequently referred to as a parliament, has two bodies, a Senate, the members of which the king appoints, and an elected Chamber of Deputies. Jordan, however, has not enjoyed true democracy in its modern history, as there have not been regular elections in the past few decades, and there have been severe restrictions on political parties. Chapter Four, Article 34, gives the king the power to dissolve the Senate and the Chamber of Deputies.

Jordan conducted its most recent General Census of Population and Housing of Jordan in 1994; thus more recent population statistics are estimates. The Department of Statistics estimates that the population in 1999 was 4.9 million, of which 52.3 percent was male and 47.7 percent was female. Jordan has experienced rapid urban growth due to migration from rural areas, and in the early 1990s the population was 79 percent urban.

Less than 6 percent is nomadic. The life expectancy at birth for a male is 68.6 years, and 71 years for a female. Infant mortality (before age one) during the five years preceding the 1997 Jordan Population and Family Health Survey was 28.5 deaths per 1,000, while the mortality rate for children aged one to four was 5.9 per 1,000. The total fertility rate is 3.61 births per woman.[2]

OVERVIEW OF WOMEN'S ISSUES

The official web site of King Abdullah of Jordan presents an impressive, cutting-edge web design, in which photographs and weighty quotes swirl around the monitor. It pronounces that "women are half the society and partners of men."[3] As will be seen, the impression the kingdom presents to the world about the status of women is quite different from the day-to-day reality of their lives in Jordan.

The status of women in Jordan today is painted against the backdrop of a conservative, traditional Islamic society governed by a hereditary male monarch. Women's groups have made some progress in a few areas during the past few decades, but women lack many individual liberties. Jordan's geopolitical and economic situations have been important variables in determining how women there currently live, and this chapter will touch on these issues as it considers areas such as employment and politics and law. Jordan's Islamic culture permeates almost all aspects of a woman's life, and Islamic political and cultural forces are a determining factor in the advances woman have enjoyed and hope to enjoyed in the future.

One's impression of Jordan in the United States, is greatly influenced by media coverage, which focuses on the role of the past and present kings of Jordan in mediating peace in the region and on the glamorous royal family, educated abroad and supporting politically correct issues. The media give a superficial impression of a progressive country. Jordan is far from a democracy. Underneath this glossy surface is a country with a very traditional Islamic way of life, with an autocratic form of government, where one of the leading woman activists, who is the only woman ever elected to parliament, is frequently harassed by the government and has been imprisoned. Jordan is not as overtly restrictive for

Two women walking on a street in Amman, one in traditional dress, the other wearing modern clothing. Photo © TRIP/H. Rogers.

women as certain other Arab countries, where a woman cannot drive a car and must cover her face, but there are many forms of constraints on women's lives. While many programs exist in Jordan to improve the lives of women, there must be deeply rooted changes to the current social power structure, which is a hereditary monarchy that imposes restraints on civil liberties and where power is held by a relatively small circle of elite families, before there are substantial changes in the status of women.

The women of Jordan, like those anywhere, are not a homogeneous group, do not enjoy one single way of life, and do not share the same concerns about women's issues. There are differences between urban and rural women and among the poor, the professional, the educated elite, and the elite elite, who are from families with close ties to the royal family. There are the leftist leaning, the Islamists, and the conservative traditionalists. There are cultural and religious differences among the Transjordanian, Palestinian, and Christian women that influence their views on politics, family, and law. These categories are not mutually exclusive. For many women, day-to-day life is a struggle, but some are well-to-do and employ maids from other, poorer countries to do the housework and raise their children.

EDUCATION

Opportunities

Girls are accorded the same opportunities for education as boys, but traditional and economic barriers to equality remain. With the adoption of the amended constitution in 1952, nine years of education became compulsory. This meant that the government had to provide education, but attendance is not enforced.[4]

Enrollment rates are quite low for boys and girls. In 1999, the net primary enrollment rate (as a percentage of the relevant age group) was 63.3 percent for males and 64.6 percent for females. Net secondary enrollment rates were 57.6 percent for males and 61.6 percent for females. From the statistics from the government of Jordan on education levels of those aged fifteen and above, it appears that many children enrolled in primary and secondary schools do not complete their education, even if we assume that the 1994 census numbers in Table 7.1 had improved somewhat by 1999.[5] The most recent statistical information regarding the education of women is from the 1994 census. The Department of Statistics publishes a breakdown of the population aged fifteen and above by level of education and sex.

According to the United Nations Educational, Scientific, and Cultural Organization (UNESCO), primary education in Jordan begins at age six and lasts for ten years, while secondary education begins at age sixteen and lasts for two years. UNESCO does not use the term "preparatory" edu-

Table 7.1
Distribution of Population Living in Jordan 15 Years of Age or Older by Educational Level and Sex

Education Level	Total Population 15+	Male	Percentage of Total Males	Female	Percentage of Total Females
Illiterate	360,202	125,317	9.9	234,885	20.6
Read and Write	171,297	99,870	7.9	71,427	6.3
Elementary	375,498	210,186	16.7	165,312	14.5
Preparatory	646,250	353,515	28.1	292,735	25.7
Secondary	416,848	222,757	17.7	194,091	17.0
Intermediate Diploma	232,222	115,746	9.2	116,476	10.2
B.Sc.	144,369	97,604	7.7	46,765	4.1
Higher Diploma	6,218	4,719	0.4	1,499	0.1
M.A.	12,186	9,861	0.8	2,325	0.2
Ph.D.	5,960	5,316	0.4	644	0.1
Unspecified	28,448	14,645	1.2	13,803	1.2
Total	2,399,498	1,259,536	100.0	1,139,962	100.0

Source: See population statistics at: www.dos.gov.jo. Statistics published by the government of Jordan are rather sketchy. The Department of Statistics web site does not define these educational levels, nor give any explanatory notes.

cation (Table 7.1). Preparatory education is probably part of the ten years that UNESCO includes as primary education. The Ministry of Education runs approximately 4,500 schools; there are 500 private schools and a certain number run by the United Nations Relief and Works Agency for Palestine Refugees in the Near East (UNRWA). UNRWA provides education, health, relief, and social services to the 3.9 million registered Palestinian refugees in Jordan, Lebanon, the Syrian Arab Republic, the West Bank, and the Gaza Strip. The UNRWA schools use the same curriculum as the schools in the host country. In 1999–2000, girls represented 50 percent of the students in UNRWA schools.[6]

Women fare almost as well as men in obtaining a secondary education; 17.0 percent of women have a secondary education, compared to 17.7 percent of men, and 10.2 percent of women have an intermediate diploma, compared to 9.2 percent of men. Students who want to attend university in Jordan must stand for the *tawjihi* exam, which determines university admission.[7] While women are less likely than men to have a college-level education or advanced degree, the percentage of men with a college or advanced degree is quite low as well. In 2000, Jordan University in Amman had 23,000 undergraduates, of whom 70 percent were women.[8] It is a public university and thus affordable for many Jordanians.

Economic resources and birth order are factors in determining how much education a girl receives. The family, typically the father, will decide whether a child attends school. A girl will not attend school if her father does not value education, or if she must work to assist in providing income for the family. Thus economic class will likely determine the amount of schooling a girl receives. When a mother needs to work outside the home to help support the family, the daughters, especially the older ones, stop attending school in order to perform the work in the home.[9] Even when mothers do not have outside employment, it is still common for daughters to substitute for the mother in running the household. In addition to the substitution of daughters for the mother in running the household in poor areas, a family may not have the resources to educate all the children, in which case the sons are given more education. At around age fourteen, girls may stop school in order to help at home. When the minimum legal age of marriage was fifteen, many girls left school to marry. This may change with a recent change in the minimum age for marriage.[10] Although the older son is given an opportunity for a high-school education, if he does not do well and there are younger brothers, he is encouraged by the parents to drop out of school and start work around age fourteen. It has been noted that "there is therefore an 'exchange pattern' between siblings with the situation of each age-group determining that of their younger siblings. This variability in access to education and employment for girls likewise explains the variety of opinions expressed on whether 'in general' girls should or should not, do or do not, study and work. In fact, the household aspires to strike a balance between income-generating members at a given moment and those being prepared for and expected to generate income in the future."[11]

In spite of the difficulties girls from poor families may face in receiving an education, statistics gathered from the squatter areas in Amman show that the number of girls completing primary school was vastly different in the mid-1980s (82 percent) than among their grandmothers' generation in 1942 (1 percent). In the mid-1980s, 89.5 percent of males attending school completed a primary education, as compared to 34 percent in 1942. While it would be ideal to have more recent data, nevertheless, the trend these data show is significant and has implications for the situation women face today.

In rural areas, where women do much of the farming work, there are limited educational opportunities for girls, who have to help with the housework or farming. Many girls never attend school, and those who do leave after the first six or nine years. Another issue in rural education is the availability of schools. In the villages in the Jordan Valley, until the end of the 1970s, the schools went through only the first nine years. Students who wanted to continue their education had to travel to the city of Creak, a burden for most.[12]

Table 7.2 captures general attitudes toward the education of a group of women in Amman. When asked for reasons for an education, their responses were divided among those who felt that it was a good idea for a

Table 7.2
Survey among Women of Amman Regarding Reasons for Education

	Yes	No	All
Is it a good idea for mothers to work?	66.7	33.3	100.0
What are the main reasons for women's education?			
To be a good mother	31.7	23.3	55.0
To have a good job	3.3	0.0	3.3
To marry well	0.0	0.0	0.0
To have a fulfilling life	31.7	10.0	41.7
Other	0.0	0.0	0.0

Source: I. Papps, "Attitudes to Female Employment in Four Middle Eastern Countries," in *Women in the Middle East: Perceptions, Realities and Struggles for Liberation*, ed. H. Afshar (New York: St. Martin's Press, 1993), 96–116.

mother to work and those who did not.[13] Traditional Islamic values influence these women strongly: those who value education do so because it can make a woman a better mother.

Literacy

The illiteracy rate is much higher among women (20.6 percent) than among men (9.9 percent) (Table 7.1). Illiteracy rates have declined somewhat since 1994: in 2000, the illiteracy rate was 4.9 percent among men aged fifteen and above and was 16.1 percent for women. A subset of this group, youth aged fifteen to twenty-four, had much lower illiteracy rates in 2000, and the rate was not higher among women: 0.7 percent for men and 0.7 percent for women.[14]

The Ministry of Education has embarked on a project with UNESCO to improve education, with a completion date of 2015. Its main objective is to reduce the illiteracy rate to 6 percent of the population. Schools in remote and rural areas are greatly disadvantaged compared to those in Amman; they have insufficient teachers and poor physical conditions. To address this issue, the ministry is assigning 3,500 new teachers to work in undeserved areas. The teachers assigned to remote and rural areas will receive a monthly bonus.[15]

EMPLOYMENT AND ECONOMICS

Jordan is considered a middle-income Arab state, not one of the wealthy, oil-producing countries in the region.[16] It has been an exporter of workers to the oil-producing Gulf States and is greatly affected by the conditions in the oil industry in terms of unemployment rates and remittances from those working abroad. Like other countries in the region, Jordan benefited from the oil boom in the 1970s and then suffered from the oil recession in the late 1980s.

Jordan also has a high level of external debt; it owes $7 billion to other governments. It spends more on debt service than on education, and twice as much as on health care.[17] The high level of debt has serious implications for the government's ability to pay for programs that will benefit women. The embargo on trade with Iraq following the Gulf War in 1991 meant that Jordan could not continue to trade with one of its largest trading partners if it wanted to support the United States in this embargo, thus creating another blow to its economy.

Beginning in the late 1980s, Jordan has had to work with the International Monetary Fund (IMF) to reschedule its high levels of debt. The IMF typically requires strict economic reforms in conjunction with debt rescheduling, which are often a source of economic pain and social discontent in any rescheduling country. The government has been working closely with the World Bank and the IMF on various economic reforms. Economic growth was good in the early 1990s, suffered in the late 1990s, but has begun to improve in the past couple of years. Jordan's economic problems are linked to the peace process, declining oil prices, which reduced demand for Jordanian exports in the region, and the overall economic slowdown in Asia.[18] In April 1989, the government's decision to end subsidies on important items such as bread, certain beverages, and fuel led to rioting in the south among those who had traditionally been loyal to the regime. These economic measures were part of the IMF austerity requirements for rescheduling. Fear on the part of the regime led to a period of liberalization that benefited women.

Decades of unrest in the region are another significant factor in the country's economic condition. The influx of approximately 275,000 refugees during the Gulf War in 1991 worsened the situation, added to the high unemployment, and strained the country's social services, including the water supply and the health-care system. The standard of living fell, and almost one million Jordanians were below the poverty line.[19] Continuing economic problems also led to King Hussein's decision to enter into a peace agreement with Israel.[20]

The human development index looks at data other than purely economic indicators to add a more qualitative nature to the analysis of development. The United Nations Development Program (UNDP) uses a version of this index, which includes measures of life expectancy, literacy, schooling, per capita gross domestic product (GDP), lifelong knowledge acquisition, women's access to power, and human freedom. The UNDP recently released its first report focusing on the Arab region, titled *Arab Human Development Report 2002*.[21]

The *Jordan Human Development Report 2000* ranks Jordan 94th of 174 developing countries in human development.[22] Among other Arab states with a medium ranking, it has one of the lowest female economic activity rates. Jordanian women hold only 3.4 percent of senior government positions, less than in Algeria, Syria, and Tunisia. One startling statistic in the report is that 21 percent of households live in poverty. Urban areas have a higher standard of living than rural areas.[23] Urban areas have lower fertility rates, a lower percentage of low-income households, better access to health care, and the highest adult literacy rates.

Job/Career Opportunities

The number of variables affecting career opportunities for women leads to a highly complex situation that cannot be generalized. Economic opportunities for women in Jordan differ among various economic classes, between urban and rural areas, and among generations. The structure of Jordanian families adds another layer of complexity to opportunities for women.

The economic cycles of the oil industry have affected career opportunities for women in Jordan. Another factor affecting women is Jordan's position as an exporter of labor, which increased significantly in the early 1970s with the oil boom.[24] While this affected employment opportunities for women, including rapid occupational mobility, Jordan experienced replacement migration from Egypt and Asia. Men from these countries took the jobs left by Jordanian men, and jobs as domestic maids and child-care providers for the more affluent sectors of society are now held by women from other Asian countries. As oil prices declined in the late 1980s, leading to unemployment in the oil-producing states and the return of Jordanian men to their homes, rising unemployment in Jordan led some policy makers to advocate that women withdraw from the workforce to reduce unemployment.

Jordanian society is rife with favoritism (*wasta*), which negatively affects women's chances in the job market. *Wasta* has become an institutionalized outgrowth of the country's social structure that emphasizes the significance of kinship and family relationships. It is a frequent subject of newspaper articles and speeches by government officials.[25] In an employment arena that is male dominated, and where men show favor in granting positions, women have an even harder time breaking into the workforce. When the press criticizes the government for corruption, the government harasses the media rather than improve the situation.[26]

Economists recognize that measures of economic activity, such as the gross national product (GNP), do not capture the labor of women who are part of the informal labor system. A woman who works at home does not receive wages that are reported, and her economic output, whether it is cooking, cleaning, child care, or volunteer work, does not fall into any category of national accounts. Much of women's nondomestic labor is not captured in government statistics, which track only those employed in certain fields in the formal labor force. Many women in Jordan engage in

Table 7.3
Jordan Labor Statistics

Year	1991	1993	1994	1995	1996	1997	1998	1999	2000	2001 Preliminary
% of Population Unemployed	17.3	19.2	15.5	15.0	13.0	14.4	12.7	13.4	13.7	14.7

Source: The NIS does not offer an explanation for providing figures only for 1991, 1993–2000. Statistics from the IMF on unemployment for 1998, 1999, and 2001 are included.

cottage-type industries or microbusinesses, which most likely are not included in statistics from the Jordan Department of Statistics. In 1999, the World Bank's labor-force activity rate showed that 43.8 percent of men in Jordan were active, compared to 14.5 percent of women.[27] The unemployment rate in Jordan has been high since the early 1990s (Table 7.3). The Jordan National Information System (NIS) does not provide these data based upon sex; however, the World Bank GenderStats database indicates that in 2000, female unemployment was 20.7 percent of the female labor force, an improvement over 28.5 percent in 1995. The numbers give one a sense of the difficulty women face in finding career opportunities. In the early 1990s, Jordan suffered the effects of declining employment in the oil industry, the upheavals from the Gulf War, and another influx of refugees. We can see the effect of these events on the high unemployment numbers, which have declined only slightly.

These government statistics are quite sketchy and lacking in definitions. Thus it is more helpful to consider numbers from researchers in the field, though these estimates tend to vary widely.[28] Table 7.4 shows that in urban areas, most working women are in the service sector. One study done in the late 1980s estimated that 65 percent of working women were employed by the government, 50 percent as teachers and 15 percent in banks. Those women who were employed in the manufacturing sector tended to be young, single, and poorly educated. As the public sector in Jordan has grown, educated women in urban areas may find it easier than men to find jobs, as the demand for teachers, clerical workers, and typists has increased. In conjunction with this trend, there has been a large increase in two-year community colleges in Jordan.

Information from fieldwork in the mid-1980s in two poor squatter areas of Amman called the Wadi and the Jabal gives a better sense of employment opportunities among the urban poor than do government statistics. The squatter areas and refugee areas make up about 25 percent of the households in Amman, and the inhabitants do not differ from the overall urban poor in terms of occupation or income.[29]

The squatter houses are made of concrete and corrugated metal, and their inhabitants are mainly Palestinian refugees from the wars in 1948 and

Table 7.4
Distribution of Jordanian Females Aged 15 and Above by Occupation and Urban/Rural Status, 1998

Occupation	Urban	Rural	Total
Legislators, senior officials, and managers	0.1	0.0	0.1
Professionals	3.1	1.8	2.8
Technicians and associate professionals	4.1	3.2	3.8
Clerks	1.9	0.8	1.6
Service workers, shop and market sales workers	1.2	0.5	1.0
Skilled agricultural and fishery workers	0.2	1.1	0.4
Craft and related trades workers	0.9	0.5	0.8
Plant and machine operators and assemblers	0.2	0.1	0.2
Elementary occupations	0.9	1.1	0.9
Total	100.0	100.0	100.0
Total (actual numbers)	17,140.0	6,110.0	23,250.0

Source: Department of Statistics Jordan, DOS-NIS: Population and Housing. Accessed September 2, 2002 from http://www.dos.gov.jo.

1967. These squatter areas grew on vacant land next to refugee camps established by UNRWA in 1948. In the camps, each family was given a plot of land on which shacks were built. In the squatter areas, the families had no legal claim to the land they inhabited; they wanted to be close to their relatives in the camps and to UNRWA facilities for refugees. There would have been serious political consequences if the landowners or the government had tried to evict the squatters, either by force or legally through the court system. The city of Amman has grown around these areas over the decades.[30]

The women in these communities form "special-purpose units" that engage in a single task, like a cottage industry. Women divide their labor in the production of traditional Palestinian dresses, based upon their area of expertise. One woman may specialize in cutting out the dress, another in sewing it together, and another in the embroidery. It is not clear whether compensation is involved, although there are income-generating activities among the social units in this area. Other activities the women engage in to earn money are peddling, running microgroceries from their homes, and food preparation for selling.

The work of women and their economic strategies are crucial to the survival of the poor households in Amman, emphasizing that the household, not the individual, is the main economic unit, due to the economic class of this population. Groups of women related by kin share in domestic work in the areas of child care, daily chores, shopping, and activities that generate income. While not all of these activities generate income, they represent an exchange of value and improve the ability of these poor women to accomplish their daily activities. Perhaps this arrangement can be considered a type of economic barter.

Also, as refugees, sometimes twice displaced, these families have experienced disrupted labor patterns. Most originated in rural Palestine and have had to adapt to urban occupations. A 1985 survey revealed that the main occupations of women who were in the formal labor force were, in descending order, janitors and maids, skilled clerical workers and teachers, seamstresses, nurses and midwives, sellers and peddlers, and unskilled clerical workers. The survey also shows the role of marital status in employment. The highest percentages of working women were the divorced, separated, and widowed. These women had low-paying jobs, such as janitors, seamstresses, and peddlers. Of those women surveyed, only 41.4 percent had regular monthly wages with full benefits, an indication of the precarious economic situation of these women, particularly considering their marital status.[31]

The labor force of poor urban women changes over a woman's lifetime. The older generation of women who were the original refugees has low levels of education and works in unskilled jobs as domestic servants or janitors. Younger generations of women are more highly educated and are in more highly skilled professions.

The traditional family structure adds yet another layer of complexity to the area of employment among urban society. Unmarried, educated women in the workforce are not necessarily improving their own future economic security: "Their increased earning capacity may subject them to exploitation rather than emancipation. To make sense out of the emerging patterns, one has to abandon the view of women as individuals making career decisions and look at the household as the main economic and decision-making unit."[32] A single woman does not typically live on her own in Jordan, but lives with her parents or perhaps with a married brother's family. There are several cases of women teachers from Jordan working in Saudi Arabia or the Gulf States for several years. They were accompanied by their fathers, who were unemployed, acting as guardian. When these women returned to Jordan, the money they had earned would be invested in a house or business in the father's name. These women would sometimes remain unmarried, work for their families, and get no property or financial security.

The Jordan Valley Authority carried out an irrigation project in conjunction with a statutory redistribution of land in 1988. The changes in landownership led to changes in agricultural labor. A minimum landholding size was specified, and the smallest landowners, who represented more than half the landowners, lost their lands. These smallest holdings were family farms, where women did most of the farming. The creation of larger farms through consolidation led to a demand for wage laborers. After the land redistribution, there were three types of land use, each necessitating a different form of women's labor. Also, the introduction of modern irrigation techniques made agricultural work much easier for men and women, thus allowing men to find work off the farm.

The family farm was the prevailing type of land use, and the size of the farm was a factor in how much women participated in agricultural labor. Typically, if the men found nonagricultural work, the women and children carried on most of the farm work, except for the marketing of production. If the men did not work off the farm, then the women contributed mainly during times of high labor demand. In a large family, an educated son would join the army or civil service to supplement family income. Only a small number of women in the villages worked outside agriculture; eight women were in the civil service and two were teachers. The village also had small groceries that were a common family enterprise, where the women and children often did the work.[33]

The next type of farm labor is sharecropping, where families without land work on larger farms in return for a share of the production. The division of labor and the participation of women on a sharecropping farm were similar to that of a family farm. A woman would enter into a sharecropping arrangement with a farm owner only if he were a relative.[34]

The third type of agricultural labor is wage labor, which is found on larger landholdings. Permanent monthly wage labor is performed by Egyptian men, who are willing to work for low wages. Local men engage in permanent daily wage labor, and the women do only seasonal labor. Seasonal labor is restricted to widows and unmarried women; married women only engage in family labor. Single women are attracted to wage labor because they can keep some of their earnings for themselves. On a family farm, a single woman would not be paid for her work, although she would be expected to work on the family farm if the men worked outside the farm.

There is another division of agricultural labor based on gender. The men generally handle the irrigation, use of chemical pesticides and fertilizers, and the marketing of production. The use of chemicals requires knowledge of the metric system, and this is "believed to be beyond the understanding of women accustomed to traditional measures."[35] Women are reluctant to do the marketing due to their low levels of literacy, as marketing requires dealing with different marketing agents and bills. If a woman is the head of a farming household, she will rely on a relative or neighbor to handle her marketing. Even though men still handle certain aspects of agricultural production, farmers feel that the introduction of modern irrigation has led to the "feminization of agriculture," and that men should find employment in other areas.

Another significant aspect of women in the workforce is the attitude toward female employment among both women and employers, that is, men, in Jordan.[36] In 1989, the Jordanian Royal Scientific Society surveyed five women from twelve segments of society in Amman, such as a leading employer, a director of a prominent women's nongovernmental organization (NGO), teachers, teenagers and their mothers and grandmothers, and women employed in various sectors of the economy. To determine the attitudes of employers, the society surveyed employers from at least five firms in fifteen different businesses in both the services sector, such as financial services, the hospitality industry, and sales establishments, and the manufacturing sector.

The women interviewed had an average of more than eleven years of schooling, so the results do not represent the attitudes of the population as a whole, but rather of the more educated segments. The women interviewed also had lower fertility rates than the average population. Thirty-five percent of the women interviewed thought that children approved of working mothers, and 66.7 percent approved of working mothers themselves. It is interesting that 93.3 percent thought that husbands and fathers approved of working mothers. The very high number of women who felt that their husbands and fathers approve of working mothers may come as a surprise, but may be explained by the high education levels of these women.

In the same survey, 28.3 percent listed the attitudes of others as a constraint on women working. Other constraints included conditions of job (21.7 percent), family circumstances (73.3 percent), job availability (20.0 percent), and transport difficulties (11.7 percent). Even though a majority of the women in the survey had a positive attitude toward working mothers, when asked for the three most suitable jobs for a woman, with no answers supplied, the women responded teaching, medicine, and secretarial work. This may simply reflect the reality of the current job market for women in Jordan.

In examining the characteristics of these women, sorted by their attitude toward working mothers, those with a positive attitude toward employment for unmarried women and married women before they have children were on average younger, had fewer children, had younger children, and were more likely to have a university education than those with a negative attitude. Probably most surprising is that the women with a negative attitude were not more religious than those with a positive attitude. Thus religious beliefs did not appear to play a major role in shaping these attitudes, at least with this small sample of women.[37]

The firms that were selected for the survey about attitudes toward women working tended to have a higher proportion of female workers than the national labor force. Thus there is a certain bias in these answers as well. However, the percentage of firms willing to hire women was not necessarily correlated with whether or not the firm already employed women, as is shown in Table 7.5.

The reasons firms gave for not increasing female employment were probably not unique to Jordan; only 18.8 percent of the firms cited religious reasons. Employers who did not currently employ women were more than twice as likely to cite insufficient education and training (13.8 percent) as

Table 7.5
Percentage of Firms by Occupation Willing to Hire Women to Fill Vacancies

Occupation	% Firms employing women	% Firms not employing women
Professional managerial	47.5	28.6
Professional technical	72.5	100.0
Technician	81.3	100.0
Skilled clerical	27.5	14.3
Skilled manual	32.5	14.3
Unskilled clerical	3.8	100.0
Unskilled manual	21.3	14.3

Source: Department of Statistics Jordan, DOS-NIS: Population and Housing. Accessed September 2, 2002 from www.dos.gov.jo.

those employers who were currently employing women. They also cited a woman's low work motivation because of home responsibilities (47.5 percent) as another reason against hiring women. Firms also gave advantages for employing women, such as that women were less expensive to employ than men (15 percent) and were more efficient (13.8 percent); that the company had women in management (5 percent); that work could be done in a single-sex environment (11.3 percent); and that their clientele were women (11.3 percent).[38]

To sum up what is known about employment and economic issues for women in Jordan today, it is safe to state that studies on the issue of women in the labor force in Jordan are generally lacking and overly simplistic.[39] They do not show geographical and class differences and do not include changes in occupational history over the lives of the women surveyed. Also, they do not provide a picture of how work has changed women's status and roles in their communities and in society as a whole. Research on women that is related to national economic development and planning contains its own biases and attempts to reflect national goals that want to integrate "women in development without causing fundamental changes in the social structure on the level of the family or the legal system as a whole." Another woman researcher contributes this observation: "There is most resistance in the Arab world to change anything to do with the family."[40]

Pay

Chapter Two, Article 23, of the constitution states: "The State shall protect labor and enact legislation therefore based upon the following principles: a) Every worker shall receive wages commensurate with the quantity and quality of his work.... d) Special conditions shall be made for the employment of women and juveniles." Apparently these special conditions are part of the civil laws, as the constitution does not elaborate further. This wording suggests that women are like children in needing special protection.

According to the U.S. government's *Country Reports on Human Rights Practices—2000—Jordan*, civil law says that women shall receive equal pay for equal work, but this law is often not followed in practice.[41] There were reports during 2001 from various private-sector employers that women were being paid less than the legal minimum wage, and that union leaders and the Ministry of Labor were not enforcing the law.

Working Conditions

Sexual Harassment

The English-language literature to date on working conditions for women in Jordan does not deal with the issue of sexual harassment. Currently the main focus of the literature is to describe the extent to which women have entered the workforce and hindrances to employment of women, and to discuss how employment for women can be increased in the future. It is likely that sexual harassment is a secondary issue at this time. It may become a topic of discussion and research in the future when greater numbers of women enter the workforce.

Support for Mothers/Caretakers

In late 1993, children became eligible to obtain health insurance through their working mothers and not just through their fathers.[42]

Maternal Leave

In 1995, the cabinet amended the Civil Service Law to give women ninety days of maternity leave instead of sixty. New laws were passed in 1996 giving working mothers improved benefits. Establishments with ten or more workers must give a woman an unpaid year of leave to raise a child, and the woman has a right to return to her job after a year as long as she has not worked for pay elsewhere during that time. A woman cannot be terminated from her job beginning with the sixth month of pregnancy or during maternity leave. During a child's first year, the mother has one hour each day to nurse.

Daycare

Child care, other than from a family member, is not available for most women in the formal labor force in Jordan. If an employer has at least twenty married female employees, and as a group they have at least ten children under the age of four, the employer must provide a nursery.⁴³ Ninety percent of the women surveyed thought that more women would work if child care were available. Most women (95 percent) preferred a family member as a child daycare provider, but many also endorsed a nursery in the workplace (78.3 percent). Preference for private nurseries was next (73.3 percent), followed closely by government nurseries (68.3 percent). Only 20 percent of interviewed women thought that leaving a child with a servant was acceptable.⁴⁴

Inheritance and Property Rights

The laws regarding inheritance and property rights are not entirely clear and are difficult to sort out without access to the laws of Jordan in English or an interpretation by a legal scholar. The main issues are that there remain cultural and social impediments to women's rights, and there have been legal attempts to reduce the rights women do have.

Historically, ownership of land was limited to men. In the 1930s, the land was privatized, and women were given the right to inherit land. Nevertheless, traditional practices that prohibited women from owning land prevailed until the late 1980s, fifty years after the change in the law. There were few women landowners, and their holdings were typically small. There is also a cultural reluctance on the part of women to inherit land, because after a woman dies, her husband or children inherit, but they belong to another kin group. Therefore, the land then "goes to a stranger." Thus in order not to anger her brothers, a woman would give them her land inheritance. Widows, however, could inherit land without any social stigma because a widow has lost the man who is responsible for her, and when a widow dies, her sons inherit the land, thus keeping it within the family. Another cultural impediment to landownership by women is the tradition that a woman is not responsible for her own living; if she is married, it is her husband's responsibility, and if she is single, it is her father's or brother's.

In 1990, a law was passed changing the formula for inheritance of state land. Women and men previously had equal inheritance rights. According to the U.S. government's *Country Reports on Human Rights Practice—2000—Jordan*, under traditional Islamic law (shari'a), a female heir receives half the amount of a male heir's inheritance. If a daughter is the sole heir of her parent's estate, she receives half, and the remainder goes to designated male relatives. This law does not affect a large percentage of people in Jordan, perhaps because it refers only to state land, which is owned by the government, and most land does not fall into this category, or because most of the population of Jordan is urban and thus not landowners.⁴⁵ The non-Muslim widow of a Muslim spouse has no inheritance rights, but a male Muslim heir has the duty to provide for all family members who need assistance. It is not clear from the report whether this is actually codified into law or remains a cultural tradition.

Social/Government Programs

Social and government programs to benefit women are quite numerous. The National Development Plan of 1975–1980 included a policy of integrating women into the development process and increasing their participation in the labor force. It appears that the motivation behind this policy was not simply to benefit women, but to reduce Jordan's dependence on non-Jordanian labor.[46]

The Urban Development Department (UDD), established in 1980, was the first agency in Jordan to provide low-income housing. Its first projects, to upgrade conditions in the squatter areas of Amman in the early 1980s, were funded by the World Bank. The UDD improved housing conditions in the areas and built community centers, health clinics, schools, shops, and workshops. The UDD is now part of the Ministry of Municipal and Rural Affairs, and its role has grown to encompass social work and community development. It has organized vocational training programs and lectures for women and has set up daycare centers.[47]

The Noor Al Hussein Foundation, the patron of which is Queen Noor, the American-born wife of the late King Hussein, supports many projects in the area of economic development for women. A complete listing may be found on the foundation's web site.[48] The foundation's Jordan Design and Trade Center features traditional handcrafted products and markets them throughout Jordan and abroad. The Aqaba Women's Center trains unemployed women, both secondary-school graduates and poor women, to produce marketable tourist items, home furnishings, and handicrafts. The foundation established an industrial sewing workshop in Mafraq where it trains and employs low-income rural women. It has a medicinal herbs project that helps women grow and market herbs from their kitchen gardens. The foundation also provides microfinance to microentrepreneurs.

The U.S. Agency for International Development (USAID) has many programs in Jordan due to its strategic importance to U.S. interests in the area, especially in the Middle East peace process. In fiscal year 2000, the amount of aid was $200 million, which included $50 million for the Wye River Peace Accord.[49] Its projects have three main focuses: development of water resources, economic opportunity, aimed particularly at sustainable businesses for women, and health and population.

Sustainable Development

Many international NGOs are active in Jordan and work closely with local NGOs. Many of the international aid programs benefit women by helping the population as a whole, but certain programs are aimed specifically at women.

The United Nations Development Fund for Women (UNIFEM) currently has two projects in Jordan that fall within its economic empowerment initiatives. Begun in 2001, a two-year program, aimed at women entrepreneurs, will give technical support to local NGOs, development programs, and financial institutions that help micro and small enterprises. A second two-year program, begun in 2002, benefits women in the tourism industry. Its objective is to increase the participation of women in this sector, to raise awareness of employment opportunities in tourism, and to open up educational opportunities related to tourism.

Welfare and Welfare Reform

Until 2001, the legal system discriminated against women in the area of pension and social security benefits. According to the U.S. government's *Country Reports on Human Rights Practices—2000—Jordan*, the Jordanian social insurance system continues the pension payments of deceased male civil servants to their heirs, but discontinues payments of deceased female civil servants. The Social Security Law was amended in 2001 and now allows women to pass on benefits to their children. The government also amended the Income Tax Law in 2001 to give female heads of households the same fiscal exemptions as male heads.

In 1995, when Islamists had a greater voice in politics, there was a proposal to allow a man tax exemptions for multiple wives under the Income Tax Law; the law had allowed an exemption for only one. The Islamists argued that this would be a protection of women's and children's rights, and that polygamy is an existing Jordanian tradition. Toujan Faisal, in leading the opposition, argued that polygamy should not be encouraged, and that if a man wanted a second wife, he should be able to afford one. The proposal was defeated.[50]

In spite of the 2001 amendments, there may still be problems for woman in the social security system. The Jordanian social insurance system appears to offer old-age, disability, and death benefits only to those men who have been employed, assuming apparently that a woman who is or has not been employed will be cared for by her husband or another male relative. Also, employees in certain categories are explicitly not covered: agricultural workers, domestic servants, the self-employed, and family labor.[51]

FAMILY AND SEXUALITY

Kinship is the basis of most social interaction in Jordan, permeating all aspects of life. Kinship starts with the family, which receives more emphasis in Jordanian culture than the individual. The Jordan National Charter, chapter five, paragraph three, states: "The family is the principal block of society. It is the natural environment for the rearing, education and personality growth of the individual."

Kinship ties the family to larger groups of relatives. Most inhabitants of Jordan are descended from the nomadic Bedouin tribes, whose tribal societal structure is still apparent. A collection of Bedouin families constitutes a clan, the center of social life, and a number of clans make up a tribe. The leader of the tribe is a sheikh, which is a hereditary position.

Gender Roles

The Jordan National Charter, chapter five, paragraph six, states: "Women are men's partners and equals in contributing to the growth and development of Jordanian society. This requires an affirmation of women's constitutional and legal right to equality, guidance, training and employment as a means of enabling them to play their proper role in the growth and development of society." At this time, this statement seems more like a future goal than a reflection of current conditions for women in the family.

There are three basic types of households in squatter areas of Amman.[52] These types of typical households may also be found in other economic strata of society, in both urban and rural areas. The simple family household (SFH) is a married couple or a single parent, with or without children. An extended family household (EFH) includes a married couple, children, and parent(s) or sibling(s) of the father, and sometimes of the mother. A multiple family household (MFH) is the combination of SFHs or EFHs, usually when a son marries and he and his family live with his parents.

In multiple household dwellings (MHDs), several families, either SFH or EFH, live together in one house. While there are many reasons for the formation of EFH and MHD, one reason is cultural norms that do not permit single people to live alone, especially women, the young, and the very old. Regardless of the financial situation of an unmarried woman, whether single, widowed, or separated, she typically lives with next of kin. The reasons behind MFH are typically economic: a son and his family do not have the resources yet to establish their own household. The structure of a household changes over time with the cycle of births, marriages, and deaths.

Patriarchy in Jordan extends beyond the division of households.[53] The roles of men and women are quite sharply delineated in Jordanian families. The man is the head of the household, and married sons also have a certain authority. The men are responsible for things outside the home, such as earning an income, place of residence, and the relationship with other heads of households within the kinship group. The women decide how the income is spent, living conditions, and daily interaction with kinfolk. In low-income urban households, the men turn their wages over to their wives or mothers and keep a small amount for "cigarette money." The woman must figure out how to make the money last until the next payday. In upgraded areas where families might borrow money to improve their homes, the women handle payment of loan installments. The women are by no means confined to the home, and their own economic activity is often necessary for low-income families to survive. The women form "mutual aid units," usually based on kinship, with other households, where the women help one another with housework, shopping, child care, and financial aid in emergencies.[54]

A case study reveals the delicate balance of the relationship between women in the same household. A woman in Amman named Muna is single and works to support two younger brothers. They live with the family of another brother who is married. Muna and her brothers form one household within this MFH. Her sister-in-law is not in the formal labor force, one source of differences between her and Muna. The study illustrates the complex relationships and roles within an MFH, and the resulting tensions. For example, each household cooks for itself, but on Fridays, Muna's day off, she cooks for both. Her sister-in-law does most of the household work, including washing; thus cooking for both households on Fridays is one way Muna repays her. Muna sews her own clothes and sews for a younger married sister, her sister's sister-in-law, and her cousin's daughter-in-law, but not for her brother's family. This shows how mutual aid units are based on kinship, but are formed selectively. Certain relatives may be excluded due to family tensions. In Muna's words, "Education is important even if a woman is married, for she may be divorced or widowed and if she cannot work, then she will live a life of humiliation at the mercy of her sister-in-law."[55]

The existence of EFHs and MFHs means that many women have to deal with other women in the household day to day, often in a subordinate role. The oldest woman in a household has authority within the women's domain. A woman's status and authority may also result from factors other than age: her own financial resources, the number of children she has, and the quality of her relationship with her husband. A woman who has a source of income thus improves her status in the household and may also enable her family to afford to live apart from her in-laws. A working woman will typically need to rely on relatives for child care. Society expects working women to have as many children as nonworking women.

Traditionally, women have been responsible for child rearing, but there are government efforts to get fathers more involved. The Better Parenting Project, a joint effort of various ministries, NGOs, UNRWA, and UNICEF, begun in 1994, aims to help parents of young children, particularly those with low incomes and little education. The project has reached more than 16,000 participants in more than 100 community centers to date. The program stresses the role of fathers in raising children. Many women participants have recommended that their husbands and sons take part in the sessions.[56]

Marriage

The 1997 Jordan Population and Family Health Survey (JPFHS) found that the median age of first marriage for women aged twenty-five to forty-nine was 21.5 years. For women with no formal schooling, the median age was 18.9, compared to 24.7 for those with a higher education. Women aged twenty-five to twenty-nine at the time of the survey married at a median age of 23.1; women aged forty-four to forty-nine at the time of the survey married at a median age of 19.4.[57]

Society is uncomfortable with the idea of an unmarried, young career woman. Young people do not date, as it is unacceptable for a young woman to be alone with a man. Any questionable behavior brings shame on the family and may result in honor killings. A Jordanian woman of Palestinian descent, university educated in the United States and unmarried at thirty, is a subject of confusion in her family, and her extended family frequently asks when she will marry. "In Jordan, everyone watches you and knows what you are doing," she says.[58]

An educated, unmarried woman who works at Jordan University explains that to propose marriage, a man must go to court to obtain a contract for marriage. After several visits at the home of the woman's parents, he brings a contract to propose marriage. She feels that Jordanian values regarding the protection of sexuality and its link to family honor are good and that Jordan respects its women. Before marrying someone, there is insurance that the man will not have been seeing other women.[59]

The 1997 JPFHS found that 7 percent of married women in Jordan were in polygynous marriages. The frequency of polygyny differed by education, age, and location. The occurrence of polygyny was 2 percent for those aged fifteen to nineteen, but 9–10 percent for women aged forty or above. Of women with no education, 19 percent were in polygynous marriages, compared to 2 percent of women with a higher education. Among rural women, the frequency of polygyny was 10 percent, versus 6 percent in urban areas. In an account of her life, Jawazi al-Malakim, a Bedouin woman who settled near Amman in the late 1960s, says, "The practice of polygamy is needed for the nomadic life, they [she and her husband] both feel, but is demoralizing to the woman in the city."[60] It is likely that polygyny made it easier to survive the hardships of the Bedouin way of life, as there would be more women to carry on the tasks of the household.

Women's groups have fought to have the laws regarding polygamy changed since such groups became active. In the 1950s, the Arab Women's Federation unsuccessfully demanded that polygamy and arbitrary divorce be made illegal.[61] In 1995, the Jordanian Women's Union began a campaign to lobby legislators to change or repeal discriminatory laws, including the Civil Personal Status Law, to restrict polygamy and arbitrary divorce.[62]

Reproduction

There have been several periodic surveys on demography and health in Jordan.[63] USAID has been funding the JPFHS as part of its worldwide Demographic and Health Surveys program.

The 1997 survey included 5,448 ever-married women aged fifteen to forty-nine: 96 percent were married, 97 percent practiced Islam, 84 percent lived in urban areas, and 53 percent had a secondary education. It found that women's fertility rates had dropped from 7.4 births per woman in 1976 to 4.4 births in 1997, but that the decrease varied from region to region and with the level of education. The study also found that the decline in fertility had accelerated over time. The greatest decline in fertility was among the group of women aged fifteen to nineteen, which had 71 births per 1,000 women in 1976, compared to 43 in 1997. The median age of first birth differed among age groups: for women aged twenty-five to twenty-nine the median age was 24.7, compared to 21.1 for women aged forty-five to forty-nine. Thus women are waiting longer to have children than in the past. For the group as a whole, the median age of first birth was 23.2 years.

Fertility was significantly higher among rural women than among urban women, with a rate of 5.0 births compared to 4.2. Women who had an education beyond secondary school had 3.7 children in their lifetime, compared to 4.5 for other women. The intervals between births were longer in 1997 than in 1996, although this also differed among women; younger and low-parity women had shorter intervals than older and high-parity women. Better-educated women also had shorter intervals, probably due to later marriages and an attempt to "catch up" in childbearing.

The study noted that women had a preferred family size of 2.9 children per woman, compared to the actual rate of 4.4. Rural women and those with less education had the highest levels of unwanted fertility. Fifty-one percent of the currently married women in the study did not want any more children or had been sterilized.[64]

Sex Education

The government promotes family planning through the Ministry of Social Development, which recently sponsored a five-day workshop on premarital services, which include counseling before and after marriage, promotion of thalassemia testing, and the use of contraceptives for family planning. The severe shortage of water in the region is one reason for the government's concern over family planning to control population. Johns Hopkins University helped to sponsor the workshop as part of its program called "Arab Women Speak Out," which it began in 1999. The forty women participants were representatives from the Jordanian Hashemite Fund for Human Development and the Jordan Association for Family Planning and Production and social workers from the ministry.

International conferences on population have recommended that husbands and wives share in the responsibility of birth control. As a result, the Jordan Population Commission has begun to consider targeting men for family-planning services. The University of Jordan funded research to measure men's knowledge of and attitudes toward family planning. It found that men with at least a secondary education and with a higher income were more positive toward birth spacing and contraceptive use. Culturally sensitive family-planning services designed specifically for men in Jordan would increase their involvement in the use of contraceptives.[65]

Contraception and Abortion

According to the 1997 JPFHS, all currently married women knew of at least one contraceptive method, and 53 percent used one. The preferred methods of modern contraception in Jordan are the intrauterine device (IUD), the pill, or tubal ligation, that is, sterilization. Of the 53 percent of women who used contraceptives, 23 percent used an IUD, 7 percent took the birth-control pill, 4 percent had been sterilized, and 7 percent relies on withdrawal.

Seventy-nine percent of the women surveyed had practiced contraception. Women in urban areas and with higher levels of education were more likely to use contraception. The more children a woman had, the higher the rate of contraception use: 48 percent of women with four or more children used a modern contraceptive.

Women may obtain contraceptives from a variety of health-care providers. Private medical providers were the source for 72 percent of women (family-planning clinic 24 percent, private physician 19 percent, private hospital 8 percent), while public sources were the source for 28 percent of women (government maternal health center 11 percent, government hospital 7 percent, government health center 7 percent). A large number of women discontinued contraceptive use within the first year, roughly 49 percent. The rate was highest with diaphragm use (82 percent) and also surprisingly high with the pill (68 percent). The reasons cited for discontinuance were method failure (14 percent) and side effects (11 percent).[66]

The Jordan Population Commission has overseen research into the attitudes of Islamic leaders toward family planning and contraception, as there is a perception that religious leaders present an obstacle to family planning. Surprisingly, the surveys found that 82 percent of male religious leaders and 98 percent of female religious leaders believe that family planning is in keeping with the teachings of Islam. Surveys of the general public regarding their belief found that 80 percent of men and 86 percent of women believed that family planning is in keeping with the teachings of Islam.[67]

The results of the surveys noted that Islamic leaders had different reasons than the general public to justify the use of contraceptives, but they were just as likely to approve of family planning as the rest of the population. Indeed, religious leaders tend to be better educated than the public as a whole and thus may have a better understanding of family planning and how it fits into religious teachings, and how religious teachings are separate from tradition. Because religious leaders tend to be respected members of the community, some studies suggest that they can be good advocates of family planning. With regard to the acceptability of different types of contraception, the study found that both the religious leaders and the general population had insufficient knowledge about certain modern methods of contraception, such as implants and injectables.

Abortion in Jordan is illegal from the perspective of both criminal law and Islamic (shari'a) law. Shari'a does allow abortion when the mother's life is at risk from the pregnancy. The head of the penalties panel at the Jordan Medical Association has called on jurists and clerics to consider legalizing abortion for psychological reasons, as in cases of rape or incest. The Ministry of Health estimates that more than 500 illegal abortions were performed in private clinics during the first eight months of 2002. A physician who performs abortions faces prison terms of three to ten years if convicted, and a woman who undergoes an abortion can be sentenced to jail for six months to three years. In an interesting twist on crimes of honor, apparently a woman's sentence may be reduced if the abortion is done to protect the woman's honor.[68]

Teen Pregnancy

The 1997 JPFHS surveyed teenage fertility among Jordanian women and reported that the level of fertility among teenagers is low and varies with age and education. At the time of the survey, 6 percent of women aged fifteen to nineteen had had a child or were pregnant. One percent of women started bearing children at age fifteen, and one in seven began by age nineteen. (There is no mention of children born to unwed mothers.) As previously noted, the age group fifteen to nineteen had the largest decline in fertility of any age group between 1976 (71 births per 1,000 women) and 1997 (43 births). The report noted that more than half of the women in this age group left school to get married, and that teenage mothers and their children were more likely to suffer from illness and death.[69]

HEALTH

Information about the status of women's health in Jordan is generally lacking. It is not clear whether the government does not collect certain data or simply does not release them.[70] There is anecdotal evidence that smoking is increasing among women in Jordan, now that it is more socially acceptable than it was in the past. Women would not usually smoke in public, but it is possible to see women doing so today. The Ministry of Health does not have statistics on smoking-related illnesses on its web site.[71]

Health Care Access

The Jordan Association for Family Planning and Protection, an NGO, has begun to offer services such as screening and management of sexually transmitted diseases, early detection of breast and cervical cancer, infertility counseling, and information for young people. The government publishes the number of health-care workers per 100,000 population. The most recent information from the World Health Organization, for 1997, is that in Jordan there are, per 100,000 persons, 166 physicians, 296 nurses, 49 dentists, and 77 pharmacists.[72] These statistics do not give one a sense of the prevalence of accessible health care. Several respondents to a survey on reproductive health noted that many women in rural areas are embarrassed to see a male physician and consequently do not seek out reproductive health services, thus underscoring the need for more female physicians.[73] The infant mortality rate in 2000 was 31.3 per 1,000. The child mortality rate in 1999 was 7.0 per 1,000 for boys and 5.0 for girls. Maternal mortality numbered 41.4 deaths per 100,000 live births. The main causes of death were hypertension disorders in pregnancy, hemorrhage (excluding abortion), pulmonary embolism, and sepsis. The study determined that 82.4 percent of the deaths would have been preventable through adequate prenatal care.[74] A separate study, published in 1996, found that rural, older, less educated women and women with a higher number of children were more likely to have "poor attendance at the prenatal clinic," and these same women were more likely to have home deliveries.[75]

The 1997 JPFHS found that in the five years prior to the survey, 4 percent of mothers did not receive any prenatal care. Sixteen percent of women with no formal education fell into this category, compared to 2 to 7 percent of women with at least a primary education. Eight percent of women in rural areas did not receive prenatal care, compared to 3 percent in urban areas. During the same period, 93 percent of births took place at a health facility. Those who had home births typically were older, had six or more previous births, or lived in rural areas. Physicians attended 65 percent of births, nurses or trained midwives 32 percent, and a traditional birth attendant or a relative was present at the remainder.

Diseases and Disorders

AIDS

At a Red Crescent workshop to highlight AIDS awareness in Jordan in August 2002, it was reported that 300 cases of the disease had been discovered in Jordan since the diagnosis of the first case, and 127 people are currently infected. Sixty-eight percent of the cases were contracted outside the country, and 32 percent in Jordan. Of the 127 cases, more than half are the result of sexual transmission. The first case in Jordan, which was discovered in 1986, was the result of a blood transfusion. Of the 300 cases to date in Jordan, 123 have been Jordanians, and 171 foreigners. The number of men in Jordan with the disease is four times higher than the number of women.[76]

There is a social stigma attached to AIDS sufferers in Jordan and widespread ignorance of how the disease is transmitted, leading many to shun AIDS patients.[77] It is also difficult for patients to obtain the expensive medicines for AIDS treatment from the Ministry of Health.

The Office of Publication and Family Health US-Jordan works to educate Jordanians about the disease, to spread awareness, and to fight the spread of the disease. According to the 1997 JPFHS, 98 percent of ever-married women were aware of the disease, and most had knowledge of how it was transmitted and how to prevent its spread. Only 2 percent of the women, however, reported using condoms. While condom use was higher among women in urban areas and with higher levels of education, no more than 4 percent of women in any of the survey categories used them.[78]

Anemia

Anemia due to dietary problems is widespread in Jordan among women and children. Thirty-five percent of women experience anemia during pregnancy and breast feeding, and as many as 28 percent suffer from it after childbearing, because of a lack of iron in the diet.[79] The World Bank GenderStats database estimated anemia in pregnant women at the alarming rate of 50 percent in 1999. In June 2002, the Ministry of Health initiated a program to add iron to flour to combat this problem. The ministry will supply the iron supplement to all bakeries.

Anemia is also a symptom of the inherited condition of thalassemia that is frequently found in Jordan and other countries of the Mediterranean region. Testing for thalassemia is one of the health services the government is trying to emphasize for couples before they marry: if both partners carry the condition, there may be serious implications for their children. Thalassemia has several forms, with varying degrees of symptomatic severity. Depending upon the genes one inherits, symptoms range from none in a silent carrier to mild anemia, severe anemia, or anemia so severe that the person would die without transfusions. Thalassemia can also cause death in utero.

Cancer

Information about the occurrence of cancer among women in Jordan is lacking, as is information about treatment of the disease. The *Jordan Times* reported that 3,250 cancer cases were diagnosed in Jordan in 2000, of which 50.2 percent were women. Breast cancer accounted for almost one-third of the reported cases in women. The Ministry of Health is working with the World Health Organization and other organizations to increase prevention programs. The Jordan Association for Family Planning and Protection offers services for early detection of breast and cervical cancer.

In 1999, the Hashemite University conducted a study of 400 women university students and employees aged nineteen and above to learn about their beliefs about breast cancer and breast self-examination. The results of the survey are still under analysis. The purpose of the study was to determine educational needs about breast cancer in order to ensure early detection and a decrease in mortality from the disease.

Depression

Government sources in English do not disclose statistics on mental illnesses. However, it appears to be publicly acceptable to discuss certain aspects of mental illness. The *Jordan Times* published a lengthy article by Adi Issam Arida, a physician, titled "The Disease of This Century—Depression" on September 10, 2002. The article touches on many types of mental illness (depression, warning signs of suicide, anxiety disorders, panic disorder, social phobia, agoraphobia, post-traumatic stress disorder, obsessive-compulsive disorder, schizophrenia, and eating disorders), describing their symptoms and treatments. It did not, however, discuss the prevalence of these problems in Jordan.

POLITICS AND LAW

Literature on various aspects of Jordanian law notes its roots in tribal customs, such as exile from the tribe, the code of honor of total loyalty to the clan and tribe to ensure its survival, and vengeance killings to maintain the tribe's honor. Evidence of this evolution of tribal customs into law may be seen in the prevalence of honor killings of women and the structure of the judicial system in Jordan. The National Charter states that Jordan can be ruled only by the Hashemites, the family that claims descent from the house of the prophet Muhammad, and their legitimate male heirs. The traditional structure of Jordanian society makes it difficult for women in the political arena.

Many women's groups in Jordan are working to change discriminatory laws, a process that can take years. These groups have focused on laws that discriminate against women in many aspects of life, including inheritance, taxes, voting, and divorce.[80] The monarchy is very involved in women's issues, not necessarily for the sake of the advancement of women, but perhaps due to concern about its image in the world.

There have been three periods of greater political liberalization in Jordan during its modern history. The first was 1954–1957, shortly after King Hussein assumed the throne. A coup attempt in 1957 led the king to ban political parties, and they were not allowed to function again until the early 1990s. The second period began after the 1967 war with Israel and ended with the civil unrest of September 1970, which led to the expulsion of the Palestinian resistance movement from Jordan. The third period began in 1989 after the rioting and lasted until 1994, when Jordan signed a peace treaty with Israel, which many in the country oppose. These periods of relative freedoms were significant for changes in the status of women, both positive and negative.[81]

Suffrage

In 1974, women acquired the right to vote and stand for election.[82] This was relatively late in comparison with other countries in the region.

The Arab Women's Federation (AWF), which was established in June 1954, shortly after King Hussein ascended to the throne, first raised the issue of the right to vote. During the first of the three periods of political liberalization,[83] the AWF sent a memo to the prime minister requesting an amendment to the Elections Law to give women the right to vote in municipal and parliamentary elections, as well as the right to run as candidates. The government published a proposed change whereby only educated women would enjoy these rights. This caused an uproar, as there was no such requirement for a man to vote or hold office. The AWF continued its efforts for several years, and eventually the government agreed to look at the issue again. This first fight for suffrage ended when an attempted political coup in 1957 ended the growth in political freedoms and led to the imposition of martial law, a ban on political parties, and the suspension of elections until 1989.

In 1966, the king raised the issue of voting in a letter to the prime minister, but the question was once again not resolved, and the 1967 war with Israel and the influx of Palestinian refugees became the focus of the country's attention. Finally, in 1974, the king issued a letter on the vote that included a royal decree amending the Elections Law, giving women the right to vote.

It should be stressed that suffrage did not come about through democratic means in the parliament, but rather through a decision from the palace. The king's action was likely in anticipation of the UN Decade for Women, which was to begin in 1975.[84] Women from Jordan would soon be meeting to form a committee for the UN conference. However, the regime was not holding regular parliamentary elections, and thus women did not get to exercise this right until 1989.

Political Participation

The absence of true democracy in Jordan makes it difficult for women and men to participate in the political process. Political parties are a subordinate partner in their relationship with the government.[85] The palace ignores parties when it is forming the government; the king does not negotiate with the parties before appointing the prime minister. The only say the members of parliament have in the process is through a vote of confidence on the newly formed government. The palace has exercised its power to dissolve parliament on many occasions during Jordan's modern history.

Elections were not held between 1967 and 1989. One excuse the palace used for not holding elections was that West Bankers were not able to participate in them.[86] There were also rumors that Palestine Liberation Organization head Yasir Arafat discouraged Jordanian Palestinians from voting in 1989 to avoid any claims that Jordan is Palestine in the fight for a Palestinian homeland.[87] After elections were held in 1989, they were again held in 1993 and 1997, although the parliament had been dissolved prior to the 1997 elections.

Again in 2001–2002, there was a clampdown on human rights and democracy in Jordan after the attack on the United States on September 11, 2001, and because of the ongoing Palestinian Intifada in Israel. In May 2001, the government reacted with violence toward protesters supporting the Intifada and imposed a ban on demonstrations. After the latest dissolution of parliament in June 2001, the government postponed general elections for at least one year and issued many additional temporary laws that impinge on civil rights such as having public gatherings or exercising one's freedom of speech individually or in the press. Nevertheless, there were protests in April 2002 against Israeli actions against the Palestinians.

The current regime has introduced a truly repressive atmosphere in which violations of many laws are considered to threaten the security of the state and carry harsh penalties. Even criticism of the royal family is outlawed. In a country where the royal family has its hand in every women's organization and institution, this makes it difficult for women to operate freely. Finally, in August 2002, the king announced that elections would be held in the spring of 2003. In the meantime, the parliament remains inactive.

Kings Hussein and Abdullah have had to walk a tightrope in the middle of politics in the region. Jordan is highly dependent on U.S. aid, which funds many programs that benefit women. When King Hussein remained neutral during the Gulf War, the United States cut aid to Jordan. In the fall of 2002, King Abdullah faced a similar situation as the United States threatened to attack Iraq. During the recent conflict with Iraq, King Abdullah continued to support the United States despite unrest in the population over U.S. actions.[88]

The many temporary laws issued by royal decree in 2001 included amendments to the Elections Law. Many had hoped for quotas for women in the elections, but this was not a feature of the amendments. A former woman senator, Na'ela Rashdan, who had run and lost in the 1989 election, supports temporary quotas as a way for a woman to prove that she can do the job. When Rashdan announced her candidacy for the 1989 elections, her own party would not back her because she is a woman. However, another observer of politics in Jordan feels that quotas for women are not a solution to increasing their political involvement. A former woman candidate and journalist, Fardous Mash, has commented that the current one-person, one-vote system, which has not always been the case in Jordan, strengthens tribalism because a voter is limited to choosing one candidate, and no woman will win an election until the law is changed.

Although Jordan has a parliament with an upper and a lower house, elections determine only the members of the lower house; the king appoints the senators, and the Senate has veto power over decisions made by the lower house. The prime minister chooses his cabinet, which first included a woman in 1979. In'am al-Mufti, an educator, was the first minister of the new Ministry of Social Development.[89] There have been only a few women in such positions of political power. Layla Sharaf became minister of information in 1984. It was not until 1993 that another woman attained the level of cabinet minister when Rima Khalaf became minister of trade and industry. In 1995, a new cabinet contained two women for the first time when Salwa Damen al-Masri became minister of social affairs, joining Rima Khalaf, who later moved to the Ministry of Planning in a cabinet shuffle. Khalaf not only headed two important ministries, but was professionally qualified to run them. On the judicial side, the prime minister appointed the first woman judge in 1996. King Hussein appointed several women to the Senate: Layla Sharaf (1989, 1993, 1994), Na'ila Rashdan (1993), Rima Khalaf (1997), and Subeiha Ma'ani (1997).

Women have had mixed luck in their races for seats in the lower house of parliament. They first ran for office in 1989, the first elections to be held in twenty-two years. Twelve women ran in this election, but none of them won. Islamists won thirty of the eighty seats in this election. Some Islamists openly questioned the candidacy of the women, but the press criticized the Islamists for this. Outside Amman, women strongly supported the male Islamist candidates. In the 1997 elections, seventeen women ran for the lower house, but all lost, in spite of strong support in all levels of society. It has been noted that "the substantial, organizational, financial and political support for female parliamentary candidates was characterized by direct, sustained, very public, and virtually unprecedented, combined support by the royal family, state institutions, Jordanian and international nongovernmental organizations, research centers, women's groups, the mass media, and other institutions."[90] But the women were not experienced politicians, had no experience with political rhetoric, and, like most of the male candidates, also lacked political credibility.

Toujan Faisal received international attention prior to the 1989 elections when it became known that Islamists had tried to intimidate her into not running.[91] Faisal had been a television broadcaster for eighteen years and was also known for her writings. In her career, she had covered women's affairs and had questioned certain Islamic and tribal practices. She was running for the Circassian seat in the Fifth District. Faisal received visits from some men who demanded that she apologize for a certain article and withdraw from the election. She refused and later received a subpoena to appear in a shari'a court, where she was charged with apostasy.

Public outrage was strong, and the educated elite submitted a petition denouncing the charges to the king. The story received international attention after it was reported by the Jordanian press. The king engaged in damage control and at a press conference "warned against a trend toward extremism" and against those who "exploit religion for political designs." Five days before the election, the Amman shari'a court ruled that the case was beyond its jurisdiction. The plaintiffs appealed, and eventually a shari'a appeals court found Faisal not guilty of apostasy. Faisal won in the 1993 lower-house elections and became the first woman elected to parliament—to this day the only woman ever elected. She served in the lower house from 1993 to 1997. The Islamists lost many of the seats they had won in the 1989 elections.

Support from the regime for women should not be interpreted at its face value. King Hussein was not a feminist but rather needed to appear to be progressive in the eyes of the West. He also could not allow Islamists to gain too much power because they opposed the peace process and normalization of relations with Israel, which the regime greatly supported.

Faisal's troubles continue to this day and are widely covered by the Jordanian press. In May 2002, she was sentenced to eighteen months in prison for "seditious libel" and "spreading information deemed harmful to the reputation of the state." She had written an open letter to the government accusing Prime Minister Ali Abu Ragheb of benefiting personally from a new temporary law, called essential to the country's security, that doubled car insurance premiums. She had noted in the letter that the prime minister's family dominates the car insurance industry in Jordan. Once again Faisal was pardoned by a royal decree, although not until she had spent time in prison; her pardon does not overturn her conviction, but merely releases her from prison. Under one of the 2001 temporary laws, she is now ineligible to run for public office because she was convicted of a nonpolitical crime and received a prison sentence of more than one year.

Women's Rights

The constitution in use today was ratified in 1952. In 1990, King Hussein convened work on a National Charter, intended to supplement the constitution. The sixty-member royal commission that drafted the document included four women: lawyer Asma Khadr, educator 'Eida Mutlaq, senator Layla Sharaf, and civil servant and columnist Muna Shuqayr.[92] The introduction to the National Charter states that women and men are equal under the law, but it is clear from an examination of various laws in the areas of inheritance, property, and women's rights that this statement does not hold in practice.

Much of family law is codified in the Personal Status Law. Until the end of 2001, the legal age of marriage was fifteen for females and sixteen for males. As part of an amendment to the Personal Status Law regarding divorce, the law raised the legal age of marriage to eighteen for both sexes. The king approved the amendment based on recommendations from a royal human rights commission.

The law does not prohibit polygyny. A man must treat all his wives equitably, provide each a separate dwelling, and disclose the existence of other wives in the marriage contract. Another 2001 amendment to the Personal Status Law gives a woman the right to initiate divorce proceedings. Under the old law, a woman had a much harder time obtaining a divorce. She would have to prove that her husband was abusive either emotionally or physically, and that he would continue; that her husband had been absent or imprisoned for one year or more; or that he had refused to pay living expenses.

Until 1994, if a woman was arbitrarily divorced by her husband, which is allowed under the law, she risked being thrown out of her home with the children. A change to the Landlords and Tenants Law in 1994 provided that a divorced woman or a widow could remain in the family apartment after the divorce or death of her husband. In the event of divorce, the man must leave the apartment in order for the woman to stay.

The new amendment was issued in the form of a temporary law, meaning that it will face debate in the next parliament, which may question its constitutionality.[93] Under the amendment, the woman loses all rights to financial compensation from her husband after the divorce. Therefore, women with no financial means of their own cannot afford to lose their financial support. Moreover, the amendment requires the woman to pay back the dowry payment. As of 2002, only two women had received a divorce under the amendment, and about 500 cases were waiting to be heard.

Women suffer discrimination in the area of citizenship rights and passport law. Citizenship is conveyed to children through the father, not the mother. A married woman cannot petition for citizenship for a non-Jordanian husband; the husband can apply himself after fulfilling a fifteen-year residency requirement. According to the U.S. government's *Country Reports on Human Rights Practices—2000—Jordan*, in practice, non-Jordanian husbands have difficulty in obtaining citizenship, and the children of these couples become stateless and lack the rights of Jordanian children, such as the right to attend school or receive other government services. A married woman must obtain her husband's permission to obtain a passport. In 1994, there were discussions in the parliament to amend the passport laws, but there is no indication that they have been amended.

Jordan's Civil Status Law requires everyone to have a document called a "family book" for almost all official transactions. The family book is needed to vote or be a candidate, to obtain food assistance, to register children in school or university, and for civil service jobs. When a woman marries, she is transferred from her father's family book to her husband's. If a woman is divorced or deserted by her husband, she must reregister on the family book of her father or a brother in order to function in society.

Some of these legal concerns are not applicable to the average woman in Jordan. For example, the issue of passing on citizenship to her children is most likely a concern of a well-to-do woman who has married a foreigner. The average woman is most concerned with the struggle of living day to day.

During the period of liberalization in the early 1990s, the Islamist parties had some successes in elections and in receiving cabinet posts and tried to implement shari'a in various aspects of life in ways detrimental to women.[94] The first was an attempt in 1990 by the Ministry of the Interior to ban male hairdressers under the pretext that it would increase women's chances for employment. Women's groups recognized it as the first step to ban mixing of the sexes, and public outcry led to a withdrawal of the ban. A second attempt to limit women's rights was a law changing the formula for inheritance of state land. In 1991, the five members of the Muslim Brotherhood Party who were in the cabinet began to segregate their employees by sex. The public response led to a swift downfall of the cabinet only six months after it had been formed. In 1993, Islamists in the government tried to segregate the sexes in sports and recreational facilities governed by the Ministry of Youth banning the government from licensing such facilities if they did not practice separation. On many occasions when such laws were voted upon in the parliament, even non-Islamist deputies would support them so as not to appear to oppose Islamic law. Islamists next tried to pass a bill to have segregation in the schools, but did not meet with success. During the debate, the minister of education, who opposed the bill for economic reasons, argued that most Jordanian schools were segregated, and that coeducation existed primarily in remote areas.

The Islamists had focused their efforts in the areas of society and education, as opposed to the economy. These are areas where they could have a strong impact on the status of women, and where other legislators did not want to appear to oppose the "party of God." With the end of political liberalization becoming apparent in 1994, the Islamists, who opposed the peace process with Israel, began to lose their political clout because of efforts by the palace. The king had to muffle the Islamists' opposition to the peace process, and in so doing he helped to delay more changes that would have affected women and the family.

Feminist Movements

The Jordanian women's movement is not one of like-minded women. There are women with more secular leftist leanings, those who are in step with the Islamist parties, and the elite, who tend to be conservative royalists. It appears that in recent times the political disagreements among various factions have been muffled by the role of organizations controlled by the palace. Future political change does not necessarily mean social change in Jordan. Activists stress the need to discuss issues within Islamic and societal traditions in order to gain acceptance with most Jordanian women.[95]

Women's groups have been active since the 1940s in Jordan, although their focus has shifted over time.[96] The early women's organizations tended to be more charitable in nature, primarily concerned with improving the education of women and the health of children and raising women's awareness about health and welfare issues. Since the late 1990s, women's groups have become more political in their concerns.

The focus on the Palestinian struggle until the army drove the Palestinian resistance movement out of Jordan in 1970–1971 after major violence erupted between the army and the resistance tended to divert attention away from many women's concerns, but the participation of women in the resistance movement was the beginning of liberation for many women. Women's groups have been affected by periods of political liberalization and subsequent reversals, as other political movements have.

Women's groups that tend to be more charitable in nature have had an easier time operating in Jordan than those with a more political, progressive outlook. During periods of political freedoms, women's groups thrived. The government has tried to centralize control over women's groups or demobilize women and obstruct their efforts at independent organizing. In its attempts to control women's groups, the palace has more or less taken over many of them. Women's organizations that are not political parties are governed by the Charitable Societies Law, which does not allow them to engage in political work. The government has designated the leaders, who tend to come from the elite families of Jordan, especially the royal family, and are not necessarily qualified for their positions. These women receive much publicity at home and abroad, but are not in step with the average woman in Jordan. Most women are uncomfortable saying anything that appears to disagree with the ideas of the royal women or taking up issues on their own. On the positive side, a person like Princess Basma, the sister of the late King Hussein, has the ability to bring attention to certain issues and get things done, for example, by going over the heads of local UN officials direct to UN headquarters.[97]

In 1992, Princess Basma established the Jordanian National Committee for Women (JNCW) at the request of the minister of planning. The JNCW works closely with external NGOs, and its objective is to implement programs and conduct research on women's issues and to raise awareness about women's rights in society. The JNCW has taped awareness-raising programs on women, family, and the law along with Jordanian broadcasting; it has established nurseries for working women; it holds meetings to raise awareness about health care; and it has commissioned studies on poverty, female-headed households, and child rearing.

The development of women's groups has also been linked with external movements, where Jordan needed to have representatives and to appear to be progressive in its efforts. These movements included the UN Decade for Women, which began in 1975 and the Beijing conference in 1995. The UNIFEM Post-Beijing Follow-Up Project for the region is based in Amman. It is working with the JNCW on implementing the action plans that arose from the Fourth World Conference on Women (FWCW) in Beijing.

The Jordanian Women's Union (JWU) has a more political orientation than certain other women's groups. Asma Khader, the lawyer who has been very involved in issues such as honor killings, was its president during the 1990s. The JWU has focused on changing laws that discriminate against women and on family relations and domestic violence. It has opened several legal advice centers, two of them in refugee camps. The JWU has had confrontations with the government over its work and its positions.

The Sisterhood Is Global Institute (SIGI) was established in 1998. Its goal is promote and support women's rights through education, skills training, and modern technology. Its programs include a human rights education program, a program to combat violence against women and girls, a training course on using the Internet, and a cultural events program that features the experiences of women leaders. Asma Khader is the director of SIGI, and the journalist Rana Husseini is one of its advisors.

Lesbian Rights

The English-language literature to date on women's rights does not deal with the subject of lesbian rights. Perhaps this is because women in Jordan continue to struggle with the most basic of human rights, such as having a voice in politics in a country without democratic freedoms and eliminating honor killings. In addition to this, the patriarchal structure of Jordanian families, where is it unusual for women to live alone, likely inhibits lesbian relationships.

Military Service

The military is another area of society where the royal elite are leading the way for change for women. In 1996 women made up 4 percent of the Jordanian army, serving in areas such as engineering and computer analysis. Women at this time were restricted to administrative, educational, and medical positions. Three female members of the royal family are working to increase the presence of women in the military. Princess Basma has toured U.S. military facilities and considers American military women to be role models for Jordanian women. In 1996, one Jordanian woman was attending the U.S. Naval Academy. The royal women have been commissioned officers in the army; all three have attended Sandhurst Royal Military Academy in England, following in the path of male Jordanian royals.

RELIGION AND SPIRITUALITY

Women's Roles and Religious Practices

In 1989, almost 40 percent of women in Jordan "were prepared to admit that they did not actively practice their religion."[98] Sixty percent of the surveyed women who had a positive attitude toward working women gave religious instruction to their children. Interestingly, only 65 percent of women who were negative toward working women provided religious instruction to their children. The percentage of women giving their children religious instruction is not terribly high for either group, although the sample was quite small and may not be representative of the country as a whole.

Religious Law

Religious courts are one of the three branches of the Jordanian judicial system. The religious courts uphold Islamic law (shari'a) and have jurisdiction over marriage, divorce, and inheritance. Other religious communities in Jordan have their own system. There are both primary and appellate religious courts.

VIOLENCE

The Arab Women's Human Rights Programme in the Context of CEDAW (the Convention on the Elimination of All Forms of Discrimination against Women), which began in 2000 and was to take two years, was targeted at the judiciary, lawyers, human rights advocates, and NGOs involved with human rights. Its objectives are to build an expert group on women's human rights, ensure that information on this topic is available to groups working in this area, and to make information available online for use in training sessions. Jordan ratified CEDAW in 1992, although it voiced reservations about certain pronouncements of the document.

UNIFEM maintains the Global Trust Fund in Support of Actions to Eliminate Violence against Women, which funded a field study in 1998 on the causes and prevalence of violence against women in Jordan. The Human Forum for Women's Rights carried out the study. A second project funded by the Global Trust Fund began in 2001 to help women victims of sexual abuse in Jordanian and Palestinian society and to develop greater awareness and sensitivity within the judicial system toward sexual abuse.

Domestic Violence

Domestic violence in Jordan ranges from spousal abuse to honor killings. An honor killing is the murder of a woman by a male relative for her perceived immodest behavior or sexual misconduct, such as premarital or extramarital sex. Victims of honor killings are often victims of sexual violence and abuse, such as rape or incest, because even then they are considered to have dishonored the family. These crimes are found in both Transjordanian and Palestinian populations and affect all economic classes, although they are more frequently reported among the poor. Another motivation for honor killings that is less discussed is economics.

Most of the literature on violence against women focuses on honor killings, and less exists on other forms of domestic violence, which ironically are considered an internal family matter and are not commonly discussed in public. A project was launched in 2000 to raise people's awareness of domestic violence and to improve services for its victims. The Jordan Family Protection Project is being financed by the United Kingdom with cooperation from the government, NGOs, and human rights groups. The project intends to create a shelter for women and children who have either been abused or deserted.

One recent example of an honor killing motivated by immodest behavior occurred in the town of Urfa, where a friend of a girl had requested a song from a local radio station and dedicated it to her. Her family considered this to be a disgrace, since the song was a love song and thus implied that the girl was involved in a love affair. The girl was pushed under a tractor and killed.[99]

Apparently there is great social pressure on men by other men in the community. Male relatives of a woman who has behaved disreputably may be subject to teasing and heckling by other men, who frequently ask them "whether they have cleansed their honor or not." According to one source, the male relatives will have a boy between the ages of fourteen and sixteen carry out the murder, as he will be subject to a lighter jail sentence than an older man. The killing may take place in public to serve as a warning to other girls and women in the community.

An issue not mentioned frequently in the literature is the attitude of female family members toward these killings. Even the mothers of the victims approve because the family worries that the other daughters will never be married if the family does not cleanse its honor. Women are complicit in these crimes for another reason as well, fear of retribution.

Many sources on these topics acknowledge that there is an underreporting of incidents because of cultural norms that discourage victims from seeking medical or legal help, or because crimes that are reported are not recorded as "crimes of honor." Rights activists outside the country are outraged by the situation and document it each year in various reports issued by the U.S. government, Amnesty International (AI), and the press. AI has covered this topic in its last few annual reports on Jordan. There were at least nineteen honor killings in 2001 and at least twenty-one in 2000. The U.S. government's *Country Report on Human Rights Practices—2000—Jordan* cites a forensic medical examiner who estimates that 25 percent of all murders committed in Jordan are honor crimes. Annually this U.S. report cites examples of honor killings, as well as reduced sentences for the perpetrators.

Honor killings have been the subject of much recent public debate in Jordan, and the Jordanian parliament has vacillated on the issue. Public debate centers on Articles 340 and 98 of the Jordanian Penal Code. Under these laws, a person who kills to protect family honor is given a reduced sentence in the range of three months to three years, or even no sentence. This is in contrast to first-degree murder, where the maximum punishment is the death penalty, and second-degree murder, where the maximum punishment is fifteen years. Someone who kills on the spot, in a fit of fury or surprise, will be given a reduced sentence. There is no requirement that the murderer be correct in his assumption about the woman having actually engaged in sexual activity outside the bonds of marriage. One may read cases where the murder was committed based on rumors that turned out to be false.

In December 1999, the National Committee to Eliminate Crimes of Honor delivered a petition to both legislative houses signed by 15,000 citizens, demanding an end to crimes of honor and the legislation that protects perpetrators. In December 2001, the parliament repealed the exemption from the death penalty for those who commit honor killings. The Jordanian royal family has supported the campaign against honor killings. The late King Hussein mentioned the problem in an address to parliament in 1997. This was the first public mention of honor killings by an Arab leader.[100] The Jordanian National Committee for Women, headed by Princess Basma, campaigns against honor killings. In January 1999, more than 250 women, including Princess Basma, demonstrated in Amman against domestic violence after the arrest of a father who had killed his daughter after she eloped with her boyfriend. During the same month, an international conference held in Amman called for judges to impose heavier penalties for crimes of honor. King Abdullah supports legislative reform, and his younger brother and cousin have been involved in the debate. In February 2000, Prince Ali bin Hussein and Prince Ghazi bin Mohammed led a protest of more than 5,000 persons to demand that the legislature repeal Article 340.

The *Christian Science Monitor* interviewed the Amman female attorney Asma Khader, who is involved with many of the country's honor killings. In one case mentioned, a married woman was murdered by her brother because some of his friends had raped her four years before, and she had "sullied her family's honor." The murdered woman's husband had come to the attorney to prosecute the brother. Khader points out that this in fact is progress; the man is seeking justice and will not drop the charges against his brother-in-law. In the past, husbands would have supported their wives' killers, but now she is seeing more men ask for protection from relatives for their wives.[101]

Women who are potential victims of honor crimes because they are victims of rape or incest or because they refuse an arranged marriage are regularly imprisoned for their own protection. The government has the authority to detain these women if it feels that releasing them will probably result in death at the hands of their families. The women in protective custody are held in a section of the Center, a type of prison, separate from women convicted of crimes. The U.S. government's *Country Reports on Human Rights Practices—2000—Jordan* states that up to forty women were held in this manner that year. As of the end of 2001, Jordan's Public Security Department was trying to find alternative, safe arrangements for these women.

The Women's Correctional and Rehabilitation Center is located in Jewideh, south of Amman. Woman are now managing and operating the facility for the first time. The center can hold more than 900 inmates and provides vocational training and academic education such as dressmaking, embroidery, knitting, ceramics, sewing, flower arrangement, typing, computer work, hairdressing, tailoring, and interior decorating. The center has a health center, including specialists to provide psychological, dental, and gynecological care. The prison also provides social care, a nursery for inmates' children, a supermarket, a canteen, a public library, and offices for lawyers. When a woman first arrives at the prison, she receives medical care and meets with a social worker who reviews the woman's case, then places the inmate with others convicted of a similar offense.

Criminal offenses include becoming pregnant out of wedlock and committing adultery, which carry two-year prison terms. While the women inmates are allowed three visits per week, the families of these women neglect them because of the shame deriving from criminal convictions. However, men who commit crimes, such as murder or theft, enjoy the support of their families and are able to reintegrate into society upon release. Women, on the other hand, pay for a conviction for their entire lives and are not reintegrated into society due to lack of family support.

Rape/Sexual Assault

According to AI, the Penal Code was amended in 1988 to make rape a capital offense. In its annual report on Jordan covering 1996, AI reported that two men were executed for raping minors, and that these were the first executions under the amendment.

Trafficking in Women and Children

Information on the incidence of trafficking in women and children in Jordan is generally unavailable. The U.S. State Department's second annual *Trafficking in Persons Report*, released in June 2002, does not even include Jordan in the list of countries it examines. It is likely that there are cases of coercive labor and sexual exploitation among young women from other countries who come to Jordan to work in domestic positions, as occurs in other countries in the Middle East.

OUTLOOK FOR THE TWENTY-FIRST CENTURY

The status of women in Jordan will likely continue to improve at the slow pace seen since the 1980s. It is unlikely that there will be radical changes to Jordanian society that would bring about quicker progress. The country will continue to be a true monarchy, ruled only by male heirs of the Hashemites. Jordan will always have a precarious geopolitical position in the world, wedged between Israel and Iraq, with a large Palestinian refugee population. Women will likely continue to benefit from the close scrutiny Jordan receives in the United States and abroad due to its role in the peace process, and from the more progressive attitudes of the European-educated royal family.

NOTES

1. One kilometer equals approximately 0.6 miles.
2. Department of Statistics Jordan, DOS-NIS: Population and Housing, DOS-NIS: Population. *Statistical Year Book 2000*. Retrieved September 2, 2002 from http://www.dos.gov.jo/sdb_pop/pop_changes2000_e.htm.
3. The King Abdullah II web site is a Government of Jordan web site, www.kingabdullah.jo/.
4. Laurie A. Brand, *Women, the State, and Political Liberalization: Middle Eastern and North Africa Experiences* (New York: Columbia University Press, 1998).
5. World Bank, *The Hashemite Kingdom of Jordan Country Assistance Strategy*, 2001, http://lnweb18.worldbank.org/mna/mena.nsf/all/D4D46C2B71E7CA6C8525694 D0056435D?OpenDocument.
6. http://www.dos.gov.jo.
7. The Department of Statistics Jordan web site does not provide definitions of terms. The "intermediate diploma" category in the table probably refers to a diploma for passing the *tawjihi* exam.
8. J. Miller, "Women and Family Honor: The Face of Feminine Identity in Jordan," *Isis—A Journal About Women* (spring): 12+. Retrieved September 9, 2002 from RDS Contemporary Women's Issues database.
9. All references to education in the squatter areas of Amman and in rural areas are from the fieldwork of Seteney Shami and Lucine Taminian, "Women's Participation in the Jordanian Labor Force: A Comparison of Rural and Urban Patterns," in *Women in Arab Society: Work Patterns and Gender Relations in Egypt, Jordan, and Sudan* (Prov-

idence, RI, and Oxford: Berg and UNESCO, 1990), 1–86. The nature of the squatter community is discussed further under "Employment."

10. S. Shami, "Domesticity Reconfigured: Women in Squatter Areas of Amman," in *Organizing Women: Formal and Informal Women's Groups in the Middle East*, ed. D. Chatty and A. Rabo (Oxford and New York: Berg, 1997), 81–99; Shami and Taminian, 1990.

11. Shami and Taminian, 1990.

12. Ibid.

13. All references to the research of Ivy Papps are from I. Papps, "Attitudes to Female Employment in Four Middle Eastern Countries," in *Women in the Middle East: Perceptions, Realities, and Struggles for Liberation*, ed. H. Afshar (New York: St. Martin's Press, 1993), 96–116. Her research is discussed further under "Employment."

14. World Bank, 2001.

15. G. Joha, "Back to School: What about the Remote Areas?" *Star* 12(109) (August 29–September 4, 2002), http://star.arabia.com.

16. For more detail about Jordan's economy, see the World Bank and International Monetary Fund (IMF) web sites, www.worldbank.org and www.imf.org.

17. R. Naiman, "No Jubilee for the Middle East," *Middle East Report* 213 (winter 1999), www.merip.org/mer/mer213/213_naiman.html.

18. World Bank, 2001.

19. A. Amawi, "Democracy Dilemmas in Jordan," *Middle East Report* 174 (January/February 1992): 27.

20. K.J. Cunningham, "Jordan's Information Revolution: Implications for Democracy," *Middle East Journal* 56 (spring 2002): 240–56.

21. M. LeVine, "The Arab Human Development Report: A Critique," *Middle East Report*, Press Information Note 101, July 26, 2002, www.merip.org/pins/pin101.html.

22. http://www.undp-jordan.org/publications_jhdr/publications_jhdr.html.

23. Ibid.

24. The discussion of employment draws heavily on the research of Seteney Shami and Lucine Taminian published in Shami and Taminian, 1990, and Shami, 1997. Information about employment among the urban poor and in rural areas is from their research.

25. The Arab Archives Institute, based in Amman, has recently published a book on the topic, *Wasta: The Declared Secret*, March 2002. The institute also held a three-day conference on this subject in April 2002 under the patronage of the prime minister.

26. G. Joha, "Book in Review: The Wild Wonderful World of *Wasta*," *Star* 12(94) (May 16–22, 2002), http://star.arabia.com.

27. World Bank GenderStats database, CPIA Indicators, http://genderstats.worldbank.org/CPIA.

28. Shami and Taminian, 1990, cite these various studies by other researchers in their publication.

29. Shami, 1997.

30. Ibid.

31. Ibid.

32. Shami and Taminian, 1990, 58.

33. Field research conducted by Lucine Taminian, in Shami and Taminian, 1990.

34. Ibid.

35. Ibid.

36. For a discussion of the methodology see Papps, 1993, 98–101.

37. Ibid.

38. Ibid.
39. Shami, 1997.
40. Shami and Taminian, 1990, 67.
41. U.S. Government, *Country Reports on Human Rights Practices-2000-Jordan*. Retrieved September 9, 2002 from RDS Contemporary Women's Issues database.
42. Brand, 1998, 135.
43. Ibid., 136.
44. Papps, 1993, 104.
45. Ibid., 134.
46. Shami and Taminian, 1990, 3.
47. Ibid., 40–43.
48. Noor Al Hussein Foundation web site, www.nhf.org.jo.
49. USAID, *USAID Assistance to Jordan*. Retrieved September 28, 2002 from http://www.usaid.gov/press/releases/fs991112.html. Additional information about aid to Jordan may be found using the web site search function.
50. Brand, 1998, 137.
51. U.S. Social Security Administration, *Social Security Programs throughout the World*, 1999, www.ssa.gov. This publication is based on data as of the beginning of 1999, or the last date for which the SSA received information from each country.
52. The discussion of types of households and gender roles is drawn from Shami and Taminian, 1990, 36–46.
53. Ibid.
54. A discussion of the mutual aid units may be found in both Shami and Taminian, 1990, and Shami, 1997.
55. Ibid.
56. L. Khader, "UNICEF Releases Parenting Report," *Star* 12(107) (August 15–21, 2002), http://star.arabia.com.
57. USAID.
58. Miller, 2001.
59. Ibid.
60. E. Hazleton, "Jawazi al-Malakim: Settled Bedouin Woman of Jordan," in *Middle Eastern Muslim Women Speak*, ed. Elizabeth Warnock Fernea and Basima Qattan Bezirgan (Austin: University of Texas Press, 1977), 263–70.
61. Brand, 1998, 122.
62. Ibid., 166.
63. The 1976 Jordan Fertility Survey, the 1983 Jordan Fertility and Family Health Survey, the 1990 Jordan Population and Family Health Survey (JPFHS), and the 1997 JPFHS. See Alan Guttmacher Institute, "Fertility Levels among Jordanian Women Have Fallen Sharply, but Unwanted Childbearing Remains High," *International Family Planning Perspectives* 25(4) (1999): 203–8, for a summary of the 1997 JPFHS.
64. The workshop on premarital services was reported in the *Jordan Times* on September 10, 2002. The article did not give the date of the workshop, but it probably took place shortly before the article appeared. D.A. Wakeel, "Family Resources Seen as Central to Preservation of Resources," *Jordan Times*. Retrieved September 23, 2002 from http://www.jordantimes.com.
65. W. Petro-Nustas, "Men's Knowledge of and Attitudes toward Birth Spacing and Contraceptive Use in Jordan: Part 1 of 2, the Jordanian Context," *International Family Planning Perspectives* 25(4) (1999): 181–85.
66. Alan Guttmacher Institute, 1999. The full text of the publication may be found on the Institute's web site: www.agi-usa.org, using the search function for Jordan.

67. C. Underwood, "Islamic Precepts and Family Planning: The Perceptions of Jordanian Religious Leaders and Their Constituents," *International Family Planning Perspectives* 26(3) (September 2000): 110–17.

68. A. Nsour, "Illegal Abortions Remain Source of Official Concern," *Jordan Times*, September 13–14, 2002, www.jordantimes.com.

69. R. Awwad, *Jordan Times*, November 30, 1999.

70. The Jordan Ministry of Health web site, www.moh.gov.jo/, has a section titled Health Research Directory, which gives abstracts of research studies conducted in Jordan in various health-related fields. It also has a section on Islamic Health Studies; these studies examine the Qur'an's statements on health issues, such as the amount of time a woman should nurse a child (two years).

71. *Star*, www.star.arabia.com, Jordan's English-language weekly.

72. World Health Organization. Retrieved September 23, 2002 from www.who.int/reproductive-health/publications.

73. K. Hardee et al., "Reproductive Health Polices and Programs in Eight Countries: Progress since Cairo: Part 1 of 2," *International Family Planning Perspectives* 25 (January 1999).

74. Ministry of Health, Health Research Directory, Biostatistics, Mortality, abstract of *Maternal Mortality Study*, www.moh.gov.jo/research/. The abstract of the study does not give a date, but it is after 1990 because it refers to WHO statistics for that year. The study was done independently of the Health Information Center of the Ministry of Health, as the authors of the study noted the ministry's inadequate record keeping on both maternal mortality and all causes of death.

75. Ministry of Health, Health Research Directory, Maternal Care, abstract of *Determinants of Infant Mortality and the Use of Maternity Services in Jordan*, www.moh.gov.jo/research/community_health_care/maternal_care.htm.

76. Ali Asad, director of the Jordanian Program for Protection from AIDS, the Ministry of Health.

77. *Star*, www.star.arabia.com, Jordan's English-language weekly.

78. Ibid.

79. "Anti-Cancer Campaign Strategies Developed," *Jordan Times*, September 12, 2002. Retrieved September 12, 2002 from www.jordantimes.com.

80. Brand, 1998.

81. Ibid.

82. The discussion of suffrage and family law is largely based on the research of Brand, 1998.

83. Brand, 1998, refers to these periods as "openings," which she covers in her book.

84. Brand, 1998.

85. E.M. Lust-Okar, "The Decline of Jordanian Political Parties: Myth or Reality?" *International Journal of Middle East Studies* 33(4) (2001): 545–69.

86. Amawi, 1992, 26.

87. Brand, 1998, 101–2.

88. J. Schwedler, "Don't Blink: Jordan's Democratic Opening and Closing," *Middle East Report*, Press Information Note 98, July 3, 2002, www.merip.org/pins/pin98.html.

89. See Brand, 1998, for a discussion of the appointments of women to different branches of government and an analysis of all the political maneuverings between the regime and various political parties during the past few decades.

90. R.G. Khouri, "Beyond Gender and Genes: Election Lessons," *WIN Magazine*, May 1998, RDS Contemporary Women's Issues database.

91. Brand, 1998, chapter 6.
92. Ibid., 104.
93. The *Star* interviewed the lawyer Asma Khader, who specializes in women's legal issues.
94. This discussion of women's rights is based on the research of Brand, 1998.
95. Ibid.
96. This summary of the women's movement is based on the research of Brand, 1998.
97. See the detailed discussion of the role of Princess Basma in Brand, 1998, 158–64.
98. Ivy Papps, "The Role and Determinants of Bride Price: The Case of a Palestinian Village," *Current Anthropology* 24 (1989): 203.
99. The *Jordan Times*, www.jordantimes.com, the English-language daily newspaper, frequently has articles concerning women's issues. Rana Husseini, who went to school in Kansas and then returned to Jordan, began reporting on honor crimes and violence in 1994.
100. I.R. Prusher, "One Woman Tackles 'Honor' Crimes in Jordan," *Christian Science Monitor*, August 10, 2000, RDS Contemporary Women's Issues database.
101. Ibid.

RESOURCE GUIDE

Suggested Reading

Brand, L.A. *Women, the State, and Political Liberalization: Middle Eastern and North African Experiences*. New York: Columbia University Press, 1998. Description of recent periods of political liberalization in Jordan, Morocco, and Tunisia and the status of women's movements. The section on Jordan is an excellent, critical overview of the political situation as the context for the women's movement, primarily during the period 1989–1994. Brand's research is based on many interviews with women who have been key figures in the women's movement in Jordan.

Hazleton, E. "Jawazi al-Malakim: Settled Bedouin Woman of Jordan." In *Middle Eastern Muslim Women Speak*, ed. Elizabeth Warnock Fernea and Basima Qattan Bezirgan, 263–70. Austin: University of Texas Press. A brief profile of an elite Bedouin woman, the wife of a tribal sheikh, whose family left nomadic life to settle near Amman in 1968.

Husseini, R. "Jordan: Women and Politics." *Al-Raida* 18(92) (Winter 2001). RDS Contemporary Women's Issues database.

Miller, J. "Women and Family Honor: The Face of Feminine Identity in Jordan." In *Iris: A Journal about Women*, spring 2001. RDS Contemporary Women's Issues database. Miller is a Fullbright scholar who arrived in Jordan in August 2000. This article gives her thoughts and impressions on many aspects of women's lives in the country and includes interviews with Jordanian women.

Shami, S. "Domesticity Reconfigured: Women in Squatter Areas of Amman." In *Organizing Women: Formal and Informal Women's Groups in the Middle East*, ed. D. Chatty and A. Rabo, 81–99. Oxford and New York: Berg, 1997. Shami conducted field research in the squatter areas of Amman and describes the intricate family groupings and ways of life among the urban poor.

Shami, S., and L. Taminian. "Women's Participation in the Jordanian Labor Force: A Comparison of Rural and Urban Patterns." In *Women in Arab Society: Work Patterns and Gender Relations in Egypt, Jordan, and Sudan*, 1–86. Providence, RI, and Oxford: Berg and UNESCO, 1990. The authors include an extensive bibliography of studies published in the 1970s and 1980s on women in Jordan. The two case studies give a vivid portrayal of urban and rural life in Jordan.

Shryock, A., and S. Howell. "Ever a Guest in Our House: The Emir Abdullah, Shaykh Majid al-ʿAdwan, and the Practice of Jordanian House Politics, as Remembered by Umm Sultan, the Widow of Majid." *International Journal of Middle East Studies* 33(2) (2001): 247–69. A fascinating account of dinner at the home of an elite family in Jordan, where the men and women ate separately. Shryock and Howell both kept detailed notes of their respective dinner conversations, which they published in this article. This account gives insights into gender roles, politics, and the characteristics of the ruling elite in Jordan, including elite women from these families.

Videos/Films

The following videos are available from the Library Video Company, www.libraryvideo.com.

The 50 Years War: Israel and the Arabs. 1999. PBS Home Video.
Inside the Palace Gates. 2002. National Geographic.
Jordan. 1995. Video Visits the Middle East Series.
Jordan: Kingdom of the Desert. 1999. Geographical Odysseys Series.
Queen Noor: Between Two Realms. 1999. A & E Biography Series.

Web Sites

Alan Guttmacher Institute, www.alanguttmacher.org.
This institute has conducted research on family-planning-related issues in Jordan. The full text of articles related to reproductive issues in Jordan, listed in the Selected Bibliography and published in *International Family Planning Perspectives*, is available on the web site.

Department of Statistics Jordan, www.dos.gov.jo.
Statistics published by the Department of Statistics Jordan are rather sketchy. The Department of Statistics web site does not define its categories or give any explanatory notes.

Embassy of the Hashemite Kingdom of Jordan in Washington, DC, www.jordanembassyus.org.
This web site provides links to numerous web sites of interest, including those of the royal family, various government ministries, and local NGOs. The embassy web site has an extensive news archive, but no search function. It is possible to locate articles in the archive using an Internet search engine.

JordanDevNet, www.jordandevnet.org/.
This web site maintains a database of hundreds of development organizations in Jordan. Many of these organizations do not have their own web sites. The reader can obtain a list of organizations by sector, including dozens of women's organizations.

The organizations are not listed in alphabetical order. The site gives details about each organization.

Jordan Times, www.jordantimes.com.
This English-language daily newspaper frequently has articles concerning women's issues. Rana Husseini writes for this paper about honor killings. The web site archives only one week of issues. The Embassy of the Hashemite Kingdom of Jordan in Washington, DC, web site contains an extensive archive of articles from the *Jordan Times*, which may be accessed using an Internet search engine.

King Abdullah II website, www.kingabdullah.jo/.
This government of Jordan web site contains the text of several important documents, including the constitution and the National Charter.

The King Hussein web site, http://kinghussein.gov.jo/people1.html.
This government of Jordan web site, contains background information about the country and its people.

Noor Al Hussein Foundation, www.nhf.org.jo.
This web site provides information about the many programs the foundation sponsors to benefit women and to promote sustainable economic development.

Star, www.star.arabia.com.
This English-language Jordanian weekly frequently has articles concerning women's issues. The web site has an extensive archive of back issues, but does not have a search function. To retrieve a specific article, one must have the date of the issue.

United Nations Development Fund for Women, www.unifem.org.jo/.
The web site's search function will list programs in Jordan.

SELECTED BIBLIOGRAPHY

Alan Guttmacher Institute. "Fertility Levels among Jordanian Women Have Fallen Sharply, but Unwanted Childbearing Remains High." *International Family Planning Perspectives* 25(4) (1999): 203+. RDS Contemporary Women's Issues database.

Amawi, A. "Democracy Dilemmas in Jordan." *Middle East Report*, January/February 1992, 26–29.

"Anti-Cancer Campaign Strategies Developed." *Jordan Times*, September 12, 2002. www.jordantimes.com.

Arida, A.I. "The Disease of This Century—Depression." *Jordan Times*, September 10, 2002. www.jordantimes.com.

Asman, M. "Jordan Week." *Star* 12(97) (June 6–12, 2002). http://star.arabia.com.

Awadat, I. "Divorce Rights Granted to the Fairer Sex." *Star* 12(95) (May 23–29, 2002). http://star.arabia.com.

Awwad, R. *Jordan Times*, November 30, 1999. The Jordan Fertility and Family Health Survey from the web site of the U.S. Jordanian Embassy, www.jordanembassyus.org.

Brand, L.A. *Women, the State, and Political Liberalization: Middle Eastern and North African Experiences*. New York: Columbia University Press, 1998.

Cunningham, K.J. "Jordan's Information Revolution: Implications for Democracy." *Middle East Journal* 56 (spring 2002): 240–56.

Dabbaheh, S.M. "Jordanians with HIV: Anonymity Is Part of Daily Life." *Star* 12(102) (July 11–17, 2002). http://star.arabia.com.

Department of Statistics Jordan, DOS-NIS: Population and Housing, DOS-NIS: Population. *Statistical Year Book 2000*. www.dos.gov.jo/sdb_pop/pop_changes2000_e.htm.

Edut, T. "Rana Husseini." *Hues* 4(3) (summer 1998): 41. RDS Contemporary Women's Issues database.

Ghattas, K. "Gender—Jordan: 'Honor Killings' under Review." Interpress Service, December 8, 1999. RDS Contemporary Women's Issues database.

Hardee, K., K. Agarwal, N. Luke, E. Wilson, M. Pendzich, M. Farrell, and H. Cross. "Reproductive Health Policies and Programs in Eight Countries: Progress since Cairo: Part 1 of 2." *International Family Planning Perspectives* 25 (January 1999): S2+. RDS Contemporary Women's Issues database.

Harvard Medical School Joint Center for Sickle Cell and Thalassemic Disorders. http://sickle.bwh.harvard.edu/index.html.

Hazleton, E. "Jawazi al-Malakim: Settled Bedouin Woman of Jordan." In *Middle Eastern Muslim Women Speak*, ed. Elizabeth Warnock Fernea and Basima Qattan Bezirgan, 263–70. Austin: University of Texas Press, 1977.

Husseini, R. "Imprisonment to Protect Women against 'Crimes of Honor.'" *Al-Raida* 19(95/96) (fall 2001). RDS Contemporary Women's Issues database.

———. "Jordan: Women and Politics." *Al-Raida* 18(92) (winter 2001). RDS Contemporary Women's Issues database.

Institute for Women's Studies in the Arab World. "Islamic Family Law Tabulated." *Al-Raida* (93–94) (spring 2001). RDS Contemporary Women's Issues database.

International Monetary Fund. "IMF Concludes 2002 Article IV Consultation with Jordan." 2002. www.inf.org/external/np/sec/pn/2002/pn0251.htm.

Joha, G. "Back to School: What about the Remote Areas?" *Star* 12(109) (August 29–4, September 2002). http://star.arabia.com.

———. "Book in Review: The Wild Wonderful World of *Wasta*." *Star* 12(94) (May 16–22, 2002). http://star.arabia.com.

"Jordanian Women Gain Right to Divorce." *We!* May 2002. RDS Contemporary Women's Issues database.

Jordan Judicial Branch of Government. www.lawresearch.com.

Jordan National Information System, Human Resources, Labour, Statistics-Time Series. www.nic.gov.jo.

"Jordan: No Death Penalty Exemption for Honor Killings." *Off Our Backs* 32(3–2) (March 2002). RDS Contemporary Women's Issues database.

"Jordan's Democracy Is Still Half Way." *Star* 12(112) (September 19–25, 2002). http://star.arabia.com.

"Jordan: Women Held in Jail to Save Them from Their Families." *Off Our Backs* 31(10) (November 2001). RDS Contemporary Women's Issues database.

"Jordan: Women March against Violence against Women." *Off Our Backs* 29(1) (January 1999). RDS Contemporary Women's Issues database.

"Jordan: Women Protest Crimes of Honor." *Women Envision* 3 (March 1999). RDS Contemporary Women's Issues database.

Joseph S. "Gender and Citizenship in Middle Eastern States." *Middle East Report* 26(1) (January–March 1996): 4–10.

Khader, L. "Uncovering the Numbers: The AIDS Reality Examined in Amman." *Star* 12(94) (May 16–22, 2002). http://star.arabia.com.
———. "UNICEF Releases Parenting Report." *Star* 12(107) (August 15–21, 2002). http://star.arabia.com.
———. "Workshop Highlights AIDS Awareness Campaign." *Star* 12(106) (August 8–14, 2002). http://star.arabia.com.
Khouri, R.G. "Beyond Gender and Genes: Election Lessons." *WIN Magazine*, May 1998. RDS Contemporary Women's Issues database.
LeVine, M. "The Arab Human Development Report: A Critique." *Middle East Report*, Press Information Note 101, July 26, 2002. www.merip.org/pins/pin101.html.
Lust-Okar, E.M. "The Decline of Jordanian Political Parties: Myth or Reality?" *International Journal of Middle East Studies* 33(4) (2001): 545–69.
Miller, J. "Women and Family Honor: The Face of Feminine Identity in Jordan." *Isis: A Journal about Women*, spring 2001, 12+. RDS Contemporary Women's Issues database.
Minerva Center. "Royal Jordanian Women Work to Open Military to Women." *Minerva's Bulletin Board* 9(1) (spring 1996). RDS Contemporary Women's Issues database.
Mitani, M. "Smoking among Women Is Becoming 'Normal' in Jordan." *Star* 12(107) (August 15–21, 2002). http://star.arabia.com.
Naiman, R. "No Jubilee for the Middle East." *Middle East Report* 213 (winter 1999). www.merip.org/mer/mer213/213_naiman.html.
Nsour, A. "Illegal Abortions Remain Source of Official Concern." *Jordan Times*, September 13–14, 2002. www.jordantimes.com.
Papps, I. "Attitudes to Female Employment in Four Middle Eastern Countries." In *Women in the Middle East: Perceptions, Realities, and Struggles for Liberation*, ed. H. Afshar, 96–116. New York: St. Martin's Press, 1993.
Petro-Nustas, W. "Men's Knowledge of and Attitudes toward Birth Spacing and Contraceptive Use in Jordan: Part 1 of 2, the Jordanian Context." *International Family Planning Perspectives* 25(4) (1999): 181+. RDS Contemporary Women's Issues database.
Prusher, I.R. "One Woman Tackles 'Honor' Crimes in Jordan." *Christian Science Monitor*, August 10, 2000. RDS Contemporary Women's Issues database.
Sawalha, F., and A.S. Hamzeh. "Human Rights Gets Mixed Review." *Jordan Times*, December 20, 2001. Middle East News Online, www.middleeastwire.com. This news service ceased operations on August 23, 2002. The *Jordan Times* archives only the past week on its web site. One can still access its archives.
Schwedler, J. "Don't Blink: Jordan's Democratic Opening and Closing." *Middle East Report*, Press Information Note 98, July 3, 2002. www.merip.org/pins/pin98.html.
Shami, S. "Domesticity Reconfigured: Women in Squatter Areas of Amman." In *Organizing Women: Formal and Informal Women's Groups in the Middle East*, ed. D. Chatty and A. Rabo, 81–99. Oxford and New York: Berg, 1997.
Shami, S., and L. Taminian. "Women's Participation in the Jordanian Labour Force: A Comparison of Rural and Urban Patterns." In *Women in Arab Society: Work Patterns and Gender Relations in Egypt, Jordan, and Sudan*, 1–86. Providence, RI and Oxford: Berg and UNESCO, 1990.
Shryock, A., and S. Howell. "Ever a Guest in Our House: The Emir Abdullah, Shaykh Majid al-ʿAdwan, and the Practice of Jordanian House Politics, as Remembered

by Umm Sultan, the Widow of Majid." *International Journal of Middle East Studies* 33(2) (2001): 247–69.

Underwood, C. "Islamic Precepts and Family Planning: The Perceptions of Jordanian Religious Leaders and Their Constituents." *International Family Planning Perspectives* 26(3) (September 2000). RDS Contemporary Women's Issues database.

UNESCO Institute for Statistics. www.uis.unesco.org.

United Nations Development Program. *Jordan Human Development Report 2000*. 2001. www.jordan.undp-jordan.org/soundbites/soundbites.html.

U.S. Agency for International Development. *USAID Assistance to Jordan*. 1999. www.usaid.gov/press/releases/fs991112.html. Additional information about aid to Jordan may be found using the web site search function.

U.S. Department of State, Bureau of Near Eastern Affairs. *Background Note: Jordan*. January 2002. www.state.gov/r/pa/ei/bgn/3464.htm.

U.S. Government. *Country Reports on Human Rights Practices—2000—Jordan*. 2001. RDS Contemporary Women's Issues database.

U.S. Social Security Administration. *Social Security Programs throughout the World*. 1999. www.ssa.gov. www.genderstats.worldbank.org/CPIA provides a link to this publication.

Wakeel, D.A. "Family Resources Seen as Central to Preservation of Resources." *Jordan Times*, September 10, 2002. www.jordantimes.com.

"Women's Shelter Remains Focus of Protection Project." *Jordan Times*, September 19, 2002. www.jordantimes.com.

"Working against 'Honor Killings.'" *Off Our Backs* 31(1) (January 2001). RDS Contemporary Women's Issues database.

World Bank. GenderStats database. www.genderstats.worldbank.org.

———. *The Hashemite Kingdom of Jordan Country Assistance Strategy*. 2001. http://Inweb18.worldbank.org/mna/mena.nsf/all/D4D46C2B71E7CA6C8525694D0056435D?OpenDocument.

World Health Organization. www.who.int/reproductive-health/publications.

8

LEBANON

Sima Aprahamian and Julie M. Koivunen

PROFILE OF LEBANON

Lebanon is a small country of 10,452 square kilometers (4,036 square miles). The Lebanese Republic is divided into six regional governments: Beirut, North Lebanon, Mount Lebanon, South Lebanon, the Bekaa Valley, and Nabatiyeh. The country has a diverse geography. The fertile mountains and plains are legendary, and its natural resources include limestone, iron ore, salt, water, and fertile land. Lebanon is bordered on the west by the Mediterranean Sea, on the south by Israel, and on the north and east by Syria.

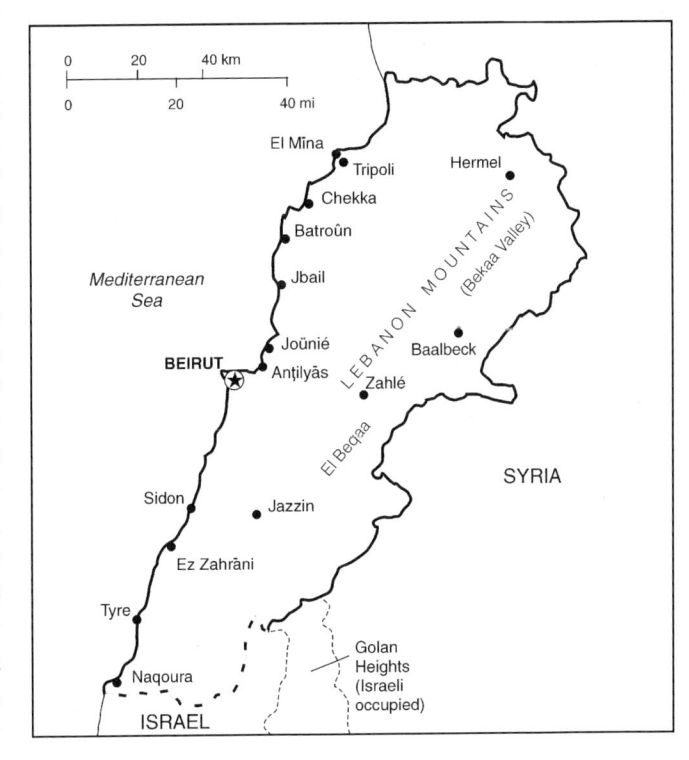

"Lebanon's database ranks among the world's poorest, be it in terms of main economic indicators, socio-economic data, or most specifically, demographic variables. In fact, since 1932 no comprehensive demographic census has taken place."[1] Its population is estimated to be between 3.6 million and 4.3 million. The population growth rate is estimated to be 1.38 percent, and the majority of the population is concentrated in the capital of Beirut, which is also its main port. Approximately 10 percent of the population are Palestinian refugees, most of whom have been denied Lebanese citizenship. There are also many ethnic minorities, including Armenians and Kurds. Muslims are estimated to comprise 70 percent of the population (including Shi'ite, Sunni, Druze, Ismailite, Alawite, or Nusayri), and Christians (including Orthodox Christian, Catholic, and Protestant) represent 30 percent. In the recent past, there has been an influx of workers from various countries such as Sri Lanka, the Philippines, and Syria. Arabic is the official language of Lebanon, but French and English are widely spoken as well.

The history of Lebanon has been marked by major influences and occupations including Roman, Greek, Byzantine, Arab, Ottoman, and European. The modern history of Lebanon has been marked by several phases. The first phase, which began in the mid-nineteenth century and continued until 1913, ended with the confessional unity of the bourgeoisie. The next phase, from 1920 to 1943, was the era of the French Mandate, and the end of this period was marked by the reconstitution of the bourgeoisie to form the National Pact. In addition, this second phase corresponded to the post-Ottoman Turkish and French mandate rule and was influenced by a gradual nationalist trend that led to the independence of Lebanon in 1943. The French authorities formed the Lebanese Republic on an institutionalized confessionalism that was inherited from the Turkish Ottoman domination, and consequently, the economy was affected by a decline in agriculture, weak industrialization in the cities and countryside, and an overreliance on the service sector. In the years after independence from 1943 to 1958, there was a gradual break in the unity of the financial-commercial bourgeoisie, as well as a period of political gain for women, as universal suffrage was eventually adopted in 1951.

Lebanese women began to organize during the nineteenth-century renaissance (*'asr el nahdat*) of the Arab world. The issues raised then were marked by European trends, as well as specific influence from the French, in terms of a focus on equality and a goal of the unity of all Arab women. During the second phase, the constitution of the newly formed state guaranteed the rights of women and those of all citizens. The constitution also formed a multireligious, multiethnic legislative and judiciary system within which each religious community had internal autonomy with respect to the regulation of educational, social, and judicial concerns. This system eventually led to a crisis that erupted into war in 1975. "The Lebanese did not go to war to change their political system; they joined a war fought on their land by the Arab states, Israel, and the superpowers to defend certain policies and ideologies. The war in Lebanon has been described as communal war between Christians and Muslims, a continuation of the 1845, 1860, and 1958 clashes, a class war between the rich and poor, a struggle for identity of Lebanon, whether Mediterranean or Arab."[2]

The war impacted the Lebanese people tremendously, and many became migrants and refugees in their own country. It is estimated that 700,000 people fled from their homes, and many have still not returned, even after many years. Approximately 25 percent of the population in Lebanon at the time emigrated during the war to safer areas of Lebanon and to other countries as well. By the end of the war, many people were still displaced from their communities, and 52.6 percent of their homes had been destroyed during the ravages of war. By 1986 alone, the devastation and cumulative losses were estimated to be $11.6 billion. In 1974, the minimum wage was about 70 percent of the average per capita income; in 1986, that fell to only 20 percent. The middle class in Lebanon suffered the most from these poor economic times and consequently has virtually disappeared.[3]

The war was a pivotal point in the history of Lebanon and dramatically affected all facets of society. Many women's organizations were impacted, and while most had been geared toward helping the impoverished people in the country, during the war they began to provide other assistance as well. Women worked to uphold the structures of Lebanese society. Many women volunteered in national and international social welfare organizations and worked to open schools that had closed during the war. Many women also entered the labor market to provide additional financial assistance to their families.[4]

Growth rates of the Lebanese population since the war have been between 2.4 and 5.3 percent, with the variation being due to fluctuations in fertility, migration, and life expectancy. The life expectancy for females, which is greater than that of males, increased from 58 years in 1970 to 70 years in 1990. Currently, the life expectancy for men is 69 years of age, and for women it is 74 years of age. Other population statistics include the following: the birth rate is estimated to be 20.16 births per 1,000 people, and the death rate is approximately 6.39 deaths per 1,000 people. The infant mortality rate is approximately 28.35 deaths per 1,000 live births, and the fertility rate is 2.05 children per woman.[5]

OVERVIEW OF WOMEN'S ISSUES

Current women's issues in Lebanon are intricately linked to the socioeconomic experiences of its diverse communities. Many of the issues facing women in Lebanon are rooted in the historical experiences of the Lebanese people and stem from a system inherited from the period of Ottoman Turkish domination.

The emerging debates center around issues of the inclusion of women in the political and economic spheres as well as creating changes in personal status and family laws. Other issues of concern include pay equity, additional visibility in public politics, creating an awareness of women's health issues, and domestic violence against women. In addition, while Lebanese women have made progress in some areas of society, including the fields of writing and literature, women have struggled to permeate societal boundaries in other disciplines. For example, women are not well represented in Parliament, and the Lebanese Women's Council indicates that

Palestine women talk while at the Bourj al Baragent Camp in Beirut. Photo © TRIP/H. Rogers.

while women have made notable achievements over the past century, additional progress is needed.[6]

The post-1975 phase of the Lebanese women's movement was characterized by the attempt to encourage the First Lady to lead a unified movement. A recent publication, *Women of Lebanon: Interviews with Champions for Peace* by Nelda LaTeef, attempts to give a voice to this movement by presenting interviews with influential Lebanese women, including former First Lady Mona Haraoui, member of Parliament Bahia Hariri, and other women working in the fields of government, social work, and literature and the arts. Mona Haraoui is the wife of the tenth president of the Republic of Lebanon, Elias Haraoui, who took office in 1989, upon the assassination of President René Moawad. First Lady Haraoui has been a model for other Lebanese women in that, "working alongside her husband, she does volunteer work and fundraising to support countless charities that assist children, the elderly, and the handicapped."[7] Bahia Hariri is a member of Parliament representing Sidon and the south of Lebanon. She also is the chairwoman of the Parliamentary Committee on Education and had worked as a teacher and administrator prior to her years in the Parliament. She states, "I believe the education of our children is one of the most vital tasks of national recovery and development. I felt I could do more for the Lebanese educational system being on the inside of government rather than on the outside."[8]

In addition, the text documents various perspectives held by Lebanese women, including their strong commitments against "national ideological projects" that, in the past, have led to devastation such as that during the Lebanese civil war. One writer, Emily Nasrallah, adopted the notion of "humanist nationalism" and sought to promote national solidarity, peace, and nonviolence in an attempt to stop the war.

During the time of war, other Lebanese women also wrote various novels from "their own particular perspectives," which contributed to the postwar healing process as well as to the history of Arabic literature.[9] According to one observer, the editor of *Al-Raida*, a leading women's periodical, during the 1975–1990 war, "Lebanese women's voices became more prominent than they had ever been before."[10] However, after the war, women's voices were heard less frequently, and "with the exception of the discussion of the recent Beijing conference, women's voices have been relatively quiet in post-war Lebanon. Following the resurrection of the state government, and the reconstitution of a central authority in Lebanon, the voices most heard in public are those emanating from the center, and these voices invariably belong to men. In spite of their crucial war-time contributions to the survival of the basic unit of Lebanese society, the Lebanese society, women are still at the margins."[11]

EDUCATION

In Lebanon, young women have been provided formal education since 1835, when the first school for girls was established. In the 1930s, women began to be accepted to study at universities, concentrating in education, arts, social sciences, and health sciences such as nursing and public health. Historically, women's choices of educational study have been constrained by local cultural beliefs and practices.

Opportunities

Lebanon has both a public and a private system of education. However, access to higher education is contingent upon one's geographical location, among other factors. Universities in Lebanon are concentrated in and around Beirut, thus limiting the general population's access to university-level educational opportunities. In addition, historical factors in Lebanon continue to affect various cultural and societal values and norms. Being a Middle Eastern country and a former territory of the Ottoman Empire, Lebanon is influenced by Middle Eastern culture and customs. However, having also been a French colony and a country frequented by Western missionaries, Lebanon has been impacted by Western culture as well. Because of these various historical influences, "Lebanese women have been influenced by this mixed cultural and behavioral milieu. Whereas school programmes and especially university curricula are based on Western models which presuppose equality between men and women, women nevertheless have to interact within a male dominated society."[12] Thus educational attainment for women is affected not only by the structure and function of the educational entities that exist in the country, but by the beliefs and expectations that are held by society of the importance of education for women.

Another important consideration is that "although Lebanese women have had opportunities and access to all levels of formal education, the informal aspect of their education is so strong it manipulates their gains and situates them at a lesser standing than men. Despite the many differences between Lebanese women of the late twentieth century and those of the early nineteenth century, both share similar conditioning as to what their fundamental duty is to society: to be a wife and mother."[13]

Literacy

In 1997, the literacy rate (defined as those fifteen years of age and older who can read and write) was 86.4 percent for the total population, 90.8 percent for the male population, and 82.2 percent for the female population.

EMPLOYMENT AND ECONOMICS

The Lebanese economy is based on free-market capitalist production and distribution. Economic growth in Lebanon has continued despite the civil war; growth rates in the economy have risen sharply since the end of the war in 1992 and peaked at 8 percent in 1994.

Job/Career Opportunities

"The participation of highly educated (college educated) women in the labour force increased between 1970 and 1990; nearly doubling in both absolute and relative terms between 1970 and 1980, and tripling between 1975 and 1990."[14] College-educated women are often employed in the fields of medicine, nursing, teaching, midwifery, social work, and other types of civil assistance. Another sector that has seen an increase in the number of women employed is wholesale and retail trade, as well as hotel and restaurant service. However, the participation of highly educated women in the field of manufacturing and the areas of finance, insurance, business, and real estate, while increasing since 1975, has been slight compared to the other sectors of the economy. This reflects the Lebanese society's tolerance of women advancing in only certain fields that have been deemed "acceptable" for women and consequently reveals a gender gap in career opportunities for women. To summarize, "in 1990, 50 percent of highly educated economically active females worked in community, social, and personal services, compared to 1 percent in the agricultural sector."[15] This is an

Young woman works on her computer at a store in Beirut. Photo © TRIP/H. Rogers.

indication that specific employment sectors have a disproportionate number of highly educated, economically active population.

Currently, discourse regarding the issues of women's employment is continuing in Lebanon. Public discussions are bringing increased attention to the issue of the gender gap in the various employment sectors in the Lebanese economy. However, there is also a realization that although changes are being made in Lebanon, this may not be the case for the other areas of the Arab world.[16]

Pay

Lebanese women still are paid less than men and have less access to more prestigious, secure positions that pay more. In women-dominated professions, such as teaching, men still hold the top, supervisory positions. Unequal pay has been an issue for Lebanese women and gained attention as early as 1943. In that year, a committee advocating equal rights for women met with the prime minister and the president of the republic and petitioned for assistance in regard to the working conditions of Lebanese women. They advocated for shorter working hours for women and salaries and conditions that were comparable to those of men's. During that time, women also participated in various marches and demonstrations, seeking equal opportunities in pay and better working conditions.

Working Conditions

During the 1990s, Lebanon experienced a growing inclusion of women in the employment sectors. According to the United Nations Department Program (UNDP) Human Development Report of 1993, women constitute approximately 27 percent of the labor force in Lebanon. Various Lebanese women's organizations and unions have been calling for an increase in the opportunities for women's participation in wage work, as well as an improvement in work environments. In December 1994, the Lebanese Women's Council established the Working Women's League as an advocacy group for working women's rights, which has been dedicated to ending the "discriminatory laws related to pension, retirement age, indemnity, maternity protection, child care facilities, and sexual harassment."[17]

A recent study on work values among Lebanese workers used a sample of sixty-one men and forty-two women from Beirut who worked in corporations, including financial institutions, auditing firms, and information systems companies. Their findings indicate that religiosity may be a significant factor for job satisfaction among Lebanese workers, in that organizational policies that were counter to the worker's religious values were found to have an overall adverse effect on the worker's job satisfaction. The researchers argue that their results support those of earlier findings that suggest the importance of religiosity in the culture at large and its subsequent effects on the daily lives of those in the society.[18]

Support for Mothers/Caretakers

Maternal Leave

The "Social Security Law gives an expectant mother the right to medical cover before, during, and after delivery. The medical service includes care and tests, necessary medications, hospital stay, and surgical operations. The law even compensates a woman for any temporary disability resulting from maternity."[19] Further, women are entitled to ten weeks of partially or fully paid maternity leave, which protects her job and allows her to remain at home for a time to care for her new infant. Additional laws pertaining to employment support women at the time of retirement. Upon reaching the age of fifty-five (compared to age sixty for men), women are eligible for their "end-of-service indemnity."[20]

Inheritance and Property Rights

In 1954, a committee was formed to campaign for the right of equality in compensation for women as compared with men, which was eventually granted in 1955. In 1956, the committee that had campaigned for equal pay for women sought equality for women in inheritance. On February 24, 1959, a law was passed granting non-Muslim Lebanese equality in inheritance. However, one observer in 1989 noted that still in Lebanese society, "marriage, divorce, separation, custody of children, inheritance, and the like are all resolved according to one's confession."[21]

FAMILY AND SEXUALITY

Gender Roles

The family is a crucial aspect of Lebanese society and an important site of specific, gendered activity. In terms of gender roles in the family, women are "socialized in a system that legally places them in a childlike incompetent category; an economic system that views them with much distrust as permanent temporaries with very few rights and benefits; and a social system that is often hostile and violent to them unless they are sexually passive, subservient, and available to men and men's wishes."[22] Although there are variations in family types and practices, young women are expected to respect their elders, particularly fathers, brothers, grandparents, and other male relatives, while young men are taught to assume responsibility for women in the family.[23] A 1999 study of Lebanese culture notes that "although there has been a tremendous increase of women attending universities, participating in the labor force and the political sphere, there is little change in the way society views women as 'wives and mothers.' "[24] Additionally, the researcher contends that in studying Lebanese society, one must not underestimate the significant role of religious authorities in reinforcing the "strict division of labor and gender roles between the sexes."[25]

In addition to appropriate gender roles, sexual identity is also developed early in the child's life. Female sexuality is viewed as being nonautonomous, and fathers and brothers have significant influence on the development of their daughters' or sisters' sexuality and bodily self-esteem. The importance of chastity among women is paramount, and the honor of the family is closely related to female virginity.

Additional research on the family indicates that "most of the research on family life in the Arab world, stressing the cultural ideals of patriarchy, patrilineality, patrilocality, and patrilineal endogamy, has focused on relationships among males. . . . scholars have paid less attention to brother/sister or other key male/female relationships."[26] While much of the research on the family focuses on the husband/wife relationship, other gender issues relevant to socialization practices are present in other relationships in the family, most notably in the brother/sister relationship. One researcher who studied brother and sister relationships in Lebanon noted that fathers and brothers are considered responsible for the protection and overall well-being of their daughters and sisters. Women are expected to uphold the honor of the family, and should a woman bring shame to her family, the closest male relative is responsible for disciplining her, thereby restoring honor to the family. As this mentality is replicated in the brother/sister relationship, men in the culture learn that to love or care for a woman is connected to controlling her, and women learn that to love or care for a man is to submit to him. Thus children learn that love and power are intricately connected. The researcher found that brother/sister relationships serve as a means of socializing children and youth into specific gender roles.[27] This analysis suggests that "the brother/sister relationship was a connective relationship built on the duality of love and power expressed psychodynamically, social structurally, and culturally. It was second only to the mother/son relationship in evoking love."[28]

Marriage

Because Lebanese culture strongly values personal connectivity, women's roles as mother and wife are foremost. A recent study of women in Lebanon found that 25 percent of women indicated that being married fulfilled all of their life's ambitions, and more than 60 percent stated that being married partially fulfilled their life's expectations. In addition, 40 percent of unmarried women said that working was a means of meeting potential husbands, and 53 percent of the married women said that they would stop working if their husbands asked them to do so.[29]

Marriage is considered to be extremely important in Lebanon as well as in other Arabic countries. It has been noted that "under Islam, women's roles in the family have been given a higher value than their roles outside the family. In addition to the role of religion in reinforcing the centrality of marriage and the family in women's lives, it has been argued that the economic pressures and the unavailability of governmental assistance coupled with the societal expectation that unwed women must remain in their parent's home, all lead to a situation in which single women are seen as financial burdens on their families."[30] This leads to increased pressure for women to marry, even at a young age. Other studies have revealed that marriage serves as economic security for women, is the only acceptable way to express sexuality, and also serves as a protection against sexual transgressions by other men.

Career women in Lebanon often must sacrifice professional aspirations for the husband and family. However, increasing attention is being given to creating changes in personal status and family laws that would benefit women. In the existing law, marriage remains under religious domination, and women are not given the opportunity to have a civil marriage.

A recent study on marriage in Lebanon found that in Lebanon, as in other Arabic countries, female sexual activity is restricted to marriage. "In Lebanon, extramarital sex (zina) is punishable by civil and religious laws, carries a prison sentence, and is considered haram, an impermissible act against God. In contrast, sex within marriage is revered, and a wife's disobedience and refusal to 'surrender herself' to her husband's rights under marriage is grounds for divorce."[31] Sex in marriage is encouraged and revered; however, premarital sex for women in Lebanon is considered to be a "crime of honor" to the family, and a woman is then considered to be unmarriageable.

In addition, a woman's virginity is not something that she herself is entitled to; rather, it is a family issue in that her virginity is meaningful and important to the men in her family. A sister or daughter who loses her virginity prior to marriage can have negative ramifications for the family in that losing the family honor may jeopardize their relationships with other families in the area, which may then affect social and economic interactions with others. Women face violence and murder by male relatives for sexual transgressions: Article 562 of the Lebanese Penal Code indicates a lighter sentence for men who kill family members without premeditation, and who are attempting to defend their family's honor—whereas the Article suggests higher sentences for murders not fitting this description. "Resistance to removing this article has been attributed to the fear that women will gain sexual freedom if they know that their extra-marital sexual acts will no longer be punished with a legally sanctioned consequence as grave as murder."[32]

In addition, divorced and separated women in Lebanon are relegated to scorn and disdain. They are considered to be "used" or "damaged goods" because they are no longer virgins and therefore are devalued. Divorced/separated women are seen as being more open to sexual advances and harassment. If such a woman is raped, the attitude is that she asked for it.

Contraception and Abortion

Several discriminatory laws have been repealed, including the penal law against contraception, which was repealed in 1983. Increased attention is being given to women's health-care issues such as birth control and other forms of contraception.

HEALTH

Health Care Access

Lebanese women's organizations, often in collaboration with organizations such as UNICEF, have worked to disseminate information on health education, preventive care, child-care issues, and prenatal and postnatal health care for women. In addition, women have also been active in introducing proposed reforms to various aspects of health-care issues in postwar Lebanon that would allow women greater access to health care.

Mental Health

While women have enjoyed an increased role in employment and educational opportunities, there are many "psychological, social, and physical stresses, brought on by the dual roles of women."[33] The effects of working in the public sphere and the responsibilities of women in the private sphere may result in additional stress, which may adversely impact some women's mental and physical health. In addition, scholars have researched the psychological impact of war, posttraumatic stress disorder, substance abuse, and the incidence of depression and anxiety, and the resulting negative outcomes for women and their children in Lebanon.

It has been shown "that the incidence of post-traumatic stress disorder, varied psychological illnesses, and substance use and abuse have significantly increased during the war years. Women tended to succumb to psychiatric illnesses more than men, probably because of the higher number of stressor elements they were exposed to."[34] Thus the war in Lebanon has had a significant impact on health issues for women in terms of their psychological and physical health.

AIDS

The prevalence of HIV and AIDS among the adult population in Lebanon is approximately .09 percent.

POLITICS AND LAW

Lebanon is a democratic republic and has been an independent country since 1943. It has a parliamentary system of government and a cabinet headed by the prime minister. The Lebanese constitution is based on the separation of executive, legislative and judicial powers, with a president elected for a six-year term, and the 128 members of parliament are elected for a four-year term.

"Until 1975, Lebanon was the only stable and developed democratic system in the Arab world. It held regular elections in an arena of diverse political parties and open competition, changed governments peacefully, and elected its president according to the specifications of the 1926 Constitution."[35] After the war, the country's economy and infrastructure were severely damaged. Adversely impacted by the war, "displaced mothers or homemakers struggled to bridge the gap between work in the home and in the marketplace, between life in the private sphere of the family and the public sphere of economics and politics."[36]

Political Participation

"Traditionally Lebanese women have had few actual practiced legal rights; nonetheless, they have accomplished much and are found in every sector of public and private life. Although these women have had many opportunities and have had access to education, they have had no voice in the political and economic system."[37] Currently, Lebanese women have been working among individual religious communities as well as at state and grassroots levels to introduce legal reforms in the areas of family and personal status laws. They are also seeking to end discriminatory legislation in the governing of business transactions. The Lebanese Women's Council has recognized three areas in which reforms are needed: violence against women, sexual harassment in the workplace, and the existing laws that discriminate against women. The council notes that while women have achieved much over the last century, since 1953, only four women have been elected to serve in Parliament. The same minimal participation is evident at the municipal level, where only 3 out of 300 municipal councils are headed by women. The Lebanese Women's Council argues that women need to be represented in the political arena, and that effective legal reform would address the social, political, and economic aspects of these and other issues.

Women's Rights

Feminist Movements

Since the 1940s, Lebanese women have been agitating for equal rights from the government, participating in marches and demonstrations for shorter working days and salaries and working conditions that were on par with those of men. In 1945, the first woman worker, Saada Nassif, joined a labor union. The Lebanese Council of Women dates from the 1950s. A new committee succeeded in winning important rights for women such as equality in inheritance. Women's activism then declined, but in 1960, women won the right to choose their nationality if they married a foreigner, and they were granted the right to travel in 1974.

No feminist movement exists in Lebanon to this day. The Lebanese Council of Women represents approximately 130 organizations from various religions, regions, and ideologies, but in the eyes of some it has "failed to carry the banner of women in their struggle for freedom, equality, and the right to be heard in matters of national concern. Thus once they won the right to vote in parity with men, they were lulled into complacency and turned their attention to 'feminine' and social affairs. In short, the Lebanese Council of Women has failed to act as a pressure group for the advancement and development of women."[38]

RELIGION AND SPIRITUALITY

Throughout different historical epochs, Lebanon has been considered to be a refuge for religious minorities fleeing persecution. It is now a multireligious, multidenominational society. There are eighteen officially recognized religious groups in Lebanon. The Shi'ite and Sunni Muslims are believed to constitute the largest religious groups, while the Maronite and Greek Orthodox Christians were the majority at the time of the last official census, which was held in 1932. These four groups, along with the Druze (an offshoot of Islam), are the largest religious groups in the country.

Religion and politics are intertwined in Lebanon, and religion is part of one's ethnic identity. All Lebanese must follow a religious confession. Atheism is not considered a choice and is not recognized. While the Lebanese republic does not have a state religion, the political system is still based on the old Ottoman "millet" system, in which each religious community has internal autonomy with respect to the regulation of educational, social, and judicial concerns.

Women's Roles

Women represent diverse roles in their respective religious communities and organizations. In some sects, women are allowed to be religious specialists.

VIOLENCE

The legitimate and illegitimate use of violence in Lebanon is male dominated. Further, one year of military service is required for all Lebanese males. The Lebanese armed forces consist of 67,900 troops, including 27,400 conscripts. There are also 13,000 paramilitary troops that constitute the Internal Security Force, commanded by the Interior Ministry. In addition to the armed forces, there are militia forces, including the Shi'ite Muslim Hizbollah (party of God), which is supported by Iran and Syria and has about 3,000 active members. Its rival, the Amal movement, also has a core of fighters. In addition, there is a presence of foreign armed forces. The United Nations Interim Forces in Lebanon (UNIFIL) has 5,602 troops who are stationed in the south and an estimated 35,000-member Syrian force as well.

Domestic Violence

Violence against women in Lebanon is not well documented. *Al-Raida* has published articles discussing issues of violence in the family and violence against women. In recent years, women's organizations have been creating a forum for discussing the issue of domestic violence and its effects on women. Increasingly, discourse is also focusing on gendered socialization practices, notions of masculinity and femininity, and the differential treatment of male and female children.

Rape/Sexual Assault

Rape in Lebanon has been documented by journalists, and activists have been calling for empirical investigations about this and other forms of violence against women. One such study included in-depth interviews with activists, community figures, and other women in Beirut and sought to determine the links between social interaction, marriage, and marriageability and sexual assault and rape in present-day Lebanon. The author stated that "an understanding of rape within Arabic contexts needs to be undertaken conjointly with an understanding of the importance placed on virginity, marriage, and the distinction between pre-marital and marital sex."[39]

The value that is placed on a woman's virginity and its relevance to marriage are important in considering perceptions of consensual sex or rape in Lebanese society. "If consent is perceived to be tied to fear of the consequences, and specifically to becoming unmarriageable, then the corollary to this equation is that women who are conceived of as already unmarriageable are seen as having 'nothing to lose' and hence believed to be consenting to sex."[40] When a disabled or divorced woman is raped and described it as such, people may be skeptical that it in fact was a rape.

Research indicates that others may actually believe that the woman agreed to consensual sex because she does not have an opportunity to gain sexual pleasure elsewhere. Having minimal chances of getting married, disabled and divorced women are often seen as having nothing to lose by consenting to sex outside of marriage and are considered to be wanting male attention, companionship, and intimacy. In Article 512 of the Lebanese Penal Code, a sentence for a man who has raped a virgin is higher than that for a rape where the victim is not a virgin.

In addition, married women are thought to be protected from sexual assault by their husbands and by other men. Implicit in this assumption is that rape does not occur in the context of marriage, and official state law states that marital rape does not exist.[41] Women's organizations in Lebanon are working to change public perceptions of rape and sexual assault in their society.

OUTLOOK FOR THE TWENTY-FIRST CENTURY

Lebanese women have been increasingly involved in the political, social, literary, and economic domains since the late nineteenth century. As early as 1928, the Council of Lebanese Women was formed to coordinate the activities of the nearly 100 women's organizations that were present at the time. In the 1990s, more Lebanese women began voicing concern and becoming active in the global women's movement(s), advocating the elimination of all forms of discrimination against women. At the local level, women are active in the struggle to overturn discriminatory legislation, to allow women to conduct business transactions without male endorsement, and to improve government services in the health and educational sectors, as well as to take part in the debates on national security and the economic stability of Lebanon.

NOTES

1. Samih Boustani and Nada Mufarrej, "Female Higher Education and Participation in the Labor Force in Lebanon," in *Gender and Development in the Arab World: Women's Economic Participation: Patterns and Policies*, ed. Nabil F. Khoury and Valentine M. Moghadam (London: Zed Books, 1995), 98.

2. Lamia Rustum Shihadeh, ed., *Women and War in Lebanon* (Gainesville: University Press of Florida, 1999), 11.

3. Ibid.

4. Ibid.

5. Boustani and Mufarrej, 1995.

6. Jean Said Makdisi, "The Mythology of Modernity: Women and Democracy in Lebanon," in *Feminism and Islam: Legal and Literary Perspectives*, ed. Mai Yamani (Berkshire: Ithaca Press, 1996), 231.

7. Nelda LaTeef, *Women of Lebanon: Interviews with Champions for Peace* (Jefferson, NC: McFarland and Company, 1997), 165.

8. Ibid., 172.
9. Lauri King Irani, "Recovering Women's Voices in Post-war Lebanon," *Al-Raida* 12(70–71) (1995): 12.
10. Ibid.
11. Irani, 1995, 12–13.
12. Boustani and Mufarrej, 1995, 99.
13. Mirna Lattouf, "The History of Women's Higher Education in Modern Lebanon and Its Social Implications" (Ph.D. diss., University of Arizona, 1999), 21.
14. Boustani and Mufarrej, 1995, 107.
15. Ibid., 110.
16. May Farah, "Globalization Finds a Place for Women: UN Report Finds That Far-Reaching Changes Are Slowly Leveling the Playing Field," (Beirut) *Daily Star*, November 11, 1999.
17. Myriam Sfeir, "Iqbal Doughan: President of the Working Women League in Lebanon," *Al-Raida* 15(82) (1918): 44.
18. Yusuf Munir Sidani and William Gardner, "Work Values among Lebanese Workers," *Journal of Social Psychology* 140(2000): 597–607.
19. Boustani and Mufarrej, 1995, 102.
20. Ibid.
21. Erelyne Accad, "Feminist Perspectives on the War in Lebanon," *Women's Studies International Forum* 12 (1989): 92.
22. Lattouf, 1999, 18.
23. Suad Joseph, "Gender and Family in the Arab World," in *Arab Women: Between Defiance and Restraint*, ed. Suha Sabbagh (New York: Olive Branch Press, 1996), 194–202.
24. Lattouf, 1999, 13.
25. Ibid.
26. Suad Joseph, "Brother/Sister Relationships: Connectivity, Love, and Power in the Reproduction of Patriarchy in Lebanon," *American Ethnologist* 21 (1994): 52.
27. Ibid., 66.
28. Ibid.
29. Kabbanji and Attat, 1997.
30. Webhi, 2002, 291.
31. Ibid, 297.
32. Ibid, 292.
33. Shehadeh, 1999, 67.
34. Ibid., 330.
35. Ibid., 8.
36. Ibid., 49.
37. Lattouf, 1999, 22.
38. Shehadeh, 1999, 35.
39. Wehbi, 2002, 297.
40. Ibid., 294.
41. Ibid.

RESOURCE GUIDE

Suggested Reading

Boustani, Samih, and Nada Mufarrej. "Female Higher Education and Participation in the Labor Force in Lebanon." In *Gender and Development in the Arab World:*

Women's Economic Participation, Patterns and Policies, ed. Nabil F. Khoury and Valentine M. Moghadam, 97–124. London: Zed Books, 1995.
Irani, Lauri King. "Recovering Women's Voices in Post-war Lebanon." *Al-Raida* 12(70–71) (1995): 12–13.
Joseph, Suad. "Gender and Family in the Arab World." In *Arab Women: Between Defiance and Restraint*, ed. Suha Sabbagh, 194–202. New York: Olive Branch Press, 1991.
———. *Intimate Selfing in Arab Families: Gender, Self, and Identity*. Syracuse, NY: Syracuse University Press, 1999.
LaTeef, Nelda. *Women of Lebanon: Interviews with Champions for Peace*. Jefferson, NC: McFarland and Company, 1997.
Shehadeh, Lamia Rustum. *Women and War in Lebanon*. Gainesville: University Press of Florida, 1999.
Wehbi, Samantha. "'Women with Nothing to Lose': Marriageability and Women's Perceptions of Rape and Consent in Contemporary Beirut." *Women's Studies International Forum* 25 (2002): 287–300.

Videos/Films

Feature Films

The Broken Wings. 1962. Yousef Malouf, director. 90 minutes.
In the Shadows of the City. 2000. Jean Chamoun, director. 102 minutes.
Once upon a Time: Beirut. 1994. Jocelyne Saab, director. 101 minutes.
A Suspended Life. 1984. Jocelyne Saab, director. 90 minutes.
Tango of Yearning. 1998. Mohammed Soueid, director. 70 minutes.
Time Has Come. 1994. Jean-Claude Codsi, director. 85 minutes.
The Tornado. 1992. Samir Habchi, director. 90 minutes.
West Beirut. 1998. Zaid Doueiri, director. 105 minutes.

Documentaries

All Is Well on the Border Front. 1997. Akram Zaatari, director. 43 minutes.
Children of Shatila. 1998. Mai Masri, director. 50 minutes.
Crazy of You. 1997. Akram Zaatari, director. 26 minutes.
Hostage of Time. 1994. Jean Khalil Chamoun, director. 50 minutes.
Lebanon: Imprisoned Splendour. 1996. Daizy Gedeon, director. 61 minutes.
Nightfall. 2000. Mohamed Soueid, director. 70 minutes.
Sharfouna. 1997. Andre Simon, director. 27 minutes.
Suspended Dreams. 1992. Jean Khalil Chamoun and Mai Masri, directors. 50 minutes.
War Generation Beirut. 1988. Jean Khalil Chamoun and Mai Masri, directors. 50 minutes.
The War of Lebanon. 2000. Omar Al Issawi, director. 12 hours.
Wild Flowers, Women of South Lebanon. 1986. Jean Khalil Chamoun and Mai Masri, directors. 75 minutes.

Short Films

Beirut Palermo Beirut. 1998. Mahmoud Hojeij, director. 17 minutes.
The Dead Weight of a Quarrel Hangs. 1996–1999. Walid Ra'ad, director. 17 minutes.
The Red Chewing Gum. 2000. Akram Zaatari, director. 10 minutes.

Web Sites

Lebanon Tourism, www.lebanon-tourism.gov.lb/country.htm.

Al-Raida, al-raida@lau.edu.lb.
Periodical for women.

Middle East and Arab Countries Population and Human Settlements, arabnet.com.

Organizations

Development Studies Association
DPI PO Box 1085
Beirut, Lebanon
Middle East and Arab countries development policy and international economic cooperation.

Lebanese Association of Human Rights
DPI PO Box 1085
Beirut, Lebanon
Middle East and Arab countries development policy and international economic cooperation.

Lebanon Family Planning Association
DPI PO BOX 118240
El-Maskan Building, Mazraa
Beirut, Lebanon
961 1 311978 961 1 318575
Middle East and Arab countries population and human settlements.

United Nations Association of Lebanon
UNA PO Box 92
Hazmieh
Beirut, Lebanon
961 1 455 027 961 1 494 317
Middle East and Arab countries United Nations association.

SELECTED BIBLIOGRAPHY

Abu Nassr, Julinda, Nabil F. Khoury, and Henry T. Azzam, eds. *Women Employment, and Development in the Arab World*. Berlin: Mouton, 1985.

Accad, Evelyne. "Feminist Perspectives on the War in Lebanon." *Women's Studies International Forum* 12 (1989): 91–95.

Boustani, Smith, and Nada Mufarrej. "Female Higher Education and Participation in the Labor Force in Lebanon." In *Gender and Development in the Arab World: Women's Economic Participation: Patterns and Policies*, ed. Nabil F. Khoury and Valentine M. Moghadam, 97–124. London: Zed Books, 1995.

Farah, May. "Globalization Finds a Place for Women: UN Report Finds That Far-Reaching Changes Are Slowly Leveling the Playing Field." (Beirut) *Daily Star*, November 11, 1999.

Farhood, Leila. "War Trauma and Women: Predisposition and Vulnerability to Adverse Psychological Health Outcomes." In *Women and War in Lebanon*, ed. Lamia Rustum Shehadeh, 259–71. Gainesville: University Press of Florida, 1999.

Irani, Lauri King. "Recovering Women's Voices in Post-war Lebanon." *Al-Raida* 12(70–71) (1995): 12–13.

Joseph, Suad. "Brother/Sister Relationships: Connectivity, Love, and Power in the Reproduction of Patriarchy in Lebanon." *American Ethnologist* 21 (1994): 50–73.

———. "Gender and Family in the Arab World." In *Arab Women: Between Defiance and Restraint*, ed. Suha Sabbagh, 194–202. New York: Olive Branch Press, 1996.

———. *Intimate Selfing in Arab Families: Gender, Self, and Identity*. Syracuse, NY: Syracuse University Press, 1999.

Kabbanji, Jack and As'ad Attat. *Al-mar'a al-'amila fi lubnan: Nata'ij midania wa tahlilia* (The Working Woman in Lebanon: Field Results and Analysis). Beirut: Sharikat al-matbou'at lil-tawzi'wal-nashr, 1997.

LaTeef, Nelda. *Women of Lebanon: Interviews with Champions for Peace*. Jefferson, NC: McFarland and Company, 1997.

Lattouf, Mirna. "The History of Women's Higher Education in Modern Lebanon and Its Social Implications." Ph.D. diss., University of Arizona, 1999.

Makdisi, Jean Said. "The Mythology of Modernity: Women and Democracy in Lebanon." In *Feminism and Islam: Legal and Literary Perspectives*, ed. Mai Yamani, 231–50. Berkshire: Ithaca Press, 1996.

Maksoud, Hala. "The Case of Lebanon." In *Arab Women: Between Defiance and Restraint*, ed. Suha Sabbagh, 89–94. New York: Olive Branch Press, 1996.

Sfeir, Myriam. "Iqbal Doughan: President of the Working Women League in Lebanon." *Al-Raida* 15(82) (1998): 44–45.

Shehadeh, Lamia Rustum, ed. *Women and War in Lebanon*. Gainesville: University Press of Florida, 1999.

Sidani, Yusuf Munir, and William Gardner. "Work Values among Lebanese Workers." *Journal of Social Psychology* 140 (2000): 597–607.

Wehbi, Samantha. " 'Women with Nothing to Lose': Marriageability and Women's Perceptions of Rape and Consent in Contemporary Beirut." *Women's Studies International Forum* 25 (2002): 287–300.

9

LIBYA

Amy J. Johnson

PROFILE OF LIBYA

Libya is located in North Africa. It is bordered by Egypt to the east, Sudan to the southeast, Tunisia to the northwest, Algeria to the west, and Chad and Niger to the south. Libya is the fourth-largest country in Africa, occupying 1,759,540 square kilometers, an area somewhat larger than the state of Alaska.[1] The vast majority of Libya is desert; 8 percent of Libya is pastureland, and only 1 percent of the country is used for farming. The Sahara Desert continues to encroach upon pastures and farmland. While the coastal areas have a Mediterranean climate, the interior desert climate can be extreme. Dust storms and sandstorms are common.

Berbers and Arabs make up 97 percent of Libya's population; the remaining 3 percent includes many foreign groups, such as Greeks, Maltese, Italians, Egyptians, Pakistanis, Turks, Indians, and Tunisians. The overwhelming majority of Libyans (97 percent) are Sunni Muslims. Arabic is the official language, though Italian and English are understood in major cities.

The country is officially called al-Jamahiriyyah al-Arabiyyah al-Libiyyah al-Shaabiyyah al-Ishtirakiyyah (in English, the

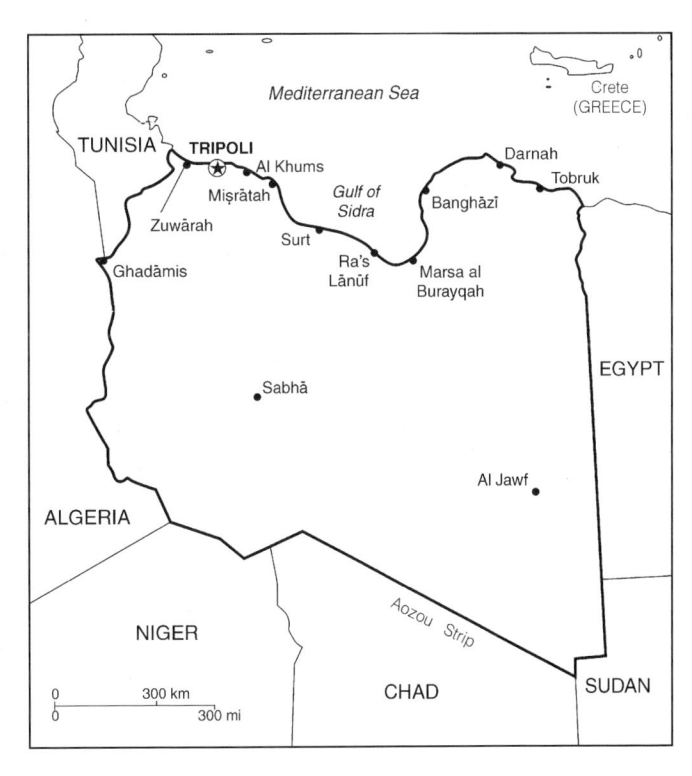

Socialist People's Libyan Arab Jamahiriyyah). *Jamahiriyyah* is a neologism coined by Libyan leader Mu'ammar al-Qadhafi that is often translated as a "state of the masses" where, in theory, the population governs through local councils. The government, however, operates essentially as a dictatorship led by Qadhafi and is heavily influenced by the military. The capital of Libya is Tripoli.

Libya has three primary natural resources: petroleum, natural gas, and gypsum. Its economy is based upon its petroleum resources. Oil accounts for almost all export earnings and approximately 25 percent of the country's gross domestic product (GDP). Per capita GDP is $7,900, one of the highest in Africa. Because of the lack of arable land, Libya must import some three-quarters of its food. The economy is socialist in orientation. Most imports come from European countries, including Italy, Germany, the United Kingdom, and France. The currency of Libya is the Libyan dinar (LD).[2]

Libya has a population of approximately 5.2 million, with a slightly higher percentage of males than females (1.06 males for each female). Its population growth rate is 2.42 percent. The country has a birth rate of 27 births per 1,000 population and a death rate of 4 deaths per 1,000 population. Libya has a total fertility rate of 3.6 children born per woman. Its infant mortality rate is 29 deaths per 1,000 live births. Overall life expectancy is 75 years. Male life expectancy is 73 years, while female life expectancy is 77 years.[3]

In order to understand the position of women in Libya, one must know the country's history. Modern Libya was created after World War II when the regions of Tripolitania, Cyrenaica, and the Fezzan were united. In the sixteenth century, Libya had become part of the Ottoman Empire when the Ottomans seized the area from the Knights of St. John. While enjoying substantial autonomy within the empire, particularly under the Karamanli dynasty from 1711 to 1835, Libya remained under Ottoman control until the early twentieth century. According to Ottoman practice, each religious community was governed by its own religious laws. Hence Muslim women in Libya were governed by Islamic law, Christian women in Libya by Christian law, and Jewish women in Libya by Jewish law.

In 1911, Italy began a campaign to seize North African lands; the campaign was particularly directed against Tripolitania and Cyrenaica, areas that had been provinces of ancient Rome. The colonial period in Libya was one of conflict because the Italian government (most notably under dictator Benito Mussolini) encouraged Italians to move to Italy, a policy known as demographic colonization. This policy resulted in the indigenous people losing much of their land, large numbers being forcibly relocated to concentration camps, and up to 50 percent of the population dying in the camps and in armed resistance to colonization. These colonial practices affected both men and women as families lost their agricultural land and were forcibly relocated. Although it was primarily men who died in armed resistance, both men and women died in the camps. The area became a battleground during World War II, serving as a main part of the North African theater from 1941 to 1943. The war brought an end to the Italian settlement of Libya.

Throughout the colonial period, resistance to Italian rule had been led by the Sanusiyyah Sufi order, founded in 1837, which believed, among other things, in the right to interpret religious law, the value of meditation and hard work, a return to the beauty and simplicity of the early Muslim community, and the importance of missionary work to spread these ideas. In addition to organizing resistance to colonial rule, the order helped create a sense of religious and political unity among the various tribal groups of the three regions. In 1902, Sidi Muhammad Idris al-Mahdi al-Sanusi became the order's leader; though he was in exile in Egypt during World War II, he remained a key political figure in Libya.

After the war, the United Nations debated what was to happen to formerly Italian Libya; while many solutions were offered, the British suggestion of immediate independence for all three provinces was eventually adopted. Representatives of the three provinces agreed to form a constitutional monarchy, and the United Kingdom of Libya became independent in 1951. The king of the new state was Idris I, the man who had been the leader of the Sanusiyyah brotherhood. Although the monarch was supported by conservative tribesmen, younger, more radical elements objected to the king's Western orientation in foreign policy, to his ban on political parties, to his preferential treatment of the Cyrenaica region, and to what they saw as his corrupt regime.

In 1969, Idris was deposed by an army coup modeled on Egypt's 1952 Society of Free Officers coup and led by Colonel Mu'ammar al-Qadhafi. The new government abolished the monarchy, declared Libya a republic, nationalized portions of the ten-year-old oil industry, severed ties with Britain and the United States, and embraced pan-Arabism. Since 1969, Libya has been ruled by Qadhafi, who is referred to as the "leader of the revolution" but who holds no formal government office.

Domestically, the new government transformed Libya from a group of conservative tribes into a more unified state guided by Qadhafi's unique blend of socialism, Islam, militarism, and Arab nationalism. Oil revenues allowed the leader to fund infrastructure and social service projects, including expanded health-care and educational systems. Internationally, Qadhafi's government first embraced pan-Arabism, pursuing but not achieving formal unions with other Arab countries. The new government acted upon its anti-Western and antimonarchical views, offering support to a wide variety of guerrilla and revolutionary movements in the Middle East and Africa as well as aid to the Black Panthers in the United States and the Irish Republican Army (IRA) in Northern Ireland. Libyan relations with the United States were affected by the sponsorship of such groups, which the United States deemed terrorist in nature, and by Libyan intelligence agents seeking out and assassinating regime opponents abroad. Libya has also had difficult relations with its African neighbors, particularly Chad. The two countries' border disputes resulted in sporadic warfare in the 1970s and 1980s. In recent years, as Libya has become less of a player on the Arab political stage, Qadhafi has turned to African nations and advocated pan-African ideas, including the formation of a United States of Africa.

OVERVIEW OF WOMEN'S ISSUES

Social policy in modern Libya, particularly with regard to gender, remains substantially influenced by Libya's religious traditions, but it is also heavily influenced by Qadhafi's unique ideology, called "the Third Universal Theory" and codified into his statement of political philosophy, *The Green Book*.[4] While the book states the equality of worth of all citizens, it also stresses the "natural" activities and predilections of each gender.

Despite this ideology, women in Libya have made clear gains in education, health-care access, employment in the public sphere, and involvement in politics since the 1969 revolution. Women enjoy a wide variety of rights, including the right to vote and to run for public office, to own and dispose of property, to be educated, and to work outside the home. Women have also made some limited gains in traditionally male sectors of the economy. Overall, however, women remain secondary to men in the labor force. Their literacy rates are lower than those of their male counterparts, and they are less educated overall in comparison to men.

Revisions in marriage and divorce law likewise have made family relationships more equitable since the revolution, though in both categories, males have a broader array of rights. The revolutionary government has significantly increased access to basic health care as well. As Libya moves into the twenty-first century, it can be expected that the ideology of Qadhafi and the country's religious traditions will continue to influence women's roles, but women continue to demand and to receive more of a voice in Libyan society.

EDUCATION

Opportunities

Qadhafi, in *The Green Book*, takes an interesting view of education, arguing that compulsory education suppresses freedom, since it negates individual choice of whether and what to learn. In his view, "to force a human being to learn according to a set curriculum is a dictatorial act. Compulsory and methodized education is in fact a forced stultification of the masses."⁵ In his view, a society should provide its members with access to all types of education and should give them the freedom to choose which types they wish to pursue.

However, Qadhafi maintains that education should also be appropriate to one's gender. Women, he argues, should not be educated for jobs that are unsuited to their more delicate physical and psychological nature. Any education that prepares women for such work is "unjust and cruel."⁶

Group of women accompany schoolchildren on a field trip. Photo © TRIP/TH-Foto Werbing.

Despite these pronouncements, primary education in Libya is free and compulsory for both boys and girls. In the early 1990s, approximately 1.3 million children were enrolled each year in primary school. At the same time, more than 200,000 were enrolled in higher education annually—in secondary, vocational, and teacher-training schools.⁷

Education in Libya was rapidly expanded after the country obtained independence in 1951. The government of King Idris funded new schools and encouraged attendance by both boys and girls; in fact, education was deemed a right of all Libyans after independence. The expanded educational programs led to more enrollments of previously underrepresented groups, including girls, Bedouins, children from the countryside, and adult learners. It also led to the establishment of the country's first university only four years after independence.

After Qadhafi's coup, the new government made an effort to "Libyanize" the educational system by providing more teacher-training courses. Previously, many teachers had been recruited from other Arab countries. The government also expanded educational facilities by building more schools, providing mobile classrooms, and arranging for desert areas to be provided with tents in which classes could be held.

Despite the efforts of postindependence governments to increase educational opportunities for girls and women, female attendance in schools at all levels has remained lower than male attendance. Rural girls are less likely to attend school and less likely to continue their education past the primary level than urban girls. Available data on attendance and dropout rates in the 1970s and 1980s indicated that "many parents sent their daughters to school only long enough to acquire basic skills to make them attractive marriage partners." Likewise, female enrollment at higher educational institutions has not expanded on the same scale that male enrollment has. However, in the 1980s, female participation in higher education began to increase, going "from 9 percent of total enrollments in the 1970–71 period, to 20 percent in the 1978–79 period, to 24 percent in the early 1980s." Despite the continuing gender gap in education and literacy in Libya, the country has made significant improvements in its educational system and in the promotion of literacy since independence, when school attendance nationwide was a mere 34,000 and literacy rates were no higher than 20 percent of the population over age ten.

Literacy

According to 1995 estimates, literacy (defined as those aged fifteen and older who can read and write) is 76.2 percent. Given that an estimated 90 percent of the population was illiterate at independence, this literacy rate is commendable. There is a gender gap in literacy, however, with an estimated 87.9 percent of males being literate, compared with 63 percent of females being literate.[8]

EMPLOYMENT AND ECONOMICS

According to Qadhafi's ideology, men and women are equal, since both are human beings; therefore, he argues, "discrimination between man and woman is a flagrant act of oppression without justification."[9] Nevertheless, he says, men and women are different and have different roles in society. Women, in his view, are made feeble once a month during menstruation. They are further weakened during and immediately after pregnancy. Once they have given birth, they must feed and care for their children. All of these, he says, are natural roles for women, and men cannot replace women in these roles.

Job/Career Opportunities

However, Qadhafi says, the natural roles of women mean that women are prevented in part or in full from participating in other activities (for example, jobs outside the home) during those times. Likewise, any work that takes women away from this natural function or involves undue physical strain is unsuitable. In Qadhafi's view, women would never freely choose to abandon their natural roles. In *The Green Book*, he argues that "the belief, including the woman's own belief, that the woman carries out physical labour of her own accord, is not, in fact true. For she performs the physical work only because the harsh, materialistic society has placed her, without her being directly aware, in coercive circumstances. She has no alternative but to submit to the conditions of that society while she thinks that she works of her own accord."[10]

Not only should women be "protected" from doing physically difficult work, they should also be "protected" from "dirty work, which stains [their] beauty and detracts from [their] femininity."[11] In Qadhafi's words, "man's work disguises the woman's beautiful features which are created for female roles. They are exactly like blossoms which are created to attract pollen and to produce seeds."[12] Therefore, according to Qadhafi, the question is not whether women should be allowed to work. Rather, "work should be provided by the society to all able members—men and women—who need work, but on the condition that each individual should work in the field that suits him, and not be forced to carry out unsuitable work."[13]

In Libya, the service and government sectors of the economy employ the majority of the labor force (54 percent), while industry and agriculture employ 29 percent and 17 percent, respectively, according to 1997 estimates.[14] The country has an estimated unemployment rate in 2000 of 30 percent.[15] Rising oil prices in 1999 led to higher earnings from exports, and since United Nations sanctions on Libya were suspended in 1999, the country has been actively seeking more foreign investment to revitalize its economy. It is hoped that the lifting of sanctions will also provide jobs, thus reducing the unemployment rate.

In recent years, Qadhafi's government has attempted to increase female participation in the economy while still remaining true to its leader's philosophy and to cultural and religious norms concerning male and female employment. Official census figures continue to report women's economic activity as minimal, but researchers estimate that the real numbers are much higher than actually reported. Some reports estimate that women make up more than 20 percent of the active labor force of the country; in rural areas, women may make up more than 40 percent of the labor force.[16] Those women not working in agriculture are most often employed in fields traditionally considered suitable for women—as educators, nurses and other health-care workers, clerical workers, and domestic workers. Despite continuing gains in education at all levels, Libyan women have not entered traditionally male jobs such as medicine, engineering, and law in significant numbers.[17]

Pay

Shortly after the 1969 revolution, the new government began passing a variety of laws regarding employment, including laws stipulating equal pay for equal work. However, this law has not significantly increased women's earnings, given that women who are employed outside the home are generally employed in lower-level jobs.

Working Conditions

Given the cultural constraints on female employment, working conditions for women can be difficult. Although the government has encouraged women to work outside the home and to enter traditionally male sectors of the economy, women have not done so in large numbers, primarily because of the continuing cultural norm that women's primary "job" is to be mothers and wives.

Support for Mothers/Caretakers

Despite Qadhafi's philosophical aversion to work that takes women away from their natural roles as mothers, the government passed legislation providing women with numerous inducements to remain in the labor force after bearing children. These policies made some practical sense, given Libya's low population and small labor force. While high birth rates are encouraged, women are also a valuable source of labor for the economy. The inducements offered included giving each mother a cash bonus for bearing her first child and providing daycare at no charge.

Maternal Leave

Women working for the government are entitled to maternal leave. Women are also entitled to menstrual leave each month, in accordance with Qadhafi's views that menstruation makes women weak. However, because women are an important source of labor in the Libyan economy, women are encouraged to remain in the workforce even after having children.

Daycare

Daycare is free. In Qadhafi's view, alternatives to mothers being the primary caregivers of children are disadvantageous; he likens nurseries and daycare centers to poultry farms, where children are crammed together and not cared for properly.[18] Since "motherhood is the female's function," Qadhafi argues that "any attempt to take children away from their mother is coercion, oppression, and dictatorship."[19]

Inheritance and Property Rights

In addition to having rights to education, work, and equal pay, women in Libya have the right to own and dispose of their own property. Inheritance law in Libya is influenced by Islamic law, which gives standard portions of a family member's property to other family members upon her/his death. Generally, the inheritance of a male is double the inheritance of a female. This is based on the religious idea that men are economically responsible for the women in their families; hence they require a larger share of inheritance to fulfill these obligations.

Social/Government Programs

Sustainable Development

Sustainable development and economic diversification have been serious dilemmas for the government. Because most of the country is desert, one of Libya's biggest challenges is developing adequate water resources. Its main answer to the problem has been the development of the Great Man-Made River Project (begun in 1983), a $25-billion project designed to pipe water out of aquifers below the Sahara Desert to irrigate new agricultural land along the Mediterranean coast in the north and to increase water resources to already settled areas. While international observers are critical of the project, the government remains committed to it and optimistic about its potential benefits. Likewise, the government has attempted to diversify its economy, a difficult task given its limited natural resources. Most diversification has taken place in petroleum-related fields, such as petrochemicals.

The expansion of farmland envisioned by the Great Man-Made River Project could create more jobs in agriculture and could increase the percentage of GDP agriculture currently claims. By creating more agricultural jobs, it could expand women's employment, though women's agricultural work is often unpaid, family-based labor that is un- or underreported in employment statistics.[20] Diversification in the petroleum-related industries seems unlikely to open up new job opportunities for women, given their limited gains in such male-dominated economic fields to date. Despite the irrigation and diversification plans, oil remains the backbone of the Libyan economy and will remain so in the absence of the development of new resources.

Social Benefits

Oil has provided revenue that the government has used to expand the array of social services it offers to its citizens. Free education, expanded health-care access, and infrastructure development were all begun on unprecedented scales after the 1969 revolution. In addition to the benefits offered to working mothers, Libyan women have the right to retire at age fifty-five and are eligible for government pensions thereafter.

FAMILY AND SEXUALITY

Gender Roles

According to some studies, popular opinion in Libya strongly endorses the idea of gender equality. However, there remains a gap between commitment to equality in principle and commitment to equality in practice.[21]

Libyan society is patrilineal and largely patriarchal. A daughter traditionally remains in the home of her father until marriage, at which time she joins her husband's extended family. Often a married son remains in his father's household until his father's death. While Qadhafi's ideology and the policies of his government introduced a number of changes in Libya, altering the structure and importance of the family were not among them. Indeed, *The Green Book* argues that the family is the basis of the nation.

Within the family, gender roles traditionally have been distinct, with men being financially responsible for the family and women being responsible for child rearing and household chores. As more Libyan women have entered the paid labor force, demands on their time have increased. The traditional view of women's roles in the family and the household has not substantially altered. Thus women working outside the home not only perform their paid jobs but also are still considered responsible for their traditional duties within the household.

Veiling

Since the mid-1980s, Islamist movements (political movements that make use of Islam, sometimes called Islamic fundamentalist movements) have gained a wider audience in Libya. One manifestation of this is the trend among younger Libyan women to veil (to cover their hair and dress modestly, actions that some believe are religiously required). Though Qadhafi has attacked this trend verbally, arguing that women should protect themselves with education, not veils and that the presence or absence of a particular item of clothing says nothing about a woman's virtue or religiosity,[22] educated women continue to don the veil in larger numbers.

Female Genital Cutting

While female genital mutilation is uncommon in Libya, it is still practiced by some nomadic tribes, particularly in the southern regions. However, as the practice is not Islamic nor culturally indigenous to Libya, the number of women involved in the practice is extremely low.

Marriage

In *The Green Book*, Qadhafi stresses that women and men both have the right to choose and reject marriage partners as a "natural rule of freedom."[23] Likewise, neither can force the other into marriage nor capriciously divorce their spouses. Qadhafi also argues that in a divorce, the house should go to the wife, since ownership of the home "is one of the suitable and necessary conditions for a woman who menstruates, conceives, and cares for her children."[24] Libyan marriage and divorce law largely follows Qadhafi's ideology; it is also heavily influenced by Islamic law.

Traditionally, marriages were arranged by parents or extended families, and, as is the case throughout much of the Arab world, the customarily preferred marriages were between first cousins. Other preferred matches were between other (religiously permitted) extended family members or, barring that possibility, between members of the same tribal background. These norms have been rapidly changing as women enter the public sphere in greater numbers and hence come into contact with unrelated men, and as young people prefer to marry mates of their own choosing.

Marriages are legal contracts between consenting parties, and both the groom and the bride must consent in order for the marriage to occur. After the 1969 revolution, the new government set the minimum age for marriage at sixteen for females and eighteen for males. A girl who is a minor (between the ages of sixteen and twenty-one) must have her father's consent to marry. However, if the girl's father refuses permission for her to marry a man whom she has chosen for herself, the girl has the legal right to petition a court for permission to marry.

Religious law influences the marriage relationship as well. Prior to the marriage, the groom must provide a dowry, the amount of which is negotiated between the families. This can be an obstacle if the young man and his family are not well off. The accumulation of the dowry can take years, often resulting in delayed marriages for young men. Polygamy is legally permitted but rarely practiced in modern Libya, with only 3 percent of marriages being polygamous, according to estimates in the 1980s.[25]

Divorce law differs based on gender as well. While both partners can legally initiate divorce proceedings, the husband can legally divorce his wife by saying to her three times in front of witnesses, "I divorce you," whereas a wife must seek recourse in the courts to obtain a divorce. Nevertheless, the state has marginally increased Libyan women's divorce and marital rights by making it easier to gain divorces in cases of abandonment or mistreatment; by requiring a man to obtain his first wife's permission if he wishes to marry a second wife; by making it illegal for a divorced man to marry a foreign woman; and by prohibiting male employees of the state from marrying non Arab women.[26]

Despite Qadhafi's view that marriage is a natural state of affairs for men and women, in 1981, he began a group called the Revolutionary Nuns. Women who joined this group (envisioned by Qadhafi as comprising up to 5 percent of the female population of Libya) were to remain single and to dedicate themselves to the service of the revolution and the progress of Libyan and Arab society. His remarks on the founding of this new organization were provocative and not in keeping with Libyan tradition. As he said, "Marriage places responsibilities on other people, it leads to successive problems. What value does (traditional) marriage have today? In the end you study for a diploma to give yourself to a nobody who only sees in you a maid, a cook, and a breeding-machine."[27] This speech and this organization illustrate Qadhafi's sometimes contradictory gender policies—on the one hand, he must be careful not to alienate religious conservatives, and on the other, he has tried to increase women's involvement in public life.

In accordance with Islamic tradition and legal precedent, child-custody law heavily favors the father, who has the right to custody upon divorce, though in some circumstances courts can award custody to the mother. In addition, Libyan children must have the consent of their fathers to travel abroad, even if they are legally in the custody of their mothers. Similarly, Libyan husbands are legally permitted to prevent their wives from leaving the country without their consent. Citizenship is accorded patrilineally, with children of Libyan fathers being considered Libyan citizens regardless of their place of birth. Such is not the case for children born to Libyan mothers outside the country.[28]

Reproduction

Sex Education

Sex education is not routinely provided to children in Libya. Although women may learn about methods of contraception in informal venues, Qadhafi's ideology concerning contraception and abortion (discussed in the next section) and Libya's desire to increase its population combine to prevent regular, reliable access to information on sexual activities and contraceptive measures.

Contraception and Abortion

According to Qadhafi's ideology, interventions to prevent conception as well as interventions to terminate pregnancies are actions tantamount to murder, since they intervene against the natural course of human life.[29] Accordingly, abortion is not legal in Libya. Families are encouraged to have many children, and working mothers are offered benefits to remain in the workforce after having children.

Teen Pregnancy

As noted earlier, girls typically remain in the homes of their fathers until marriage. Gender mixing in Libyan society occurs with less frequency than in Western European or North American societies, and accordingly, there is less opportunity for young men and young women to develop relationships. In general, sexual activity outside of marriage, including sexual activity prior to marriage, is not socially acceptable for men or women. However, the social stigma attached to such sexual activity tends to be stronger for women than for men. The Libyan government does not routinely keep or publish statistics on teen pregnancy rates.

HEALTH

Health Care Access

Since the 1969 revolution, the Libyan government has made great strides in expanding health-care access to all its citizens. Access to basic medical care is good; it is estimated that 95 percent of Libyans have access to basic health-care services. This is due in large part to government policy, which has resulted in substantial subsidies for medical care. However, access to advanced health-care services and critical-care facilities is limited.

Diseases and Disorders

Libya has managed to dramatically reduce the infection rates of many of the diseases that have historically been public health threats. By the 1960s, malaria had been virtually eliminated in the country. In the 1970s, a variety of diseases were common in Libya, including typhoid, hepatitis, schistosomiasis, whooping cough, chicken pox, mumps, and measles. However, the government mounted sustained efforts to combat these diseases and claimed to have them under control by the mid-1980s. Given the amount of resources allocated to the expansion of health care throughout Libya, these claims are not unreasonable. In addition, although tuberculosis had formerly been a significant health problem in Libya, government establishment of centers devoted to care and treatment of the disease combined with efforts to stop new cases from developing dramatically reduced infection rates by the mid-1980s.

AIDS

According to a 1999 estimate, the adult prevalence rate of HIV/AIDS is 0.05 percent. There are no reliable statistics on the number of people living with HIV/AIDS or the number of deaths from HIV/AIDS.[30] Although HIV/AIDS does not pose a major public health threat in Libya, the nation has been involved as a prominent advocate for HIV/AIDS prevention and treatment in Africa. In 2000, Libya hosted a three-day symposium on the AIDS challenge in North Africa. In addition, the government has established a national center for assisting people living with HIV/AIDS and funded the Qadhafi Human Rights Prize for efforts in the fight against this pandemic.

POLITICS AND LAW

Suffrage

Men and women both have the right to vote; in fact, for all Libyans aged eighteen and over, voting is compulsory. While women have had voting rights since the early 1960s, very few women made use of these rights before the 1969 revolution.

Political Participation

In addition to increasing women's educational and economic opportunities, Qadhafi has also encouraged women to become more active in politics and law. Beginning in 1989, women for the first time were legally permitted to enter the judicial occupations. The government began appointing women to positions as "judges, public prosecutors, and case administrators."[31] Women were likewise urged to claim their rights within the political system. However, very few female candidates ran, and few of those who did were elected. While some were appointed to diplomatic posts overseas, only five women in the period 1979–1999 were elected to posts within the ruling legislative body.[32]

In addition to appointing women to judicial positions, the regime began three women's organizations, the goals of which are to increase women's participation in the public sphere: the Female Guards, who are dedicated to protecting Qadhafi and the revolution, the Women's Revolutionary Committees, who aim to increase belief in the leader's philosophy, and the Revolutionary Nuns, discussed in the "Marriage" section.[33]

Women's Rights

Women in Libya have a broad array of legal rights, including the right to own and freely dispose of property, the right to education, the right to employment, the right to marry and divorce, and the right to vote and run as candidates for political office.

Feminist Movements

Like all political activity in Libya, feminist activities take place primarily within governments-sponsored organizations. Organizations such as the Revolutionary Nuns, the Female Guards, and the Women's Revolutionary Committees, all of which provide women with political outlets and activities, can be considered feminist in orientation. It has often been debated whether Qadhafi himself or the actions and policies of his government can legitimately be considered feminist. Nevertheless, it remains evident that the Libyan government has attempted to provide more avenues for education and employment for women and has encouraged women to become politically active. In this regard, government activities (such as including women in the armed forces and the judiciary) have often outpaced demands for change. The result has been that demands for an improvement in women's status and women's rights in Libya often come not from Libyan women or the Libyan people but from the government, whose actions and policies often challenge cultural and religious norms.

After independence, women in Libya also gained the right to "form their own associations, the first of which dated to 1955 in Benghazi. In 1970 several feminist organizations merged into the Women's General Union, which in 1977 became the Jamahiriya Women's Federation. Under Clause 5 of the Constitutional Proclamation of December 11, 1969, women had already been given equal status under the law with men. Subsequently, the women's movement has been active in such fields as adult education and hygiene. The movement has achieved only limited influence, however, and its most active members have felt frustrated by their inability to gain either direct or indirect political influence."

Lesbian Rights

Homosexual activity is officially illegal in Libya. Homosexual acts are punishable by three to five years in prison. While monarchical Libya also criminalized homosexual activity, the basis for the law following the revolution was explicitly said to be religious. The Military Code likewise imposes a penalty of up to five years in prison for actual and attempted homosexual acts by members of the armed forces. The country has opposed including sexual orientation as a criterion of nondiscrimination in international forums, for example, at the United Nations Fourth World Conference on Women in Beijing in September 4–15, 1995.

Military Service

Qadhafi's philosophical pronouncements on gender-suitable work notwithstanding, he has urged women to become directly involved in the armed forces; he is often photographed with his all-female bodyguard corps. Arguing that "women of the Arab world live in a subjugated state and must be liberated from oppression and feudalism,"[34] the Libyan leader presents women's involvement in the military as consistent with religious and family life.

In 1978, Qadhafi publicly announced plans to include women in conscription, though at the time, this was not entirely implemented. The next year witnessed the opening of a women's military college in the capital city, which trained "volunteers aged 13 to 17 in basic military subjects and the use of various weapons."[35] In 1983, the college was closed following disturbances involving students who wished to leave the school.[36] Nevertheless, boys and girls were directed to study military science and undertake programs of military training appropriate to their age, beginning in primary schools and continuing through university. Though university military training has not been in effect since 1990, students must serve in the military for one year after graduation.[37]

Despite Qadhafi's efforts, the idea of women in the military has not met with much popular acceptance. In 1984, Qadhafi introduced a new law for passage by the General People's Congress (GPC) that included female conscription; the GPC refused to pass the law, a rare step for a body that normally approves its leader's proposals. Not content with this outcome, Qadhafi organized "spontaneous" demonstrations of women who demanded their rights to participate in the armed forces and used these demonstrations as evidence of popular demand to introduce female conscription. Nevertheless, the women's military college in Tripoli remained closed, and no clear steps toward universal female military training were taken.[38]

RELIGION AND SPIRITUALITY

Islam arrived in Libya in the mid-seventh century when Arab Muslim armies invaded much of North Africa, including Cyrenaica, Tripolitania, and the Fezzan. Originating in the Arabian peninsula, Islam is a religion that emphasizes morality, charity, submission to the will of God, and the equality of all believers. The so-called five pillars of the faith (the statement of faith, prayer, charitable giving, fasting during the month of Ramadan, and pilgrimage to Mecca) reinforce this notion of equality, as all Muslims are to perform these acts.

One of the first acts of the new government after the 1969 coup was to disband the Sanusiyyah Islamic order, a logical step given the position of the deposed king in that order. However, this did not signal a change from Libya's Islamic traditions. In fact, Qadhafi stresses the role of Islam in Libyan society in his speeches and has attempted to merge Islamic and socialist ideas in his state. In 1973, displeased at the lack of popular enthusiasm for the revolution thus far, Qadhafi declared that all law would be replaced by Islamic law (shari'a) and that Libya should rid itself of everything contrary to pure Islamic principles. Qadhafi's attempts to infuse Islam into his government and policies have met with resistance from some religious leaders who believe that he manipulates Islam for his own purposes.

Women's Roles

While women do not have formal roles within the religious structure, such as leading Friday communal prayers, women have served other women in religious capacities throughout Islamic history, helping them learn the Qur'an, giving religious advice, making charitable endowments, and leading prayers for other women, among other things.

In interpreting Islamic law (shari'a), jurists rely primarily on the Qur'an, the collection of revelations to the prophet Muhammad, and the sunna, the received custom regarding Muhammad embodied in the Hadith reports. Women do not typically serve as jurists in Islamic countries; Qadhafi's encouragement and appointment of women to judicial positions in Libya were revolutionary for that country.

Rituals and Religious Practices

There are some special provisions for women, such as the prohibition on fasting for women who are pregnant, breast feeding, or menstruating. Women are not exempt from this religious duty; instead, they must fast an equivalent number of days when they are physically able.

VIOLENCE

Libya is a signatory to a number of international documents concerning women's rights and violence against women. It has signed the African Charter on Human and People's Rights, the International Covenant on Civil and Political Rights and its optional protocol, the International Covenant on Economic, Social, and Cultural Rights, the International Convention on the Elimination of All Forms of Discrimination against Women, and the Convention on the Rights of the Child.

Domestic Violence

Statistics on violence against women are not routinely kept, and the extent of the problem is not known. It is generally agreed that violence against women occurs, especially within the family structure. However, these issues are seldom discussed in public or by the government, as they are viewed as private, family matters. Traditionally, such issues have been addressed through the mediation of family members and neighbors.

Rape/Sexual Assault

Statistics on rape and sexual assault are likewise difficult to obtain. Traditionally, a woman's chastity, or honor, was of primary importance to herself and her family. Women who were not chaste before marriage, whether by choice or by force, were considered to have violated the honor of the entire family. While neither the religious nor cultural norms of Libya condoned rape, these traditional attitudes have affected open discussion of and governmental action on the issue.

War and Military Repression

Libya's war with Chad in 1980–1989 took a toll on the country. Women served in the military in Chad, including some command positions. With Qadhafi's encouragement of female involvement in military training in schools and in the armed forces, women, like men, have been and will continue to be involved in conflict. Libya is infested with antipersonnel mines, many left over from the North African campaign during World War II. It has sought assistance from the United Nations and the international community in removing these mines, which it believes pose a serious health threat to its citizens.

OUTLOOK FOR THE TWENTY-FIRST CENTURY

Qadhafi's power has been challenged domestically by opponents within the military who attempted several coups in the 1980s and 1990s. Islamist groups could also pose a threat to the regime; in 1997, government forces clashed with members of Islamist groups in the eastern region of the country. While a successful military coup would likely not radically alter women's positions within Libya, an Islamist government could significantly change gender policy in the country. In order to counter this threat, Qadhafi has attempted to appease Islamist groups by stressing his own piety, by referring often to Islam's place in the Libyan government, and by sponsoring various religious gatherings. The government continues to try to balance traditional religious norms and its own version of modernity, especially with regard to women's roles in society. Libya's future after Qadhafi remains uncertain, but given the long-term trends in women's rights, it seems likely that barring a radical change in government orientation, Libyan women will continue to gradually expand their economic, educational, and political opportunities in the years to come.

NOTES

1. One kilometer equals approximately 0.6 miles.
2. "Libya," *CIA World Factbook*, www.cia.gov/cia/publications/factbook/geos/ly.html.
3. Ibid.
4. *The Green Book* was released in three sections, one in 1976, one in 1978, and one in 1980. The contradictions between the philosophical ideas about gender in the work and actual policy in Libya can be partially explained by this, as the section dealing with women was not published until 1980.
5. Muammar Qaddafi, *Qaddafi's Green Book* (Buffalo: Prometheus Books, 1988), part III.
6. Ibid.
7. Kwame Anthony Appiah and Henry Louis Gates, eds., *Africana* (New York: Basic Civitas Books, 1999), 1166.
8. "Libya," *CIA World Factbook*.
9. *Qaddafi's Green Book*, part III.
10. Ibid.
11. Ibid.
12. Ibid.
13. Ibid.
14. "Libya," *CIA World Factbook*.

15. Ibid.
16. "Libya," Library of Congress country study, http://memory.loc.gov/frd/cs/lytoc.html.
17. Ibid.
18. Ibid.
19. Ibid.
20. Some experts believe that if the project succeeds, it will irrigate too much land, and Libya, with its small labor force, will be forced to recruit agricultural workers from abroad.
21. Amal Obeidi, *Political Culture in Libya* (London: Curzon Press, 2002), chap. 7.
22. Ibid., 177.
23. *Qaddafi's Green Book*, part III.
24. Ibid.
25. "Libya," Library of Congress country study.
26. Ibid.
27. Quoted in Obeidi, 2002, 177.
28. "Libya," Library of Congress country study.
29. *Qaddafi's Green Book*, part III.
30. "Libya," *CIA World Factbook*.
31. Obeidi, 2002, 175.
32. Ibid.
33. Ibid., 176.
34. "Libya," Library of Congress country study.
35. Ibid.
36. Ibid.
37. Obeidi, 2002, 175.
38. "Libya," Library of Congress country study.

RESOURCE GUIDE

Suggested Reading

Arnold, Guy. *The Maverick State: Gaddafi and the New World Order*. London: Cassell Academic, 1997. Discusses the Libyan state and Libyan society and confronts popular misconceptions about the country.

el-Kikhia, Mansour O. *Libya's Qaddafi: The Politics of Contradiction*. Gainesville: University Press of Florida, 1998. Focuses on ethnic groups in Libya and their relationships with the state. Also includes discussion of the impact of oil on politics and government and discussion of Qadhafi's political philosophy.

Obeidi, Amal. *Political Culture in Libya*. London: Curzon Press, 2002. Discusses topics such as regime success, gender issues, Arab nationalism, and politics in Libya.

Simon, Rachel. *Change within Tradition among Jewish Women in Libya*. Seattle: University of Washington Press, 1992. Discusses the women of the Jewish community of Libya from the nineteenth century until Qadhafi's 1969 revolution, when most Jews left Libya.

Simons, Geoff. *Libya: The Struggle for Survival*. New York: Palgrave, 1996. Discusses U.S. policy toward Libya, the Lockerbie bombing in 1988, and modern Libya.

St. John, Ronald Bruce. *Libya and the United States: Two Centuries of Strife*. Philadelphia: University of Pennsylvania Press, 2002. Explores U.S.-Libyan relations and the reasons for the historical conflict between the two nations.

Vandewalle, Dirk. *Libya since Independence: Oil and State-Building*. Ithaca, NY: Cornell University Press, 1998. Deals with the influence of oil wealth on the building of political institutions in Libya since independence in 1951.

Videos/Films

Africa: Tunisia, Libya, Egypt. 1994. Our Developing World: Regional Political Geography series. Deals with women's issues, health, and population growth in these three countries.

Great TV News Stories: Muammar Qaddafi—Libya's Radical Ruler. 1986. ABC News production. Deals with Libyan leader Qadhafi.

Lion of the Desert. 1981. Directed by Moustapha Akkad. Deals with Libyan resistance to Italian colonization.

Web Sites

ABC News profile of Libyan leader Mu'ammar al-Qadhafi, www.abcnews.go.com/reference/bios/gadhafi.html.

CIA World Factbook, entries on Libya, www.cia.gov/cia/publications/factbook/geos/ly.html.

Library of Congress country study on Libya, http://memory.loc.gov/frd/cs/lytoc.html.

Permanent mission of Libya to the United Nations, www.libya-un.org/index_f.html.

U.S. Department of State Consular Information Sheet on Libya, http://travel.state.gov/libya.html.

World Center for Studies and Research of the Green Book, www.greenbookstudies.com/index_en.html. Includes full text of *The Green Book*.

Organizations

Libyan-American Friendship Association
PO Box 471
Merrifield, VA 22116
Phone: 703-425-9350
Email: lafa@lafa.org
Web site: www.lafa.org
Organization concerned with improving ties between the peoples of Libya and the United States.

Libyan Midwife Association for Mother and Childhood Care
PO Box 83405
Tripoli
Libyan Arab Jamahiriya

Phone: 00128 21 602334
Maternal and child-care organization.

Permanent Mission of Libya to the United Nations
309–315 East 48th Street
New York, NY 10017
USA
Phone: 212-752-5775
Email: info@libya-un.org
Libya's representatives at the United Nations in New York.

Society for Libyan Studies
c/o The Institute of Archaeology
31–34 Gordon Square
London WC1H 0PY
UK
British organization dedicated to the study of Libya, including its history, archaeology, law, sciences, geography, geology, and education.

Al Wafa Association for Human Services
Sidi Almasri University Road, PO Box 91522
Tripoli
Libyan Arab Jamahiriya
Phone: (218-21) 600871; c/o UNDP (218-21) 3330856
General social service organization in Libya.

SELECTED BIBLIOGRAPHY

Das, Man Singh, ed. *The Family in the Muslim World*. New Delhi: M.D. Publications, 1991.
Graeff-Wassink, Maria. *Women at Arms: Is Ghadafi a Feminist?* Edinburgh: Darf, 1993.
el-Kikhia, Mansour O. *Libya's Qaddafi: The Politics of Contradiction*. Gainesville: University Press of Florida, 1998.
Monti-Belkaoui, Janice, and Ahmed Riahi-Belkaoui. *Qaddafi: The Man and His Policies*. Brookfield, VT: Ashgate, 1996.
Obeidi, Amal. *Political Culture in Libya*. London: Curzon Press, 2002.
Qaddafi, Muammar. *Qaddafi's Green Book*. Buffalo: Prometheus Books, 1988.
Vandewalle, Dirk. *Libya since Independence: Oil and State-Building*. Ithaca, NY: Cornell University Press, 1998.
Zoubir, Yahia H., ed. *North Africa in Transition: State, Society, and Economic Transformation in the 1990s*. Gainesville: University Press of Florida, 1999.

10

MOROCCO

Kim Shively

PROFILE OF MOROCCO

The Kingdom of Morocco, located in northwestern Africa with an area of 458,730 square kilometers, is a rugged mountainous country that has coasts on both the Mediterranean Sea and the Atlantic Ocean. Unlike other countries of the Mahgreb (North Africa), Morocco remained independent until the twentieth century, when the country was colonized by the French in 1912. This history of independence has allowed the country to develop a strong traditional character that blends the native Berber, Arabic-Islamic, and African cultures that dominate in Morocco. An overwhelmingly Muslim country, Morocco is ruled by one of the oldest continuous monarchies in the world, and the current ruling dynasty traces its ancestry to the Muslim prophet Muhammad. After independence from France in 1956, Morocco became a constitutional monarchy in which the king is head of state and is supported by a democratically elected parliament. Morocco's market economy has traditionally been highly centralized, though in the 1980s and 1990s the state sought to liberalize the economy by privatizing many state industries and opening the borders to foreign investment, export, and tourism.

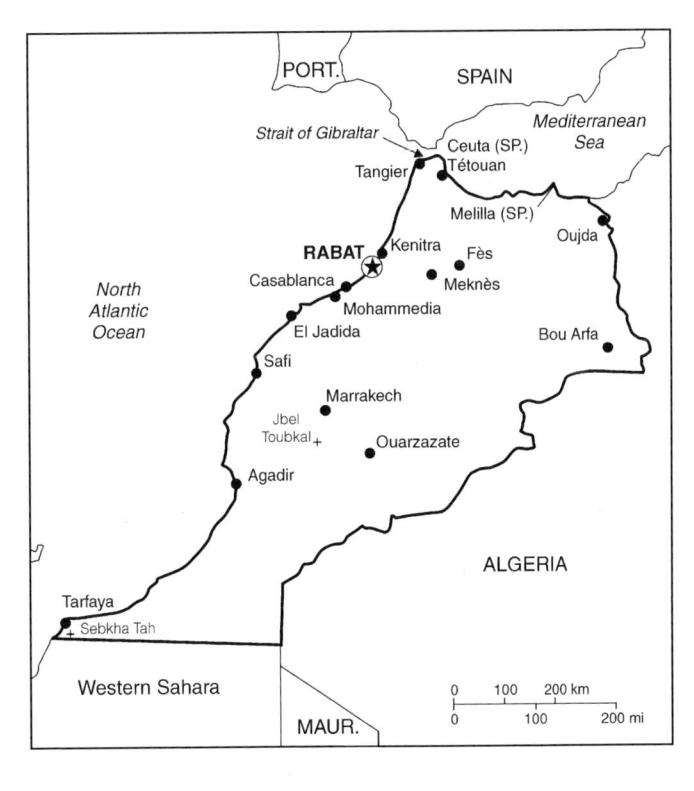

In 2001, Morocco had a population of 30 million, though the rate of population growth is still relatively robust and the population itself is quite young (35 percent of the population is under fifteen). The total fertility rate is somewhat high, at an average of 3.4 children born to every woman, though this rate is not as high as in many other developing countries.[1] Infant and maternal mortality are also quite high but declining. By the late 1980s, 330 out of 100,000 women died in childbirth, 80 out of 1,000 babies died before the age of one, and 119 children out of 1,000 died before reaching age five.[2] Indeed, childhood diseases are the most frequent cause of death in Morocco. Even with these grim statistics, life expectancy is quite respectable for both men and women: in 1999, men lived to an average of 66.6 years and women to an average of 71.1 years.[3]

OVERVIEW OF WOMEN'S ISSUES

Morocco's constitution explicitly provides for gender equality, but in reality, women's participation in socially engaged and productive activities is severely limited both by traditional conceptions of gender roles and by legal restrictions embedded in Morocco's Personal Status Code. Most Moroccans see women's primary social roles as housekeeper and childbearer, and many are unwilling to provide the education and job opportunities to women that would threaten to expand these roles into traditionally male domains, such as scholarship, political activity, and employment. Furthermore, women are treated both practically and legally as legal and social dependents on their fathers or husbands: they can conduct few legal or financial activities, such as divorce, business ventures, or employment, without consent from their husbands, fathers, or other male relatives. Moroccan religious tradition reinforces these restrictions on women: the Personal Status Code that treats women as legal minors is derived directly from Muslim law. Furthermore, many believe that women and men simply have different but complementary natural capacities—men for breadwinning and leadership, women for nurturing and caring—that require men to take care of women and women to be obedient to men. While many Moroccans accept these assumptions of gender capacities, there is a growing women's movement that challenges the status quo and seeks to better the legal and social condition of women in Morocco.

EDUCATION

Opportunities

Education and literacy are perhaps two of the most important factors contributing to women's improved status and economic position in Morocco and in any society. The more education a woman receives, the greater are her chances of obtaining a job and the higher her earning capacity, whereas a lack of education dramatically limits a woman's ability to enter the workforce. Within the family context, when a woman has less education than her husband, her decision-making role may be weakened relative to her husband's preferences, thus giving her less control over her reproductive life and over the resources available to children and leading to a less healthy family. Education also leads to lower fertility since educated women have better knowledge of and access to contraceptives. This is a reflection of a worldwide trend in which increased education and wealth are linked to smaller family sizes and to better health overall and lower rates of infant and child mortality.

In more general terms, education is an avenue for change for women, since schooling provides exposure to the outside world, to nonfamilial institutions and contacts, and to opportunities to establish nonfamilial networks of potential support. Education is also an important source of social recognition and self-esteem for women and has a great impact on women's perception of and confidence in themselves, their reproductive and familial roles, and their place in the economic system and society at large.

Like many other countries in the Middle East, Morocco has set a goal of universal primary-school enrollment, but this country has a consistently poor record in this regard, especially concerning girls. From 1985 to 1990, primary-school enrollment rates actually fell from 79 percent to 66 percent, the lowest rate in the region, and girls are more likely than boys to drop out of primary school before finishing. Morocco also has one of the lowest secondary-school enrollment rates in all of the Middle East and North Africa, with only 29 percent of high-school-age girls enrolled in high schools in 1995. Overall, the average time of schooling for Moroccan men was 4.1 years in 1990, but only 1.5 years for women. In vocational schools, girls fare better and on average make up more than half of all students enrolled in commerce and service training programs, but the type of training they tend to receive revolves around traditionally "feminine" occupations, such as secretarial and beautician training. Women make up only 10 percent of all students in industrial and engineering training and are thus at a disadvantage in the increasingly technologically oriented labor markets of the late twentieth and early twenty-first centuries.[4]

Several factors inhibit many women from pursuing even a primary education. Two of the most important are cost and the socialization of girls for family life. For poor and rural families, not only is the expense of actually sending a girl to school prohibitive, but also the loss of labor can be the greatest economic impediment to sending a girl to school. From an early age, girls tend to contribute much more than boys to household economic production and activities, and the loss of that labor can create enough difficulties for the family that it chooses to keep daughters at home. Furthermore, the socialization of girls revolves around the acceptance of traditional gender roles with the goals of marriage and a family, not education and employment. Even among those women who do go on to take jobs before or during marriage, most obtain only low-skill, low-wage jobs for which education has little benefit. For many parents, then, it seems truly unnecessary and costly to send a girl to school, whether she marries or not. This attitude, combined with the burden of educational fees, might explain in part why only 57 percent of Morocco's primary-school-age girls are enrolled.[5]

A related factor impeding the education of girls is the simple issue of geographical distance. Many parents are unwilling to send their daughters to faraway schools where they are exposed to both moral and physical risks. Families, especially male relatives, take full responsibility for the protection and reputation of girls and women in the family and so are reluctant to relinquish or jeopardize that responsibility by exposing girls, especially older girls approaching womanhood, to potential harm either to the girl herself or to the girl's (and hence the family's) reputation.

National education policy and funding also play important roles in promoting the education of girls, but Morocco has never formulated policies that seek to guarantee gender equality in education. Rather, Moroccan policy has focused more heavily on gender differentiation by promoting separate schools and curricula for boys and girls, though this stance may be understandable given many families' reluctance to send girls to schools in which they would mix with boys. If schools are segregated by gender, families may be more willing to allow their girls to attend for longer periods. Still, segregated schools tend to be unequal since more economic resources are allocated to boys' schools than to those for girls, a problem exacerbated by the fact that Morocco spends a rather small percentage of its gross national product on education, compared to other countries in the region.

The low caliber of schooling for girls may lead many families to question further the value and expense of educating girls. The quality of instruction, class size, teacher training and experience, and the condition of school buildings are often quite inferior, especially in rural areas. Textbooks are often unavailable, other sorts of educational tools are simply lacking, and there are no resources for specialized educational facilities, such as libraries, laboratories, and cafeterias. Teachers are often overworked and underpaid; female teachers are in short supply (many families prefer women teachers to instruct their daughters); and the teaching profession is often devalued, especially at the primary level, thus contributing to low teacher morale. All of these problems affect girls much more than boys, since girls often have fewer and poorer schools, inferior supplies, and less competent teachers.

Issues of social class affect the constraints on educating girls, since families with sufficient resources are able to send their daughters to high-quality private schools where the female students are closely supervised and receive a competitive education. Indeed, the number of girls in private schools is close to that of boys, but this option is available only to the wealthiest Moroccans.

Literacy

Given the poor educational prospects for girls in Morocco, the literacy rate is quite low—one of the worst in the Middle East and North Africa. A full 69 percent of all women were illiterate in 1995, compared to approximately 43 percent of all men.[6] There is a persistent urban-rural gap in literacy, in that women living in rural areas tend toward higher rates of illiteracy, but poorer women in urban areas are also less likely to attain literacy or adequate levels of education. The effects of illiteracy on women's lives can be harsh; it leaves women at the mercy of those around them who can, by being able to read and write, better negotiate bureaucratic, legal, and many social obstacles in obtaining resources and opportunities for themselves and their children.

EMPLOYMENT AND ECONOMICS

Although Morocco faces a number of economic difficulties typical of many developing countries—excessive government spending, burdensome constraints on private activity and foreign trade, and unstable economic growth—it has been somewhat successful in attracting foreign investment, liberalizing its economy, and establishing robust export markets (largely to the European Union) that allow for higher levels of employment. In fact, Morocco has high levels of employment of women in comparison to other countries in the Middle East and North Africa, though many of these women lack essential education and skills, which restricts them to low-wage, low-security jobs. Some of the most significant challenges to the equitable employment of women are educational opportunities for girls and social attitudes that militate against women working outside the home.

Job/Career Opportunities

Moroccan women make up a full quarter of the country's labor force and are especially prominent in tourism and manufacturing, as well as in public and private services such as banking and insurance. Probably the economic sector with the greatest participation of women is the export-focused manufacturing industries, especially textile, garment, and leather production. Most of these goods are produced by women; this labor generally garners very low wages and requires little formal education. The presence of so many women in the labor force may be traced to a number of factors, probably the most significant of which are general economic instability and the need for extra income in Moroccan households, as well as the increase in export manufacturing, especially textile production, that has heightened the demand for uneducated labor.

Another important sector that relies on significant levels of female labor is agriculture, which employs approximately 40 percent of the Moroccan population.[7] But farming is generally a risky business in a dry country such as Morocco, and income from agriculture is unstable. Indeed, drought conditions in the 1990s depressed agricultural conditions in Morocco, leaving many rural families impoverished and driving many others to seek employment in urban centers, though favorable rainfalls in 2000 have improved this situation.

Pay

Women in the labor market often garner lower wages than men due to the types of employment that women commonly engage in—informal jobs in the unregulated job market that yield low or even no wages. But even in the formal, "official" job market, most women tend to have lower wages, are underemployed, and are at risk for poverty, especially if they are the principal breadwinners in the household. This situation can be traced to two major factors:

> In the late twentieth century in Morocco, there was a sizable decrease in the wages of all workers, especially in the textile, leather, and agricultural sectors—sectors that attract many female workers. Thus the general drop in wages hit women particularly hard because of the types of jobs they tend to hold.

> The population and hence the labor force has been growing at a rate that outpaces the creation of new jobs, thus leading to higher unemployment and reduction in wages. Since women are often involved in jobs with little long-term security, they are often subject to wage reductions or job loss. Indeed, in 1992, unemployment was measured at 13 percent for men and at 25.3 percent for women, with higher rates of unemployment in urban areas.[8] Low wages provide some benefits for the Moroccan economy in general, since they attract foreign investment and the establishment in Morocco of factories of foreign companies that are looking for cheap labor. But the laborers themselves, especially women workers, are directly exposed to the underside of foreign investment since they are often forced to take low-paying jobs that put them at risk for poverty.

Even when women hold jobs that are commonly held by men, they are vulnerable to wage discrimination, since Morocco has no law that guarantees equal pay for men and women. As in many other parts of the world, women in jobs on average receive a lower wage than equally qualified men in the same positions.

In the context of agricultural labor, rural women are most often unpaid family laborers who work on their fathers' or husbands' farms, and women's agricultural work may simply be seen as part and parcel of their general household work. Such women rarely secure any sort of job in which they are paid their own wages, though some women may be hired out along with their families to work on farms during labor-intensive periods, such as planting or harvest. Even in these situations, women and men tend to work separately, as dictated by social customs regarding gender segregation, and women often receive lower wages than men. In most cases, though, women farmers see their own agricultural labor as undifferentiated from other sorts of household labor associated with female adulthood, and therefore they do not expect any remuneration.

This situation in which women work as unpaid "family helpers" rather than hired wage-earning employees is quite prominent in urban settings in Morocco as well. In developing countries around the world, what economists call the "informal sector" is an important, if often underestimated, economic engine and employer. In the 1980s, informal employment constituted 57 percent of all nonagricultural jobs in Morocco, and most newly created employment was associated with informal, unregulated work.[9] Workers in the informal sector may include the self-employed, unpaid family laborers (usually women), part-time workers who are "off the books," or laborers in small-scale enterprises (usually ten workers or fewer) that commonly hire casually and skirt employment regulations.

In both urban and rural areas, women are heavily involved in informal wage labor, such as carpet weaving, pottery production, sewing and embroidery work, leather work, and hairdressing. Often these women have little access to their own wages since any income they generate is seen as contributing to a general household "coffer" that is most often overseen by the male head of the household. Even those women who do preserve some independence over their wages can often use their earnings only for self- or family maintenance and have little hope for true economic autonomy since they have no access to credit with which to build or expand an independent business. Finally, those women who work in family-owned businesses are in much the same position as rural women working in agriculture: they receive no wages since their labor is seen as part of family household work. While the informal sector provides many employment opportunities for poorly educated women, the unregulated nature of most informal jobs leaves these workers vulnerable to exploitation resulting from underpayment, poor working conditions, and long work days.

Working Conditions

As in much of the developing world, Morocco has established labor standards and social insurance that benefit only a small portion of the working population—generally those employed in the formal job market, especially in the public sector. In 1993, Morocco signed the United Nations Convention on the Elimination of All Forms of Discrimination against Women, part of which was designed to improve working standards for women. But other Moroccan legal codes have led to inconsistencies in the application of fair labor laws. For instance, the Personal Status Code, which gives preferences to men in inheritance, family, and household financial matters, foils any equality established in labor laws or in the constitution. Even though laws are in place to protect women from inequality in the workplace, enforcement is haphazard or even nonexistent, pointing to a severe gap between law and reality in Moroccan life.

On the other hand, Morocco does have fairly substantial social insurance programs for those who work in the formal economy, providing decent if not generous compensation for medical care, including maternity needs, disability, work injury, and family allowances, though these benefits do not include unemployment compensation. But since relatively few women work in the formal sector, most women do not benefit from these social programs.

Sexual Harassment

The issue of sexual harassment in the workplace has only occasionally been addressed publicly in Morocco. Publicity concerning this problem increased after a 1995 case in which women employees at the Manufacture du Maroc textile factory outside Rabat made a public complaint about harassment in the workplace and their case was taken up by the Democratic Association of Moroccan Women (ADFM). The female workers went on a two-week strike to protest repeated violence against several women employees, including the arbitrary dismissal of the general secretary of the factory's women worker's union, her subsequent rape by a foreman, and the dismissal of seventeen women who protested. The ADFM mobilized human rights organizations and women's organizations in defense of these workers. This instance not only shows that women are vulnerable in the workplace, but also demonstrates that women are organizing and gaining ground in their ability to protest inequality and harassment, suggesting that working conditions for women may improve in the future.

Support for Mothers/Caretakers

Maternal Leave

A number of labor policies concerning pregnancy and maternity leave have been established to protect women's jobs. Morocco offers maternity benefits to women workers, but only to those women who work in the formal sector, and even then, the benefits are not especially generous. Employed women are entitled to twelve weeks of maternity leave at full pay, though they then receive no medical benefits. Similarly, workplaces with at least fifty women workers over the age of fifteen are required to provide nursing rooms, although this law is rarely enforced. Because these policies apply only to women in the formal economy, the majority of women in the informal economy have no sort of maternity leave benefit or job protection.

Daycare

There are very few formal daycare centers, and those that do exist are confined largely to the wealthier parts of urban centers. Most women who work and need child-care services rely on family, older children, or neighbors to look after their small children. Since many women live near their own families or their husband's families, they can easily call on extended family members to assist with child care.

Inheritance and Property Rights

Laws concerning the inheritance of wealth and property are based on Moroccan family law, which stipulates that a woman is allocated half of a male's share of inheritance, but in many instances the woman's share is forfeited. From an economic perspective, this not only guarantees lower personal wealth for women, but also impedes women from drawing on family wealth to start up or expand their own businesses.

Unmarried women have very little control over any property other than, perhaps, the trousseau that a woman prepares in anticipation of her marriage. Once a woman is married, she is presumed to have control over certain items of movable property, such as kitchen utensils, clothing, and, most important, jewelry, which is often seen as a woman's independent source of wealth to be stowed away for potential future needs. All other property, including land and housing, is assumed to be the husband's unless the wife can prove otherwise. In sum, laws on inheritance and property rights ensure that women are de jure economic minors vis-à-vis their male relatives.

Social/Government Programs

Welfare

During the early 1990s, the World Bank carried out a number of poverty assessments in Morocco. These studies found that approximately 82 percent of the Moroccan population lacks formal social security programs, such as basic health care, schooling, and fundamental infrastructure services, for example, waste disposal and potable water systems.[10] A number of austerity programs in the 1980s coupled with an increase in military spending resulted in a decline in public welfare services throughout the country.

Rural dwellers appeared to suffer the most from this lack of state antipoverty programs, in that a full 95 percent of them have no social insurance or welfare to draw on in times of need.[11] Rural wage earners are the hardest hit, and rural women suffer disproportionately. In urban areas, most poor workers, including women, are self-employed and gain some income, but rural women rarely have this advantage and have to rely mainly on precarious agricultural bounty for financial well-being and access to wage jobs in agriculture.

FAMILY AND SEXUALITY

Gender Roles

Gender roles in Morocco tend to be distinctly defined for both men and women. Work and social roles are largely segregated, so that men are often seen as naturally fit for some types of work, such as breadwinning labor, while women are seen as naturally fit for other kinds of work, such as child rearing and housework, and are thought to be naturally subordinate to men. It is important not to overstate this separation of labor and roles, since women do sometimes take work outside the home and demonstrate leadership. Nevertheless, the stereotypical gender roles of man as head of household and woman as dependent and housekeeper are seen by many Moroccans as essential to gender identity.

One factor that contributes to the relatively rigid separation of gender roles is a widespread morality that requires the spatial separation of unrelated men and women and the division of labor associated with this division of space. In many areas of Moroccan society, men work and spend much of their time with other men, while women spend the bulk of their time with other women and children. Men's work and social interactions are most commonly associated with the public sphere of economic, political, legal, and communal recreational activities. Women's work and social life tend to focus more on the private home and on the immediate neighborhood or homes of close relatives. Interaction between men and women, especially between unrelated men and women, is generally restricted and regulated. When women must venture away from the home, they most often wear the *hijab*, a head-to-toe form of veiling

Veiled and unveiled women walk together in Tangier. Photo © TRIP/ H. Rogers.

consisting of a veil and a sheet or robe that covers the whole body and hides the woman from the view of strangers.

The separation of the sexes extends to many aspects of social life. For example, cafés are visited exclusively by men and bar women from entering, and most stores or marketplace stalls are run by men only. The few women who do work outside the home in shops or in the marketplace will often do so because either male relatives cannot or there are no male relatives. The women's stores or stalls are relatively sheltered, out of the way of the main market, and exclusively serve other women.

This social order that requires the separation of men and women also defines roles for each family member in their respective realms of interaction: the household leader and breadwinner is the father, while the mother's primary duty is seen as maintaining the household and raising and educating children. Many Moroccans, though not all, believe that these roles are divinely ordained and are necessary for the smooth functioning of a peaceful, blessed society, while deviations from these roles are sometimes seen as inviting divine displeasure and social chaos. This popular concept of preordained gender roles prohibits many women from expanding their gender roles to include political involvement or wage-earning economic activity, even if the family is in need of the extra income, since women may themselves feel that their participation in public political or economic activities goes against the natural order of things. The degree to which men and women are separated varies considerably according to the education and wealth of the family—wealthier, Western-educated families may practice little segregation, and many well-educated Moroccan women are taking on positions of authority and leadership. But the division of space into gendered spheres that require specific gender roles is quite common throughout Moroccan society.

Though this division of space and gender roles seems to put women directly under the command of men, the separation of men from women actually means that women are seldom directly supervised or controlled by men. In reality, the subordination of women to men derives from social structure rather than direct manipulation. Women are expected to act in certain ways that give deference to men, and women are socialized by their mothers and female kin to accept and maintain this deference. Indeed, the supervision of women is most often carried out by other women or by the constraints that a woman might place on herself. Thus women's self-image and their images of their own sex and of men are essential in perpetuating women's subordination in much of Moroccan society.

Marriage

For most Moroccan women, marriage is a social obligation and is essential to adult female identity. Indeed, the idea of a menstruating and unmarried woman has long been alien to Moroccan family ideology, though economic and social developments are changing this mindset as job insecurity and educational goals induce many men and women to postpone marriage to an older age. Previously, many Moroccan women married before the age of fifteen. Current Moroccan family law has established the minimum age for marriage at fifteen for women and eighteen for men, but by the 1980s, the average age of a woman at marriage rose to twenty-two for women and twenty-five for men, though many still marry at younger ages.[12]

Many or even most Moroccan women have little legal input into the choice of a husband, for it is the woman's father or other male relative—a marriage tutor or guardian (*wali*)—who is approached by suitors and who chooses a future husband for the woman. The suitors often wrangle with the father or *wali* over the amount of money and goods that the groom's family will contribute to the new household and over when and where the girl is to be married. It is also the father or *wali* who validates a wedding contract in court, though technically the woman is supposed to give her own consent. As such, a Moroccan woman, no matter how old she is when she marries, cannot contract her own wedding and is put into a position of inferiority vis-à-vis her male relatives. This does not mean that women do not have some real input into their choice of a husband, and a young woman may try to persuade her father or *wali* to consent to a particular suitor. But the final decision lies with the men, not with the bride herself. However, women who have already been married, such as widows and divorcées, have fewer restrictions when they seek a husband, and they are no longer required to be represented by a male. But many such women opt not to represent themselves due to modesty or simple ignorance and may choose a male relative, even a son, to negotiate a marriage contract for them.

Moroccan family law allows for polygyny (where a man takes more than one wife), though the law also requires that the husband must be able to treat all wives equally and fairly, which is a difficult condition. A wife does have the right to stipulate in the marriage contract that the husband take no second wives, but these rights are often ignored or can be circumvented in many cases. In reality, the vast majority of Moroccan marriages are monogamous, since most men cannot afford to maintain two wives, and a wife will often not tolerate a second wife in the household.

An important aspect of a Moroccan woman's first marriage is the issue of virginity, and the notions of premarital sex or loss of virginity prior to marriage are socially unacceptable. The very word for "girl" or "daughter"—*bint*—also means "virgin," suggesting that virginity is fundamental to the identity of unmarried girls. Thus an important component of many Moroccan wedding ceremonies is proof or disproof of the bride's virginity, which traditionally includes a public display of bloodied sheets after the consummation of the marriage.

Because of the extreme importance of virginity at the time of marriage, mothers will often check to assure that their daughters are indeed virgins or will have a doctor examine the girl and issue a certificate of virginity in case there is some doubt as to her purity. Similarly, the groom's family often views the signs of defloration on the wedding night as essential to its honor. A groom may become enraged if he finds that his bride is not a virgin and will call the marriage into question. The situation can be saved if witnesses—usually other women or doctors who examine the bride— affirm that the young woman is actually a virgin. But lack of virginity at the time of marriage is an acceptable reason to cancel the wedding. Such an action is extreme, since both families invest heavily in weddings, the dishonor of the bride translates into dishonor and humiliation for her entire family, and the groom's family may be subject to stigma as well. Thus many grooms may not make the lack of blood an issue, and certainly the lack of blood on the wedding night may also result from his own impotence, often due to nervousness at having his sexual performance under such scrutiny. Grooms sometimes create an appearance of successful defloration to protect all those involved, perhaps by cutting themselves or the bride, or by sacrificing a bird and spilling its blood on the sheets. The essential symbol of the wedding night is spilled blood, and very few question how the blood is actually spilled.

Once the couple is married, they may set up an independent nuclear household or, as is also common, they may live patrilocally, meaning that they will live with the groom's family in a traditional extended family arrangement. In the patrilocal household, the new bride is expected to be subservient to the men and to her mother-in-law, the female family member who often has greater access to family wealth and who holds more power in the household. Daughters-in-law will often compete with each other and with the unmarried daughters of the house (the groom's sisters) for power and respect. Thus there are many sources of household conflict, and women are often portrayed as contentious and even unpleasant. A number of Moroccan proverbs portray women's household relationships in negative terms, as can be seen in the saying "The wife of one brother only loves the wife of another brother if she is one-eyed or flat broke." This popular view that women are contentious, however, is contradicted by the many instances in which daughters-in-law and mothers-in-law get along relatively harmoniously, and it ignores the fact that many families also experience tensions among the household men, such as when fathers and sons or brothers vie for control over household resources.

In the context of marriage, gender roles are to some extent reinforced by law in the Moroccan Personal Status Code (*Mudwanna*), which specifies a husband's and wife's respective marital rights and duties. This code was enacted in 1957 after Moroccan independence from France and is based primarily on the shari'a, the Islamic law based on the Maliki school of Islamic law that prevails in the Maghreb.[13] In Article 36 of the Mudwanna, for example, the wife is obliged to maintain fidelity to her husband, remain obedient to him according to accepted social standards, breast-feed children if possible, manage and organize the household, and maintain deference to the husband's father, mother, and close relatives. Thus the married woman's legal duties focus on housekeeping, reproduction, submission, and family responsibilities. On the other hand, the husband's responsibilities, according to Article 35 of the code, include financial support of his wife and children (food, clothing, housing, and the like), equal treatment of wives in the case of polygamy, authorization for the wife to visit and receive visits from her parents within socially acceptable limits, and protecting the wife's exclusive control over her own possessions.

In sum, a man's duty to his wife is primarily material—he must maintain her physically—and this ability to maintain his wife is largely gained from work outside the house. The woman's obligation to her husband is largely moral, with the focus on her activities within the private household and on her submission to his legal and moral power over her. In reality, many Moroccan women work outside the home, contribute to family wealth, and are heads of the household, but the legal codes do not reflect this reality and do not protect women in these less traditional positions.

In Moroccan law, either the husband or the wife may request divorce, but a woman must take her case before a judge with specific reasons for the divorce, such as a husband's extended desertion. In general, the woman has been required to show that she is subject to substantial danger or injustice. The husband, however, has few constraints on his request for a divorce and must merely petition the court as he desires. For women, this imbalance can represent a substantial hardship, since taking their case before a judge requires significant financial outlay when they have little or no financial independence, and judges are often sympathetic to male defendants in divorce cases, making it unlikely that a woman will obtain a divorce even if she should have a case brought before the court. These hardships prevent many women from actually initiating divorce cases, since the prospects for success are bleak and the financial damages could be overwhelming.

Even if a woman should obtain a divorce, she faces a number of obstacles. Though the husband is required to support his ex-wife and children financially, enforcement of these requirements is minimal at best. Most women do not know their rights and are reluctant to take alimony cases to court, again due to the poor prospects for success and the financial resources such an action would require, though a 1992 law exempted women from paying legal fees in alimony cases. Furthermore, a divorced woman can maintain custody of her small children only if she remains unmarried, even though the social stigma of being an unmarried divorced woman is quite severe. Should she remarry, she loses custody of her children, and in any case, men obtain legal guardianship of all children once they are past puberty, though the mother often continues to care for them.

The husband incurs no penalty if he remarries. There has been ongoing discussion in political circles about the need to reform and equalize the divorce laws, especially since divorce rates in Morocco are relatively high (around 50 percent of all marriages end in divorce), but only a few minor changes have taken place thus far, such as the waiving of legal fees in alimony cases.[14]

Reproduction

Morocco has been experiencing a demographic transition that has become common throughout many developing countries. This has involved a shift from high fertility, high birthrates, and high mortality to patterns of low fertility and low mortality, though Morocco still has a higher total fertility rate—3.4—than many other developing countries.[15] During the 1980s, Morocco's maternal mortality rate stood at 330 per 100,000 live births—the highest rate in the Middle East and North Africa—yet mortality rates were decreasing, leading to an increase in population.[16]

High fertility is linked with the cost or value of having children and the status of women. Women's lower status is associated with low levels of female education and employment, making their primary roles those of childbearer and housekeeper. This is clearly a class issue, since women from wealthy families have access to education, employment, and good medical care and have knowledge of contraception, thus leading to low fertility rates among the elite. But especially among poorer women with little or no economic independence or education, having sons who will care for them in the future is a highly prized form of social security. For rural farmers, children of both sexes are needed to assist in agricultural labor, leading to a pattern of large families in rural communities. In sum, the cost of children and the status of women varies from class to class, though the overall tendency in Morocco is toward relatively high fertility rates.

Apart from material benefits of childbearing, such as the need for family workers or future support, motherhood is often essential to many women's self-identity. A pregnant woman or mother gains a more elevated social status than a woman without children, and women are heavily socialized into seeing motherhood as the most important, sometimes even sacred, role that women play in society. The symbolic significance of motherhood cannot be overestimated and should be understood to play an important role in high fertility rates.

However, childbearing is viewed positively only in the context of marriage. Any woman who has a child outside of marriage suffers a number of penalties. For example, a woman who tries to register a child that no father claims can be arrested and sentenced to a six-month jail term. For a Moroccan woman to prove paternity, she must produce twelve witnesses who will testify to the fact that she had sexual relations with the father of her child. An unwed mother who tries to abandon her child in order to avoid imprisonment is also subject to prosecution. In sum, the penalties for premarital sexual intercourse for women, even when it is against their will, are quite high, while men are rarely held accountable for their premarital sexual activities.

Sex Education

There is little or no formal sex education in Morocco, since discussion of sexual matters in public or private schools is considered a breach of decency and morality. In particular, there is a strong notion that exposing girls or women to explicit sexual information would negatively affect their morals, suggesting that women are less able to withstand sexual temptation and men are better able to resist potential corrupting influence. This does not mean, however, that girls or young women do not receive more informal information about sexual matters, perhaps from female relatives, friends, or various forms of media. Nevertheless, many young women only learn of sex on their wedding night, making the act of defloration particularly frightening and confusing.

Contraception and Abortion

Though most Moroccan women are aware of various forms of contraception, contraceptive use is still not common in Morocco. Only about 30 percent of all women have ever used any form of contraception.[17] Even those who are interested in using contraception cannot always gain access to it, since medical facilities or dispensaries are not readily available, affordable, or accessible. Many women would like to limit their family size, but are frustrated in finding the means to prevent further pregnancies. Abortion is also not a viable option. Many women find abortion repugnant or see it as a violation of God's will, but in any case, abortion is illegal, even if the pregnancy is the result of rape or incest. Women who have abortions can be and are prosecuted.

Teen Pregnancy

Many Moroccan women marry and have children while they are still in their teens, so any problems associated with teen pregnancy relate to the more general issue of having children out of wedlock, which carries a high social and legal penalty in Morocco. As noted earlier, any female, whether a teen or not, who has a child outside of marriage—even if the child is conceived as a result of incest or rape—can be sentenced to a six-month jail term, on the presumption that the unwed mother is a prostitute (that is, unwed mothers receive the same legal treatment as prostitutes).

HEALTH

Health Care Access

In 1956, Moroccan health-care services were extremely sparse and difficult to access. There were only about 700 health-care practitioners to care for a population of millions. Since then, the Moroccan government has actively worked to improve health-care services. By 1992, at least some level of health care had become available to about 70 percent of the population.[18] Yet most health-care services are available in urban centers; rural residents must rely on traditional herbalists and other practitioners to deal with often complicated health problems. To deal with this disadvantage, the Moroccan government supports mobile medical teams and scattered pharmacies and clinics, though these are still inadequate. There have also been concerted efforts to teach basic hygiene to children and adults alike, but infant and childhood diseases remain serious health threats. Also, difficulties in providing reliably safe drinking water and dealing with waste disposal have impeded Morocco's efforts to improve health care. Still, the average life expectancy in Morocco is a respectable 66.6 years for men and 71.1 years for women.

Particular problems with health-care access arise for women, since many women are largely dependent on male relatives to gain access to public services. Women often need the permission or assistance of related men to contact medical personnel or to go to clinics or pharmacies and may therefore be subject to the time constraints or whims of their relatives. This problem is exacerbated by economic considerations. Although the government may provide many basic services to the general public, better, more extensive health care is often available only to those who can pay for it. Even in wealthy families, a woman often cannot gain access to her own or her family's wealth except through male relatives, again making her dependent on men for access to good health care.

Diseases and Disorders

AIDS

While the incidence of AIDS in Morocco has not reached epidemic proportions, the number of HIV-positive people has been steadily increasing and probably exceeds 15,000, though this figure actually represents a very small proportion of the Moroccan population—approximately .01 percent.[19] It has been extremely difficult for the Moroccan health ministry, the World Health Organization, and other health-related watch groups to obtain accurate figures on HIV- or AIDS-affected people. Several factors inhibit the accurate reporting of AIDS: many physicians do not report AIDS cases they diagnose, perhaps in order to protect the patients from the stigma that AIDS carries; many doctors do not have a thorough knowledge of the disease and therefore misdiagnose it; and the only laboratories that are equipped to analyze blood samples for HIV are located in Rabat and Casablanca, which causes a shortage of diagnostic facilities. Furthermore, data on certain high-risk groups for AIDS, such as prostitutes or drug users, are virtually nonexistent, thus contributing to the underrepresentation of AIDS and HIV patients in national statistics.

While most AIDS patients are men, pregnant women also constitute a significant proportion of reported AIDS cases, partly because the World Health Organization conducted a study on pregnant women and AIDS. Still, the incidence of HIV or AIDS among other female populations is unknown and needs attention.

In terms of treatment, the Moroccan health ministry contributes approximately half of the cost of individual treatment, which, considering the high cost of AIDS drugs, can still make treatment prohibitively expensive. The Moroccan government has turned to foreign resources for help, and some organizations, such as the French government, are extending material assistance in the treatment of AIDS. The current sultan of Morocco, King Mohammed VI, had an address on the issue read on his behalf before the 2001 United Nations General Assembly special session on AIDS, requesting international cooperation and assistance in the fight against AIDS.

Cancer

The rate of breast cancer, as well as ovarian cancer, among Moroccan women has been steadily increasing to a rate of approximately 2 percent of the female population.[20] Even though great progress has been made in the treatment of breast cancer, issues related to exposure to environmental carcinogens and ability to pay for cancer treatment severely limit the recovery rate for many Moroccan women.

Compared to women in the United States, for example, Moroccan women are exposed to higher levels of pesticides and phosphates in the environment and to contaminants in the water. Also, women may be exposed to higher levels of cadmium, an element that has been shown to accelerate the growth of abnormal cells in the breast. Thus women in Morocco are especially vulnerable to breast cancer.

Among the problems facing women with breast cancer and other forms of "women's cancer" such as ovarian and cervical cancer is an extreme shortage of diagnostic methods, such as mammograms and sensitive biopsy techniques, that would help in the early detection that is crucial in the successful treatment of the disease. Also, much cancer treatment requires significant financial outlay by the women's families—a financial burden that many women simply cannot afford.

Depression

Like many other developing countries, Morocco does a poor job of treating depression and other mental illnesses. Morocco invests very few resources toward the treatment of any mental illness, let alone depression, which disproportionately affects women. Morocco does have some resources available within its general health clinics, and some private mental health-care practitioners and facilities are available to those few Moroccans who can afford such treatment. But the many Moroccans who are poor and who suffer from depression are stuck in a vicious circle from which there is no easy escape without assistance: poverty itself exacerbates the effects of mental illnesses and also prevents sufferers from getting treatment, which often leads to increased poverty due to lost wages or property from increased disability. Even when treatment is available, people who suffer from depression are often too ashamed to seek professional help due to the stigma attached to mental disorders. Thus not only are improved treatment facilities necessary on a large scale to combat depression, but a public education campaign about mental disorders would perhaps encourage more sufferers to seek help.

POLITICS AND LAW

Morocco's political system is a constitutional hereditary monarchy in which the king is the head of state. He is also the head of the armed forces and appoints the prime minister and the other members of the government. Morocco has had a parliamentary system since its independence from France in 1956, but the parliament in general is a largely conservative body of supporters of promonarchy parties that rarely challenge the king's rule. Power is heavily concentrated around the king and his supporters, and in fact the king has the power to order the review of legislative measures and to disband the Legislative Assembly. Still, there have been a number of opposition parties and trade unions, many of which have supported an expansion of women's rights, but these have played relatively minor roles in political life and have had little effect on the nature of Morocco's politics.

Suffrage

Women over the age of twenty-one have enjoyed the right to vote since 1956, and this right is explicitly supported in Article 8 of the current Moroccan constitution, last revised in 1992. While most eligible women actually vote, most do so because it is a legal obligation, and few have a sense that their participation is in any way consequential. This sense comes from the fact that the Moroccan electoral process has long been accused of being corrupt and open to fraud and tampering. Periodically, campaigners attempt to introduce legal and electoral reform through national referenda, but they have been repeatedly stymied by the electoral fraud and voting irregularities that they have fought against. For most voters, the sense of political stagnation and corruption leads to a sense that voting is an empty gesture.

Political Participation

The nature of the Moroccan government and electoral process makes change extremely difficult, and for women who wish to be involved in politics, this may be highly frustrating. There have been very few women in positions of political leadership, partly because leadership has been associated with men for so long, and partly because mobilizing support for female candidates has proven difficult. Not only must women political leaders be accepted by men, but they must succeed in mobilizing women for support, a daunting task considering that few women are involved in politics at any level in the first place. King Hassan of Morocco (who died in 1999) himself was also generally opposed to the mobilization of women. To those women who demanded greater equality, King Hassan made minor concessions in order to appease his European allies, but he refused to make any significant changes to include more female candidates, which would challenge Moroccan traditions or Muslim law, for fear of opposition from the large conservative political sector.

Yet there have been a number of women who have run for political positions at the local level ever since the 1970s, though it was not until 1993 that women gained seats in the national parliament in opposition parties. The 1993 elections proved to be a particular watershed for women in politics, since the success of the women candidates sprang in part from a publicity effort around proposals for changes in the Personal Status Code (Mudwanna) in favor of more rights for women. Yet even in this context, only two female candidates actually gained parliamentary seats. Because Morocco has no opinion polling organizations, it has been difficult for any candidates to understand why voters choose one candidate over another. Furthermore, the centrist and conservative parties, which support no women candidates, have considerably more funds at their disposal than the opposition parties, many of whom include female candidates. These factors all work against including women in national politics, though clearly some gains have been made as of the 1993 elections.

Women's Rights

In the 1980s, Morocco came under increased criticism for its poor human rights record, especially for its arbitrary detention of political prisoners and use of torture. By the early 1990s, King Hassan supported a number of human rights initiatives—largely due to pressure from internal opposition parties and from foreign governments—and political debates became dominated by discussions of human rights and democratization.

Yet the issue of women's rights has remained outside these discussions of human rights, and little headway has been made in the legal position of women as independent and equal citizens. The Moroccan constitution (last modified in 1992) has included clauses supporting the equal rights of men and women. Article 5, for instance, states that "all Moroccans are equal before the law," Article 8 guarantees men and women equal political and civil rights, and Article 12 stresses that both sexes are equal in the exercise of public employment and working conditions. But this equality does not extend to other areas, especially those rights and duties covered in the Personal Status Code (Mudwanna).

Probably the greatest criticism that is leveled against the legal position of women in the Mudwanna is that women are technically treated as legal minors rather than fully independent adults. For instance, women are not permitted to enter into their own marriages without the supervision of a male tutor. In labor laws, there are a variety of restrictions on employment, such as exposure to toxic materials, that pertain to children under sixteen and to all women, and there are prohibitions against women working in environments that would be injurious to their "morals." The penal code is also highly discriminatory. For example, a woman must get permission to initiate a civil suit against her husband, but the husband has no such constraint. Any man who murders or assaults a wife who has committed adultery benefits from considerations of extenuating circumstances, considerations that a wife in similar circumstances is not permitted.

Reforms in personal status law in favor of women's equality have been extremely difficult to carry through and face numerous obstacles. In Morocco, the control of women and the production of children are crucial parts of the male-dominated social order in general, and legal changes that threaten that order come under intense opposition, especially from the large religious conservative populations in both the urban and rural sectors of Moroccan society. Furthermore, notions of what actually constitutes women's rights are somewhat different in Morocco from those in many Western countries. In the West, concern about gender equality has been at the center of the struggle for women's rights, but in Morocco, such ideas often seem irrelevant. For most Moroccan women, gender roles are considered to be naturally divided so that men and women have specific duties that they carry out in separate social domains. This division of roles is further based on the ideas that the sexes are not truly equal but complementary, that men and women do not compete for and fulfill the same social roles, and that greater social harmony is achieved through lack of competition and resentment. Indeed, some Moroccan women have criticized the West's focus on role competition—the idea that women and men can hold the same roles—as a means of women's liberation. They see a more authentic Muslim identity as one grounded in commitment to family and social needs rather than in individual desires and aspirations.

Feminist Movements

Many women have fought for legal changes that would make them more fully independent. Though women's movements were important in the anticolonial movements that led to the independence of Morocco from French rule, they faded in importance after independence was gained and did not become reestablished until the late 1960s. Many of these women's groups have associated themselves with opposition parties, since few resources were available for such organizations outside of the political network. Even then, opposition parties have tended to be chronically short of funds, and the women's groups within these parties were not generally considered to be a top priority. It was not until 1983 that a woman's organization established itself outside of a political party, and such independent organizations have had to rely on funding from abroad to carry out their sociopolitical work. This external funding, however, often brings the organizations under criticism for being the pawns of foreign powers and concerns.

Furthermore, the number of women actually involved in feminist and women's rights movements is quite small, and participants are usually limited to major urban areas such as Rabat and Casablanca, while the rural population is left outside of these movements. Other factors that discourage women from becoming involved in these movements include family and social pressures to work in the home and for the family, rather than for broader social goals. Most women also carry a tremendous workload both within the house and in other employment situations, which leaves little time for other activities. Women who do participate in such movements are often accused of neglecting their children and their families. Also, given the general restrictions on women's mobility, it is difficult for women to get to meetings, rallies, or other organizational activities. Other problems include the fragmentation of the women's movements themselves, as each movement has its own political structure and organization that begets rivalries and prevents highly coordinated movements in support of particular rights and legislative changes.

Yet in the early 1990s, women's movements did come together to pressure for reforms in the Personal Status Code that would lead to greater rights for women. In 1992, a women's organization launched what was called "the Million Signatures Campaign" that sought to make a number of major changes in the Mudwanna, including the outlawing of polygamy, equal share in inheritance, equal rights in divorce cases, eliminating the woman's need for a tutor in establishing marriage contracts, and the general establishment of women's full legal competency upon reaching the age of maturity (that is, women will no longer be treated as legal minors). Yet even the opposition parties were lukewarm to these proposals, and the religious conservative leaders (*ulama*) strongly opposed the proposed changes since they saw them as violations of their relatively narrow interpretation of Muslim law. Indeed, many conservatives also saw the proposed changes as a form of Westernization that introduced foreign elements into Moroccan society.

In the end, the opposition was so overwhelming that only minor changes were actually made to the Mudwanna in 1992—changes that were suggested by the *ulama* and signed into law by the king. For example, women were exempted from paying for legal fees in cases related to getting alimony, though none of the divorce laws themselves were liberalized. Also, the parliament shortened the work period required of women before retirement from twenty-one years to fifteen years, thus giving women earlier access to their pensions—though some women saw this as a way of getting women out of the workforce. The husband was required to inform his first wife if he wished to take a second wife and was required to get a judge's permission to contract a second marriage. With regard to custody, the mother was considered primary custodian of all sons under the age of twelve and all daughters under the age of fifteen, and after these ages the children were permitted to choose which parent they would stay with. In 1995, the parliament also voted to cancel a law that forbade married women from concluding commercial transactions without their husbands' consent. All of these reforms have been fairly minor, and given the majority conservative opposition to reforms of personal status law, significant changes may be a long time in coming. In general, women's movements in Morocco are working in a difficult environment for any sort of legislative reform, especially in the areas of women's rights.

Lesbian Rights

All same-sex sexual relationships are criminalized under Section 489 of the Penal Code as of November 26, 1962. Any couple—including lesbian couples—caught engaged in homosexual acts is subject to a penalty of between six months' and three years' imprisonment and to an additional fine of 120 to 1,000 dirhams (Morocco's currency unit) for "lewd or unnatural acts with an individual of the same sex." In this legal context, any acknowledgment of female homosexuality is simply not possible, and this legal situation is reinforced by a social order in which women's primary social-sexual roles are defined within the context of the patriarchal family group. While there may be same-sex relationships between women, these are by necessity kept from public knowledge: any discussion of homosexual or lesbian rights is simply outside the bounds of acceptable public discourse in Morocco.

RELIGION AND SPIRITUALITY

Women's Roles

Virtually all citizens of Morocco profess adherence to Islam, and though there are tiny Jewish and Christian minorities, this discussion will focus exclusively on women's experience of Islam in Morocco. In general, Moroccans adhere to the tenets of Islam to differing degrees, depending on individual living circumstances and economic and educational experiences. Most Moroccan women consider themselves to be relatively devout Muslims and are careful followers of Islamic practice, requirements, and devotional traditions.

In basic terms, religious expectations for men and women are virtually identical. Men and women are considered equal before God and must observe the "five pillars" of Islam: they must profess their faith in God and in Muhammad as God's messenger, pray five times a day, give alms to the poor, fast during the month of Ramadan, and take part in the the annual pilgrimage to the holy sites in Mecca and Medina (*hajj*) at least once in their lifetime. But how women carry out these practices and others differs considerably from men's experience of Islam. Probably one of the greatest general distinctions between men's and women's practices is that women's religious observances tend to be heavily focused around the home and immediate community, while men's practices and experiences tend to be in the public arena. Mosques, for example, are almost exclusively frequented by men, though there are usually spaces in the back for women, which are generally infrequently used. Most women feel that they can best protect their own modesty and reputation by praying at home.

This informal but widely acknowledged restriction on women's religious observances contributes to the lack of formal leadership roles that women may obtain, at least in the public sphere. Religious law also prevents women from taking on leadership roles: all prayer leaders (imams) and preachers must be men, and most religious education beyond the rudimentary level is reserved for male scholars. Women learn to recite the Qur'an, and many strive to memorize major parts of it (recitation of the Qur'an is a fundamental part of Muslim devotion), but more in-depth understanding of interpretations of the Qur'an the Hadith (the sayings of the prophet Muhammad), and religious law are almost exclusively the province of men. Women's religious roles focus on personal or family devotion, and they are seen as the primary religious educators of small children. Though women's religious roles are highly circumscribed, women undertake a number of more active religious roles within particular ritual contexts.

Rituals and Religious Practices

In day-to-day religious practice, men and women generally express their devotion in separate spaces, and while this separation of the sexes persists during the major religious holidays, holidays are also a time when the strictures on gender interaction may be lifted somewhat. For instance, during Ramadan, when Muslims must fast from the first light of the day until evening darkness, the fast is usually broken with a celebratory meal called *l-fṭûr* that is shared by the entire family and guests, both male and female. Ramadan is also a time when the whole family will attend the mosque together for prayers and for socializing. During the Feast of the Sacrifice (*l-ʿîd l-kabîr*), when a ram or other large animal is sacrificed to commemorate Ibrahim's (Abraham's) willingness to obey God's command to sacrifice his son, men and women work together in the sacrifice process and eat the first meal of the sacrifice together, though men and women are assigned separate tasks. For instance, men are in charge of the actual sacrifice — women are not permitted to cut the animal — and women divide the animal into portions, cook the food, and may help to distribute meat to poor neighbors.

Once in their lifetime, men and women are both enjoined to go on the pilgrimage to Mecca (*hajj*), and married couples will often travel together and share living quarters with others. Also, many stations during the pilgrimage experience are attended by both sexes together. But the ritual requirements for men and women are somewhat different, and there are times when men and women are separated from each other. One example is that during the circling of the Ka'ba (the great structure at the center of Mecca toward which all Muslims pray, believed to mark the grave of Ibrahim), men circle in the area adjacent to the structure, while women must circle further out, away from men.

But by and large, men and women have markedly different experiences of religious practice, and this separation of the sexes has allowed women to develop a number of rituals centered around women. One of the most important rituals available to women in distress is a sojourn at one of the various sanctuaries that house a particular Muslim saint. These sanctuaries are common throughout the Maghreb and vary in size from just a small pyramid of stones to a large, ornate building. Each sanctuary is believed to house the presence of the particular saint who is hosted there, usually because the structure covers the saint's tomb, a place he or she once lived in, or a site of an important event in the saint's life. Many women go to these sanctuaries in order to seek solutions to their problems, to cure illnesses in themselves or in their children, to ward off potential evil, or to seek solace in times of grief or difficulty. Though women are the most frequent and numerous visitors to sanctuaries, men may visit the sanctuaries as well, but they keep to a separate area.

Most Moroccan saints are male, and the few women saints who are recognized tend to be poorly elaborated figures and are largely asexual. For example, most female saints are virginal or removed from human society, while male saints are not expected to be either sexually abstinent or reclusive. But all saints are believed to confer blessing and possibly solutions to problems, if approached properly. Women may come and stay at the sanctuaries for hours or even days (some sanctuaries have rooms to rent), during which time they may pray, fast, commune with other female visitors, and conduct a number of rituals to seek peace or aid. Some rituals may require that the woman hold some object, such as a cloth, stone, or plant, associated with the saint and make her plea in colloquial Arabic or Berber.[21] The supplicant will often come up with her own answer in the presence of the saint, who is believed to impart the solution, and if the solution is successful, the woman pilgrim may give the saint a gift or perform a sacrifice in the saint's name. Many women literally find sanctuary from the difficulties of everyday life at the sanctuaries of the saints. The sanctuaries are an egalitarian arena in which women can temporarily escape from the patriarchal, hierarchical social order to which they are subject in everyday life.

Another important religious ritual available to poorer women, especially in urban areas, involves ceremonies of night trance dancing (*lîla* or *derdeba*), performed during Shaban (the month prior to Ramadan in the Arabic calendar). These trance performances are organized by the Gnawa, a popular Sufi order (Islamic mystics and ascetics) that is held in some disdain by educated and orthodox Moroccans as being less theologically sound than other internationally recognized orders. The trances that trance dancers experience are attributed to possession by a whimsical spirit (*jinn*), who may cause possessed individuals to fall ill or have visions or dreams in which they are addressed by the spirit. When a woman (or man, though women are by far the most common participants in this ritual) fears that she has been possessed, she will visit a Gnawa leader—male or female—who will then diagnose which *jinn* has possessed the client. A frequent way in which the possessing spirit may be placated, if not exorcised, is to organize a night of trance dancing in the *jinn*'s honor.

The first segment of the ritual consists of the sacrifice of an animal, such as a sheep or goat, which is believed to make the entire *lîla* efficacious. The Gnawa member leading the trance night drinks the blood of the animal in order to enter a trance state, and it is in this state that the leader becomes a conduit through whom the spirits speak and convey their wishes. The trance dancing itself begins after the final prayers at sundown. After a number of small rituals are conducted, such as the eating of special foods, a group of musicians play rhythmical music, and eventually the active participants fall into trances, allowing the spirit to take full possession of the participants' bodies. A woman in trance may faint or shriek, crawl or roll about, or dance wildly. Some trance dancers may perform acts that are potentially dangerous to themselves, but the observing audience members are always on guard to protect the trancers from hurting themselves or others. The overall goal of the dancing is to establish a workable relationship with the possessing spirit by fulfilling its wishes and behaving in a way that corresponds to the individual spirit's nature, though final exorcism is considered to be generally impossible.

In general, the trance dancers act in ways well outside normal Moroccan behavior, but this antisocial behavior is attributed to the women's possessing spirits, not to the women themselves. Many analysts have speculated that such trance behavior is a way in which women may release pent-up antisocial feelings in a socially acceptable way, and it allows the participants to behave in ways that society would never allow in other circumstances. In a society in which women's behavior, appearance, and movement are highly constrained, the need for such an outlet is understandable.

Religious Law

Much of Moroccan family law is based on Muslim religious law (shari'a), which enunciates clearly distinct legal rights and duties for men and for women based on the idea that men and women have different potentials and capabilities. It has already been noted that beliefs about men's and women's natural abilities have translated into a legal code in which a man has legal responsibilities as breadwinner and head of the family, while a woman is required to maintain the household, care for children, and serve her husband. Other aspects of religious law reinforce this hierarchical relationship between men and women by maintaining that women are both intellectually inferior (they have a weaker intellect or *a'qel*) and morally inferior to men, especially in the ability to control sexual desire. Both of these propositions regarding women's capabilities are part of the basis by which women are treated as legal minors or dependents of related men. The laws that have established this dependent position of women as intellectual and moral inferiors require the guardianship and control of more intelligent and more constrained men, much as children do.

VIOLENCE

Domestic Violence

Domestic violence is common in Morocco but generally goes unreported. Many Moroccan women experience abuse at the hands of their husbands as a regrettable but inevitable reality, especially since the Qur'an itself states that a husband may beat his wife if she is disobedient. Given the general acceptance and religious justification of domestic violence, wife beating is normalized and seen as part of everyday family life. Some conservatives have even argued that the Personal Status Code allows the husband to beat his wife and to kill her in cases of adultery, though this is a very broad interpretation of Moroccan family law. In any case, there have been few public resources available to women who wish to escape an abusive husband, though in the 1990s centers for battered women opened in Casablanca and other urban centers. However, most women turn to their own families for help and support if abuse gets out of hand, but this is generally only a temporary solution since a woman's family may also see domestic violence as a normal part of marriage.

Rape/Sexual Assault

The incidence of rape and other sexual assault in Morocco is not well known, again because of underreporting. Few women who have been subject to such assault will come forward to authorities, and many may not admit it to their own families, given the stigma and potential legal punishments attached to rape victims. If a woman bears a child conceived out of rape, she can be sentenced to up to six months in jail, which is the same as the sentence for a woman found guilty of prostitution.

As is normal with rape victims around the world, many emotions—shame, embarrassment, guilt, fear—may militate against a woman discussing her experience with others, let alone seeking medical help or law-enforcement assistance to track down the perpetrator. In Morocco, moreover, a woman's sexual activity is tightly bound to the family context, and family honor rests in part on this containment of sexuality of the women of the family. Rape is thus seen as a violation not only of the woman's personal integrity but also of the integrity and honor of the entire family. Thus even when the family knows of the sexual assault on one of its female members, it may be loath to publicize it in any way, even by reporting it to the police, due to the negative social effects it has on the family as a whole.

This tendency to treat rape as a taboo subject was weakened when the "Thabit affair" became widely publicized in 1993. Hadj Mohammed Mustapha Thabit was a police commissar for an area near Casablanca when two women filed a complaint against him charging him with abduction and rape. Over the course of the investigation, Thabit himself revealed that he had raped approximately 500 women over the course of about thirteen years. He would sometimes lure his victims with promises of assistance—to obtain a passport, for instance—or would abduct women by force, take them to an apartment, and rape them. He himself recorded these events on videotape. It was also revealed that several of Thabit's colleagues knew about his actions and even condoned them. Ultimately, Thabit was sentenced to death, and several of his colleagues received lesser sentences.

While the official state media did not report the affair, other media outlets kept the scandal on the front pages, thus making rape and violence against women a topic for public discussion. Indeed, many of the shelters for abused and battered women opened after this scandal became public, but rape and sexual abuse still remain relatively taboo subjects in Moroccan society, and few resources or programs are available to victims of sexual abuse.

Trafficking in Women and Children

While there is little evidence that Morocco is involved in any sort of international trafficking in women and children, there is a tradition of child servitude in Morocco that puts children, especially girls, in the path of sexual and physical exploitation. Many female orphans or girls from poor families may become child servants who work in Moroccan homes (*petites bonnes*). While many *petites bonnes* may simply serve these families without incidents, others are subject to physical and sexual abuse at the hands of their employers, and the girls have no recourse to protection other than flight. It is not unusual for a *petite bonne* to become pregnant after sexual assault, and given that unmarried mothers are subject to legal penalty and jail sentences, this puts the *petites bonnes* in extremely difficult situations, especially since they have no family to turn to. Many may flee and hide, seek abortion, or dispose of their babies, and there have been few institutions who will offer them support. One exception is the Association of Women's Solidarity, an organization that provides services to single mothers, such as jobs that allow the women keep their babies and earn incomes without resorting to prostitution. This type of agency is rare, and most former *petites bonnes* and other single mothers have few resources to draw on.

OUTLOOK FOR THE TWENTY-FIRST CENTURY

Clearly, much work needs to be done in order to improve the lives and prospects of Moroccan women. The feminist and women's movements have made significant headway in bringing issues of women's equality into public consciousness and into popular discourse, but the reality is that few concrete changes have been made to challenge the legal and social traditions that have cast Moroccan women as legal minors and social inferiors. In the coming century, a major task for women's groups is to seek further changes in the Personal Status Code that subordinates women to their male relatives, but given the highly conservative nature of the Moroccan legislative body and social leaders, these changes may be a long time in coming. But as more and more Moroccan women join the workforce and participate in political activity, the Moroccan people may gradually adjust to the idea of women as less dependent and more self-determining individuals. Similarly, exposure to Western media in which women take on leadership roles may also lead to a gradual loosening of gender roles in Morocco, though this can also have the opposite effect of casting women's equality as a Western imperial import to be rejected as alien. In any case, a liberalization of women's roles is a distinct possibility, several years or even decades of hard work may be required to bring about the changes that would improve the lives and opportunities of Moroccan women.

NOTES

1. World Health Organization, *Epidemiological Fact Sheet on HIV/AIDS and Sexually Transmitted Infections, Morocco, 2002 Update*, www.who.int/emc-hiv/fact_sheets/pdfs/Morocco_EN.pdf.
2. Valentine M. Moghadam, *Modernizing Women: Gender and Social Change in the Middle East* (Boulder, CO: Lynne Rienner Publishers, 1993), 123.
3. "Les Soins Medicaux," University of Toronto, http://cwr.utoronto.ca/Cultural/fre/morocco/health.html.
4. Valentine M. Moghadam, *Women, Work, and Economic Reform in the Middle East and North Africa* (Boulder, CO: Lynne Rienner Publishers, 1998), 31, 33, 41–44.
5. Ibid., 43.
6. Ibid., 54.
7. Laurie A. Brand, *Women, State, and Political Liberalization: Middle Eastern and North Africa Experiences* (New York: Columbia University Press, 1998), 33.
8. Ibid., 57. In general, unemployment figures count individuals who are currently unemployed and are actively seeking work. Thus women who work at home and are not seeking outside employment are not included in unemployment figures.
9. Ibid., 61.
10. Moghadam, 1998, 61.
11. Ibid.
12. Moghadam, 1993, 126.
13. Four schools of Islamic jurisprudence have persisted in the Muslim world, and each school of law takes different attitudes toward the rights and duties of women. The Maliki school, named after Malik Ibn Anas (d. 796), prevails in most of Africa, including Morocco. Other schools include the Hanafi school, which is dominant in all areas of the former Ottoman Empire (Turkey, the Balkans, and most of the Arab Middle East) as well as in central Asia, India and Pakistan; the Shafi school, whose adherents are found in East Africa, Indonesia, Lower Egypt, Iran, and Iraq; and the Hanbalite school, which prevails in Saudi Arabia.
14. Brand, 1998, 62.
15. World Health Organization, *Epidemiological Fact Sheet on HIV/AIDS and Sexually Transmitted Infections*. The "total fertility rate" refers to the number of children a woman would bear if she experiences throughout her lifetime the rates that prevailed during the period of the WHO fertility survey.
16. Moghadam, 1993, 121.
17. Ibid., 123.
18. "Les Soins Medicaux," University of Toronto at http://cwr.utoronto.ca/cultural/fre/morocco/health.html.
19. World Health Organization, *Epidemiological Fact Sheet on HIV/AIDS and Sexually Transmitted Infections*.
20. "Breast Cancer in Morocco on the Rise, Medical Magazine Says," *Morocco, Health*, 7/22/1999, http://www.arabicnews.com/ansub/Daily/Day/990722/1999072250.html.
21. The language of formal, orthodox Islam is literate Arabic—often inaccessible to largely illiterate Moroccan women. The fact that the saints are approachable in colloquial languages makes them seem all the more inviting and friendly.

RESOURCE GUIDE

Suggested Reading

Baker, Alison. *Voices of Resistance: Oral Histories of Moroccan Women.* Albany: State University of New York Press, 1998.
Buitelaar, Marjo. *Fasting and Feasting in Morocco: Women's Participation in Ramadan.* Oxford and Providence, RI: Berg, 1993.
Combs-Schilling, M.E. *Sacred Performances: Islam, Sexuality, and Sacrifice.* New York: Columbia University Press, 1989.
Davis, Susan S. *Patience and Power: Women's Lives in a Moroccan Village.* Cambridge, MA: Schenkman Books, 1983.
Dwyer, Daisy Hilse. *Images and Self-Images: Male and Female in Morocco.* New York: Columbia University Press, 1978.
Kapchan, Deborah. *Gender on the Market: Moroccan Women and the Revoicing of Tradition.* Philadelphia: University of Pennsylvania Press, 1996.
Maher, Vanessa. *Women and Property in Morocco: Their Changing Relation to the Process of Social Stratification in the Middle Atlas.* London and New York: Cambridge University Press, 1974.
Mernissi, Fatima. *Beyond the Veil: Male-Female Dynamics in Modern Muslim Society.* Bloomington: Indiana University Press, 1987.
———. *Doing Daily Battle: Interviews with Moroccan Women.* Translated by Mary Jo Lakeland. London: Women's Press, 1988.

Videos/Films

The Bride Market of Imilchil. 1988. Steffen Pierce and Christian Pierce, directors. Explores the Imilchil shrine in Morocco, where every September men and women gather to choose mates and marry in a nearby tent.
A Door to the Sky. 1989. Farida Benlyzaid, director. Nadia, a young Moroccan émigré, returns from Paris to Fez to visit her dying father. At his funeral, she befriends a spiritual Muslim woman, and together they decide to turn the father's palace into a Muslim women's shelter.
My Heart Is My Witness. 1996. Louise Carré, director. Explores the status of women in Islam through interviews with women from Morocco, Algeria, Tunisia, and Mali.
Saints and Spirits. 1976. Melissa Llewelyn-Davies, director; Elizabeth Fernea, producer. Examines the effects of Muslim teachings and traditions on the lives of some Muslim women in Marrakech, Morocco. Filmed by an all-woman crew.
Some Women of Marrakech. 1977. Melissa Llewelyn-Davies, director; Elizabeth Fernea, producer. An overall survey of the life and conditions of Muslim women in Marrakech, Morocco, especially in light of Islamic teachings.
Women's Wiles. 1999. Farida Benlyzaid, director. A modern fairy tale about a Moroccan merchant's daughter who must use her wiles to capture the attention, heart, and respect of a prince.

Web Sites

American-Moroccan Forum, www.amfor.com.
A web site devoted to American and Moroccan relationships. The links are especially useful.

Marrakesh Express, www.marrakeshexpress.org.
An illustrated study of Moroccan textiles, plus an online textile store, with an emphasis on women's involvement with weaving. Includes an annotated bibliography on Morocco.

Moroccan Ministry of Culture and Communication: Moroccan Women, www.mincom.gov.ma/english/generalities/mwoman/.
The official Moroccan statement on women, culture, and the state.

Morocco: Arab-esque Dance Project, www.arab-esque.org/morocco/morocco.html.
Web site with information and links about all types and aspects of Moroccan folk dance.

World Health Organization, Epidemiological Fact Sheet on HIV/AIDS and Sexually Transmitted Infections, Morocco, 2002 Update, www.who.int/emc-hiv/fact_sheets/pdfs/Morocco_EN.pdf.

SELECTED BIBLIOGRAPHY

Brand, Laurie A. *Women, the State, and Political Liberalization: Middle Eastern and North African Experiences.* New York: Columbia University Press, 1998.
Buitelaar, Marjo. *Fasting and Feasting in Morocco: Women's Participation in Ramadan.* Oxford and Providence, RI: Berg, 1993.
Combs-Schilling, M.E. *Sacred Performances: Islam, Sexuality, and Sacrifice.* New York: Columbia University Press, 1989.
Dwyer, Daisy Hilse. *Images and Self-Images: Male and Female in Morocco.* New York: Columbia University Press, 1978.
Hessini, Leila. "Wearing the Hijab in Contemporary Morocco: Choice and Identity." In *Reconstructing Gender in the Middle East*, ed. Fatma Müge Göçek and Shiva Balaghi, 40–56. New York: Columbia University Press, 1994.
Mernissi, Fatima. "Women, Saints, and Sanctuaries in Morocco." In *Unspoken Worlds: Women's Religious Lives*, ed. Nancy Auer Falk and Rita M. Gross, 112–21. Belmont, CA: Wadsworth, 1989.
Moghadam, Valentine M. *Modernizing Women: Gender and Social Change in the Middle East.* Boulder, CO: Lynne Rienner Publishers, 1993.
———. *Women, Work, and Economic Reform in the Middle East and North Africa.* Boulder, CO: Lynne Rienner Publishers, 1998.

II

THE OCCUPIED TERRITORIES

Stephanie Hargrave

PROFILE OF THE OCCUPIED TERRITORIES

The land of the Palestinian people is currently disputed. The political and social leaders of the Palestinian people are in negotiation with Israel and other nations, as well as with the United Nations, to reestablish the boundaries and the recognition of the country. Historically, a mandate by the League of Nations and subsequently the United Nations created two separate areas, one to be known as Israel, one to be known as Palestine. Subsequent to these mandates, the area designated as Palestine was occupied, and now the area that is under negotiation to reestablish sovereignty as Palestine consists of two separate spaces, the West Bank and the Gaza Strip. Israel claims the space between these areas.

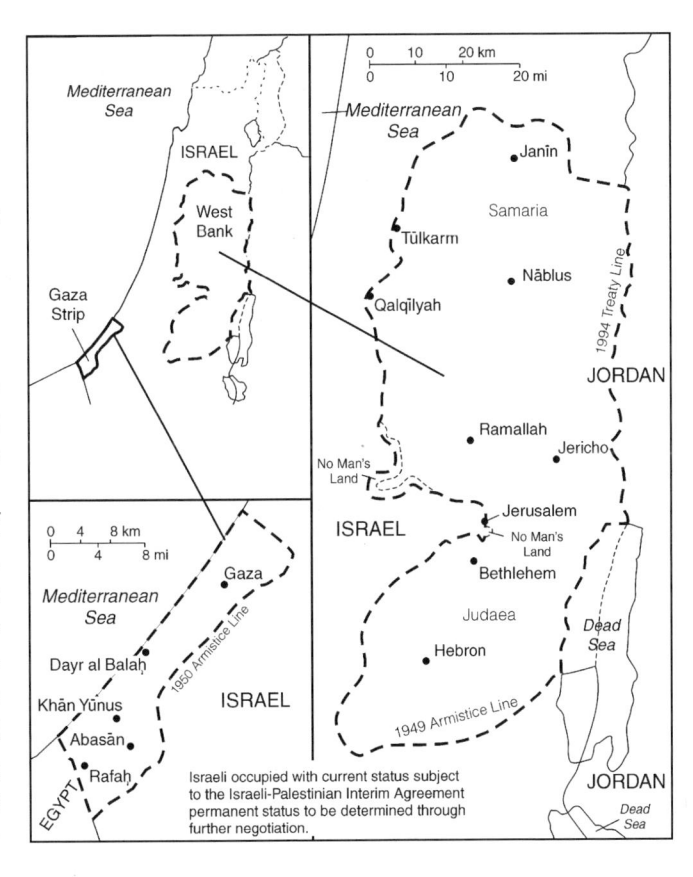

The West Bank consists of 5,860 square kilometers, an area roughly the size of Delaware. It has a rugged terrain with 27 percent arable land and no permanent crops. The climate is temperate, with temperature and precipitation amounts varying with altitude. It has elevations from the Dead Sea at 408 kilometers below sea level and mountain ranges in excess of 1,000 miles above sea level. The Gaza Strip is less than 360 square kilometers, which is slightly more than twice the area of Washington, DC. It has sand and dunes on its flat coastal plain. Thirty-nine percent of the land in the Gaza Strip is used for permanent crops, as approximately 120 square kilometers are irrigated.[1] Current environmental issues in both areas include irrigation and fresh water availability, both for crops and for the people, and sewage and sanitation issues. A large portion of the population in both areas resides in camps created by the United Nations Relief and Works Agency for the Palestinian Refugees in the Near East (UNRWA) after the 1948 Arab-Israeli conflict. Because these camps were created as temporary shelters and have been in use for more than forty-five years, the issues of water and sanitation need to be addressed on a permanent basis.

The government of the West Bank and the Gaza Strip is currently unsettled. Leadership of the Palestinian Authority is organized under a president and a cabinet of ministers. The Palestinian Authority has limited power over the disputed territories of the West Bank and the Gaza Strip and is the recognized negotiating body for the establishment of the Palestinian state by the Israeli government and the United Nations.

Since the late twentieth century the economy of the West Bank and the Gaza Strip has been in turmoil due to the uprising in the territories. Unemployment rates are high in both areas, and trade has been severely disrupted.

In 2000, the population of the West Bank was estimated at nearly 2,100,000 and that of the Gaza Strip at nearly 1,180,000. In addition to the Palestinian people in these areas, an estimated 335,900 Israeli settlers are living in the West Bank and the Gaza Strip. There are some variations between the West Bank and the Gaza Strip residents, with the West Bank identifying approximately 83 percent as Palestinian and other Arabs and 17 percent as Jewish, and the Gaza Strip identifying more than 99 percent as Palestinian and other Arabs. Palestinians are primarily Muslim, 75 percent in the West Bank and 98.7 percent in the Gaza Strip, with a strong minority of Christian Palestinian Arabs, approximately 8 percent in the West Bank and almost 1 percent in the Gaza Strip.[2] The predominant language is Arabic, but Hebrew and English are widely used and understood in both areas.

The male-to-female population ratio is approximately 1.05/1 for Palestinians under the age of sixty-five. The life expectancy for men and women in the West Bank is 70.58 years and 74.07 years, respectively. In the Gaza Strip, the life expectancy is somewhat lower, with men at 69.76 and women at 72.32 years, based on 2001 estimates. The fertility rate in the West Bank and Gaza Strip was estimated at 5.9 in 1999 and dropped to approximately 4.3 in 2001. Infant mortality is estimated at approximately 22 deaths per 1,000 live births in the West Bank and approximately 26 deaths per 1,000 live births in the Gaza Strip. Maternal mortality rates are not available.[3]

OVERVIEW OF WOMEN'S ISSUES

War and conflict are the overriding aspects of life in the Occupied Territories of the West Bank and the Gaza Strip. Paradoxically, this has both hampered and enhanced the situation of women in the territories. International attention to the territories, an increase in women in the workforce due to economic necessity in traditional households or the need for women to step into a traditional "male" role of breadwinner when the male heads of households are detained, injured, killed, or unemployed due to continuing conflict with Israel, and an increase in women intellectuals due to access to education have all had profound effects on the roles and expectations of women in Palestine. Related to these topics, health-care issues and an emphasis on family and political issues have increased the visibility of women in the Occupied Territories.

EDUCATION

Opportunities

Historically, women were expected to hold to traditional roles and responsibilities in Palestine. This meant that women remained in the home, and educational opportunities were afforded primarily for the males of the population. This situation and these expectations have taken some large turns toward modernity since the twentieth century. Women are now being educated at relatively high rates in all levels of education, including the high percentage pursuing university degrees.

The political and social unrest of the region has led to a lack of funding for state-run education for all students. The UNRWA created some schools in the refugee camps throughout the region, but limited funding initially resulted in limited opportunities. However, education became an important aspect of Palestinian existence, and women soon made up between 35 and 55 percent of the university population.[4] After the first Intifada (uprising), with the creation of the Palestinian Authority to serve as an interim government during final negotiations for statehood, education became a "national" priority. This meant the creation of new schools and the opportunity for education to large centers of the population in both the West Bank and the Gaza Strip. This is in addition to the schools operated by Israel and attended by Palestinian children in the territories and in Israel.

A discrepancy exists between the literacy rates reported for females in the West Bank and the Gaza Strip for the age groups between fifteen and forty-four. The rates in the West Bank average 9.05 percent for females in this age group. In the Gaza Strip, the average is 5.6 percent. Girls leave school at a higher rate in the West Bank than in the Gaza Strip, with dropout rates of 2.39 percent in the West Bank and 1.42 percent in the

Gaza Strip. The school dropout rates for boys are higher in the West Bank than in the Gaza Strip as well.

Preprimary schools in the Occupied Territories are supported by the private sector. Data on specific numbers of children utilizing these services are unavailable. Of children aged six through eleven, attendance at primary-level schools is estimated at more than 91 percent for girls and more than 90 percent for boys. Boys drop out of the primary level slightly more frequently than girls. This is reflected in the slightly higher illiteracy rates for boys aged fifteen through nineteen. In the secondary level of education, the dropout rates for girls exceed those of boys.

At the university level, between 45 and 53 percent of the students are women. Women teachers at the university level make up approximately 12 percent of the faculties as a whole. The Palestinian Ministry of Higher Education identifies ten Palestinian universities and several community colleges. These include Birzeit University and Hebron University in the West Bank and Al-Azhar University in Gaza.

Education in the Occupied Territories has become a precious resource with the onset of the most recent clashes between Palestinians and Israel. Economic pressures as well as physical barriers to access to education through roadblocks and checkpoints force many students to drop out of their studies. Universities have been affected by this turn of events as well; some are struggling to stay open, while others are closing their doors for the time being. The time schedules of those staying open are subject to curfew restrictions placed on areas in the territories. Accelerated and intensive courses are one way that some universities deal with these pressures. Lack of opportunity and economic resources for education has serious ramifications for future generations. The lack of political power of the Palestinian Authority since the recent uprising in the territories has resulted in a lack of control over many state-run systems, including education. The curfew imposed on the Occupied Territories by Israel during the current uprising has made it difficult in some areas and impossible in others for children to attend school. If and when the current crisis is settled, the Palestinian government will have the task of reestablishing the educational system and restoring its quality and scope.

Literacy

If illiteracy rates across both the West Bank and the Gaza Strip are averaged, an estimated 91 percent of all women are enrolled in education. Of those aged fifteen to nineteen, illiteracy rates for males are larger than rates for females, averaging 3.4 percent for males and 2.5 percent for females. As age increases, the disparities between illiteracy rates for male and female members of the population change dramatically. For Palestinians aged twenty to twenty-four, female illiteracy averages 4 percent, and male illiteracy averages 3.5 percent. The gap widens for the age group twenty-five to thirty-four, with females averaging 7 percent and males averaging 3.8 percent. The age group thirty-five to forty-four finds female illiteracy at 16 percent and male illiteracy at 5.2 percent. For the age group forty-five to fifty-four, the census information shows a female illiteracy rate at 50 percent and the rate for males at 10.3 percent. The age group from fifty-five through sixty-four has female rates of illiteracy of more than 81 percent and male rates at 31.4 percent, and the age group of sixty-five and older sees female illiteracy rates of more than 90 percent, with male rates approaching 46.2 percent.[5]

EMPLOYMENT AND ECONOMICS

The mid- to late 1990s experienced a growth rate of Palestinian gross domestic product (GDP) that reached 6 percent in 1999. This growth rate was expected to continue at a more modest level into the year 2000, making the stability of Palestine and the possibility of final negotiations of the Oslo peace accords feasible for the Palestinian Authority as it inherited the responsibility for civil services in the territories of the West Bank and the Gaza Strip.

Job/Career Opportunities

In 1999, the unemployment rate in the Occupied Territories was at a low of 11.8 percent.[6] Of these employed Palestinians, approximately 14 percent were women. Of the population of men and women in the Occupied Territories, 91 percent of men aged twenty-five to thirty-four were employed, as compared with 16 percent of women in that age group.[7] The majority of jobs were in the service industries, with craft and trade work following closely behind in percentage of the workforce. The majority of women were employed in the services and agriculture.

Women held professional jobs throughout the territories as well. Women were teachers in relatively high percentages, ranging from 33.4 percent in secondary schools to 50.5 percent in basic school education. Of the dentists working in the territories, approximately 22 percent were women. Women made up 12 percent of physicians, 4 percent of veterinarians, 26 percent of pharmacists, 8 percent of lawyers, 7 percent of engineers, and 8 percent of journalists throughout the territories.

The economy of the Occupied Territories continued to be closely tied to those of Israel and some other Arab countries, such as Jordan and Egypt. The Palestinian economy had some small industries that produced goods for export to these countries, such as olives, citrus and other fruits, and dairy products. The economy relied on imports of food, consumer goods, and construction materials, primarily from a trade partner in Israel. Additionally, a growing percentage of Palestinians were employed in Israel, traveling to and from their places of employment daily through checkpoints.

In this growing economic workforce, women who had thirteen or more years of schooling were more likely to be employed. Nearly 13 percent of women were self-employed, and 1 percent of women were employers, having one or more employees.

Aid from the international community continued to play a part in the overall economic situation of the territories. This was utilized to improve infrastructure in the territories, such as roads and services, as well as to increase investment from foreign countries. An estimated U.S. $410 million was distributed from international aid pledges in 1995. The optimistic outlook on economic growth and sustainability was devastated by the outbreak of the Al-Aqsa Intifada in 2000, due to the breakdown of the peace process and the final negotiations of the Oslo Accords.

Pay

Women earn approximately 66 percent of the salaries of men. Before the Al-Aqsa Intifada, the estimated median monthly income stood at 2,500 new Israeli shekels (NIS), which had decreased to an estimated 1,200 in 2002. This leaves an estimated 66 percent of Palestinians living at or below the poverty line of U.S. $2 per day.

Inheritance and Property Rights

Tradition and the laws associated with Islam, known as shari'a, continue to guide the rights of inheritance of women in the Occupied Territories, despite the large minority of Christian Palestinians in the territories. According to Islamic law, if a husband dies, his wife is entitled to one-eighth of his estate if he had children and one-fourth if he was childless. Daughters are entitled to one-half the inheritance of their brothers. If there are no male heirs, one daughter would receive half of her father's estate, and two or more daughters would share two-thirds of his estate.

Females are considered to be the responsibility of their male kin. Responsibility for a daughter lies with her father and subsequently her brothers until she is married. When she is married, this responsibility passes to her husband.

At marriage, it is a common practice for a woman to renounce her inheritance rights to her father's estate in order to maintain familial harmony. This is related to the woman's need to secure her future support should her marriage not survive. If she is divorced, a woman becomes dependent again on her father or brothers. If she demanded the right to her inheritance, this support would likely be denied if it should become needed.

Brothers who receive their sister's inheritance often send their sisters presents as a show of support. These are often related to the inheritance, such as olive oil from olive grove owners or produce from farmers. Society views women who demand their inheritance somewhat unfavorably, particularly in rural areas. A survey conducted in 1999 by the Palestinian Central Bureau of Statistics indicates that more than 67 percent of women do not get their share of inheritance. These figures differ according to where the woman and her family live. Rural women renounce their inheritance at a rate of more than 82 percent, while women in camps have the lowest percentage of renouncing their inheritance at approximately 57 percent.

Tradition and practice of inheritance in Palestine follow necessity. Women must think of their future needs and act accordingly. By maintaining their relationships with their brothers, they assure that they have a place to return to should their marriage dissolve or their husband die. Increased absence by heads of households due to arrests, injuries, or deaths associated with the struggle against Israel means that women are more aware of the need to maintain family support. Living in urban areas may allow women better opportunities to support themselves in these situations, making it easier to demand their share of inheritance. Women in rural areas are more bound to traditional practices and are more likely to renounce their inheritance to their brothers to ensure their future support.

Government and International Programs

It is estimated that the gross domestic product of the Occupied Territories has decreased by as much as 19 percent since 2000. Estimates of the unemployment rate in Palestine in the year 2002 range from 33 to 38 percent. This increase in unemployment has come from a variety of sources. The United States Agency for International Development (USAID) estimates that 75,000 jobs held by Palestinians in Israel have been lost due to closures, limitations to mobility in and around Israel, increased restriction of permits to work, and increased political discord between Israel and the territories. This job loss in Israel alone is expected to affect more than 750,00 Palestinians throughout the territories as sources of economic support are lost.

Unemployment is also related to destruction of infrastructure and closures in the territories. The retaliation of Israel against acts associated with the Al-Aqsa Intifada include increased control over the mobility of Palestinians in and around the territories. Curfews have been in effect for long periods of time since 2000, effectively keeping Palestinians in their homes for these periods. During curfew, people cannot be on the streets in the territories, making the normal activities of daily life impossible. These include shopping for food, going to work or school, and visiting friends and family.

Closures of lines of transportation have been severe at times, affecting up to 75 percent of the territories with regard to mobility and business operation. Military checkpoints limit the number of people and vehicles that enter and leave areas of the Occupied Territories, making the transportation of goods, people, and aid difficult. Individuals have attempted to circumvent this system of checkpoints by traveling routes off of the main roads. This has resulted in increased time and costs associated with getting goods to and from areas in the territories. Also hindered are such services as trash removal and the delivery of fresh water supplies normally dependent on tanker trucks.

Finally, a large increase in damage to infrastructure has been reported. This includes the destruction of the Gaza International Airport's runway and damage to roads, sewage lines, water supply lines, and houses throughout the territories.

These events have had a huge impact on the incomes of the Palestinian people. USAID estimates that total income losses are around U.S. $2.4 billion, with more than $300 million in infrastructure damage. This translates to a median decrease in income in the territories of more than 50 percent.

International aid has risen in the wake of the Al-Aqsa Intifada. Estimates of 2002 levels of international aid exceed $900 million. These funds take several forms. Infrastructure development has improved sanitation and water supplies to areas of both the West Bank and the Gaza Strip. Cash and food aid to individual families has increased, and larger amounts of medical supplies and larger numbers of health-care professionals have been sent to the region.

International aid has also taken the form of microcredit loans to begin or support businesses in the territories, according to USAID. These loans are made primarily to women. Women are particularly vulnerable to the economic hardships because they are traditionally dependent on the male heads of households for support. A 1999 survey estimated that only 12 percent of the women in the workforce contributed to their household income. These microcredit loans are a form of development in the territories.

FAMILY AND SEXUALITY

The family is a basic unit in Palestinian society. It is an important component of identity and defines the roles and responsibilities of both women and men in the society. Scholars have identified three separate types of family structures among Palestinians living in the West Bank and the Gaza Strip. Differences between these family structures are related to the social conditions around the family, including whether the family lives in the West Bank or the Gaza Strip, whether it lives in a refugee camp or in a town, and the relative wealth of the family, among other things.

The three types of family structures are the nuclear family, the transitional family, and the extended family. The nuclear family, as in the West, consists of a married couple and their unmarried children. This family unit is becoming more common and is primarily found in the West Bank towns; it is much less common in the camps of the Gaza Strip. The relative wealth of individuals and families living in the West Bank as compared to the Gaza Strip makes this family structure possible, as there is less necessity for family support. The poorer conditions of the Gaza Strip necessitate adherence to a larger base of people for family support.

The transitional family is a hybrid between the nuclear family and the extended family. It consists of the married couple and their unmarried children, but also includes part of the extended family, such as grandparents and parents of the couple and/or siblings of the couple. This maintains the integrity of the family unit, but is more flexible than the traditional extended family. This type of family structure can be found in the more rural parts of the West Bank and in the camps of the Gaza Strip.

The traditional extended family encompasses up to five generations under one roof. Typically, it includes the descendants of a common grandfather and their wives and children. It is believed that this is the most common family structure throughout the Occupied Territories, as it maintains the historical family structure most fully. The members of an extended household create a strong financial base for the support of the other family members, and this strength leads to social influence over family members and decisions on values and norms of the family that are passed down from generation to generation. This type of family structure is most evident in villages and smaller population centers throughout the territories, but is found less and less in the towns and in the camps.

Gender Roles

Families help to shape girls and boys into appropriate gender roles. As in most Arab countries, laws and traditions are largely based in Islamic law (shari'a), which applies generally to the population. These traditions shape the expectations of both boys and girls in the society. Girls are expected to stay in the home and not to engage in public activities. Adolescence is a time of strong pressure by the family to adhere to religious or traditional dress and behavior, particularly for girls. Sexuality and sexual information about body development and other matters are considered taboo, and girls are punished for discussing these topics in public. The information that is received outside of the educational environment is often distorted, leading to confusion and possibly even fear in the young girls. Traditional roles place women in the home and men in the public sphere. Interpretations of the Qur'an (the Islamic holy book) suggest that a woman should be covered, showing her beauty only to her husband or her family.

Some differences are noted in the ability and encouragement of girls to complete the educational process based on where they live. Girls living in towns and cities are more likely to attend school and complete their education, including attaining university degrees, than are girls from rural areas or the refugee camps. Economics is only one of the reasons for this discrepancy. Also involved are the influences of conservative aspects of the society, which are stronger in the rural areas than in the cities. It has been noted that the West Bank is much more accepting of educated women than is the Gaza Strip, in large part because of the influx of influences from the West through nongovernmental organizations (NGOs) and other international groups, which are concentrated in and around Ramallah and Jerusalem in the West Bank.

Marriage

Shari'a also dictates marriage customs throughout the Occupied Territories, but different circumstances and changing times create the opportunity for different interpretations of this law. For example, traditional marriage customs are still very prevalent in the territories. This is typified by the choice of a bride by the groom's parents, with the "ideal" wife identified as the daughter of the father's brother, or the groom's first cousin. The marriage is a contract entered into by the parents of both the bride and the groom. The bride and groom are expected not to see one another until the wedding day, and the bride is not to refuse the match that her parents have agreed to. However, this traditional structure has been adapted to allow the potential groom to select his wife. The contract is negotiated through a liaison whom the groom picks to represent him to the family. The potential bride is often asked for her input regarding the acceptance or rejection of the suitor's request.

Because the population is dense in the Occupied Territories, it is likely that the potential bride and groom know one another prior to an arrangement being made. Both families' financial situations, as well as their religion and practices and social ties to the community, are considerations. Boys and girls are with one another in school, in the streets of the towns and camps, and in other social settings, so the future couples have more opportunity to talk prior to being involved in traditional, chaperoned courtship. Increasingly, so-called love marriages are being entered into without the traditional negotiations of the families. These arrangements are much more prevalent in the West Bank than in the Gaza Strip, again because of the influence of the outside culture in this part of the territories.

In a survey conducted in 1995, nearly 27 percent of the women in both the West Bank and the Gaza Strip had been married prior to age seventeen. The percentage is much higher (ranging from 30 to 54 percent) for women over the age of fifty and is at a low of 14.1 percent for those currently in the age group fifteen to nineteen.[8] The women's movement in the Occupied Territories has been active in encouraging the emerging government to create laws limiting early marriage. While these efforts were initially considered effective, the current political status of the territories makes these seemingly trivial points of law pale in comparison to the larger issue of statehood. Thus this issue is not being considered as readily as it was prior to the current escalation of violence, and its outcome is uncertain.

After marriage, Palestinian girls often move from their parents' house either to the independent home of their new husband or to the home of his family. The laws and customs of the shari'a dictate that men are responsible for the financial support of women, so new brides are dependent on their husband for support. Preparations for married life are often minimal for the new wives, and demands often exceed expectations for these women. Physical force and violence within the married couple's home are not uncommon occurrences. Some shifting of these traditional roles occurred during the first Intifada, when men were detained, hurt, or killed in the fighting with Israel, and women were forced into roles as heads of household in large numbers. The recent conflicts have again made women into heads of households at much higher rates than previously.

Tradition in Palestinian society dictates a strong advocacy for an extended family relationship, which may or may not be reflected in residency patterns. If the parents of the husband do live in a family's home, this has the potential to be either beneficial or detrimental to the wife. A tradition-bound in-law can make life difficult for a new bride, particularly since little preparation for married life is offered prior to marriage regarding the expectations of the woman in the home. However, a more liberally minded in-law can benefit the woman by providing support either in learning the duties and responsibilities of a wife or in maintaining the home while simultaneously working outside the home. Working women are not an uncommon occurrence in the territories, though their prevalence has been curtailed by political and military constraints subsequent to the Al-Aqsa Intifada.

Women have the right of divorce in Palestine. The laws, largely based on shari'a, provide that a woman can divorce her husband if he fails to fulfill his duties. However, tradition dictates that women receive two dowries at marriage, one in the form of household items, such as furniture, and another to be set aside in case of a woman's husband seeking to divorce her. If the husband divorces the wife, she receives this second part of her dowry, called a *mahr*. Social pressures make divorce a situation to be avoided. Divorced women have little ability to live on their own and often must return to the houses of their parents or brothers for support. Custody of any children from the marriage is mandated to the father for sons at the age of nine and for daughters at the age of eleven. Remarriage is rare for divorced women, and they often are reliant on their relatives for the rest of their lives.

Reproduction

Sex Education

Formalized sex education in the primary and secondary schools is a goal of the Ministry of Health, and sexual and reproductive health has been identified as a central theme of the developing Palestinian Health Plan.

Contraception and Abortion

Efforts have been made to inform women about contraceptives, and an estimated 98 percent of women are familiar with the use of birth-control methods. However, a 1996 estimate placed the percentage of women who do not use contraceptives throughout the Occupied Territories at roughly 52 percent of the female population, and a 1999 estimate from the Palestinian Ministry of Health estimated that this had decreased to 45.2 percent.[9] Laws concerning abortion are contradictory, sometimes allowing abortion if the mother's life is in danger, but the laws do not take into account the cause of the pregnancy.

Teen Pregnancy

Given the traditional aspect of the society, teenage pregnancy is not a profound problem. Debates continue regarding the continued existence of "honor killings," murders of young women by their family members for apparent disgrace of the family with regard to matters of virginity and chastity within the community, for young women who "disgrace" their families. It is considered that the stories surrounding these "honor killings" are used to scare young girls into compliance with tradition and cultural expectations of gender. Girls may marry as young as twelve to fourteen years of age in the territories.

HEALTH

Health Care Access

Access to health-care facilities in the Occupied Territories was improving prior to the recent uprisings. According to figures provided by the UNRWA, a total of fifty-one primary health-care facilities were in operation in the West Bank and the Gaza Strip in September 2002 due to the combined efforts of UNRWA, grants from international sources, NGOs, and the Palestinian Authority. These facilities had a total staff of 1,702 health-care workers attending to more than 4.7 million patient visits in 2001. In the West Bank, the average daily consultation per medical officer was 104; in the Gaza Strip, the average was 109.[10]

The accessibility of these UNRWA clinics allowed several of the health concerns of the region to be addressed. In its 1999 survey, UNRWA estimated that between 97 and 99 percent of pregnant women in the Occupied Territories were immunized against tetanus during their pregnancy. Between 95 and 99 percent of the baby deliveries were attended by trained personnel in the territories. Despite these statistics, it is believed that approximately 20 percent of women do not receive any prenatal care, and more than 80 percent do not receive any postnatal care.

An estimated 49 percent of Palestinians are uninsured. This results in a need for free or reduced-cost services, such as the clinics provided by UNRWA in both the West Bank and the Gaza Strip. UNRWA also plays a large part in the health of Palestinians by providing shelters in the refugee camps and maintaining access to safe water and sewage facilities in these areas. Safe water and sewage facilities are factors that are directly linked to the health of individuals in the Occupied Territories. Access to these services is tied to social and economic features of the territory and is subject to external pressures. The 2000 uprising known as the Al-Aqsa Intifada and the subsequent Israeli response has resulted in lowered access to these services, which leads to increased health concerns for the people of the territories.

Diseases and Disorders

A 2000 survey of health indicators indicated that approximately 6 percent of the population suffered from a chronic disease. These diseases included diabetes, which was found in more than 2 percent of the female population and 1.7 percent of the male population; high blood pressure, found in 3.3 percent of the female population and 1.6 percent of the male population; and cardiac disease, which affected men and women nearly equally at approximately 1.2 percent of the population. The survey results indicated that approximately 48 percent of the males in the West Bank and the Gaza Strip are smokers, while only 3 percent of the women in the territories identified this habit.[11]

Health concerns that are increasing in the Occupied Territories include malnutrition, anemia, and diarrhea, as well as mental health problems such as depression and anxiety. The current situation of the territories is one of forced closure and curfew imposed by Israel. This means that the inhabitants of specific areas of the West Bank and the Gaza Strip are not allowed out of their homes unless the curfew is lifted. Closures are the transportation closings of roads and other methods of movement from one place to another. Checkpoints, armed guards, and large physical barriers are placed on the roads leading into and out of these areas, limiting the ability of people and cargo to pass from one area to another. Limited as well are the humanitarian aid efforts and the health-care transports, such as ambulances. With no ability to get to the sick or to remove them to hospitals that are located outside the closed areas, people are suffering in much greater numbers than before the uprising.

Current states of curfew and closure in areas have contributed to difficulty in accessing safe water. In some areas, the only source of safe water is tanker trucks, which are not allowed to pass the closure sites. Other issues include trash removal and access to hospitals on the other side of roadblocks or checkpoints. As these conditions continue, increases in communicable diseases are possible, including cholera.

Outbreaks of diarrhea have been reported throughout the territories since the beginning of the Al-Aqsa Intifada. These are also related to the infrastructure problems of access to safe water and sewage removal in the territories. These outbreaks are often traced to contaminated water supplies and are often correctable. However, the continued closures can hamper the epidemiological investigations to find the source of the contamination as well as detain the supplies necessary for repair of the problems identified.

Food shipments are stopped in the closures as well, leaving many Palestinians hungry. Recent survey results suggest that more than 63 percent of randomly selected households from both the West Bank and the Gaza Strip are facing difficulty maintaining an adequate food supply because of a combination of loss of family income and curfew as well as lack of availability. Comparison of recent statistics with ones from 2000 indicates an increase of children suffering from stunting (defined as low height for age) with a 22.6 percent increase, moderate underweight conditions (defined as low weight for age) with a 36 percent increase, and moderate wasting (defined as low weight for height) with a 50 percent increase. Anemia is also identified as an increasing problem. Children are estimated to be suffering from mild to severe anemia at a rate of 50 percent. The prevalence of anemia among women aged fifteen to forty-nine is estimated at 48 percent (March through June 2002).

The percentage of pregnant women giving birth with a doctor or midwife in attendance has decreased. The Palestinian Ministry of Health estimates an increase in home deliveries of 100 percent since closures began. Stillbirths are estimated to have increased by 56 percent due to the lack of attendance of medical personnel at births.

AIDS

A statement made in 2001 to the United Nations by Nasser Al-Kidwa, ambassador to the Permanent Observer of Palestine to the United Nations, indicated that the AIDS rate in the Occupied Territories was very low and asserted that those diagnosed were receiving full free care due to the small number of cases.

Cancer

Cancer is a rare occurrence, with a 0.1 percent rate of treatment. Ulcers and asthma are found in less than 1 percent of the population, respectively, and epilepsy has a prevalence rate of 0.3 percent for the territories.[12]

Depression

In 2000, 53 percent of women surveyed suffered from crying attacks, 45.6 percent suffered from a fear of loneliness, and 45.8 percent suffered from a feeling of hopelessness and frustration. Men surveyed had a 44.6

percent response regarding suffering from a feeling of hopelessness and frustration. Headache was a common health problem reported, with nearly 30 percent of women and 24 percent of men reporting suffering headaches in the survey. Women also had a relatively high incidence (15.6 percent) of abdominal and stomach complaints.[13] A more recent article by USAID stated that a survey of households found 87 percent reporting psychological difficulties in one or more family members. The area suffers from an inadequate number of mental health-care facilities to treat these disorders.

POLITICS AND LAW

Suffrage

Women first voted in the Occupied Territories in the election of the first Palestinian Legislative Council. Registration of all Palestinians in the Occupied Territories over seventeen years of age began in November 1995. The election day was January 20, 1996. The women identified as members of the Palestinian Authority were elected in this poll.

Political Participation

Women have been active participants in political activities since the occupation of Palestine in 1948. By maintaining family structure and keeping social welfare efforts going, women were able to support resistance against the occupation as well as protect the national identity of Palestine and the Palestinians. These social welfare projects included fundraising activities as well as food and monetary support of the Palestinian people in and around the population centers. Social welfare efforts were stratified by the economic situation of the people. The wealthier women were philanthropic in their efforts and were largely in charge of these welfare activities. While they were necessary and helpful to maintaining the social structure, they lacked the ability to make opportunities available for the community, and specifically for the women to improve their own situations.

Eventually, these welfare efforts changed to more overtly political activities. As the number of women attaining education increased, so did their political consciousness. Women began taking part in demonstrations and sit-ins and eventually in international efforts at highlighting the plight of the Palestinians through such activities as hijackings. Leila Khaled is one of the most famous Palestinian women activists. She participated in the hijackings of two airplanes in 1969 and 1970. While she was certainly not the only woman involved in these highly publicized political activities during this period, she became a symbol for the activities of women in support of Palestine. These highly publicized events encouraged other women's groups to unite in a women's movement in support of Palestine.

These groups began as part of larger, male-dominated political groups.

The first Intifada began in 1987, and women participated in large numbers. The behavior of the participants fell well outside of traditional expectations, since women were involved in confrontations with Israeli military personnel, demonstrations in the streets, and even, in some cases, violence. These activities resulted in women being hurt, imprisoned, and even killed. Scholars indicate that this was a period of relative freedom in the lives of Palestinian women as they worked along with men to achieve a civil society in Palestine.

A second phase of the Intifada resulted in women pulling back from the confrontation with Israel and turning toward a more formalized structure of the efforts of women in the territories. This had two effects on the status of women in Palestine. First, the relative freedom of women during the initial phases of the Intifada was replaced by a more rigid form of structure implemented after the popular uprising of the people was constrained by the political parties in the region. This constraint tended to exclude women, resulting in a decrease of their activity. Second, women retreated from active life and returned their efforts in social welfare, focusing on education, health, and food production as a support for the political efforts.

The Intifada resulted in international recognition of the situation in the Occupied Territories and Israel and helped lead the way to the signing of the Oslo peace accords and the subsequent final status talks that were to take place. The final status negotiations were tied directly to the development of laws and policies regarding the civil society of Palestine, including laws pertaining to women.

Women's Rights

Committees were formed to identify necessary laws and policies regarding women as the development of Palestinian laws was discussed. While the society was based largely on traditional shari'a, additional laws were necessary, including laws associated with personal status. These included questions of divorce rights, inheritance, and laws surrounding the marriage contract. In order to understand social expectations associated with the roles of women, as well as to encourage support of laws specifically designed to improve the role and status of women in Palestinian society, the women's groups utilized a "model parliament" approach. These mock sessions allowed an open debate on the status of women and how the implementation of laws would be accepted in these communities. Religious and social leaders were invited to participate in an effort to give these activities a "national" feeling as opposed to the feeling that they were just about questions pertaining to women. Workshops were held in these areas to help clarify existing laws and problems and to identify the ways that particular laws and the modification of existing laws might address these issues.

The question of citizenship of women was a major issue. Laws were suggested to allow women to carry their own passports and to be able to list their children on their passports. It was also stressed that the signature of a male relative should no longer be necessary for women to travel within and outside of Palestine. A woman's ability to vote, her ability to divorce, and her improved ability to claim inheritance rights were issues associated with the development of a civil law code for Palestine subsequent to the final status negotiations.

The Palestinian Authority was identified as the negotiating body to represent the Occupied Territories in the negotiation process. Women took on roles in the Palestinian Authority during these negotiations, with nearly 6 percent on the Legislative Council, 7.5 percent on the National Council, and 9 percent on the Ministry Council.[14] Questions of women's citizenship became important in these status talks, and women's committees and NGOs took on important roles as consultants in the process of civil law development.

One of the larger questions surrounding these efforts by women's committees was the right of return of the refugees who had fled the territories after the occupation in 1948. Also related is the method utilized for counting refugees. Currently, nationality is only achieved by men, with wives and daughters being dependent, but not identified as Palestinian in the full sense of the spirit of citizenship. The count of refugees reflects the count of those identified as Palestinian and underestimates the number of those in exile due to the lack of women represented in the numbers. Additionally, women cannot pass on nationality to their offspring, and if a woman marries a man who is not a Palestinian national, she loses any ability to claim citizenship.

After the Al-Aqsa Intifada in 2000, these decisions and questions were deferred to the renewed question of statehood. The Israeli retaliation to the Al-Aqsa Intifada has involved partial reoccupation of areas of the territories, closure of areas throughout the West Bank and the Gaza Strip, and implementation of curfews throughout the region at different times. With mobility severely limited in some areas, and the destruction of the structures associated with the Palestinian Authority, the discussion of civil laws has diminished. The legal status of women in the Occupied Territories, therefore, has been placed on hold.

Lesbian Rights

The common law of the Occupied Territories in its present state makes no mention of rights for lesbians or homosexuals. The law is a document and nonenforceable in its present state, having only gone through three readings in the Legislative Council since its inception due to the Intifada and ongoing negotiations with Israel for sovereignty.

Military Service

The women's movement in the Occupied Territories has had a huge impact on the development of questions of civil law, as well as in the maintenance of Palestinian identity not only in the Occupied Territories, but also among Palestinians living throughout the world. The image of the mother is often invoked to represent Palestine, and having a son or daughter martyred for the cause of Palestine raises women to a special status in the society. A large percentage of the individuals performing suicide bombings in Israel have been women. Although there is no formal military force for the Occupied Territories, women have been attempting to make a difference in the struggle for the independence of Palestine.

RELIGION AND SPIRITUALITY

Women's Roles

Women's roles in Islam are highly prescribed. The Qur'an states that men and women are complementary to one another, with the men responsible for the financial support of the household, existing in the public sphere, and the women responsible for the domestic sphere and support of the husband and family.

Modesty is prescribed by Islamic law, including modesty in dress and expression. Women are expected to cover their beauty, showing it only to their husbands and family members that they will not marry, such as brothers and parents. Women are expected to conform to the traditional law (shari'a) regarding decisions on marriage and other personal status issues.

As more women are being educated in the Occupied Territories, these religious practices are being questioned. Many women choose not to cover their heads or faces in public. This is met with a variety of reactions. Some areas use social pressure to ensure that the custom of covering the head is maintained, with taunting of the uncovered women undertaken by community members. Many women who choose to cover do so as a way of ensuring their relative freedom. By being covered, they no longer bring attention to themselves and are allowed to go to school unhampered by social pressures.

Social custom and traditional law in Palestine are not as strict as in other Arab countries. Strict penalties are not enacted into law to keep women covered. More highly educated women tend to forgo the covering, particularly those living in urban areas in the West Bank.

Custom and religious practices maintain the social roles of men and women in an effort to balance the society, according to some scholars. The traditions help to solidify the family unit as an important part of life. This ensures that all members of a family are supported as well as possible.

Religious Law

The religious laws are not so strict as to demand a particular interpretation, nor are they inflexible to the needs that new contexts require. Scholars of the Qur'an identify an important aspect of understanding Islam, namely, that the interpretation of tradition and religious law, as performed by those outside of Islam (that is, "the West"), is often biased against Islam. The role of women under Islamic law is compared to the role of women under secular law in the West. Opponents arguing against Islam as antifeminist often overlook the distinction. The laws, which are considered to be inequitable for men and women in the Palestinian society, are created by a particular interpretation of the Qur'an and not as a literal translation of the religious document. A second aspect of this argument is that the roles of women across nations are vastly different, and comparing the role of women in an Arab country to the role of women in the United States is kin to comparing apples to oranges.

Women embrace Islam not only as a religion, but also as a way of life and a tradition that give particular meaning to their lives. The Christian Palestinians living in the Occupied Territories are subject to many laws and traditions based in Islam. These provide a base for the identification of the Palestinian identity and character.

VIOLENCE

Women in Palestine encounter violence from many sources on a daily basis. This has profound effects on their psychological and physical health, as well as on their ability to fulfill their roles in the society. External pressures, such as occur in war and occupation, as well as pressures from overcrowding, overpopulation, a high fertility rate, and generalized frustration among the Palestinian population, result in a violent environment that has little chance of improvement in the near future.

Domestic Violence

Domestic violence is common in the Occupied Territories. Beatings of wives by husbands frequently occur. The gender roles and expectations inherent in marriage support this in many ways. Additional pressures associated with a rising birth rate coinciding with a rising unemployment rate make violence increase in the domestic sphere. Perceived inability to fulfill obligations to society and family makes men particularly vulnerable to taking this method of release.

Threats to personal safety, insufficient food supplies, a lack of freedom to move about due to curfew and closure, and a general feeling of hostility associated with the experience of occupation take their toll on men in the territories. Women are responsible for more and more obligations as men are hurt or detained in the ongoing political arena outside of the domestic sphere, which causes an increase in pressure within this gender group as well.

In addition to violence in marriage, activities outside of marriage are attributed to causes of violence against women. Male relatives continue to practice what has been termed "honor killings" in Palestine and the refugee camps of Palestinians. Although the actual rate of this practice is unknown, and some sources doubt that it continues to exist, the threat or rumor of this practice has consequences for women in the territories. Behavior is severely modified to accommodate expectations of modesty and family honor identified by male members of family units. In addition to the physical murder of women, violence can take the form of forced marriage to a partner chosen by male relatives without the consent of the woman. This is a method of maintaining family honor in many instances, squelching rumors of immoral behavior on the part of women suspected of not maintaining traditional roles.

Rape/Sexual Assault

Rape is not reported widely in Palestine, but many scholars believe that this is due to the social pressure against premarital or extramarital sexual contact by women. If a woman is raped, it reflects poorly on her family, and so it is suspected that these occurrences are not acknowledged publicly in order to avoid scandal.

War and Military Repression

The military activities of Israel in the Occupied Territories since the mid-1960s have been violent to women. In some instances, women are particular targets for Israeli aggression. This can be seen in the destruction of the homes of suspected terrorists or terrorist supporters or sympathizers. Women have been denied the ability to cross checkpoints in order to reach a hospital on the other side of the closure zones. This has resulted in the documented deaths of women due to complications of childbirth or heart attack because they were refused medical attention.

Women are traumatized by seeing loved ones hurt or killed in the ongoing military activity. Women and children are being beaten, shot, arrested, and killed in the Occupied Territories. This has resulted in much psychological and emotional distress in both the women and the children of the territories.

Women have begun to participate in the violence in numbers not previously seen. In 2002, the first Palestinian woman suicide bomber carried out an attack in Israel. While women had been involved in attacks such as hijackings, this was the first documented case of a suicide bombing activity undertaken by a woman. This has resulted in a renewed effort by Israel to "profile" the Palestinians and stop activities such as suicide bombs in Israel. However, profiling is becoming more and more difficult as the range of Palestinians willing to sacrifice themselves for the cause of the end of occupation grows. This may have an adverse effect on the treatment of Palestinians by the Israeli military, as any Palestinian can be suspected of being a suicide bomber.

Palestinian women carrying food supplies pass by a street damaged by an Israeli army bulldozer in the West Bank town of Ramallah, March 2002. AP/Wide World Photos.

OUTLOOK FOR THE TWENTY-FIRST CENTURY

Traditional roles that keep many women in the domestic sphere continue in the Occupied Territories, although the female militant, as in the late 1960s and early 1970s, has become romanticized. The periodic reoccupation of the territories, the implementation of curfews, and the limitation of mobility, as well as the almost daily violence, place the women of the Occupied Territories in a unique and stressful position. Although opportunities and the overall situation of women have been seen as improving since, the violence and uncertainty within the territories takes its toll on all Palestinians.

NOTES

1. United Nations Relief and Works Agency (UNRWA), CIA World Factbook, Arabia.net, Palestinian Central Bureau of Statistics, Worldbank Gender Statistics.
2. CIA World Factbook.
3. Ibid.
4. All statistics within this section are from the Palestinian Central Bureau of Statistics, Palestinian Academic Network.
5. Palestinian Central Bureau of Statistics.
6. Statistics are estimates by the Palestinian Central Bureau of Statistics.
7. All statistics for this section are derived from the Palestinian Central Bureau of Statistics, the UNRWA, and the United States Agency for International Development (USAID).

8. Palestinian Central Bureau of Statistics, Palestinian Ministry of Health, and Health Development Information and Policy Institute for Palestine.
9. Ibid.
10. All information for this section has been derived from the United Nations (UNRWA), Palestinian Central Bureau of Statistics; Oxfam International; United Nations, Palestine Monitor, Carnegie Council on Ethics and International Affairs; Palestinian Ministry of Health; and Health Development Information and Policy Institute for Palestine.
11. The survey was conducted by the Palestinian Central Bureau of Statistics.
12. Palestinian Central Bureau of Statistics.
13. Ibid.
14. Palestinian Central Bureau of Statistics.

RESOURCE GUIDE

Suggested Reading

Butt, G. *The Arabs*. London: I.B. Tauris Publishers, 1997. Provides a good, general introduction to the Arab world, including history and current debates.

Fernea, E.W., and B.Q. Bezirgan, eds. *Middle Eastern Muslim Women Speak*. Austin: University of Texas Press, 1977. A good source for authentic women's voices from the region.

Hourani, A.H. *A History of the Arab Peoples*. New York: Fine Communications, 1997. An accessible book outlining the history of the region and the impact that its history has on current conditions and conflicts.

Jad, I. "Claiming Feminism, Claiming Nationalism: Women's Activism in the Occupied Territories." In *The Challenge of Local Feminisms: Women's Movements in Global Perspective*, ed. Amrita Basu, 226–48. Boulder, CO: Westview Press, 1995. Provides a good overview of the role of women in negotiating for the reestablishment of Palestinian sovereignty as a nation.

Videos/Films

Jerusalem: An Occupation Set in Stone? 1995. Marty Rosenbluth, writer/director/producer. Hillsborough, NC: Insightment Video Productions.

Letter from Palestine. 1989. Steve York, writer/director, and D. Fanning, executive producer. Washington, DC: York Zimmerman.

Palestinian Portraits. 1989. Simone de Bagno, director. Brooklyn, NY: First Run/Icarus Films.

Web Sites

Arabic News, www.arabicnews.com.
Provides the latest information about the region in general.

Arab Women Connect, www.arabwomenconnect.org/awc/e_links.asp?link_cat=3.
All links to women's committees and issues related to Palestinian women are available through this site.

CIA World Factbook, www.ca.gov/cia/publications/factbook.
Includes historical information about the region as well as statistical data. West Bank and Gaza Strip are separate searchable entries in the database.

Health Development Information and Policy Institute for Palestine, www.hdip.org.
Provides links to maps and publications regarding the Occupied Territories, including archives of health-related issues.

Palestine Chronicle, www.palestinechronicle.com.
Up-to-date information on events in Palestine and the Middle East.

Palestine Monitor, www.palestinemonitor.org.
Self-identified as the "Voice of Civil Society," this site provides information and links to many sources on issues of the Occupied Territories and women's issues.

The Palestinian Central Bureau of Statistics, www.pcbs.org.
Provides statistics on Palestinian life, including gender statistics and health, education, and work-related information.

United Nations Relief and Works Agency for Palestinian Refugees in the Near East, www.un.org/unrwa.
Information about official counts of Palestinian refugees living in the Occupied Territories, as well as in the refugee camps in the surrounding countries, and a good source of photographs of refugee camps as well as recent news regarding Palestine.

World Bank, http://genderstats.worldbank.org.
Searchable site for specific information from a reference external to the current conflict in the Occupied Territories.

Organizations

Birzeit University
PO Box 14
Birzeit, West Bank, Palestine
Phone: +972-2-298-2000
Fax: +972-2-281-0656
Birzeit provides an academic base for research regarding the Occupied Territories and issues of gender and Palestinian statehood. This is one of the few Palestinian universities.

Institute for Palestine Studies (IPS)
Washington, DC 20007
3501 M Street N.W.
Phone: (800) 874-3614 or (202) 342-3990
Fax: (202) 342-3927
A U.S.-based agency focusing on questions and issues of the Occupied Territories and the current social and political condition of the Palestinians.

Israel/Palestine Center for Research and Information
PO Box 9321
Jerusalem 91092
Phone: 972-2-676-9460
Fax: 972-2-676-8011
The center is a joint venture by Israelis and Palestinians committed to finding a peaceful resolution to the current state of the region. It provides a balanced view of the activities by both sides regarding the quest for an end to the occupation.

United Nations Relief and Works Agency for Palestinian Refugees in the Near East (UNRWA)
UNRWA Liaison Office, New York
Chief, Liaison Office, Maher Nasser
One United Nations Plaza, Room DC1-1265
New York, NY 10017
Phone: (+1 212) 963-2255, (+1 212) 963-1234
Fax: (+1 212) 935-7899
The primary organization created to serve the Palestinian refugees in the area after the occupation. UNRWA runs hospitals, shelters, and other services vital to the survival of Palestinian refugees.

SELECTED BIBLIOGRAPHY

Central Intelligence Agency. *CIA World Factbook*. www.cia.gov/cia/publications/factbook. 2000.

al-Faruqi, L.L. *Islamic Traditions and the Feminist Movement: Confrontation or Cooperation*. 2002. www.jannah.org/sisters/feminism.html.

Hammami, R., and E. Kuttab. "The Palestinian Women's Movement." *News from Within* 15(4) (1999): 3–9.

Hansel, S., and J. Mashal. *Restricted Mobility and the Threat to Health*. Carnegie Council on Ethics and International Affairs, 2001. www.carnegiecouncil.org/themes/hrd_hanselmashal.html.

Hargrave, S. "Negotiating Borders: A Quasi-ethnographic Inquiry of Women, War, and Identity in Novels by Arab Women Writers." Master's thesis, Wichita State University, Wichita, Kansas, 2001.

Holt, M. *Women in Contemporary Palestine: Between Old Conflicts and New Realities*. Jerusalem: PASSIA, 1996.

Kuttab, E. "Palestinian Women in the Intifada: Fighting on Two Fronts." *Arab Studies Quarterly* 15(2) (1993): 69–85.

Oxfam Community Aid Abroad. *Palestine: Australian-funded Aid Impacted by Conflict*. 2002. www.caa.org.au/pr/2002/palestine.html.

Palestinian Central Bureau of Statistics. *Gender Statistics and Indicators*. www.pcbs.org.

12

SAUDI ARABIA

As ad Abu Khalil

PROFILE OF SAUDI ARABIA

Saudi Arabia occupies the bulk of what historically is known as Arabia, or the Arabian peninsula. It has been shaped mostly by its strong association with Islam (it houses the two holiest sites in Islam) and the presence of oil: most of the proven oil reserves of the world are located in the country. It is a vast country, more than one-fifth the size of the United States. Most of its land is desert, and agriculture is only possible in the southwest of the country. The discovery of oil in the 1930s gave a boost to the political status of the kingdom and to its founder, King ʿAbdul-ʾAziz, and his successor descendants.

Saudi Arabia is an unusual country and truly a land of contradictions. It is ruled ostensibly according to the strict rules of a particularly conservative brand of Sunni jurisprudence, yet it has been rapidly modernized due to the influx of oil revenues. Its educational system is governed by an obscure group of Wahhabi clerics, yet it imports the latest products of Western technology and weaponry. Its official ideology is based on exclusivism and religious intolerance, yet troops from the United States are now permanently deployed on its territory. Saudi Arabia is a country that represents all the exoticisms of ancient Arabia, but it is also a country that has been undergoing tremendous changes and transformation. Oil wealth has changed the kingdom, and not necessarily always in a favorable manner, as was beautifully illustrated in Abdul-Rahman Munif's novel *Cities of Salt*.

The kingdom does not reveal much in its data. For instance, it is estimated that the population is more than 22 million, but no exact figure is known. There are only estimates of the number of foreign workers (mostly in oil) in the country. The profile of the population is shown in Table 12.1.

Table 12.1
Population Profile Table

Age structure:
  0–14 years: 42.52 percent (males, 4,932,465; females, 4,743,908)
  15–64 years: 54.8 percent (males, 7,290,840; females, 5,179,393)
  65 years and over: 2.68 percent (males, 334,981; females, 275,505) (2001 est.)
Population growth rate:
  3.27 percent (2001 est.)
Birth rate:
  37.34 births/1,000 population (2001 est.)
Death rate:
  5.94 deaths/1,000 population (2001 est.)
Net migration rate:
  1.32 migrants/1,000 population (2001 est.)
Sex ratio:
  at birth: 1.05 males/female
  under 15 years: 1.04 males/female
  15–64 years: 1.41 males/female
  65 years and over: 1.22 males/female
  total population: 1.23 males/female (2001 est.)
Infant mortality rate:
  51.25 deaths/1,000 live births (2001 est.)
Life expectancy at birth:
  total population: 68.09 years
  male: 66.4 years
  female: 69.85 years (2001 est.)
Total fertility rate:
  6.25 children born/woman (2001 est.)

Source: Central Intelligence Agency, www.cia.gov/cia/publications/factbook/, Saudi Arabia, 2002.

OVERVIEW OF WOMEN'S ISSUES

Saudi Arabian women face many of the same problems as women from other parts of the world. Who among women cannot identify with issues of rape, domestic violence, gender discrimination, commodification of women in popular culture, the stress of fathers' frequent disregard of parenting responsibilities, sexual harassment, monopolization of political office by men, and the general sexism of the state and society? But there are some concerns that are peculiar to Saudi Arabia and a few other Muslim countries: fear of the harassing morality police, the inequities of access to public space, the requirement of male permission for female travel, the absence of females from the political elite, the persistence of traditional culture, the promotion of a particularly conservative and sexist interpretation of Islam, the small percentage of women in the labor force, and the ban on female drivers. All of these issues are in addition to the general problems faced by women everywhere around the world.

Two women and a girl at a beach in Dahran. Photo © Abbas/Magnum Photos.

For some, Saudi Arabia has become a symbol for the plight of Muslim women and has been used to highlight gender issues in the Middle East for purposes of the denigration of Islam and the peoples and cultures of the Middle East. For example, it receives disproportionate attention, and a simple search on Lexus-Nexus will produce far more articles on women in Saudi Arabia than in Egypt, the most populous Arab country. Any news that evokes images of the mystique of the Arabian Nights and the Middle East harem captures the imagination of Westerners regardless of whether it is true.

Issues of women in the Middle East have often served as effective propaganda for purposes of Western colonization and domination. This is very well articulated by the notion of "colonial feminism."[1] Colonial feminism developed during the nineteenth- and twentieth-century era of Western colonialism, and traces of it can still be observed in the current discourse on Afghanistan and Saudi Arabia despite the official waning of the colonial era. During the nineteenth century, colonial officers were not reluctant to condemn sexism in Middle Eastern countries, yet these same men refrained from paying attention to sexism and misogyny in their own lands. Their contemporary counterparts, who are often but not always men, exhibit similar behavior. For example, news stories during 2001–2002 often campaigned on behalf of Muslim women, yet there exist within European and U.S. societies harsh realities of domestic abuse and rape, especially in the United States, where domestic violence may mean death at the hands of a woman's husband or boyfriend. But it is easier to identify injustice in some distant land than in one's own, where one has to confront more immediate challenges that are often obscured behind the thick layers of national pride and patriotism.

Saudi Arabia and its women attract so much attention in the Western press and in Western popular culture because Saudi Arabia, like the Taliban of recent years, represents the most extreme version of contemporary Islam, which makes it all the more exotic and consequently authentic. As a British colonial ruler once observed, reformed Islam is no more Islam. Mainstream Islam, many people and organizations in the West believe, is not Islam. Saudi Arabia serves as a useful example of how oppressed women are "over there," perhaps to remind women in the West of how "lucky we are here." Such sentiments have been heard loudly recently as the United States justified its war against Afghanistan by references to the plight of women under the Taliban, even as the U.S. president demonstrated his less than optimal attention to the American gender question, especially when he withheld payments and aid to international agencies that provide birth control for poor women for fear of supporting abortion choices.

In the Arab world, Saudi Arabia also receives attention, partly because Saudi propaganda campaigns are always lavish to try to soften the negative coverage of Saudi policies and practices, and partly because Saudi Arabia is truly an extreme version of fundamentalist Islam and most Muslims cannot identify with it. This is true even of the Muslim fundamentalists who decry the hypocrisy of the Saudi royal family.

EDUCATION

Opportunities

Gradually but steadily, women in Saudi Arabia have been increasingly represented in various educational levels and tiers, although the fields of Islamic theology and jurisprudence elude them because the clerics insist that they are to be kept out of those fields. Education has been a staple of Islamic teachings; a famous Hadith, deeds or body of utterances attributed to the Prophet after his death, states that people should "seek knowledge even if you have to go all the way to China." Education was known among women early in Islam, and ʿAʾishah, the Prophet's favorite wife, was quite learned although she could not write. The prophet Muhammad encouraged women to learn about religion and made available a special gate at his house for women who wanted to learn about religion and made available a special gate at his house for women who wanted to learn about Islam.[2] The struggle for learning in Saudi Arabia has been fought by men and women alike: higher education for men in Saudi Arabia was not available until 1957. The clerics were adamantly opposed to the education of women for decades after the founding of the kingdom. They argued that education would corrupt morals and bring a breakdown of the family.[3] King Faysal and his wife championed the cause of women's education and pushed the clerics to change their minds. The first official primary school for girls was first founded in Riyadh in 1960.[4] After King Faysal assumed the throne in 1964, he presented a series of what were then considered reforms, many of which were rejected by the clerical establishment. But the compromise that Faysal reached with the clerics stipulated that the affairs of women's education would be in the hands of a committee staffed by the senior clerics and their representatives. The percentage of girls and women in school kept steadily increasing until it exceeded that of men in some areas (table 12.2). In 1988/1990, for example, "69,054 female students graduated from secondary schools compared with 65,086 males."[5]

Although progress has been made in the field of education, issues of sexism still mar the process of women's education in the kingdom. Men are more likely to receive state support to study abroad than women, although family and tradition may also serve as strong barriers for women's quest of foreign education. Furthermore, the rising unemployment in the kingdom and the decline of oil wealth are adding pressures to the social system and may lead to a backlash against women's education and labor.

But the subject of education has to be related to the curriculum, which is still tied to the interests and propaganda of the clerical establishment. There is evidence that the education of women is widespread in Saudi Arabia and elsewhere in the region. In one comprehensive survey, some 90 percent of Saudi women surveyed maintained that education is "obligatory because it is so urged by religion."[6] The clerical establishment injects a heavy dosage of religious indoctrination into the curricula and allow only their conservative and consistently sexist interpretations of religious texts. It is also unclear whether the increasing education of women will increase the pressure on the state to provide jobs for the new graduates. Moreover, as segregation in education is strictly enforced by the government, one suspects that more resources are assigned to men's schools than to women's. One would also need to see the extent to which scientific fields receive support in women's schools and colleges, in comparison to those of men. In other words, the figures regarding the expansion of female educational opportunities should not necessarily be read as signs of a reduction of gender inequity in all fields and at all levels.

Table 12.2
Women and Education in Saudi Arabia

Educational Level	1970	1975	1980	1983	1995
Elementary Level	31 percent	36 percent	39 percent	41 percent	48 percent
Secondary Level	20 percent	33 percent	38 percent	39 percent	46 percent
College Level	8 percent	20 percent	28 percent	32 percent	46 percent

Source: Central Intelligence Agency, www.cia.gov/cia/publications/factbook/, Saudi Arabia, 2002.

Literacy

While there have been important strides in combating illiteracy among women, there is still a gap in literacy between men and women, according to 1995 estimates by the CIA: male, 71.5 percent; female, 50.2 percent.[7]

EMPLOYMENT AND ECONOMICS

The Saudi government has been increasingly allowing more women in the workforce. The ability of the clerical establishment to confine women to their houses has suffered because of the advanced educational attainments by women. In addition, the kingdom has increasingly tried to reduce the size of the foreign workforce, which, according to figures from the Saudi Ministry of Planning, stood at 3.56 million in 1989.[8] The size of the foreign workforce in the kingdom became an issue for both political and economic reasons. Politically, the government became subject to criticism for allowing such a large number of foreigners, mostly non-Muslims. This is always a sensitive issue to the royal family, especially when it came under attack by dissidents enraged over the presence of U.S. troops in the kingdom. Second, the presence of foreign workers has become an issue of economic and political stress, at least since the 1990s, with the advent of the economic downturn and the rising unemployment in the kingdom. Unlike the image from the past, many Saudis are now willing to accept even what used to be considered "dirty jobs" for the benefits of economic security.

Job/Career Opportunities

The 1989–1990 Five Year Development Plan focused on increasing the female participation rate in the civilian economic sector to 6 percent by 1994–1995.[9] More and more women are pursuing careers, perhaps because their ability to rely on men in the family has been diminished with the economic problems that the kingdom has been facing for years. While the *Economist* estimates the number of working women to be around 250,000, it has reported increasing desires by women to enter the business sector.

In two cities alone, Riyadh and Jeddah, 6,000 business licenses were issued to women in 1998.[10]

There is evidence of an increasing societal support by and for women to work outside the home. However, some factors may inhibit the willingness of women to admit support for more women in the labor force. Such a view may indicate a lower-class status, as rich women may associate women in the workplace with need and poverty. Some high-ranking members of the government are quite open about their support for women's work. The second deputy commander of the National Guard, for example, asserted that there is "nothing in Islam that forbids a woman from working; in fact, the contrary is true. To arbitrarily prevent a woman from working is against Islam."[11]

Few data exist on women and work in Saudi Arabia. The public sector remains the largest employer of women (and men), and "the vast majority who work are in the sex-segregated education system where their numbers are growing as Saudis replace foreign nationals."[12]

Pay

As women make up less than 7 percent of the labor force in the kingdom, and they are confined to the female realm of businesses, the state does not have accurate statistics on inequity of pay for comparable work. In other words, the state needs first to provide equal work opportunities before the issue of equal pay can be addressed and studied.

Working Conditions

Women face tremendous obstacles in the workplace: they cannot deal directly with men; they must have a male "guardian" sponsor; and they cannot drive and therefore have to depend on a man for their transportation.

Sexual Harassment

Women are not visible in public places to the same degree that men are. Women are also required to adhere to conservative dress that passes as the Islamic traditional dress in the kingdom. The state is quite strict in dealing with sexual harassment issues when they occur, but it does not provide statistics in this area. Also, the fact that women are always required to go out accompanied by a male "guardian" may minimize the problem.

FAMILY AND SEXUALITY

Gender Roles

A version of Islam and patriarchy exists in Saudi Arabia that is extreme and harsh in its assumptions and applications, even by the standards of conservative Muslim scholars in the Middle East. This peculiar version of fundamentalist Islam must be understood by making special references to the official religious doctrine in Saudi Arabia (Wahhabiyyah) and to the political arrangement that has governed the affairs of the state since the founding of the kingdom early in the twentieth century. Wahhabiyyah is named after its founder, Muhammad Ibn Abdul-Wahhab, who led an eighteenth-century religious reform movement that became the official state religion in Saudi Arabia. Wahhabiyyah is a quintessential Salafiyyah movement, in the language of Islamic fundamentalism. Salafiyyah is from Arabic *salaf* (the exemplary predecessors). The movement is so named because its adherents want to fully emulate the life and lifestyles of the "good predecessors" (*as-salaf as-salih*), who were very close to the path of the prophet Muhammad, or sunna. It is the ultimate goal of Sunni Muslims to live their lives following in the footsteps of Muhammad.

Muhammad Ibn Abdul-Wahhab was fixated on returning to the early simplicity and purity of original Islam and focused on preaching the concept of strict monotheism, the most important concept in Islam and the one around which most theological debates revolved. Abdul-Wahhab was active in Saudi Arabia and fought against what he considered to be "innovations," which meant whatever came to pass as Islam but was not, in his opinion, Islam. But there is no such pure Islam, as the faith spread by virtue of its practical flexibility and its ability to meld into local cultures and settings. When the House of Saud, the royal family of Saudi Arabia, was fighting to win control of what is today Saudi Arabia, it formed an alliance with the movement, and adopted it as its useful ideology around which young men of zeal gravitated.

In the twentieth century, the victorious Saudi royal family constructed a delicate arrangement by which it ruled, while the Wahhabi took control of the religious establishment and the educational system of the kingdom. The Wahhabi religious establishment espoused, preached, and taught a conservative and exclusivist doctrine that did not bode well for the welfare of Saudi women and their equality with men.

The best representative of the Wahhabi doctrine and its impact on women is the influential Mufti Shaykh ʿAbdul-ʿAziz Bin Baz, who until his death in 1999 was the highest religious figure in the kingdom. Bin Baz was the epitome of obscurantist thought; he never believed that a man set foot on the moon, and he held that the earth is flat for a very long time.[13] On the subject of women, Bin Baz was, like other theologians of Wahhabiyyah, most inflexible. In their minds, any part of the woman, including for some her voice—not unlike some branches of Orthodox Judaism—was a pudendum that should never be exposed except to a very small number of family members. Bin Baz prohibited arts and photography, and the theologians of Wahhabiyyah did not want radio and television in the kingdom but later changed their minds once they became convinced that they could be used for purposes of religious indoctrination, which explains the unpopularity of Saudi television with its heavy dosage of Islamic "evangelism." The Saudi religious elite believes in strict and rigid segregation, and for that reason women are still prohibited from driving cars lest they find themselves freely roaming public space in the company of "strange" men. On this subject, Bin Baz was quite unequivocal: "The *hadiths* points out what we have been saying about the dangers of mixing boys and girls at all levels of instruction. The evidence for that from the *Quran, sunnah* and the experience of the *ummah* today are many but I do not wish to mention them all here in order to be brief. The knowledge of our government, may Allah give them understanding, as well as the Minister of Education and the President of the Directory for Girls Education is sufficient for us to go into this matter here. I ask Allah to grant us all what is good for this *Ummah*. And to make us and our male and female youth good. And to give them happiness in both this life and the Hereafter. He is the Hearer, Responder. And peace and blessings be upon our Prophet Muhammad and his family and Companion."[14]

Segregation

Segregation is another staple of Saudi society, although forms of segregation exist in all societies, including Western societies. Segregation in Saudi Arabia is legally enforced, and the power of the state, through the fearsome "morality police," is employed to impose harsh set of rules and regulations pertaining to social habits and dress. To be sure, these rules apply to both men and women, but are more stringent on women than on men. Segregation in other societies exists whenever males gather together and feel that there are certain things that should not be shared with women, for example, in bars or strip joints. Segregation in Saudi Arabia is more extreme and leaves women at a great disadvantage because through segregation the clerical establishment and the royal family have kept women out of major decision-making bodies that often rule on issues dealing with women themselves. Also, the ability to violate rules of segregation is greater for a man than for a woman because the penalties of violation for women are always harsher and deal with the issues of honor and chastity. It is in that context that the Saudi government is still very keen on imposing the ban on female driving.

Veiling

Much attention is paid in the Western literature to the issue of veiling. In the West, veiling has become a symbol for the oppression of women in the Middle East. Just as the dress of women in the West is not indicative of whether they are oppressed, the existence of the veil itself should not necessarily imply conditions of oppression. Events in Afghanistan during 2001 and subsequent years have focused much attention on the veil (in its various forms), often implying that discarding of the veil is the true measure of the liberation of women and of gender equality. Such a view is too superficial to be taken seriously. Some Western feminists place excessive emphasis on veiling, as if dress is useful to summarize the life and conditions of women.

This is not to say that veiling is nonsexist: it is when it is enforced by a patriarchal state or by a male member of the family. It is also sexist because it implies a sexual objectification of women: they have to be covered to reduce the chances of male sexual arousal. Similarly, or conversely, women in the West are now expected to dress to reveal and to induce male sexual arousal, which means that in both cultures, where males design and determine women's dresses, sexism is at the root of the dress system. In the West, the state does not enforce a dress code, but social enforcement may be as strong as any law. Women who do not follow the fashion trends in schools and colleges in the United States are punished socially and often severely.

Whereas in Saudi Arabia the dress code, mandatory veiling, is imposed by the state and women do not have the option of rejecting it, evidence from other Arab and Muslim countries indicates that veiling may occur for a variety of reasons: to avoid a fashion competition on college campuses frequented by the upper class; to reduce the threat of verbal and physical sexual harassment on the streets, although women should be immune from that regardless of how they dress; to express a belief that religious devoutness requires veiling; to achieve the ability to roam freely in public space, especially in rural areas; to succumb to pressures from members of the family; and to follow traditions or laws in a particular place.

Marriage

In matters of marriage, there is still an emphasis on the traditional marriage and the traditional family institution, which often imply the perpetuation of patriarchal structure through the family. As in other Muslim Arab countries, polygamy is permitted in Saudi Arabia, although polygamous marriages in the kingdom, as elsewhere in the region, are a small percentage of all marriages. Only the wealthy members of the royal family and their business partners can afford to indulge in this traditional "luxury." Statistics about this practice and about attitudes toward it are lacking.

Traditional marriages still exist in Saudi Arabia and elsewhere in the region, although specific data in this regard are unavailable. Traditional marriages entail an agreement between parents, often for business or political purposes, to marry off their daughters and sons, often with little consultation with them. Younger urban members of society are more likely to insist on their right to choose their own partners in marriage. In a survey of Gulf Arab women, Saudi women were the most insistent on selecting their own husbands (Table 12.3).

Table 12.3
Preference for Selecting One's Own
Husband among Gulf Arab Women,
1981–1982

Country	Percentage
Bahrain	77.8
Kuwait	84
Qatar	90.3
UAE	87.5
Saudi Arabia	90

Source: Ahmad Jamal Dhahir, *Al-Mar'ah fi Duwal al-Khalij al-'Arabi: Dirasah maydaniyyah* (Women in the Arab Gulf States: An Empirical Study) (Kuwait: Dhat as-Salasil, 1983), 194.

Table 12.4
Preference for Meeting Future Husband
before Marriage

Country	Percentage
Kuwait	68.2
Qatar	82.3
Bahrain	66.7
UAE	87.5
Saudi Arabia	70

Source: Ahmad Jamal Dhahir, *Al-Mar'ah fi Duwal al-Khalij al-'Arabi: Dirasah maydaniyyah* (Women in the Arab Gulf States: An Empirical Study) (Kuwait: Dhat as-Salasil, 1983), 194.

According to the same study, a large majority of women in Arab Gulf countries also favor meeting their future husband before marriage, as is illustrated in Table 12.4. This should put to rest the Western stereotypical view of Middle Eastern women relishing their own inferior status, and it should also challenge the Islamic fundamentalist assumption regarding women's willingness to embrace traditions. The percentages derived from the study indicate a measure of sociopolitical anticonformity that may eventually put stress on the political system and in the long run bring about important changes. We cannot view the statements by the crown prince of Saudi Arabia regarding changes in the status of women, and his decision to consult with women's delegations—an unprecedented political gesture—without taking into consideration the ways in which women in Saudi Arabia have expressed, by whatever means available, their views and opinions.

Reproduction

Contraception and Abortion

In Islam, abortion and contraception are not the controversial issues that they are in Christian societies, as Islam was pioneering in devising methods for contraception and abortion centuries ago. In fact, because Islam (unlike Christianity and Judaism) allows sex for sex purposes, and not merely for procreation, Muslim jurists have allowed flexibility in this area. Yet the ability to obtain contraception and abortion is entirely a matter of class: women of upper-class status may obtain whatever they need, unlike poorer women who do not have access to the elite doctors who are willing to perform abortions, or who cannot afford to go to Lebanon to obtain access to such procedures.

Teen Pregnancy

Teen pregnancy is strictly frowned upon, especially if the girl is not married. In such a case, it will be considered illicit adultery punishable by the state. Some early marriages may cause teen pregnancy, but it is not the same problem that exists in Western societies. No statistics in this area are available.

HEALTH

Information on the health conditions of women in Saudi Arabia is scarce. Investigation of such matters offends the intention of the clerics to keep such information private. The kingdom has had first-rate medical care, which is provided free to all citizens. It is not known what particular diseases afflict women, although reports of health problems and overweight problems due to the change of diet after the introduction of fast food have been published. AIDS cases are shrouded in secrecy, although they are still less than 0.01 percent of the population.

POLITICS AND LAW

Whereas many Muslim countries have incorporated Western laws into their code and have allowed some reforms in the application of laws, Saudi Arabia remains quite inhospitable to the notion of legal reforms in the realm of gender for fear of instigating a rift between the royal family and the religious elite. The nature of the alliance between the two sides is such that the royal family is allowed to rule (and sin), while the religious establishment exercises a monopoly over issues of religion and education.

The nature of the political formula of governance in Saudi Arabia allows the religious establishment to have the final say on the subject of gender

Table 12.5
Women and Support for Minority Rule

Country	Percentage
Bahrain	55.6
Kuwait	49.8
Qatar	59.7
UAE	50
Saudi Arabia	70

Source: Ahmad Jamal Dhahir, *Al-Mar'ah fi Duwal al-Khalij al-'Arabi: Dirasah maydaniyyah* (Women in the Arab Gulf States: An Empirical Study) (Kuwait: Dhat as-Salasil, 1983), 194.

and sexuality. When the government tried in 2001 to introduce identity cards for women to facilitate their further incorporation into the workplace, a furor ensued when the religious establishment decreed that it is impermissible to have a woman's picture on the identity cards.[15] The royal family had to postpone the procedure until further notice.

Suffrage

Saudi Arabian women cannot vote.

Political Participation

Neither men nor women have political rights in Saudi Arabia. However, there is evidence that Saudi women are becoming more vocal in demanding their rights. In the proliferating Arab satellite media, one often hears Saudi women callers arguing passionately over political issues. For example, one survey indicates that Saudi women are quite supportive of minority rule, as is illustrated in Table 12.5.

The same survey also indicates that some 60 percent of Saudi women reject the notion that politics should be the exclusive concern of men, and that men should be in charge of political affairs.[16] Such figures and surveys, often published and conducted in Arabic, are missing from the literature on the subject, which thereby promotes the stereotype of Saudi women passively and silently endorsing their own exclusion.

Women's Rights

The notion of guardianship in Saudi Arabia is rooted to a phrase or two in the Qur'an. It stipulates that women are legally incomplete or inferior entities and that a male (a father, husband, brother, uncle, or any other male relative) is legally in charge of the woman "under him." Thus a woman in Saudi Arabia must obtain written permission from the male guardian to be allowed outside of the country. Other Arab countries also have that principle, although it is not strictly enforced in most of them.

The climate of oppression affects everybody concerned in the kingdom, and human rights organizations have documented cases of arbitrary arrests, regular executions, and torture.[17] But where there is power, as the French philosopher Michel Foucault stressed, there is opposition. The government is based on institutionalized prejudice and sexism, both of which are embedded in many of the laws. These law explicitly discriminate "against women in almost all aspects of life: decision making, employment, education and family relationships."[18] The Basic Law that founded the consultative council ignored the presence of women in the population, although women did express their defiance against the state on a number of occasions, especially after the invasion of Kuwait, when some women took to cars to protest the ban against women drivers. The participants, many of whom were university professors, were severely punished: they were called whores in mosques; they were taken to hospitals and tested for semen, alcohol, and drugs; several lost their jobs; their passports were confiscated; and they received harassing calls at their homes for months.[19] Ironically, outside of the kingdom, Saudi women can pursue more opportunities commensurate with their talents and skills. In October 2000, United Nations Secretary General Kofi Annan appointed Saudi Arabian Thuraya Ahmad Obeid as an executive director for the United Nations Development Program (UNDP). It is certain that Obeid would be unable to work as a staff member of such an important organization inside the kingdom.

Lesbian Rights

Lesbian rights have not been studied, although a novel by Hanan Al-Sheikh discussed lesbian relations in Gulf countries. There is no reliable information on this matter.

Military Service

Women have no access to military service of any kind in the kingdom.

RELIGION AND SPIRITUALITY

It is often mistakenly assumed that the lives of Middle Eastern women are shaped solely by Islam and by its restrictive law (shari'a). In reality, no society is exclusively shaped by religion, and there is no such thing as a uniform religion. Islam, like other religions, assumes the culture and traditions in the region and environment in which it finds itself. The historic and cultural setting of Saudi Arabia has its own peculiarities; the

Table 12.6
Women Who Think That Traditions Obstruct Women's Progress

Country	Percentage
Kuwait	34.9
Qatar	43.3
Bahrain	44.3
UAE	5
Saudi Arabia	50

Source: Ahmad Jamal Dhahir, *Al-Mar'ah fi Duwal al-Khalij al-'Arabi: Dirasah maydaniyyah* (Women in the Arab Gulf States: An Empirical Study) (Kuwait: Dhat as-Salasil, 1983), 236.

birthplace of the prophet Muhammad and the location of the two holy sites in the kingdom, Mecca and Medina, have added a heavy religious and clerical dimension to the local culture. The political arrangement in the kingdom between the House of Saud and the Wahhabi clerics also reinforces the role of religion in society and upholds the exclusive monopoly of the shari'a in all matters of personal status laws. Other Arab countries are similar in this regard, although the Saudi system of jurisprudence follows the strictest version of Sunni Islam.

Tradition weights heavily on the ways in which shari'a is interpreted and applied in the kingdom. The clerical establishment often invokes traditions in order to press on society and the government the imperative of sticking rigidly to its own version of Islamic legal and theological interpretations. At least some women in Saudi Arabia seem to be aware of the ways in which "traditions" have been used to justify and perpetuate male supremacy in the kingdom, as is seen in Table 12.6.

The very question of traditions is a controversial one; the clerical establishment and many Middle East governments have succeeded in preaching that tradition and religion are one and the same. Those women who express a willingness to challenge traditions are also challenging religion, regardless of whether they know it.

Women's Roles

Islam allows equality of piety between the genders, although menstruation is considered a disqualifier. Women do partake in all religious services and practices, but under rigid conditions of segregation. They are also prohibited from holding judgeships or clerical positions.

OUTLOOK FOR THE TWENTY-FIRST CENTURY

It is unlikely that democratic change will come to the kingdom of Saudi Arabia soon. There is a danger that political exploitation of the subject of Muslim women by Western powers, especially the United States, can only increase the suspicious among many in the region toward Western feminism and eventually help in discrediting local feminists who are linked to the colonial and domineering interests of Western powers. The struggle for gender liberty and equality is a Saudi one. But the presence of oil and Western support for the oppressive Saudi government only make the struggle more difficult.

NOTES

1. Leila Ahmed, *Women and Gender in Islam* (New Haven, CT: Yale University Press, 1992).
2. 'Abdul-Muta'ali al-Jabri, *Al-Mar'ah fi-t-tasawwur al-Islami* (Women in the Islamic Perspective) (n.p., n.d.).
3. See the information section in Mona AlMunajjed, *Women in Saudi Arabia Today* (New York: St. Martin's Press, 1997), 59–80.
4. Ibid., 62.
5. Ibid., 65.
6. Ahmad Jamal Dhahir, *Al-Mar'ah fi Duwal al-Khalij al-'Arabi: Dirash maydaniyyah* (Women in the Arab Gulf States: An Empirical Study) (Kuwait: Dhat as-Salasil, 1983), 140.
7. Central Intelligence Agency, www.cia.gov/cia/publications/factbook/, Saudi Arabia, 2002.
8. As cited in AlMunajjed, 1997, 81.
9. Cited in AlMunajjed, 1997, 82.
10. *Economist*, "Putting Saudi Women to Work," September 24, 1998.
11. Cited in W. Powell, *Saudi Arabia and Its Royal Family* (Secaucus, NJ: Lyle Stuart, 1982), 140.
12. Eleanor Abdella Doumato, "Women and Work in Saudi Arabia: How Flexible Are Islamic Margins?" *Middle East Journal* 53(4) (autumn 1999): 569.
13. See Salih Al-Wardani, *Ibn Baz: Faqih al Sau'ud* (Ibn Baz: The Theologian of the House of Saud) (Cairo: Dar Husam, 1998).
14. From a fatwa by Bin Baz, www.uh.edu/campus/msa/articles/fatawawom/know.html#seeking, January 7, 2002.
15. "Getting Their Cards," *Economist*, January 3, 2002.
16. Dhahir, 1983, 194.
17. *Amnesty International Public Document*, AI Index MDE 23/036/2000, News Service Nr. 84, May 10, 2000.
18. Amnesty International, *Women in Saudi Arabia*, www.amnesty-usa.org/countries/saudi_arabia/women/index.html.
19. These accounts are based on written descriptions written by the activists themselves and smuggled outside the kingdom. They were read by this author.

RESOURCE GUIDE

Suggested Reading

AlMunajjed, Mona. *Women in Saudi Arabia Today*. New York: St. Martin's Press, 1997.

Altorki, Soraya. *Women in Saudi Arabia: Ideology and Behavior among the Elite*. New York. Columbia University Press, 1986.

Amnesty International USA. *Saudi Arabia: Gross Human Rights Abuses against Women*. New York: Amnesty International USA, 2000.

Arebi, Saddeka. *Women and Words in Saudi Arabia. The Politics of Literary Discourse*. New York: Columbia University Press, 1994.

Doumato, Eleanor Abdella. *Getting God's Ear: Women, Islam, and Healing in Saudi Arabia and the Gulf*. New York: Columbia University Press, 2000.

Videos/Films

Arab Diaries. 2001. Deborah Davies, producer. Icarus Films.
My Journey, My Islam. 1999. Kay Rasoul, director. Women Make Movies.

Web Sites

Amnesty International, www.amnesty-usa.org/countries/saudi_arabia/women/index.html.

ʿAbdul-ʿAziz, fatwa, Bin Baz, www.uh.edu/campus/msa/articles/fatawawom/know.html#seeking.

NISAA, www.nisaa.org/.
NISAA is a regional project of the Arab Women's Forum, AISHA. Women's Center for Legal Aid and Counselling/Jerusalem (WCLAC), a Palestinian NGO, is responsible for the coordination and implementation of this Web Site.

United Nations Development Fund for Women (UNIFEM), www.arabwomenconnect.org/.

U.S. Central Intelligence Agency, http://www.cia.gov/cia/publications/factbook/.

SELECTED BIBLIOGRAPHY

Ahmed, Leila. *Women and Gender in Islam*. New Haven, CT: Yale University Press, 1992.

AlMunajjed, Mona. *Women in Saudi Arabia Today*. New York: St. Martin's Press, 1997.

Dhahir, Ahmad Jamal. *Al-marʾah fi Duwal al-Khalij al-ʿArabi: Dirasah maydaniyyah* (Women in the Arab Gulf States: An Empirical Study). Kuwait: Dhat as-Salasil, 1983.

Doumato, Eleanor Abdella. "Women and Work in Saudi Arabia: How Flexible Are Islamic Margins?" *Middle East Journal* 53(4) (autumn 1999): 569.

Geertz, Clifford. *Islam Observed: Religious Development in Morocco and Indonesia*. Chicago: University of Chicago Press, 1971.
al-Jabri, ʿAbdul-Mutaʾali. *Al-Marʾah fi-t-tasawwur al-Islami* (Women in the Islamic Perspective). N.p., n.d.
Mackey, Sandra. *The Saudis: Inside the Desert Kingdom*. Boston: Houghton Mifflin, 1987.
Powell, W. *Saudi Arabia and Its Royal Family*. Secaucus, NJ: Lyle Stuart, 1982.
al-Wardani, Salih. *Ibn Baz: Faqih al Saʿud* (Ibn Baz: The Theologian of the House of Saud). Cairo: Dar Husam, 1998.

13

SYRIA

Naji Abi-Hashem

PROFILE OF SYRIA

Syria is located at the eastern edge of the Mediterranean Sea. It is surrounded by Turkey to the north, Iraq to the east, Jordan to the south, and Lebanon to the west. Syria has a small border with Israel, mainly the Golan Heights located in the southwest. The nation is officially known as the Syrian Arab Republic or the Arab Republic of Syria. It is home to many diverse ethnic, sociocultural, and religious groups, including the Kurds, the Armenians, the Assyrians, the Alawites, the Shiites, the Arab Christians, and the Arab Druze. The majority of the population, however, is from the Arab Muslim Sunnis.

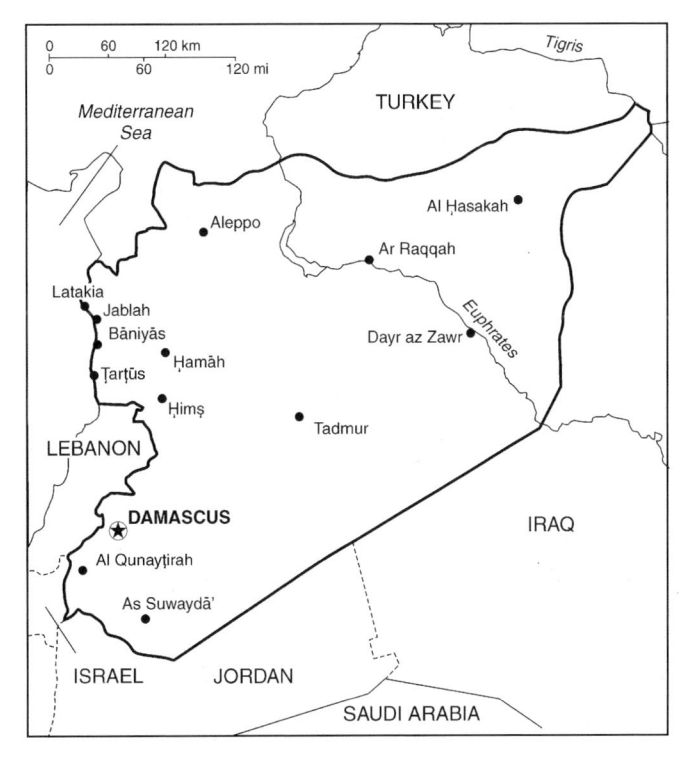

Syria is extremely ancient and has a rich cultural heritage. It was part of many old civilizations. Once the center of the Islamic Empire, Syria covers a wide area that has experienced occupations and invasions over the centuries by almost all great empires that came into the region, from the Romans and the Mongols to the Crusaders and the Turks. Because it was strategically placed at the gate of the Near East, many ancient Syrian writers, poets, and thinkers have influenced the surrounding cultures through the years. Syria is also known for its agriculture. It is a land of rolling hills, wide plains, fertile valleys, and barren deserts. It stretches over approximately 71,500 square miles (185,180 square kilometers) and is located at the western end of a rich farmland called the Fertile Crescent.

The ancient and larger Syria was an Arab kingdom long before the Arab-Muslims achieved glory with the coming of Islam. Syria has long been the home of Arab nationalism. Before becoming, under the Omayyads, the capital of the Muslim world, Syria had for fifteen centuries spoken and written a language that consists of modern Arabic. Ancient Syria, along with other places in the Middle East (like Phoenicia and Mesopotamia), was the cradle of civilizations where the greatest human achievements were established. The secrets of agriculture and the very first alphabet were invented there. Religious thought, the language of trade, human philosophy, systems of urban development, and diplomatic and cultural exchanges also had their roots there. Today Damascus, Aleppo, and Hama pride themselves on being the oldest continuously inhabited cities in the world. Major cities in Syria are Damascus, Aleppo, Homs, Latakia, and Hamah.

The capital, Damascus, is the largest city in Syria. It is situated in an oasis at the foot of Mount Kassyoon. Throughout history, Damascus has been famous for its trade, culture, intellect, and religious heritage. The present territory of Syria does not coincide with the ancient Syrian boundaries. The country has three major geographical areas: the coast, the mountains, and the plains. Each region has a unique climate and character, which obviously shape the temperament, mentality, and subculture of its people. The main river in Syria is the Euphrates.

The rural settlement is very traditional. The choice of a village site was usually determined by the availability of water, fertile land, and defense fortifications. Community living is very dense, and village streets are usually narrow. A mosque or a church normally stands in the middle of the settlement or is built on higher ground nearby so it can provide a reference point and a broad view of the surroundings. This type of close living has advantageous and disadvantageous effects on the structure of Syrian marriages and families around the country. Life is normally characterized by a strong sense of collectivism and communal bonding, yet at the same time, it provides little privacy or personal space. Individual welfare and personal comfort are usually sacrificed for the sake of the family and the community.

Syria is predominantly Arab (some 90 percent of the people are Arabic speaking).[1] The ethnic composition of the country is Syrian Arab, 74.9 percent; Bedouin Arab, 7.4 percent; Kurds, 7.3 percent; Palestinians, 3.9 percent; Armenians, 2.7 percent; and others, 3.8 percent.[2] The religious background and affiliation as of 1992 were Sunni Muslim, 74 percent; Muslim Alawite, 11 percent; Christian, 10 percent; Druze, 3.0 percent; and others, 2.0 percent. The largest minority is the Kurds, about one million people, mostly in the northeast region. In addition, there are smaller groups, confessional and linguistic in nature, who are ethnically non-Arabic, but have gradually integrated Arabic into their culture. Chief among them are the Armenians, with more than 300,000 living in the city of Aleppo, and other smaller scattered groups of Turks, Assyrians, Gypsies, and Aramaic-speaking communities.[3] The predominant Arabic language spoken across Syria indicates that most of the migrations over the centuries to Syria have been from Semitic-speaking people originating in Arabia. The amalgam of all immigrants, including some groups from Asia (and a very few from Europe), have produced present-day Syria's tribes, persons, villagers, and city dwellers. Today, the Arabic character and national type are more noticeable in Syria than in any other modern Arabic or Middle Eastern nation.

During most of its recent history, Syria has had an upper class and ruling society consisting mainly of two interlocked segments, absentee landlords and urban bourgeoisie. The latter group consisted of the large-scale merchants and rentiers. After the country's independence in 1946, the wide privileges of the ruling elites were curtailed by the nationalists and socialists who came to power. The government's attention shifted to those officers and technicians working for the country's institutions, the military, or the state.

The population is mostly divided among urban industrial and rural agricultural. Among the rural dwellers are small minorities known as nomadic and seminomadic herders. Most of the peasants live in villages and work on their farms year-round. Although the government has improved the living conditions in the countryside by building roads, local schools, electricity lines, and health-care clinics, it has not totally eliminated the landlessness and poverty in many places.

Syria's population is nearly 16,730,000 and is expected to double in twenty-seven years.[4] The distribution of urban versus rural population is 54 percent to 46 percent.[5] Males comprise 51.3 percent of the population and females 48.7 percent.[6] The average fertility rates were 3.6 live births per urban woman and 5.1 live births per rural woman.[7] In 1994, women-headed households accounted for about 9 percent of Syrian families, and the age of most female heads was greater than forty-five.[8] The population density is approximately 85 people per square kilometer (compared to 238 in Great Britain).[9] The annual growth rate in the 1990s was 3.6.[10] The monetary unit is the Syrian pound, which is roughly equivalent to U.S. $0.52.

Work in rural and desert areas is seasonal and follows the agriculture rhythm of the land. Women generally share in all field work except plowing. When machinery was introduced after World War II, many farmers lost their share of work and migrated in large numbers to nearby cities, especially among the young generation. These gradual migrations have been causing women more stress due to the splitting of their families, the additional financial hardships, and the subsequent adjustment to new mentalities, lifestyles, and subcultures of the larger cities.

Petroleum, natural gas, phosphate rock, asphalt, and salt are the main minerals found in Syria and exist in sufficiently large quantities for commercial exploitation. Small deposits of coal, iron ore, copper, lead, and gold exist primarily in mountainous regions. Industrialization has caused pollution of already overextended water resources. Lack or misuse of fertilizers and inefficient irrigation methods have compounded this phenomenon. Overexploitation of some areas for agriculture has also caused soil-erosion problems.

Syria gained its full independence on April 17, 1946, seceding from the French Mandate established in 1920. Prior to that, Syria was part of the Ottoman Empire under long-term Turkish rule. Today, modern-day Syria is a vital Arab republic that stands for Arab legitimacy, fervor, and steadfastness. Syria is a member of the United Nations, the Arab League, and the Organization of the Islamic Conference (OIC), as well as many other international organizations. On the national level, the body of the political system is represented by the executive, legislative, and judicial branches. The president is the head of the state and is directly elected by the people every seven years. The 1973 constitution gives the president major executive powers to appoint all vice presidents, the prime minister, and the council of ministers. The president is also the commander in chief of the armed forces and the secretary general of the present ruling party, El-Baath.

The major political parties in Syria are approved by the government itself and are represented in the People's Assembly (*majliss el-shaab*) by the direct voting of the citizens. Some of the major ones are the Arab Socialist Baath Party, the Arab Socialist Union Party, the Arab Socialist Party, the Communist Party of Syria, the Union Socialist Party, and the Union Socialist Democratic Party. All are ideologically compatible with the main ruling Baath Party. The judicial system is also based on the 1973 constitution. The Supreme Court has been established as the head body of the judicial system and consists of a chief justice and four justices who are appointed by presidential decree for a period of four years. The Syrian courts of law are divided into two juridical court systems: Courts of General Jurisdiction and Administrative Courts.

Syrians are a very hospitable people and always welcome friends and strangers into their homes. They do everything possible to make their guests feel comfortable. The hosts are pleased only when they see their guest pleased. They will offer food, drinks, entertainment, and comfort and, it has been said, will even offer the wall painting if the guest stares at it long enough. They do not accept no for an answer; saying "no" is almost an insult to them.

OVERVIEW OF WOMEN'S ISSUES

The daily social life of most Syrian women is centered around the house, the family, neighbors, and relatives. The way of life in the cities differs markedly from that of the countryside. There are also major differences between those women with modern education or training and those with traditional education and upbringing or those without any formal education at all.

There are variations of lifestyles in Syria and significant differences among its regions. For centuries, life among the tribes and villages has been unambitious, tranquil, devoted to the interests of the family and the community, and focused on matters of housing, clothing, dieting, and amusement. Life was characterized by a sense of contentment and great simplicity. But today, with the majority of the elite in power dwelling in large cities, the pattern of life has adopted foreign or Western styles. Its members, along with their spouses, play tennis and bridge, listen and dance to music, read foreign newspapers and magazines, and pursue modern professions and occupations.

Local women pose by a Roman water wheel in Hama. Photo © TRIP/J. Sweeney.

Women of all walks of life are constantly trying to make visible contributions to the development of community, social functions, education, business, and public life. Their work is presently an integral part of the global Syrian structure and economy. The fewer obstacles they face, the more contributions they are able to make. Unfortunately, there are some inconsistencies in the available resources and published reports about the condition of women in Syria. In general, there is an agreement that modern Syrian women actively participate in public life and are represented in most professions as well as in the military. The constitution clearly gives them equality to men in their rights, duties, and privileges.

On the other hand, their struggles are extended and real. Many disadvantaged women are trying hard to find their place in their community and larger society. For example, gender issues and women's empowerment are currently the primary focus of the Syrian National Committee for Women. On a positive note, it has been reported that many Syrian women often occupy high positions in society, like executive directors, lead consultants, heads of government departments, ambassadors, and other key positions. They constitute 6 percent of judges, 10 percent of lawyers, 57 percent of teachers below university level, and 20 percent of university professors. These women are effective and successful as they participate in many organizations, communal functions, and professional syndicates.

EDUCATION

Opportunities

In traditional societies, status and wealth are not directly the results of education but rather are related to family heritage, trade skills, personal connections, and prestige in the community. However, schooling is compulsory for all children eight years of age and older. Most children attend public schools that are funded and managed by the government. There are also some private schools, mostly expensive, that enjoy high academic standards. They are administered by natives and foreigners and are funded partly by tuition and partly by grants from outside mission agencies. The United Nations operates schools for the Palestinian refugee children. Basic textbooks are mainly distributed free to enrolled students. However, the Ministry of Education does control the curriculum in all schools of the country.

Education is divided into several phases: six years of compulsory primary education, three years of lower secondary education, and three years of upper secondary education. The latter years serve as preparation for either university entrance examinations or technical-vocational training. Special attention is given to the technical stream of education. Young women are encouraged to enroll in the technical-vocational schools and to pursue this career path.

Syria has four major universities, located in Damascus, Aleppo, Latakia, and Homs. The largest and oldest is the University of Damascus, founded in 1923, with current enrollment about 60,000. In university-level specializations, the female enrollment in humanities is almost equal to that of men (the gender gap is 3.6). However, women are behind in sciences (gap 18.4), medicine (gap 35.2), and engineering (gap 39.8).[11] In addition, the data collected show a huge difference between the numbers of male and female academic professors. The proportion of the female university instructors in 1998 was 20 percent, whereas the proportion of women functioning as research assistants or university administrators has increased to 48 percent. The gender equality for professorships in humanities is 0.34, in basic sciences, 0.37, in medicine, 0.21, and in engineering, 0.10.[12] Therefore, and overall, women are less likely to hold a university teaching position than their male counterparts.

Literacy

The literacy percentage of the Syrian population in 1995, for those fifteen years of age and over, was almost 75 percent. Male literacy reached 88.3 percent, while female literacy reached 60.4 percent.[13] The estimated illiteracy rate in Syria in 2000 was 11.7 percent for men and 39.5 percent for women.[14] The gender gap in literacy in 1995 was relatively narrow and reached its peak in the age group thirty-five to fifty-nine years.[15] The gender gap was much lower for the younger generation than for the older generation.

EMPLOYMENT AND ECONOMICS

Job/Career Opportunities

It was reported in 2001 that Syrian women constitute about 20 percent of the labor force and 52.5 percent of the country's services sector.[16] The percentage of employed women in agriculture is approximately 80 percent, compared to only 40 percent in the industrial sector.[17] The pattern of participation of women in work and economic activities varies by the region or area of residence. While rural females in the age group fifteen to twenty attain the peak of their involvement in the workforce, urban women of that age group are less active economically until they reach the ages of twenty-five to thirty, when they reach the peak of their involvement. Both groups, especially urban females, decrease their work activity after marriage due to homemaking and childbearing responsibilities.

Unemployment is more likely to occur among urban than among rural women. The gender gap is also elevated in the cities. Women were four times more likely to be unemployed than men. The gender gap, however, lessened between the years 1970 and 1995 for all age groups except the elderly. This is probably due to the increased participation of women aged fifteen to fifty in the general labor force.[18]

In rural areas, the women's responsibility in the family and their participation in the field work have increased lately due to the migration of males to larger cities or to neighboring countries for work, education, and training. In addition, males are required to serve in the army for several years. If soldiers are married, they have to leave behind their young families and the field work as well. This phenomenon has resulted in a greater number of women (mostly illiterate) laboring in the fields for the sake of their immediate and extended families without adequate remuneration. Poorer women are active in all phases of crop production except for grazing, which is the men's responsibility, and are completely responsible for caring for the livestock. This pattern is common in many remote parts of the Arab and Middle Eastern world. In rural Syria, farming is usually a household activity, except among wealthier landlords. Women have little role in marketing the products and little control over the resulting income in the household.

Some customs revolve around delicate and exquisite crafts. Traditional crafts are still being made today the way they used to be made thousands of years ago. For example, the skills of embroidery, ceramics, pottery, jewelry, and basketry are all carefully passed down from generation to generation. Embroidery is one of the most important crafts of Syrian women. In recent years, it has been incorporated into the high-fashion business, like elegant gowns and jackets made by traditional needlework, together with rich Middle Eastern fabrics. The survival of these skills and handmade crafts exemplifies the core values of the Syrian culture.

Pay

The constitution provides for equality between men and women, including equal pay for equal work. The underlying principles of Syrian law and equity are basically derived from Islamic jurisprudence and, to a lesser degree, from the French civil codes.

Working Conditions

Social activists have been promoting the efforts of all Syrian women, whether they are housekeepers, field workers, or educated professionals. They acknowledge the need for better work conditions and call for the modification of many traditions that historically have hindered females' progress and contributions.

Support for Mothers/Caretakers

Daycare

There is no formal daycare in Syria. Activists are suggesting the removal of social obstacles and the implementation of certain practical measures, like the creation of local nurseries for the children of working mothers everywhere. Well-equipped nurseries would not only help overworking, overworrying mothers, but also would facilitate the psychosocial development and learning experiences of the young children themselves.

Inheritance and Property Rights

Generally, the laws of Islam (shari'a) recognize the right of women to inherit land and money, but, in practice, this is not fully applied to women and has yet to catch up with other laws and regulations. Although women are not impeded from owning or managing land or other real property, most Syrian women are culturally pressured to waive their land inheritance in favor of their brothers or sons.

Inheritance for Muslims and Christians is based on civil and religious laws (like the shari'a). Accordingly, women are usually granted half of the inheritance given to male heirs. However, shari'a mandates that male heirs provide financial support to all female relatives who inherit less. For example, a brother who inherits his unmarried sister's share from their parents' estate is obligated to provide for his sister's needs and well-being. If the brother fails to do so, she has the right to file a legal claim. Evidently, such cases are rare due to a number of factors mentioned elsewhere in this chapter, like avoiding public shame, protecting the family's reputation, giving the other party enough time to change his mind, or giving the relatives a chance to intervene and resolve the matter.

Social/Government Programs

Syria gained its independence in 1946 in the midst of much political instability and turmoil. According to historians, there were constant power struggles among the internal segments of the government and much friction among the predominant social and religious groups. In 1970, General Hafez el-Assad led a bloodless military takeover of power and established an authoritarian rule. He was confirmed as president in 1971 and finally consolidated his power in 1973 under a new socialist constitution. Hafez el-Assad was hoping to make Syria a superpower in the region, to rebuild the strength and glory of the collective Arabic nations, and to regain the southwestern piece of territory lost to Israel during the war of 1967 (the Golan Heights). For that, he committed Syria to enormous spending on an arms buildup that severely strained the budget and left little resources for other essential projects and developments. This delayed important progress in many vital areas and affected unfavorably the general welfare of disadvantaged families, women, and children.

Sustainable Development

Some observers are openly pessimistic about the possibility of any major future changes in the Syrian society. They argue that given the economic and political situation in the country, it is quite difficult to gauge what the short-term future may hold for Syria. These observers perceive the current system and the state's budget as struggling for basic survival. They fear that repression may resurge again in the society. While the new current young president appears to have a genuine desire for reforms, according to analysts, there are clear limits (and internal resistance) beyond which the regime itself may not be able to expand. With unemployment conservatively estimated at 30 percent, few families have any disposable income left as they struggle to survive.

FAMILY AND SEXUALITY

In discussing the family in Syria, a differentiation must be made among the urban, the rural, and the Bedouin families. The religious faith and cultural practices of each group play a major role in determining the social nature, family structure, and personal function within that community. Consequently, there are several factors that affect the status of the family in Syria. One survey found that (a) there is a general tendency to reduce the age difference between spouses, especially among younger generations, (b) marriage outside the circle of the extended family (intermarriage) is acceptable not only within the cities but also between small towns and villages, (c) a young man is willing to marry a young woman who is less educated than he, but an educated women is not willing to marry a man who is less educated than she, (d) remarriage of the husband is mainly due to divorce or the death of his wife, and the family income is not a major factor in remarriage, (e) the number of children seems to have a strong correlation with the parents' level of education but not with their income or the size of their dwelling place, (f) the less educated parents have more children and tend to use harsh discipline and rigid socialization methods, (g) in some congested and condensed living quarters, there is no adequate space for children to play, and therefore, they tend to use the streets as their playground, (h) the use of the veil by women is mostly found among illiterate groups and those females married to illiterate or semiliterate men, and veils are less used among educated women, and (i) the family income is not a factor in veiling or unveiling of women, even though the level of income may be an indicator of their social standard in general.[19]

Socializing and eating are the major forms of relaxation in Syria. People love to visit and talk. Socializing may involve the gathering of the whole family and relatives together or the gathering of men and women separately. Leisure time for women often involves exchanging home visits and talking at length with other women friends or family members. Women usually gather to socialize around Turkish coffee or strong tea in someone's home for a morning visit called *sobhiyyeh* or an afternoon time called *ass-riyyeh*. For many families, mealtimes are the most important social events. Festive meals are extensively served as the family members and friends leisurely chat for hours and enjoy an abundance of food, drinks, a variety of desserts, and, a little later, strong coffee.

When the weather permits, many Syrians like driving to mountain resorts for the day or having picnics outdoors. Strolling and walking along main boulevards are a very common habit among all ages. Young women usually go out in groups, frequently wearing their best clothes, as they stroll together for the evening. On mild evenings, city parks are normally full. These activities are especially popular on Thursday night (before Friday, a formal holiday), which is the beginning of the weekend in Syria.

Gender Roles

In many Arab-Muslim nations, many established housewives enjoy high status and are very well treated and never abused. They are the queens of their household and family. Usually, the house and its surroundings are the woman's territory alone. She is referred to as the lady of the dwelling (*sit el-daar*). Such women normally have a strong presence and are considered the family manager and the ultimate overseer, caregiver, and boss. Men usually keep a low profile around the house, as if they are second-class citizens, and spend most of their time outside the home, either at work, in coffeehouses (street cafés), or in town squares.

A challenge facing many urban women and homemakers is the acute shortage of housing. This is due to a number of factors: the average Syrian household size, which is about five people per family; the fast pace of change in the country from an agricultural to an industrial economy; the pursuit of education or job opportunities by young adults within the cities, especially males, who have been increasingly moving out of their original family residence into their own tiny places; the increase in urban population; and greater social mobility. This shortage is forcing many families, at times, to share the same residential units, even though in some cases they are not relatives, and make special arrangements on how to use each part of their dwelling space.

In communities that are more religiously strict, culturally traditional women tend to favor a high level of privacy. However, women who are more educated and less strict religiously (including the minority of Christian and Jewish women) tend to favor less outer protection. In recent decades, women's visibility in public domains has increased, mainly due to the substantial number of young educated women entering the workplace and traveling abroad. Several documentaries have indicated that some urban women in Syria are fashionably secular. These women can dress, work, and travel as they please. Little research exists examining how modernization has affected Syrian females in their personal life, family status, and role in their homes, neighborhood, and other internal domains.

Regarding home privacy, most Syrian women prefer to have visual privacy and protection from the eyes of strangers while in their homes. Women in Damascus, from both the traditional and the modern settings, expressed in a survey that they desire more visual privacy at home from the eyes of outsiders and passersby. Women who live in modern neighborhoods often modify the original design of their house in order to increase the level of privacy. The creation of male and female turfs, as an Islamic tradition, was perhaps the most important element in the structure of towns and cities in which separation of the sexes and the observance of residential visual privacy were important.

Islamic civil laws regulated the design and architecture of many communities and guided social relationships in most neighborhoods. Traditional dwellings were inwardly oriented, with blank outer walls at the pedestrian level. Windows that faced the street were built at higher levels and were frequently accompanied by wood lattice screens (*mash-rebiyya*) to ensure a one-way view, so women could see outside but passersby, especially men, could not see inside. In addition to providing privacy, the screens reduce glare and facilitate air circulation. This sensitive matter of moral decency and female protection highlights the role of customs and cultural norms in Middle Eastern societies, whether women live in a traditional or a modern neighborhood. It is similar to the notion of reputation or social image (*summa'ah*), masculine obligation to honor and protect the female members of the family or tribe (*a'areddh*), honor or a sense of an ascribed pride (*sharaf*), common sense in public, social decency, or common morality (*haya*), and dignity or self-respect (*karaameh*).

In general, it is believed that women's beauty, when displayed more than the minimum necessary in public, could cause societal disruption or communal trouble (*fitnah*). Therefore, many traditional communities around the Middle East, with the guidance and encouragement of their elders (both males and females), try to encourage precautionary measures in order to prevent unnecessary exposure of their treasured women.

Women dress modestly in general, especially outside urban cities. In small towns and villages, women almost always go out in groups of two or three or accompanied by men. Covering the head and veiling are traditional signs of respect, appropriate manners, and social status. This practice is now rare among the young female generation. However, due to the resurgence of Islamic sentiment in the Arabic and Muslim worlds, many women have begun to wear a form of scarf covering part of the hair or thrown around the neck (*hijab*) as a symbol of Islamic solidarity and political protest. It is almost a position of affirmation of their roots, femininity, and social status. Also, it is an act of opposition to the Western culture and political corruption invading their countries.

Children and youth are encouraged to play sports and participate in cultural activities. Soccer is the most popular sport in Syria. Children often play the game in the streets. Men usually attend games at a local stadium while it is simultaneously shown live on television. Women have been gradually allowed to participate in outdoor sports events. Today, more Syrian women are playing sports and taking part in competitions. Ghada Shouaa, a Syrian female athlete, won the gold medal at the Atlanta Olympics in 1996 for the heptathlon, a seven-event competition.[20] The victory caused a major celebration in the whole country at that time and served as a great inspiration to the younger generation of Syrian women.

Marriage

A woman is expected to be chaste before marriage and loyal to her husband and his family, that is, parents-in-law and the significant elders on his side of the family. Single women from the middle and upper classes usually begin to marry after the age of eighteen. Single women from the working class and from rural areas usually marry between the ages of fourteen and eighteen. Bedouin girls typically marry before or no later than the age of fourteen. However, there have been several attempts to change the status of younger women in such areas through new legislation in order to facilitate their involvement in appropriate community agencies, educational programs, and public organizations.

Regarding marriage and divorce laws, the minimum age for marriage is eighteen years for males and seventeen for females. Marriage may be allowed by judicial discretion for males fifteen years of age and for females thirteen years of age.[21] Any local judge may withhold permission to marry if the court finds any major incompatibility in age between betrothed parties. If both parties are underage, they need the permission of the family sponsor or guardian (*wali*). The *wali*'s objection to any girl's marriage when she is under seventeen years of age may be overruled by the judge.[22]

Polygyny is legal, but only a minority of Muslim men actually practice it. Under shari'a, a husband has the right to take up to four wives without asking the consent of his existing wife or wives. However, he is supposed to treat and support them equally. The first wife or any subsequent wife has the right to seek a divorce when she discovers that her husband has taken an additional wife.

A judge may also refuse approval of a polygamous marriage unless the man provides proof that his case is legal and lawful. Financial coverage and capacity to care for the wives should also be established before the polygamous marriage is approved. Therefore, when a man desires or seeks to care for more than one wife, it is up to the judge to verify the man's readiness and ability to give support and fair treatment equally to all of his wives.

The word "divorce" (*talaaq*) has its own power in marriages. When it is uttered while the husband is disoriented, intoxicated, enraged, under coercion, in the course of grave or fatal illness, or simply to pressure and coerce his wife, it is deemed ineffective. According to the Islamic civil and religious laws to which the power of a number is attached, saying the word *talaaq* (divorce) or *taal-ka* (you are divorced) shall be considered single and irrevocable (except third of three).[23] Some sources report that Syrian women in general have the right to initiate a divorce if they are unfairly treated and to seek compensation if they are divorced by their husbands.

Sex Education

Female children are taught early in life to be cautious about touching their body, especially the private parts, and must protect and cover them in order to remain safe, clean, and innocent. Sexual education is still a taboo subject in Syrian families and schools. Sometimes, in great secrecy, a close friend or a relative might explain to the girl certain facts about menstruation, sexual relationships, and reproduction. Most circles consider the topic disrespectful, shameful, and totally inappropriate for children. For a girl to openly acknowledge her sexual feelings to anyone, except to close and trustworthy friends, or to flirt in public is considered very risky behavior. This may be viewed as consciousness-raising, which threatens to place her under accusations that she has actually experienced premarital sex or, even worse, has desired to do so. Most urban men are now becoming more understanding and less judgmental of these sensitive adolescent matters.

Contraception and Abortion

Like many other communities around the Middle East and the world, for most conservative Syrian men, sexual abstinence is an act of nobility and religious obligation. But for many other Syrian men, licentiousness and sexual experiences are symbols of pride, manhood, and virility. Not all Syrian women practice abstinence either. Before many marriages, medical procedures are performed to stitch the remains of the hymen in order to restore lost virginity. Therefore, when some marriages are consummated, the virginity of the bride is artificial.

Teenage Pregnancy

In the majority of Syrian societies, the virginity of young women is still of great moral, religious, and cultural significance. In physical terms, and depending on the particular subculture, the actual intact hymen is a strict requirement and a moral rule that applies to marriage-age women alone. The virginity of young women has been historically considered a treasure and was equated with honor, dignity, purity, and high family reputation. To offer a virgin means to offer the best of the community. It has been an essential part of all religions and anthropologies. Virginity has a deep psychological meaning. In the Arab-Muslim world, it has a major human value and stands as a philosophical and religious symbol, almost like the myth of motherhood. Breaking the virginity, in many cultures, represents an important rite of passage from girlhood to womanhood.

Syrian families in general have to deal with the increasing sexual threats to teenage girls from the outside world. Many young Syrians have access to uncensored magazines, satellite television channels, and Internet pornography. Unequipped with skills or adequate knowledge about open sex, young women are increasingly at risk to act out what they see or to copy their favorite heroine characters they read about. Already, many girls as young as thirteen proudly walk the streets of Damascus wearing heavy makeup, a carefully styled hairdo, and sometimes even revealing clothing.

HEALTH

Health Care Access

Improving the health of women and the welfare of families in Syria still requires, first of all, a great deal of education and care for all women across their age span. This especially means protecting underserved mothers from poverty, ignorance, fears, and illnesses. There have been many attempts to provide women with basic education, health care, and social security. In many parts of Syria, health awareness and family planning are still badly needed. However, many concerned urban women have been campaigning on the national level in addition to their family duties. They are able to spare enough energy to participate in national affairs and to achieve personal goals outside the home.

Health facilities in Syria include state hospitals, sanatoriums, private hospitals, and outpatient clinics of the armed forces. In addition, there are a number of public and private clinics, maternal and child-care centers, antituberculosis and malaria centers, and rural health-care clinics.

According to a 1998 count, there are about 22,300 physicians in Syria, almost one physician for each 700 persons. In the year 2000, the birth rate per 1,000 people was about 31.1, while the death rate was 5.3. In 1995, the marriage rate per 1,000 was almost 8.4. The total fertility rate of the average births per each childbearing woman in the year 2000 was 4.1.[24] Around 20 percent of births were delivered by untrained hands.[25] Finally, in 2000, the life expectancy at birth for the male was 67.4 years and for the female 69.6 years.[26]

Diseases and Disorders

Although most endemic diseases have been eliminated, relatively high child mortality in some areas is still caused by measles, digestive and respiratory diseases, tuberculosis, and trachoma, which are particularly spread among the Bedouins, peasants, and residents of city slums. Physicians are concentrated in large cities, and this denies poor people in remote areas most needed medical services and attention. Otherwise, health conditions and sanitation in the cities, towns, and larger villages are satisfactory.

Depression

Among the factors that are found to cause most low-income women major mental distress are the physical abuse they experience, their inability to pursue enough education, the polygamy situations they find themselves entangled in, the quality of their residence or dwelling, the age of marriage, and their current aging process. Among these, women's illiteracy, polygamy, and physical abuse were the strongest determinants of mental distress leading to further emotional distress and psychological disturbances.

POLITICS AND LAW

Suffrage

Syria is a republic, defined by its constitution as a socialist popular democracy. Citizens eighteen years of age and older, both male and female, can vote. Literate women theoretically have full political rights.

Political Participation

Given the nature of the Syrian political system, women have made remarkable progress in the areas of public service, leadership, and politics. There are two females in the Cabinet of Ministers and twenty-four females in the People's Assembly, 10.5 percent of the total number of representatives.[27] The participation of women in the cabinet has been limited to the Ministries of Culture, Health, or Education. There are those who argue that women are underrepresented in the government because they are not allowed to occupy more seats in the People's Assembly or hold key ministerial positions in the cabinet. Repeatedly, various analysts say that women in Syria have equal rights under the law and have a full access to education, but they are poorly represented in politics and in state employment.

Women's Rights

As of 1992, Syrian law provided for the equal rights of women. The government has continued to make efforts to counter most of the discrimination against women that is culturally conservative or religiously inspired. The government encourages women to enroll at all levels of education, and its policies include equal pay for similar work. However, traditional concepts of male guardianship continue to be strong and to counter the official policies. These concepts and expectations, especially among Muslims, often limit a woman's rights in the areas of marriage, divorce, child custody, inheritance, and personal determination. Moreover, the government accords the right for spiritual authorities and religious courts to rule on the majority of social and interpersonal matters.

Although the government has sought to overcome traditional discrimination against women and to encourage women's pursuit of education and well-being, according to some parties, the People's Assembly has not yet changed personal status retirement or social security laws that unfairly treat women. In addition, some civil and secular laws have a tendency to discriminate against women. For example, according to certain legal analysts, the punishment for dignity and adultery crimes for females is twice as harsh as it is for males. Similarly, husbands may easily claim adultery as a ground for divorcing their wives, but women face more obstacles in proving the same evidence or in carrying the same argument. If a woman requests a divorce from her husband, she may not be entitled to child support in some instances, even if she finally obtained the divorce and was able to keep the children. Under the same laws, mothers lose their right to custody of boys when they reach the age of nine and girls when they reach the age of twelve.

Women over the age of eighteen basically have the legal right to travel without the permission of male relatives. Technically, though, a husband may file a request with the office of the Ministry of Interior to prohibit his wife from leaving Syria. Similarly, a father or a brother may request that his unmarried sister or daughter be restricted from traveling abroad even if she is over eighteen years old.

In 1998, the Syrian Family Planning Association generated a study titled "Arab Syrian Women's Perspectives: Women's Legal Rights and Gender Equality Issues in Syria."[28] It tried to analyze women's status in Syria from a gender-equality perspective and looked into ways in which legislation affects the rights of women in the political, economic, social, cultural, and health domains. The study also focused on women's legal status, which affects their sexuality and reproductive rights. The Syrian Family Planning Association has chosen as its goals to increase awareness of women's rights in general, especially their right to equality and free informed choices in the various walks of life; to encourage male involvement in improving women's sexual and reproductive health status, sharing household responsibilities, taking care of children, and promoting gender equality; and to advocate, with the support of the media, for changes to legislation, policies, attitudes, and values that prevent these goals from being attained.

Feminist Movements

There are a number of highly influential women in Syria, but critics claim that qualified women who are Western educated and are among the brightest of their generation are not given the full chance or the right opportunity to make their impact on the highest level of the social echelon. Most of these female critics live and voice their objections outside Syria.

They blame the lack of women's improvement on the stagnation of political systems and on the male-oriented interpretations of the Islamic laws and ultimately the Qur'an (which tends to be fundamentalistic at times). Muslim feminists tend to challenge the laws and constitutions governing Muslim women everywhere and label such laws as merely un-Islamic. They believe that true Islamic teachings grant women better social rights and higher standards of living. They call on women to break their own bubble before they can change any social system or civic laws.

However, the average and moderate Syrian women do not all agree with the criticism of the extreme feminists. They believe that these feminists are writing about sensitive and complex issues based on few cases and, therefore, are publicizing a negative image of Syrian women that the Western media want to see.

RELIGION AND SPIRITUALITY

The overwhelming majority of the Syrian population is Sunni Muslim. They are divided into several sects. The Sunnis constitute 74 percent of all the Muslim groups[29] and of the whole Syrian population.[30] The Alawites, a subbranch of the Shi'ite sect, are the next largest Muslim group and are mostly centered around the chief port of Latakia. The Alawites include the Imamis (an orthodox Shi'ite group), who live mostly in the southwest. The Alawites are followed by the Druze, who are loosely connected to Islam and are mainly found in the south of the country. They are mostly a mystic sociocultural religion characterized by strong ethnic and communal bonds. The Druze's belief system tends to incorporate elements of Judaism, Islam, and Christianity along with some Eastern religious philosophy. The Christian community constitutes about one-tenth of the total population, almost 1.5 million people.[31] It has been said that the Christians are one of the most important spiritual and cultural minorities in Syria's history.

Although Christian groups are geographically dispersed, they tend to favor modern ways of life. These Christian communities include the Catholics (Eastern Rites, Melchites, Chaldeans, Latins), the Orthodox (Greek, Syrian), the Monophysites (Jacobites, Armenians), the Protestants and Evangelicals (several denominations), and the Assyrians (Nestorians). It is believed that there is still a small Jewish group, a few hundred in number, who survived the wars and migrations. At one time, there were about 30,000 Jews living in the country.[32]

Syria is mainly a traditional country with a culturally and religiously oriented society. The family, community, education, self-discipline, and respect are morally and ethically strongly valued. Syrians place a high degree of emphasis on spirituality and present themselves well both at home and abroad. It is normal to find Syrian families all over the world who still live their lives and customs as if they were in their old beloved country.

Women's Roles

The dedicated life, service, and spirituality of some Christian women in the ancient Near East and the issues of gender in general in Christianity have become a significant focus of recent study and scholarship. Devoted nuns and monks are still living and serving today in remote areas and monasteries, located in the deserts and on top of hills. Mainly, they carry on the same early Syriac Christian traditions that have been known for centuries. On the other hand, the practice of Sufism, a form of contemplative spirituality in Islam, and dedication to monastic and meditative life by Muslim women have almost disappeared in modern Syria. However, many Christian and Muslim urban women are very active in their own religious circles in the cities and small towns across the nation, dedicating themselves to worship and a life of teaching, helping, and caring for the poor, sick, and needy.

Since 2001, several female delegations representing Western mainstream churches and denominations have visited Damascus and met with various women's groups there. Together they have discussed ways to cooperate and network as they have exchanged views about their coexistence among the divine religions. They also affirmed their mutual contribution toward progress and rapprochement among all peoples. The Western delegations expressed a willingness to develop special friendships with all Syrian women and to help them achieve their own goals of justice, peace, welfare, and equality.

Religious Law

Although Syria has no official religion, Islam or one of its derivatives has been required to be the religious persuasion and affiliation of the head of state and the basic guide for the civil and legal system. However, that religious preference or inclination is basically different from being an Islamic nation itself where all the laws and social regulations are a direct application of the teachings of the Qur'an and shari'a, as is the case in countries like Iran (mostly Shi'ite) and Saudi Arabia (mostly Sunni). Regarding marriage and divorce, for example, the rules and guidelines of shari'a tend to apply to Muslims only. Christians seem to be subject to church-canon laws in these matters, making marriages more binding and divorces more difficult to obtain.

VIOLENCE

A phenomenon in the midst of which Syrian women find themselves caught up and deeply affected is the "blood feud." It can be any endless cycle of revenge killing between rival groups or families (usually by killing one person at a time from the other party that continues for many generations). This practice is still a strong tradition in some tribal and nomadic communities. It is an ancient custom used to serve as a social mechanism to preserve honor, dignity, and justice among the Bedouin families. It is a psychosocial form of group protection or self-defense that is perceived as the sole responsibility of the males in the whole extended family. This practice has somewhat decreased in modern times due to industrialization and mobility in Syria.

The persistence of this custom has favored family structure and has bonded the members of the group together even though it promotes exclusivism. Consequently, like any other tradition, blood feud has been subject to reevaluation, rescreening, and marginalization by some rural community members who have higher levels of education, broad cultural exposure, and professional pursuits. Its decrease or, in some cases, disappearance is mainly due to a number of social factors and recent reforms, among them the strict enactment of protective progressive laws; the better settlement of Bedouins and nomads; the revision of penal, crime, and murder laws in tribal communities; and the government provision of social workers and community counselors to rural areas, especially where such practices are still present.

Domestic Violence

Wife beating and other physical abuse are known to occur, but the conservative sociopolitical and civil atmosphere in Syria discourages public discussions of such personal matters. Therefore, it is difficult to estimate the extent of such behaviors and occurrences. There are no official statistics on domestic violence or abuse. Although Syrian women can have access to the courts in order to file a claim and address any grievance caused by violent acts against them, the majority of domestic abuse cases are not pursued for a number of reasons, such as the social stigma attached to legal proceedings on personal issues; fear of the judges' bias and leaning toward male face-saving in the community; the shame attached to personal revelation and disclosure of private matters; the burden of guilt placed on the victim for exposing the whole family to public judgment that results in social rejection, condemnation, and isolation; and the interference of relatives, neighbors, and friends who usually try to help each other resolve family disputes without resorting to the police or the court system. There appear to be no laws against spousal rape. Domestic violence may be the largest single reason for family distress and marital divorce.

Studies have found that physical and sexual abuse is more prevalent in rural areas and among the less educated people than in larger cities. However, some female activists believe that thousands of Syrian women of all ages are being physically or sexually abused, particularly in the suburbs and rural areas. They base their findings on feedback from physicians, lawyers, teachers, and caregivers because of the lack of official estimates of domestic violence. These activists claim that the current laws offer little protection for women and tend to ease the path to mistreatment and violence.

Battered women apparently have the legal right to seek redress in court, but few women pursue such action due to the social stigma attached to it. A few social services, like the Syrian Women's Federation, offer help to battered wives and try to intervene in solving family problems. Some private groups, including the Family Planning Association, have organized seminars on domestic violence that have actually been reported by the national media and press. This coverage was clearly a positive and supportive step from the government. Unlike in the West, there are no designated public shelters for battered women in Syria who seek safe havens from their aggressive husbands or other abusive family members. A few women escape to a distant relative or friend, go back to their parents' home, or seek shelter at a religious institution or monastery. However, this behavior could be culturally interpreted either as an act of mercy and salvation to the troubled woman and her young children or as a sign of failure on her part as a wife and a homemaker. In the Middle East, males' misbehaviors apparently are more tolerated and dismissed than those of women.

Rape/Sexual Assault

There are no official estimates on rape, and the law provides inadequate restitution for victims. Most controversial is a law, common in many Arab societies, that a rapist can be acquitted if he marries his victim. In this case, the woman appears to suffer three times, first when she is raped, second when she is married to her rapist, and then again when he inevitably divorces her after a short period of time, especially if there is a child involved.

OUTLOOK FOR THE TWENTY-FIRST CENTURY

Educators, caregivers, politicians, and concerned thinkers have strongly felt an increasing need to promote women's status in Syria. The first department to be established at the Arab Center for Strategic Studies in Damascus was the Women and Family Affairs Department. Goals are being set to improve the condition of women beyond their role as housewives and homemakers, to mobilize their potentialities, to enhance their coping skills, and to prepare them adequately to face the upcoming challenges of the twenty-first century.[33] For example, the Federation of Syrian Women played an important role in advancing awareness of women's issues and in integrating their concerns within the country's national agenda. Likewise, the Syrian Women's Union, in collaboration with the Family Planning Association and the Syrian Lawyer's Association organized a major conference that brought together accomplished women from various professions (female writers, professors, lawyers, former diplomats, and others).[34]

They openly discussed possible strategies to advance the current rights, status, and welfare of women in the country of Syria.

The main objectives of the Arab Center for Strategic Studies are the following:

- Affirm the present role and contribution of all Syrian women
- Promote the importance of education to women as the best guarantee for a better and healthier future
- Encourage the utilization of other human vital resources in order to create more balanced and well-integrated families
- Help improve the status of women in society by confronting the prevalence of false stereotypes about them and their real assets and abilities
- Enlighten women about their civil, political, and legal rights and about their own social duties and responsibilities as well
- Investigate any discriminatory acts against women in general, especially those working in various fields and occupations
- Educate women about their many options and empower them to overcome the main obstacles constantly facing them
- Facilitate women's access to health education as well as to other sociocultural awareness programs and social services around the country
- Inform women about current political trends and local changes and how these new developments may affect women's life and well-being
- Conduct research and organize conferences on timely subjects related to child, marriage, and family issues
- Set up key training programs to equip women of all levels and walks of life with basic and necessary skills
- Implement action programs, create social bodies, and pursue new policies that further boost the role and status of women in society
- Cooperate with similar Middle Eastern, Arab, and international organizations and network closely with both governmental and nongovernmental agencies in order to meet these declared goals of better serving, understanding, and improving the conditions of women in Syria.[35]

Social and economic planners are calling for the acknowledgment of all hardworking women in Syria, both in the rural and urban areas, for the removal of the major hindrances they face, and for the facilitation of their growth and actualization. Thus far, Syrian women have been an essential part of the livelihood, welfare, and progress of all Syrian communities. Undoubtedly, they will continue to make their vital contributions toward more positive change and social development and to build a healthier home environment and a better family life for all Syrians.

NOTES

1. S. Sherman, "Syria," *New Internationalist* 336 (July 2001): 36, http://web1.epnet.com.
2. "Syria," *Britannica Book of the Year 2002* (Chicago: Encyclopedia Britannica, 2002), 736.
3. Sherman, 2001, 36.
4. "Syria," *Britannica Book of the Year 2002*, 736.
5. Ibid.
6. Ibid.
7. United Nations, "Economic and Social Commission for Western Asia," *Women and Men in the Syrian Arab Republic: A Statistical Portrait* (New York: United Nations, 2001).
8. Ibid.
9. Sherman, 2001, 36.
10. The Syrian Arab Republic (Al-Jamhouriya al Arabia as-Souriya), www.syriagate.com/.
11. United Nations, 2001.
12. Ibid.
13. "Syria," *Britannica Book of the Year 2002*, 736.
14. United Nations, "Estimated Illiteracy Rates in Selected Countries," 2000, http://web1.epnet.com.
15. United Nations, 2001.
16. "Syrian Women Constitute 20 Percent of the Labor Force," December 23, 2001, www.syrialive.net/.
17. Ibid.
18. United Nations, 2001.
19. M.S. Akhras, *Family Status in Syria* (Kuwait: Arab Institute for Planning, 1976).
20. "Sports and Recreation," n.d., http://cwr.utoronto.ca/Cultural/english/syria/sports.html.
21. "File: Islamic Family Law Tabulated," *Al-Raida* 18–19(93–94) (spring/summer 2001): 64–69. For a full statement on the scope and results of this study, see www.law.emory.edu/ifl.
22. Ibid.
23. Ibid.
24. "Syria," *Britannica Book of the Year 2002*, 736.
25. United Nations, 2001.
26. "Syria," *Britannica Book of the Year 2002*, 736.
27. "Women and Human Rights: Syria, Near East, and North Africa," *Women's International Network News* 24(2) (spring 1998): 29.
28. "Women's Perspectives in Syria," *Contemporary Women's Issues Database*, March 1, 1998, 7.
29. "Syria," *The New Encyclopaedia Britannica* (Chicago: Encyclopaedia Britannica, 2002), 28: 361–74.
30. The Syria Arab Republic (Al-Jamhouriya al Arabia as-Souriya), www.syriagate.com/; "Syria," *The Encyclopedia Americana: International Edition* (Danbury, CT: Grolier, 1999), 26: 188–97.
31. F. Lawson, "Syria," *Collier's Encyclopedia* (New York: Macmillan Educational, 1992), 22: 3–25.

32. "Syria," *The Encyclopedia Americana*, 1999, 26: 188–97.
33. M. Sfeir, "Focus: Women's Centers," *Al-Raida* 17–18(90–91) (summer/fall 2000): 35–38. See also www.lau.edu.lb/centers-institutes/iwsaw.html.
34. "Women and Human Rights: Syria, Near East, and North Africa," *Women's International Network News* 24(2) (spring 1998): 29.
35. Sfeir, 2000, 35–38. See also www.lau.edu.lb/centers-institutes/iwsaw.html.

RESOURCE GUIDE

Suggested Reading

Akhras, M.S. *Family Status in Syria*. Kuwait: Arab Institute for Planning, 1976.
Culture. 2002. www.cafe-syria.com/.
al-Kodmany, K. "Residential Visual Privacy: Traditional and Modern Architecture and Urban Design." *Journal of Urban Design* 4(3) (October 1999): 283–312. http://web1.epnet.com.
Minai, N. *Women in Islam: Tradition and Transition in the Middle East*. New York: Wiley, 1981.
Schneider, H. "Letter from Syria: The World's Commotion Arrives on Internet." *Washington Post*, June 20, 2000, A17.
"Syria: Abuse of Women Sanctioned by Tradition and Government." *Women's International Network News* 25(3) (summer 1999). Also see www.unfoundation.org.
Syrian-American Women Association. www.syrianamericanwomen.org/.

Web Sites

Café-Syria, www.cafe-syria.com/.
A private NGO whose objective is to promote Syria.

Castalia Systems, Syria Gate, www.syriagate.com/.
Information resource about Syria.

Jabri Group, Syria Live, www.syrialive.net/.
Offers guides and services for Syrian travel, business, entertainment, media, lifestyle, and literature.

Syrian Arab News Agency, www.sana-syria.com/.

Syrian Computer Society, www.syrianminds.org/.
One of the affiliated activities of the society.

Organizations

Arab Institute for Human Rights
26 av. Moheiddine Klibi
2092 Tunisia

Committee for the Defense of Democratic Freedom and Human Rights in Syria
33 Rue P.V. Couturier
92240 Malakoff, France

Institute for Women's Studies in the Arab World
Lebanese American University
PO Box 13-5053
Chouran Beirut 1102-2801, Lebanon

Women and Family Affairs Department
Arab Center for Strategic Studies
PO Box 36843–36844
Damascus, Syrian Arab Republic

Women's Studies
Centre for Middle Eastern and Islamic Studies
University of Durham
South Road
Durham DH1 3TG, United Kingdom

SELECTED BIBLIOGRAPHY

Akhras, M.S. "The Syrian Woman: Her Role and Status in the Process of Social Change." *Al-Raida* 3(14) (1980): 15. See also www.lau.edu.lb/centers-institutes/iwsaw.html.

Brock, S.P., and S.A. Harvey. "Holy Women of the Syrian Orient" [book review]. *Journal of Near Eastern Studies* 60(3) (1987): 204–6. www.ucpress.edu/books/pages/2081.html.

"Estimated Illiteracy Rates in Selected Countries." United Nations. 2000. http://web1.epnet.com.

"File: Islamic Family Law Tabulated." *Al-Raida* 18–19(93–94): (spring/summer 2001): 64–69. For a full statement on the scope and results of this study, see www.law.emory.edu/ifl.

Kannout, M. *Women 2000: Gender Equality, Development, and Peace for the Twenty-first Century*. New York: 23rd Special Session of the General Assembly of the United Nations, June 7, 2000. www.un.org/womenwatch/daw/followup/beijing+5stat/statments/syria7.htm.

Maziak, W., T. Asfar, F. Mzayek, F. Fouad, and N. Kilzieh. "Socio-demographic Correlates of Psychiatric Morbidity among Low-income Women in Aleppo, Syria." *Social Science and Medicine* 54(9) (2002): 1419–27. www.elsevier.com/inca/publications/store/3/1/5/.

"Muslim Women Gather to Discuss Responses to Militants." *Morning Edition*, National Public Radio (NPR), May 13, 1996.

Sfeir, M. "Focus: Women's Centers." *Al-Raida* 17–18(90–91) (summer/fall 2000): 35–38. See also www.lau.edu.lb/centers-institutes/iwsaw.html.

Sherman, S. "Syria." *New Internationalist* 336 (July 2001): 36. http://web1.epnet.com.

"Sports and Recreation." N.d. http://cwr.utoronto.ca/Cultural/english/syria/sports.html.

Syrian Women Constitute 20% of the Labor Force. December 23, 2001. www.syrialive.net/.

The Syrian Arab Republic (*Al-Jamhouriya al Arabia as-Souriya*). http://www.syriagate.com/.

United Nations Economic and Social Commission for Western Asia. *Women and Men in the Syrian Arab Republic: A Statistical Portrait*. New York: United Nations, 2001.

"US Anglican Church Delegation for Boosting Relations with Syrian Women." BBC, Religion, October 4, 1999. www.bbc.co.uk.

"Women and Human Rights: Syria, the Middle East." *Women's International Network News* 19(2) (spring 1993): 20.

"Women and Human Rights: Syria, Near East, and North Africa." *Women's International Network News* 24(2) (spring 1998): 29.

"Women's Perspectives in Syria." *Contemporary Women's Issues Database*, March 1, 1998, 7.

Syria-Women's Role in Agriculture. FAD-Office of Evaluation and Studies. Retrieved August 11, 2002 from http://www.ifad.org/gender/learning/sector/agriculture/31.htm.

Zahra, R. *Locking the Mystery: Women's Sexuality.* N.d. www.geocities.com/wellesley/3321/win24b.htm.

14
TUNISIA

Angel M. Foster

PROFILE OF TUNISIA

Situated on the North African coast of the Mediterranean Sea, Tunisia is a country with an area of nearly 164,000 square kilometers bordering Algeria and Libya. Tunisia's geography reflects its combined coastal and desert location, and thus the terrain is characterized by the mountainous north, the coastal north and northeast, the arid central plains, and the semiarid desert south.

A former French protectorate, Tunisia gained independence in 1956 and shortly thereafter became a one-party republic with nationalist leader Habib Bourguiba as its first president. Bourguiba was a popular modernizer and reformer and was appointed president for life by the Neo Destour Party in 1975. In 1987, Bourguiba was deposed in a bloodless "constitutional coup" by then Prime Minister Zine El Abidine Ben Ali, who claimed that Bourguiba was no longer fit to rule. The first national elections in the post-Bourguiba era took place in 1987, and Ben Ali, who was uncontested, was elected president with 99 percent of the vote. Ben Ali has since been elected to two additional five-year terms, most recently in 1999. The legislative branch of the Tunisian government is comprised of a 182-seat Chamber of Deputies (parliament). Recent reforms have led to limited political liberalization, and in the 1999 elections opposition parties won thirty-four parliamentary seats.

Tunisia is classified as a lower-middle-income country, with an annual per capita income of slightly more than U.S. $2,000 in 2000. Agriculture, mining, energy, tourism, and manufacturing sectors all contribute to Tunisia's economy. Following a balance-of-payments crisis in the mid-1980s, Tunisia embarked on a series of structural economic reforms that increased economic liberalization, macroeconomic stability, and private-sector investment. From 1987 to 2000, Tunisia experienced relatively constant economic growth, and in 2000 Tunisia's budget deficit dropped to 2.4 percent of total GDP.

The population of Tunisia reached 9.7 million in 2001. Approximately 60 percent of Tunisia's population lives in urban areas, with more than 10 percent concentrated in the capital city of Tunis. Although the arid and semiarid central and southern regions constitute 70 percent of the total land area, less than 30 percent of Tunisia's population lives in these regions. Tunisia's investment in health, education, and social services has contributed to its consistently strong demographic indicators.

Throughout history, Tunisia has been at the crossroads of a number of civilizations. Consequently, Tunisian culture and identity reflect Arab, Berber, African, and European influences. Arabic is the official language in Tunisia. French is widely used in higher education and commerce, and approximately 2 percent of the Tunisian population speaks Berber in the home. The overwhelming majority of Tunisians are Sunni Muslims (98 percent), with Jews and Christians constituting the remainder of the population. Approximately 75 percent of the Tunisian population is defined as being middle class, and more than 90 percent of the population has access to electricity and drinking water in their homes. Ownership of televisions, radios, and telephones increased significantly in the 1990s.[1]

In 2001, Tunisia's total fertility rate was its lowest in history at 1.99 children per woman, and the infant mortality rate was 29.04 per 1,000, thus placing Tunisia's health indicators among the best both in the Middle East and North Africa region and among lower-middle-income countries. In 2001, the overall life expectancy in Tunisia was nearly 74 years, with 72.3 years for males and 75.6 years for females.[2] The overall male-to-female ratio is 1.02, in large part due to the higher ratio of males to females at birth (1.08).

OVERVIEW OF WOMEN'S ISSUES

On August 13, 1956, five months after Tunisia gained independence, the first personal status code, the Code du statut personnel (CSP), was created. President Habib Bourguiba championed the reform in Tunisian civil law. Bourguiba was concerned about those aspects of Tunisian culture and society that he viewed as inhibiting development and progress. Consequently, social institutions, and specifically women's emancipation, became key areas of reform in the early postindependence era. Although Bourguiba saw the improvement of women's educational and economic status as integral to Tunisian development, he also viewed women's emancipation as a strategy for undermining "regressive" values, leaders, and institutions, enhancing relations with prospective European allies and donors, and strengthening his own leadership. Thus improvements in women's rights and status served multiple political and economic agendas for the national government and the first president.

Revolutionary for its time, the personal status code formally secularized civil law and granted women full legal majority with all subsequent rights and duties.[3] The CSP significantly reformed marital law through the prohibition of polygamy, the elimination of repudiation (the practice by which a husband unilaterally dissolves a marriage through oral declaration), the requirement that both the bride and the groom consent to the union, and the establishment of a minimum age of marriage (ultimately amended to twenty and seventeen for men and women, respectively). Women were granted equal rights to initiate a divorce and greater custodial rights.[4] Formal rights in the areas of political participation, education, employment, and health care were also enacted in the decade following independence. After significant lobbying from women's organizations, the CSP was further amended in 1964, 1966, 1981, and 1993. The 1993 reforms fortified a woman's right to alimony and child support, including lifelong support for disabled children, granted Tunisian women the ability to pass Tunisian nationality to their children, and made marital obligations reciprocal, although different obligations toward family income remain. Thus the Tunisian CSP is widely accepted as the most progressive civil code in the Arab world, and women's status in Tunisia is often cited as being the most elevated in the region.

The CSP has had an enormous impact on women's rights, status, and opportunities in Tunisia. Although some shortcomings in the legal system persist, the major weaknesses are related to its application. As is true of women around the world, Tunisian women suffer from violence, discrimination, and inequities in their homes, workplaces, and society. Tunisian women continue to be marginalized at the individual and collective levels through both formal and informal institutions, and barriers to gender equality are influenced by patriarchal traditions, socioeconomic realities, and political repression. Thus Tunisian women face a series of challenges with respect to the realization of their rights, opportunities, and potential.

EDUCATION

Opportunities

Since Tunisia achieved independence from France in 1956, the country has made significant advances in increasing educational opportunities for women and girls. The national education program was founded on three primary principles: nondiscrimination in access to education, universal educational opportunities, and obligatory enrollment from age six to age fifteen, inclusive. Nearly 20 percent of the national budget is dedicated to education, and through investment in infrastructure, the development

Modernly dressed teenagers encounter a pair of traditionally dressed women in Houmt Souk. Photo © TRIP/H. Rogers.

of national teacher-training programs, and reforms in educational law, Tunisian women have made considerable gains in educational status.

Since 1958, primary and secondary education has been both compulsory and free. As a consequence, enrollment statistics for girls have steadily increased since independence. In 1974–1975, girls constituted 38.6 percent of students in primary school. This percentage increased to 48.7 percent in 1994–1995.[5] During these same years, the proportion of female secondary-school pupils increased from 27 percent to 43 percent. Current enrollment statistics suggest that primary enrollment for girls is nearly universal, and secondary enrollment is approximately 49 percent.

Yet current enrollment statistics for primary and secondary education continue to reflect rural-urban and female-male disparities. Lower enrollment for both sexes is found in rural areas, and primary-school dropout rates are higher for girls than for boys in grades one through four. Progression through the Tunisian educational system is performance based, and it appears that boys are more likely to repeat a year than their female counterparts. Overall, boys and girls have identical rates of progression, with 60 percent of elementary students successfully advancing to secondary school.[6]

Since the 1980s, vocational training has become an increasingly important component of the Tunisian educational system. Of trainees in public-sector programs, 31.5 percent were female in 1997, compared to 19.5 percent in 1994.[7] However, 45 percent of vocational programs are within the private sector, and thus, overall, more than 70 percent of the vocational program enrollees are female, with most focusing on building skill sets in the service sector. From 1992 to 1997, more than 65,000 women received vocational training through public institutions, 57,000 through private institutions, and more than 21,000 through nongovernmental organizations (NGOs). Female students are concentrated in four main areas of training: computers and secretarial work (56 percent), clothing and textiles (31 percent), hair styling/cosmetology (8 percent), and electricity/electronics (1 percent).[8] Thus vocational training is providing many Tunisian women with the necessary skills for joining the formal labor force.

Women's educational achievements are not limited to grade school and vocational training. Women have also advanced significantly in postsecondary education. As a percentage of all diploma holders, women increased from 28 percent in 1981 to 43 percent in 1994.[9] In 2001–2002, women constituted nearly 54 percent of enrolled students. Women are well represented in the arts and humanities, the social sciences, and medicine, whereas they constitute a relatively small percentage of students in math and sciences (35 percent) and engineering (10.7 percent).[10]

Literacy

At the beginning of independence in 1956, nearly 85 percent of the population was illiterate, and only 4 percent of girls were enrolled in primary school, making illiteracy for both men and women the norm. However, in 1966, the male illiteracy rate was 53.9 percent compared to a female illiteracy rate of 82.4 percent. In order to address this significant gap, mass literacy campaigns specifically targeting women began in 1966. The largest women's organization in the country, the Union nationale de la femme tunisienne (UNFT), developed regional and national programs to combat adult illiteracy and held classes throughout the country on literacy, cooking, sewing, and child rearing.[11] The literacy initiatives, combined with increased primary-school attendance rates, had a profound impact on illiteracy. In 2000, the youth literacy rate among females aged 15–24 was 10.8% compared to 2.6% for males, and the literacy rate among females over the age of 15 was 39.4%, more than double that of males (18.6%).[12]

EMPLOYMENT AND ECONOMICS

Job/Career Opportunities

In 1993, the Tunisian Labor Code was amended to provide that all forms of discrimination against women in the workforce are prohibited and women are guaranteed equal salaries and opportunities. As a percentage of the total labor force, the female labor force has increased significantly, from 6 percent in 1966 to nearly 24 percent in 2000.[13] Between 20 and 25 percent of all adult women work in the formal economy, in comparison to more than 60 percent of all adult men.[14] Women are engaged in all sectors of the Tunisian economy and in 1994 constituted 17.3 percent of the service sector, 20 percent of the agricultural workforce, and 40 percent of the manufacturing sector.[15] In 1999, 40 percent of all women in the active labor force were employed in professional or skilled positions. The proportion of female magistrates increased from 10 percent in 1984 to 24 percent in 1998, and the proportion of female lawyers increased from 10 percent in 1992 to 22 percent in 1999.[16] In 1992, more than 33 percent of all physicians were women.[17] Women are also well represented in the civil service sector and in broadcast and print media.

Female-owned businesses have increased dramatically in the last decade, in part due to government initiatives to extend credit and loans to female entrepreneurs. By 2000, more than 5,000 women owned businesses in Tunisia, with 85 percent of enterprises falling into the category of industry and crafts. Further, microcredit lending programs offered through both the government and the NGO community led to a significant increase in female-headed microenterprises, from 18 percent in 1993 to 30.5 percent in 1997.[18]

Unemployment continues to be a significant problem in Tunisia, and in 1990, the national unemployment rate reached 15.3 percent. Unemployment among women has grown markedly and is greater than unemployment among men; in 1990, the unemployment rate among men was 13.9 percent, compared to 20.9 percent among women.[19] Underemployment is also a significant problem for women in the labor force, particularly those women employed in the agricultural and textile sectors. Yet in spite of the increase in unemployment and underemployment, the poverty rate in Tunisia fell from 22 percent in 1975 to 4.2 percent in 2000.[20]

Pay

Tunisian labor law guarantees equal salaries for men and women, and the Tunisian government sets the national minimum wage. The industrial minimum wage is currently set at $138 a month for a forty-eight-hour work week and $120 a month for a forty-hour work week. The agricultural minimum wage is set at $4.27 a day. The informal economy, which primarily revolves around commerce and services, is not regulated and is not subject to salary standards. More than 240,000 workers are employed in the informal workforce, and women carry out a considerable proportion of informal-sector activities.[21]

Working Conditions

The right to organize and bargain collectively is officially protected in Tunisia, and approximately 15 percent of the workforce is unionized.[22] Although antiunion discrimination is prohibited, it is widely acknowledged that discrimination against union activists does occur in the private sector. Further, many sectors, such as textiles, hotels, and construction, hire predominantly temporary workers, thereby preventing unionization and effective collective bargaining. In several predominantly female sectors of the economy, including the domestic service sector, collective bargaining does not exist.

Although the minimum age of employment in Tunisia is officially sixteen, the minimum age for "light work" in the nonindustrial and agricultural sectors is thirteen. Work hours for adolescents are regulated, and workers between the ages of fourteen and eighteen must have twelve hours of rest each day and are prohibited from working between 10 P.M. and 6 A.M. In nonagricultural sectors, children aged fourteen to eighteen may not work more than two hours per day.[23] Many teenage girls work in the informal economy, assisting relatives in the agricultural and textile sectors. Further, in lower-income communities, teenage girls have often been pushed into domestic service and their income retained by the family. However, this practice appears to be in decline, in large part due to government enforcement of both school attendance and child work laws.

Complex occupational health and safety standards exist and differ by industry. Regional labor and health inspectors are responsible for enforcing workplace conditions, hours, and adherence to the minimum wage. Pension, unemployment, workplace-injury, and death benefits apply to most segments of the labor force, although the domestic service sector is a notable exception.

Sexual Harassment

Tunisia does not have specific legislation addressing sexual harassment. However, gender-based discrimination is prohibited under Tunisian labor law, and thus sexual harassment falls under this umbrella. The enforcement of antidiscriminatory policies sometimes occurs in the public sector but is virtually absent in the private sector. For example, the Tunisian government assesses compliance with equal opportunity policies as a standard part of the audit of all government entities and state-owned enterprises. This same monitoring does not occur in the private sector. Yet in spite of these government efforts, research conducted in North Africa in the 1990s found that sexual harassment was pervasive throughout Tunisia and was rarely reported to employers or civil authorities.[24]

Support for Mothers/Caretakers

Tunisian employment law explicitly guarantees the protection of the working woman both as a woman and as a mother. Although the Labor Code codifies the equality of men and women in all aspects of employment, women can be prohibited from certain positions in order to ensure their protection from occupational exposures (including operating certain machinery and heavy lifting), carcinogens, and overnight work.[25] These laws are often more rigorously enforced if a woman is pregnant or is of reproductive age. Tunisian law also affords a woman with young children the option of taking a leave of absence or choosing part-time employment in order to assist the woman in reconciling her professional and familial responsibilities. Finally, a woman is allowed to retire with full benefits after fifteen years of service if she has three children under the age of fifteen or a child with a severe disability. While these laws accord many benefits to working mothers, a number of Tunisian feminists have charged that they also serve to implicitly support the primacy of motherhood over participation in the workforce and thereby reaffirm traditional concepts of gender roles.

In 1992, the Association tunisienne des mères (ATM) was established as the Tunisian branch of the Mouvement mondial des mères. Dedicated to assisting mothers in achieving their full familial, social, economic, and political potential, the ATM engages in research on the role of mothers in various aspects of Tunisian policy and society. Through its regional committees, the ATM works to integrate mothers into the development process and to meet the basic needs of mothers in rural communities.

Maternal Leave

Tunisian law requires that the public sector provide women with two months of maternity leave at full salary. Further, in 1992, Tunisian legislation was enacted that guaranteed a mother's right to breast-feed. Tunisian law requires that breast-feeding mothers who work full-time be given two hours per day to breast-feed for six months following maternity leave.

The private sector has different regulations regarding maternity leave. Private-sector employers are required to grant women maternity leave for thirty days at two-thirds of the daily wage. Maternity leave can be extended if warranted by medical circumstances, and a woman's position will remain protected. Further, private-sector employers are required to provide women with one hour per day to breast-feed. If the private-sector organization employs fifty or more women, a special room designated for breast feeding must be established. Government enforcement of breast-feeding laws in the private sector is minimal.

Daycare

Most working mothers prefer to rely on extended family for child-care assistance. However, rural to urban migration, the distance between family members, and the overall decrease in family size have led to changes in the structure of the Tunisian family. Thus for many women, using family for support is impractical or impossible. Consequently, an increasing number of private daycare facilities have been created in large urban centers to meet the needs of women with young children who work outside of the home. To date, daycare is not used extensively outside of the capital, and employers are not required by law to provide daycare facilities.

Family and Medical Leave

Although Tunisian legislation has made significant strides toward providing a supportive environment for working mothers, limitations persist.

Tunisian law guarantees neither paid nor unpaid paternity leave. Thus the responsibility for early child care is designed to rest almost exclusively with the mother. Further, there are no provisions in Tunisian labor law for job protection for caregiving responsibilities other than parenting. However, Tunisian labor law represents a significant achievement in the promotion of gender equality and remains among the most progressive policies in the Middle East and North Africa.

Inheritance and Property Rights

Prior to independence, Islamic law (shari'a) strictly regulated inheritance rights in Tunisia. According to shari'a, a daughter receives one-half the share of her brother. After Tunisia gained independence, the CSP required that if the deceased had no male children, the female children would receive the entire inheritance. This represented a departure from shari'a, as previously male relatives, not the female children, had been next to inherit. However, the CSP did little to address the inequality in inheritance law, in part because of the significant cultural and religious support for the continuation of traditional inheritance practices.

Women in Tunisia have equal rights in the ownership of property and have the unrestricted ability to enter contracts and invest their wealth and earnings. Further, women, regardless of marital status, have equal access to credit under Tunisian law. However, in practice, women are often unable to take advantage of these economic rights. Traditional cultural and religious values influence many women's decisions regarding property and land. Consequently, many women "give" their ownership rights to male relatives. Women are also less likely than men to make long-term investments with their earnings. Women often direct their income to daily family expenses, such as school fees, food, clothing, and medicine, whereas men are more likely to invest in home ownership, vehicles, or farm equipment.[26] In the absence of investments or co-ownership with their spouse, women are often in an economically disadvantageous position in the event of divorce. Finally, women's access to credit is often limited because most women are unable to commit property substantial enough to guarantee a loan. In order to address this shortcoming and assist women in taking advantage of their economic rights, a number of government- and NGO-sponsored credit lending programs have been established.

Social/Government Programs

Sustainable Development

Beginning in 1993, environmental issues were officially integrated into Tunisia's development policies. National development plans, generally set at five-year intervals, are now expected to explicitly address the issue of sustainability. In Tunisia, women occupy 36 percent of the staff positions in the Ministry of the Environment and Land Use Planning, and a representative from the UNFT serves on the national commission dedicated to sustainable development.[27] Environmental programs in Tunisia have targeted soil erosion, desertification, deforestation, water pollution, and waste treatment. There is one principal NGO committed to environmental issues in Tunisia, l'Association tunisienne pour la protection de la nature et de l'environnement. This organization has initiated information and educational campaigns for both secondary schools and the general public.

Welfare

Dedicated to striking a balance between promoting economic efficiency and ensuring basic social services for all, social welfare programs have played a critical role in the development of human resources in Tunisia. In 2001, the Tunisian government spent more than 5.58 billion dinars (approximately U.S. $4.3 billion) on social welfare programs. That same year, social welfare programs constituted 51.6 percent of the national budget, and in 2000, the monthly allocations per household averaged 221 dinars. Coverage is nearly universal, and in 2000, 84 percent of Tunisian citizens received some form of benefit.[28]

FAMILY AND SEXUALLY

Gender Roles

Historically, gender roles in Tunisia have reflected a division between the private, domestic female sphere and the public male sphere related to procreative responsibility and economic power. Prior to Tunisian independence in 1956, Tunisian society was largely agrarian, and women were relegated to the status of legal minors. Women had essential and demanding caregiving, agricultural, procreative, and domestic responsibilities that were essential for familial and societal functioning and yet were often used as a pretext for confining their sphere of activity. Islamic law governed familial relationships, and thus polygamy, repudiation of a wife by her husband, and child marriage were permitted. The financial, familial, and religious pressure to provide heirs and security through childbearing influenced both fertility and son preference. A woman's conduct reflected on the honor of her extended family, and thus women's chastity and fidelity were mandated and monitored.[29]

Yet the private/public dichotomy has never been rigid. Throughout Tunisian history, women have worked outside the home. They actively participated in resisting French colonization and contributed to the political and economic development processes. Furthermore, the historical evidence suggests that individually and collectively, women used "female spaces," the home, the public bath (*hammam*), and saint's tombs, to achieve a considerable amount of autonomy and power in spite of social restrictions.[30] Women have also held significant power within the family, particularly after raising their own children. Thus within the larger patriarchal framework, gender roles in Tunisia have demonstrated considerable variability.

Women's rights and status have evolved noticeably since Tunisia gained independence. The changes in Tunisian law and the advancement of social services have afforded women educational, professional, and economic opportunities. These legal reforms and the dedicated actions of numerous women's organizations and feminist activists have helped to break down the once dominant private/public dichotomy. While these achievements are notable in improving the status of women and promoting gender equality, the growing role of Tunisian women in the public sphere has not relieved them of the burden of the conventional gender roles in the domestic sphere. Thus while there is growing acceptance in Tunisia of women as policy makers, wage earners, and professionals, societal expectations continue to hold women responsible for primary caregiving and child-rearing responsibilities.

Marriage

The promulgation of the Code du statut personnel (CSP), which formally divorced civil law from Islamic law had a profound impact on marital law through the prohibition of polygamy, the requirement that both the bride and the groom consent to the union, and the establishment of a minimum age of marriage for both men and women. Further, the Islamic tradition of a man being able to repudiate his wife was eliminated, and both spouses were granted the right to initiate divorce proceedings, with or without cause. In 1981 and 1993, amendments to the CSP granted custody in the best interest of the child, strengthened women's rights to alimony and child support, and fortified women's equality within the family. Although the institution of marriage continues to be influenced by cultural, familial, and religious law, Tunisian law guarantees women full rights with respect to marriage and divorce.

Marriage in Tunisian society continues to be nearly universal, with almost all women marrying at least once over the course of their lifetime. However, increased educational, economic, and professional opportunities for women have influenced the timing of marriage in Tunisia. The average age of first marriage for women has been steadily increasing since the 1960s, from 20.8 years in 1966 to 24.3 years in 1984 and 26.5 years in 1994.[31] Regional and educational disparities exist, with urban, educated women marrying, on average, more than a year later than their rural, less educated counterparts. Approximately 6.2 percent of first marriages end in divorce, and nearly 40 percent of divorced women remarry (with urban and rural remarriage rates of 32 percent and 52 percent, respectively). However, as a consequence of divorce, widowhood, single parenting, and male labor migration, the number of female-headed households in Tunisia is increasing.

Although consanguineous marriages are becoming less frequent in younger generations, approximately 28 percent of all Tunisian women are married to a first cousin.[32] In rural communities and among older generations, marrying within kin groups remains highly valued. Nearly 60 percent of Tunisian women are married to men completely outside of the familial network.

Reproduction

Sex Education

The introduction of sexual health education into public secondary schools began in the early 1990s. Throughout the 1980s and 1990s, studies indicating poor levels of sexual health knowledge among adolescents came to the attention of government and nongovernment health representatives. By 1994, reproductive health issues were introduced into the third-year natural sciences curriculum throughout the country, thereby affecting all students aged thirteen to fifteen. The sexual health curriculum focuses on basic information about fertilization and conception, the microbiology of sexually transmitted diseases, and the mechanisms of HIV transmission and prevention. More in-depth sexual health education is integrated into the experimental science track, available to select students aged seventeen to twenty-one years.[33] Student support for the reproductive health components of the curriculum has been nearly universal.[34] Significant variation in the quality of sexual health education exists between regions and among schools, depending on the acceptability of sexual health education in the surrounding community and the comfort and interest levels of individual teachers.[35]

Sexual health education is also available to adult women through a variety of different community and national efforts. In 1995, the Ministry of Public Health required that all couples obtain a prenuptial health certificate before marriage and enacted national standards for the examination. In addition to the physical exam and testing, physicians are encouraged to discuss the results with the couple (both individually and as a unit) and provide counseling and information on reproductive health issues. Further, a number of NGOs have established sexual health education programs targeting adult women. These programs focus not only on contraception and family planning, but on sexuality, legal rights, and infertility as well. However, these efforts are highly variable in both quality and availability.

Contraception and Abortion

As early as the 1960s, family planning was viewed as an important component of Tunisia's social and economic development plan.[36] In 1962, the

Tunisian government initiated an experimental family-planning program after first legalizing contraception the previous year. In 1966, the Tunisian national family-planning program became the first family-planning program both in Africa and in the Arab world. The development of a national family-planning program was coupled with legal reforms guaranteeing women's access to contraceptives and abortion. Consequently, programs designed to increase the number of family-planning centers, provide training to health service professionals, and educate the population about the benefits of family planning ensued. As the cornerstone of the women's health program, the family-planning program in Tunisia remains one of the most comprehensive and successful programs in the world.

Contraception is widely available and accepted throughout Tunisia. The contraceptive prevalence rate increased from 9.1 percent in 1966 to 31.4 percent in 1978 and to more than 70 percent in 1999.[37] Although rural and less educated women are less likely to use contraception than their urban and educated counterparts, contraception is used among all demographic groups in the country. Most methods of contraception are widely available in Tunisia, including oral contraceptive pills, intrauterine devices (IUDs), and condoms. Tubal ligation is an available surgical option for women, but male sterilization (vasectomy) is not available. The family-planning program in Tunisia has focused almost exclusively on married women of reproductive age. There remains a significant unmet need for contraception among unmarried and never-married women.

Tunisia remains the only country in the Middle East and North Africa to have fully legalized abortion. In 1965, Article 215 of the penal code was amended to provide that an abortion performed by a licensed physician in an authorized hospital or clinic was permissible if a woman had five or more children or if the pregnancy endangered her health. In 1973, the law was further amended to provide that all women, regardless of their number of children, are able to obtain first-trimester abortions for medical or social reasons. After the first trimester, abortions are permissible if continuation of the pregnancy threatens the woman's physical or psychological health or if the fetus suffers from a serious illness or deformity. By the beginning of 2000, medical abortion through the drug mifepristone (RU486) had also become available on a limited basis in Tunis.[38] Abortion is widely available through both the public and private health sectors and is free for poor and lower-income women. The overall rate of abortion in Tunisia, as reported in 1995, was 96.2 abortions per 1,000 live births.[39] Most women seeking abortions are married, and 35 percent of abortions are obtained by women in the age cohort thirty to thirty-four, most of whom cite contraceptive failure as the reason for their unintended pregnancy.

Teen Pregnancy

As the average age of marriage and access to contraception and family-planning services have increased, adolescent pregnancy has been in steady decline. Statistics from the 1990s indicate that approximately 3 percent of women aged fifteen to nineteen have ever been married.[40] The fertility rate among women aged fifteen to nineteen in 1995 was 32 births per 1,000 women. This represents a decrease from 50 births per 1,000 women in 1993.[41] Information on the rate of out-of-wedlock pregnancies in Tunisia is difficult to obtain. One study estimated that approximately 1.4 percent of all deliveries are by unmarried women, with 31 percent of these by adolescents.[42]

Adoption

In 1958, the Tunisian government legalized adoption. Tunisia remains the only Arab country to have formally enacted such legislation. Transitional placement is also available to children who are not eligible for adoption. Adoptive parents are required to be at least fifteen years older than the child, socioeconomically sufficient, of good moral standing, and married. Although a family court judge can make an exception for a widowed or divorced prospective parent, adoptive rights to not extend to gay and lesbian Tunisians.[43]

HEALTH

Health Care Access

The development of a national public-sector health system has been a priority for the Tunisian government since independence. Legislation institutionalized the concept of health as a right of the Tunisian population, and in 2000 more than 8 percent of the national budget was spent on health care.[44] Primary health services are available throughout the country, and it is estimated that more than 90 percent of the population has ready access to a primary care facility. Infrastructural development has been a priority of the Tunisian government, and by 2000 there were 167 hospitals and 1,981 primary health centers distributed throughout the country. The Tunisian government has also tried to expand the population of health service providers. In 1962, there were 460 physicians.[45] Through the creation of four medical schools and numerous midwifery, nursing, and paramedical training programs, the pool of health service providers has expanded dramatically. By the year 2000, nearly 7,500 physicians and more than 27,000 paramedical personnel were practicing in Tunisia.[46]

Women's primary health services are widely available and accessible, with the poor receiving free services. Government health facilities provide prenatal, maternal, postnatal, and family-planning services to all women. The total fertility rate decreased from 7.2 children per woman in 1962 to under 2.0 children per woman in 2001.[47] The percentage of women seeking prenatal care increased from 54 percent in 1984 to 85.3 percent in 1998, and the percentage of women delivering in health facilities increased from 56 percent to 86 percent during the same period.[48] These improvements in perinatal services are partially responsible for Tunisia's achievement in lowering the maternal mortality rate to 69 per 100,000 live births in 1994.[49] While regional, rural-urban, and educational disparities continue, Tunisian women's health indicators are consistently among the best in the Middle East and North Africa.

Although primary health services are widely available, tertiary and specialist health services tend to be more regionally concentrated. Infertility treatment, for example, is available only in the large cities of Tunis, Sousse, and Sfax, and most of the service providers practice through the private sector. Further, the women's health program has concentrated on the health needs of married women of reproductive age and their children. Unmarried, young adult women are generally not targeted by the health system, and most do not receive routine medical care or preventive services.

Diseases and Disorders

AIDS

The first case of HIV/AIDS was documented in Tunisia in 1985. Between 1985 and 1992, 130 cases of AIDS and 250 cases of HIV were recorded.[50] The number of cases of HIV continued to rise steadily throughout the 1990s, and by July 1995, 378 cases of HIV and 255 cases of AIDS had been registered.[51] Young men represent the most vulnerable cohort within Tunisian society: 70 percent of cases occur within the age group twenty to forty, and the ratio of men to women is nearly four to one.[52] Heterosexual intercourse and injection drug use appear to be the most common routes of transmission, and in a significant proportion of the cases it appears that the virus was contracted abroad. Beginning in 1987, the Ministry of Public Health sponsored public education campaigns dedicated to HIV/AIDS awareness and mechanisms of transmission and prevention. In addition, several hotlines and NGOs have been established in Tunis and the Sahel to provide information and promote sexual health education and confidential testing. Although there is a general consensus within the medical community that HIV/AIDS has been underreported, HIV/AIDS remains a relatively limited health problem in Tunisia. However, there is also a general consensus that other sexually transmitted diseases, particularly gonorrhea, herpes, and chlamydia, are considerably more prevalent in all age cohorts.

Eating Disorders

Information on eating disorders in Tunisia is limited. Traditional concepts of female beauty place value on voluptuousness, a body type associated with fertility and maternity. Indeed, a recent study found that approximately 22.7 percent of women in Tunisia are obese, and more than 50 percent of women were found to be overweight or obese.[53] However, in part due to the infusion of Western media images, fashion and concepts of beauty appear to be changing among young urban women. Many young women report desiring "model" bodies, lighter hair, and fairer skin, and dieting and exercise have become more commonplace among young women in Tunis.[54] However, to date, there is no documentation of compulsive exercising or eating disorders.

Cancer

The Tunisian population is entering a period of epidemiologic transition in which the burden of disease shifts from infectious and deficiency diseases to chronic noncommunicable diseases. In tandem with this transition, there has been a recent increase in research dedicated to noninfectious illnesses, including cancer. Detailed epidemiological information on the prevalence and incidence of breast and cervical cancer in Tunisia is not available. However, a study conducted from 1993 to 1997 found that the incidence of breast and cervical cancer were 19.7 per 100,000 and 4.8 per 100,000, respectively. This study revealed that breast cancer was the most common and cervical cancer was the third most common type of cancer affecting Tunisian women.[55]

Studies conducted on breast and cervical cancer in the early 1990s revealed a significant need for both national awareness-raising campaigns and health service provider training programs.[56] In response to emerging research, the government embarked on a series of national campaigns to promote the early detection of breast cancer. Public radio and television announcements have focused on the technique of self-examinations, and in-service trainings have provided health service practitioners with greater knowledge of early detection and screening. Current national guidelines recommend monthly breast self-exams and annual mammographies for women over forty years of age. Finally, as health services and resources continue to improve and expand, treatment for breast cancer is becoming more effective.

Cervical cancer has not received the same level of attention. Currently, there are no national standards regarding cervical cancer screenings (Pap smears). As the etiology of cervical cancer is associated with the human papilloma virus, a sexually transmitted disease, public discussions on risk factors, prevention, and early detection have been limited. However, the Association tunisienne de lutte contre le cancer (ATCC) has been extremely proactive as an advocate for information, prevention, and research on all forms of cancer.

Depression

Only recently have mental health issues formed an active area of research in Tunisia. In 1990, the Association tunisienne pour la santé mentale (ATSM) was established to develop a more comprehensive understanding of mental health issues in Tunisia and to provide better resources to patients suffering from mental illness. Statistics on the prevalence of depression are not available. However, recent studies from Tunisia have identified depression, anxiety, and suicidal ideation as priority areas in both research and treatment.[57] Consistent with studies in other regions of the world, depression among women in Tunisia appears to be multifactorial, with physiological, societal, socioeconomic, and familial contributors. The development of clinical depression among Tunisian women has been associated with the death of a spouse, divorce/separation, domestic violence, a stressful work environment, infertility, and the loss of virginity.[58]

Services for women suffering from depression are limited. In Tunis and other large urban centers, psychologists, psychiatrists, and professional counselors are available through both the public and the private sector. However, in rural areas, few services are available. The ATSM has advocated for additional resources to be dedicated to research, education, and multiple treatment modalities in order to better address depression in Tunisia.

POLITICS AND LAW

Suffrage

In 1957, Tunisian women were granted the right to vote and the right to stand for elections at all levels of government. The first woman was elected to parliament in 1959. Created on June 1, 1959, the Tunisian Constitution states that all citizens have the same rights and duties and are equal before the law.

Political Participation

Women's participation in Tunisian politics has been increasing significantly. In 1989, 4.3 percent of the Tunisian Chamber of Deputies was female. In 1999, women constituted 11.5 percent of the Chamber of Deputies, with twenty-one elected members. In 2001, a number of women held high-profile positions within the national government: two women as ministers, three women as secretaries of state, and one woman as vice president of the assembly (Chamber of Deputies). Women have even greater representation at the municipal level. In 1957, 1.3 percent of elected municipal officials were female, compared to nearly 21 percent in 2000. However,

Tunisia effectively remains a one-party system, particularly at the national level. This lack of political pluralism inhibits the political participation of and the political discourse available to both women and men.

In addition to formal political participation, much discussion has taken place about how to better integrate women into development initiatives in Tunisia. Several women's organizations are dedicated to ensuring that women's voices and interests are integrated into the decision-making process.

Women's Rights

Feminist Movements

Feminism has a long and varied history in Tunisia. Tahar Haddad, an early-twentieth-century Islamic scholar, is often credited as the founder of modern Tunisian feminism. Like Egypt's Qasim Amin, Haddad argued that Islam was a dynamic and progressive religion and that adherence to arcane social customs formed a significant impediment to Tunisia's modernization. According to Haddad, laws enforcing women's secondary status represented a distortion of Islam and its fundamental values. In a book published in 1930 titled *Notre femme dans la loi et dans la société*, Haddad advocated for women's education, reform in marital law, and the advancement of women's status. Although Haddad was criticized by many Islamic clerics, his ideas appealed to many leaders of the budding independence movement and became a starting point for the development of modern Tunisian feminism.

Throughout the colonial period, women actively participated in the resistance efforts and mobilized for independence. The first women's organization was formed in 1936 and was dedicated to promoting women's education. Subsequent women's organizations focused on the nationalist struggle, labor rights, and social issues. These organizations were largely created by women of elite backgrounds, many of whom had been influenced by the European feminist and Communist movements. Throughout the 1930s and 1940s, women's organizations became more focused on the struggle for independence, and women's issues took a secondary position on the agenda.

In 1956, the Union nationale de la femme tunisienne (UNFT) was formed with the explicit goal of elevating the cultural, social, economic, and political status of Tunisian women.[59] As a women's auxiliary to the national party, the UNFT was primarily responsible for communicating, supporting, and implementing the Neo Destour Party's initiatives and policies.[60] Among the early initiatives of the UNFT were literacy and education campaigns and awareness-raising programs about the personal status code and women's rights. The UNFT became a prominent organization in the years after independence, with nearly 14,000 members in 1960 and more than 38,000 members in 1969.⁶¹ By 2000, the UNFT remained the largest women's organization in Tunisia, with more than 135,000 members throughout the country.

However, the UNFT remains directly tied, and often subordinate to, the Neo Destour Party. The development of an autonomous feminist movement began to take shape in the late 1970s. In 1978, a group of women formed the Club d'études de la condition des femmes (CECF), an organization dedicated to examining critically the significant disparity between the theoretical and the actual status of women in Tunisia. Through discussions, consciousness-raising groups, cultural and artistic exhibitions, and the organization of events on International Women's Day (March 8), the CECF began to draw attention to the continued gender-based inequities in Tunisian law, policy, and society.⁶² Although the CECF disbanded in 1982, it represented a turning point in feminist organizing and mobilization in Tunisia. By 1989, more than twenty women's organizations were officially registered in Tunisia. These organizations represent a wide array of positions and focus on a variety of issues. Some are dedicated to political and economic rights, some to health and education, and others to issues such as violence against women and human rights. As is more broadly the case in the current political climate, the Tunisian government continues to enact barriers to the development of organizations with an activist and/or political agenda. However, organizations like the Association tunisienne des femmes démocrates (ATFD) have been able to creatively overcome many government-imposed obstacles and are creating space for public discussions about more controversial areas surrounding women's rights, status, and participation in Tunisia.

Lesbian Rights

Homosexuality is illegal in Tunisia. Under Article 230 of the Penal Code, consenting adults face up to three years' imprisonment for engaging in sodomy. Sodomy laws apply to gay men, lesbians, and bisexuals. Although enforcement of the law is uncommon, the illegal status of homosexuality impedes lesbian, gay, and bisexual communities from lobbying for protection from discrimination. To date, the lesbian, gay, and bisexual community has no legal rights with respect to housing, employment, or parenting. Adoption rights are not extended to gay individuals or couples.

Transgender rights are not protected in Tunisia. In 1993, Tunisia made international headlines when an appeals court ruled that a transsexual man would not be allowed to legally change his name through the civil courts. The plaintiff had received a sex-change operation in Europe and sued for permission to officially change his civil status. Drawing upon Islamic jurisprudence and equating transsexualism with homosexuality, the appeals court ruled that sex reassignment was an elective surgery and, as such, could not justify a change in civil status.

Military Service

Tunisia enacted mandatory military conscription in 1956. At the age of twenty, all men are required to serve for twelve months in the military, whereas women are not required to serve. Exceptions to conscription can be obtained for students, family income earners, and those residing abroad. However, it is expected that men fulfill their military duties by age twenty-eight. Men likely receive some valuable skill-building and employment experience while serving in the military that women are unable to take advantage of. Although the military continues to be a predominately male institution, women are employed in all branches of the military and as uniformed police officers.[63]

RELIGION AND SPIRITUALITY

Rituals and Religious Practices

Rites of passage are an important component of Tunisian women's social identity and experience. Engagement, marriage, childbirth, and male circumcision are but a few of the events that are widely celebrated within families as well as the larger community. The manner in which these events are celebrated differs by region of origin, rural-urban residence, and socio-economic level, yet throughout the country, these events carry both socio-cultural and religious significance and symbolize important relationship changes in the lives of women.

The public bath (*hammâm*) continues to play an important role in women's lives in many areas of the country. Particularly for women in rural areas, the *hammâm* represents a female space in which women socialize, discuss personal issues, and exchange information, particularly in the area of women's health and sexuality. The *hammâm* remains a primary venue for many female rituals and plays an important role in engagements, weddings, and pregnancy. The *hammâm* also continues to be integrated into traditional medicine and traditional healing practices throughout the country.

The *hammâm* also plays an important role in postpartum celebrations. Accompanied by her newborn and female kin, a woman returns to the *hammâm* for the first time forty days after giving birth and engages in a ceremonial cleansing denoting her reintroduction into the female social network, her ability to perform household responsibilities, and the resumption of the conjugal relationship. Recognizing the importance of caring for both the child and the mother in the postpartum period, a small group of physicians capitalized on this culturally significant tradition by implementing a fortieth-day postpartum consultation program. Women in Sfax were encouraged to return to a health service center forty days after giving birth, at which time pediatric, gynecological, and family-planning services were offered. This integrated program achieved notable success and was later expanded to other regions of the country. The physician-initiated program received international acclaim for its success in providing much needed services through the integration of maternal and child health, family planning, and local traditions.

Although a number of religious and cultural rites of passage remain universally important for Tunisian women, there are also many regionally specific rituals. One example, *tasfih*, although no longer widely practiced, remains important in several communities within the center and south of Tunisia. *Tasfih* has historically served to symbolically restrict premarital sexual desire among women and girls. Occurring in an exclusively female milieu, *tasfih* involves inserting seven small incisions on the knee of a premenstrual girl, recitation of ritual phrases, soaking raisins with the blood from the wounds, and consumption of the raisins. This ritual is believed to promote chastity and reinforce sexual discretion. Prior to marriage, the scarification ritual is repeated, with incisions made in the opposite direction. The second event releases the woman's sexual desires and allows the woman to engage in conjugal relations. Female circumcision or genital cutting is not practiced in Tunisia.[64]

VIOLENCE

Domestic Violence

According to an analysis of Tunisian family court proceedings, approximately 4,000 complaints of domestic violence are filed each year.[65] However, there are no reliable statistics measuring the extent of violence against women in Tunisia, and there is a general consensus that the number of reported incidents represents a significant underestimate of the prevalence of abuse.

Prior to 1993, domestic violence was not explicitly illegal, and domestic abuse fell under more general assault and battery law. The murder of a wife caught in the act of adultery by her husband was legally differentiated from other murders, carrying a penalty of only five years. This same exception was not accorded to a woman who found her husband in a similar compromising position.[66] Further, until 1981, a wife was criminally liable for adulterous behavior, whereas a husband was not.

However, reforms in both the penal and civil codes have significantly affected the status of abused women. In 1993, Article 207 of the Tunisian penal code was amended to provide that murder by a spouse was no longer differentiated from other murders. Under Article 218, a person who causes injury to, hits, or otherwise assaults or attempts to assault a spouse is punishable by up to five years' imprisonment and a fine. Abuse of a spouse or a descendant is considered an aggravating factor, and thus the penalties are more severe. The threat of assault is punishable as well. Domestic violence law falls under the category of assault and battery and is thus limited to physical assault and physical injuries. Sexual violence is addressed through rape law. However, unlike other crimes of violence, criminal proceedings in domestic violence cases can be halted at any time by the withdrawal of the victim's complaint.

Civil law has also affected the status of abused women. The CSP granted women full legal majority and required that the bride consent to a union. Further, the CSP abolished both polygamy and repudiation of a wife, actions that in and of themselves, some have argued, constitute forms of violence against women.[67] Finally, a 1993 amendment to the CSP granted women the right to pass Tunisian nationality to their children, thus influencing child custody in cases of divorce.

Although shortcomings in the penal and civil codes continue to exist, the application of existing laws appears to be the most significant problem for abused women. In practice, many women have found it difficult to obtain a divorce on the grounds of abuse, and family judges often require formal attempts at reconciliation, which may include cohabitation, before granting a divorce.[68] Further, many women have found that in spite of the laws, police, medical personnel, and judges are dismissive of the abuse and are disinclined to intervene. Thus many women feel that reporting the abuse would be futile. Finally, in spite of the awareness-raising campaigns conducted by several women's organizations and NGOs, many women are unaware of their legal rights with respect to domestic violence. This has an enormous impact on women's use or nonuse of the judicial system.

Domestic violence is more commonly addressed through informal familial, kin, and community networks. By confiding in male relatives, seeking refuge with extended family members, and involving neighbors in domestic disputes, abused women often draw on these networks for sanctuary and assistance. A survey on domestic violence conducted by the UNFT found that more than 50 percent of female respondents stated that they would turn to familial assistance as their first resource.[69]

NGOs have been instrumental in addressing the issue of domestic violence in Tunisia. In 1989, the ATFD was founded as an autonomous activist women's organization dedicated to the elimination of all forms of discrimination against women and the defense and expansion of women's political and civil rights. In 1993, the ATFD opened the first domestic violence center in Tunisia, staffing both a listening center and a hotline. Between 1993 and May 1997, the ATFD opened dossiers on 438 abused women in Tunis. Several other women's organizations, including the UNFT and the Association tunisienne du planning familial (ATPF) have sponsored educational campaigns, informational sessions, and research on domestic violence.

Rape/Sexual Assault

The penalty for rape can be severe, depending on the age of the victim and the relationship between the victim and the perpetrator. Child molestation carries a sentence of five years, and the sentence is doubled if the perpetrator is a relative of the victim. The use of a weapon during a rape and the rape of a child may be punishable by death.[70] Tunisian legislation does not recognize marital rape; in particular, marital rape falls outside of domestic violence law. In practice, few cases of rape and child molestation are reported, and few services exist for women who have been sexually assaulted.

Trafficking in Women and Children

The 1995 Code for Protection of Children includes protection against all forms of mistreatment and abuse. Policy in this area focuses on prevention, and the establishment of a women's and children's rights monitoring organization has been proposed. The Tunisian government has also created a rapid-reaction task force. Under the direction of a family court judge, this task force is dedicated to intervention in case of emergency. Tunisia is also a signatory, without reservation, to Articles 34 and 35 of the Convention on the Rights of the Child, which cover the right of children not to be exploited for sexual purposes. All forms of child abuse, including neglect, are illegal in Tunisia. Habitual mistreatment of a child is punishable by five years in prison and a fine. If the abuse occurs within the family, the child can be taken into custody by the state.[71]

Tunisian law prohibits both bonded labor and slavery. Further, prostitution is prohibited by the Tunisian penal code. Although prostitution exists, charges against prostitutes are rarely initiated in practice. There have been no reported cases of trafficking, forced prostitution, or sex tourism in Tunisia.

War and Military Repression

Tunisia is a politically stable country, is not currently engaged in civil or foreign war, and is not involved in any military campaigns.

OUTLOOK FOR THE TWENTY-FIRST CENTURY

Since independence, Tunisia has made enormous strides in improving the status of women and codifying legal equality. Tunisian women have achieved a status and position almost unparalleled in the Middle East and North Africa. As the twenty-first century unfolds, Tunisian women will continue to assert themselves in political participation, economic development, and social reform with the aim of capitalizing on past successes to actualize and expand formal rights and opportunities.

NOTES

1. www.tunisiaonline.com.
2. www.tunisiaonline.com; United Nations Statistics Division, *The World's*

Women 2000: Trends and Statistics (New York: UN Publications, 2001); World Bank, *World Development Report* 2000/2001 (Washington, DC: World Bank, 2001).

3. Although the CSP divorced civil law from Islamic law, many scholars have noted that the CSP was construed in light of Islamic principles. A. Mayer, "Reform of Personal Status Laws in North Africa: A Problem of Islamic or Mediterranean Laws?" *Middle East Journal* 49(3) (summer 1995).

4. S. Galal, "Women and Development in the Maghreb," in *Gender and Development in the Arab World*, ed. N. Khoury and V. Moghadam (London: Zed Books, 1995), 63–64.

5. Ministère des affaires de la femme et de la famille, *Rapport national sur la femme* (Tunis: Ministère des affairs de la femme et de la famille, 1995), 25.

6. www.worldbank.org/gender/info/tunisia.html.

7. www.tunisie.com/femmes.

8. www.worldbank.org/gender/info/tunisia.html.

9. Ibid.

10. Ibid.

11. Galal, 1995, 59.

12. www.genderstats.worldbank.org.

13. www.tunisiaonline.com.

14. www.genderstats.worldbank.org.

15. S. Abderrahim, *La condition de la femme en Tunisie et sa santé reproductive et sexuelle* (Tunis: ATPF, 1996), 44.

16. www.tunisie.com/femmes.

17. Ministère des affaires de la femme et de la famille, 1995, 43.

18. www.insnat/tn.

19. www.worldbank.org/gender/info/tunisia.html.

20. www.tunisieinfo.com.

21. www.worldbank.org/gender/info/tunisia.html.

22. www.acdi-cida.gc.ca.

23. www.eireir/freedata/hrcodes/TUNISIA.htm.

24. www.arabicnews.com.

25. Ministère des affaires de la femme et de la famille, 1995, 40.

26. Abderrahim, 1996.

27. www.un.org/french/womenwatch.

28. www.tunisieinfo.com.

29. L. Labidi, *Çabra Hachma: Sexualité et tradition* (Tunis: Dar Annawras, 1989).

30. This is consistent with researchers' concepts of patriarchal bargaining, a term "intended to indicate the existence of set rules and scripts regulating gender relations, to which both genders accommodate and acquiesce, yet which may nevertheless be contested, redefined, and renegotiated." D. Kandiyoti, "Islam and Patriarchy," in *Women in Middle Eastern History: Shifting Boundaries in Sex and Gender*, ed. N. Keddie and B. Baron (New Haven, CT: Yale University Press, 1991), 40.

31. ONFP, *La santé de la mère et de l'enfant* (Tunis: Ministère de la santé publique, 1996), 175.

32. Ibid., 182.

33. The Tunisian educational system is modeled after the French educational system. Third-year students are generally between thirteen and fifteen years of age and are roughly equivalent to freshmen in U.S. high schools. After the sixth year of secondary schools, students are assigned a track (experimental sciences, humanities, economics, mathematics, or technical sciences). Through the sixth year, all students take

the same courses. During the seventh year, students focus their course work on the subjects covered in their track. Thus only students in the experimental science track will receive additional sexual health information.

34. N. Gueddana et al., *Les jeunes au quotidien: Environnement socio-culturel et comportements de santé* (Tunis: ONFP, 1996), 50.

35. A. Foster, "Young Women's Sexuality in Tunisia: The Health Consequences of Misinformation among University Students," in *Everyday Life in the Muslim Middle East*, ed. D. Bowen and E. Early, 2nd ed. (Bloomington: Indiana University Press, 2002), 100.

36. A. Daly, "Tunisia: The Liberation of Women and the Improvement of Society," in *Family Planning Programs: An International Survey*, ed. B. Berelson (New York: Basic Books, 1969).

37. ONFP, *Impact du programme national de planning familial* (Tunis: ONFP, 1997).

38. E. Batya et al., "Can Women in Less-Developed Countries Use a Simplified Medical Abortion Regimen?" *Lancet* 357(9266) (2001), 1402–5.

39. This may represent an underestimate, as private-sector abortions are likely to be undercounted in national statistics.

40. www.un.org/unsd/demographic/ww2000.

41. www.worldbank.org/gender/info/tunisia.html.

42. A. Triki, speech given at "la Journée de la santé de la reproduction" conference, Gammarth, Tunisia, April 3, 1999.

43. www.juristetunisie.com.

44. www.tunisiaonline.com.

45. G. Rossignol, "Les médecins en Tunisie," *Servir: Revue tunisienne du service public* 5 (1969): 32.

46. www.tunisiaonline.com.

47. ONFP, *La santé de la reproduction et le planning familial en chiffres* (Tunis: ONFP, 1998); www.tunisiaonline.com.

48. www.tunisiaonline.com.

49. Ministère de la santé publique, *La mortalité maternelle en Tunisie* (Tunis: Ministère de la santé publique, 1994), 12.

50. Z. Fekih, "La situation épidémiologique du SIDA dans les pays du Maghreb," in *Santé de la femme et de la famille*, ed. ONFP (Tunis: ONFP, 1993), 31.

51. M. Masmoudi, "Connaissances, croyances, et attitudes des jeunes lycéens à propos du SIDA." Ph.D. diss.,(thèse pour le diplôme d'état de doctorat en médecine, Faculté de médecine "Ibn El Jazzar" Sousse, 1996).

52. Fekih, 1993, 32.

53. N. Mokhtar et al., "Diet Culture and Obesity in Northern Africa," *Journal of Nutrition* 131(3) (2001): 887–92.

54. A. Foster, unpublished survey results.

55. M. Hsairi et al., "Estimation à l'échelle nationale de l'incidence des cancers en Tunisie, 1993–1997," *Tunisie médicale* 80(2) (2002): 57–64.

56. M. Njah et al., "Connaissances, attitudes, et comportements des femmes tunisiennes à propos des cancers gynécologiques," *Sozial- und Präventivmedizin* 39(5) (1994): 280–86.

57. S. Douki, M. Taktak, and S. Ben Zineb, "Femmes et santé mentale," paper presented at the Seminaire sur femme, santé mentale, et société, Tunis, March 28, 1998.

58. Ben Abid, J., A. Belhadj, and S. Douki, "Femme et santé mentale," in *Santé de la femme et de la famille*, ed. ONFP (Tunis: ONFP, 1993), 113–19.

59. There is some debate about the date of the UNFT's creation. The UNFT resulted from the fusion of several precursor organizations, including the Union Musulmane des Femmes Tunisiennes, which was established in 1936. Women's cells that had been affiliated with the Neo Destour Party also formed the new state-sponsored women's organization. While most of the literature states that the UNFT was created in 1956, the first congress was not held until 1958. I. Marzouki, 1993.

60. S. Ferchiou, 1996.

61. L. Brand, *Women, the State, and Political Liberalization: Middle Eastern and North African Experiences* (New York: Columbia University Press, 1998), 206.

62. Ibid.

63. R. Curtiss, "Women's Rights: An Affair of State for Tunisia," in *Arab Women: Between Defiance and Restraint*, ed. S. Sabbagh (New York: Olive Branch Press, 1996), 33–37.

64. A. Eschen and M. Whittaker, "Family Planning: A Base to Build on for Women's Reproductive Health Services," in *The Health of Women: A Global Perspective*, ed. M. Koblinsky, J. Timyan and J. Gay (Boulder, CO: Westview Press), 105–31.

65. www.state.gov/g/drl/rls/hrrpt/2001/nea/8303.htm.

66. Daoud, 1994, 47.

67. E. Ben Miled has noted that as domestic violence is essentially about power, both repudiation and polygamy are forms of violence against women. Indeed, the threat of these activities often caused women fear, anxiety, and psychological morbidity.

68. ATFD, 1994, 58.

69. UNFT, 1992, 37.

70. Chtioui Aouij, 1992, 28.

71. République Tunisienne, *Rapport de la Tunisie sur l'application de la Convention Internationale sur les Droits de l'Enfant* (Tunis: Groupe Ikone, 1995).

RESOURCE GUIDE

Suggested Reading

Afkhami, M., and E. Friedl, eds. *Muslim Women and the Politics of Participation: Implementing the Beijing Platform.* Syracuse, NY: Syracuse University Press, 1997.

Bowen, D., and E. Early, eds. *Everyday Life in the Muslim Middle East.* 2nd ed. Bloomington: Indiana University Press, 2002.

Brand, L. *Women, the State, and Political Liberalization: Middle Eastern and North African Experiences.* New York: Columbia University Press, 1998.

Chatty, D., and A. Rabo, eds. *Organizing Women: Formal and Informal Women's Groups in the Middle East.* Oxford: Berg, 1997.

Hejaiej, M. *Behind Closed Doors: Women's Oral Narratives in Tunis.* London: Quartet Books, 1996.

Holmes-Eber, P. *Daughters of Tunis: Women, Family, and Networks in a Muslim City.* Boulder, CO: Westview Press, 2003.

Keddie, N., and B. Baron, eds. *Women in Middle Eastern History: Shifting Boundaries in Sex and Gender.* New Haven, CT: Yale University Press, 1991.

Khoury, N., and V. Moghadam, eds. *Gender and Development in the Arab World.* London: Zed Books, 1995.

Makhlouf-Obermeyer, C., ed. *Family, Gender, and Population in the Middle East.* Cairo: American University in Cairo Press, 1995.

Murphy, E. *Economic and Political Change in Tunisia*. London: Macmillan, 1999.

Sabbagh, S., ed. *Arab Women: Between Defiance and Restraint*. New York: Olive Branch Press, 1996.

Videos/Films

Bent Familia. 1997. Directed by Nour Bourzid. Three women explore friendship, relationships, and self-awareness in this moving and award-winning film. Distributed by Arab Film Distribution.

Halfaouine: Boy of the Terraces. 1990. Directed by Ferid Boughedir. Comedy that explores the coming of age of a thirteen-year-old boy in the Tunis neighborhood of Halfaouine. Distributed by Arab Film Distribution.

Man of Ashes. 1986. Directed by Nouri Bourzid. Examines traditional concepts of masculinity in Tunisia. Distributed by Arab Film Distribution.

My Heart Is My Witness. 1996. Directed by Louise Carré. Explores the status of women in Islam through interviews with women from Morocco, Algeria, Tunisia, and Mali. Distributed by Women Make Movies.

The Silences of the Palace. 1996. Directed by Moufida Tlati. Award-winning feature film set in 1950s Tunisia that offers a dramatic examination of memory, motherhood, and sexual and political power. Distributed by Capitol Entertainment & Home Video.

Web Sites

Association tunisienne des mères, www.atm.org.tn.
Contains information on women's status, women's political participation, and women's organizations in Tunisia.

www.juristetunisie.com.
Offers direct excerpts from sections of the Tunisia personal status and penal codes.

Tunisia Globe, www.tunisiaglobe.com.
Latest news and information on Tunisia, including political updates.

Tunisia Online, www.tunisiaonline.com.
Official web site with links to Tunisian census data, United Nations statistics, and numerous Tunisian organizations.

United Nations Development Program, www.undp.org/hdr/2002/indicator.
Contains the 2002 Human Development Report online.

Organizations

Association des femmes tunisiennes pour la recherche et le développement (AFTURD)
Cité Sprols Bloc 9
Rue 7301 El-Menzah
Tunis, Tunisia
Phone: 216-1-870-580
Web site: www.macmag-glip.org/French/focaux.htm. AFTURD is dedicated to study-

ing the integration of women into economic development programs and improving women's participation in the decision-making process.

Association tunisienne des femmes démocrates (ATFD)
6 Rue de Liban
Tunis, Tunisia 1000
Web site: http://web.tiscali.it/WIN/035.html. Founded in 1989, the ATFD is committed to eliminating all forms of violence against women and promoting the equality of women in all parts of Tunisian society.

Association tunisienne du planning familial (ATPF)
9 Rue Essoyoutin
El Menzah
Tunis, Tunisia 1004
Phone: 216-1-232-419
Web site: http://ippfnet.ippf.org/pub/IPPF_regions/IPPF_CountryProfile.asp?ISOCode-TN#ATPF. The ATPF is the Tunisian branch of the International Planned Parenthood Federation and is dedicated to improving the quality and accessibility of comprehensive reproductive health services and information.

Centre de recherche d'étude, de documentation, et d'information sur la femme (CREDIF)
5 Rue Fatma
Ennachi
El Menzah J
Tunis, Tunisia
Web site: www.ministeres.tn/html/ministeres/tutelle/femme.html. Founded in 1990 under the auspices of the Ministry of Women and Family Affairs, CREDIF serves as a clearinghouse for information on women and gender and is dedicated to promoting research on the status of women in Tunisian society.

Union nationale de la femme tunisienne (UNFT)
56 Boulevard Bab Bnet
Tunis, Tunisia
Phone: 216-1-560-178/216-1-560-181
Web site: www.unft.org.tn. As the oldest and largest women's organization in Tunisia, the UNFT is dedicated to providing economic, social, and cultural support for women throughout the country through direct service provision and to improving the status of women through the promotion of economic and legal reforms.

SELECTED BIBLIOGRAPHY

Batya, E., S. Hajri, N. Nhu Ngoc, C. Ellertson, C. Ben Slama, E. Pearlman, and B. Winikoff. "Can Women in Less-Developed Countries Use a Simplified Medical Abortion Regimen?" *Lancet* 357(9266) (2001): 1402–5.
Brand, L. *Women, the State, and Political Liberalization: Middle Eastern and North African Experiences*. New York: Columbia University Press, 1998.
Curtiss, R. "Women's Rights: An Affair of State for Tunisia." In *Arab Women: Between Defiance and Restraint*, ed. S. Sabbagh, 33–37. New York: Olive Branch Press, 1996.
Daly, A. "Tunisia: The Liberation of Women and the Improvement of Society." In

Family Planning Programs: An International Survey, ed. B. Berelson, 102–13. New York: Basic Books, 1969.

Eschen, A., and M. Whittaker. "Family Planning: A Base to Build on for Women's Reproductive Health Services." In *The Health of Women: A Global Perspective*, ed. M. Kablinsky, J. Timyan, and J. Gay, 105–31. Boulder, CO: Westview Press, 1993.

Foster, A. "Young Women's Sexuality in Tunisia: The Health Consequences of Misinformation among University Students." In *Everyday Life in the Muslim Middle East*, ed. D. Bowen and E. Early, 2nd ed., 98–110. Bloomington: Indiana University Press, 2002.

Galal, S. "Women and Development in the Maghreb." In *Gender and Development in the Arab World*, ed. N. Khoury and V. Moghadam, 49–70. London: Zed Books, 1995.

Kandiyoti, D. "Islam and Patriarchy." In *Women in Middle Eastern History: Shifting Boundaries in Sex and Gender*, ed. N. Keddie and B. Baron, 23–42. New Haven, CT: Yale University Press, 1991.

Khoury, N., and V. Moghadam, eds. *Gender and Development in the Arab World*. London: Zed Books, 1995.

Mayer, A. "Reform of Personal Status Laws in North Africa: A Problem of Islamic or Mediterranean Laws?" *Middle East Journal* 49(3) (summer 1995): 432–46.

Mokhtar, N., J. Elati, R. Chabir, A. Bour, K. Elkari, N.P. Schlossman, B. Caballero, and H. Aguenaou. "Diet Culture and Obesity in Northern Africa." *Journal of Nutrition* 131(3) (2001): 887S–892S.

United Nations Statistics Division. *The World's Women 2000: Trends and Statistics*. New York: UN Publications, 2001.

World Bank. *World Development Report 2000/2001*. Washington, DC: World Bank, 2001.

French Bibliography

Abderrahim, S. *La condition de la femme en Tunisie et sa santé reproductive et sexuelle*. Tunis: ATPF, 1996.

Ben Abid, J., A. Belhadj, and S. Douki. "Femme et santé mentale." In *Santé de la femme et de la famille*, ed. ONFP, 113–19. Tunis: ONFP, 1993.

Douki, S., M. Taktak, and S. Ben Zineb. "Femmes et santé mentale." Paper presented at the Seminaire sur femme, Santé Mentale, et Société, Tunis, March 28, 1998.

Fekih, Z. "La situation épidémiologique du SIDA dans les pays du Maghreb." In *Santé de la femme et de la famille*, ed. ONFP, 31–34. Tunis: ONFP, 1993.

Gueddana, N., et al. *Les jeunes au quotidien: Environnement socio-culturel et comportements de santé*. Tunis: ONFP, 1996.

Hsairi, M., R. Fakhfakh, M. Ben Abdallah, R. Jlidi, A. Sellami, S. Zheni, S. Hmissa, N. Achour, and T. Nacef. "Estimation à l'échelle nationale de l'incidence des cancers en Tunisie, 1993–1997." *Tunisie médicale* 80(2) (2002): 57–64.

Labidi, L. *Çabra Hachma: Sexualité et tradition*. Tunis: Dar Annawras, 1989.

Masmoudi, M. "Connaissances, croyances, et attitudes des jeunes lycéens à propos du SIDA." Thèse pour le diplôme d'état de doctorat en médecine, Faculté de médecine "Ibn El Jazzar" Sousse, 1996.

Ministère de la santé publique. *La mortalité maternelle en Tunisie*. Tunis: Ministère de la santé publique, 1994.

Ministère des affaires de la femme et de la famille. *Rapport national sur la femme*. Tunis: Ministère des affaires de la femme et de la famille, 1995.

Njah, M., R. Hergli, J. Gloulou, S. Bent Ahmed, and M. Marzouki. "Connaissances, attitudes, et comportements des femmes tunisiennes à propos des cancers gynécologiques." *Sozial- und Präventivmedizin* 39(5) (1994): 280–86.

ONFP. *Impact du programme national de planning familial*. Tunis: ONFP, 1997.

———. *La santé de la mère et de l'enfant*. Tunis: Ministère de la santé publique, 1996.

———. *La santé de la reproduction et le planning familial en chiffres*. Tunis: ONFP, 1998.

ONFP, ed. *Santé de la femme et de la famille*. Tunis: ONFP, 1993.

République Tunisienne. *Rapport de la Tunisie sur l'application de la Convention Internationale sur les Droits de l'Enfant*. Tunis: Groupe Ikone, 1995.

Rossignol, G. "Les médecins en Tunisie." *Servir: Revue tunisienne du service public* 5 (1969): 32–45.

15
UNITED ARAB EMIRATES

Carolyn I. Wright

PROFILE OF THE UNITED ARAB EMIRATES

The United Arab Emirates is located on the Arabian Gulf between Qatar, Oman, and Saudi Arabia, forming the "big toe" of the Arabian peninsula beside the Strait of Hormuz. Before the 1970s, native Emirates based their economy on pearl diving, agriculture, boat building, and fishing. Many were nomads, known as Bedouins. They wandered with their camels and small animals in constant search of pasture and water. Many of the Emirate women of today are daughters and granddaughters of those Bedouins, and their grandparents who never recorded their ages.[1]

The UAE celebrated its thirtieth anniversary as a federal system of government on December 2, 2001. The United Kingdom, originally in treaty relations with what had formerly been the Trucial States, encouraged the development of a new government as it withdrew from the Persian Gulf. The leaders of the seven original sheikdoms or emirates formed aSupreme Council that is the top policy-making body of the new UAE. The Supreme Council elected a president in 1971, Sheikh Zayed bin Sultan Al Nahyan, who continues as president into the new millennium.[2]

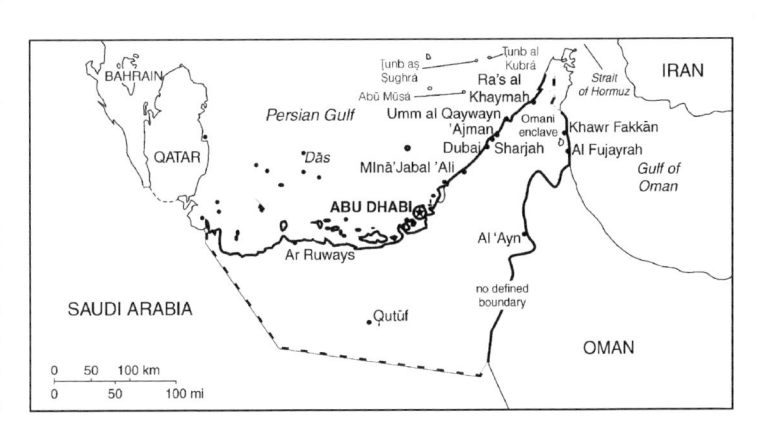

The United Arab Emirates (UAE) has a population of approximately three million people with an anticipated growth of only 2.9 percent within the next quarter of a century. Only 20 percent of the population (approximately 600,000 people) is native-born Emirates.[3] Cultural traditions are based upon an Islamic and Arabian heritage. Although 96 percent of the UAE's population is Muslim and its official language is Arabic, the UAE tolerates other religions, and English is commonly spoken and is taught in all public and private schools.[4] The UAE does not embrace new inhabitants. One does not become an Emirate by choice or design; one is born an Emirate or is not an Emirate.

There is a distinct difference between those who are considered expatriates and those who are considered nationals. Only nationals may own property, receive free housing, or obtain treatment at specific government-sponsored hospitals staffed currently by Canadian doctors. While the UAE is generous to refugees and displaced persons, they can never become nationalized citizens.

It now is easy for urban dwellers in the UAE to forget that they are in a desert. Large desalination plants were built to irrigate with seawater. The UAE irrigates for vegetation and has an abundance of coconut, date, and palm trees, dairy, tree, and vegetable farms, and grassy parks with multiple large fountains.[5] Thirty million date palms are cultivated in the UAE. The Abu Dhabi municipality alone produces 1.5 million sapling trees, 20 million flowers, and 30,000 plants a year. Most buildings are less than twenty years old and are air conditioned. Cities are modern and cosmopolitan. Six-lane highways span the country. A major industrial sector, a media center, and Internet City have emerged. The Burj Al Arab seven-star hotel was recently voted the best in the world. The UAE is a member of the Wildlife Federation and has won awards for preservation of its sea turtles. It works in conjunction with American institutions, such as Cornell University, to bring new ideas and agricultural technology to the country. It has a broad social welfare system, and its natives have one of the highest per capita incomes in the world.

The production of oil, which was reorganized in 1973, has its main long-term market in Japan and South Korea.[6] The profit from the sale of oil and the leadership of President Zayed are responsible for facilitating the development of the UAE's infrastructure and its people. President Zayed's vision was to create a healthy, educated society. It was done in thirty years.

As of 2001, the population of the United Arab Emirates was 2,445,989. The birth rate was estimated at 18.3 births per 1,000 and 3.9 deaths per 1,000. There are approximately 3.16 children born per woman. The infant mortality rate is 16.1 deaths per 1,000 live births. Life expectancy is 77.1 years for women and 72 years for men.[7]

OVERVIEW OF WOMEN'S ISSUES

The rise of the Islamic women's movement in the UAE does not exclude a focus on Islamic texts and teachings, interpreted by men, to argue for the enhancement of the rights of women. But UAE women are not silent and inactive.

The UAE is a contradictory society. It loves its daughters and, like an overprotective father, restricts them. The diversity of female college students is a prime example of what the UAE says that it wants for its young women. However, Emirate women are limited by the decisions of men, who are by tradition and belief the leaders of their world. By today's Western standards, Emirate women are submissive and without full authority.

The UAE government has surpassed Western governments in the quickness of passing laws that acknowledge the rights of women. The UAE is clear that all women should be educated and that women should take their place in the workforce. The UAE Constitution guarantees that women enjoy the same legal status, claim to titles, access to education, and right to practice professions as men, regardless of their marital status.[8] With their hair tied back in *shelas*, they jump from airplanes and shoulder assault rifles. They ride jet skis in abayas, and they jog along the Arabian Corniche in running shoes with veils on. Still, women are limited in their choices. As one student said, "Why do we need to learn critical thinking in college? We will never use it at home."[9]

EDUCATION

Opportunities and Literacy

Female students are in the majority at all educational levels in the country. Education for women has been a priority in the UAE since its inception. In 1973, the Abu Dhabi Society for the Awakening of Women was founded by Sheikha Fatima bint Mubarak to eradicate illiteracy and train women in the trades.

Free education, including books, is provided for all citizens from preschool through the fourteen government-sponsored colleges. English is taught throughout the educational process and is considered both the language of business and the second language of the country.

The government-sponsored colleges include the Gulf Medical College in Ajman, which admits both men and women. Women in the UAE attend gender-segregated schools of higher learning. This means that while schools may have both male and female teachers, male and female students do not share the same classrooms. In the 2000–2001 academic year, more than 95 percent of female students entered higher education in the UAE.[10]

Female students are comfortable working in all female groups. They sit and talk in places specifically set apart for them. Nothing about school is private from their fellow classmates. These are not artificially created consciousness-raising groups, but natural groups developed over centuries of watching older women share and work together. While Western students often express difficulty about working in teams, the women of the UAE often express difficulty about working independently.

In spite of this seemingly enlightened attitude toward women and education, there are obstacles for women. The male head of their family, who is often a father or husband, must give permission for college women to go on field trips or even stay after class to work on projects. While males may go to college outside the country, females do not study abroad unless they are accompanied by their husbands, brothers, or fathers. Although this is beginning to change, today women are seldom allowed to travel to another country alone to get an advanced degree. Even within the UAE, women seldom obtain an advanced degree. In 1996, of the 143 graduates of Dubai's Women's College, only eight pursued higher studies. In spite of this figure, women were the first to graduate from Emirates University with a master's degree in environmental sciences.[11]

Women must negotiate with their fathers what major to choose. Often fathers do not want daughters choosing a career that results in their working alongside males after graduation. Many students are eager to study to become teachers of special education, although there are not yet programs for them to study in.

Colleges and universities have rules that give mixed messages. Many female students are married and often are mothers. Students are allowed to attend school while pregnant. Women are encouraged to nurture the next generation as well as complete their education in order to enter the workforce. Yet women students who give birth are allowed only twenty days (including weekends) to be with their newborns. At Zayed University, after twelve missed classes, they are given a "withdrawn-failed" from class. Infants are not allowed on campus at all. Some new mothers reported being called by the university while still in the maternity ward, asking when they would return to school. Domestic servants, usually from such countries as Sri Lanka and the Philippines, become caretakers of the infants.

Many students choose to breast-feed infants while attending school full-time. There are no medical offices or child-care or breast-feeding rooms on college campuses, in malls, or in other public places.

Each student is required to purchase a laptop computer. The university system is more technologically advanced than many U.S. universities. The Internet is used by each student in and outside of class.

In 1975, 70 percent of the UAE's female population was illiterate. In 1998, 33 percent was illiterate. The figure today is about 7 percent among all people aged fifteen to forty-five.[12] Continuing education and literacy classes are available to women at no cost at public schools. Illiteracy has also been a target of the Women's Federation. More than seventy-four free adult education centers have been created throughout the country for women.

EMPLOYMENT AND ECONOMICS

Job/Career Opportunities

Historically, women of the UAE have always worked. Before the 1970s, women in the mountains and oases of the UAE played an important role in agriculture. In the coastal areas, women brought up children, cared for the old and ill, and looked after farms and livestock while their husbands served as fishermen and pearl divers.[13]

President Zayed has been quoted as saying, "Nothing could delight me more than to see Women taking up her distinctive position in society.... Nothing should hinder her progress.... Like men, women deserve the right to occupy high positions according to their capabilities and qualifications."[14] In spite of the obvious advances of UAE women, they are given mixed messages about education, career choices, and opportunities. First, women are encouraged to obtain higher education in order to take leadership roles in government. However, leadership roles often mean research and support positions, mostly in government bureaucracies.[15] College-educated women often apply for or are offered the job of an administrative assistant.

Despite major advances toward the emancipation of women in the UAE, obstacles persist. A major concern is the lack of employment for women in spite of their advanced degrees. Low employment may be due to several factors, such as employment being a choice rather than a necessity, lack of employment opportunities, a narrow focus on where women work, and training in areas that are not in demand. In addition, childbearing and a lack of child-care centers, along with the traditions and customs that say that mothers are the best caregivers, discourage attempts at working outside the home. Solutions include a movement toward Emiratization, or the movement to hire nationals first. Retraining, maternity-leave regulations, family-friendly work hours, and support for developing home businesses are in process.

In spite of the perceived lack of employment opportunities for women, some women have made a powerful difference in the lives of UAE female citizens. The General Women's Union, an autonomous organization with its own budget, includes a Heritage work group. It was founded by Sheikha

Women in Dubai go over paperwork at a bank. Photo © TRIP/H. Rodgers.

Fatima bint Mubarak, wife of the president, in 1975. The Heritage group was developed to support low-income or widowed Emirate women by providing workspace for them to make traditional crafts. They produce wares and sell them at a retail shop on-site, thereby earning an income. Emirate women work in research, banks, education, communications, and medicine. They are businesswomen, police officers and soldiers, physicians, computer operators, tellers, teachers, professors, and security guards.

Support for Mothers/Caretakers

Maternal Leave

Under Islamic law (shari'a) and under the UAE civil law, women are entitled to forty-five days of paid maternity leave and maybe considered for up to ninety days of leave. Another proposal would allow for a two-year reduced-salary leave to enable mothers to nurse infant children. If a woman is a widower, she is given a paid four-month and ten-day leave upon request.

Inheritance and Property Rights

Religion and religious teachings and interpretations guide economics, as they do every major area of UAE life. UAE women may independently own property and sponsor expatriates willing to build businesses in the UAE. They are entitled to and may manage their own money, including their dowries, which are forever theirs, and inheritances. No man may claim it. They manage their households and real estate and buy, sell, mortgage, or lease any or all of their properties regardless of whether they are single or married and whether the properties were obtained before marriage or after. They bargain vigorously in the open-air markets (*souqs*). However, most of their decisions are guided by the men in their families.

The amount of one's inheritance is usually divided according to sex. The woman's share is half of the man's share. This division is justified on the grounds that the male is primarily responsible for the maintenance of his wife or wives, all of his children, and in some cases dependent female family members. His responsibility remains the same regardless of his wife's wealth. Women have no obligation to spend money on their family. Women are entitled to alimony in the case of divorce. Men, however, are seen as the rational thinkers and decision makers of Emirate families and are asked their opinion on all family matters, including economics.

Social/Government Programs

Welfare

The Ministry of Labor and its Social Affairs office, headed by the country's top female civil servant, and the General Women's Union, headed by the wife of the president, Sheikha Fatima bint Mubarak, are the two official bodies that specifically address women's issues in the UAE. The Social Security Law of 1977 includes unmarried women, divorced and separated women, and women married to foreigners in its list of those entitled to financial aid. More UAE women than men receive assistance.

The UAE government has a housing program for citizens. The federal Ministry of Public Works and Housing has built 7,839 low-cost homes for distribution to UAE citizens as well as 920 residential units. All citizens are entitled to free or heavily subsidized housing. In 1999, approximately 175 million dollars were appropriated to provide loans for citizens with a monthly income of less than 2,700 dollars. Citizens were provided up 500,000 dirhams interest free to be paid back over a twenty-five-year period. The Residential Loans Corporation of Abu Dhabi was established in 1991 with a fund of 4.4 billion dirhams to enable citizens to build their own homes. Loan programs have been established in each emirate.[16]

FAMILY AND SEXUALITY

Gender Roles

Islam regards a woman's role in society as a mother and a wife as the most sacred. It has been written that "neither maids nor babysitters can possibly take the mother's place as the educator of an upright, complex-free, and carefully reared children. Such a noble and vital role which largely shapes the future of nations, cannot be regarded as 'idleness.'"[17] This does not mean that women should not work. There is no Islamic decree forbidding employment for women if the work fits her nature and the society needs her work. Questions may arise as to what fits a woman's nature and who has the power to say.

Unlike Saudi Arabian women, the women of the UAE are allowed to both drive and own cars. However, they may do so only with the signed permission of their fathers, husbands, or the male head of their family, who may even be a younger brother. However, until 2001, UAE female police officers could not pull over traffic violators if they were male. The law has been changed to make it possible for female police officers to have authority over male drivers. Female security guards must wear scarves that cover the head (*shelas*).

The question of a woman's covering (*hijab*) is controversial in the West.[18] It is often taken as a sign of women's submission. However, in the UAE, there is no law mandating *hijab*, and some women do not wear *hijab* at all. In many cases, the *abaya* (a long, black, wrinkle-free overgarment) is a status symbol among adolescents. Young students wear *abayas* and, like the youth of America, want a favorite store or brand name embroidered in a bright-color thread near the hem of their garments. The brand name is seen as a status symbol. Wearing the *abaya* itself is a status symbol because it identifies the wearer as a citizen. *Shelas* are often removed during class and are put back on only before reentering the hallway or if a male enters the classroom.

Marriage

Marriage is the goal of all women citizens, but if they are presumed to be sexually impure, even by rumor, they will not be chosen as wives. Emirate women are not to be tainted by the look or touch of men, even if they are experiencing a medical crisis. For example, there should be no Heimlich maneuvers, no lifting of fainting women, and no putting an arm on a student's shoulders for comfort or in friendship. To do so would ostracize the student and damage her reputation. It would make her unmarriageable, and in the UAE, an unmarriageable woman is a spinster who must live with her parents or siblings or who may become a second or third or fourth wife.

Parents arrange marriages. It has been common for women to marry a first cousin, thus keeping the bloodline pure or within the family. A partner is discussed by the parents and then usually, although not always, introduced to the daughter. Theoretically, young women have the right to reject a marriage partner. If they accept the decision of their parents, and most do, a contract is negotiated with the future husband and his family. This contract can include such items as permission for the young woman to continue her education, to work, or to visit her parents as she desires. The contract may be looked upon as a premarital agreement by Western eyes, but it is the marriage. Not until the contract is signed can the couple "date." A woman does not take the names of her husband after marriage but retains the name of her father. A name such as Noora bint Salem means Noora, daughter of Salem. The children of the new union also take the names of their father.

The average age of marriage for women has increased with the modernization of the country. A study by the Ministry of Health revealed that currently it is between age twenty-five and twenty-nine for women, with a positive correlation between education and the age of marriage. Women who are illiterate marry between the ages of fifteen and nineteen. Women living in rural areas marry younger as well, at an average age between twenty and twenty-four years. "It has also been noted that decisions of educated women about when and who to marry are less influenced by the traditional forces that have favoured early marriage and marriage to a relative."[19]

The marriage ceremony, which appears rather like a Western wedding reception, is a women's party. No men attend with the exception of perhaps the groom late in the evening or early in the morning. He may or may not come in to walk down the runway and be looked over by the guests. He then takes the bride to the marriage room, where the marriage is consummated. It is not unusual for 500 or more guests to attend the wedding. Increasing the number of guests increases the prestige of the family. Lavish weddings have been discouraged by the government but still exist. The number of camels killed to serve the guests has been limited by the government to four regardless of the number of people attending. Lamb and sometimes goat are also served. Music, dancing women, and sometimes transvestites are used to entertain the female guests. The males have their own wedding party that only men attend.

The Marriage Fund was established in 1993 "to assist the UAE's youth to marry and start a family with the least possible financial burden."[20] This was a direct attempt to keep citizen men from marrying foreign wives for whom large dowries and lavish wedding ceremonies would not be necessary. The increasing interest in foreign wives was leaving Emirate women single and destabilizing UAE society. The Marriage Fund gives up to 70,000 dirhams, by request, to young UAE men wishing to marry UAE women, and an additional 20,000 dirhams if they are over age thirty. What was seen as an answer for unmarried UAE women has a downside; some men request the money and never marry.

Mass weddings are also encouraged, and special marriage halls have been built to provide inexpensive space for weddings. Legal sanctions have also been established limiting the amount of money one can spend on a wedding without paying a large fine or enduring a prison sentence. Individuals of high social class seem to be exempt from these rulings.

The groom or his family pays for the marriage ceremony and also gives his wife a dowry. She is entitled to keep this money as her own to do with as she likes, even in the case of a later divorce. Potential grooms who do not have the money to pay for the marriage and dowry may use the Marriage Fund.

Polygamy is legal in the UAE, but young women do not choose to be second wives unless they have no alternative. They have the legal right to say no to husbands who wish to take a second wife but seldom have the power to keep this from happening. Illness of a first wife and barrenness are legitimate reasons for husbands to take another wife. According to the Qur'an and the prophet Muhammad, only four wives are allowed, and each wife must be treated equally. If a husband cannot do this, then he must not take additional wives.[21] In reality, wives do not believe that they are treated equally, and husbands sometimes take more than four wives.

A woman has a legal right to end her marriage. Because women are seen as more emotional than men, they are encouraged to take their concerns about their marriage before a judge. Men have merely to notify their wives that they want a divorce, either directly or by inference. There has been some controversy about the divorce rate in the UAE, and the actual divorce rate is unknown. Newspapers reported a figure of 2 per 1,000 in 1995.[22] However, the Marriage Fund does give grants to divorcées. The government has acknowledged that families have been negatively impacted by economic developments that created nuclear families, replacing extended families. According to shari'a law, children over age eight became the property of husbands upon divorce. However, the Dubai courts have developed a mutual consent agreement to help resolve child-custody issues. In 2001, the Dubai courts handled more than 2,000 family disputes in the first nine months, many of which were over a lack of family support or adultery.[23]

Reproduction

Women are encouraged to marry early and to have large families (the current average is twelve children) to increase the population of citizens, even as they are encouraged to complete their college education. Both male and female children are eagerly welcomed into the family. UAE women are quick to say that both male and female children are treated equally, up to a point. They loudly complain that young males are allowed to do much more than young females even though they also carry the burden of family responsibility much earlier. While some defend this position as appropriate preparation for males who will become leaders of their families, others claim that it is not appropriate or desirable. Adoption in the UAE is not an issue because it would not keep the bloodline pure.

Sex Education

School textbooks are censored for sexual content, which may include pictures of married couples holding hands, and no chapters on cohabitation or homosexuality are allowed. Women gather together in informal same-sex meetings and may discuss marriage and its rituals.

Contraception and Abortion

The Qur'an forbids female infanticide. Both girl and boy babies are eagerly welcomed into the family. Contraception is available but not freely discussed. Some females are afraid that if they use contraception, they will become barren. Many married women no longer see their families on a regular basis. They live with their husband's family and may not feel comfortable discussing birth control with their mothers-in-law. It is known that as the education of women increases, the birth rate decreases. This may be because women are waiting longer to get married, or because they are waiting longer to have children, or both. No information is currently available regarding abortion in the UAE.

HEALTH

Health Care Access

At the present time, the UAE government funds 81 percent of health-care services in the UAE. Pharmaceuticals are subsidized by the government, and this lowers the cost of both over-the-counter and prescription medications.[24] As of February 2002, doctor prescriptions were not needed to obtain medications at the licensed pharmacies.[25]

The Ministry of Health now manages 30 hospitals, 115 primary healthcare centers, and 9 preventative medicine centers. The numbers of hospitals and primary care facilities continue to increase.[26] Sheikha Fatima was instrumental in starting the first obstetrical hospital in Abu Dhabi. However, some hospitals, staffed by Western physicians and nurses, are available only to citizens, who are only 20 percent of the total UAE population.

In the past, children born with birth defects were hidden away by their families. Birth defects, seen as genetic, would discourage marriage between their daughters (seen as the cause of the defects) and men from desirable families. This has changed, and special schools for children with birth defects, such as Down syndrome, have been created. Three centers for rehabilitating children were opened in the UAE in 2001. On occasion, parents will be seen with special-needs children shopping in supermarkets and malls.

Physically and mentally disabled adults are cared for in the Zayed Centre for the Rehabilitation of the Handicapped, which opened in 1995 as an experimental center housing only twenty people with the support of the UN Development Program in conjunction with the Abu Dhabi government.[27] A center for fitting artificial limbs and an elderly center were created with support of the UAE Women's Federation, "an active lobbyist for full legal safeguards for the right of the disabled to work."[28]

Diseases and Disorders

Chronic illnesses include diabetes and heart disease for both men and women. The UAE is paying special attention to health promotions and screenings for these illnesses.

AIDS

AIDS has been recognized as a problem for the UAE and its citizens for several years. In spite of the lack of reporting on sexual issues and concerns, HIV/AIDS has been discussed in the media and in government documents and protocols. A program to prevent the spread of AIDS was established by the Department of Health and Medical Services in 1984. All entering expatriates on work visas are required to have an HIV/AIDS test. In 2001, public health education included information on HIV/AIDS. Beginning in November 2002, this public health program included an awareness campaign for prison inmates using lectures in various languages given by physicians.[29] While there are no statistics available on HIV/AIDS in the UAE, the deportation of those who are discovered to have the disease is not uncommon.

The increased use of illegal drugs by youth is being reported more frequently in UAE newspapers. Nationals are encouraged to raise their children with traditional religious values and to make use of family counselors as a deterrent to social misbehaviors.[30] There have been frequent reports of stiff penalties for the sale, use, or possession of drugs by expatriates. None of the reports mention citizens by name.

Cancer

Studies by the UAE government found that 71 out of every 100,000 women are cancer patients, which is less than in the United States. Three specialized centers for cancer treatment have been created.

POLITICS AND LAW

UAE citizens are covered under both civil and shari'a law. Civil law includes civil service law, labor law, and criminal law and covers non-family-related issues. Shari'a law is family law or what is equivalent to the family court system. The UAE Constitution provides that under the civil law, women are equal to men.

Suffrage

The UAE is not a democracy, and therefore its citizens do not vote.

Political Participation

Women are not given the opportunity to run for office and are not elected to government offices. While the Qur'an does not forbid women becoming judges, there are no female judges. It is believed that women are not appointed judges because they think with their hearts and not their heads. Women's "emotional nature" increases doubt about their fitness for the post.[31] Men make the best decision makers. This, however, is not to be seen as the fault of Islam. Both in the Qur'an and in history, women have participated in serious political discussions, even with the prophet Muhammad himself. In spite of this, interpretations have made women ineligible for the position of head of state due to perceived differences in the biological and psychological makeup of men and women. According to Islam, the head of state leads people in prayers and is responsible for the well-being of his people.

> This demanding position, or any similar one, such as the Commander of the Army, is generally inconsistent with the physiological and psychological make-up of women in general. It is a medical fact that during their monthly periods and during pregnancies, women undergo various

physiological and psychological changes. Such changes may occur during an emergency situation, thus effecting her decision, without considering the excessive strain which is produced. Moreover, some decisions require a maximum of rationality and a minimum of emotionality—a requirement which does not coincide with the instinctive nature of women. . . . It is more logical to explain the present situation in terms of the natural and indisputable differences between man and woman, a difference which does not imply any "supremacy" of one over the other. The difference implies rather the "complementary" roles of both the sexes in life.[32]

In spite of what are seen as the biological and psychological differences between men and women, five women were appointed to the Sharjah Consultative Council in 2001, a first and important movement toward allowing women to participate in the country's governmental system.

Women's Rights

Women are governmentally influential in both direct and indirect ways. Sheikha Fatima bint Mubaraks created the Women's Federation in 1973 for the purpose of developing opportunities for women. These opportunities include fostering education and eliminating illiteracy, developing women's self-image and self-esteem, encouraging the organizing of women to play an increasingly active role in social development, and influencing social policy.[33] The federation now consists of six women's groups with thirty-one branches in all parts of the UAE. Some groups publish magazines, while others compete in international chess championships. Some groups conduct research on women. The federation, which has its own charter, is supported by the UAE government. It has the right to represent the women of the UAE in discussions with all government departments, institutions, and ministries obtain needed research statistics from these departments and suggest possible solutions, and propose new laws.[34] Women's lack of education was one concern. The Marriage Fund was a suggested solution to expensive weddings. The federation's research center on women's issues has focused on health concerns, maternity and child care, and cultural and social issues.

In an unprecedented move children of UAE citizen women who were previously married to expatriates were granted citizenship in January 2002. While this presidential decree covered only widows and those separated and divorced from expatriates, there is hope that it will be expanded to all children born of citizen women married to noncitizen husbands.[35]

Feminist Movements

The women of the UAE have attended every international conference for women since their inception in New Mexico in 1975. UAE women believe that Islam offers them a guarantee of rights that can be a model for the world. The UAE was elected to a four-year membership on the Women's Committee of the fifty-four-member UN Economic and Social Council beginning in 2002. It expressed its full support of the Arab Women Organization and established a national database on UAE women, one of its kind in the Arab world.[36]

Military Service

Women in the armed forces were not originally trained by UAE male soldiers. Instead, U.S. armed services women trained UAE women in the armed services. This eliminated problems due to gender segregation that prevented men from physically coming into contact with women.[37]

Still, in 1992, fifty-nine UAE women soldiers graduated from the Khawla bint al Azwar military training college after completing the six-month practical and theoretical military training. After having completed the course conducted by the Dubai Police College, twenty women were asked to join the VIP Protection Corps, a crack team of bodyguards.[38]

RELIGION AND SPIRITUALITY

UAE citizens are both Sunni and Shi'ite Muslims, with the majority being Sunni. Their cultural values are reflective of their religious beliefs and are seen in the valuing of family, modesty for women, segregation of the genders, the belief that men are rational decision makers and the best family leaders, and the belief that parents know what is best for children.

Women's Roles

Religion is passed down through fathers, but the teaching of religion is the responsibility of mothers. Women cannot marry non-Muslims. Men can but their wives must convert to Islam. Older males are responsible for both the safety and behavior of women.

The history of Islam and its implications for women, as in most religions, are based on interpretation. Islamic history is rich in women of great achievements, Islamic law has given women clear-cut legal rights, and women's reputation, chastity, and maternal roles are and have been important to both of the above.

Rituals and Religious Practices

Mosques are everywhere in the UAE, and the call to prayer is heard several times a day. Prayer rooms are clearly labeled in the modern shopping malls, and it is common to see men, but not women, occupy them when the call to prayer is heard. It is usual to see hundreds of men kneeling toward Mecca, heads bowed in prayer, from the footbridge of the outdoor *souq*. Women have fewer religious obligations than men. Women do not have to pray every day and do not need to fast when menstruating, during pregnancy, while breast feeding, and for forty days after birthing.

Religion impacts dress. Muslim women of the UAE observe the covering of the head and the body (*hijab*) because they believe that Allah has told them to protect themselves from the unwanted advances of men.

Religious Law

The Qur'an holds that men and women are equal and that all followers must search for knowledge. According to Islamic law, women have the freedom to reject a marriage proposal. In marriage, the male is to be the leader, but both are responsible to one another. It has been noted that, "this refers to the sexes which entitles the weaker sex to protection. It implies no superiority or advantage before the law."[39]

VIOLENCE

Domestic Violence

Family advisors with the Dubai courts found that many complaints of abuse and assault were filed by husbands. There are no known laws to protect either men or women. Cases brought before the family advisors are mediated.[40]

Child abuse is another issue. Boys over age nine are often beaten for not praying. However, this is not considered abuse, but rather normal behavior. No other information on this topic in the UAE is available.

Rape/Sexual Assault

No information is available regarding rape or sexual assault of UAE citizen women. No incidents of a sexual nature, with the exception of adultery, are reported in the daily newspapers, and none concern citizen women. The sexual violation of any woman would, by custom, be seen as harmful to her reputation and end her availability for marriage. Women are seen as responsible for their sexuality and the sexuality of men. One reason for wearing the *hijab* is to prevent the wandering eye and sexual attention of males. One goal of the UAE is to work hard to maintain "the privacy of women in public places."[41]

Adultery is attended to by family law and historically has treated women more harshly than men. Jailing or stoning of the offending party has been reported as punishment,[42] but only a few cases regarding expatriate women and their punishment have been given notoriety. Because that notoriety offended foreign governments and affected business, reporting of such incidents has all but ended.⁴³ Therefore, when adultery, even by consenting adults, is discovered, punishments are now being distributed on a more equal basis.⁴⁴

OUTLOOK FOR THE TWENTY-FIRST CENTURY

With the oil money, society has moved in only thirty years from a culture subsisting in the desert by herding goats to one of cities, high-tech hospitals and schools, an infrastructure of superhighways, and air and sea networks. Young women live in a completely different world from that of their grandmothers, who might have given birth in a tent and lived as nomads.

UAE women have been involved in the international women's movement while still paying special attention to traditional cultural and religious differences. UAE women students believe that *patriarchal* means separate but equal: It affords them protection but does not step on their individual rights. Women's roles, which include homemaking and child care, are seen by college students as equal with men's roles of wage earner and decision maker. They think that men equally value all roles as they do.

Female students are aware of and angry about the difference in the treatment of male and female children but see it as a cultural phenomenon. They understand about androgyny but wonder about its impact on their culture and are confused about how society could or should be altered when they are not aware of any particular benefits from the altering.

Younger women have a privileged lifestyle now with villas and servants. The feminist movement is helping them come together to gain self-respect and respect, and self-empowerment and power. It is keeping women focused on the family at the same time it is helping them to focus on themselves. The goal is to take responsibility for their families for themselves, as well as take responsibility for themselves.

The women of the UAE want to make their country better because they love it. They are learning, as they move toward global education, to fearlessly acknowledge and clearly state how they want to see their country change. They are beginning to understand that critiquing and acting on that critique make their country stronger.

Their questions are similar to women's questions in the West. "Should I work after I have a child?" "How do we encourage fathers to participate more in child care?" "How do we prevent domestic accidents?" "How do we better care for our elderly?" "How do we provide public health information in the most effective manner?" "What do we do about domestic violence and child abuse?" "How do we best support families and reduce the incidence of divorce?" These are universal dilemmas.

NOTES

1. Conversations with female students at Zayed University, Abu Dhabi. Students were assigned genograms as a class assignment, but came back stating that they could

not fill their grandparents' ages on the genogram because their grandparents did not know when they were born. When they were asked their ages, they would just say "old."

2. Ministry of Information and Culture, *United Arab Emirates Yearbook, 2000–2001* (London: Trident Press, 2001), 73–82.

3. Ibid., 30.

4. Ibid.

5. Ministry of Information and Culture, *The United Arab Emirates Facts and Figures* (Abu Dhabi, UAE: Ministry of Information and Culture, n.d.), 17.

6. Ministry of Information and Culture, *United Arab Emirates Yearbook, 2002* (London: Trident Press, 2002), 17; G. Brooks, *Nine Parts of Desire: The Hidden World of Islamic Women* (New York: Doubleday, 1995). The UAE has the world's third-largest proven oil reserves (98.2 billion barrels in 1999, or 9.5 percent of the world's crude oil reserves), but the nonoil sector of the UAE's economy contributes more than twice as much as the oil sector to the gross domestic product. Ministry of Information and Culture, *The United Arab Emirates Facts and Figures*.

7. World Fact Book 2002, CIA, United Arab Emirates.

8. UAE Government, "Women and the UAE Constitution," n.d., www.arab.net/uae/govt/ue_womenconstitution.html.

9. Email communication, conversation with a female faculty member at Zayed University, Abu Dhabi, UAE, spring 2002.

10. Ministry of Information and Culture, *United Arab Emirates Yearbook, 2002*, 213.

11. Emirates Center for Strategic Studies and Research, "The Education of Women," 2001, www.ecssr.ac.ae.

12. Ministry of Information and Culture, *United Arab Emirates Yearbook, 2002*, 217.

13. Arab Net, UAE Culture, *The Role of Women*, n.d., www.arab.net/uae/culture.ue_womenrole.html.

14. Ibid.

15. Women represent 40 percent of all UAE employees. Women represent 100 percent of all nursery-school teachers, 55 percent of primary teachers, 65 percent of intermediate and secondary-school teachers, and 47 percent of all government employees, including 40 percent of senior positions. They represent 15 percent of all professors in higher education and 54.3 percent of hospital employees. "Government" includes teaching in public schools and working in hospitals. Ministry of Information and Culture, *United Arab Emirates Yearbook, 2002*; UAE Government, www.arab.net/uae/govt/ue_womenemploy.html.

16. Ministry of Information and Culture, *United Arab Emirates Yearbook, 2002*. U.S. dollars have a greater value than UAE dirhams. While the rate changes slightly according to the market and by institution, dividing the dirham by 3.678 gives the approximate value in dollar terms.

17. Ibid., 21–22.

18. Ibid. The word *hijab* comes from the Arabic word *hajaba*, meaning to hide from view or conceal. See also E. Fernea, *In Search of Islamic Feminism: One Woman's Global Journey* (New York: Doubleday, 1998), 421.

19. Ministry of Information and Culture, *United Arab Emirates Yearbook, 2002*, 229.

20. Ibid., 228.

21. M. Ali, "Who Practices Polygamy?" (Chicago: Institute of Islamic Information and Education, n.d.), www.usc.edu/dept/MSA/humanrelations/womeninislam/whatishijab.html. Retrived July 15, 2002.

22. D. Zeitoun, "High Cost of Living Ups Divorce Rate," *Gulf News*, May 5, 2000, 13.

23. E. Abdullah, "Dealing with Family Disputes," *Gulf News*, October 19, 2001, 5.

24. Ministry of Information and Culture, *United Arab Emirates Yearbook*, 2002, 235.
25. Personal experience.
26. Ministry of Information and Culture, *United Arab Emirates Yearbook*, 2002, 230–34.
27. Ibid.
28. UAE Government, "Women in the UAE," *Social Welfare*, n.d., http://www.arab.net/uae/govt/ue_womenwelfare.html. Retrieved July 16, 2002.
29. "Drive to Educate Inmates on Personal Hygiene," *Gulf News*, November 3, 2002, www.gulfnews.com.
30. T. Fleihan, "Parents Urged to Teach Children Moral Values," *Khaleej Times*, November 19, 2002, www.khaleejtimes.co.ae/uae.htm.
31. I. Badawi, *The Status of Woman in Islam* (Al Ain, UAE: Zayed Welfare Centre for New Muslims, 1980), 22.
32. Ibid.
33. Emirates Center for Strategic Studies and Research, "Women's Organizations," 2002, www.ecssr.ac.ae. Retrived July 15, 2002.
34. UAE Government, *The UAE Women's Federation*, n.d., www.arab.net/uae/govt/ue_womenfederation.html.
35. Emirates News Agency, "Ray of Hope for National Women Wedded to Expats," *Middle East News*, January 11, 2002, www.middleeastwire.com/uae/stories/20020199_meno.shtml.
36. Ministry of Information and Culture, *United Arab Emirates Yearbook*, 2002, 235.
37. Brooks, 1995.
38. Emirates Center for Strategic Studies and Research, *Employment of Women*, 2001, www.ecssr.ac.ae.
39. Badawi, 1980, 18.
40. Abdullah, 2001, 5.
41. Fleihan, 2002.
42. Stoning involves burying the living body up to the breast (in the case of a woman) or neck (in the case of a male) and hitting them with stones until they are decapitated.
43. Presentation by the German ambassador to Zayed University business students in lecture presentation, fall semester, 2001.
44. "Two Jailed for Adultery," *Gulf News*, June 24, 2002, www.gulfnews.com.

RESOURCE GUIDE

Suggested Reading

Brooks, G. *Nine Parts of Desire: The Hidden World of Islamic Women*. New York: Doubleday, 1995.

Fernea, E. *In Search of Islamic Feminism: One Woman's Global Journey*. New York: Doubleday, 1998. This book does not cover the UAE specifically but does give general information and a firsthand account of the author's experiences with feminist issues in the Middle East.

al-Suwaidi, J., ed. *Annual Report*. Abu Dhabi, UAE: Emirates Center for Strategic Studies and Research, 2001.

United Arab Emirates Ministry of Information and Culture. *United Arab Emirates Yearbook*. London: Trident Press, 2002.

Web Sites

Arab Net, www.arab.net/uae.
A collection of articles written by leading journalists and editors in the Middle East. It is owned in part by Saudi Research and Marketing.

Emirates Center for Strategic Studies and Research, www.ecssr.ac.ae.
(See Organizations.)

Gulf News, www.gulfnews.com.
Daily newspaper in English.

Institute of Islamic Information and Education, www.usc.edu/dept/MSA/human relations/.
Seeks to provide information about Muslims, especially in North America.

Khaleej Times, www.khaleejtimes.com.
Daily newspaper in English.

Middle East News, www.middleeastwire.com.
Emirates news agency.

Middle East Report, www.merip.org.
A nonprofit organization established thirty-one years ago, based in Washington, DC, with no links to government, religious, or political groups.

UAE Interact, http://uaeinteract.com/default.asp.
Official web site for the Ministry of Information and Culture, UAE.

Organizations

Association for Women's Development
Executive Director, Aisha Abdallah Eissa Al-Darbi
Ras al-Khaima, UAE
Phone: 971-7-362778 or 971-7-333778
Fax: 971-7-362033
This organization works on economic and social development, children and youth, and reproductive issues.

Emirates Center for Strategic Studies and Research
PO Box 4567
Abu Dhabi, UAE
Web site: www.ecssr.ac.ae
This independent organization, established in 1994, is a focal point for scholarship on issues of significance for the UAE. It conducts and sponsors empirical research and international conferences on such topics as economics, stability, oil, social issues, international law, globalization, and energy.

General Women's Union
PO Box 130

Abu Dhabi, UAE
Phone: 02 447-5333
Fax: 02 445-5202

Institute of Islamic Information and Education
PO Box 41129
Chicago, IL 60641
Phone: (773) 777-7443
Fax: (773) 777-7199
Web site: www.iiie.net
This nonprofit institution strives to provide accurate information about Islamic beliefs and history from proven sources.

UAE Federal Ministries

Ministry of Agriculture and Fisheries
The Minister: Saeed Mohammed Al Raqbani
Undersecretary: Hamad Abdullah Al Mutawa
Abu Dhabi POB: 213
Phone: 02 6662781
Fax: 02 6654787
Dubai POB: 1509
Phone: 04 2958161
Fax: 04 2957766
Email: maf@uae.gov.ae
Web site: www.uae.gov.ae/maf

Ministry of Communications
The Minister: Ahmed Humaid Al Tayer
Undersecretary: Abdullah Ahmed Lootah
Abu Dhabi POB: 900
Phone: 02 6651900
Fax: 02 6651691
Dubai POB: 1131
Phone: 04 2953330

Ministry of Defence
The Minister: Gen. Sheikh Mohammed bin Rashid Al Maktoum
Abu Dhabi POB: 46616
Phone: 02 4461300
Fax: 02 4463286
Dubai POB: 2838
Phone: 04 3532330
Fax: 04 3531974

Ministry of Economy and Commerce
The Minister: Sheikh Fahim bin Sultan Al Qasimi
Undersecretary: Abdul Raoof Al Mabarak
Abu Dhabi POB: 901

Phone: 02 6265000
Fax: 02 6215339
Dubai POB: 3625
Phone: 04 2954000
Fax: 04 2951991
Email: economy@emirates.net.ae
Web site: www.economy.gov.ae

Ministry of Education and Youth
The Minister: Dr. Abdul Aziz Sharhan
Undersecretary: Dr. Jamal Al-Mehairi
Abu Dhabi POB: 295
Phone: 02 6213800
Fax: 02 6313778
Dubai POB: 3962
Phone: 04 2994100
Fax: 04 2994535
Web site: www.education.gov.ae

Ministry of Electricity & Water
The Minister: Humaid bin Nasir Al Owais
Undersecretary: Saeed Majid Al Shamsi
Abu Dhabi POB: 629
Phone: 02 6274222
Fax: 02 6269738
Dubai POB: 1672
Phone: 04 2626262
Fax: 04 2690064

Ministry of Finance & Industry
The Minister: Sheikh Hamdan bin Rashid Al Maktoum
Minister of State: Dr. Mohammed Khalfan bin Kharbash
Undersecretary: H.H. Sheikh Ahmed bin Zayed Al Nahyan
Abu Dhabi POB: 433
Phone: 02 6726000
Fax: 02 6663088
Dubai POB: 1565
Phone: 04 3939000
Fax: 04 3939738
Email: mofi@uae.gov.ae
Web site: www.fedfin.gov.ae

Ministry for Foreign Affairs
The Minister: Rashid Abdullah Al Nuaimi
Abu Dhabi POB: 1
Phone: 02 6652200
Fax: 02 6668015
Dubai POB: 3785
Phone: 04 2221144
Fax: 04 2280979
Email: mofa@uae.gov.ae

Ministry of Health
The Minister: Hamad Abdul Rahman Al Madfa
Undersecretary: Dr. Sheikh Saud Al Qasimi
Abu Dhabi POB: 848
Phone: 02 6334716
Fax: 02 6726000
Dubai POB: 1853
Phone: 04 3966000
Fax: 04 3965666
Email: postmaster@moh.gov.ae
Web site: www.moh.gov.ae/intro

Ministry of Higher Education and Scientific Research
The Minister: Sheikh Nahyan bin Mubarak Al Nahyan
Undersecretary (acting): Saif Rashed Al Suwaidi
Abu Dhabi POB: 45253
Phone: 02 6428000
Fax: 02 6427262
Email: mohe@uae.gov.ae
Web site: www.uae.gov.ae/mohe

Ministry of Information & Culture
The Minister: Sheikh Abdullah bin Zayed Al Nahyan
Undersecretary: Saqr Ghobash
Abu Dhabi POB: 17
Phone: 02 4453000
Fax: 02 4452504
Dubai POB: 5053
Phone: 042615500
Fax: 04 2635807
Email: mininfex@emirates.net.ae
Web site: www.uaeinteract.com

Ministry of Interior
The Minister: Lt. Gen. Dr. Mohammed Saeed Al Badi
Undersecretary: Major General Sheikh Saif bin Zayed Al Nahyan
Abu Dhabi POB: 398
Phone: 02 4414666
Fax: 02 4414938
Dubai POB: 4333
Phone: 04 3980000
Fax: 04 3981119

Ministry of Justice, Islamic Affairs and Awqaf
The Minister: Mohammed Nukhaira Al Dhahiri
Undersecretary: Sultan Saeed Al Badi
Abu Dhabi POB: 260
Phone: 02 6814000
Fax: 02 6810680
Dubai POB: 1682
Phone: 04 2825999
Fax: 04 2825121

Ministry of Labour and Social Affairs
The Minister: Mattar Humaid Al Tayer
Undersecretary (Labour Affairs): Ahmed Atiq Al Jumairi
Undersecretary (Social Affairs): Mohammed Eisa Al Suwaidi
Abu Dhabi POB: 809
Phone: 02 6671700
Fax: 02 6665889
Dubai POB: 4409
Phone: 04 2691666
Fax: 04 2668967

Ministry of Petroleum & Mineral Resources
The Minister: Obeid bin Saif Al Nassiri
Undersecretary: Nasser Mohammed Al Sharhan
Abu Dhabi POB: 59
Phone: 02 667 1999
Fax: 02 6664573
Email: mopmr@uae.gov.ae

Ministry of Planning
The Minister: Sheikh Humaid bin Ahmed Al Mu'alla
Undersecretary: Ahmed Abdulla Mansoor
Abu Dhabi POB: 904
Phone: 02 6271100
Fax: 02 6269942
Dubai POB: 207
Phone: 04 3531060
Fax: 04 3536240
Email: mop@uae.gov.ae
Web site: www.uae.gov.ae/mop

Ministry of Public Works and Housing
The Minister: Rakad bin Salem Al Rakad
Undersecretary: Ali Hamad Al Shamsi
Abu Dhabi POB: 878
Phone: 02 6651778
Fax: 02 6665598
Dubai POB: 1828
Phone: 04 2693900
Fax: 04 2692931
Email: mpwh@uae.gov.ae

Ministry of State for Cabinet Affairs
The Minister: Saeed Khalfan Al Ghaith
Secretary General: Juma Butti Al Bawardi
Abu Dhabi POB: 899
Phone: 02 6811113
Fax: 02 6812968
Dubai POB: 5002
Phone: 04 3967555

Fax: 04 3978884
Email: moca@uae.gov.ae
Web site: www.uae.gov.ae/moca

Ministry of State for Financial & Industrial Affairs
The Minister: Dr. Mohammed Khalfan bin Kharbash
Dubai POB: 1565
Phone: 04 3939000
Fax: 04 3939738
Email: mofi@uae.gov.ae
Web site: www.uae.gov.ae/mofi/

Ministry of State for Foreign Affairs
The Minister: Sheikh Hamdan bin Zayed Al Nahyan
The Minister of State: H. H. Sheikh Hamdan bin Zayed Al Nahayan
Undersecretary: Saif Saeed bin Sa'ed
Abu Dhabi POB: 1
Phone: 02 444 4071
Fax: 02 4494994
Dubai POB: 3785
Phone: 04 222 1144
Fax: 04 2280979
Email: mofa@uae.gov.ae

Ministry of State for Supreme Council Affairs
The Minister: Sheikh Majed bin Saeed Al Nuaimi
Undersecretary: Yousuf Ahmed Abu Al Reesh
Abu Dhabi POB: 545
Phone: 02 6323900
Fax: 02 6344225

SELECTED BIBLIOGRAPHY

Abdullah, E. "Dealing with Family Disputes." *Gulf News*, October 19, 2001, 5.
Ali, M. "Who Practices Polygamy?" Chicago: Institute of Islamic Information and Education, n.d. www.usc.edu/dept/MSA/humanrelations/womeninislam/whatishijab.html.
Arab Net. UAE Culture. The Role of Women. N.d. http://www.arab.net/uae/culture.ue_womenrole.html.
Badawi, I. *The Status of Women in Islam*. Al Ain, UAE: Zayed Welfare Centre for the New Muslims, 1980.
Brooks, G. *Nine Parts of Desire: The Hidden World of Islamic Women*. New York: Doubleday, 1995.
"Drive to Educate Immates on Personal Hygiene." *Gulf News*, November 3, 2002. www.gulfnews.com.
Emirates Center for Strategic Studies and Research. "The Education of Women." 2002. www.ecssr.ac.ae.
———. "Employment of Women." 2002. www.ecssr.ac.ae.
———. "Women's Organizations." 2002. www.ecssr.ac.ae.
Emirates News Agency. "Ray of Hope for National Women Wedded to Expats."

Middle East News, January 11, 2002. http://www.middleeastwire.com/uae/stories/20020199 meno.shtml.

Fernea, E. *In Search of Islamic Feminism: One Woman's Global Journey*. New York: Doubleday, 1998.

Fleihan, T. "Parents Urged to Teach Children Moral Values." *Khaleej Times*, November 19, 2002. www.khaleejtimes.co.ae/uae.htm.

Fleischmann, E. "Women and Gender in Middle East Studies: A Roundtable Discussion." *Middle East Report*, October–December 1997. www.merip.org/mer/mer205/ellen.htm.

Hajjar, L. *Middle East Report*, summer 1998. www.merip.org/mer/mer207/lisa207.htm.

Ministry of Information and Culture. *The United Arab Emirates, Facts and Figures*. Abu Dhabi, UAE: Ministry of Information and Culture, n.d.

———. *United Arab Emirates Yearbook, 2000–2001*. London: Trident Press, 2001.

———. *United Arab Emirates Yearbook, 2002*. London: Trident Press, 2002.

Saliba, T. "Arab Feminism at the Millennium." *Signs* 25(4) (summer 2000): 1087–92.

Sharoni, S. "Women and Gender in Middle East Studies: Trends, Prospects, and Challenges." *Middle East Report*, October–December 1997. www.merip.org/mer/mer205/simona.htm.

"Two Jailed for Adultery." *Gulf News*, June 26, 2002. www.gulfnews.com.

UAE Government. *The UAE Women's Federation*. N.d. www.arab.net/uae/govt/ue_womenfederation.html.

———. Women in the UAE: Social Welfare. www.arab.net/uae/govt/ue_womenwelfare.html.

Zeitoun, D. "High Cost of Living Ups Divorce Rate." *Gulf News*, May 5, 2000, p. 13.

YEMEN

Susanne Dahlgren

PROFILE OF YEMEN

The Republic of Yemen lies in the southernmost tip of the Arabian peninsula. It has an inhabited area of 555,000 square kilometers excluding the Empty Quarter, the large desert area that reaches to Saudi Arabia. Yemen has borders with Saudi Arabia to the north and east and with Oman to the east. The southern part of the country has a thousand-kilometer-long sandy coast along the Indian Ocean, and in the west it has a coastline on the Red Sea. Yemen is a country with spectacular views ranging from steep mountains with terrace cultivation to beautiful green valleys with mud-brick houses. The oldest skyscrapers in the world (The "Chicago of the Desert") are said to lie in Yemen; seven- to ten-floor tall and narrow mud houses of the town Shibam are single-family households and date back as early as the fifteenth century. Yemen is often called the country of the Thousand and One Nights, with elements of culture that have barely changed through the centuries.

Present-day Yemen is a republic with a multiparty system and parliamentary democracy. It was formed in 1990 when the Yemen Arab Republic (YAR, North Yemen) and the People's Democratic Republic of Yemen (PDRY,

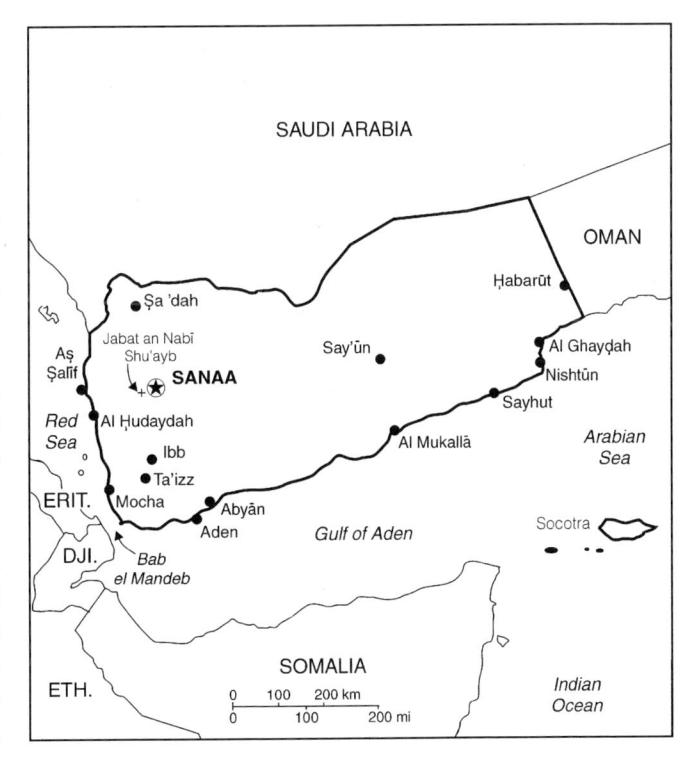

South Yemen) united to form the Republic of Yemen, which had not been under a common ruler since the sixteenth century. Women have full political rights, making Yemen and Bahrain the only countries in the peninsula that have granted women, among other things, the right to vote and run as candidates in all levels of elections. However, women's role in politics is nothing new in Yemen; this is the country of the Queen of Sheba, who reputedly ruled justly and made her country an outstanding power in the ancient world.

Yemen is a country of contradictions, with a population whose living conditions range from archaic poverty to modern lifestyles. Women's situation varies from countryside to town and from area to area; while some women live in harsh circumstances in mountainous areas without running water and electricity, in some towns women have taken an active role in politics and professions, acting as leaders, managerial directors, and even as judges.

The Yemeni people consist of an ancient South Arabian population and Arabs who immigrated after the ninth century. Contacts with Africa and the Indian Ocean were always close. These trading and other contacts have brought people from the African coast and from various parts of Asia who to a great extent have now mixed with the original population. The vast majority of Yemenis are Muslims. The country is roughly divided along a north-south axis into Shi'as of the Zaidi school in the north and Sunnis of Shafei doctrine in the south. A small Jewish population lives in northern areas of the country.

Today's Yemenis get their livelihood from agriculture, fishing, manufacturing, and a growing service sector. In recent years, oil production and refining have replaced agriculture as the major revenue-generating activity for the state. However, Yemeni oil reserves are modest in comparison to those of other peninsular countries and are doomed to decrease in the future. Per capita income was U.S. $360 in 1999 due to high population growth and slow gross national product (GNP) growth. This indicator rates Yemen as one of the poorest countries in the world.

Yemen has one of the highest rates of population growth in the world; the population is expected to rise from the present 18.7 million to 49.4 million by the year 2031.[1] About 48 percent of the population is below fifteen years of age, with a gender ratio of 105.1 males for every 100 females.[2] Health indicators locate Yemen among the least developed countries in the world. While considerable improvement has taken place since 1990, life expectancy at birth is only 59.8 years. Maternal mortality has decreased and is now at 351 per 100,000 live births. While fertility is high with 6.5 live births per woman, child mortality reaches 81 per 1,000 live births.[3] Health services vary around the country, and in particular, people in remote areas of the countryside suffer from poor care.

YEMEN

OVERVIEW OF WOMEN'S ISSUES

Yemen's ancient and medieval history reports two prominent female rulers, Queen Bilqis of the Sabaean Kingdom (probably around 1000 B.C.) and Queen Arwa, who ruled from 1091 to 1138. When present-day Yemenis talk about history, they always mention these two rulers, considered as predecessors of today's parliamentary democracy. These two names often come up when Yemenis discuss the role of women in politics; it is affirmed that Bilqis and Arwa have demonstrated how capable a leader a woman can be.

Women's road to present-day politics, however, has not been easy. While the country was still divided with imams (Islamic leaders) ruling the North and British colonialism in the South, women had very little access to what happened outside their homes. Women first gained voting rights in the early 1970s in both parts of the then-divided country. However, women's access to rights has always been curtailed by their social position and attitudes prevalent in their own families and has been influenced by the strong urban/rural divide. While reforms in the South improved the position of women of low social status remarkably at times, wealthy women in elitist families always have had less trouble promoting a political career or studying abroad. After the unification, only two women in both the 1993 and 1997 elections were elected to the national parliament, all four of them from the South. The first female full cabinet member was nominated in 2000.

In today's Yemen, several women's organizations, human rights groups, and other nongovernmental organizations (NGOs) promote women's rights, and some political parties have women in their leading bodies if not in the highest leadership. One of the topics discussed in civil society is violence against women and what it means in terms of customs and traditions, family life, and women's participation in the public sphere.

The major problems women face today vary according to the area in which they live, social class, and attitudes prevalent in their own families. While illiteracy among women in the countryside is still very high, in towns women struggle with the deteriorating economy that has impoverished even middle-class families. In such circumstances and provided the family has traditional role expectations, girls risk not finishing even primary education.

Yemeni women talk in Sanaa. AP/Wide World Photos.

[439]

Yemen has one of the largest gaps in the world between boys' and girls' school attendance rates.

In the countryside, every third family lives in absolute poverty, whereas in the towns the figure is every fourth.[4] Anemia, malnutrition, and consecutive pregnancies are the health hazards of poor women in particular, while ignorance of causes of health problems, long distances, and high out-of-pocket expenses prevent women from seeking help in public health clinics.

Women's right to equality, granted in the constitution, is severely curtailed by poor access to services and resources. The official interpretation of Islamic law (shari'a) as reflected in legislation limits women's rights further. The family legislation manifests a traditional reading of Islamic law with considerable differences in men's and women's duties and rights, to the benefit of the former. Perhaps the biggest impediment to women receiving benefits similar to those of men from all social resources has to do with the customs and traditions that degrade women and present them as mentally deficient persons and thus dependent on male guidance and control. While women experienced considerable progress in their access to education, work careers, health care, and equality in marriage during the PDRY era from 1967 to 1990, these rights have been seriously eroded since the Yemeni unification.

One particular problem that Yemeni women face has to do with the mild narcotic shrub *qat*, which most males consume, often on a daily basis in societal gatherings, thus draining the family budget. The number of women in the habit of chewing *qat* is considerably lower than that of men. Official statistics indicate that up to 50 percent of the family income may be allocated to daily *qat* needs of the household head alone. An average of 1,460 hours is wasted annually for the consumption of *qat* on a daily basis.[5]

EDUCATION

Opportunities

In the Law of Education (1992), girls and boys are granted equal rights to education. In practice, however, education is one of the fields in which government spending does not meet the needs of the growing population.[6] The country does not have enough classrooms to accommodate the rapidly growing school-age population. The difficulty of recruiting female teachers to the countryside contributes to girls' decreased ability to continue their studies after the primary level. As a result, girls' possibilities to go to school have been increasingly reduced. While some schools have introduced a two-shift system where boys attend classes in the mornings and girls in the afternoons, in some areas the authorities have advised parents to favor boys' school attendance when the number of seats in a classroom is limited. However, girls' percentage among primary-school students varies considerably according to area. While Aden town has the highest percentage of girls, 45 percent of all primary-school pupils, in the northern Sada Province the figure is only 14 percent.[7]

At the secondary-school level, a three-year curriculum that follows the nine years of primary education, girls' number among all pupils decreases further. In the early 1990s, in Shabwa-Province in the south, only seventeen girls out of 2,515 secondary-school attendees continued their education after primary level.[8] It is usually the case that secondary schooling of girls requires special arrangements. First, parents in more traditionally minded areas expect complete segregation of the sexes, particularly after the primary level. This means separate schools for boys and girls. Second, parents are often unwilling to allow a male teacher to teach girls in puberty. Since female teachers in the country make up only about 17 percent of all teachers, a female teacher is often not available to instruct girls. Third, in case a school is not situated in a nearby area, parents might be unwilling to allow their daughters to travel long distances to the nearest secondary school. During the PDRY era, school buses operated in areas where distances were long.

In the northern part of the country, girls' access to primary education in major towns dates back to the time of the Ottoman occupation, which lasted until 1918. Some schools included separate instruction for girls on, among other subjects, home economics and needlework. Religious themes, language, and history were among the topics in these schools' curricula. In other areas, girls could attend religious schools adjacent to local mosques. Still, only a fraction of girls had the benefit of basic education until the 1970s.[9] Only after the 1962 revolution in the north that overthrew the imamic rule did girls' secondary education and chances to continue to higher levels and to vocational training really emerge. Still, in the mid-1980s, girls' percentage among secondary-school pupils was less than 10 percent.[10] The number of female students in northern universities has steadily increased since 1985 when they were first allowed to enter higher education.

In the southern part of the country, women's access to education dates back to British colonial times. Since the declared policy of the colonial rule was not to touch issues considered as belonging to "custom and religion," in particular, matters that had to do with the family and women, the British were not eager to establish public schooling possibilities for girls. Therefore, girls obtained the chance to receive education much later than boys did. After some administrative changes in the late 1930s, primary education was opened to girls in Aden in public schools and schools run by various Christian missions and welfare societies. About the same time, girls' schools were opened in Hadhramaut, in the eastern part of the country. By 1958, girls in Aden had only three secondary schools, while in most of the countryside girls' education stopped at the primary level. In Hadhramaut, a few intermediate schools were reserved for female students, but they had no secondary-level classes. After independence, public schooling expanded outside Aden, and girls' numbers in both primary and secondary levels increased rapidly. While in some parts of the countryside parents remained reluctant to allow girls to proceed to the secondary level, in statistics covering the whole southern part of the country in the mid-1980s, girls' number in secondary schools reached about a third of that of boys.[11]

In today's Yemen, many women continue their studies up to the university level. During the 1980s, the number of female students was higher than that of male students in some departments of Aden University. During the 1990s, this tendency seems to have been reversed.[12] The present problem does not lie in women's access to university education, but in female students dropping out of public life after graduation. This has to do partly with the lack of child-care facilities in almost all regions of the country and partly with traditional role expectations prevalent among young people, men and women alike. Many female university graduates tend to leave the decision regarding their professional careers to the husband. The idea that once a woman has children, she has to drop her career has reemerged in areas of the country where during the 1980s attitudes were more favorable for women's employment even if they had young children.

Separate from the public school system, religious establishments maintained religious schools where aspects of Islamic faith, law, and history were taught. In 2001, these institutions were integrated into the public school system. In the mid-1980s, Islamic girls' schools had some 25,000 pupils throughout the northern part of the country, 5,000 in the capital Sana'a alone.[13] However, in some provinces of present-day Yemen, religious schools have no female students at all.[14] This situation contributes to the lack of religious knowledge among women and, in particular, leaves the socially important field of religious interpretation to male scholars only.

Yemen has a female adult literacy rate of 23 percent, which is among the lowest in the world.[15]

EMPLOYMENT AND ECONOMICS

Job/Career Opportunities

Labor laws provide equal rights for men and women in the workplace, but official statistics point to low female participation in the labor market due to the misconception of work applied in the statistics. In rural areas, where the family work norm prevails, women engage in various kinds of work both inside and outside the house. Where male labor migration to wealthier countries in the Arabian peninsula is high, running the household and taking care of the farming and cattle might be entirely on women's shoulders. Even in households rich in land, women usually work in the fields.

In the rural areas, a strict division of labor according to sex prevails.

Women's duties include harvesting, guarding crops, grinding grain, fetching firewood, and carrying water. Women also take care of animals. As a rule, men are involved in heavier and more dangerous work and in work that involves commercial aspects outside the home, while the lighter, repetitive, internal managerial and domestic tasks are women's responsibility. Men dominate all aspects of the production and marketing of *qat*, which is the major cash crop in many areas.

In towns, women's job opportunities vary according to the professional field. Earlier, nursing and teaching were considered suitable tasks for women provided they worked with women only. Since the 1980s decades, the variety of job opportunities has widened extensively. Women can now engage in almost any work, and women's attitudes concerning suitable work for women signal less societal restraint. According to social stratification that varies locally, socially lower-class women engage in jobs considered unsuitable for women of other categories. Such professions include street hawkers, sweepers, housemaids, and other servile work. In bigger cities, such as Sana'a, Aden, and Taizz, women's actual job opportunities are much wider than in other areas. Factory work as such is not considered improper for women, but due to long working hours and relatively low income, factory women tend to be from the lower social categories. Factory women are often illiterate and lack formal education. In southern cities, women with university degrees work in factories as supervisors, accountants, legal advisors, and heads of departments.

Lower-middle-level professions include nursing, clerical work, and other tasks that require vocational training or special skills, such as newspaper editors. In cities, women more often occupy these professions than men, even though nursing is also a rather popular profession among men. In pay scale, these jobs stand in the middle between manual laborers and professionals with higher degrees.

Women who complete higher education work in administration, supervising, engineering, teaching, medicine, public service, including the judiciary, and production. Only a few women now work in courts as judges. Before the unification, the judge's profession was open to women only in South Yemen. At that time, female judges presided over commercial and magistrate courts in southern towns. In North Yemen, women were restricted from working in professions that were considered to require "rational judgment," such as judges and parliament members. After unification, judge training was concentrated in Sana'a, and there have been no female students since then, even though no law restricts women from entry to the Judicial Institute. The few female judges who remain work presently in commercial and juvenile courts in the southern part of the country.

In overall labor statistics, professional women's number is low, but in cities their role in production, services, and finance is substantial. The examples of women in high government positions and that of the first female full cabinet member, nominated in 2000, are significant. Women are also engaged in running nongovernmental organizations, and their role in political organizations is visible wherever they are given the chance. A few women work as artists, writers, and poets, but these professions, even though they are highly respected, do not provide steady income.

Women and Art

Women display artistic aspirations in several art forms. Women have acted as poets, singers, artists, and writers. Among the most prominent old poets are Ghazal al-Magdashiyya, who lived during the late nineteenth century, and Nadra Ahmad al-Salahiyya, born in the mid-twentieth century. Both Ghazal and Nadra have composed traditional oral poetry of the *zamil* and *balah* type, and Nadra even the most prestigious kind of poetry in the Arab world, called *qasida*. Poetry allowed these rural women also to express political views in a society where women otherwise had little access. Among the present-day generation, Nabila al-Zubeiry, Ibtisam al-Mutawakil, Arwa Abduh Uthman, Ameena al-Nusairi, Huda Abalan, and Huda al-Attas are popular poets, and some of them also write novels. Women writers often work as journalists and write novels and short stories along with their journalistic work. These include Amal Abdullah, Salwa Yahia al-Iriyani, and Shafiqa Zuqriyya. Ittidal Dairiyya and Shafa Munassir have also written children's short stories.

Several women have become renowned nationwide as singers. Classical singers include Fattoom Nasser, Nabiha Azim, Sabah Monassar, Raja'a Ba-Sudan, and Iman Ibrahim. Among the present-day popular singers are Fat'hia al-Saghirah, Kafa Iraqi, and Amal Ko'del.

Plastic art is a new art form in Yemen, and most artists are trained abroad. Women artists are few but are respected equally with male artists. Due to the lack of government support for art, artists have to have another job to support themselves. One of the best-known artists is Ilham al-Arashi, who also chairs the Aden branch of the Yemeni Plastic Artists Syndicate. She has exhibited her work both locally and abroad.

Pay

In Yemen, men and women receive equal pay.

Working Conditions

A majority of women in Yemen work at home taking care of running the household, bringing up children, and supervising the domestic compound. In extended family households, often a strict division of labor prevails where the senior female member of the household supervises minor members, such as daughters and daughters-in-law, who perform the heaviest and most time-consuming tasks. Running errands outside the home, such as shopping, is the responsibility of the husband and younger children. Women tend to spend most of the day busy in household chores while male members of the family take their rest, but women's domestic work is not counted in official labor statistics. This makes most of women's productive activity invisible in society at large.

In public services and administration, women tend to have considerably longer working hours than men do. This is partly due to the fact that women as a rule get up earlier than their male family members to make breakfast and get children ready for going to school or daycare. In any government office, women who work in clerical positions arrive earlier than men with senior positions. Men also leave the work earlier; the habit of chewing the mild narcotic *qat* drives men to the market before lunchtime to buy the daily ratio of *qat* because the best-quality *qat* tends to sell out early. If the workplace provides transportation to its employees, women often are more dependent on it than men. Consequently, they have to respect the official working hours and both arrive earlier and stay longer at work than men usually do.

Many working women experience the problem of double shifts. Even though there are some men who participate in household chores and taking care of the children, these tasks tend most often to be left on women's shoulders. While men rest after working hours, women start preparing meals for the family, attending to children's needs, and cleaning the house. Earlier, when working weeks included only one free day, the Muslim holiday Friday, working women had no day just for rest because Friday tended to be the day for washing laundry. In 2000, a law was issued to make two days of the week, Thursday and Friday, the weekend. This reform has considerably reduced the working woman's workload.

Sexual Harassment

Traditional and customary ideas that women lack rationality and are incapable of taking care of their morality sometimes hinder women in working in places where as part of work, they have to meet men who are not close relatives. While in many areas of the country no such thinking prevails, in general, the attitude limits women's choice of profession. Though no statistics exist on sexual harassment in working life, those who have studied working women have not reported such incidents as widespread.[16] Men tend to respect women in work, with the exception of women who work, in restaurants and hotels, where they are subjected to harassment on a regular basis. This is probably due to the thinking that no decent woman works in service professions and in particular in places that serve alcohol.

Support for Mothers/Caretakers

The family is the principal support for working mothers. This custom is also established in the Social Care Law (no. 31 of 1996), which rules that the family takes full responsibility in providing all basic needs to the child inside and outside the family. Special provision is made for children who are deprived of family care, but nurseries and kindergartens are reserved only for such cases.

The most common family type in Yemen is the extended family, in which a senior couple shares the household with children and their spouses and offspring. Often the household also accommodates other family members who do not have a family of their own, such as unmarried, separated, or widowed sisters of the husband or the wife. Elderly people live with their son's or daughter's family. A household may include three or four generations and accommodate more than twenty people.

Maternal Leave

Labor laws in former North and South Yemen differed to some extent in regard to maternity leave. While the northern law (1970) granted pregnant women seventy days for maternity leave with 70 percent of their salary, the southern law (1978) allowed women sixty days with full salary. A special provision in the latter law granted an additional twenty days' leave in strained circumstances or for the delivery of twins. It also granted the right to a six-hour working day (the normal working day was eight hours in production) for breast-feeding mothers during the first six-months after delivery and a seven-hour working day after that. The present Labor Law (no. 5 of 1995) followed the southern law in respect of maternity leave of sixty days with full pay and an additional twenty days' leave in case of complications in pregnancy. Working hours for a pregnant woman from the sixth month of pregnancy until the sixth month after the delivery are five hours a day. The law prohibits overtime work for women during these two periods.

Daycare

Since the mid-1980s, in larger cities, the nuclear family has emerged alongside the extended family, and in such households working mothers often experience severe problems in child care. Whenever female family members live long distances from each other, a working mother has to spend a long time every working day transporting her children to a female relative. This is the duty of the mother more often than that of the father.

Public and private child care is a rare phenomenon in Yemen, even though the women's movement has raised this issue since the 1970s. According to official statistics from the mid-1990s, the country had only sixty-two kindergartens spread unevenly in larger towns and in district centers in the southern part of the country.[17] Most of the child-care centers are run by a factory or a government office, with access restricted to employees' children only. Professional child attendants and teachers in the kindergartens number about 600 people, nearly all of them women.[18]

Inheritance and Property Rights

Even though the constitution provides equal rights to the sexes, men and women are not treated equally in inheritance and property rights. Following Islamic principles, only men are obliged to support the family. As women do not have economic obligations in a marriage where the husband is alive, her income and property remain under her control. According to this principle, no law can force a woman to use her property to support the family even if the husband is incapable of maintaining it. This duty falls on the woman's or husband's male relatives. Still, in practice, women often do support the family from their salaries. In case the woman acts as the head of the household, she has the actual obligation to support her family.

Inheritance laws follow Islamic law (*shari'a*) which grants a woman half the share of a man. This principle is motivated by the man's obligation to use his income and property to maintain his family. Men also often carry the responsibility, legislated as their duty, of economically supporting their elderly parents. However, as women's involvement in wage labor has increased during the past decades, many women support their retired or disabled parents. The principle of guaranteeing a woman her property during marriage favors the woman, but actual circumstances often prevent her from benefiting from this rule.[19] A woman often leaves her share of an inheritance to the control of her brother with the agreement of taking a benefit whenever need arises.

In Islam, women are guaranteed equal rights to men in possessing and managing property that they have obtained through marriage payments or inheritance or have acquired by engaging in economic activities or by borrowing. The most widespread type of women's property is jewelry and cash she obtained from her husband when contracting marriage. In rural areas, women might possess land, whereas in towns women's property is sometimes in the form of houses. Some women possess houses as part of a housing society, or through government donation. The latter group includes both widows of martyrs (men who have died in a battle) and women in influential political positions.

Very few women are involved in business activities or managing properties. Traditional values that tend to view women as needing male guardianship do not support women acting as legal persons.

Social/Government Programs

In government and donor programs, gender inequality is acknowledged as one of the principal hindrances to economic and social development of the country. Programs to strengthen economic reforms, ensure food security, guarantee basic education, improve public and reproductive health, and address the water crisis put special emphasis on increasing female participation in various aspects of development. In particular, reforms in health care and education aim at involving rural women.

The National Population Action Plan (adopted in 1991 and updated in 1996 and 2000) addresses women's rights in order to develop legislation on mother and child rights along the lines of Islamic principles. It also calls for the creation of labor and welfare bills to ensure an appropriate environment for working women and enhance women's awareness about their legal rights. The Social Welfare Bill was passed in 1996 to provide financial assistance for orphans, poor women and children with no supporters, families of prisoners, and people with disabilities.[20] Various women's nongovernmental organizations, human rights groups, and the trade unions are active in addressing women's rights issues in government policies and in raising awareness among women about their legal rights as well as resources available in the society to improve the family's economic situation.

FAMILY AND SEXUALITY

Gender Roles

Traditional role expectations present the family as the basic unit of care and support in society. Men assume the role of the head of the family, and women and children are presented as being under their guidance and command. According to this familial ideology, men and women complement each other in family. While men are responsible for providing for the family and making the decisions, women take care of running the household and bringing up the children. By sacrificing their own needs and aspirations to the benefit of the happiness of the family, women contribute in raising a new generation to serve their country.

Sexual segregation is an overall principle that organizes the society. In everyday life, men's and women's spheres of life are separate in order to prevent men and women who are not close kin from meeting. This principle is based on the understanding that women are not supposed to spend time in nonkin male company because that might cause a breach of sexual morality. In its strictest forms, this ideology prevents a woman from moving freely outside her home and participating in mixed education or working with male colleagues. As the strictness of this rule varies from rural to urban areas and from one province to another, so do its actual manifestations differ. Rural women often enjoy more freedom of movement than their urban sisters. This is manifest in the dress a woman wears: rural women in general veil less than women in towns. While a rural woman might not wear any overcoat and hold her head scarf loosely, in some towns women cover themselves from head to toe, leaving no skin visible.

In women's lives, sexual segregation has both negative and positive aspects. The negative aspects subject the woman to strict familial control and direct at her societal pressure and harassment when she moves outside her home, which often results in women's self-imposed restrictions on both physical movements and aspirations. Men also suffer from strict sexual seclusion. When women veil heavily, men do not see women other than their closest family members, a matter of complaint among many men. Seclusion of women limits men's access to homes; while women receive their guests in a house, men have to stay outside and kill time hanging around. Attitudes toward gender segregation vary among men the same way they do among women.

Even though gender segregation is usually presented in the West entirely in negative terms, women in Yemen also acknowledge positive aspects to it. Women might feel more relaxed and confident in an all-female group where they do not have to compete with socially better-equipped men. Some teachers point out that in mixed education, female students find it hard to concentrate if male students are present. Some women mention also the disturbing staring and harassment they occasionally experience from men in public places and acknowledge that veiling allows them to move freely in such spaces. A veiling woman can control her contact with men and limit the choice of addressing a man to herself alone because men tend to respect women in *purdah*.

Marriage

A new phenomenon in matchmaking involves a decreased level of parental choice and guidance in contracting a marriage. Since the last decades of the twentieth century when modern phenomena have influenced lifestyles in larger towns in particular, new family roles have emerged alongside the traditional familial ideology. While the traditional family is an extended family with several generations and family units sharing the household, among younger people in larger cities, the nuclear family is increasingly the ideal. In the latter family type, the role expectations might be the same as in a traditional family, often depending on how the marriage was contracted. As women's participation in higher education and working life has increased, more and more women have tended to choose their spouses themselves, especially among work colleagues or fellow students. This kind of marriage is commonly called "love before wedding," in contrast to the traditional matchmaking principle of parental supervision, called "love after wedding." It is noteworthy that both types of marriage are expected to bring happiness and love between the spouses. The free-choice marriage often brings role expectations in the family based on companionship and equal sharing, in contrast to the idea of complementary gender roles.

Young women's increasing participation in movements of the Islamic call (*dawa*) also brings new role expectations in marriage. While the Islamic call often means a heightened personal awareness in practicing Islam in daily life, women activists in Islamic movements raise the issue of how to be a proper Islamic wife and mother. This ideology differs from the traditional family ideal in addressing women directly as agents of spreading Islamic understanding. Thus it grants women an active role in transforming the society in an Islamic direction. In emphasizing men's and women's separate fields and the need for sexual segregation, this ideology differs from the "modern" family ideal that deemphasizes gender separation.

Marriage is a norm in Yemen. Both men and women aspire to get married and receive support for their aspirations from the family. Social attitudes stigmatize women who have not married, while men can go on with their lives unmarried without societal pressure. A recent phenomenon among highly educated women indicates that the marriage norm might be challenged in the future. Provided that her parental family is supportive, a working woman in particular can now consider the option of remaining unmarried. As the culture emphasizes family support, living single in a separate apartment, however, is not an option yet, even if a woman can fully support herself by wage labor. Little societal or family pressure is directed at a divorced or widowed woman in case she is self-supporting or has a place to return to after her marriage is over, such as her parental home.

Reproduction

Population statistics show that Yemen is among the countries in the world with the highest rates of population growth. The fertility rate in Yemen is currently 3.5 percent, while in the beginning of the 1990s it was up to 3.7. This means a decline from 7.8 live births to 6.5 children born alive.[21] In practical terms, this shows that an ordinary Yemeni woman experiences a few miscarriages during her fertile years. Still, as this is the statistical average, some women experience successive pregnancies throughout their fertile period. This phenomenon is reflected in the popular saying "Out goes the baby, in comes the man!"

In towns and among educated women, fertility rates are much lower. A recent ideal is that of the family with only two to three children, provided that at least one of them is a boy. Men often insist on having boys because the traditional ideology presents men as carriers of the family lineage, while women are married away. A preference for boys might result in less care of a female infant when a desperate woman who has given birth to too many girls tries to please her husband. This is reflected in statistics that show an unbalanced gender ratio in young age groups to the benefit of boys, while in society at large the number of women exceeds the number of men.

Contraception and Abortion

United Nations statistics show that some 35 percent of women would prefer not to give birth to more children. Still, the official contraceptive prevalence is only 12 percent.[22] Yemeni women use both traditional and modern contraceptives. Traditional methods include both harmful and harmless methods. Among the harmful methods are inserting salt into the vagina and drinking water mixed with charcoal, whereas harmless methods include herbs and fruit. However, even the latter can cause medical problems. Seeds of a fruit called *hadaj* are boiled and drunk. This folk remedy is also used for constipation and causes extreme dehydration.

As a rule, men refuse to use condoms, leaving the responsibility of birth control to women. Most women who use modern contraceptive methods take the pill. A widespread misconception about intrauterine devices that the uterus will swallow the device prevents women from using this method. Problems related to family planning are most serious in areas with meager access to health care and where women's illiteracy is high. A husband's consent is required for an abortion to be performed in a public health center.

Teen Pregnancy

Early pregnancies are another problem in Yemen. While marital age has steadily increased throughout the country, in remote areas in the countryside, girls are still married off at an early age, between fourteen to sixteen years of age or even younger. Since 1999, when age limits were removed from the Personal Status Law, there has been no minimum age of marriage for either sex. Among the most urgent tasks in health education declared in national health plans is to spread awareness about the dangers of early pregnancies. As health authorities understand that it is difficult to prevent people from marrying off their daughters at an early age, the message directed at young married husbands is to delay pregnancy until the wife reaches at least eighteen years of age.

Female Genital Cutting

Female genital cutting is a serious health danger, although it is not practiced throughout the country. It is mainly prevalent in the coastal areas with historical migration to and from the Horn of Africa, where the custom is more widespread. This traditional practice is motivated by arguments related to virginal chastity, marital loyalty, physical purity, and religion. Some people say that it is ordered by Islam (sunna); some claim that it does not look nice if a girl is not circumsised, or that she will desire sex if she is not cut, which would be shameful for her and her family. The method of circumcision involves what is called a milder version.

The circumciser is often an elderly woman who acts also as a traditional birth attendant, and the procedure is done at home. She lifts the tips of the two labia minora with a needle and thread. The thread is then tied and lifted to cut the small tips with a razor. Then the thread is removed, and a raw egg that acts as an antiseptic is applied to the cut part. A piece of cotton is soaked in sesame oil and placed between the two cut parts to prevent a fusion. Black powder that is believed to heal wounds is also applied to prevent bleeding and fusion. Occasionally the two cut parts grow together, and a woman whose circumcision is done improperly has to be cut open in delivery.

This practice causes pain for a woman in sexual intercourse and reduces her enjoyment. Infections and bleeding are other health risks. In childbirth, bleeding and pain might be accompanied by the risk of prolonged labor. Even though Islamic preachers and learned men no longer speak in favor of this violent custom, as some of them did in earlier times, they do not participate with the health authorities to eradicate it. As female circumcision is not believed to be the most urgent women's health problem in Yemen, it has not been the main target of women's movement's activities even though it is condemned and discouraged in different organizations' programs. In the 1997 demographic survey, its prevalence was indicated at 22 percent in the age category forty-five to forty-nine years and 20 percent among women aged fifteen to nineteen years. About 97 percent of female circumcisions are performed at home by local elderly women or traditional birth attendants, and the remaining 3 percent at health facilities.[23]

HEALTH

Health Care Access

The prevalent gender inequality in Yemen is strongly manifested in access to health care. Lack of female medical and nursing staff and customary attitudes prevent women in some rural areas from attending a clinic and obtaining treatment. Long and arduous distances in the countryside often cause women with pregnancy complications to die on the way to the faraway health unit.

Diseases and Disorders

Customary attitudes that degrade women and present them as dependents of men subject women to inferior status in the family. The usual manifestations are disregard of her health, successive pregnancies, too much heavy household work, and malnutrition because men eat the best part of the food available at home. Among pregnant mothers, malnutrition and anemia are the most common health hazards.

Typical causes of postnatal mortality among mothers include pre- and postdelivery bleeding, embrial toxication, puerperal fever, oval detonation (breaking of the ovaries), and surgeon effects on delivery. A high rate of hepatitis also contributes to the high maternal mortality rate of 351 per 100,000 live births. Only one-fifth of deliveries take place in the presence of skilled birth attendants.[24] In some parts of the country, a woman in labor is left on her own in a room to deliver and is assisted only after the baby is born. In other areas, a local traditional birth attendant assists in delivery and provides postdelivery care. Women usually give birth on the floor with some cloth underneath, some in a squatting position leaning on a female relative or a rope, and some in a lying position holding a relative woman's hand. In hospitals and delivery units, women are made to deliver in the typical Western position lying on the delivery bed, a fact that decreases the popularity of hospital delivery.

In both urban and rural areas, the economically most vulnerable people are subjected to various diseases caused by poor sanitary conditions and environmental hazards. Such health problems include acute respiratory infections, diarrhea diseases, malaria, and tuberculosis. Cholera is rare in Yemen, but there are occasional outbreaks in limited areas. Also, Rift Valley fever appears in Yemen occasionally. In particular among infants and children, meningitis and measles are serious diseases that could be prevented by vaccination. Because several governmental and donor organizations have engaged in comprehensive vaccination campaigns throughout the country, remarkable success has been achieved in eradicating polio and some other diseases preventable by immunization. People with disabilities usually remain without professional care. Among women, the most widespread cancer type is breast cancer. Elderly women often suffer from incontinence, osteoporosis, and problems linked to dysmenorrhea.

AIDS

Official data indicate a low prevalence rate of HIV. In the year 2000, only 806 cases were reported, of which 196 were suffering from AIDS.[25] Still, it is likely that the disease remains underdiagnosed and underreported given that access to health care is limited. As sexually transmitted diseases are common in Yemen and the risk of stigmatization often prevents people from visiting a doctor, HIV/AIDS rates must be much higher than so far reported. Available studies indicate that the major mode of transmission is sexual and that HIV spreads in Yemen basically from the Horn of Africa, where transmission rates of HIV are very high, and from the Gulf countries with labor migration.[26]

Depression

Not only external circumstances prevent women from seeking professional help for health problems, but also psychological factors. From childhood, girls in many areas of the country learn to believe that they are less wanted and inferior to their brothers. This attitude contributes to low self-esteem among women and influences a woman's conceptions about herself and the needs of her body. Since many women spend most of their lifetime inside four walls performing household tasks in a squatting position, backache tends to be widespread. Being such a common symptom, it is often considered natural and thus requiring no treatment. In older age, many women are basically incapable of moving in an upright position without help, which further curbs their ability to enjoy life and perform their duties. Depression is reported to be more common among women than men. This is linked to stress and fatigue in their daily life and to low self-esteem, which makes women undervalue themselves and their potential.

POLITICS AND LAW

Suffrage and Political Participation

Women obtained suffrage in southern Yemen by virtue of the constitution of the former People's Democratic Republic of Yemen (South Yemen) enacted in 1970. This basic law required the state to guarantee equal rights for men and women in all fields of political, economic, and social scope and to provide the conditions necessary for realizing that equality. By 1981, women held 6 seats out of 111 in the highest legislative organ, the Supreme People's Council, and about 10 percent of the seats in local people's assemblies throughout the country.[27] During this period of one-party rule, the General Union of Yemeni Women had an official role, secured in the constitution, in promoting women's rights and engaging women in all fields of public life.

In the northern part of the country, women also gained voting rights in the constitution enacted in 1970. Even though women could run as candidates for the People's Assembly and local councils, no for many reason, no women ever were elected. First, the state apparatus did not support public roles for women, and legislation banned women from serving in the judiciary and, in certain official institutions, and in the police. Second, female candidates were reported to have experienced harassment and official pressure to withdraw their candidacy. Third, women's participation in the extradomestic labor force, education and, civil society remained low throughout the Yemen Arab Republic.

When North and South Yemen unified in 1990 and a multiparty system was introduced for the first time in both parts, women's political rights were secured in the new constitution, enacted in 1991. Still, in the unified country's legislative body, the parliament, women's number has remained very low. In parliamentary elections held in 1993 and 1997, only two women in each election were elected to the 301-member legislative body, all four of them from the south. While the number of female candidates dropped from forty-eight in 1993 to twenty-three four years later, women's number among registered voters increased considerably, from 16 percent in 1993 to 28 percent in 1997.[28]

Even though Yemen is officially a parliamentary democracy, large areas of the country remain outside central government control. Locally prominent tribes rule these areas, which include the northern part of the country, except its coastal strip, and some areas in the south and east. Some of these tribes and their prominent leaders also have an important position in national politics. The tribal system as it exists in Yemen relies on customary law that varies from area to area and differs both from statutory law and from Islamic law. The principal values of tribal ideology (*qabyala*) include personal autonomy, courage, hospitality, mutual cooperation, and generosity. It is often emphasized that tribal society is egalitarian. This principle, however, does not apply to women. As the tribal system is based on genealogy counted according to the male line, women reckon genealogy not directly but through relationship to a significant male. As a woman's behavior, modesty, and chastity directly influence her male guardian's honor, women often are kept under strict control by their families. In the tribal society, women are not autonomous actors and are left outside all formal decision making.

Women participate in national politics through political parties, various nongovernmental organizations, and as intellectuals who contribute to debates in the media. Three of the largest political parties, the People's General Congress, Islah (Reform), and the Yemeni Socialist Party, have women in their leading bodies if not in the leadership. Still, none of these parties nor other parties presently raise women's issues as strongly as was the case during the 1970s and 1980s in the former South Yemen (ruled by the Yemeni Socialist Party) when women's liberation (*tahrir al-mar'a*) was on the official agenda. Even though all political agents acknowledge the public role women must be given for the country to develop, official initiatives tend to be limited and modest. Still, high expectations are placed on the first female full cabinet member, who holds the human rights portfolio. Since 1996, the government has nominated the National Women's Committee to promote women's issues nationwide, to act as the official women's body in various international venues, and to coordinate cooperation with international donors.

Women's Rights

Yemen has signed several international human rights conventions, including the Convention on the Elimination of All Forms of Discrimination against Women (1984), the Convention on the Political Rights of Women (1987), and the Convention on Consent to Marriage, Minimum Age for Marriage, and Registration of Marriage (1987).[29] The constitution provides women equal rights with men in most fields of life, but in actual practice women face obstacles that prevent them from exercising their rights. In the women's movement, these obstacles are acknowledged, and seminars and workshops are organized to tackle these problems. Many of these problems have to do with women's participation in extradomestic work, access to education, and participation in elections. Working women often face child-care problems and have a double shift. As a solution to this problem, women's organizations have demanded establishment of more public daycare centers. Also, women activists believe that attitudes among men need to be changed regarding household work. The women's movement has also raised voices against the trend of a decreasing number of girls in education. During the local elections in 2001, women's organizations held training courses to involve more women as voters and candidates and to encourage women to vote for a female candidate. As the election statistics show, very few women are elected.

All women's groups and human rights organizations agree that the problem in Yemen with regard to women's rights is not legislation as such, but the implementation of the laws, which does not benefit women. This is partly because of prevalent attitudes that belittle women and partly because women themselves do not know their rights.

Women's initiatives that both have an awareness-raising aspect and contribute to women's well-being range from welfare activities for poor women, development projects that concentrate on increasing women's involvement, and training courses that instruct women in income-generating activities to initiatives to raise women's awareness of their rights. During the local elections campaign in early 2001, women's activities reached a new level. Several initiatives were taken to raise women's participation in voting and candidacy. Governmental and nongovernmental women's organizations, including the National Women's Committee, the Yemeni Women's Federation, and the Women's Forum for Research and Training, organized training courses for women and men. In these meetings, legal advice was delivered and practical aspects were discussed. Among the topics raised were the problems that an individual woman faces with her family when deciding for whom to vote and when trying to run for election. Particular role plays were organized among participants to rehearse possible situations in families when male family members try either to stop the woman from running for office or to force her to vote for a male candidate. The participants and organizers of these meetings considered this kind of empowerment of women as vitally important. It was explained that male pressure in families is a serious form of violence against women.

An important platform for women's participation in politics is newspapers and the media. Yemen has a large number of prominent female journalists and editors. During the PDRY era in the south, the General Union of Yemeni Women had a weekly radio program called "The Family" that informed women about all kinds of issues related to women and children. For several years, the women's union also hosted a television program devoted to women. The union published a woman's magazine called *Nisa' al-Yaman* (Women of Yemen), which wrote about various political, social, and cultural issues. The most active branches of the union also had their modestly printed local journals for women. Its sister organization in the North, the Yemeni Women's Association, also had its own radio program. Since the mid-1960s, women have joined Sana'a and Taizz radio stations as announcers, journalists, and producers.

In present-day Yemen, several women's magazines are published. *Arwa*, a magazine devoted to family and social affairs, was established in 1990 and is run entirely through the efforts of its founder, Arwa Muhammad Qa'id Saif. The Sana'a-based newspaper *al-Mar'a* (Woman) is also devoted to women's issues, with Sayyida al-Hailamah as chief editor. The official National Women's Committee publishes a newspaper called *al-Yamaniyya* (Yemeni woman) with much of coverage of politics, pathbreaking women in new professions, and social issues. Progressive men also contribute to this newspaper. Other magazines edited by women include *Mutab'at 'ilmiyya* (Scientific newsletter), which addresses media research, and *al-Shaqa'iq* (Sisters), which covers women's religious issues. The Empirical Research and Women's Studies Center at Sana'a University published for some time a theoretical journal on women's studies called *Majallah al-Dirasat al-Niswayyah* (Women's studies magazine). Several women work as announcers on the two national television channels. While the country was still divided, Sana'a television did not have bareheaded female announcers like those on Aden television, but slowly during the 1990s women there too cast away their veils while working on-screen. The most popular television announcer, Sofia, who moved from Aden television to Sana'a after unification, has maintained her personal style and has never veiled on the air. Many women consider the example of these popular television personalities as crucial to how women's presence in the public at large is influenced.

Feminist Movements

During the 1940s, the first voices were heard against the "inferiority of women" and in support of "liberating the woman from her shameful position as the object of pleasure for men only." These voices belonged to liberal and leftist male intellectuals who in the course of the fight against the British colonial power in Aden also raised the issue of women's liberation. At the same time, several charities and welfare associations run mainly by European women engaged in drawing local women from their homes for strictly *purdah* bandage-making parties and visiting needy women in their homes.

In 1951, the first women's society was established in Aden. The wife of the British chief secretary set up the Aden Women's Club with modernizing aims such as teaching the local women dressmaking, embroidery, "simple home nursing" cooking, and hygiene. In the beginning, however, few local women attended because their husbands considered that wives had too much freedom if they joined a club. The Aden Women's Club later radicalized when local women took the leadership, and other women's organizations joined the fight for education, job opportunities, and improved health care for women. While this was happening in Aden, other parts of present-day Yemen remained untouched by calls to liberate the woman from "customs that degrade her." After independence in 1967, the General Union of Yemeni Women (GUYW) was established in 1968, and its activities, such as literacy and sewing classes, health education, and empowerment courses on women's rights, gradually reached all corners of the country.

In the Yemen Arab Republic in the north, the first women's organization, the Yemeni Women's Association (YWA) was established in 1965. The organization had branches in all major cities. Even though conditions in various areas of the country differed, the main task of the association was to promote literacy among women. In the 1975 census, women's illiteracy was measured at 97.2 percent.[30] The YWA never gained a political role in the state, nor were its campaigns politically supported by the government. After the Yemeni unification, the YWA and its sister union in the south, the GUYW, were joined to form the Yemeni Women's Federation (YWF). Putting together two organizations with such different backgrounds was not an easy task in the first place, and the hegemony of Islamist women in the Sana'a branch of the federation further complicated the process.

Islamist women have been active in the women's movement since the 1980s, and their goals do not differ entirely from those of other women's rights activists. The principal distinction has to do with the role Islam is seen to play in guaranteeing women their rights. Islamist women are active in welfare work and promote women's general and religious education and literacy. Women in Islamic organizations emphasize the special role women have in spreading the cause of Islam as mothers and activists.

Women's studies is part of the program in some of Yemen's universities. In Sana'a University, gender issues have been taught and studied in the Empirical Research and Women's Studies Center, which also, as noted earlier, published a scholarly journal. In the late 1990s, the center's activities were, however, reorganized, and feminist teachers were discharged. The proclaimed reason was the heavy pressure that came from some of the conservative circles in the society.

The word "feminism" is not used as such in Yemen, but the way women's rights advocates define their causes and issues is clearly feminist. During the PDRY period, politics to improve women's situation in society and the family were officially called women's emancipation (*tahrir al-mar'a*). In recent years, discussions on women's problems in society have centered on the concept "violence against the woman." This notion refers to a number of problems women face in their everyday life. First, it is about the negative attitudes women face at home when trying to pursue education, decide about going to work outside the home, or choose a husband. These attitudes are viewed as part of the persisting negative customs and traditions that degrade and belittle women. Second, it is about negative attitudes and structural limitations in society at large that prevent women from benefiting from the resources available in society or claiming their legal rights. Third, it is about the question of women's different treatment from men in society and denying women the same human rights. Last, it is about physical violence to which women are subjected inside and outside their homes.

Women's organizations and human rights groups constantly debate these issues from different angles in seminars, workshops, and the media, making Yemen a country with a lively debate on women's issues. Still, feminism is nothing new in Yemen. As Leila Ahmed has asserted, Yemen has an old tradition of strong, active, and independent women. While this ancient tradition has died away in other areas of the Middle East, women in the southernmost part of the Arabian peninsula continue to act out of this indigenous tradition of feminism. According to Leila Ahmed, this feminism is manifest in illiterate women not exposed to Western thought who show awareness of patriarchy and its oppression and who know that Islam has also been misused as an ideology to control women.[31]

Lesbian Rights

Even though human rights organizations also address women's rights in their agenda, lesbian rights are not acknowledged as a human rights issue yet. It will be some time before matters of sexual identity can be addressed publicly in a country where matters related to sex are considered shameful to discuss in public and where the heterosexual family forms the corner stone of society. However, sexual relationships between people of the same sex are rather common even though homosexual sex constitutes a criminal offense.

Military Service

During the independence struggle against the British in the southern part of what is now Yemen, women participated in armed struggle in some areas of the countryside. Some of them became martyrs remembered with respect similar to that for male fighters who died in the battle. During the rule of the PDRY, women worked in the military in desk offices but were not entitled to military training. After the unification, conservative forces tried to impose a law banning women from the military, but failed. Women preserved their right to work in the military forces, and that right is considered in the women's movement as a victory for the women's cause.

RELIGION AND SPIRITUALITY

Women's Roles

Among the major Islamic schools in Yemen, the Sunni of the Shafei school and the Shi'a of the Zaydi doctrine, women are not allowed to enter the mosques but must pray at home. Among the two minority Shi'a schools, the Ismailis and the Bohras, women have a separate space in mosques and celebrate major Islamic festivals together with men. Few women act as religious scholars, and their role in Islamic jurisprudence is small. In women's Qur'anic study groups, female religious scholars act as speakers and lecturers. In many women's everyday life, the five daily prayers structure the day. The day starts before sunrise with the first early morning prayer. When praying, a woman covers her head with a scarf, and if she is wearing a short skirt or trousers, she also covers her legs with a cloth. Some women perform the small or big pilgrimage (*hajj*) to the holy city of Mecca.

During the 1990s, young women in particular responded to the Islamic call (*dawa*) and joined Islamic activism. For these young women, religion is a matter of building consciousness and a process toward deeper spirituality. The so-called Islamic dress, a head scarf (*hijab*) and a loose overcoat, represents to these women a symbol of religious consciousness. Even though this outfit has spread widely among the younger generation, representing the common dress of some 99 percent of young women in some major cities, most women do not see it in such religious terms as the Islamic activists do.

Rituals and Religious Practices

Women practice religion in different ways. A modern phenomenon that has emerged in Yemen during the last decades is to keep religion and faith as a private matter and not to expose religiosity in any physical way. Traditional practices include various forms of spirit possession (*zar*), spiritual healing (*sihr*), and different Sufi (Islamic mysticism) orders. Veneration of local saints is also of ancient origin and is widespread in the Sunni areas of Yemen. All these traditional forms of spirituality and religion have been severely suppressed in recent years by different groups of Islamists and other "purifiers" of popular Islam who consider these practices "un-Islamic." Women in particular have played a role in these traditional practices, acting as saints (*waliyya*), zar-ring leaders (*'alaqa*), and various kinds of healers. Women also organize celebrations to invoke blessings, such as *mawlid* where the birthday of a holy man or the prophet Muhammad is celebrated, and parties where a vow (*nadhr*) is made to promote health and invoke good fortune.

Women's Qur'anic study groups (*nadwa*) are an important part of women's informal networks among the Islamic activists. These gatherings form a link in the transmission of knowledge from senior religious scholars to younger generations. The biggest Islamic party, Islah, is active in universities in particular, and the party's female activists come to the campus and organize lectures and celebrations on special religious occasions.

Religious Law

Religious law is in particular applied in the Personal Status Law (no. 20 of 1992 as amended in 1998 and 1999), which consists of family law and provisions that have to do with inheritance and other aspects of women's rights in marriage and divorce. The law reflects a conservative interpretation of Islamic law (shar'ia), and the disparity in men's and women's duties and rights in marriage is manifested in many provisions of the law. First, only the bride's guardian can sign the marriage contract; the bride's consent, however, is in normal cases required for marriage. Silence is considered a token of consent. As witnesses in the contract ceremony, two men or one man and two women are enough. Thus a woman's witness counts as half that of a man. A husband is entitled to marry up to four wives provided he treats them equally. The law allows a husband an unconditional right to divorce by repudiation (*talaaq*). The wife cannot reverse such a divorce but was in the initial version of the law (1992) entitled to compensation provided she took the case to court and the court found the divorce unjustified. This stipulation was abolished in 1998. As for the wife, the only way to leave an unsatisfactory marriage is either to appeal to a court on dissolution of the marriage (*faskh*) according to one of the clauses stipulated by the law, such as the husband's prolonged absence, or by gaining the husband's consent to a no-fault divorce (*khul*). The custody of children in divorce is normally given to the mother until the age of nine for boys and twelve for girls, but if she exhibits "misconduct," she risks losing her children after they reach the age of five.

The gender discrepancy in the law is most evident in the duties men and women have in marriage. The wife's duties are to allow the husband free sexual access, obey him in all matters, and ask for his permission whenever leaving the house. The husband has no similar obligations. Instead, his duties include maintaining her and their common children, respecting his wife's standard of living to which she was accustomed prior to marriage, and treating all his wives equally. The Personal Status Law in its original 1992 form can be considered to include some improvements compared to the law that prevailed in the former North Yemen (law no. 3 of 1978). However, women's rights were further weakened in the amendments that the parliament made to the law in 1998 and 1999. All in all, the Personal Status Law represents a clear setback to women's rights when it is weighed against the Family Law (no. 1 of 1974) of the former South Yemen. The latter provided women, among other rights, similar rights in divorce to those of men, stipulated that extrajudicial divorce was illegal, and put limitations on the practice of polygamy.

VIOLENCE

Domestic Violence

There are no surveys or statistics on domestic violence against women. According to the Personal Status Law, physical or psychological harm and duress are legal causes for a woman to seek judicial dissolution of her marriage. Such divorce cases are rarer than the actual occurrences of domestic violence against women since many factors prevent a woman from leaving a marriage that is her economic safeguard. The idea that rape can occur in the family is alien in Yemen, where social attitudes pertaining to modesty prevent people from talking about sibling rape or sexual abuse committed by a husband. Amnesty International maintains in its reports that women face severe discrimination in criminal law and procedures. After the promulgation of a new penal code in 1994, flogging and amputation became applicable to the whole of unified Yemen. Earlier such punishments were in force only in the former YAR. Flogging is prescribed for offenses of a sexual nature, such as premarital sex and adultery (*zina*). In the latter case, death by stoning is also applicable. There is little information on how many incidents are brought to court, how many sentences have been passed and upheld by higher courts, and which ones have actually been executed. Considerable opposition to applying these punishments prevails among the judiciary. As a legacy from the former YAR moral order, some people might be accused of unjustified meeting with no third party present between an adult man and a woman who are not close relatives (*khilwa*). Even though *khilwa* is not mentioned in the new penal code, in practice people are occasionally harassed and arbitrarily arrested on suspicion of *khilwa*.

OUTLOOK FOR THE TWENTY-FIRST CENTURY

In Yemen, there is a strong sense of understanding that women's full participation is vital to the overall development of the country. Still, much needs to be done to enable women to use the available resources and to derive full benefits from their rights. Combating illiteracy and improving the living standard of rural women in particular still remain among the most urgent tasks. Women will need to be encouraged to take political roles at both national and local levels, and their role will need to be strengthened in the administration to address the particular problems women face in pursuing education, participating in the labor market, and accessing health services. Even though Yemen has a strong female potential with many capable women and a large male population to support the women's cause, the underlying attitudes that traditionally underestimate women remain to be combated in all levels of society.

NOTES

1. United Nations in the Republic of Yemen Common Country Assessment (Sana'a: 2001).
2. Yemen. Human Development Report 1998 (Sana'a: Ministry of Planning and Development).
3. United Nations in the Republic of Yemen Common Country Assessment (Sana'a: 2001).
4. Ibid.
5. Human Development Report.
6. Common Country Assessment, Republic of Yemen. Women National Committee, Status of Woman in Yemen, Sana'a, 1996, and Republic of Yemen, Women National Committee, National Report on the Implementation Level of the Convention on Elimination of All Forms of Discrimination against Women, Sana'a, 1999.
7. Status of Woman in Yemen.
8. Ibid.
9. Farouk M. Luqman, *Yemen 1970* (Aden: 1970).
10. Paul Dresch, *A History of Modern Yemen* (Cambridge: Cambridge University Press, 2000).
11. People's Democratic Republic of Yemen, Central Statistical Organisation, *Statistical Yearbook 1988* (Aden: 1990).
12. National Report on the Implementation Level of the Convention on the Elimination of All Forms of Discrimination against Women.
13. Dresch, 2000, 175.
14. Status of Woman in Yemen.
15. Common Country Assessment. The figure is for 1998.
16. Susanne Dahlgren, "Islam, the Custom and Revolution in Aden: Reconsidering the Changes of the Early 1990s," in *Yemen into the Twenty-first Century: Continuity and Change*, ed. Kamil Mahdi and Anna Wuerth (Reading: Ithaca Press, forthcoming).
17. Amat al-Aleem al-Soswa, *Yemeni Women in Figures* (Sana'a: 1996).
18. Ibid.
19. Martha Mundy, *Domestic Government: Kinship, Community, and Polity in North Yemen* (London: I.B. Tauris, 1995).
20. Republic of Yemen, *Ten Years of Achievements, 1990–2000* (Sana'a: Ministry of Planning, n.d.).
21. Common Country Assessment.
22. Ibid. The information is from 1998 and based on UNFPA Yemen Office's Programme Review and Strategy Development Report. See also Status of Woman in Yemen.
23. National Report on the Implementation Level of the Convention on the Elimination of All Forms of Discrimination against Women.

24. Common Country Assessment.
25. Ibid.
26. Ibid.
27. Helen Lackner, *P.D.R. Yemen: Outpost of Socialist Development in Arabia* (London: Ithaca Press, 1985).
28. National Report on the Implementation Level of the Convention on the Elimination of All Forms of Discrimination against Women.
29. Status of Woman in Yemen.
30. Richard F. Nyrop, ed., *The Yemens: Country Studies*, Foreign Area Studies, American University (Washington, DC: U.S. Government Printing Office, 1986). See also Mundy, 1995, on particular circumstances.
31. Leila Ahmed, "Feminism and Feminist Movements in the Middle East, a preliminary Exploration: Turkey, Egypt, Algeria, People's Democratic Republic of Yemen," in *Women and Islam*, ed. Azizah al-Hibri (Oxford: Pergamon Press, 1982).

RESOURCE GUIDE

Suggested Reading

Clark, Janine A. "Women and Islamic Activism in Yemen." *Yemen Update* 39 (1997): 13–15. Publication of the American Institute for Yemeni Studies. www.aiys.org/. Outlines women's recent activism in the name of Islam.

Dahlgren, Susanne. "The Chaste Woman Takes Her Chastity Wherever She Goes: Discourses on Gender, Marriage, and Work in Pre- and Post-unification Aden." *Chroniques Yéménites*, 1998/1999. www.univ-aix.fr/cfey/chronic/susan98.html. Everyday living patterns of three generations of women in Aden town.

Dorsky, Susan. *Women of 'Amran: A Middle Eastern Ethnographic Study*. Salt Lake City: University of Utah Press, 1986. Study of women's living spheres in the early 1980s in one of the most traditional areas of the country.

Mahdi, Kamal, and Anna Wuerth, eds. *Yemen into the Twenty-first Century: Continuity and Change*. Reading: Ithaca Press, forthcoming. Proceedings of a 1998 conference on Yemen; specialists on Yemeni studies cover all fields of life.

Makhlouf, Carla. *Changing Veils: Women and Modernisation in North Yemen*. Austin: University of Texas Press, 1979. Elite women's lives in 1970s Sana'a.

Miller, W. Flagg. "Public Words and Body Politics: Strategies of Two Women Poets in Rural Yemen." *Journal of Women's History* 14(1) (spring 2002). Two women poets' life stories, poetry, and terms of female artistic expression.

Videos/Films

The Architecture of Mud. 1999. Directed by Caterina Borelli. Produced by Anonymous Productions. Description of traditional construction techniques, architecture and town building in the renowned valley of Hadhramaut. The video may be bought ($195) or rented ($60) from Documentary Educational Resources, 101 Morse St., Watertown MA 02472, or http://der.org/docued.

Bab al Yemen: Gateway to Yemen. 1993. Directed by Walther Grotenhuis. 40 minutes. Olympic Films. Distributed by Filmmakers Library, 124 East 40th Street, New York 10016. Rental $55, purchase $250. Drawing on the symbolic opening of

Bab al-Yaman in Sana'a (the gate to the old town), this cinéma vérité montage portrays socioeconomic change through contrasting images of daily life.

Murshidat: Female Primary Health Care Workers Transforming Society in Yemen. 1999. Produced and directed by Delores Walters. Walters is an anthropologist who has also written about these low-status women in coastal Yemen. The documentary tells the story of twenty women making home visits and performing daily routines in Mother and Child Health Center. 35 minutes. To order, contact Syracuse Alternative Media Network, www.samn.org, phone: (315) 425-8806.

Web Sites

Bab Al-Yemen, www.al-bab.com/yemen.
Numerous links to articles and material on Yemen.

American Institute for Yemeni Studies, www.aiys.org.
Much information on research and studies. The AIYS journal, *Yemen Update*, can be accessed in web form.

French Institute for Archaeology and Social Sciences in Sana'a, www.univ-aix.fr/cfey.
Similar resource pool to that of the American Institute for Yemeni Studies. English pages include the institute's journal, *Chroniques Yéménites*.

Tele Yemen, www.y.net.ye.
Links to various Yemeni sites, including newspapers.

Yemen Times, www.yementimes.com.
The leading English-language weekly newspaper in Yemen in full web form, critical but Western minded.

Organizations

Empirical Research and Women's Studies Center at Sana'a University
PO Box 1802
Sana'a University
Yemen
Email: research@y.net.ye
Academic gender studies institute that publishes the *Dirasat Niswayah* journal (Journal of Women's Studies).

Forum for Civil Society
PO Box 19458
Sana'a, Yemen
Phone: 967-1-207 650
Email: fcs@y.net.ye
Human rights organization promoting democracy and strengthening civil society. Publications concern women's rights, among other issues.

Women National Committee and Supreme Council for Women, www.yemeni-women.org.ye.
Two committees established by the government to coordinate the nation's women

politics and to make surveys and reports, still not entirely governmental. The web site includes the women's paper *al-Yamaniyya* (Yemeni Woman).

Women's Forum for Research and Training, www.geocities.com/ taralws/wfrt.htm.
A Taizz-based women's human rights organization devoted to training men and women in women's rights. Works in close cooperation with Human Rights Information and Training Center, which publishes the bilingual *Our Rights* magazine. Email: hritc@y.net.ye

Yemeni Women's Federation
PO Box 5096
Aden, Yemen
Phone: 967-2-251 453
Fax: 252 657
Email: wida@y.net.ye
The oldest women's organization in Yemen, with activities in most regions of the country. Active branches include the Aden branch.

SELECTED BIBLIOGRAPHY

Carapico, Sheila. *Civil Society in Yemen: The Political Economy of Activism in Modern Arabia*. Cambridge: Cambridge University Press, 1998. A composite view of Yemeni civil society, social activism, and history of the modern era.
Lackner, Helen. *P.D.R. Yemen: Outpost of Socialist Development in Arabia*. London: Ithaca Press, 1985. A comprehensive study of the country that was South Yemen.
Meneley, Anne. *Tournaments of Value: Sociability and Hierarchy in a Yemeni Town*. Toronto: University of Toronto Press, 1996. Women's visiting and socializing patterns in Zabid, a town with strict sexual segregation.
Mundy, Martha. *Domestic Government: Kinship, Community, and Polity in North Yemen*. London and New York: I.B. Tauris, 1995. Classic study of the role of the household in the community economy and politics and the thick ethnography of a small town north of Sana'a.

INDEX

Abaya: in Bahrain, 52; in UAE, 417–18. *See also* Veiling

Abortion: in Algeria, 25; in Bahrain, 53; in Egypt, 82; in Iran, 122; in Iraq, 158; in Israel, 176; in Jordan, 213; in Libya, 270; in Morocco, 296; in the Occupied Territories, 324; in Saudi Arabia, 348; in Tunisia, 392–93; in UAE, 420; in Yemen, 451

Abuse. *See* Children, molestation of; Children, trafficking in; Murder, of women; Prostitution; Rape; Violence

Activists, female, 10; in Egypt, 87, 97; in Iran, 108, 128; in Jordan, 191; in Lebanon, 252; in the Occupied Territories, 328; in Syria, 362, 374–75; in Tunisia, 391; in Yemen, 450, 458, 460, 461. *See also* Feminism; Organizations

Adolescents. *See* Children; Pregnancy, adolescent; Teens

Adoption by homosexuals: in Tunisia, 394

Adoption: in Egypt, 81; in Tunisia, 394; in UAE, 420

Adultery: in Algeria, 37 n.27; in Egypt, 84; in Jordan, 227, 228; in Morocco, 307; in Saudi Arabia, 348; in Syria, 371; in Tunisia, 400, 401; in UAE, 420, 425; in Yemen, 462. *See also* Fidelity; Honor, family; Murder, of women

Agriculture and gender roles: in Iran, 112; in Israel, 174; in Morocco, 287, 295; in Syria, 361; in Tunisia, 390; in Yemen, 442–43. *See also* Migration, male labor

Agriculture and women's income: in Jordan, 200, 201; in Libya, 265, 267; in Morocco, 286; in Tunisia, 389

Agriculture, female workforce in: Algeria, 18–19; in Iran, 114, 118; in Jordan, 194, 200–201; in Lebanon, 244; in Libya, 265, 267, 277 n.20; in Morocco, 285–86; in Syria, 361; Tunisia, 385, 386, 388; Tunisian minimum work age, 387; in UAE, 415; in Yemen, 442. *See also* Migration, male labor; School, dropout rates; School, work versus; Teens, school v. work

AIDS. *See* HIV/AIDS

Al-Aqsa Intifada. *See* Palestinians

Alimony: in Egypt, 88, 89, 92; in Iran, 121; in Jordan, 221; in Morocco, 294, 303; in Tunisia, 391; in UAE, 416

Amnesty International (AI): in Jordan, 227, 228

Anemia: in Jordan, 215; in the Occupied Territories, 325, 326; in Yemen, 440, 453. *See also* Diseases and disorders

Antidiscrimination policies: in Tunisia, 387

Arab League: Bahrain, 46; Syria, 358

Arab Revolt, participation in: Jordan, 190; Lebanon, 240

Arts, control of: in Saudi Arabia, 345

Arts, women in the: in Yemen, 444

Assassination. *See* Murder, of women

Assault: in Algeria, 21; in Iran, 134. *See also* Death, by violence; Fundamentalism; Rape; Violence

Ba'th (Baath): in Iraq, 151, 153, 154, 157–58, 160, 161; in Syria, 358

Baha'is: in Iran, 137–38

Banking. *See* Credit, obtaining; Investments, business

Bargaining, collectives: in Iraq, 152; protection of in Tunisia, 386. *See also* Unions

Beauty, concept of: in Tunisia, 395–96

Bedouins: in Jordan, 190, 207–8, 210; in Libya, 262, 263; in Syria, 364, 367, 369. *See also* Feuds, blood; Nomads; Tribes, laws and traditions of

Beijing +5, effect on women: in Algeria, 36

Beijing, Fourth World Conference, effect on women: in Jordan, 224; in Libya, 273. *See also* UNIFEM

Benefits. *See* Welfare, programs in

Berbers: in Algeria, 32. *See also* Nomads; Tribes, laws and traditions of

Betrothal: in Iran, 119; in Jordan, 210. *See also* Bride price; Contracts, marriage; Dowry

Birth defects: in Israel, 176; in UAE, 421

Birth, rate of: in Algeria, 17, 24–25, 26; in Bahrain, 44; in Egypt, 68; in Israel, 176; in Lebanon, 241; in Libya, 260; in Saudi Arabia, 338; in Syria, 369; in Tunisia, 400–401; in UAE, 412. *See also* Fertility, rate of; Pregnancy; Reproduction

Bisexuals, rights of: in Tunisia, 399. *See also* Rights, transgender

Bombings, suicide: in the Occupied Territories, 330, 332–33. *See also* Palestinians, resistance movement of

Breast cancer. *See* Cancer

Breastfeeding during employment or school: in Bahrain, 50; in Egypt, 72, 82; in Iraq, 154; in Jordan, 204; in Morocco, 288; in Tunisia, 388; in UAE, 414, 416, 425; in Yemen, 446

Bride price: in Bahrain, 52; in Egypt, 77; in Iran, 119

Business, female owned: in Algeria, 24; in Tunisia, 386. *See also* Crafts; Contracts, women entering; Entrepreneurs; Self-employment

Cancer: in Bahrain, 54, 55; in Iran, 124–25; in Israel, 177; in Jordan, 214, 215–16; in Morocco, 298; in the Occupied Territories, 326; in Tunisia, 396; in UAE, 422; in Yemen, 453. *See also* Diseases and disorders; Health

CEDAW, effect of: in Algeria, 20, 21, 34; in Bahrain, 58; in Egypt, 93; in Jordan, 225; in Libya, 275; in Morocco, 287; in Yemen, 455–56

Cervical cancer. *See* Cancer

Chador. *See* Veiling

Charities: in Algeria, 36 n.36. *See also* NGOs; Organizations; Poverty

Chastity: in Lebanon, 246, 248; in Libya, 275; in Morocco, 292, 293; in the Occupied Territories, 324; in Syria, 367; in Tunisia, 390, 401; in UAE, 418. *See also* Circumcision, female; Fidelity; Genitals, cutting/mutilation of; Honor, family; Marriage; Murder, of women; Pregnancy; Sexuality

Checkpoints: in the Occupied Territories, 320, 325

Child care: in Algeria, 22; in Bahrain, 49; in Egypt, 72; in Iran, 116; in Iraq, 154; in Israel, 175, 176; in Jordan, 204–5; in Libya, 266; in Morocco, 289; in Syria, 364, 369; in Tunisia, 388–89; in UAE, 415; in Yemen, 442, 446–47, 456. *See also* Family, support for working women; Work

Child health. *See* Health-care programs; Mortality, child rate

Child-rearing, responsibility for: in Algeria, 24; in Egypt, 74; in Iran, 115, 118; in Israel, 175; in Jordan, 209, 225; in Libya, 268; in Morocco, 290, 307; in Saudi Arabia, 417; in Syria, 371; in Tunisia, 391; in Yemen, 446. *See also* Child care; Gender; Leave, maternal and paternal

Children as workers: in Morocco, 295, 309; in Tunisia, 387. *See also* School, drop-out rates; Teens, school v. work

Children, custodial rights concerning: in Algeria, 24; in Bahrain, 51, 52–53, 61; in Egypt, 78, 89, 92; in Iran, 121; in Libya, 270; in Morocco, 294, 303; in Syria, 371; in Tunisia, 383, 391; in UAE, 419–20. *See also* Alimony; Citizenship, transfer of; Divorce

Children, disabled: in Bahrain, 59; in Tunisia, 383, 387–88

Children, molestation of: in Algeria, 34; in Jordan, 226, 228; in Tunisia, 402–3. *See also* Health, mental; Murder, of women; Rape; Violence against women and children

Children, religious responsibility for: in UAE, 424

Children, rights of: in Tunisia, 402; in Yemen, 448. *See* Law, Islamic; Inheritance, right of; Marriage, minimum age of; Property, right to own

Children, support after divorce: in Egypt, 88, 89; in Iran, 121; in Jordan, 221; in Libya, 270; in Syria, 371; in Tunisia, 391. *See also* Alimony; Children, custodial rights concerning

Children, trafficking in: in Algeria, 34; in Tunisia, 403

Christianity, Coptic: in Egypt, 88, 94, 99 n.17

Christianity: in Algeria, 32; in Iran, 106; in Morocco, 304; in the Occupied Territories, 314, 318, 331; in Saudi Arabia, 348; in Syria, 362, 372, 373. *See also* Laws; Rights

Circumcision, female: in Egypt, 76–77, 99 n.17; in Libya, 268; in Morocco, 304; in Tunisia, 401. *See also* Chastity; Genitals, cutting/mutilation of; Honor, family; Pregnancy; Sexuality; Virginity

Citizenship, denial of women's: in Algeria, 17, 20, 24, 27, 28, 35; in the Occupied Territories, 328–29; in UAE, 423

Citizenship, fight for: in Algeria, 33; in UAE, 423

Citizenship, transfer of: in Egypt, 88; in Jordan, 221, 222; in Lebanon, 251; in Libya, 270; in Tunisia, 383. *See also* Children, custodial rights concerning

Civil war. *See* War, civil

Clans: in Iraq, 157, 161; in Jordan,

208. *See also* Bedouins; Feuds, blood; Tribes, laws and traditions of
Code du statut personnel (CSP), Tunisian, 382, 389, 391, 402, 404 n.3. *See also* Personal status code
Code, Algerian Family, 15, 17, 23, 24, 26, 36; v. citizenship, 33; fight to abolish, 27, 29–30; and work, 21, 22, 34; and marriage, 23. *See also* Equality; Fundamentalism; Gender; Law, Islamic
Code, penal: Algerian, 21; Tunisian, 401
Code, personal status (CSP): in Morocco, 282, 287–88, 293, 300, 303, 307; Tunisian, 382, 398, 402, 404 n.3. *See also* Law, personal status
Code, Tunisian Labor, 385, 387
Colonialism, feminism and: in Algeria, 17, 23, 36 n.5; in Egypt, 88; in Saudi Arabia, 340; in Tunisia, 398; in Yemen, 457
Colonialism, independence from: Algeria's, 15, 28–29; Bahrain's, 43; Iraq's, 150; Lebanon's, 240; Libya's, 261; Morocco's, 281, 293–94; Syria's, 357; Tunisia's, 381, 390; Yemen's, 459. *See also* France; French Mandate; Freedom fighters; Great Britain; Italy; Ottoman Empire, part of
Communism: in Tunisia, 398
Condemnation (*kofr*): in Algeria, 20
Contraception: in Algeria, 23, 25; in Bahrain, 53; in Egypt, 83; in Iran, 121–22, 123; in Iraq, 158; in Israel, 176; in Jordan, 211–12; in Lebanon, 249; in Libya, 270; in Morocco, 295, 296; in the Occupied Territories, 324; in Saudi Arabia, 348; in Tunisia, 392–94; in UAE, 420; in Yemen, 451
Contracts, marriage, 3; in Algeria, 23; in Egypt, 78–80, 88; in Iran, 119, 135; in Jordan, 210, 221; in Libya, 269; in Morocco, 292, 303, 328; in the Occupied Territories, 322; in UAE, 418; in Yemen, 449, 461. *See also* Betrothal, Marriage
Contracts, women entering: in Algeria, 28; in Bahrain, 62; in Morocco, 303; in Tunisia, 389
Convention on the Elimination of All Forms of Discrimination against Women. *See* CEDAW; Health, CEDAW's influence on
Coptic church. *See* Christianity, Coptic
Coup, political: in Syria, 363; in Tunisia, 381. *See also* War, civil
Crafts: in Bahrain, 46; in Iran, 106; in Jordan, 199, 206; in the Occupied Territories, 317; in Syria, 361–62; in Tunisia, 386; in UAE, 416; in Yemen, 458. *See also* Earnings, woman's control of; Entrepreneurs, women as; Self-employment
Credit, obtaining: in Tunisia, 389
Crimes against humanity: in Algeria, 17. *See also* Children; Fundamentalism; Violence
CSP. *See* Code du statut personnel
Curfew: in the Occupied Territories, 316, 319, 325, 329, 331–32

Day care. *See* Child care
Death benefits, workplace: in Jordan, 207; in Tunisia, 387
Death, by violence: in Algeria, 16, 17; in Bahrain, 58. *See also* Fundamentalism, religious, violence and oppression via; Honor, family; Murder, of women
Decision making, political: in Egypt, 86; in Israel, 178; in Saudi Arabia, 345; in Tunisia, 398; in UAE, 422; in Yemen, 455. *See also* Gender, and decision making
Depression. *See* Health, mental; Violence, domestic
Development, policies and progress: in Algeria, 22; in Bahrain, 46, 51; in Egypt, 72–73, 85, 86–87; in Iran, 127–28; in Iraq, 155; in Israel, 172; in Jordan, 196, 202, 206; in the Occupied Territories, 317, 319–20; in Saudi Arabia, 342–43; in Syria, 363; in Tunisia, 382, 389, 390, 392, 398; in UAE, 423; in Yemen, 448. *See also* Environment, policies and issues regarding; Health, access to; Law, civil; Politics, participation in; Reform; Sustainable development
Devices, intrauterine (IUDs). *See* Family planning
Disabilities, women with: in Algeria, 29; in Jordan, 207; in Yemen, 448, 453. *See also* Children, disabled
Discrimination, gender-based: in Algeria, 17, 22, 26; in Bahrain, 48; in Iran, 109, 113–14; in Iraq, 162; in Israel, 171, 173, 179; in Jordan, 197, 216, 221; in Lebanon, 245; in Morocco, 286; in Syria, 376; in Tunisia, 383, 387, 402. *See also* Law, religious; Harassment; Unions; Women, unmarried, health care for; Workplace, condition of
Discrimination, of migrants: in Iran, 137–38; Iranians, 138; in Jordan, 197
Diseases and disorders: in Algeria, 26; in Bahrain, 54; in Iraq, 158, 160; in Israel, 177; in Jordan, 214, 215; in Libya, 270; in Morocco, 282; in the Occupied Territories, 325–26; in Syria, 369; in UAE, 421; in Yemen, 452–53
Diseases, sexually transmitted (STDs): in Algeria, 26; in Egypt, 83, 84; in Jordan, 214; in Tunisia, 392, 395, 396; in Yemen, 453. *See also* HIV/AIDS
Disorders. *See* Diseases and disorders; Eating disorders; Health, mental; Illness, mental
Divorce: in Algeria, 23, 36; in Bahrain, 51, 52, 61; in Egypt, 80, 81, 84, 88–89, 91–92, 94, 97; in Iran, 119, 135; in Iraq, 157, 158, 162; in Israel, 175, 182; in Jordan, 221, 222; in Lebanon, 249, 253; in Libya, 268, 269,

INDEX

270; in Morocco, 294, 295, 303; in the Occupied Territories, 318, 323; in Syria, 367, 371, 373, 374; in Tunisia, 383, 389, 391, 392, 402; in UAE, 419; in Yemen, 450, 461. *See also* Alimony; Children, custodial rights concerning; Contracts, marriage; Dowry; Law, Personal Status; Repudiation; Polygyny

Doctors. *See* Physicians

Domesticity, gender roles within. *See* Gender, public v. private roles

Dowry (*rahr*): in Algeria, 23; Egypt, 78, 89; in Jordan, 221; in Libya, 269; in Morocco, 292; in the Occupied Territories, 322, 323; in UAE, 416, 419. *See also* Betrothal, gift to woman; Bride price

Drop-out rates, school. *See* School, drop-out rates

Drug use: in Iraq, 156; in Lebanon, 249; in Morocco, 298; in UAE, 422; in Yemen, 440, 445. *See also* HIV/AIDS

Earnings, woman's control of: in Egypt, 69, 75, 77, 93; in Iran, 110, 114; in Jordan, 201, 208–9; in Morocco, 285, 286, 287, 290, 291; in Saudi Arabia, 200; in Syria, 361, 370; in Tunisia, 383, 389; in UAE, 416; in Yemen, 447, 450. *See also* Gender, division of labor by; Pay; Women, unmarried

Eating disorders: in Algeria, 26; in Egypt, 85; in Iran, 124; in Saudi Arabia, 348; in Tunisia, 395–96. *See also* Fertility v. eating disorders; Infertility; Malnutrition

Economic development. *See* Development policies and progress

Economics. *See* Gross Domestic Product (GDP); Gross National Product (GNP); Reform, economic

Economy, as influenced by oil production: in Algeria, 15, 24; in Bahrain, 47, 48; in Iran, 106; in Iraq, 159. *See also* Oil industry

Economy, formal: in Bahrain, 47; Egyptian women in, 93; in Jordan, 196; in Morocco, 287–88; Tunisian women in, 385

Economy, informal: in Morocco, 287–88; Tunisian teens in, 387

Education programs: in Bahrain, 44–45; 59; in Egypt, 93; in Iran, 124, 131; in Iraq, 151, 156, 157; in Israel, 170; in Libya, 263; in Tunisia, 383, 404 n.33. *See also* Health-care programs; School; Sex, education programs regarding; Violence, domestic

Education, access to: Bahrain, 45, 59; in Egypt, 75, 76; in Iran, 110–11; in Israel, 170; in Jordan, 192–93, 221; in Lebanon, 243; in Libya, 262–63; in the Occupied Territories, 315; in Tunisia, 383–84, 398, 399; in Yemen, 441. *See also* Politics, participation in; School

Education, government investment in: in Algeria, 18; in Bahrain, 44; in Iran, 110–11, 127; in Jordan, 192; in Morocco, 284; in Saudi Arabia, 341–42; in Tunisia, 383; in UAE, 413

Education, private-sector: in Bahrain, 44; in Iran, 110; in Iraq, 151; in Lebanon, 243; in Morocco, 284; in the Occupied Territories, 316; in Syria, 360; in Tunisia, 384

Education, public-sector: in Bahrain, 44; in Iran, 110; in Iraq, 151; in Jordan, 193; in Lebanon, 243; in the Occupied Territories, 315; in Syria, 360; in Tunisia, 384; in UAE, 414; in Yemen, 441–42

Education, religious: in UAE, 424; in Yemen, 441, 442. *See also* Rituals, religious

Education, women in postsecondary: Algeria, 18; Bahrain, 45, 48; in Iran, 111, 122; in Iraq, 151; in Israel, 170, 171; in Jordan, 193; in Lebanon, 243; in Libya, 262–63; in Morocco, 283; in the Occupied Territories, 315, 316; in Syria, 360; Tunisia, 385; in UAE, 413, 414; in Yemen, 441, 442

Education, women's status within: Iranian, 110–11, 127; in Israel, 170; in Jordan, 193, 195, 222; in Lebanon, 243; in Libya, 263, 264; in Morocco, 283; in the Occupied Territories, 315, 321; in Saudi Arabia, 341–42, 345, 376; Tunisian, 382, 398; in Yemen, 440, 441. *See also* Reform, education

Educational systems, types of: in Algeria, 17, 32; in Bahrain, 44; in Egypt, 86; in Iran, 110, 131; in Iraq, 151; in Israel, 170; in Lebanon, 243; in Morocco, 284; in Tunisia, 404 n.33; in Yemen, 441

Elections: in Israel, 178; in Jordan, 218; in the Occupied Territories, 327; in Yemen, 454, 456

Electoral process: in Bahrain, 57; in Iran, 125, 126–27, 138; in Iraq, 161; in Israel, 178; in Jordan, 217, 218–19; in Morocco, 299–300; in Tunisia, 381

Embargo: against Iraq, 153, 154, 159; against Libya, 265

Employment, domestic service sector: in Egypt, 70, 73; in Iran, 112, 113–14, 135; in Jordan, 197, 200; in Tunisia, 386, 387; in Yemen, 443. *See also* Rape

Employment, right to: in Algeria, 21, 24, 29, 34; in Bahrain, 58; in Egypt, 70; in Iran, 113; in Israel, 171–72, 174; in Lebanon, 248; in Morocco, 300; in UAE, 417. *See also* Entrepreneurs, women as; Labor, laws regarding; Manufacturing; Military, service in; Migration, male labor; Pay; Police; Textiles; Tourism; Training; Work

Employment, service sector: in Algeria, 19; in Jordan, 198; in

INDEX

Libya, 265; in Morocco, 285; in the Occupied Territories, 317; in Syria, 361; in Tunisia, 385; in Yemen, 443

Employment, women as professionals: in Egypt, 70; in Iran, 112; in Iraq, 155, 162; in Israel, 170, 172; in Jordan, 198, 200, 210; in the Occupied Territories, 317; in Saudi Arabia, 342–44, 350–51; in Tunisia, 385–86; in UAE, 427 n.15; in Yemen, 440, 441, 443, 457. *See also* Health care, professionals in; Training; Work

Entrepreneurs, women as: in Algeria, 24; in Iran, 111; in Jordan, 197–98, 199, 200, 206; in Morocco, 289, 290; in the Occupied Territories, 318; in Syria, 361–62; in Tunisia, 386. *See also* Loans, monetary

Environment, policies and issues regarding: in Algeria, 23; in Bahrain, 50–51; in Egypt, 74; in Iran, 117; in Tunisia, 389, 390; in UAE, 412. *See also* Education, environmental; Organization for Economic Cooperation and Development (OECD)

Equality, gender: in Algeria, 21, 29; in Bahrain, 58; in Egypt, 85; in Iraq, 152–53, 161, 163; in Israel, 171, 178, 179; 182; in Jordan, 220–21; in Libya, 267; in Morocco, 282, 301; in Saudi Arabia, 344–45; in Syria, 362, 370, 371; in Tunisia, 391, 399; in UAE, 422. *See also* Code, Algerian Family; Gender; Laws; Rights

Family Code, Algerian. *See* Code, Algerian family

Family planning: in Algeria, 23; in Bahrain, 53; in Egypt, 80–81; in Iran, 122; in Jordan, 211–12; in Syria, 371; in Tunisia, 392–95, 400–401. *See also* Health, reproductive; Pregnancy, prenatal care; Family planning

Family, extended: in Bahrain, 51; in Egypt, 93; in Iran, 120; in Iraq, 156; in Israel, 174, 180; in Jordan, 199, 208; in Morocco, 293; in the Occupied Territories, 320–21; in Yemen, 444–45, 446

Family, Jewish law: in Israel, 175

Family, Muslim law: in Egypt, 90–92, 94; in Iraq, 157; in Jordan, 205; in Morocco, 307

Family, place in society: in Egypt, 73–74; in Iraq, 157; in Israel, 173–74, 175; in Libya, 268; in the Occupied Territories, 320–21; in Syria, 372, 376. *See also* Gender; Honor, family

Family, support for working women: in Iraq, 154, 156; in Israel, 173, 174; in Jordan, 199, 208–9; in Lebanon, 248; in Libya, 265–66; in Morocco, 289; in the Occupied Territories, 323; in Tunisia, 387, 388; in Yemen, 446–47

Family, support from abuse: in Egypt, 96–97; in Iran, 133; in Israel, 183; in Libya, 275; in Morocco, 307–8; in Tunisia, 402. *See also* Violence; Women, shelters for

Feminism, tradition and: in Lebanon, 250, 251; in Morocco, 301–2; in Tunisian workplace, 388

Feminism: in Algeria, 29–30, 33; in Egypt, 88, 89; in Iran, 127–28, 131; in Iraq, 162; in Israel, 177, 178; in Jordan, 223; in Lebanon, 242, 251; in Libya, 272; in Morocco, 302; in Syria, 362, 371, 372; in Tunisia, 391, 398; in UAE, 423–24; in Yemen, 457, 458–59. *See also* Colonialism, feminism and; Gender; Religion, women's rights and

Fertility v. eating disorders: in Tunisia, 395–96. *See also* Infertility; Malnutrition

Fertility, rate of: in Algeria, 16; in Bahrain, 44, 53; in Egypt, 68, 80–81; in Iran, 107, 122; in Israel, 176; in Jordan, 190, 202, 211; in Lebanon, 241; in Libya, 260; in Morocco, 282, 295; in the Occupied Territories, 331; in Syria, 357, 369; in Tunisia, 382, 394; in Yemen, 450. *See also* Reproduction

Feuds, blood: in Syria, 373–74. *See also* Tribes, laws and traditions of; Violence

Fidelity: in Morocco, 293; in Tunisia, 390. *See also* Adultery; Repudiation

Food availability: in the Occupied Territories, 326, 331. *See also* Anemia; Malnutrition

France, colonialism by: of Algeria, 15, 23, 36 n.5; in Lebanon, 240; of Morocco, 281, 282; in Syria, 357; of Tunisia, 381, 390

Freedom fighters, women as: in Algeria, 17, 29, 30, 35. *See also* Palestinians, resistance movement of; War, civil

Freedoms. *See* Laws; Rights

French Mandate: Lebanon, 240; Syria, 357. *See also* Colonialism, independence from

Fundamentalism, religious, and employment, 6; in Bahrain, 48; in Egypt, 73, 75; in Saudi Arabia, 342–43

Fundamentalism, religious, and politics: in Algeria, 17, 27, 30, 32; in Egypt, 100 n.29; in Iran, 126, 127, 128, 131; in Jordan, 220; in Saudi Arabia, 344–45, 346; in Syria, 371–72. *See also* Hamas (Movement of Islamic Resistance)

Fundamentalism, religious, violence and oppression via, 33; in Algeria, 17, 20, 33; in Iran, 137

Gay. *See* Homosexuality; Lesbianism

Gender, decision making and: in Egypt, 74; in Israel, 172; in Morocco, 283; in Saudi Arabia, 350; in Tunisia, 390; in UAE, 416, 424. *See also* Decision making, political

Gender, division of labor by: in Egypt, 75; in Iran, 108, 115, 118; in Israel, 175; in Jordan, 208–9;

INDEX

in Libya, 268; in Morocco, 286, 287, 290, 291; in Yemen, 442–43, 444–45. *See also* Agriculture; Family; Households, female-headed; Work

Gender, equality of. *See* Benefits; Equality, gender; Inheritance, right of; Law, Islamic; Pay; Property, right to own

Gender, family responsibilities and: in Algeria, 24; in Bahrain, 51; in Egypt, 74; in Iran, 108, 118; in Lebanon, 246; in Libya, 266, 268; in Morocco, 285, 293, 294, 307; in the Occupied Territories, 323; in Syria, 365; in UAE, 424. *See also* Family; Gender, public v. private spheres; Households, female-headed

Gender, public v. private spheres: in Bahrain, 51, 60–61; in Egypt, 85; in Iran, 118; in Iraq, 156, 161; in Israel, 175; in Lebanon, 250; in Libya, 264; in the Occupied Territories, 321; in Tunisia, 390, 391. *See also* Equality, gender

Gender, roles defined by: in Algeria, 23–24, 28, 35; in Egypt, 74, 93–94, 95; in Iran, 118; in Iraq, 156, 161; in Israel, 170–71; in Jordan, 208, 209; in Libya, 265–66, 269; in Morocco, 290, 293; in the Occupied Territories, 321, 330, 331; in Saudi Arabia, 343–45, 349; in UAE, 417; in Yemen, 448

Gender, work and: in Egypt, 75; in Iran, 114–15, 118; in Jordan, 209; in Lebanon, 245; in Libya, 264, 268, 276 n.4; in Morocco, 283, 290; in Tunisia, 388, 389

Genitals, cutting/mutilation of: in Egypt, 76, 87; in Libya, 268; in Tunisia, 401; in Yemen, 451–52. *See also* Chastity; Circumcision, female; Pregnancy; Sexuality

Government, and women's organizations: in Tunisia, 398–99. *See also* Organizations

Government, as employer: in Bahrain, 48, 49; in Egypt, 73; in Iran, 111, 112–13; in Jordan, 198; in Libya, 265; in Tunisia, 385–89, 390; in UAE, 427 n.15. *See also* Politics, participation in

Government, credit programs by: in Tunisia, 389

Government, form of: Algerian, 26; in Bahrain, 55; in Egypt, 68; in Iran, 107, 138; in Iraq, 160; in Israel, 169; in Jordan, 190, 218–19; in Libya, 260; in Morocco, 281, 299; in the Occupied Territories, 314; Tunisian, 381, 398; in Yemen, 437

Government, representation in: in Algeria, 27–28; in Egypt, 86; in Jordan, 218–20; in Morocco, 300; in Tunisia, 397

Great Britain, colonialism by: of Bahrain, 43; of Iraq, 150; in Saudi Arabia, 340; in Yemen, 438

Gross Domestic Product (GDP): of Algeria, 16; of Bahrain, 48; of Jordan, 196; of Libya, 260, 267; in the Occupied Territories, 317, 319; of Tunisia, 381–82

Gross National Product (GNP): of Algeria, 16; of Iraq, 155; of Jordan, 197; in Yemen, 438

Guardian, male (*iwaliī*): in Algeria, 23, 25, 33; in Iran, 118, 134–35; in Jordan, 200; in Lebanon, 246; in Morocco, 284, 292, 307; in the Occupied Territories, 318; in Saudi Arabia, 344, 350; in Syria, 367; in UAE, 414; in Yemen, 447, 455. *See also* Law; Marriage; Law, Personal Status; Rights; Segregation and separation; Transportation, women's access to; Travel, women's right to

Gulf War, effect of: on Jordan, 198

Hamas (Movement of Islamic Resistance): in Algeria, 32

Hammân (public bath): in Tunisia, 391, 400. *See also* Women, meeting places of

Harassment, in the workplace: in Algeria, 21; in Bahrain, 49; in Iraq, 153; in Israel, 171; in Jordan, 204; in Lebanon, 250; in Saudi Arabia, 344, 350; in Yemen, 445

Harassment, sexual: in Egypt, 75–76, 97; in Iran, 109, 114–15; in Israel, 179; in Jordan, 204; in Morocco, 288; in Saudi Arabia, 344, 345; in Tunisia, 387; in Yemen, 454. *See also* Rape; Violence, sexual

Healing, traditional practice of: in Algeria, 31–32; in Tunisia, 400–401; in Yemen, 460–61

Health, CEDAW's influence on: in Algeria, 26

Health, mental: in the Occupied Territories, 326–27, 332; in Syria, 370; in Yemen, 454. *See also* Illness, mental

Health, reproductive: in Algeria, 23; in Israel, 176; in Jordan, 214; in Syria, 369, 376; in Tunisia 392, 394–95. *See also* Reproduction; Pregnancy, prenatal care

Health, safety standards at work: Tunisian, 387. *See also* Leave

Health, sexuality and: in Lebanon, 249; in the Occupied Territories, 323; in Syria, 371; in Tunisia, 392, 400. *See also* Family planning; Genitals, cutting/mutilation of; HIV/AIDS; Sex, education programs regarding

Health care programs: in Bahrain, 54; in Iran, 123; in Iraq, 159; in Israel, 172, 176; in Jordan, 204, 214, 216; in Lebanon, 249; in Morocco, 297, 298, 299; in Syria, 369; in Tunisia, 392, 396, 400–401; in UAE, 421. *See also* Family planning; HIV/AIDS; Poverty; Sex, education programs regarding; Water, access to clean; Waste treatment

Health care, access to: in Algeria, 26; in Bahrain, 54; in Egypt, 82; in Iran, 123; in Iraq, 156, 157, 159; in Israel, 176; in Jordan, 214; in Lebanon, 249; in Libya, 270; in Morocco, 296; in the Occupied Territories, 324–25, 327, 332; in Saudi Ara-

INDEX

bia, 349; in Syria, 369; in Tunisia, 394–95, 400–401; in UAE, 420–21; in Yemen, 452. *See also* Healing, traditional practice of; Medicine, access to; Mortality

Health care, professionals: in Egypt, 76; in Israel, 176; in Morocco, 297; in the Occupied Territories, 325; in Syria, 369; Tunisia, 392–93, 394–95, 396; in Yemen, 452. *See also* Genitals, cutting/mutilation of; Physicians

Heterosexuality and STDs: in Egypt, 84; in Tunisia, 395

Hijab. *See* Veiling

HIV/AIDS: in Algeria, 25, 26; in Bahrain, 54–55; in Egypt, 84–85; in Iran, 121, 123, 124, 129; in Jordan, 214–15; in Lebanon, 250; in Libya, 270; in Morocco, 297, 298; in the Occupied Territories, 326; in Saudi Arabia, 349; in Tunisia, 395; in UAE, 421; in Yemen, 453

Homosexuality: in Bahrain, 60; in Egypt, 84; in Iran, 129; in Iraq, 163; in Israel, 179–80; in Libya, 273; in Morocco, 303; in the Occupied Territories, 329; in Tunisia, 399; in UAE, 420; in Yemen, 459. *See also* Adoption by homosexuals; Rights, transgender

Honor killings. *See* Adultery; Chastity; Fidelity; Murder, of women; Violence

Honor, family: in Bahrain, 52; in Egypt, 75–76, 97; in Iran, 115, 123; in Iraq, 153, 165; in Jordan, 210, 224, 226–27; in Lebanon, 246, 248, 249; in Libya, 269, 275; in Morocco, 292, 293, 307; in the Occupied Territories, 324; in Syria, 363, 366, 374; in Tunisia, 390. *See* Abaya; Adultery; Chastity; Fidelity; Murder, of women; Veiling; Violence, domestic; Virginity

Hotlines, for domestic violence: in Tunisia, 402. *See also* Women, shelters for

Households, female-headed: in Algeria, 24; in Iran, 120; in Jordan, 207; in Morocco, 286; in the Occupied Territories, 319, 320, 323; in Syria, 357; in Tunisia, 391–92; in Yemen, 447

Housing: in Syria, 365–66. *See also* Family, extended; Women, unmarried

Human Rights Watch: in Bahrain, 56

Human Rights. *See* Rights, human

Illiteracy: in Algeria, 18; in Bahrain, 45, 46, 47; in Egypt, 69; in Iran, 126; in Iraq, 151–52; in Jordan, 195; in Libya, 264; in the Occupied Territories, 316–17; in Saudi Arabia, 342; in Syria, 360–361, 364; in Tunisia, 385; in UAE, 414, 418; in Yemen, 439. *See also* Literacy

Illness, mental: in Algeria, 25, 26; in Bahrain, 55; in Iran, 125; in Israel, 176; in Jordan, 216; in Lebanon, 249; in Morocco, 298; in Tunisia, 397, 406 n.67

ILO. *See* International Labor Organization

Immigration: to Israel, 179. *See also* Refugees

Immunization. *See* Medicine, access to

Incest: in Iran, 123, 134; in Jordan, 226, 228; in Yemen, 462. *See also* Children, molestation of; Violence

Income. *See* Earnings, woman's control of; Pay

Independence, achievement of political: Algeria from France, 15, 29; Bahrain from Great Britain, 44; Tunisia from France, 381, 390

Industry: in Algeria, 17–18, 19; in Iran, 117; in Israel, 174. *See also* Manufacturing; Textiles

Infanticide, female: in Algeria, 16, 26; in UAE, 420

Infants, postnatal care: in Tunisia, 394. *See* Mortality, infant rate

Infertility: in Egypt, 81, 84; in Iran, 122; in Tunisia, 392, 395, 397. *See also* Divorce; Repudiation

Inheritance, right of: in Algeria, 22; in Bahrain, 50, 61; in Egypt, 72, 77; in Iran, 116; in Iraq, 154, 162, 164; in Jordan, 205; in Lebanon, 245; in Libya, 266; in Morocco, 288, 289; in the Occupied Territories, 318–19; in Syria, 362–63; in Tunisia, 389; in UAE, 416; in Yemen, 447. *See also* Law, Personal Status; Property, right to own

Injury, workplace compensation from: in Bahrain, 51; in Tunisia, 387

International Conference of Population and Development (ICPD, 1994), participation at: Egypt, 77, 82, 87

International Labor Organization (ILO), effect of: in Bahrain, 49

International Monetary Fund (IMF): in Egypt, 87; in Jordan, 196

International Women's Day: in Tunisia, 399

Intifada. *See* Palestinians, resistance movement of

Islam. *See* Hamas (Movement of Islamic Resistance); Fundamentalism; Law; Population, religious; Rights; Shi'ism; Sunni; Veiling

Italy, colonialism by: in Libya, 260

IUDs (intrauterine devices). *See* Contraception; Family planning

Judaism: in Egypt, 94; in Iran, 137; in Israel, 169, 174, 175; in Morocco, 304; in the Occupied Territories, 314; in Saudi Arabia, 348; in Syria, 372; in Yemen, 438

Judges, women as: in Egypt, 88, 92; in Iran, 113; in Jordan, 219; in Libya, 272; in Saudi Arabia,

[473]

352; in Syria, 359; in UAE, 422; in Yemen, 438, 443

Kidnapping, of women and children: in Algeria, 34. *See also* Children, trafficking in; Children, molestation of; Trafficking; Slavery; Violence

Labor Code: Tunisian, 385
Labor, laws regarding: in Bahrain, 48–49; in Yemen, 446. *See also* Child care; Gender, work and; Reform, legal; Work
Labor. *See* Employment; Work; Workforce
Language, in commerce: in Tunisia, 382; in UAE, 413
Language, in education: in Iran, 110; in Iraq, 151; in Tunisia, 382; in UAE, 412, 413
Language, predominant: in Algeria, 19, 30; in Iraq, 150; in the Occupied Territories, 314; in Syria, 357; in Tunisia, 382; in UAE, 412
Language, societal and political choices in: in Egypt, 90; in Morocco, 310 n.21
Law, civil: in Algeria, 22; in Bahrain, 51; in Iraq, 160; in Israel, 179, 182; in Jordan, 203, 204, 216, 220–21, 222; in Morocco, 300, 307; in the Occupied Territories, 328, 329, 330; in Tunisia, 382, 389, 391, 401, 402–03, 404 n.3; in UAE, 416, 422
Law, Islamic (*shari'a*): in Algeria, 15, 22, 23, 26, 31, 37 n.24; in Bahrain, 50, 56, 60, 61, 62; in Egypt, 73, 77, 91, 94, 97; in Iran, 127, 128, 133, 135; in Iraq, 160, 163, 164; in Jordan, 220, 222, 225; in Libya, 260, 274; in Morocco, 293, 300; in the Occupied Territories, 318, 321; in Saudi Arabia, 351; in Syria, 362; in Tunisia, 389, 390, 391, 404 n.3; in UAE, 416; in Yemen, 440, 447, 461. *See also* Citizenship; Gender; Fundamentalism; Law, civil;

Marriage; Polygamy; Religion; Shi'ism; Sunnism
Law, Jewish: in Israel, 175, 176, 182
Law, Personal Status (PSL): in Egypt, 85, 87, 88, 91, 92, 96; in Jordan, 221; in Morocco, 301, 303; in the Occupied Territories, 328; in Saudi Arabia, 351; in Yemen, 451, 461–62. *See also* Code, Algerian Family; Code, Personal Status
Law, religious: in Algeria, 22, 26, 27; in Israel, 182–83; in Jordan, 222; in Libya, 260, 274; in Morocco, 300, 304, 310 n.13; in the Occupied Territories, 331; in Syria, 373. *See also* Law, Islamic
Law, tribal. *See* Tribes, laws and traditions of
Leave, family and medical: in Tunisia, 388–89
Leave, maternal and paternal: in Algeria, 22; in Bahrain, 49, 50; in Egypt, 71, 72; in Iran, 115; in Iraq, 153, 154; in Israel, 174; in Jordan, 204; in Lebanon, 245; in Morocco, 288; in Tunisia 388–89; in UAE, 414; in Yemen, 446
Lesbianism: in Algeria, 31; in Bahrain, 60; in Egypt, 93; in Iran, 129; in Iraq, 163; in Israel, 179; in Jordan, 224; in Libya, 273; in Morocco, 303; in the Occupied Territories, 329; in Saudi Arabia, 351; in Tunisia, 399; in Yemen, 459. *See also* Adoption by homosexuals
Life, expectancy rate: in Algeria, 16; in Bahrain, 44; in Egypt, 68; in Israel, 176; in Jordan, 190; in Lebanon, 241; in Morocco, 282, 297; in the Occupied Territories, 314; in Saudi Arabia, 338; in Syria, 369; in Tunisia, 382
Literacy campaigns: in Bahrain, 46, 47, 59; in Iran, 110; in Iraq, 151–52; in Jordan, 195; in UAE, 414
Literacy, effect on employment:

in Bahrain, 45, 46; in Lebanon, 244; in Morocco, 285; in Saudi Arabia, 341. *See also* Illiteracy
Literacy, politics and: in Iran, 127, 129; in Iraq, 151–52; in Tunisia, 398
Literacy rates: in Algeria, 18; in Egypt, 69; in Iran, 112; in Iraq, 152; in Lebanon, 244; in Libya, 264; in the Occupied Territories, 315; in Saudi Arabia, 342; in Syria, 360–61; in Tunisia, 385; in Yemen, 442
Living, arrangements of. *See* Family; Housing
Loans, monetary: in UAE, 417. *See also* Credit, obtaining; Government, credit programs by

Malnutrition: in Algeria, 26; in Yemen, 440, 453. *See also* Anemia; Food availability; Health
Manufacturing, employment in: in Jordan, 198; in Lebanon, 244; in Morocco, 285; Tunisian women in, 385; in Yemen, 443. *See also* Industry; Textiles
Maraboutism: in Algeria, 31–32, 33. *See also* Religion; Rituals
Marriage, arranged: in Iran, 135; in Iraq, 156; in Jordan, 228; in Libya, 269; in the Occupied Territories, 322, 332; in Saudi Arabia, 346–48; in UAE, 418; in Yemen, 449
Marriage, civil law regarding: in Bahrain, 52; in Egypt, 91; in Iraq, 164; in Israel, 175; in Libya, 268; in Tunisia, 391, 392. *See also* Dowry
Marriage, consanguineous: in Egypt, 78; in Syria, 364; in Tunisia, 391; in UAE, 418
Marriage, delay of: in Algeria, 24; in Bahrain, 45; in Iran, 136; in Jordan, 210; in Morocco, 292; in the Occupied Territories, 322; in Syria, 367; in Tunisia, 391
Marriage, family income and: in Bahrain, 48; in Israel, 171–73; in Morocco, 291; in Tunisia, 383, 389. *See also* Earnings, woman's control of; Inheri-

[474]

tance, right of; Pay; Property, right to own

Marriage, minimum age of: in Egypt, 83; in Iran, 123, 135; in Jordan, 194, 209–10; in Libya, 269; in Morocco, 291–92; in the Occupied Territories, 322, 324; in Syria, 367; in Tunisia, 383, 390, 393–94; in UAE, 418; in Yemen, 451

Marriage, religious law and: in Algeria, 23; in Bahrain, 52, 61; in Egypt, 77, 91; in Iran, 119–20; in Iraq, 164; in Lebanon, 248; in Libya, 268; in the Occupied Territories, 318, 322; in Tunisia, 390, 391, 398. *See also* Contract, marriage; Betrothal; Divorce; Dowry

Marriage, temporary: in Algeria, 33; in Iran, 120, 129, 135. *See also* Kidnapping; Slavery, sexual; Trafficking, of women

Marriage: in Bahrain, 52; in Lebanon, 246; in Morocco, 292; in the Occupied Territories, 318; in Saudi Arabia, 347–48; in Syria, 373; in UAE, 418, 425; in Yemen, 449–50, 461. *See also* Adultery; Chastity; Children, custodial rights concerning; Contracts, marriage; Divorce; Fidelity; Households, women as heads; Housing; Gender; Murder, of women; Remarriage; Ritual, marriage as; Virginity; Violence; Women, unmarried

Media, as feminist tool: in Iran, 126, 128, 129; in Jordan, 220; in Morocco, 308; in Yemen, 455, 458

Media, control of: in Bahrain, 56; in Egypt, 87; in Jordan, 191, 197, 220; in Saudi Arabia, 345; in Yemen, 456–57

Medicine, access to: in Algeria, 26; in Iraq, 159; in Morocco, 297, 298; in the Occupied Territories, 324; in Saudi Arabia, 348; in UAE, 420–21; in Yemen, 452–53. *See also* Health

Menstruation, rituals and: in Egypt, 95, in Iran, 131–32; in Libya, 265; in Morocco, 291–92; in Saudi Arabia, 352; in UAE, 425

Menstruation, work and: in Libya, 265

Migration, male labor: in Egypt, 83; in Iran, 120; in Jordan, 195, 197; in Syria, 361. *See also* Diseases, sexually transmitted; HIV/AIDS; Households, female-headed

Military campaigns. *See* Checkpoints; Curfews; Travel; Water, access to fresh; Waste, treatment of

Military, repression by: in Algeria, 35; in Iran, 136–37; in Iraq, 165

Military, service in: Algeria, 20, 31; Bahrain, 60; Egypt, 93; in Iran, 129; in Iraq, 152, 163; in Israel, 180–82; in Jordan, 224–25; in Libya, 271, 272, 273–74, 275–76; in Saudi Arabia, 350; Tunisia, 400; in UAE, 424; in Yemen, 459–60

Mining: in Syria, 357–58

Mortality, child rate: in Egypt, 82; in Iran, 122; in Iraq, 159; in Jordan, 191, 214; in Morocco, 282, 283; in Syria, 369; in Yemen, 438

Mortality, infant rate: in Algeria, 17, 26; in Egypt, 68; in Iran, 107; in Iraq, 158, 159–60; in Jordan, 190; in Libya, 260; in Morocco, 282, 283, 295; in the Occupied Territories, 314; in Saudi Arabia, 338; in Tunisia, 382; in UAE, 412

Mortality, maternal rate: in Algeria, 17; in Egypt, 68, 82; in Iran, 107; in Morocco, 282, 295; in the Occupied Territories, 314–15; in Tunisia, 395; in Yemen, 438, 453

Mothers. *See* Breastfeeding, during employment or school; Children; Family; Gender; Leave, maternal and paternal; Work

Moudjahidates. *See* Freedom fighters

Murder, of women: in Algeria, 33, 35; in Egypt, 96, 97; in Iraq, 164–65; in Jordan, 210, 216, 224, 226–27; in Lebanon, 248; in Morocco, 301, 307; in the Occupied Territories, 324, 332; in Tunisia, 401. *See also* Honor, family; Violence

Narcotics, use of. *See* Drug use

Nationals vs. expatriates: in UAE, 412. *See also* Citizenship

NGOs and credit programs: in Tunisia, 389, 390

NGOs and environmental issues: in Tunisia, 390

NGOs and health programs: in Bahrain, 54; in Jordan, 225; in Tunisia, 392, 395

NGOs and literacy programs: in Bahrain, 461–70

NGOs and social services: in Iran, 117, 134; in Jordan, 201–2, 206, 223–24; in Syria, 376; in Yemen, 448

NGOs and women's organizations: in Algeria, 30; in Jordan, 206–7, 223–24, 225; in the Occupied Territories, 321

NGOs as support from domestic violence: in Egypt, 97–98; in Jordan, 225; in Tunisia, 402

Nomads: in Iran, 118; in Jordan, 190; in Libya, 268; in UAE, 425. *See also* Bedouins; Berbers; Clans; Tribes, laws and traditions of

Non-governmental organizations. *See* NGOs

Nursing. *See* Health care access

Obesity: in Egypt, 85; in Tunisia, 396

OECD (Organization for Economic Cooperation and Development), influence of: in Bahrain, 51

OECD. *See* Organization for Economic Cooperation and Development

[475]

INDEX

OIC (Organization of the Islamic Conference): in Syria, 358
Oil industry: in Algeria, 15, 24, 35; in Bahrain, 47, 48, 51; in Iran, 111; in Iraq, 152, 154, 161; Jordan's export of workers to, 195, 197; in Libya, 261, 267; in Saudi Arabia, 337, 338; in UAE, 412
Organizations, Algerian women's, 27, 29–30
Organizations, Bahrainian women's, 47, 54, 58, 59, 60
Organizations, Egyptian women's, 87, 89–90
Organizations, Iranian women's, 117
Organizations, Iraqi women's, 151, 154, 162
Organizations, Jordanian women's, 216, 223, 224. *See also* UNIFEM (United Nations Development Fund for Women)
Organizations, Lebanese women's, 241, 245, 250, 251
Organizations, Libyan women's, 269, 272, 273
Organizations, Moroccan women's, 302, 309
Organizations, Palestinian women's, 327–28
Organizations, Saudi women's, 348
Organizations, Syrian women's, 359, 373, 375–76
Organizations, Tunisian women's, 385, 388, 390, 398, 399, 402, 406 n.59
Organizations, UAE women's, 412, 413, 414, 415, 421, 423
Organizations, Yemeni women's, 439, 454, 455, 456, 457, 458
Orphanages: in Iran, 117
Ottoman Empire, part of: Algeria, 32; Jordan, 190; Lebanon, 240, 241, 243; Libya, 260; Morocco, 310; Syria, 358; Yemen, 441
Ownership. *See* Property, right to own

Palestinians, as refugees: in Jordan, 193, 198–99; in Lebanon, 239

Palestinians, resistance movement of: in Jordan, 223; in the Occupied Territories, 315, 318, 323, 325, 327–28, 329. *See also* Bombings, suicide
Parties, political: Algeria, 30; in Iraq, 151, 153, 154, 157–58, 160, 161; in Jordan, 217–18; in the Occupied Territories, 328; in Syria, 358; in Tunisia, 381, 397–99, 406 n.59. *See also* Communism; Organizations
Patriarchy: in Israel, 175, 177; in Jordan, 208–9; in Libya, 268; in Saudi Arabia, 344–45, 346–47. *See also* Gender, public v. private roles
Pay, formal workforce: in Iran, 113, 114; in Iraq, 152–53; in Israel, 171, 172; in Jordan, 200, 202, 203–4; in Lebanon, 241; in Morocco, 282, 286; in Syria, 362; in Tunisia, 386; in Yemen, 438, 444
Pay, informal workforce: in Jordan, 198, 199; in Morocco, 286, 287; in Tunisia, 386; in UAE, 416, 417
Pay, minimum wage standards of: in Egypt, 71; in Israel, 173; in Jordan, 204; in Morocco, 286, 287; in the Occupied Territories, 318; in Tunisia, 386, 387
Pay: in Algeria, 20, 21; in Bahrain, 48, 49; Egypt, 77; in Iran, 110, 114; in Iraq, 152, 153; in Israel, 171, 173, 174; in Jordan, 201, 203–4; in Lebanon, 245; in Libya, 265; in the Occupied Territories, 318; in Saudi Arabia, 343–44; in Yemen, 444. *See also* Benefits, work; Earnings, woman's control of; Employment; Leave, maternal and paternal; Teens, school v. work
Penal code. *See* Code, penal
Pension, benefits: in Iraq, 154; in Israel, 171; in Jordan, 207; in Libya, 267; in Morocco, 303; in Tunisia, 387. *See also* Retirement
Personal status code. *See* Code, personal status (CSP)

Physicians and sexual health: in Egypt, 78; in Jordan, 214; in Tunisia, 392–93
Physicians: in Israel, 176; in Jordan, 214; in Saudi Arabia, 348; in Syria, 374; in Tunisia, 386, 394, 400–401. *See also* Health care access; Health care, service professionals in
Pilgrimage, religious: from Egypt, 95; from Iran, 130, 132–33; from Libya, 274; from Morocco, 304, 305, 306; from Yemen, 460. *See also* Menstruation, rituals and; Rituals
Police, women as: in Algeria, 20, 31; in Iraq, 152, 163; in UAE, 417, 424
Political organizations. *See* Organizations, women's political; Parties, political
Politics, participation: in Algeria, 27–28, 29; in Bahrain, 57–58; in Egypt, 85–86, 90; in Iran, 108, 109, 126, 127; in Iraq, 161, 162; in Israel, 177; in Jordan, 217–18, 219, 220; in Lebanon, 250; in Libya, 271; in Saudi Arabia, 349–50; in Syria, 370–71, 376; in Tunisia, 385, 397–98; in UAE, 423; in Yemen, 454–55
Politics. *See* Fundamentalism, religious, and politics; Law, Islamic; Organizations, women's political; Reform, political; Religion and politics
Pollution. *See* Environment, policies and issues regarding; Waste treatment; Water, access to clean
Polygamy: in Algeria, 24; in Bahrain, 52, 61; in Egypt, 79–80, 84, 90, 91–92; in Iran, 120, 125; in Iraq, 156, 164; in Jordan, 207, 210, 221; in Libya, 269; in Morocco, 292, 294; in Saudi Arabia, 347; in Syria, 367; in Tunisia, 383, 390, 406 n.67; in UAE, 419; in Yemen, 461, 462. *See also* Law; Marriage
Polygyny. *See* Polygamy
Population, religious: in Algeria, 15; in Bahrain, 43; in Iran, 130; in Iraq, 150; in Israel, 169; in

[476]

INDEX

Lebanon, 240; in the Occupied Territories, 314; in Syria, 356, 372; in Tunisia, 382; in UAE, 412

Population, sex ratios of: in Algeria, 16, 25–26; in Bahrain, 44; in Iran, 107; in Israel, 169; in Jordan, 190; in Libya, 260; in the Occupied Territories, 314; in Saudi Arabia, 338; in Syria, 357

Population: in Egypt, 67; in Iraq, 150; in Lebanon, 239, 241; in Libya, 259; in Morocco, 282; in the Occupied Territories, 314; in Syria, 356; in Tunisia, 382. *See also* International Conference of Population and Development

Poverty: in Jordan, 197; in Morocco, 299; in the Occupied Territories, 318; in Tunisia, 386. *See also* Health; Malnutrition; Waste treatment; Water, access to clean

Pregnancy, adolescent: in Algeria, 25; in Bahrain, 54; in Egypt, 82; in Iran, 123; in Jordan, 213; in Libya, 270; in Morocco, 296; in the Occupied Territories, 324; in Saudi Arabia, 348–49; in Tunisia, 393–94; in Yemen, 451

Pregnancy, out-of-wedlock: in Algeria, 25; in Israel, 176; in Jordan, 213, 228; in Morocco, 295–96, 309; in Saudi Arabia, 348; in Tunisia, 394. *See also* Women, unmarried, health care for

Pregnancy, prenatal care: in Algeria, 24–25, 26, 37 n.33; in Iraq, 166; in Jordan, 214, 215; in the Occupied Territories, 324; in Tunisia, 394. *See also* Family planning; Health, reproductive; Reproduction

Pregnancy, work and. *See* Health, safety standards at work

Property, right to own: in Algeria, 22, 23; in Bahrain, 50; Egypt, 77, 93; in Iran, 116; in Iraq, 154, 164; in Jordan, 205; in Lebanon, 245; in Libya, 266; in Morocco, 289; in Tunisia, 389; in UAE, 416; in Yemen, 447. *See also* Dowry; Inheritance, right of

Prostitution: in Bahrain, 62; in Egypt, 83, 98; in Iran, 128, 134, 135; in Morocco, 296, 298, 308; in Tunisia, 403. *See also* Pregnancy, out-of-wedlock; Slavery, sexual

PSL. *See* Law, Personal Status (PSL)

Public, women in. *See* Gender, public v. private roles

Qat. *See* Drug use

Qu'ran, interpretation of: in Bahrain, 61; in Egypt, 78, 86; in Iraq, 163; in Morocco, 304; in the Occupied Territories, 330; in Syria, 372; in UAE, 419, 420

Ramadan: in Egypt, 95; in Iran, 132; in Iraq, 163; in Libya, 265, 274; in Morocco, 304, 305, 306

Rape: in Bahrain, 62; in Egypt, 97; in Iran, 134, 137; in Iraq, 165; in Israel, 176; in Jordan, 226, 228; in Lebanon, 249, 252; in Libya, 275; in Morocco, 296; in the Occupied Territories, 332; in Syria, 375; in Tunisia, 402–3; in UAE, 425; in Yemen, 462

Rape, marital: in Iran, 133, 134; in Jordan, 226; in Lebanon, 252, 253; in Morocco, 308; in Syria, 374; in Tunisia, 403; in Yemen, 462

Reform, economic: in Bahrain, 62; in Iran, 107; in Jordan, 196; in Syria, 363; in Tunisia, 382

Reform, education: in Iran, 107, 110–11, 127; in Jordan, 192; in Tunisia, 384

Reform, legal: in Bahrain, 61; in Iran, 122, 127; in Iraq, 156; in Lebanon, 250; in Morocco, 301; in Saudi Arabia, 349; in Tunisia, 382, 384, 385, 388, 390, 392. *See also* Environment, policies and issues regarding

Reform, political: in Egypt, 86, 90; in Iran, 127; in Iraq, 156; in Lebanon, 250; in Tunisia, 381

Refugees: in Jordan, 193, 198–99, 200; in Lebanon, 240, 251; in the Occupied Territories, 314, 320–21; in Syria, 360. *See also* Palestinians, as refugees

Religion, law and. *See also* Law, civil; Law, Islamic

Religion, politics and: in Bahrain, 57–58; in Iran, 133; in Jordan, 222, 224; in Saudi Arabia, 340–41, 342, 344–45, 348, 350; in Syria, 373; in Yemen, 460. *See also* Fundamentalism, religious, and politics; Organizations, women's political; Reform, political

Religion, women's rights and; in Egypt, 93, 94, 95; in Iran, 127–29; in Israel, 174; in Jordan, 212, 222, 225; in Lebanon, 246, 251; in Libya, 274; in Saudi Arabia, 340, 341–42; in Tunisia, 391; in Yemen, 460

Remarriage: in Morocco, 292, 294, 295; in the Occupied Territories, 323; in Syria, 364; in Tunisia, 391

Repression: in Iran, 137–38; in Iraq, 155, 156, 157, 162; in Jordan, 218, 219–20; in Saudi Arabia, 346, 348–49, 350

Reproduction: in Algeria, 24–25; in Bahrain, 53; in Iraq, 153, 157; in Israel, 175, 176; in Jordan, 209; in Tunisia, 390, 391–94; in UAE, 420; in Yemen, 450–51. *See also* Family planning; Fertility, rate of; Health, reproductive; Infertility; Pregnancy, prenatal care

Repudiation: in Algeria, 23; in Egypt, 78; in Libya, 269; in Syria, 367; in Tunisia, 383, 390, 391, 406 n.67; in UAE, 419; in Yemen, 461. *See also* Divorce

Retirement, benefits: in Algeria, 21; in Bahrain, 51; in Egypt, 71; in Iraq, 153; in Israel, 182; in Jordan, 207; in Lebanon, 245; in Libya, 267; in Morocco, 303; in Tunisia, 387–88. *See also* Pension, benefits

Rights, constitutional: in Algeria, 23, 28, 29; in Bahrain, 44, 57; in Egypt, 91–92; in Jordan, 218.

INDEX

See also Employment, right to; Transportation, women's access to; Travel, women's right to

Rights, economic: in Algeria, 24; in Tunisia, 389. *See also* Earnings, woman's control of; Law, Islamic; Property, right to own; Social security

Rights, human: in Jordan, 218, 225; in Morocco, 300; in Saudi Arabia, 350; in Yemen, 455

Rights, transgender: in Tunisia, 399. *See also* Bisexuals, rights of; Homosexuality; Lesbianism

Rights, women's. *See* Elections; Equality, gender; Feminism; Inheritance, right of; Law; Politics, participation in; Property, right to own; Suffrage

Rights, workplace: in Iraq, 162; in Tunisia, 385, 387. *See also* Discrimination, gender-based; Employment; Family, and medical leave; Harassment, sexual; Leave, maternal and paternal; Work

Rights. *See* Children, rights of; Divorce; Suffrage; Travel, right to

Ritual, wedding as: in Israel, 175; in Morocco, 292–93; in Tunisia, 400; in UAE, 418–19

Rituals, female: in Iraq, 164; in Morocco, 304; in Tunisia, 400–401; in Yemen, 461. *See also* Maraboutism

Rituals, religious: in Egypt, 95, 100 n.50; in Iran, 130, 131, 132; in Iraq, 163–64; in Lebanon, 251; in Libya, 274; in Morocco, 304, 305, 306–7; in Saudi Arabia, 352; in Tunisia, 400–401; in UAE, 424; in Yemen, 460, 461. *See also* Healing, traditional practices of; Maraboutism; Menstruation, rituals and

Rural-urban disparities, in contraception and family planning: in Algeria, 25; in Egypt, 81, 83; in Jordan, 212; in Tunisia, 393

Rural-urban disparities, in education: in Iran, 110; in Iraq, 156; in Jordan, 194; in Libya, 263; in Morocco, 283, 285; in the Occupied Territories, 321; in Tunisia, 384

Rural-urban disparities, in health: in Egypt, 82; in Jordan, 197; in Morocco, 297; in Tunisia, 395, 397; in Yemen, 438, 453

Rural-urban disparities, in marriage: in Egypt, 83; in Saudi Arabia, 347; in Syria, 364; in Tunisia, 391, 392; in UAE, 418

Rural-urban disparities, in rituals and events: in Iran, 130–31; in Syria, 373; in Tunisia, 400; in Yemen, 448–49

Rural-urban disparities, in work: in Syria, 361; in Yemen, 448–49

Safety, work. *See* Health, safety standards at work

Salaries. *See* Earnings, woman's control of; Pay

Sanctions, against Iraq: 153, 154, 158, 159, 160, 166; against Libya, 265

Sanitation: in Syria, 369; in Yemen, 452–53. *See also* Education, environmental; Environment; Health; Waste, treatment of; Water, access to clean

School, drop-out rates: in Egypt, 69; in the Occupied Territories, 315–16; in Tunisia, 384; in Yemen, 441

School, enrollment: in Algeria, 18; in Bahrain, 44; in Egypt, 68–69; in Iran, 110, 131; in Iraq, 151; in Jordan, 192–93; in Libya, 262–63; in Morocco, 283; in Saudi Arabia, 341; in Syria, 360; in Tunisia, 384, 385; in Yemen, 440. *See* Education

School, transportation to: in Algeria, 18, 23; in Bahrain, 46; in Jordan, 194; in Morocco, 283, 284; in Yemen, 441

School, work versus: in Jordan, 194; in Tunisia, 387

Segregation and separation: in Algeria, 34, 35; in Bahrain, 60; Egypt, 78, 89, 94, 96; in Iran, 110, 111, 118, 131, 132; in Israel, 172, 174; in Jordan, 202, 222; in Morocco, 284, 286, 291, 304–5; in Saudi Arabia, 341–42, 343–44, 345–46, 352; in UAE, 413, 424; in Yemen, 441, 450, 448–49, 450. *See also* Fundamentalism; Guardians; Law, Islamic

Self-employment: in Jordan, 199; in Morocco, 290; in the Occupied Territories, 318; in Syria, 361–62; in UAE, 415. *See also* Crafts; Entrepreneurship; Workforce, informal

Service sector. *See* Employment, in service sector

Services, social: in Iran, 117; in Libya, 267; in Tunisia, 390. *See also* Welfare, programs in

Sex, education programs regarding: in Algeria, 25; in Bahrain, 53; in Egypt, 81; in Iran, 121; in Libya, 270; in the Occupied Territories, 323; in Syria, 368; in Tunisia, 392, 395

Sex, extra- and premarital: in Egypt, 83, 84; in Iran, 139; in Jordan, 226; in Lebanon, 248; in Libya, 270; in Morocco, 292, 296; in the Occupied Territories, 332; in Syria, 368; in Tunisia, 401; in Yemen, 462

Sex, tourism in: in Egypt, 84, 98; Tunisia, 403

Sexuality and identity: in Egypt, 74–75; in Iran, 118, 119; in Iraq, 157; in the Occupied Territories, 321. *See also* Gender

Sexuality. *See* Bisexuals; Chastity; Diseases, sexually transmitted; Health; Heterosexuality and STDs; Lesbianism; Rape; Rituals, religious; Rights, transgender; Sex, education programs regarding; Violence

Shari'a. *See* Law, Islamic

Shi'ism: in Bahrain, 50, 52; in Iran, 106, 116–17, 137; in Iraq, 150, 157, 161; in Syria, 372; in UAE, 424; in Yemen, 438, 460

Slavery, sexual: in Algeria, 17, 33, 34; in Bahrain, 62; in Tunisia, 403

INDEX

Slavery: in Tunisia, 403
Social security: in Algeria, 24; in Bahrain, 51; in Iran, 114, 115, 116, 123; in Israel, 173; in Jordan, 207; in Morocco, 289; in UAE, 416–17. *See also* Welfare, programs in
Socialism: in Algeria, 26
Speech, freedom of: in Algeria, 20, 27. *See also* Media; Rights, constitutional
Sports, women in: in Algeria, 20; in Iraq, 151; in Syria, 366
STDs. *See* Diseases, sexually transmitted
Sterilization: in Tunisia, 393. *See also* Contraception; Family planning
Suffrage: in Algeria, 27; in Bahrain, 56–57; in Egypt, 85–86, 90; in Iran, 108, 125; in Iraq, 161; in Israel, 177; in Jordan, 217; in Lebanon, 240, 251; in Libya, 270–71; in Morocco, 299; in the Occupied Territories, 327; in Saudi Arabia, 349; in Syria, 370; in Tunisia, 397; in UAE, 422; in Yemen, 438, 454. *See also* Electoral process; Politics, participation in
Suicide. *See* Bombings, suicide; Health, mental; Illness, mental
Sunnism: in Algeria, 32; in Bahrain, 50, 52; in Iran, 106, 137; in Iraq, 150, 157, 161; in Saudi Arabia, 344; in Syria, 372; in UAE, 424; in Yemen, 438, 460
Sustainable development: in Algeria, 22–23; in Bahrain, 50–51; in Iran, 117; in Iraq, 154; in Jordan, 206–7; in Libya, 267; in Syria, 363; in Tunisia, 390

Teachers. *See* Education; Employment; Training
Teens, marriage rate of: in Iran, 123; in Jordan, 213; in Libya, 270; in Morocco, 296; in Syria, 368; in Tunisia, 394. *See also* Chastity; Health, reproductive; Marriage; Pregnancy, adolescent; Sex, education programs regarding; Virginity

Teens, school v. work: in Jordan, 194; in Tunisia, 387. *See also* Education; Employment, domestic service sector; School
Teens, working mothers with: in Jordan, 194; in Libya, 270; in Tunisia, 387–88
Textiles, employment in: in Morocco, 285, 286; and Tunisian women, 386; minimum work age, 387. *See also* Industry, Manufacturing, employment in
Torture, of women: in Algeria, 34, 35; in Bahrain, 35; in Iran, 137; in Morocco, 300–301. *See also* Military, repression by; Violence
Tourism, employment in: in Morocco, 285; *See also* Sex, tourism in
Tradition. *See* Abaya; Circumcision, female; Equal rights; Gender; Genitals, cutting/mutilation of; Healing, traditional practices of; Inheritance, right of; Law, Islamic; Marriage; Property, right to own; Rituals, religious; Segregation and separation; Veiling
Trafficking, of women: in Algeria, 34; in Bahrain, 61; in Iran, 134–35, 136; in Iraq, 156; in Jordan, 229; in Morocco, 309; in Tunisia, 403. *See also* Children, molestation of; Kidnapping; Slavery; Violence
Training, teacher: in Algeria, 18; in Iraq, 151; in Israel, 171; in Jordan, 195; in Libya, 263; in Morocco, 283, 284; in Syria, 360; in Tunisia, 383–84; in UAE, 414
Training, types of for females: in Bahrain, 45; in Iraq, 151, 156; in Israel, 171, 182; in Jordan, 202, 206; in Lebanon, 243, 244; in Morocco, 283; in Syria, 360, 376; in Tunisia, 384, 394, 396; in UAE, 416. *See also* Employment, Work
Training, vocational: in Iraq, 151, 156; in Jordan, 206, 228; in Lebanon, 244; in Morocco, 283;
in Syria, 360; in Tunisia, 384; in Yemen, 441, 456
Transportation, women's access to: in Egypt, 76; in Iran, 111; in Iraq, 155; in Jordan, 202; in Saudi Arabia, 344, 345–46, 350; in UAE, 414, 417. *See also* Guardian, male
Travel, right to: in Algeria, 24, 29, 34; in Bahrain, 58; in Egypt, 88; in Iran, 111; in Jordan, 221–22; in Libya, 270; in Morocco, 302; in the Occupied Territories, 319–20, 329; in Saudi Arabia, 341–42, 343–44, 350–51; in Syria, 371; in UAE, 414. *See also* Guardian, male
Tribes, laws and traditions of: in Bahrain, 51, 56; in Iran, 135; in Iraq, 165; in Jordan, 207–8, 216; in Libya, 261, 269; in Syria, 359; in Yemen, 455. *See also* Bedouins; Clans; Feuds, blood; Nomads
Tubal ligation. *See* Sterilization

UAE (United Arab Emirates). *See specific entries*
UN (United Nations), activity in: in Algeria, 20, 22; in Jordan, 223; in Syria, 358, 360. *See also* specific UN organizations; Beijing, Fourth World Conference
UN Decade for Women: in Jordan, 217, 224
UN Economic and Social Council: in UAE, 424
Underemployment, among women: in Bahrain, 48; in Morocco, 286; in Tunisia, 386
UNDP (United Nations Development Program): in Jordan, 196; in Lebanon, 245; in Saudi Arabia, 350
Unemployment, women compared to men: in Egypt, 71; in Iraq, 154; in the Occupied Territories, 317; in Syria, 361; in Tunisia, 386
Unemployment: in Algeria, 29; in Egypt, 73; in Iraq, 154, 155; in Libya, 265; in Morocco, 286; in the Occupied Territories, 319;

[479]

in Syria, 363; in Tunisia, 387.
See also Welfare, programs in
UNESCO (United Nations Educational, Scientific, and Cultural Organization): in Jordan, 192–93, 195
UNICEF: in Iraq, 154; in Jordan, 209; in Lebanon, 249
UNIFEM (United Nations Development Fund for Women): in Jordan, 206–7, 224
Unions: Bahrain and, 59; in Iraq, 153, 159; in Jordan, 225; Tunisian workers and, 386. See also Bargaining, collective; Discrimination, gender-based; Harassment, sexual
United Arab Emirates (UAE). See specific entries
UNRWA (United Nations Relief and Works Agency for Palestine Refugees in the Near East): in Jordan, 193, 198–99, 209; in the Occupied Territories, 315, 324
Urban–rural disparities. See Rural-urban disparities
USAID (U.S. Agency for International Development): in Egypt, 87; in Jordan, 206, 210; in the Occupied Territories, 319, 320

Vaccinations. See Medicine, access to
Vasectomy. See Sterilization
Veiling, 3, 4–7, 9; in Algeria, 17, 33, 36 n.5; in Bahrain, 52; in Egypt, 75–76; in Iran, 110, 111; in Iraq, 156, 164; in Libya, 268; in Morocco, 290; in the Occupied Territories, 330; in Saudi Arabia, 345–47; in Syria, 364, 366; in UAE, 417, 425; in Yemen, 449. See also Abaya
Veiling, politics of: in Egypt, 75–76, 89, 90; in Iran, 114, 125, 126, 128, 136, 137; in Libya, 268; in Saudi Arabia, 346–47; in Syria, 366; in Yemen, 460
Violence against women and children: in Algeria, 26, 33; in Bahrain, 61; in Egypt, 88; in Israel, 182; in Jordan, 226; in Lebanon, 248, 252; in Libya, 275; in Morocco, 301; in the Occupied Territories, 331, 332; in Tunisia, 401; in UAE, 425; in Yemen, 459. See also Children, molestation of; Murder, of women
Violence, domestic: in Bahrain, 61; in Egypt, 96–97; in Iran, 133; in Iraq, 164; in Israel, 175, 183; in Jordan, 226 in Morocco, 301, 307–8; in the Occupied Territories, 323, 331, 332; in Syria, 374; in Tunisia, 397; 401–2, 406 n.67; in UAE, 425. See also Children, molestation of; Health, mental; Incest; Murder, of women; Rape
Violence, sexual: in Algeria, 26; in Egypt, 97–98; in Iraq, 165; in Jordan, 225–26; in Morocco, 308, 309; in Tunisia, 401–2; 403. See also Children, molestation of; Health, mental; Rape
Violence: in Algeria, 21; in Iran, 134. See also Death, by violence; Feuds, blood; Fundamentalism, violence and oppression via; Murder, of women; Rape; Repression
Virginity: in Egypt, 74, 83, 98; in Iran, 121, 123, 134; in Lebanon, 247, 248, 249, 253; in Morocco, 292–93, 305; in the Occupied Territories, 324; in Syria, 368; in Tunisia, 397. See also Chastity; Genitals, cutting/mutilation of; Rape
Vote, right to. See Suffrage

Wages. See Earnings, woman's control of; Pay
War, civil: in Algeria, 15, 20; in Lebanon, 242, 243, 249
War, civil, participation in: Algerian women, 15, 20
War crimes. See Military, repression by; Murder, of women; Rape; Torture
Waste, treatment of: in Iraq, 154, 160; in Morocco, 289, 297; in the Occupied Territories, 320, 325; in Tunisia, 390. Environment, policies and issues regarding
Water, access to clean: in Algeria, 23, 30; in Iraq, 154, 160; in Morocco, 289, 297; in the Occupied Territories, 320, 325, 326; in Tunisia, 390; in UAE, 412. See also Environment, policies and issues regarding
Weddings. See Ritual, wedding as
Welfare, programs in: in Algeria, 23; in Egypt, 73; in Iran, 114, 115, 116, 117; in Iraq, 155–56, 161; in Israel, 173; in Jordan, 204; in Morocco, 289; in the Occupied Territories, 327; in Syria, 376; in Tunisia, 387, 388, 390; in UAE, 416–17; in Yemen, 448, 456
WHO (World Health Organization): in Jordan, 216; in Morocco, 297
Widows: in Algeria, 34; in Egypt, 72; in Iran, 138; in Iraq, 152, 156; in Jordan, 205; in Morocco, 292; in UAE, 416; in Yemen, 450. See also Employment; Inheritance, right of; Retirement; Social security
Women, meeting places of: in Iran, 126, 131, 132; in Jordan, 207; in Lebanon, 246, 248; in Morocco, 290, 305–6; in Syria, 364; in Tunisia, 390–91, 400; in Yemen, 461. See also Rituals
Women, movements for. See Feminism; Organizations
Women, organizations for. See Organizations
Women, shelters for: in Algeria, 20; in Iran, 134; in Israel, 179, 183; in Jordan, 226; in Morocco, 308; in Syria, 375. See also Rape
Women, unmarried, health care for: in Algeria, 25; in Jordan, 201; in Saudi Arabia, 200; in Tunisia, 393, 395. See also Pregnancy, out-of-wedlock
Women, unmarried: in Egypt, 93; in Iran, 111, 121; in Jordan, 200, 201, 202, 208, 210; in Lebanon, 247; in Morocco, 289, 291–92,

293; in Syria, 363; in Tunisia, 393, 395; in UAE, 416, 417, 418; in Yemen, 446, 450. *See also* Earnings, woman's control of; Guardian, male; Honor, family; Pregnancy, out-of-wedlock

Work, minimum age requirement: in Algeria, 18; in Tunisia, 387

Work, mothers and: in Bahrain, 49, 51, 59; in Iran, 116; in Iraq, 153, 154; in Jordan, 194, 202, 204, 208–9, 225; in Libya, 265, 266, 270; in Tunisia, 387–88; in Yemen, 446, 456. *See also* Breastfeeding during employment or school; Child care; Family; Gender; Leave, maternal and paternal; Work

Work, outside the home: in Algeria, 34; in Bahrain, 48; in Egypt, 70, 73, 78, 88; in Israel, 172, 173; in Jordan, 194; in Libya, 265, 267; in Morocco, 291, 294; in Saudi Arabia, 342–44; in Tunisia, 390; in UAE, 415; in Yemen, 442. *See also* Breastfeeding during employment or school; Child care; Pregnancy; Work, mothers and

Work, part-time v. full-time: in Egypt, 71; in Israel, 171, 175; in Morocco, 286, 287; in Tunisia, 387

Work, unpaid: in Algeria, 18; in Egypt, 70; in Jordan, 197, 199; in Libya, 267; in Morocco, 286, 287; in Syria, 361; in Yemen, 445

Workers, foreign: in Bahrain, 44, 48, 62; in Egypt, 83; in Iraq, 155; in Jordan, 197; in Lebanon, 240; in Libya, 268; in Saudi Arabia, 338, 342–43; in Syria, 360

Workforce, formal: in Iran, 112–13; in Jordan, 199, 200; in Morocco, 286; in the Occupied Territories, 318; in Saudi Arabia, 342–44; in Tunisia, 384. *See also* Pay; Training

Workforce, informal: in Iran, 116; in Jordan, 197–98, 199; in Morocco, 287. *See also* Agriculture, workforce in; Crafts; Employment; Industry; Manufacturing; Self-employment; Textiles

Workforce, skilled: in Algeria, 18, 34; in Bahrain, 48; in Israel, 172, 180; in Tunisia, 384–85. *See also* Health, professionals in; Training

Workplace, condition of: in Bahrain, 48–49; in Egypt, 70–72, 75–76; in Iran, 113, 114, 115; in Israel, 173; in Jordan, 197; in Lebanon, 245; in Libya, 265; in Morocco, 28, 301; in Syria, 362; in Tunisia, 387, 397; in Yemen, 442. *See also* Breastfeeding during employment or school; Discrimination, gender-based; Health, safety standards at work; Unions

World Bank: in Egypt, 87; in Jordan, 196; in Morocco, 289

World War I, effect on Jordan, 190

World War II, effect on: Algeria, 31, 35; Egypt, 90–91; Israel, 174; Libya, 260, 261; Syria, 357

Zoroastrians: in Iran, 106, 137

THE MIDDLE EAST AND NORTH AFRICA

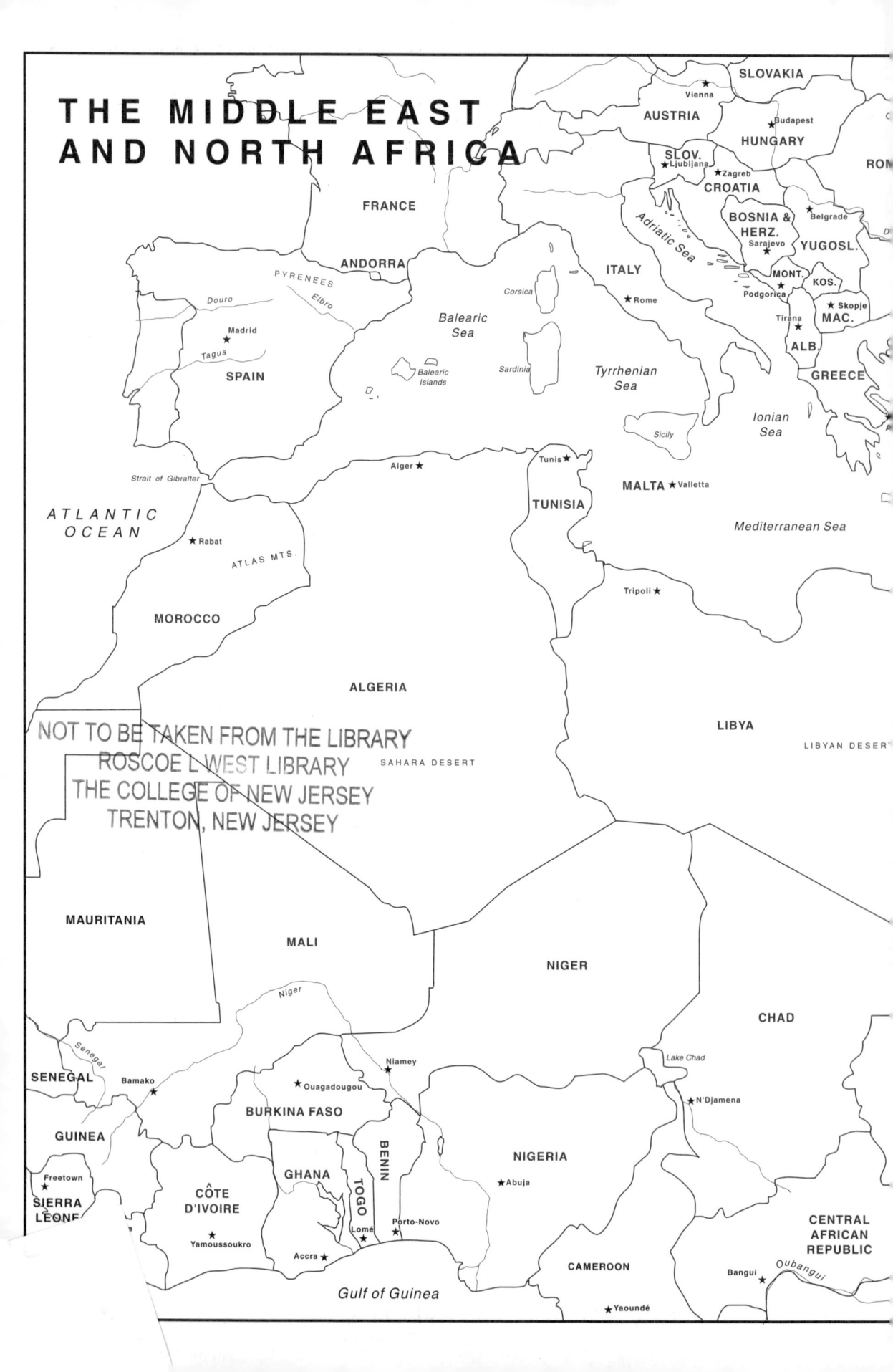